Great Voyages in Small Boats:
Solo Transatlantic

Great Voyages
in Small Boats:
Solo Transatlantic

John de Graff, Inc.
Clinton Corners, New York

GREAT VOYAGES IN SMALL BOATS: SOLO CIRCUMNAVIGATIONS

First printed 1982
ISBN 0-8286-0085-6
Library of Congress Catalogue Card Number: 80-71021
Manufactured in U.S.A.
John de Graff Inc. Clinton Corners, N.Y. 12514

CONTENTS

My Ship is So Small

by
Ann Davison

"Oh, Lord Have Mercy
Thy Sea Is So Large
And My Ship Is So Small."
from the
BRETON FISHERMAN'S
PRAYER

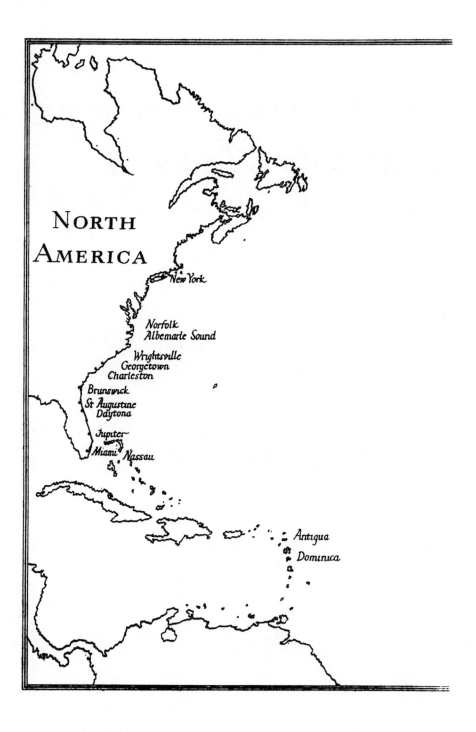

NORTH
AMERICA

New York

Norfolk
Albemarle Sound

Wrightsville
Georgetown
Charleston
Brunswick
St Augustine
Daytona

Jupiter
Miami Nassau

Antigua
Dominica

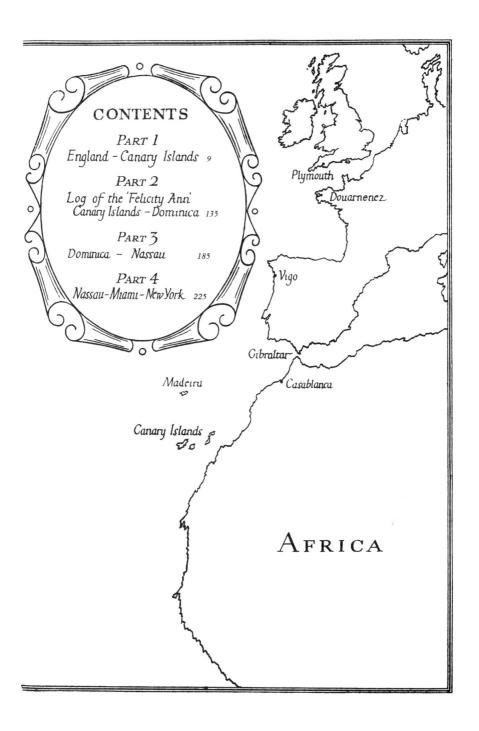

CONTENTS

Plymouth

Douarnenez

Vigo

Gibraltar

Madeira

Casablanca

Canary Islands

AFRICA

Some Sailing Terms

(Explained for the non-sailing reader)

See page 286

Illustrations

Part I

England . . . Canary Islands

Chapter I

"Two eggs!" said Grace, looking at my plate. "Look, they've given you *two* eggs—what have you done to deserve that?"

Rationing was still in force in England, and two eggs were not a normal issue for a hotel breakfast.

"It is not what she has done," said Pete sententiously. "It is what she hopes to do. You could get another egg by simply telling them you are going to sail the Atlantic. They might believe you—they are obviously a trusting lot. . . ."

He looked down at his own one-egg plate and then at the camera on the chair beside him as if he had half a mind to take a picture.

"No you don't," I warned. Professional photographers are indefatigable. To anyone else two eggs on a plate simply means a good breakfast—with perhaps a little influence in rationing times—but to a cameraman they can suggest anything from a new light on human relations to atomic warfare. Pete worked for *Life* Magazine and I was his current assignment, so he had been haunting me for days, appearing at the most incredible times in the most unlikely places, recording my every move. A very unnerving procedure for anyone unused to being a human angle.

Last evening my ship had been put out at moorings for the first time, and I had spent the night aboard, hoping at last to escape his unrelenting surveillance. But such was his devotion to duty he rowed out from the shore at dawn to portray what a woman looks like after her first night afloat, or, as the press boys would say, "on the dawn of her great adventure." Great adventure perhaps: dawn it certainly was, and for me a somewhat testy period at the best of times. . . .

11

Now I was embarking on what was likely to be the last honest, old-fashioned English breakfast I would enjoy for a long time. In comfort at any rate. Possibly the last. . . . The thought edged to the forefront of my mind . . . I considered it academically; a possibility for someone else. What would a last breakfast be like? Two eggs? The condemned man ate a hearty . . . No. That was a midnight thought, not a morning one.

"A special breakfast," I said aloud. "Not for publication."

The little hotel dining-room was crowded. Mostly on my account, I reflected with surprise. Newspaper reporters, radio and television interviewers and operators, photographers, well-wishers and sensation-seekers mingled with the sprinkling of habitués, all eating their one eggs and waiting for me to make the final move. Extraordinary, I thought. Make one step aside from the conventional and the spotlight is on you. You are isolated and observed like a goldfish in a bowl. I looked out through the dining-room window across the waterfront to where the River Tamar flowed past with the serenity of the unwitting. Or the uncaring. The ferryboat from Plymouth was just nosing into the pier in front of the hotel. A ferry I had grown to know pretty well during the past few weeks, and the last time I had crossed on it, two days . . . a lifetime . . . ago, had been at night, and I had looked up at the mast silhouetted against the dark blue sky, imagining it was *my* boat on the dark water with *my* mast swaying across the stars. But now my imagination broke down. I could not see any further ahead than the next few hours.

"If you have finished hogging all those eggs," said Grace, "I'll give you a hand to finish packing."

Pete said, "You don't pack a ship, you stow it," and picked up his camera.

As we made to pay the bill the manageress came forward, smiling. "There'll be no charge for your breakfast, Mrs

Davison," she said, and added, with an unexpectedly emotional clasping of her hands, "Oh, I do wish you the very best of luck, but I know . . . I feel sure . . . you'll make it. You'll be all right." She felt in her pocket and then held out a little bottle with a ship in it. "Will you take this along with you for luck?"

I have always wanted a ship in a bottle. And at that moment I could have wished it was the only sort of ship I ever had wanted.

"Two eggs, no charge, ships in bottles," said Grace. "There must be more in this than I thought. . . . Too late to join in as cabin boy?"

Pete said he was going down to the quay to get "some crowd shots," and the reporters rose purposefully from their tables.

"Mrs Davison, is it true you are making your first call at Madeira?"

"Mrs Davison, how long will it take you to cross the Atlantic?"

"Mrs Davison, where do you intend to land in America?"

"Why are you going alone, Mrs Davison?"

"Aren't you going to take a cat or something?"

"Why are you going, Mrs Davison?"

Mrs Davison replied with a bland assurance as though she knew the answers. I listened to my voice as if it was someone else speaking, and wondered what the reaction would be if I said I didn't know why I was going, couldn't sail a boat, was terrified of the sea, and that it would be nothing short of a miracle if I made Madeira, America, or anywhere out of Plymouth Sound. But though it pays to tell the truth, it rarely pays to tell the whole truth, so I just went on giving the stock answers as convincingly as I could.

"Ann," Grace interrupted, "you'll never be ready. . . . Come on."

"Stop chivvying," I said sharply, addressing not Grace but the inexorable Fates, appealing to the gods to stop their mills for a moment. Just a moment. I would feel braver then. Brave enough to set out on the venture I had dreamed of and worked on for so long, to sail across the Atlantic single-handed. But the gods were deaf, the mills went on grinding, and the moment of departure drew nearer minute by minute. You dream a dream and then you are stuck with it.

Grace said, not as indignantly as she might, "I am not chivvying, but do come on."

We went out of the hotel and across to the shipyard near by. The shipyard that had been home for me during the past three months whilst the ship was being fitted out, but which was now assuming the transient uncertainty of a railway-station. It was nearing high water, and the ship, my innocent accomplice, had been brought in from her moorings to alongside the stone jetty, where a multitude of people in holiday mood were milling about waiting for the spectacle I was to provide. We did not go to the ship, though, but went first to the store in a loft at the far end of the yard, to see if anything had been overlooked in the loading. This had been done the night before last by flashlight, and we had worked like beavers, for the gear—provisions and spares— when piled up on the jetty looked bigger than the ship they were going into, and even Pete lent a hand between pictures. Assured that nothing had been forgotten, we went then to the office to clear up last-minute details and ring through for a weather report. A final check on conditions—as if at that point there was likely to be any startling change—after which I retired to a quiet corner to study the chart and lay off a course. It was an Admiralty Chart, the eastern portion of the Atlantic Ocean, of a scale that usually reduces a long voyage to reasonable proportions; only nothing seemed reasonable just then. As if a record was being played over, I could hear my voice telling the reporters, "I intend to sail sou'west from here clear out into the Atlantic, and then run down for Madeira." Just like that. Good grief, Madeira was a thousand miles away. I fiddled with the dividers and parallel rule, and stared at the chart as if I had never seen anything like it before. I read the weather report again, but it might have been in Chinese for all it conveyed. I had been doing simple dead reckoning for years, having once earned my living as a flying pilot, but now my mind was blank. I doodled a few stylised ships on a stylised sea on the edge of the chart, pulled my wits together and, without thinking, laid off a course, noted some figures, rose and went to the ship. She looked smart and defiant and workmanlike, and moved me with her beauty, as she had done ever since I had first set eyes on her; but she meant no more to me then than an instrument with which I hoped to accomplish the task I had so incredibly chosen.

The shipyard was owned, managed, and worked in by the Mashford Brothers, all six of whom appeared to be on board, making last-minute additions, alterations, and modifications, lashing down and making fast on deck those items for which there was no stowage space below, and doing what were then to me incomprehensibly seamanlike things to rope.

"All for You," one of the brothers sang gaily. I smiled wanly and went below. There, with his coat off and sleeves rolled up, was Sid Mashford, designer of the ship and managing director of the firm, busily engaged in fixing a loud-speaker to a locker bulkhead. He looked round as I entered the cabin and said, "Nearly ready," in a conciliatory tone, as if I was raring to go.

I sat on the settee bunk, and wondered how many times this particular pattern had occurred in my life. It was always the same. I would work blindly and wholeheartedly towards a certain point, and when it came I would go numb. And feel sick. I felt sick now. I said so to Sid.

"Keep calm. Keep calm," he said, sweat running off his brow as he savaged the screwdriver. "You'll be all right. Just keep calm."

You don't look too calm yourself, I thought, and you're not going. . . . The responsibility, I suppose. You designed the ship and built her and fitted her out. But I'm going to sail her, and if anything goes wrong it will be my fault. And why should anything go right? All that ocean . . . And I don't know anything about sailing . . . Well, hardly anything. Sid knows that, but he never discouraged me. . . . In fact, no one has discouraged me since the beginning of this idea. . . . "Go on, Ann. You'll make it," is what they've said all along. Which is what I wanted them to say, isn't it? So what am I griping about? Because I am frightened. Face it, you fool, frightened silly. Oh, God, why must I always have to prove something?

The sudden cessation of activity aboard interrupted my reverie. The ship was ready. The moment had come.

I went ashore to say goodbye. People pressed round. People who yesterday had been my friends; people I knew and loved, whose lives and hopes and ambitions I had shared. Now they were strangers from another world. Or I was. They spoke, and it was as if I could not hear or understand what they were saying. I spoke without knowing what I said. Without looking I was aware of Pete running round in a photographic frenzy. Without listening I was aware of Grace at my elbow, reminding and anxious. Friends who had travelled far for the occasion were giving last-minute gifts and messages; but it was as if I had already gone, for between us was a barrier, invisible and impenetrable. Abruptly I turned away and climbed down on to the boat again.

Bill Mashford, another member of the firm, said, "I'll give you a hand getting under way—the launch can pick me up in the Sound."

So we started the engine and put up the sails and cast off, and ran up river a little way to sort things out. At least, Bill did most of the sorting, which was just as well, as left to myself, being as I was under an emotional anaesthetic, anything might have happened, and the onlookers provided with more of a spectacle than they bargained for. As we motored back, people in the shipyard waved. They were waving out of the hotel windows, and all along the waterfront. The ferryboat crossed ahead of us blowing her hooter, and the passengers aboard raised a small forest of arms. Mechanically I waved back. The yard launch rushed after us filled with my friends, all laughing and gay. It was as if the life I had forsaken was reaching out after me. In Plymouth Sound the launch came alongside, and Bill transferred himself aboard it.

The sun had a halo round it, and a small and fitful breeze was blowing. Sid Mashford leant over the side and called out, "Ann! Take in your jibsheet!" Jibsheet? . . . Jibsheet? . . . Ah, the staysail was flogging. I hadn't noticed. Also in the Sound was the aircraft carrier H.M.S. *Eagle*, with a vast crew aboard waving encouragement. So I was told two years later, but at the time I never saw her. If I could miss the *Eagle* I could hardly be expected to notice a little thing like a flapping staysail.

I took a pull on the sheet and belayed it with extraordinary care, and relaxed as if the day's work was done. Then suddenly bethought me of a telegram, promised but not sent. This oversight slipped into the void of my consciousness and swelled to enormous proportions. Whatever else, that telegram must go. I scribbled a note on a piece of paper and roared up to the launch in the manner of one bringing the news from Ghent, thrust the message into someone's outstretched hand, and if the launch hadn't shied away, would have torn off our topsides in the process, for it never occurred to me to slow down.

The launch kept nervously out of reach after that, and as we neared the open sea two sailboats joined the fleet. Graceful and white-winged and under full control, their burgees were dipped in elegant salute. I felt I ought to reply, but decided against it as being too difficult, so flapped an ineffectual hand and wished they would all go home and leave me to face what had to be faced. They represented the last thin thread holding me to a life that was past, and I wanted to be alone to face my future, stretching there before me, from horizon to horizon, the broad, sparkling, illimitable Atlantic, enigmatic and promising nothing. At last the boats turned away from seaward, back as it were to yesterday, whilst I kept straight on, for tomorrow.

The tenuous thread was broken and I was on my own.

*   *   *

At half-past three that afternoon, Eddystone lay abeam, close to starboard. The wind had died away, and the lighthouse, like a huge admonitory finger, pointed to heaven from a glass-calm sea. Eddystone was my departure point, and I looked at it with a lingering fascination as it slowly fell astern, the last signpost on the long, long road to Madeira.

The sky was clear overhead, but there was a thickish haze which gave a curious mirage quality to the sea that exactly matched my mood. The dark blue sails hung limp as the little ship motored through the limpid mirror of the sea, and time crept forward as the sun swung slowly across the sky to melt red in the mist on the western horizon. All colour faded as the day died; then night, darkly enveloping, spread a mantle of solitude over the sea. An immeasurable solitude that reached up from the bottom of the ocean and stretched out beyond the stars, that penetrated every particle of water and permeated the very structure of the ship, that muffled the sound of the engine, that was life and death and everywhere and nothing.

With night came the wind. It whispered first, then sang in the rigging, and kicked up little waves that grew bigger and rougher as the wind gained confidence. And it blew from the sou'west, which was awkward as that was the way I wanted to go. The little ship, grossly overladen, bucked and pitched in the head sea, and seemed to me, in my colossal ignorance, to be horribly insecure. Overly cautious, I reefed the mainsail and changed the staysail for the storm jib, a ridiculous piece of canvas for the wind that was blowing then; but there were all the long night hours ahead, and as this was the first time I had ever sailed a boat on my own I was not taking any chances.

Then I sat in the cockpit, steering south and thinking of my friends, at home now, *safe* at home, warm and dry, with roofs over their heads and the good earth solid and steady under their feet. They were on land, where there were forests and fields and flowers and roads leading with comparative certainty to a specific destination. Where the warm yellow light through windows would stab the country darkness and the glow from a whole town lighten the night sky. Where there were people, wise, sensible people who stayed at home and never let their dreams run away with them.

But land was invisible, and the sea was dark and desolate. There was not a ship in sight. My only companions were the stars and the wind and the waves, remote and impersonal. The ship heeled and water slapped her bows, lapped over the lee rail and ran searchingly aft. It was cold and the chill struck through the defences of my duffle-coat.

Cold and lonely and frightened, I wondered why I had let a dream run away with me. Why, for heaven's sake, why?

Chapter 2

THE only way to live is to have a dream green and growing in your life; anything else is just existing and a waste of breath. My dreams don't run on mink coat and diamond lines—not that I have anything against mink coats and diamonds, but they aren't much use on an island, or in an airplane, or on a boat, and those are the sort of lines my dreams run along. Rugged stuff. Adventure, some people call it, or romance, or when they are really frustrated, escapism. If anyone asked me and I was unguarded enough to reply, I would call it the pursuit of beauty or truth, and if I was honest I would admit it was largely curiosity, the urge to find out the why, the what, and the how at first hand, without simply taking someone else's word for it. Most of my dreams have come true at one time or another, so adventure and I are old buddies. We have had some rare capers together, good, bad, exciting, interesting, and, on occasion, terrible, but never at any time have they been dull. I know by now that the glitter of romance as seen from afar often turns out to be pretty shoddy at close quarters, and what appears to be a romantic life is invariably an uncomfortable one; but I know, too, that the values in such living are usually sound. They have to be, or you don't survive. And occasionally you are rewarded by an insight into living so splendid, so wholly magnificent, you can be satisfied with nothing less ever after, so that you go on hoping and searching for another glimpse for the rest of your life.

The dream-boat business came up three years before I actually set out, because I had a life going spare and wanted to use it; and the notion of sailing a small boat about the world appealed because it offered freedom, independence, travel, and a home into the bargain. It represented a variety of interests in the actual management and navigation of the ship, all fairly unknown activities to me, and it was necessary at the time for me to acquire new interests and so a new meaning in life; also it would surely provide unlimited copy with which to feed the typewriter and incidentally me, for I had degenerated into a writer of sorts through the years. The fact that I knew nothing about boats, very little about sailing, and was terrified of the sea was no deterrent to a full-scale production of a dream. I could learn, and, with knowledge, some of the fears would vanish. The decision to sail the Atlantic instead of groping round the coast as a shakedown cruise was not quite so crazy as it seems, for ships, like airplanes, are only likely to get into real trouble near land, which was one factor I knew irrefutably. Moreover, I reckoned I would know by the time I reached America whether I liked the life or not, and either way there ought to be a story in it. After all no other woman had sailed the Atlantic single-handed, or even, so far as I knew, attempted to do so, which fact did not influence me in the least, though it turned out to be a useful stick with which to goad enthusiasm in others. Enthusiasm in others is a primary necessity when undertaking an enterprise one knows very little about.

The venture had to remain at the dream stage for a couple of years from its inception, because I was starting life again from scratch with no more than the clothes I stood up in and with a fair pack of wolves howling at the door. To settle the wolves was the first consideration; money had to be made in order to feed them, and without capital or skill the quickest way to make any seemed to me to be to write a book. Just a hunch I had. However, this would not have been possible without the extraordinary generosity of two of the kindest people I know, who not only threw open their home to me, but, more important even than that, gave unstintingly their understanding and unfailing moral support. Whatever their own private doubts may have been, they never once showed them to me. Never once did they ask, as they might well have done, "What if the book is a flop?" . . . You take in a stray cat and it doesn't catch the mice. . . . But their attitude was always to talk hopefully of the prospects "when the book comes out" as if its success was a foregone conclusion, though they could have had no possible grounds for such a belief.

As a matter of fact I wrote two books, writing the second apparently unable to break off the habit whilst the first was gestating at the publishers'; and, without setting the world on fire, they did for me all I had hoped and gambled on. To drop the wolf motif, creditors were paid off, and a little was left over for dream money. But dreams, like wolves (how did they get in again?), have to be fed, so in between books or stubborn chapters, I went in search of boat lore against the time I owned one of my own. I even took a job as a hand in a boatyard for some months.

It was a small, primitive yard on the South Coast, unpretentious and unconventional, otherwise I should never have got the job, women in the boating industry being as popular as Beethoven at a jam session; and it was tucked away at the end of an obscure mud creek where the tide used to creep in and out apologetically as if sorry to disturb. Plover spun over the nearby fields, and curlew called from the saltings, wild duck paddled by the shore, and the whole setting was so rural it might have been a hundred miles from the sea, which was round the corner and way out of sight. The yard was so far from the nearest branch of civilisation only the keenest boating enthusiast could ever find it, the postman rarely and the newspaperman never.

The owner, Jake, was tall, dark and bearded, stern and withdrawn, given to sudden flashes of disarming affability. He could build a boat, renovate a wreck, a radio, or an engine with equal facility and consummate skill. He wrote articles for the technical press and novels on the side. He once remarked after a long silence and *à propos* of nothing at all, "You talk about imagination, but no one has anything on the Lord."

His wife, Carol, was small and vital, with the beauty of an eighteenth-century miniature. She ought to have worn a pompadour and patches, but instead wore pastel-coloured slacks and multi-coloured scarves and lived at the run as though time was too scarce for walking. She was talented and versatile, equally at home splitting logs with a giant axe, making elegant clothes from her own designs, weaving mats on her patent loom, or carving dolls' furniture out of scrap wood in the carpenter's shop. The dolls' furniture was for their daughter, Susan, aged five, a prodigy who could, and would, read anything. "Is the crisis over?" she would inquire from behind a formidably political paper. She crawled under the boat where I was lying flat on my back learning the boating business from the bottom up—and just how much bottom there is to a 30-foot boat has to be scraped to be appreciated—to terrify me with a string of strangely inconsequential questions. "Are you rich? Are you Spanish? Have you ever laid a baby?" The last no doubt inspired by the cackling of the hens, who enthusiastically used the entire boatyard as a nesting-box, but the others came from heaven knows what recesses of a fertile mind.

The yard employed one real hand, a red-haired, red-bearded Canadian jack-of-all-trades, known as Vancouver. He lived in a sheet-iron shack he had built himself "back up in the bush," in other words amongst six trees at the end of a field, and bought ready sliced bread because, as he said, it was one less chore to do. He worked with incredible speed and sang at his work, rarely stopping to give an order or make a remark as he usually knew a song to suit. "It looks like rain in Cherry Blossom Lane," he would carol when the clouds came over. "We had better get the covers on this old hooker, tra-la." I like to sing at my work, too, and if I happened to strike up first and he approved my choice

23

we would harmonise, otherwise he would pull out all the stops and sing me down.

In a brief non-operatic moment he once told me to make a set of wedges to slip under the ribs taking the engine bearers in a cruiser we were building out of a lifeboat hull. I asked him how, not unreasonably I thought, to which he testily replied, "Ef I'd the time to show you I could make 'em myself." When I eventually produced the wedges after an unconscionable tussle in the carpenter's shop, he said philosophically, "Guess she don't fit so good . . . but what the heck . . . I ain't a boatbuilder and you ain't a boatbuilder's mate, so what kin they expect from a coupla amachewers?"

As a matter of fact both Vancouver and Jake were very patient with my shortcomings as a boatyard hand, but neither were prepared to spend time on instruction. I asked Jake where the waterline was to come on a boat I was painting, but he simply looked sardonic as only a bearded man can and said, "Work it out for yourself." It is as good a way as any, learning by the old-fashioned method of trial and error, soaking up such knowledge gained by a sort of osmosis; provided you have the time and can stand the knocks.

I lived aboard an old forty-footer due for rehabilitation lying out on the saltings, and at high water springs had to time my entrances and exits with the tide, as there was no dinghy to spare for commuting. The old boat was exceedingly ripe, and altered shape at every tide. Sometimes a crab would scuttle across the cabinsole, giving rise to conjecture as to how it got in, and where it proposed to go out. As I lived on my infinitesimal earnings—this being a between-chapter episode—housekeeping was eked out with what was available from natural resources, such as sea spinach, samphire, and other growths flourishing on and around the saltings.

Most of the boats in the yard were old tore-outs like the one I lived in, but as it was hoped they would eventually become someone's pride and joy, they were scraped and burnt off, sanded down, stopped and cemented, painted and varnished until their own builders would not have known them. Apart from the crane on what Vancouver was pleased to call the dock, there were no mechanical aids, and all work was done by hand, the hard, bruising and basic way. We chipped and chiselled, drilled and bored. We lined up for engine installations, we steamed ribs and riveted them in. Occasionally we even got on the water, which was supposed to be our natural element seeing we were all so wild about boats we had to work amongst them.

The most memorable of these brief brushes with Neptune was when the *Golden Fleece* was brought over from Portsmouth, entailing contact with some twelve miles of open water. Jake had a back-ache that day, so Vancouver was told off to do the fetching and I was promoted to mate. Vancouver prepared for the voyage—it was a blazing hot day—by putting on oilskins, sou'wester and seaboots. Carol was going to drive us to Portsmouth, and put on some gaily coloured scarves, and at the last moment Jake decided to come too, and put on a yachting cap. "I can't *do* anything," he agonised, "I'll simply sit and direct." As befits a master mind. The usual clutter of nautical aids were flung into the back of the car and we set off. The yard car had come off the ways in '23 and was strictly an austerity model, all its trimmings having been lost in the limbo. It looked like an animated bathtub, and our progress drew the crowds like a royal procession.

We boarded the *Fleece* at her moorings in one of Portsmouth's more humble aquatic back-alleys as the tide was sweeping in. The partial conversion of the boat included a cabin, and the engine-room opened out directly on to the large cockpit. She was much hung about with gear and tarpaulins, and "For Sale" was written in large orange letters on the port bow. By the time the tide was on its way out we were still trying to start the engine. Jake ceased directing and said, "We can forget about going today." But Vancouver, that staunch individualist, simply removed his oilskins and swung the motor again, whereon it started. Jake, forgetting his back-ache, immediately sprang forward and cast off, and Vancouver, with a masterly grasp of events, leapt to the tiller. I went into the forepeak to see if the petrol tap on the tank there was turned on, having switched it on and off so frequently in the past hour or two that I had lost count, and this was no time to have it off.

Apart from running aground, having the engine, obviously in a touchy condition, stop a few times, so that there were moments when we might almost have been classified as a harbour hazard, we cleared Portsmouth without incident.

Outside the harbour there was a pleasant quartering breeze. The day was bright and sunny. Jake pointed out the Nab Tower, the Isle of Wight, the *Queen Mary*, and one or two other local landmarks, whilst the *Fleece* with her considerable tophamper rolled along with a joyous abandon. For a time we felt very gay and seagoing. Then an aircraft came screaming towards us at no height and Jake looked at it thoughtfully. "Ah yes, target area, I'd forgotten." Simultaneously Vancouver and I discovered we had the sea to ourselves and exclaimed, "Here?" with some urgency. Jake said, "We'll find that out." The plane roared over our heads, dived at the shore, climbed up on its tail and came round with the evident intention of repeating the performance *ad lib.* We pressed on uncomfortably, hoping we did not resemble a target too much.

As the entrance to the harbour leading to our home creek drew abeam, Jake pointed to a small white speck on the horizon ahead. "We go round that buoy," he directed. "We do not," said Vancouver, making to turn in, and a brisk interchange followed as to times, tides, banks, and depths which Vancouver closed by saying, "We ain't got the gas anyhow." Jake then decided to put the small amount of gas remaining in the spare can into the tank. My part in this operation consisted of assuming a Yogi attitude in the forepeak, juggling with the valves and inhaling petrol vapour whilst Jake filled the tank from deck. The motion was *awful*. My head was spinning as I tottered back to the cockpit to tell the others I was just out in time, ha ha, a few minutes more and I would have been sick.

Then the engine stopped. Without way on, and as if she had been waiting for this moment, the *Golden Fleece* cast decorum to the winds and indulged in an exhibition of free aquabatics that would have won her first prize anywhere in any company. This was her day out!

Frantic attempts to restore the engine to life were unavailing, and in desperation Vancouver rigged a jury mast with the boathook; but the tarpaulin he proposed using in lieu of a sail refused to be detached from the warps and woosies with which it was entangled on the cabin roof. I could not help him. I was sitting in the cockpit, transfixed, albeit an unwilling spectator, incapable of movement and deaf to any appeals to my better nature, for I had none, nor any feelings to spare for my fellow men, being immobilised by a great personal discomfort. Thwarted in his attempt to rig a steadying sail, Vancouver divested himself of his oilskins, sou'wester, and seaboots and returned to the starting handle with a true cave-dweller's approach to action. He did not so much swing that engine as wring its neck. He tore off the carburetter, wrenched it to pieces, reassembled it, and flung it back in place, then proceeded to strangle the engine again. His face was purple and running with sweat. For some reason he appeared to be working against time.

Meantime, the *Fleece* fought back with every trick she knew.

Jake leant against the cockpit coaming with a faraway look in his eyes.

"A little cottage," he murmured, "a little ivy-covered cottage. . . ."

"Chickens," I suggested faintly.

"Chickens," he assented turning a most horrific colour, and

adding with commendable composure, "Excuse me, I am going to be sick."

Vancouver erupted from the engine-room, flung himself flat on the cockpit floor and closed his eyes.

The *Fleece* had won hands down.

Jake recovered first: he looked sadly at the prone figure and said, "If we threw him over the side now, he would never know or care," then heroically took his aching back into the engine-room. In a few moments, surprisingly, the engine started. Vancouver leapt to life and the tiller. The engine stopped. He dropped back inert on deck. It started again. He sprang to the helm. It stopped and he dropped. Again it started and again he jumped to the tiller. It was quite fascinating. This time the engine kept on going, and he turned for the harbour entrance flat out, unheeding of buoys, banks, bars, or Jake's entreaties to watch out. Spotting a plug behaving in a rather unusual manner —it appeared to be boiling—I mentioned it, just as a matter of interest, to Vancouver, who crouched over the tiller and hissed, "For Chrissake don't tell him, he'll wanna fix it."

Then a gusty altercation broke out as we approached the bar. It was low water and Jake maintained we would not make it. But Vancouver said, "We will" in a tone implying he was of a mind to carry the boat across if necessary. With the motor hacking and coughing and a few inches to spare we cleared the bar and ploughed up our home creek in the merest trickle of water, until eventually the *Fleece* slid to a standstill about a mile from the yard in a valley of mud.

Silently Jake threw out the anchor, jumped over the side, and waded to the shore. Jake was a tall man, and noting where the mud came to on his boots, Vancouver and I agreed it was not for us and decided to walk back to the yard along the channel in the remaining water. When it reached the seat of my pants I stopped worrying about getting wet. Then we met a man grovelling in the mud of his own free will. "Saaaaaay," said

Vancouver, "Cockles. They're mighty nice t' eat." So we went on a cockle hunt, and having no other container used Vancouver's sou'wester as a basket.

Jake was prone and brooding over a resurgence of back-ache when we finally got back to the yard with a hatful of trophies. He looked at me pretty straightly. "And you," he grated, "said you wanted to sail the Atlantic. . . ."

Chapter 3

THE boatyard job came to an end when Jake decided to sell up and go abroad. He looked at one of the wrecks we were patching up as good as new if you gave it no more than a passing glance and said, "My God, if we sell that thing we'll *have* to go abroad." And although this had nothing to do with it, sell up they did and abroad they went in search of scope and sunshine; and I returned to my stubborn chapter, encouraged to have the book finished by autumn because of a belief that more of the boating business was coming my way then. Authentic sailing this time, as member of the crew of a 40-ton cutter sailing for Florida. This had come about through meeting a young couple, John and Bonnie Staniland, who were actually leading the sort of life I was aiming at. They lived on a boat and sailed the oceans unfettered, untrammelled, and unrestricted. Since the end of the war they had crossed the Atlantic five times and thought no more of it than the average yachtsman would of popping across the Channel. I read about them first in a yachting magazine. The article stated they were fitting out a 40-ton cutter for yet another transatlantic trip. Moreover, and this was the bit that held my attention, they were looking out for a volunteer crew to share expenses on the voyage. A chance to take a trial trip round the course with a competent driver? I wrote at once, making no claims to being a sailor, but mentioning my flying experience and the fact I was then employed as a hand in a boatyard, and was (of course) willing to learn. (Oh, most willing to learn, despite the sad antics aboard the *Golden Fleece*.) The expense angle was tricky, bearing in mind the present meagre earnings so soon to stop, but I skipped that. In my sort of life, who knew where and how what money was coming

Ann Davison

Trying out the twin staysails in Plymouth Sound

when, to coin a phrase—sorry, that slipped out—but to make myself clear, don't count your chickens before they are hatched but keep the incubator going. A reply was hardly to be expected; there would surely be a rush of *bona fide* crew members eager to take up the opportunity to join in with what was obviously a genuine undertaking. Nevertheless, the Stanilands wrote back. . . . "You sound eminently suitable . . ." they said, and suggested I should visit them over the weekend aboard their yacht, *Diadem*, then lying at moorings in the Beaulieu River. Me—"eminently suitable!" Nothing could stop me then. I took trains and buses and a five-mile walk through the New Forest and arrived two hours late with a toothbrush and hope running high.

The *Diadem* looked magnificent lying peaceably in the river. She was of imposing dimensions, and her 80-foot mast struck a small chill in my heart. Would I have to go up that thing? Below decks she was superb. The main cabin appeared to my goggling eyes to be no less than a scale model drawing-room complete with all the fixings including a piano. This was yachting of a very high order indeed. And her owners were no less dazzling. Despite their undeniable efficiency and experience, there was nothing salty or rugged about John and Bonnie Staniland. They were both strikingly good looking and gay, straight out of a glossy ad.—Bonnie, a tall brunette, was gorgeous enough to stop the traffic anywhere—and they had a fund of traveller's tales that had me listening agape. Place names like Funchal, Miami, and Nassau cropped up in the conversation as casually as Bournemouth, Exeter, or Brighton. They spoke of people called Bengt or Jules, and my imagination, ever ready to go to work at the drop of a hat, pictured palm trees, blue seas, white sands, and fat round Trade Wind clouds with no trouble at all. Oh yes, this was for me.

They said I could join the crew for crossing number six, fully realising my knowledge of sailing was equivalent to an aborigine's concept of the expanding universe. I was moved and not a little troubled. Conscience strikes all of us at times.

"There is something . . . I think I ought to tell you . . ." I began.

Bonnie and John exchanged glances and John said, "You don't have to—we know all about you—"

Which only goes to show the transparency of the walls we believe to have erected about ourselves.

"And it doesn't make any difference?"

John said, "In similar circumstances we should have probably reacted the way you did."

Probably not. Few people are as crazy as that.

★   ★   ★

Only Frank and I. Frank was my husband. He was killed in a shipwreck we brought on ourselves; for circumstances, however much we would like to shift the blame elsewhere, are largely of our making, which is the hardest and bitterest lesson to learn in life.

Frank was mad about boats and the sea; they had been an intermittent part of his life before we met, but we had been married eight years before sailing was woven into our joint pattern of living. We had been through a variety of ventures together, aviation, quarrying, farming; we even became islanders for three years; then Frank brought up his life ambition to sail round the world. I am always game for anything new, so we bought an old fishing ketch and converted her over two years into what we considered to be a pretty handsome vessel, providing an elegant home with the ability, so we thought, to go anywhere we wanted. We spent too much money on her and got into difficulties. Debts piled high and our efforts to meet them were unavailing. With a notice of foreclosure, and a sheriff on the way to nail a writ to the mast, we sailed out of port bound for the West Indies, knowing full well we were only postponing the inevitable, but hoping that the transoceanic crossing short-handed—she was a big ketch, 70 feet overall—would prove the ship's capabilities and increase her value, maybe to the point of covering our commitments. It was a desperate move, and it did not come off. We ran into bad conditions almost immediately, and after nineteen days of incredible hardship we lost the ship one night in a sou'westerly gale on the rocks at Portland Bill, with her sails blown out and the engine defunct, and how we got there is a long, long story. We tried to make the shore in a life-raft, but were swept out to sea through the race. The seas were terrible; the raft kept turning over. The cold was intense; it killed Frank. Fourteen hours after leaving the *Reliance*, the ironical name of the ship that had been, the raft was swept ashore and I climbed the cliffs to start life again, alone.

It was not in any spirit of defiance, or revenge, or expiation, or vindication, that I chose to return to a way of life that had barely begun before ending so disastrously. From the start, even as I climbed those cliffs, I knew I would, I *had* to, though at the time it would have been impossible to explain why, beyond, maybe, a compulsion to try and complete what we had set out to do together. But it went even deeper than that.

There was the fear . . . listening to the wind howling at nights and feeling the tendrils of fear creeping with paralysing intent about the very core of my being. A fear that had pursued me through flying, through the island years, and to the sea, where it had combined with the waves to increase its terror. Yet the shipwreck itself had neither increased nor lessened the fear. Fear comes from ignorance, of that I was aware; and forming in the back of my mind was the thought that if this fear could be faced, tackled, and overcome, I should find a key to living. A key that had been plainly lost on the way before, otherwise Frank and I would never have made the mistakes that led to our undoing. It was an amorphous thought, ever growing, developing, and changing shape, but gradually it seemed to me that a single-handed passage across the Atlantic represented life in essence. It could be that I was afraid of life and that the wind and sea were merely symbolic. If I could navigate a ship across the ocean on my own, it might be that I would be well on the way to learning how to live.

*　　*　　*

That weekend aboard the *Diadem* was the beginning of a friendship that was to be renewed at intervals in all sorts of strange places under circumstances I could only dream of then, although, in fact, the Stanilands and I were never to sail together, at least not in the way that we agreed to during that first meeting; an agreement that kept me buoyed during that long sad summer when I wrote the story of the *Reliance*. The Stanilands were cruising in the Baltic then, and it was arranged we should meet again in the autumn to prepare for the voyage to Florida. On their way back to England they encountered most evil weather, and, through a series of misfortunes, a reef off the Danish coast and a long drawn out salvage case, from all of which they managed to extricate themselves eventually; but the trip to America was off. At least postponed.

The book[1] was completed, accepted, and put into the publisher's mill for processing.

A year came off the calendar, another book[2] came off the typewriter and John and Bonnie appeared on the scene again. This time with an infant son, Ian, for whom I found myself subpœnaed as godmother, a 46-foot schooner bearing the highly provocative name of *Nymph Errant*, and more plans for an ocean voyage. Without wasting any more time than it takes to throw some denims in a holdall, I joined them at Lymington, and we took the boat round from there to moorings in the Hamble River, where John intended completing the refit of the schooner.

[1] *Last Voyage*   [2] *Home was an Island*

Ships, I may say, when not at sea, are always being fitted out or refitted or worked over in some way; they are never complete; work on them is never done, they are ceaselessly, relentlessly demanding, and if you waited until every job was finished you would never put to sea at all. The trick is to know when to down tools without jeopardising the safety of the vessel.

Within a few weeks of the date fixed for sailing I learnt that the book of the last ill-fated voyage was about to come out and a number of fierce cats would be sporting among the pigeons in consequence. I liked to think I could run away to sea and ignore the carnage, if any. But you have to live with yourself and you cannot gain a thing by running away, so the *Nymph Errant* sailed without me, and I stayed to watch the cheques whistle past my ears on their way to the creditors. Vicariously, the *Reliance* paid for herself.

★   ★   ★

This was the point, then, when it seemed desirable to take positive action if the venture was ever to be lifted out of the dream category. With the *Reliance* debts paid off and the book still making money, I set about looking for a suitable ship, in rather a desultory manner because I was not at all sure what I was looking for, though certain I would know it when I saw it. This approach, it must be admitted, added immeasurably to the interest of ship-hunting, and undoubtedly assured various brokers and shipyards that there is one born every minute. For of course one could not *explain*. The market for small ocean-going ships is negligible, so they cannot be bought off the peg, but to say that is why you want a ship when your reaction to the simplest technical question is one of blank surprise takes more moral courage than I have.

At first I was inclined towards the old-fashioned, straight stemmed, chunky, fishing-boat types, still being under the influence of the *Reliance*, which after all had been the only ship I had ever known at all intimately. Jake wrote and asked why, and suggested a small modern Bermudan rigged vessel around five tons as being more easily handled and suitable in every way. And I thought, why not, there is such a thing as progress. The old-fashioned types I had looked over had been such crates and in such a dismal state of decrepitude, so I turned my attention to elegant little modern yachts, most of which were hideously expensive, and all too sneery and unsympathetic, proudly winking their chromium plate and flashing their varnish and flaunting their laid decks in a way I knew would be beyond me either to keep up or live up to.

But in the end the right ship came along when least expected, as these things have a way of doing if not pressed too hard.

As there did not seem much sense in getting a boat unless one knew, at least in theory, how to operate it, I thought I had better take lessons in sailing. The only people I knew in the yachting world were Jake and Carol and the Stanilands, and they were all abroad, so I studied the yachting magazines and found one or two advertisers willing to take on a tyro, and chose one operating from Torquay, because I had always liked the West Country. After an exchange of letters I went down to Devonshire to stay with Commander and Mrs Lund, who lived on a red cliff-top overlooking Torbay on the outskirts of Torquay. Commander Lund had spent some twenty years as navigational instructor in the Navy, and after retirement continued teaching in a private capacity both navigation and sailing. Every morning and afternoon for a week or so the Commander and I went sailing in the Bay in his 18-foot yawl so that I could, quite literally, learn the ropes.

The Commander was a good instructor. I realised that sailing could be a pleasant orderly affair, and glimpsed what it is that gets people. The few excursions I had ever made in a sailboat previously had reluctantly induced the conclusion that the slower the transport the more the commotion, at least on the part of those involved. Look at an ox-cart . . . the squeaks and the groans and the shouting . . . much like sailing. The mildest-mannered man aboard ship will whirl about like an eggbeater and the softest spoken man curse like a trooper. "Belay there, you twit! The sheet, you bloody clot—the SHEET—you creep!" (That'd be me hauling on the wrong rope and when I am shouted at I always shout back, it is a reflex action, but never makes for harmony.) I thought this was an essential part of sailing and something I would just have to get used to, like the awful irrelevant nomenclature.

Commander Lund was different however; he did not shout. His hobby was archæology, which probably explains it; you cannot deal in æons and bother about the little things of today. He explained the different ropes and their functions with infinite patience, and watched you ravel them up and showed you how to unravel them without making you feel you were the only moron alive. When you got a bit more competent he would make a game of it to keep you on your toes. "There's fog coming down," he would say suddenly, just when you were relaxed and basking at the helm and thinking how nice it was sailing under a sunny sky. "We are trying to make for Brixham —what are you going to do about it?" So you would have to bounce out of your calm and think about times and tides and courses. Or he might say, "Look out, your port shroud's parted!" and you were expected to act as if it had. Or then again, he might throw a cork float overside and cry, "Man overboard!" and you would have to pick it up, by no means a simple operation, for if you were too long about it he would groan and say, "He's drowned by now," and you would feel pretty bad about it.

Such was his training that in a very short time, only a matter of a week or two, I felt quite like taking a small ship across the Atlantic.

The Commander knew nothing of this dark design on the

part of his pupil. I was chary of telling people. Bonnie and John knew of course, but they accepted it as a perfectly normal desire as they were doing it all the time, and Jake and Carol knew too, but they were abroad and unlikely to hold it against me because they would not set any store by it anyway. It was the sort of thing they would like to do; might get round to doing one day; it was the sort of thing a whole lot of people would like to do, if they had the time, or the money, or the initiative, or something. Saying you would like to sail the Atlantic or the Pacific or round the world amongst small boat sailors is tantamount to saying you would like to win the Irish Sweepstake; not impossible, but pretty remote.

It was not easy to tell the Commander I was learning to sail because I wanted to sail the Atlantic; but the time came when I wanted to jump from the comparative simplicities of sailing round the Bay to the deeper complexities of celestial navigation, and some explanation seemed called for. Commander Lund was not in the least surprised. He simply said, "Well, in that case, what you need to know is thus and thus . . ." which took the enormity out of the project and put the whole thing in its proper perspective. Then both he and his wife adopted the venture as if it was their own. They certainly could not have shown more interest. We spent long delightful evenings discussing ways and means, poring over ocean charts, arguing the merits of Madeira, the Azores, and the Canaries as jumping off places for the crossing, and studying winds and currents. For the first time the dream took on a gleam of reality.

Then the Commander found my ship.

I was visiting a friend in Plymouth when he called me up there in a state of great excitement. The dreamboat was lying at a yard just across the river from Plymouth. A 23-foot sloop. Too small, I said. "Come and see her," he urged, "she's just the ship for you. Practically new . . . diesel auxiliary. . . ." I pricked up my ears at that; a diesel was certainly an inducement. "And the funniest thing," he was full of enthusiasm, "what do you think she is called? *Felicity Ann*," he announced, as if that settled it.

"Oh *no*," I said, "I couldn't possibly own a ship with a name like that, everyone will think I called her after myself." (They do, too.)

But the price was right, and more to please the Commander than anything I went to see her; and as soon as I set foot on her I knew he was right, and that she was the ship for me. She was sympatico. She had a slightly aggressive air and the quality, distinguishable but indefinable, that spells reliability; adversity I felt, would bring out the best in her. But I wanted confirmation and needed advice. She looked so very tiny for all her staunchness. Lacking the knowledge, I had only a hunch to go on that she was the right boat for the job. Was she in fact suitable for such an undertaking? There would be no choosing the weather in the Atlantic, she would have to take whatever came. Could she?

Almost as if there was a predestined pattern over which I had no control, this problem settled itself too, curiously enough through the book. Among the letters that were the outcome of its publication was one from Humphrey Barton, a partner in the well-known firm of Laurent Giles of Lymington. Humphrey Barton had surveyed the *Reliance*. He wrote kindly of the book, but the fact that he wrote at all I took as an omen. No one could be better qualified to advise on the requirements of a small ship on a large sea, for apart altogether from his extensive experience as surveyor and yachtsman, Humphrey had sailed a five-tonner, the *Vertue XXXV*, direct from England to New York in 1950. Yet I doubt if I should have had the courage to approach him for advice if he had not written. He did not seem surprised when I told him what I had in mind, and agreed to survey the *Felicity Ann* with a view to her potentialities as an ocean cruiser. If Humphrey had any misgivings he kept them to himself; to me he gave nothing but encouragement and the most valuable assistance.

*   *   *

Before the war the Cremyll Shipyard, on the Cornish side of the River Tamar opposite Plymouth, built a number of 4-ton T.M. sloops that were handy, fairly fast, and able seaboats. In 1939, a new keel was laid and the hull planked up, making, possibly, the twelfth of the line, but the ship was not completed owing to the outbreak of World War II. She was tucked away in a corner and forgotten, as the shipyard became wholly engaged on Admiralty work. Ten years later, in 1949, a West Country yachtsman was looking over the yard and saw her: "Ah, just the little ship I want for a single-handed cruise to Norway." He was a knowledgable, practical man, and as this particular sloop was destined to go far in conditions varying from deep sea to calm canal, she did not turn out quite like her sisters. Her hollow silver spruce mast was stepped on deck in a tabernacle to allow for the comparative ease of unstepping it for canal work, but to obviate any weakness at sea, the deckbeams in way of the mast were doubled, and additionally strengthened by an angle-iron frame and steel knees. A 5 h.p. Coventry Victor diesel engine was installed under the bridge deck with a ten-gallon fuel tank under the cabinsole. The cabin was very simply laid out for single-handed cruising, with a settee bunk to port, a head discreetly hidden forrard amidships, and a table-locker and galley occupied most of the starboard side in the main part of the cabin. There was a zinc-lined locker under the bunk and another, unlined, under the galley. Forrard of the head was the chain locker and a wide open space up to the eyes of the ship for the stowage of sailbags, etc. She was a double-ended boat with tiller steering, and Bermudan rigged with a double track on the mast, one for the mainsail, and the other for the trysail to facilitate operations in bad weather; the theory being that you could have the trysail hanked on ready before dropping the main. The Columbian pine boom was fitted with bronze worm-type roller reefing gear so that sail could be reduced by simply winding it round the boom.

She was 23 feet overall, 19 feet on the waterline, had a beam of 7 feet 6 inches, and a draught of 4 feet 6 inches. Her ballast keel was 17 cwt of iron, and in addition there was about 3 cwt of inside ballast. Her total sail area was 237 square feet, and her working sails consisted of staysail, genoa, and mainsail which were all mildew- and water-proofed and dyed blue. There was also a spare mainsail of very heavy canvas, a storm trysail, and a storm staysail. She was built under the name of *Peter Piper* but launched as *Felicity Ann*, in September, 1949. By then, however, her owner was engaged in other matters and had no time to spare for single-handed sailing to Norway or anywhere else, so six weeks later she was hauled out again and laid up. For nearly two years she waited in the sheds, and because of her initials and peculiarly inactive life was known in the yard as "Sweet *FA*."

Then I came along and saw her: "Ah, just the little ship I want for a single-handed cruise. . . ."

Humphrey Barton went over her with the nautical equivalent of a fine tooth-comb and pronounced her sound and capable of carrying me safely across deep waters; but not, he added, without certain modifications.

In February, 1952, I became the owner of the sloop *Felicity Ann*, a registered vessel, "with all her guns and appurtenances." But after I had posted the cheque that committed me irrevocably to the practical application of a dream, I walked round and round the mail-box wondering how to get it out again and thinking, "You've done it now, me lass, there's no turning back. . . ."

Chapter 4

SID MASHFORD was sitting in the cockpit of *Felicity Ann* reading through a list of modifications that Humphrey had made out. It was a long list, and Sid was leafing a little impatiently. All yards are used to the strange whims of new owners, a race incapable of accepting a boat as she is and who must immediately set about turning her into something else, but the alterations demanded for *Felicity Ann* were outside the normal for what might be considered a weekend cruiser. Sid knew nothing of my plans. As usual I had tried to keep them under cover, cherishing a fast fading hope I might yet slip away from England when the time came without too many people knowing the reason why. Publicity has its uses, but it can be an awful humbug if your enterprise comes ·unstuck. Far better to act first; then if you succeed you can talk about it with a smug assurance none can deny, and if you fail you don't have an audience saying, "Thought 'e would, the silly so-and-so." A counsel of perfection, however, is seldom practicable.

"There's a lot of work here," said Sid, "and this is our busiest time of year. Everyone wants their boats ready and launched for Easter . . . are you sure all this is necessary?"

I thought I could detect a certain resentment. *FA* was a yard production; designed by Sid and built by the firm. There are few things a man is more sensitive about than the qualities of his boat. Humphrey had sent specifications, made out by the firm of Laurent Giles, for entirely new rigging—"as the mast is stepped on deck we cannot take any chances," Humphrey had written—and drawings for a reduced sail plan, which meant taking six feet off the mast and eight inches off the boom. There was to be a watertight and self-draining cockpit. A 25-

gallon water tank fitted under the cockpit. A spray hood for the protection of the helmsman. There were drawings, too, for high steel stanchions, "anything less than 30 inches is useless," stated Humphrey emphatically. These were for lifelines to keep the crew (me) within bounds, and a pulpit to fence in the stem-head and prevent the crew (me) from plunging headlong over the bows. There were further drawings for two beautiful staysails, twin sails for running down-wind, with appropriate specifications for the booms to wing them out, and stays to hank them on, and topping lifts to support the booms. An extra pair of steel straps was called for to strengthen the coach-roof.

They were, I could see, somewhat exaggerated requirements for anyone apparently just wanting a splash and a bobble in the Sound on a sunny Sunday afternoon.

"You see," I said at last in desperation, "I want to sail her across the Atlantic."

Sid shuffled the lists and read a paragraph through before looking up again.

"Alone?" he asked.

"Yes."

"Oh," he said, folding the lists and putting them in his pocket. "Oh. Well . . . we will have to see what we can do."

No one seemed to be surprised about the project except the one person concerned.

Fitting out is a snowball operation, increasing as it goes along. I added a few notions of my own, mostly concerning lockers. I was locker happy, and had a locker built in wherever there was an open space. I visualised sailbags and paint pots being flung about in an inextricable confusion without anything to restrain them, so lockers were put in both sides from the head forrard. An expensive bilge pump was installed in the cabin, although there was already one in the cockpit; but bilge pumps have been known to choke, and I reckoned that when you want

43

a bilge pump you want one more than anything else on earth and are not likely to count the cost. The installation of the compass, an ex-R.A.F. surplus grid type, gave us a bit of a headache. It had to be visible from the cockpit, out of the way, protected, but away from metal. It was eventually put in gimbals and screwed to a shelf in the cabin on the aft port bulkhead, through which a port was cut so that the compass could be seen from the cockpit. This meant that one always had to steer sitting on the port side. It is normal to sit on the lee side, but the advantage of being a novice is that one has no fixed habits.

All the work on *FA* was carried out by the man who originally built her, Bert, and an apprentice, Ginger, a lengthy youngster, who had to fold into the most fearful contortions when working in *FA*'s tiny cabin, but contrived, nevertheless, like Vancouver, to sing continuously at his work. Bert was a builder of the old school, a man of few words who wore his teeth on Sundays. The work was overseen by Sid officially, and the other five Mashford brothers unofficially, and anyone who happened to be passing by. For *FA* was a yard pet. Everyone, whether actively concerned in the job or not, had her welfare at heart, and was determined that *she* would not fail through any lack or oversight on the part of Cremyll Shipyard, whatever her skipper might do.

Fitting out in the yard at the same time was the *Catania*, an elegant 12-tonner, a cutter, owned by a young American, Norman Fowler, who planned to sail her home. Norman had bought the *Catania* some few weeks before I became the owner of *Felicity Ann*, and he knew as much about sailing as I did, which was a source of great comfort to both of us. Together we could discuss our forthcoming ventures in familiar non-nautical terms of one syllable and present a united front of ignorance to a world of experts. After a study of Humphrey's survey one day,

I said thoughtfully to Norman, "There is just one thing that worries me about my ship—she has only one bilge stringer."

And Norman answered, "Oh, Ann, how *awful* . . . what is it?"

Yet we were the only two people in Plymouth, that town of historic departures, who were planning long voyages.

Moreover, we both planned similar voyages. We intended to sail in April or May, straight for Madeira, none of your fiddling little port-to-port hops for us (mainly because we wouldn't know what to do with a port having made one); and at Madeira we intended to stay no longer than necessary to take on oil and water. Then, having topped up with provisions and taken a deep breath, we would sail smack across the Ocean in the Trade Wind belt to arrive in Antigua not later than the end of July, before the hurricane season set in in the West Indies. A nice straightforward itinerary with no nonsense about it. But after Antigua our ideas petered out. Norman talked largely of carrying on through the Panama and on to California, only another five thousand miles or so. I thought vaguely of spending the hurricane season refitting in English Harbour, Antigua, having heard it was the safest harbour in the area when hurricanes are about, then pottering on through the islands to Florida and on to New York, but this had an improbable, nebulous quality about it, as if I intended after the moon to go on to Mars.

Norman was highly strung, temperamental, spontaneous, and unpredictable. He would be executing a ballet dance in the sheds one minute, with giant leaps and entrechats—to the utter stupefaction of the yard hands—and talking sombrely of retiring to a monastery the next. He would discuss any subject that occurred with an impatient fluency and utter disregard of interruption that completely threw the stolid British reserve with which he was surrounded. The stolid British reserve took him very seriously and was frightened silly both by him and for him, and it was vastly relieved when he was joined for the voyage by

Edward Allcard, who had already crossed the Atlantic twice single-handed and wished to return to the States to collect a boat he had waiting there for yet more voyaging. The stolid British reserve evinced no such anxiety on my account, their faith in the national characteristic of muddling through being no doubt unimpaired.

The *Catania* sailed at the beginning of May to the usual accompaniment of press, cameras, and cheers. "Hurry up, and we'll celebrate in Madeira," said Norman, and I thought if I got to Madeira I would need to celebrate. Then a week later, when we were all speculating as to their whereabouts and figuring they must be nearing Madeira, I had a card from Norman. They were in Brest. Stress of weather. Norman said it was tough but fun. I wondered. Not for long, however; I was soon to be under way myself; preparations had reached a crescendo and the lists were getting shorter.

These lists are an inherent part of the boating business. Once you buy a boat you start making lists, and as long as she, or any other boat, is in your possession you go on making lists. I daresay once having acquired the habit it is yours for life. No voyage is complete without them, certainly no voyage *could* be completed without them. There are lists of provisions, lists of tools, lists of domestic requirements (housekeeping goes on even on a boat), lists of engine spares, lists of bosun's gear, lists of paints, fuels, and big things like anchors and lights, ropes, warps, wire, sheets, halyards, and sails, and little things like blocks, shackles, nuts, bolts, brass eyes, screws, cuphooks, and copper tacks, and lists, endless, interminable, and apparently ever-increasing, of Work To Be Done.

There are stowage lists, disclosing the oddest assortment of companions; cottonwool, batteries, disinfectant, radio spares, vitamins, and bandages, together with one tin of sausages, in one compartment. Chocolate, pepper, and spare logline in

46

another. Interspersed in the margins are terse little notes: "See Sid" (or Bert or Jim), "Tell Joe" (or Bill or Harry). Train times, from unnamed departure points to unspecified destinations. "Friday morning," heavily underlined. Telephone numbers and addresses without any names attached. Dateless weather reports—"vis. good to mod."—and simply, quite inexplicably, "Mallard," no doubt very relevant at the time.

Making out these lists, quite apart from acting upon them, brings the enterprise into focus in a way nothing else can. One wants copper tacks, but how many? Spare canvas for patching—but how much and what weight? Spare rope—but what size and how long? Nothing must be forgotten. Nothing must be overlooked. Everything must be stowed so that it is fast, immovable, accessible, and dry, *without* disturbing the trim of the ship. This is impossible. In a small ship like *FA*, things are either going to get wet, or be impossible to get at. They are going to put the ship down by the head, down by the stern, or just generally down. It is an insoluble problem which one refuses to face as such. We raised the waterline on *FA* four inches and hoped for the best.

And food—what does one need? A healthy active man leading an open air life needs about three pounds of food a day, so the book says. I worked out a beautifully balanced diet, proteins, carbohydrates, and stuff on this basis, only to discover in due course that my whole system revolted against such arbitrary regulation.

Medical supplies were reduced to drammamine, Veganin, benzedrine, acriflavine, bandages, common sense, and a reliance upon normal good health.

During the three months fitting out period I stayed at an excellent little hotel in Cawsand, one of those stone villages only Cornwall can grow straight up out of the sea as part of the local scenery, and every morning walked three practically vertical miles to the shipyard. There I got into overalls and under everyone's feet, deluding myself I was doing a job of work. I did all the painting, bottom and topsides and deck; and all the varnish work; and all the preparing and stopping and sanding, under the impression I was Getting To Know the Ship, whilst skilled men like Bert did all the serious work.

At weekends I used to take the ferry over to Plymouth and a bus from there to Torquay to dwell further upon the wonders of celestial navigation with the Commander. This used to be pretty discouraging for him, as although I can grasp the essentials of such things with fair ease I am incapable of doing the simplest arithmetic because I cannot add. I faced up to and accepted this disability about the time I realised I should never grow into the lean dark type, but it was new to the Commander and he found it alarming, for modern methods of celestial navigation, once you know your way about the tables, rely entirely upon simple addition and subtraction. Commander Lund never quite lost heart, but he looked purse-mouthed and said I had better bring the boat round to Torquay before I set off, to do some practical navigation under his supervision. I did not like to say so, but knew this would be useless. I am too suggestible. So long as people do not know or realise my limitations, so long as they show confidence in my abilities, there is a good chance that I will pull off whatever it is I am trying to do. But if anyone tells me I am no good, I can do nothing but agree, and that is fatal. To sail the boat about before departure and make a public display of my limitations would serve only to undermine my morale without contributing anything towards arithmetical accuracy. I clung to a private conviction that these errors, if not observed too closely, would cancel themselves out, and that it would be all right on the night if I was allowed to play the part my way. So I said nothing and continued to work out theoretical problems that left me stranded on a reef or in the middle of an African desert because I had forgotten to move the decimal point or carry ten.

At last the *Felicity Ann* was launched, the mast was stepped and the work on her took on a more active character. Sorties were made into the Sound to see how the ship and her equipment behaved. I did not take her out alone, of course, but always dragged one or other of the Mashford brothers along by putting the onus on them—you fixed her, you see she works—which they most certainly did. No yard could have done more or charged less. If ever I fit out again in England I will do so at the Cremyll Shipyard, though it would not surprise me in the least if, when they saw me coming, they jacked up the whole works and took to the hills. *FA* was the smallest ship in the yard that spring, but there is no doubt but that she caused more commotion than all the rest put together. Those trial trips out to the breakwater were fun, and they were revealing too. One of them for instance, was responsible for having the cockpit coamings raised and the spray hood constructed, which Humphrey had suggested but I had rejected in one of my periodic attacks of meanness as being nice to have but not essential. But Sid got wet one windy afternoon and decided it would be a whole lot wetter in the real sea, so up went the coamings and on went the hood, additions I was to be very grateful for later on.

By now, of course, my secret was known to only a few million people. Almost strangling with fright, I had been induced to mention it over the West Country radio, and press men were bobbing up all over the place. With a bludgeoning enthusiasm that startled even me, I had raised contracts from the *Sunday Chronicle* in England and *Life* Magazine in America for the exclusive story of the voyage, because even dreamers have to eat. The editors showed a lively interest in the project, mixed with an eager impatience to have me get on with the job.

I had tried to keep the venture, which was a serious one for me, out of the stunt class, and so had asked for nothing in the way of equipment. Nevertheless things came unasked. Messrs

Heinz supplied six dozen self-heating cans of soups. The makers of the Tissot watch presented a wrist watch. Smiths an alarm clock. An ex-Merchant Service officer, himself fitting out for a round the world voyage, sent a chronometer watch in gimbals. The B.K. Motor Co. of Plymouth supplied batteries for the radio and flashlights. The British Paints Co. gave paints and varnish, a little wistfully as they were always doing this and no one ever got anywhere, but you never knew. The Coventry Victor Motor Co., on learning that one of their engines was bound across the Ocean in charge of a feather-headed female, sent post haste their chief maintenance engineer to overhaul the engine and make sure it was correct to the last split pin, and provided a handsome bunch of spares.

Everyone who had a hand in getting the *Felicity Ann* ready for sea, from first to last, whether they worked on the ship, provided the gear, stores, or valuable advice, did a noble job. In the end there was nothing for me to do but go.

Chapter 5

THE actual realisation of a dream is neither better nor worse than imagined. It is entirely different. Before setting out, I thought I had no illusions about the voyage or sailing alone. I expected to be lonely. I expected to be frightened. What I did not expect was the positive panic of emotion that swamped me at the outset of the voyage. I was so lonely that whenever a ship appeared I could not take my eyes off her until she vanished. Once I turned and followed a trawler for nearly an hour, although she was apparently bound for Iceland, because I could not bear the friendless vista of an empty sea. Loneliness does not come from the physical state of being on one's own so much as from fear, the same old fear that stems from ignorance; and having thrust myself out into the unknown with only myself to rely on, I had reverted at once to the primitive. A child with a bogey round every corner. I was not only afraid of the wind and the sea. I was afraid of the ship. I was afraid of reefing the sails, or putting them up or changing them in any way. I was afraid of stopping the engine, and having stopped it, afraid of starting it again.

The numbness with which I set out wore off very slowly, and the first few days passed in a frightened haze upon which the entries in my log book throw very little light. These entries were mostly recordings of times, a sort of notch-cutting to mark the passing of hours. It is inconceivable that I did not eat for five days, but there is no mention of my having done so, and I cannot recall a single meal, not even a cup of coffee. Fortunately I was not seasick, but I had guarded against *that* contingency by repeated does of drammamine, a very effective protection against seasickness, the only snag being that it is inclined to make one drowsy. Neither do I remember actually going to sleep during those first few days, though I must have done so. I do remember feeling so tired that my only ambition was to fold up and sleep for a week.

The second night out is identifiable in my memory because of fog. Nothing particularly horrific occurred, except that a steamer loomed up astern and scared me even more witless, quite unnecessarily, as she sheered off to starboard and disappeared into the murk, wailing like a lost soul. The rest of the night was spent in clammy discomfort in the cockpit, expecting to be run down any moment.

The course I was trying to steer was sou'westerly but this was hampered by a head wind, so I made in a general southerly direction, plotting estimated positions by dead reckoning on the chart. I made several attempts to take sights with the sextant, and found it a very different proposition in real life, infinitely more difficult than taking a sight from the high cliffs of Devon with the Commander standing by with a stop watch. The high cliffs of Devon stay put on their nice firm underpinnings, but the deck of a lively little vessel offers a poor support for an inexperienced sight-taker. I concluded it was an impossible undertaking and unreasonable of anyone to think otherwise.

On the fourth day out the log read 230 miles. By then it seemed I had spent a lifetime at sea, and there was another 700 miles to go to Madeira. How embarrassing it would be if Madeira failed to turn up at the appointed time. There was, so far as I could see, very little reason why it should. And what would one do then? Turn right? Or left? Or keep straight on? Or accost a passing vessel, "Have you seen Madeira lately?"

Then, as if a kindly Fate interposed to keep me from getting too discouraged, the following night granted a few hours of sheer magic. One of those rare glorious experiences that lift you right out of the commonplace (though God knows there is little of the commonplace about being at sea single-handed) on to Olympian heights of delight. The wind had backed right round to the northeast, and *Felicity Ann* was flying before it, her boom way out and lifting, tugging at the mainsheet as if she was alive and impatient of restraint. Her mainsail, taut and straining, was silhouetted against the night sky. And the night sky was a black velvet backcloth for countless glittering stars. Wavelets tumbled in a foam of phosphorescence spilling a thousand bright jewels on the sea. A comet spanned the heavens leaving a broad white wake across the sky even as the ship sped over the waves leaving a broad white wake on the water. All the loneliness and the fears were forgotten, dissolved into nothing by an ecstasy of being so pure, so complete, that nothing else mattered or existed. There was no past, no future, only the participation of a brilliant present. An exquisite distillation of the meaning of life.

Then the kind Fate went off duty. Before dawn it was blowing all hell and I was staring in horror at the mounting waves. I reefed the main and, when that was not enough, took it in altogether and changed the staysail for the storm jib. The dawn was scowling and bleak, overhung with a canopy of low cloud. Later, the wind eased a little but left a heavy cross sea for the ship to wallow in. I was in no mood for another bout with the sails, so started the engine and plugged on towards the never-never land of Madeira.

Then the ship began to behave strangely. So much was obvious even to me. She seemed sluggish, rising to the seas with an effort, quite unlike her usual buoyancy, and she rolled with a slow deliberation as if waterlogged. I slid back the hatch and looked into the cabin. She was waterlogged. The cabin was awash, with water way up over the floor-boards and slopping from side to side, leaving an oily tidemark on the woodwork. Both bilge pumps were jammed solid when I tried to use them. Anyone else would have pulled up the floor-boards, baled the

53

ship out, cleared the pumps, found out why the water was coming in, and taken steps to stop it. I did none of these things. They never occurred to me. I was too stupid with fatigue, too tense and too tired from an excess of experience to think constructively. I was confused, and wanted to stop and take stock of the situation. I wanted to be still and free from the incessant motion, I wanted, most desperately, to sleep. The ship was half full of water which I was unable to get out by the obvious methods, therefore I must find somewhere where I could start thinking again under normal conditions. I looked at the chart and decided to make for Brest, the nearest port, about 70 or 80 miles away if my reckoning was correct.

Later on in the morning the clouds lifted and broke apart, the sun shone and my outlook improved enormously until the colour of the water changed to light green. This was disturbing, as it was different and therefore probably dangerous. Everything was suspect at that stage of my seagoing, which no amount of reassurance from the charts and reckoning could allay.

I passed two fishing boats, very gay and colourful and French, neither of them fishing, but lying to, rolling heavily, evidently waiting for the tide or weather. The fishermen, as colourful as their boats, leant over the side and watched our progress with interest. Some of them waved and I waved back, much heartened by the sight of real live people. Then it occurred to me it would be sensible to ask for a position check, so I turned back to the nearest ship, a bright blue, broad-beamed trawler called *Fends les Vagues*, which seemed a pretty appropriate choice under the circumstances. I motored round and round her trying to convey in basic French and Indian sign language what I wanted. "Où est Brest?" I shouted, that being the nearest I could get to expressing my needs. Fishermen crowded to the bulwarks, looking eager, interested, and absolutely blank. I expressed these needs several times on both sides of the fishing boat, up wind and down wind, but succeeded only in throwing the entire crew into a fever of excitement as they threshed from side to side across the deck trying to keep me in sight. I motored round to the stern of the vessel and read the port of registry. Douarnenez. All right then: "Où est Douarnenez?" I tried, with no better result, and regretted, not for the first, nor by any means the last, time in my life, having started something that was proving difficult to continue and impossible to stop. And I would have gone on my way, but a handsome young man wearing a dashing cap and chewing on a cigarette end and looking as if he had stepped straight out of a French movie, authoritatively waved me alongside, a manœuvre I accomplished with a masterly and quite unexpected precision. Several agile men then leapt down on to FA and held her off with a dramatic show of strength and dexterity. "Venez abord, Madame," invited the handsome young skipper courteously, and completely fascinated by the turn of events, I climbed up on the trawler, a fairly athletic feat, and appreciated as such by the onlookers, as the two ships were rolling wildly and inharmoniously.

"Et maintenant," said the skipper politely. "Qu'est-ce que vous desirez, Madame?"

I pointed to FA, to the chart I had had the forethought to bring with me, made a sweeping gesture in the general direction of where Brest ought to be, said "Brest" in a loud clear voice, and hoped it conveyed the general idea. The fishermen crowded round the chart, gazing intently at it as if looking for X marks the spot. "Douarnenez," said one of them suddenly, pointing it out triumphantly as if he had found the key to the problem; and the rest nodded wisely. But the skipper tapped me on the shoulder, said something I freely translated into "Radio," pointed to the wheelhouse, and beckoned. I followed him into the wheelhouse, down a companionway, and into the main cabin. This compartment, a large piratical-looking affair, managed to give the effect of guttering candles in spite of electric light. There were tiers of berths all round the sides, built-in like the old "but-and-bens" of Highland cottages, a few wooden kegs at strategic points, and if there had been a roll of parchment on the chart table I would have accepted it unquestioningly; but it was a D.F. chart, and the delicious atmosphere of Treasure Island was thrown off centre somewhat by the incongruous intrusion of a huge radio, which jutted out into the cabin and occupied most of the forward bulkhead.

The skipper went to this functional-looking machine, handed me a pair of headphones, put on a pair himself, switched on the ship-to-shore apparatus and called up Brest. I could not follow all the moves in the game, but caught the general gist. The shore operator and the skipper held an animated discussion to which I listened with admiration, wondering how they managed to communicate without seeing one another, French conversation being so visual. Then the skipper turned to me, indicating it was question time and to go ahead. I took fright at once, "Mais, je ne parle pas Français," as if he didn't know. And the next thing, there was Land's End at the other end of the phone. Small world. Feeling the situation was getting away from me, I tried to explain.

"I only want to check my position. The, er, ship, my ship . . . yacht *Felicity Ann* out of Plymouth . . . is making a bit of water and the pumps are jammed. I am going into Brest to fix things . . . just an idea, you know, to get a position check, but my, huh, French isn't up to it." Nor my English either.

"You are on board the trawler now?" The operator at Land's End sounded puzzled. "Are they giving you a tow in?"

"Oh, *no*," I said, very British and liable to give a light laugh any moment. "It is nothing serious . . . all I want is a position check. . . ."

"That I can't give you," said he briskly. "Ask the skipper . . . he'll tell you. Good luck."

Well now, I thought, that had been the idea. Still . . . "Thanks," I said, "I will."

There was an outbreak of Gallic garrulity on the air and the skipper signed off, looking pleased with himself at having given a demonstration of the modern mysteries of science. He leant over the chart table with the expression of a magician about to produce a truly enormous rabbit out of the hat, but the trick was interrupted by a great commotion breaking out on deck. Amidst the general confusion, anguished cries of "le petit bateau" were recognisable. The skipper's expression changed to one of alarm and he flew up the companionway. I flew after.

Felicity Ann had broken away and was careering off under bare poles with three fishermen aboard. They stood on deck looking helpless and rather woebegone at having been abducted. This escape produced more activity aboard the trawler than a tiger at large in a cattle market. Gesticulating men rushed to and fro, leaping up and down companionways, running into one another, and skipping over fishing gear. Ropes were thrown, orders shouted, bells rung, machinery started, and with a roar of mighty engines the trawler got under way. Cheer-leaders yelled encouragement to the men on *FA*, to me, to one another, and to everyone in earshot. With the maximum of fury and the minimum of effort *FA* was waylaid, captured, and tied up alongside.

The three men immediately climbed back on to the trawler, much relieved for themselves, but very concerned for me, having discovered the water in the cabin. "Trop de l'eau," they cried in great agitation. "Oh, trop," I agreed. And a passionate discussion took place among the men. Finally the skipper detached himself from the committee meeting to inform me of the findings. Catching about one word in ten, I understood him to say that fishing being what it was, and *FA* being in the state she was, why didn't I let them tow her into Douarnenez? Frankly, it seemed a very good idea. I had never been to Douarnenez, I had never been aboard a French trawler before,

and surely one of the reasons for coming to sea was the assimila-
tion of new experiences, so why not? Then I thought of what
tows mean in the marine world, and said the only word I knew
in the language to cover the situation: "Combien?" which the
skipper brushed aside as an insult to chivalry, and action was
taken to put *FA* in tow.

She got away again, by herself this time, and I was really
worried for a moment, but once again, amidst fearful tumult,
she was caught, and finally lashed up short under the stern so
that she had no option but to follow the trawler's every move.
When assured that "le petit bateau" was safe and under control,
the men went through a convincing demonstration of eating in
mime, and we all trooped below.

There did not appear to be a regular cook in the crew; they
all fixed their own meals, producing from personal lockers
knives, forks, plates, mugs, long loaves of bread, and bottles of
wine, then vanished one by one into the galley to reappear with
an omelette, fried fish, or whatever. They vied with one another
to fix a meal for me. Everyone contributed something, brook-
ing no refusal, and as it was a large crew I hogged the biggest
meal since the two-egg breakfast in Plymouth. The conversation
flowed as easily as the wine, so that we gathered all sorts of
interesting and doubtless entirely erroneous information about
one another, and in no time flat what remained of the afternoon
and evening was gone. Then the skipper put his hands together,
rested the side of his face on them and closed his eyes, the rest
of the crew following suit to make the meaning quite clear.
They pointed to the bunk by. the radio and said, "Pour
vous, Madame." It was the skipper's. What sailor could offer
more?

I rolled into the bunk and pulled the blanket up round my
ears, revelling in the indescribable bliss of the prospect of a whole
night's sleep.

"Bonne nuit, dormez bien," called the men. The lights went

out. All was quiet but for the muffled throb of the engine, a giant heart beating in the night, and the secret sounds of a ship moving through the water. The barely perceptible motion, a smooth lifting and rolling, was soothing, soporific: I faded out of consciousness, inexpressibly content. Lovely, lovely people ... blessed . . . blessed sleep. . . .

Chapter 6

"It is a good thing I am honest," said Georges, after the last reporter had been ferried ashore, "I could say *anything*. . . ."

"What a chance you've missed . . . or have you? The truth will out when the reports are published," I said idly, staring across the blue bay to the green hills on the far side.

"But I will only have to translate for you and you will never know," grinned Georges.

We were lazing on the deck of his boat, the *Breveertein*, a converted pilot cutter, which Georges referred to as a Plymouth hooker, moored stern on to the breakwater in the Douarnenez yacht basin. *Felicity Ann* was tied up alongside, using the *Breveertein* as a floating dock, for the tides there are enormous, having a rise and fall of between 30 and 35 feet. Strangers to the harbour are apt to leave their dinghies tied to the quay on a line that leaves them hanging by their teeth at low water. With a small ship like *FA* it is infinitely more comfortable to use some-one else's moorings under such circumstances, and rise and fall with the bigger ship on the tide.

Georges was Dutch, but spoke English so well I thought at first he was British. He also spoke French as well as he spoke English, and by acting as my interpreter since arriving in port enabled me to retire, if not with honour at least with ease, from the linguistic combat. But the day after our session with the Press he came fuming back from the shore.

"I will never believe in anyone again, never, never," he cried, climbing aboard the *Breveertein* with a batch of papers under his arm. He threw some of them into the cockpit of *Felicity Ann* where I was busy putting eyesplices in every rope's end I could lay hands on, having just learnt how to do them.

"There—see what they say—and they seemed so nice, those reporters, too."

"Translate for me, Georges."

"No. I've finished translating. You will have to learn French."

"Lon, Paul-Emile," I appealed to Georges' crew and confrères who were pottering about the deck. "Please translate for me?"

Lon leapt over on to *FA* and settled in the cockpit, picked up one of the papers and started to unfold an entirely new legend.

"Alors," he said. "This is very interesting. You have eyes of the sea . . . ah, blue, yes, that is right. But, you wear round your neck 'une cutlass énorme'—quelle femme formidable—do you?"

I showed him the clasp knife on a lanyard I wear when working on board.

My encounter with the trawler was depicted in the most stirring terms. A dramatic rescue from a watery grave. *FA* was on the point of foundering in a raging gale, but her skipper, true to the traditions of the sea, resisted all attempts at rescue, preferring to go down with the ship (like hell). However, my "saviour" dragged me, resisting all the way, from the cruel sea, and towed the sinking vessel into port. Quite a party it must have been. The *Flying Enterprise* episode was still fairly fresh in the public mind and it was unthinkable I could be any less heroic. . . .

The writer of this gallant tale had interviewed Madame aboard her tiny vessel in the port of Douarnenez where Madame was resting herself after her harrowing experience, chain smoking, the rugged hussy, amid a medley of whiskey bottles. . . .

"Rum," I said darkly, looking across at Georges. "One bottle, and he wasn't averse to it either, the ——." Georges rattled his newspaper and said nothing.

Lon continued: "Madame Davison has no . . . does not speak French, but Madame is not incommoded . . . it does not matter

61

because Georges . . ." He looked up, "Ah, Georges, you are famous now . . . acts as her interpreter, having become . . . during her short stay . . . her ami et confidant . . . why"—Lon gave a yelp of delight—"he is practically your lover!" Georges, furious, got up and went below. S'truth, I thought, I may not be a raving beauty, but he need not look quite so revolted. Lon, mistaking my expression said, "Why not? He is quite a nice fellow. Oh, listen, this is good—it says here—every evening Madame sings sad . . . plaintive Irish songs, accompanying herself on her har . . . harmonium, and it is now Georges' favourite occupation listening to her!"

"WHAT?"

"That is what it says here!"

It said a whole lot more in a similar strain quite unrelated to or restricted by anything resembling the truth. Other papers and magazines presented no less lurid accounts. *Felicity Ann* was variously described as a ketch, a schooner, a yawl, and even as a miniature replica of the *Reliance*. My motive for making this single-handed attempt at crossing the Atlantic was unanimously imputed to one of revenge. The free imagination of the French press was something I just had to learn to take, for there was nothing to be done about it. It may be controversial that a country gets the government it deserves, but it undoubtedly gets the sort of stuff it wants to read, and the French like their reading strongly spiced. They fairly lapped up the Ann Davison capers, and I tried not to notice, only it was a bit hard to stop by for an apéritif to see it all pinned up over the bar, with a picture of me looking like an angry Britannia, and have the fishermen sipping their vin rouge look up bright-eyed and eager, hoping I would live up to the brave, swashbuckling female Casanova character with which I had been endowed by the press.

The English newspapers contributed in some measure to all this by insisting on ringing me up through the local police station, thus investing the venture with an importance out of all

Felicity Ann sailing in Plymouth Sound

H.M.S. *Eagle* looks down on *Felicity Ann's* trials in the Sound

proportion, and throwing the little Breton port into yet further transports of delight and expectation; for cross-Channel calls were not so numerous that they could be lightly ignored.

Yet no one could be less like the devil-may-care death-defying daughter of the sea of their imagination than I. I was mighty glad to have the pumps and a few other things on the boat to fix as an excuse for staying in port, and I was in no hurry at all to get back to sea. This was the break I wanted—the chance to build up a stockpile of courage to go on. For, of course, I intended to go on; but in easy stages, no more ambitious thousand-mile passages until I was tougher and more able. Besides, I had acquired, in the stopover at Douarnenez, a taste for going in places. Surely the main purpose of setting sail from one place was to get to another, and with all the world at one's disposal, it seemed a pity not to see as much of it as possible, to get a slant on more new countries, customs, viewpoints, and fascinating new people.

Even without those six days from Plymouth, which would have made a Lancashire mill town look like fairyland to me, Douarnenez has charm. It is a colourful fishing port, unspoilt by tourism, lying at the end of a long, narrow inlet, narrow only by virtue of its depth inland, eighteen miles from the open sea, amid a surrounding coast and country very Cornish in character. The houses are painted in gay colours, the fishing boats are painted in gay colours, the fishermen wear sailcloth suits of blue or red, straight or mixed, and only the women are sombre in black. But they wear snowy aprons and snowy starched caps of a variety of shapes, tall, short, large or small, or conical, elaborately laced or plain, the construction being indicative of locality.

It was about six o'clock in the morning of May 24th when the trawler *Fends les Vagues* brought her strange catch into port. Word got round in no time and Authority appeared aboard with rather more alacrity than I was ever to meet again. Authority was entertained in the main cabin with the skipper and a few chosen members of the crew in attendance, and of course the inevitable bottle of wine without which no business can be properly conducted in Brittany. With its dubious assistance I touched a new high in French conversation that morning, trying to explain to Authority why I was there. However, it was all settled amicably judging by the general expressions of good will and the freedom with which the bottle made its rounds, and when it was finished and the last official paper signed and put away, I was swept away on a tide of Breton hospitality. People were called up from all over town to provide ease for a sailor: baths, food, entertainment, even money to enable me to cable to England for more and let the nation, via the press, know where I was—as if it cared. The boat was baled out and the pumps removed for cleaning and repair; their removal was not strictly necessary, of course, but things have a way of happening very quickly in a foreign language, and they were out and away before I fully realised what was taking place.

Then the tide took a literal turn and *FA* was hustled out of the fish dock, which dried out at low water, into the yacht basin which did not, and there took up her station alongside the Dutch boat, then the only other yacht in port.

Within a couple of days Douarnenez lost its strangeness and I felt not only at home but as though I belonged. This was not only due to the extraordinary friendliness on the part of the people there, but because it is part of a sailor's life and one of the attractions of seafaring. When you come into port you cut right through the preliminaries and establish a life complete with its favourite haunts, lifelong friends, and routine almost immediately. A tourist remains an outsider throughout his visit, but a sailor is part of the local scenery from the moment he arrives.

The hospitality of Douarnenez was overwhelming. Along with the boys off the *Breveertein* I was caught up in a social whirl, all the more delightful on account of its unexpectedness— social flings had not been allowed for in the original programme —and we visited sardine factories, a château, attended numerous luncheon and dinner parties, and an endless series of cocktail parties in which each hostess was on her mettle to compete with the last. It was all very delicious and civilised, and there seemed no reason why it should ever stop; the roar of the sea and the whine of the wind seemed remote and unreal. Yet, however deep a sailor's roots appear to go, there comes a time when he suddenly knows it is time to get under way again. For no particular reason; it is just time to go; and no matter how reluctant he is to leave he begins to put his things together—and goes. From some angles I guess I am a natural born sailor; anyway I was getting *FA* stored up and ready for the next bout with the ocean, when the *Daydream* came into port. Seeing strange and obviously yacht masts sticking up over the fish quay, the *Breveertein* boys and I wandered round to see what they were, driven by the seamen's insatiable curiosity. The *Daydream* was bound for Italy with an English delivery crew on board, and because we were hosts by virtue of our having arrived in port first, we asked them round for drinks aboard our boats. The skipper and two of the crew of *Daydream* came along, and first we drank aboard *FA*, but seven below in her cabin crowds things up a little so we moved aboard the *Breveertein* where we mixed drinks and some sort of meal whilst exchanging yarns and sea talk.

"And where are you bound for?" asked the skipper of the *Daydream*, addressing Georges, who looked vague.

"Oh, I don't know. We may go on to Belle Isle later on."

"They've been here seven months," I said. "The Captain hates the sea."

"No more than you," said Georges mildly. "Anyone who goes to sea for fun is crazy. This is the best part of cruising, in port talking about it."

65

The skipper of the *Daydream* looked startled.

"Oh, I wouldn't say that," he protested.

"I would," put in one of his crew, a journalist taking the trip in search of copy. "It is like banging your head against a stone wall, so nice when you stop. All yacht clubs ought to have a visiting psychiatrist."

"It is so cold," said Georges, "so uncomfortable. Look how nice it is now, with everything on the table—they would not stay like that if we were at sea."

"No," added Lon. "Somebody should warn you when you start sailing. No one ever tells you the truth. You read about it in books and it all sounds so . . . so wonderful. You listen to people talking and it is all so exciting. . . . You go into those shops—chandlers—full of things for ships, ropes that smell so good, and it is all so romantic. You walk round the docks and see all the pretty ships and you have to spend hundreds and hundreds of pounds before you find out how AWFUL it is. . . ."

The *Daydream* skipper was plainly an eager yachtsman and ready to square up in defence of the love of his life, but fortunately at this point there was a commotion on deck to distract us all. Georges looked out through the hatch and then called down, "It is Jean, a fisherman I know. He is drunk."

Jean staggered into the cabin, thrust a large flagon of vin rouge on to the table and addressed us not too amicably in an incomprehensible tongue.

"Oh dear," said Georges, "he is speaking Breton. That means he is very drunk."

"I speak very good English. Sure," began Jean and lapsed into a tirade in Breton with a wealth of descriptive gesture.

"He is not happy with his wife," translated Georges, pretty freely I should say. Jean had rolled up his sleeves to display armfuls of scars. He stretched out his hands and cracked each joint lustily.

"What an awful noise," murmured Georges.

66

The skipper and crew of *Daydream* gazed at Jean like a bunch of rabbits fascinated by a boa-constrictor. Then the journalist pulled himself together and attempted to make conversation. "When are you off?" he asked me, with difficulty keeping his eyes averted from Jean, who had produced an enormous knife and was tracing out the scars on his arm with it.

"Tomorrow or the day after," I said.

"Where to?"

Jean leant across the table and stabbed a piece of sausage with his knife.

"North Spain—Corunna or Vigo, depending on the weather and how we go."

"Good show," said the other member of the *Daydream* crew, breaking a monastic silence.

Jean tore the cork out of the bottle of red wine and attempted to top up our glasses of rum, spewing a stream of vin rouge round the cabin, oblivious of our cries of protest. "I speak very good English. Sure," he said. The skipper of the *Daydream*, obviously feeling it was high time he got his men out of here, rose to his feet.

"Nice evening. Thanks," he said. "We'd better be getting back aboard now. Early start in the morning, you know."

We trooped up on deck. It was low tide and a still, starry night, the water was as smooth and glossy as a piece of oiled silk. With an unexpected agility for one so drunk, Jean pulled the dinghy alongside. Georges said, "He says he will take you ashore." The *Daydream* crew stood stockstill. Jean gestured to the dinghy and the journalist, with the bravado of one going to meet the inevitable, climbed over the side and into the dinghy. The skipper was about to follow, but Georges stopped him. "Two in that punt is enough now," he said. Jean jumped over the side, the punt rocked precariously; he pushed off and we held our breaths.

"Goodbye, good luck," shouted the journalist as the dinghy

capsized. We watched him swim to the breakwater, climb the 40-foot steel ladder to the top and run along the quay shouting, "Bloody hell," like the little pigs, all the way home.

Breathing hard and with one hand on the upturned punt, Jean reappeared alongside. We hauled him, dripping, aboard and secured the boat. "That was clever of him, to bring back the dinghy," said Georges in a detached manner.

"Lost the oars," said Paul-Emile sadly.

"Better use the other dinghy," said Lon, bringing it round from the stern half full of water. Before we could stop him Jean leapt into it and sank it. We hauled him aboard again and dragged the dinghy up by the snout and drained it.

"Well. Goodnight," said the skipper of the *Daydream*, preparing to go overside. Jean barred his way and said something rather harshly. Georges translated, "He insists on taking you ashore now. It is a matter of honour." The skipper turned to me. "Get him on your boat whilst we slip ashore," he said.

"Not on your life," I replied promptly. "He is not coming aboard my boat."

"Christ," he said resignedly, and made to climb over the bulwarks. Georges, who had disappeared below, returned clad in oilskins, seaboots, and sou'wester. We looked at him in astonishment. "Looks like rain," he explained. "Lon, look after Jean, we will get rid of him later. I will take them ashore."

Lon and Paul-Emile engaged Jean in talk, whilst the dinghy sneaked away, the skipper and his silent crew standing in the sternsheets. They raised their arms in salute. "Goodbye," they cried in unison, vast relief in their voices. "Goodbye, Ann, *bon voyage*."

The dinghy upended and deposited the three of them in the water. . . .

68

Chapter 7

"GORGEOUS motoring weather," said Lon looking out across the harbour. The morning was bright and sunny; the water in the Bay matched the blue of the sky and there was hardly any wind. Gorgeous motoring weather. The deck of the *Breveertein* was crowded with friends who had come to see me off. Georges was fussing with the jibsheets. He came aft. "Ready?" he asked. "Then I will start the motor for you."

"I had better start it myself," I said, "and get used to the idea. There won't be anyone out there to start it for me."

"All the more reason why someone should do it now," he said climbing through the hatch. The engine started easily enough, and thumped away cheerfully after a couple of swings. I looked round the harbour, at the people aboard *Breveertein*; another little life over. "Well: I can't think of any excuse for staying longer. . . ."

It was eleven o'clock in the morning when I sailed out of Douarnenez on June 10th, down the long arm to the open sea, and it was not until a quarter past six that evening that we cleared Armen Buoy and the curious popples and overfalls outside the Bay. Two hours later I stopped the engine, reefed down and changed the jib and hove to for the night. *Felicity Ann* hove to better reefed down; with full canvas she was inclined to sail on; but also I was not very happy yet about altering sail in the dark, and as there was a smartish northeasterly breeze blowing by then I was not taking any chances. Playing jibs on the pitching foredeck was my undoing, however. I had omitted to take any drammamine and was horribly seasick all night, but by next morning had recovered and got under way, feeling a little wan but firing on all cylinders.

The Bay of Biscay did not live up to its evil reputation, and on the whole we made good time, crossing the Bay, some 300 miles, in five days. This is only an average of 60 miles a day, but a single-hander has really only half a day to sail in as he has to navigate, eat, and sleep sometime. There was a following wind, pretty fresh, most of the time, and there were torrential downpours of rain. Low black clouds dragged across the sky, and heavy grey seas humped up and grumbled after us. I did not care for the weather, but it might have been very much worse. I sailed during the day and hove to each night around eight or nine o'clock to sleep, waking at intervals to look out and see if anything was coming. Ships were many and manifest during the night and in the morning, but unaccountably disappeared during the afternoon.

I was not nearly so lonely this time, a little more knowledgeable, a little less scared, not so tired but still apprehensive and disinclined to take anything on trust. I still grasped the tiller as if holding the ship together by main force.

The radio was not operating, for reasons best known to itself, and I was unable to take any sights that made sense, through sheer lack of skill, it must be admitted; so navigation was purely by dead reckoning, and I wondered what sort of landfall we would make. I was aiming for the N.W. corner of Spain, a little east of it, actually, so as not to miss it altogether and go sailing on and on into the Atlantic. On the night of the 15th a number of insects appeared aboard: flies, moths, and a hunting wasp. I wondered what she thought she was doing out there. A pigeon flew round the ship, took its bearings and flew off. The colour of the sea changed to dark green and all the signs pointed to land near by. The following evening the mountains of Spain stood up stark and clear in the failing light. Lights blinked their signals from the shore, but I could not make them match up with the lights shown on the chart. At first I thought we had made landfall much further east than intended, and was much put out until I recognised the light of Cap Vilano, and then was so pleased at being where I wanted that I washed out any notion of going in to Corunna and decided to carry on for Vigo.

There was no sleep that night. We had joined the main road and the traffic was thick. Motoring, for there was no wind to speak of, down towards Cape Finisterre in company with a vast concourse of shipping, I felt absurdly important at being such a little ship amongst all the big ones; for here were vessels on their way to and from the Mediterranean, Africa, Panama, South and Central America; liners, tankers, freighters, tramps, and ... one small sloop.

About three o'clock in the morning a little breeze sprang up and I went below to switch off the engine. This has a short routine if done properly. You throttle back, unscrew the primer valve and remove the cap and put a rag over it; the engine blows back as it stops and clears its throat so to speak, and the operation makes for easier starting by keeping the primer clear, otherwise it gums up and you develop biceps swinging the engine to not much purpose. It is not a long operation, yet when I came out again into the cockpit the ship was enveloped in thick fog, and the world had shrunk to a radius of a few yards. Knowing the amount of shipping in the vicinity I was very alarmed. I could hear them hooting all around.

On such occasions it is well to keep busy and not dwell too much on the situation. I lit every oil lamp aboard and hung them from strategic points about the ship, lit the cabin light so that it shone through the ports, fixed a flashlight so that the beam illuminated the mainsail, and hoped that the general glow might be noticed if anything came too close. A pretty thin hope, but, if nothing else, the lights imparted a certain cheer—to me.

Through some oversight there was neither bell nor hooter aboard, and no way of making a noise other than beating the bottom of the frying pan, which made a most inadequate little sound, although I did my best, and the frying pan was never any good for omelettes afterwards.

The breeze had faded out altogether with the descent of fog and, as it seemed highly desirable to be mobile, I started the motor again. Then, with a bunch of flares Georges had given me in case of an emergency, I returned to the cockpit to steal quietly on course at quarter throttle, listening with ears like antennæ to the warnings of invisible ships.

One in particular seemed to be coming nearer. A big ship with a deep bass voice like those of the "Queens." I held my breath. It *was* coming nearer. Each hoot was louder than the last, and I could hear a throbbing. . . . It was like being under a stick of bombs during the war—would the next be on or over? I stood up in the cockpit. Suddenly the blast of her hooter nearly blew us out of the water. The whole atmosphere vibrated. I ripped off the top of a flare, nearly blinding myself with its purple brilliance, kicked the throttle wide open, and *FA* leapt from under a roar and a swoosh.

We might just as well have leapt into it, but I could no more have stopped my flight reaction than I could have stopped the progress of that ship. Her next blast came from further away, but I could hardly hear it for the blood beating in my ears, I was so scared. We romped over a monstrous wake and with ears flat back skittered westwards across the shipping-lane with the sole purpose of getting away from it as quickly as possible. For two hours we raced on, and then suddenly shot out of the fog, leaving it behind us like a wall to the eastward. By then it was dawn. I put out the lights, stopped the engine, and flopped on the cabin-sole, dead to the world.

Thirty-six hours later, well off-shore, we were hove-to off what I reckoned to be the vicinity of the entrance to Rio Vigo and the port of Vigo, but could not be certain of this as once again I was unable to make the lights I could see jibe up with the lights on the chart. In any case I was not going to attempt any entries into port at night. Vigo was to be the first port, anywhere, I had ever tried to take a ship into on my own in my life, and I wanted plenty of light on the subject. Also I did not have a detailed chart of Vigo, only a small scale chart of the peninsula (which was why I was having trouble with the lights, the ones I could see were local and not shown on the chart). But I did have the pilot-book for the area, and with the aid of this admirable but rather pessimistic publication was able to identify the river entrance in the morning.

Actually there are two entrances, the river mouth being divided by a group of islands. By the Grace of God I chose the northern one. Without a detailed chart I would have most certainly piled up in the other. It was a brilliant day with a crystal clear atmosphere throwing golden lights on the bold blue mountain tops. It was also blowing pretty hard and there was quite a sea running as we made towards the entrance. It was necessary to reef down, which surprised me as it did not look a very cross day. As we drew near the river mouth I saw a small open boat rolling as if she would roll under, a long narrow-gutted little beast with hardly any freeboard, thoroughly un-stable in appearance and behaviour. I thought she was in difficulties and moved in to see if any assistance was wanted, only to find a man and a boy fishing perfectly happily. It was the most reassuring thing I had seen in years. If they could think nothing of it in that thing, in my comparatively giant ocean cruiser what had I to worry about?

Entering the river, which is fairly wide, I dropped the sails, took in the logline, and put up the ensign and the Q and G flags. The Q to say my ship was healthy and requested free pratique, and the G for a pilot. Having found Vigo, I felt entitled to relax on a bed of laurels and hand over the responsibility of

73

getting *FA* into harbour to the professionals. What do they have pilots for, anyway?

One of the things I never seem to learn is that there is no easy way, no short cut. . . .

Several ships of various sizes overtook *FA*, looked at her indifferently, and pressed on with their affairs with not a sign of a pilot amongst them. So, as they were obviously bound for Vigo, and there seemed no point in hanging about, I decided to follow; but even the slowest of them was making ten knots and was way ahead in no time. Vigo was plain to see, a cluster of dots on the foothills, on the starboard hand about six miles up the river. I thought I had only to watch the ships carefully to see where they docked; but as each ship reached the town she vanished into thin air. So far as I could see there was a long unbroken quay wall fronting the port. I tried to make out the harbour entrance or entrances through the binoculars, but these were just for show, I could see better without them, and I could not see the entrances at all. A large steamer ploughed past, too big for a vanishing trick surely, and I watched it unwaveringly, until something caught my eye to starboard and I glanced up to see a buoy we had shaved by, my guardian angel being more alert than I, and when I looked back at the steamer it had gone. Then I saw her funnel, above and on the other side of the quay wall. Very well, if she could go straight through a concrete wall, so could I.

Hard on the wake of another ship I turned *FA* briskly to starboard and lo, there—open sesame—was the entrance to a dock. But it was not for us. Even without any Spanish I knew what they meant. So round we came and out again and into another dock. That wasn't for us either. We buzzed one or two more to no avail, and then wandered down towards the end of the town. By this time a number of interested and vocal people had gathered at various prominent points. I knew they were giving valuable information and wished I could understand them.

74

At the far end of the town was an imposing white building with tier upon tier of balconies abutting right on to the water. It might have been the local equivalent of the Hôtel Splendide, but it was shaped like a liner with a funnel on the topmost balcony, so I decided—you know my methods, Watson—that it must be the Vigo Yacht Club. A quay ran from this building parallel to the shore, and on the seaward side of it was a large glossy black yacht lying at anchor. Altogether the prospects seemed much brighter. I taxied along to the end of the quay and peeped round the corner. Sure enough, there was a narrow entrance into what was unmistakably a yacht basin, a little congested, but indubitably a haven for small stray ships. Right in the fairway was a man in a rowing boat. He waved me away.

"Damn," I thought, "no room anywhere in this hell-fired inn," and turned back.

There was a bustle aboard the black yacht. She appeared to be getting ready to get under way, but I espied the blue ensign she was flying and rushed over to her.

"Where can I tie up?"

They looked surprised and pointed to the yacht basin. . . . "In there . . . plenty of water. . . ."

"But . . ."

The anchor was up and they were away.

Disconsolately I motored back to the yacht basin where the rowing boat was still blocking the entrance. Very vigorously the man waved me away.

There was nothing for it, apparently, but to sit like a beggar outside the castle walls, and anchor.

The big fisherman anchor was lashed down on to the grid over the chain locker and covered by a number of sailbags and other bulky items that seemed to gravitate naturally to the forepeak. These I pitched on to the cabinsole, then unfastened the lashings, lying on my stomach because there isn't even sitting

75

headroom there, and fought the anchor out on to the foredeck. It was folded for stowing and wired. I went back into the cabin for the pliers, then out again to cut the wire. I tried to remove the canvas cover from the navel pipe, but the knots on the lashing were too tight for my fingers. I felt for the "cutlass énorme" but it wasn't there. So back again to the cabin for a knife.

Meanwhile FA was going round and round in circles at a speed that felt faster than light. I throttled back. The engine promptly stopped. Down into the cabin I went to start it. I put her out of gear to let her drift, but the motor without any load on screamed like an aircraft engine on a test bench, so I put her into gear and FA took a flying leap at the sea wall. I spun her round and went out into the middle of the river to cool off.

By now the quays and balconies of the Yacht Club were black with people. The whole town had turned out to watch.

The show must go on. I put the tiller over so that FA galloped round in circles again like a circus horse and went forrard to heave out the anchor chain. A fathom came out and then it stopped. I went below to see why it had jammed. A ship hooted imperatively. I scrambled out into the cockpit to find a tanker bearing down at a rate of knots no more than 30 yards away. I skated from under her bows and contemplated cutting my throat.

There was now considerable excitement ashore. Hundreds of people were shouting and waving.

I abandoned the anchor project and decided to have one last shot at the yacht basin. The man was still in the entrance waving me away but I was in an ugly mood and prepared to run him down, at which he looked inexplicably pleased and moved out of the way. Throwing check lines in all directions, I fetched up alongside the biggest yacht in the basin, and a cheer went up from the crowd.

Three men immediately jumped on board and before my very eyes started stripping the ship. With incredible rapidity they

76

whipped off the sails, removed lights, log, flags, ensign, jack-staff, boathook, twin booms, sheets, anchor, warps and such, until the deck was as clear and unencumbered as an egg. They piled the gear into the cabin so that it was crammed almost to the deckhead. I was afraid they might unstep the mast and try and put that in too, but although they looked it over searchingly, they let it stay. Later, when the dust had settled and an English-speaking Spaniard arrived on the scene so that I stopped being a deaf mute and joined the human race again, I learned that this was simply a precaution against thieving.

I also learned that the Spanish gesture for "Come on" is ours for "Go away."

More than that, I learned I had come into port flying a rather unusual signal. Being of an economical turn of mind and know-ing no better, I had flown the Q and G flags on the same hal-yard, one above the other, making a two letter signal QG, "Send all the lifeboats you have." But I could not get red in the face about it. I was in Vigo, five hundred miles from where I had started: there were stumpy little palm trees lining the promenade on the opposite side of the yacht basin, and the loud-speaker system was playing "Autumn Leaves" (which ever since has evoked that same small glow of satisfaction). I had sailed from England to North Spain alone in my own ship, and if my progress had been rather more than ragged, what of it? I had arrived. So why hadn't they sent those lifeboats—with St Bernards and brandy to boot?

Chapter 8

PEOPLE in Vigo were careful to point out to me that the north was not the *real* Spain (later, when I was in Gibraltar and making trips across the border into Southern Spain, they told me there that wasn't the real Spain either). Whatever the standards of Spanish reality may be, Vigo seemed genuine enough to me and very charming. A little white seaport tucked away up a river and incongruously set against a background of blue mountains, thriving, bustling, packed with interest, and brand new people. I was fascinated by the Spain I saw, a brilliant, boldly shadowed scene, and I was fascinated by the Spanish way of life, which was new to me fresh from an environment where equality, equal pay, and efficiency were the bywords if not the criterion.

The Spanish have all the time in the world: something attracts their attention and they can watch it for hours. They stood on the quays, massed shoulder to shoulder, silent like Cortez on that old peak of his, and studied *Felicity Ann* as if she was a visitation from outer space. Occasionally someone would hiss "Psst . . . pssssst . . . Señora!" with the hope of luring me on deck so that they could study La Navigante Solitaria as well; for a lone female sailor was the strangest thing they had ever heard of and well worth a good hour's staring time. For Spain is essentially a man's country, where everything is assessed, approached, and judged from the masculine angle. All the advertising is directed at him, even the stores put the emphasis on things like shirts and ties and shaving lotion to catch his buying eye, for the male is supreme and the women just tag along. Before marriage the girls are guarded like specie, and after marriage they are homebodies guarding their own daughters, and there is no nonsense about whether father is head of the household. Not that I have the slightest doubt but that women, being what they are, get their own way in Spain as well as anywhere else. In the really low income brackets, as they say in these bureaucratic times, the lord and master rides ahead on a midget donkey with matchstick legs, whilst his spouse, the worker bee, follows with the baggage, which she totes on her head—a practice resulting in a truly magnificent carriage. All the peasant women walk like queens and all the others like courtesans.

It was natural, then, that the advent of a lone woman sailor stretched Spanish credulity to the limit. They were far too polite to do other than stare and stare and stare, but you could see that speculation was rife.

It is a country of contrasts: light and shade: gaiety and despair: spontaneity and a rigid regard for protocol: indifference to the point of cruelty to animals and a passionate love for children. Family life seemed very close and jolly, though at first I was startled to see children along with their parents having a high old time in the cafés at one or two o'clock in the morning. But then the Spanish sleep during the heat of the day, work during the cool of the morning and evening and live at night, which is a most sensible arrangement. The language is pure music. I know exactly six words of Spanish but can listen to the rippling cadences for hours, and it is always spoken with such intensity of feeling that a perfectly simple statement like "See you same time same place Tuesday" becomes an assignation of unimaginable possibility and portent.

The Yacht Club threw open its magnificent doors to me, which was generous, because the Yacht Club was very grand and I was not. Since the social aspect had not entered my calculations in the original project, shore-going clothes had not been in-cluded in my personal gear. So for a people who set a lot of store

79

by appearance—the Spanish really go for dressing up in the grand manner—it was nice of them not to mind me padding round their marble halls barefooted and denimed. They even forgave me for mistaking the men's room for the shower the first night I arrived, presumably because such an eccentric could hardly be held responsible for her actions.

There was a charming couple who invited me to dinner in their home because he liked sailing and she came from Douarnenez, bonds obviously calling for celebration, and I discovered then how late people dine in Spain (by ten o'clock I am gnawing the furniture when no one is looking). This was the night of the festival of the bonfires, and bonfires were lit in all the streets, so after dinner we drove round the town to look at the goings-on going on. An important feature of the fiesta seemed to be jumping through the flames, which was exciting and picturesque, but the reason for it all escaped me as our combined linguistic understanding was not enough for an explanation.

Almost anything is dramatic when you don't speak the language. I changed francs into Spanish currency at a street corner with a shambling middleman and an English-speaking Spaniard as interpreter and umpire. We none of us looked at one another whilst the middleman muttered figures. I stared out across the harbour saying "No" until the magic figure was mentioned, then with a jog on my elbow from the interpreter I said "Si," and we all went into a store up the street, where the proprietor shut all the doors and just refrained from looking under the counter, and amidst garlic, wine, and strange unmentionables hanging from the ceiling, the appropriate number of the filthiest notes were counted out. The umpire took my francs and counted them; he took the Spanish money and counted that; then held out the francs in one hand and the pesetas in the other, and we reached out and took our money and counted it again. Throughout, not a word was uttered in the store, but when the transaction was complete we looked at each other and smiled, the doors were opened and life went on as before.

An Irish yacht followed *FA* into port that first night and complained we stole all her thunder, for the owner was the Spanish Vice-Consul for Bantry and a well-known figure in Vigo. Whilst she was in port there was a lot of fun eating fabulous food in exotic restaurants on mountain tops, drinking exquisite wines to the accompaniment of a fine flow of discursive Irish chatter.

And there were the two Dutch boys, Karl and Jan, of a converted Morecambe Bay prawner sailing to California on a shoestring. Karl was an engineer, dancer, entertainer, writer, poet, and owner of the boat. Jan was an artist, cook, and crew. Karl wrote articles and Jan illustrated them and so they worked their way from port to port; but the shoestring almost parted when they were run down one night by a steamer in the Bay of Biscay in a flat calm, an encounter which the little ship survived with considerable damage, and the wonder is that she survived at all. For a while they thought she would not, but they plugged and pumped and patched her up somehow to sail under jury rig to Vigo, where they promptly set about repairing ship themselves.

They introduced themselves one evening by tapping politely on *FA*'s coachroof and formally inviting me to dinner aboard their boat. "It is not good to be alone, no?"

The dinner was excellent and a triumph of resourcefulness. Three courses with all the fixings; and knowing something of what it entails preparing a meal aboard a small boat I appreciated their ingenuity and was touched by the trouble they had gone to. The *pièce de résistance* was dessert, with "Good luck, good sailing to *FA*" written on it in pink icing. When I get to the stage of making flourishes with icing sugar aboard *FA* I shall consider I have graduated with honours. After dinner Jan sang "Ma Pomme," his long fair hair falling over his eyes, and when he finished he looked from under his forelock. "It is good, yes? —Like Maurice Chevalier?"

It was, too.

Karl and Jan had plenty of work to do on their own boat, but that did not deter them from giving me a hand on mine. As has been said before, there is always something to do on a boat. They fixed the lower cross-trees, which was a great relief as I hate going up the mast, and the cross-trees had acquired an irritating habit of flying up and giving *FA* the appearance of a stout and startled fawn.

Despite its undoubted hospitality, charm, and attraction, I only stayed a week in Vigo. The success of having got there had gone to my head and I was eager to go to sea and find out if I could do it again. I would not have stayed the week even, but strong northerly winds got up and drove fishing boats in for shelter, and I saw no reason for being rash, so fussed around in a tizzy for a couple of days, trying to decipher weather reports. Then the wind moderated and the clouds, no longer pursued by an invisible fury, sauntered across the sky. Karl was fond of saying, "It is not safe to look into the future with eyes of fear," so hugging my brand new confidence born of one little triumph, I set out on the morning of June 26th for Gibraltar, five hundred miles away.

Chapter 9

THE wight that first said "Pride goeth before a fall" must have tried to reef down in a strong northerly. The winds waited until we got nicely out to sea and some forty miles on our way to Gibraltar and then, just on nightfall, said, "There she is!" and came tearing along full of vigour and rumbustiousness, at which my new-found confidence retired to let old man Caution take over again, and I turned up into wind to shorten sail. *FA* at once went into her demented see-saw act, and I crawled forrard to change jibs feeling uncommonly like an apprentice lion-tamer about to attempt the subjugation of a singularly angry lion, for, heavens, how that sail can hate. It throbs with a rage that shakes the ship and lashes out with canvas, sheets, and shackles, making a terrible noise, the embodiment of unbridled ferocity, whilst its wet and windy supporters on the sidelines scream derision and hurl great dollops of spray.

By the time I had taken in the staysail and hanked on the storm jib I was soaked, battered, and worn out.

Reefing the mainsail does not present any problems with roller reefing providing it is tackled in the proper manner, but make one false move on a ship and the resultant hurrah's nest is horrible to behold. And worse to rectify.

I didn't get the sister-hooks on the topping-lift—a tackle that takes the weight of the boom when you lower the sail—properly hooked on to the shackle on the collar at the end of the boom, so that the collar jammed and revolved with the boom instead of allowing the boom to revolve inside it, and in no time flat the mainsheet was wound round the boom, round the main-sail, and for reasons best known to itself, round the boom gallows as well. The tangle up had the Laocoon making daisy

83

chains by comparison. I was forrard of course, winding the reefing gear, paying out the main halyard, easing the mainsail down, and holding on, a simple operation, calling for only four hands. When I saw what was happening, I rushed aft, forgetting to belay the main halyard, which promptly flew out to sea and then wrapped itself round the upper cross-trees. So then I scrambled back and forth, scrabbling at the lash-up in a frenzy, swearing all I knew and a lot I didn't and achieving absolutely nothing at all, until *FA* lost patience and gave me one easy lesson in how to keep your head by nearly removing mine. She swung a classic haymaker with her boom and dropped me neatly into the cockpit.

After a while I got up and sat on the seat. *FA* had returned to her see-saw routine, rocking up and down, spitting spray and grumbling: "Why the stampede? There's all the time in the world. If only you thought what you were going to do before you did it, you would save yourself so much trouble."

Maybe she did not say it. Maybe the crack on my head just made me think she did. But I learnt something all the same.

We ran all night under reefed main and storm jib, but by seven o'clock the following morning the north winds were blowing in earnest and I had to take the mainsail in altogether and run under storm jib only. The seas were high, grey, and impressive. They came up under the ship and lifted her until all the world was spread about beneath, then they rushed on and left her to sink back into a canyon of tall, toppling waters. Stray bits of advice from quay men came percolating back from fitting out days: "Never let her run too fast, she's too fine aft." Never let her run too fast. What is too fast? A big sea curled over and broke on the quarter deck. That was enough for me. I can take a hint. Out went the sea-anchor. It was amazing the difference it made. *FA* might have been set in concrete. The anchor warp thrummed with strain. Then I dropped the jib and

FA, who had been riding by the stern, came round and lay broadside on to the seas. I did not like this, but did not know what to do about it then, so went below and left *FA* to look after herself. She knew so much better than I.

The cabin was wonderfully reassuring. It was hard to believe there was so much unpleasantness going on outside, except for the noise. The scream of the wind, the roar of the sea, the hiss of a big wave, the thrrrrrup of spray on deck, occasionally a crash when she took it green. Then the cabin would go dark, and I would look up from my book and see water solid through the portholes as though looking into an aquarium, and I would turn several pages without a notion of what I was reading.

It was quite a wind. Within the next twenty-four hours no less than four steamers hove to and hooted at us, all set for a big rescue operation. I used to slide back the hatch and wave with a false nonchalance, and dive below before too much sea got into the ship. I hated to see them go, but was inestimably comforted by their concern.

We lost the sea-anchor; it fridged through its own fastenings at the end of the warp. I reckoned we made a sou'westerly drift of about 24 miles in that blow, which eased to the merest breath after a couple of days and worked its way through east to south, leaving a lumpy and confused sea to contend with. I started the engine, because it is aggravating to hang about to no purpose, and so found the clutch was suffering from a surfeit of sea water and had frozen in gear, which made starting rather hard work. The southerly wind freshened and a shark swam round the ship which was somehow rather dispiriting, and I was very tired. Then we had a day of flat calm to recover in, but this was immediately followed by a northerly wind that blew with even greater ferocity than before.

We lay to a warp for two days. During the nights I had to keep constant watch for ships, as none of the oil lamps would stay alight in those conditions and there was not a hope of our being seen. A small ship does not even show up on the radar screen. It was frankly terrifying, but a high pitch of fear cannot be sustained for long—it turns to a state of apathetic resignation. All the same I wore myself out worrying. I worried about the gear; whether there was anything I could or should do; if there was a ship bearing down . . . they were very close by the time you could see them in those seas . . . and the more I fretted the wearier I got, and the wearier I got the more I worried.

The windage of the mast and the rigging was enough in that wind to lay the ship over, and she had a curious way of jiggling, rocking herself very quickly, until she was hit by a big sea, then she would remain perfectly still for a moment as if shocked— you can't do this to me—then she would pull herself together and start rocking again. When this happened the primus gimbals, swinging clear out of the galley over the floor of the cabin, would groan ooooh . . . ooh in the most pathetic and appropriate manner. They should have been oiled and made groan-proof, but were so amusing in a rather unfunny situation that I left them alone to state the case for me vicariously, and then it wasn't necessary. A monster sea caught the ship and threw her on her beam ends. One never quite knows what happens on these occasions. The sound of the wave breaking was like an explosion, and it felt as if FA was trying to do a barrel roll. Everything on the starboard side of the cabin broke loose and crashed over to port. Cups, plates, books, charts, navigation instruments, pepper, salt, soap detergents hurtled through the air. The entire galley, primus stove, gimbals and all, came out by the roots. Kettles, bowls, and pans tumbled about in frantic confusion. Something hit the compass and smashed it. Water poured through the sliding hatch as if it was wide open. As soon as FA came up for air I looked out to see if anything was left on deck. The cockpit was filled to the coamings and the whole ship was dripping as if she had just been fished up from the bottom of the sea, but otherwise everything was as it should be, nothing had parted or been carried away, or gone ping. I helped the self-drainers drain the cockpit by baling with a bucket, and then worked like a maniac in the cabin trying to restore order, as if doing so could prevent another big sea getting us.

Actually it did moderate after that, and about midday the clouds broke apart and bright sunshine shone down upon the water. A heartening feature; disaster never seems quite so imminent when the sun shines.

The following day we pottered along uncomfortably in a high sea that did not have enough wind to support it. I reckoned we were off Cape St Vincent by evening, and was surprisingly rewarded by the flash of its light at nightfall. We had been ten days at sea, and had covered most of the distance from Vigo at a fast drift. The wind freshened during the night again, and there were so many ships about I fidgeted and could not sleep and started the next day's work limp and nervous. We rounded the Cape and altered course for the Straits of Gibraltar, navigating by the hand-bearing compass as the other was out of commission. The sea was lumpy and confused and our progress was slow.

I hove to at six o'clock, worn out and discouraged by the small advance made for the energy expended. A steamer hove to near by and looked at us questioningly, but I waved reassuringly as usual, and she went on her way to leave us to get through another restless and uncomfortable night. It blew with gale force, and although the seas were nothing like as high as before, they were short and fast with plenty of weight in them, which made them harder to take than the bigger seas. I barely had the strength to get under way the following day, one of peculiar emptiness. The sky was hard and absolutely cloudless. There were no birds and no ships to be seen. Land was out of sight. The sea did not sparkle, it was dull and angry and leaden for all the clarity of atmosphere. I looked in the water, but even the fish seemed to be hibernating. One little cloud would have been welcome. Lonely, weary, and acutely depressed, I cast about in the lockers for something to eat, not having done so for a couple of days. Cold food in bad weather is singularly unappetising, but since the stove had gone out of action there had been no alternative. I found a tin of plum cake which I had forgotten, one slice of which held the magic of recuperation, and I was heartened enough to experiment with a self-steering device I thought I had invented. I had not, and was compelled to continue steering. The wind was nearly west by now, on the port quarter, and at nine-thirty p.m. I hove to and turned in, oblivious and uncaring of ships, seas, or anything else, and passed out cold until eleven o'clock the next day, when I woke refreshed and slightly guilty, to find gorgeous motoring weather with only the merest suggestion of air from the west. The respite did not last long, however, the weather turned squally, then the wind went into the east and blew half a gale, and so it went on, day after day, and it seemed as though I had never known and never would know anything but a life of dismal, damp endurance.

One night we were nearly run down. The seas were fierce, and we were lying to without any canvas, when suddenly a steamer appeared on the crest of a wave, a triangle of lights, port, starboard, and masthead, coming straight for us. No time to get sail up, no time to prime the engine. I swung the starting handle with strength borrowed from fear, and the engine started. We climbed out of the way as the big freighter slid by to disappear as quickly as she came, hidden by the seas.

After that there was no more sleep.

The following night the loom of a light appeared on the horizon sky ahead, and I took it to be the one I was expecting to see on the Spanish coast at the entrance to the Straits of Gibraltar. It was not possible to time the light and check it, as most of the time it was obscured by waves. None the less, I altered course to go through the Straits and plugged on all through the night, only to find we were plugging our way smack on to the African coast somewhere down by Larache in the morning. I could have kicked myself. The light had been Cape Spartel. For a moment I was almost of a mind to carry on to Casablanca, but having said I was going to Gibraltar, to Gibraltar I was going if it took the rest of my life.

We thumped north along the African coast under motor and a sweltering sun. There was no wind at all and the sea was smooth and oily; there was a thick pink haze, and I sat at the tiller, sweating and burning, acutely discomforted by the violent change of conditions. The clutch was slipping badly, so it was eight p.m. by the time we reached Cape Spartel, and I was dizzy with fatigue, having been at the helm without sleep or respite for forty-eight hours; and there had been little enough sleep or respite before then either. Life now simply resolved itself into one of imperative urges, and the most imperative urge of all was sleep. I wanted oblivion with every fibre of my being. And here we were right at the entrance to the Straits, where ships were crowding through like sheep at a gate. One might as well pull up in the middle of Broadway for a quiet nap.

Extreme fatigue does strange things. As in a dream I became aware of two other people aboard, and as in a dream it seemed perfectly natural that they should be there. One of them sat on the coachroof and the other came aft holding on to the boom quiescent in its gallows. "O.K.," he said. "You kip down. We'll keep watch." Obediently I went below and slept till morning.

Stretching and yawning and still weary, I climbed into the cockpit in the light of day. "Thank you," I said. "That was good . . ." but they had gone. Never had the cockpit looked so empty.

A small grey freighter was hanging solicitously in the offing, officers on the bridge training their binoculars on *Felicity Ann*. I was too tired even to wave.

There was a nice westerly breeze blowing, the sort of wind that makes a person say, if he likes that sort of thing, "Let's go sailing today."

"Well, don't just sit there." *FA* was rolling impatiently. "Why don't we get some sail on and use this breeze. First decent one since we left home. . . . Jeez—what I got for a skipper —or maybe you think Gibraltar will come out to you?"

I dragged the sails up by their back hair, tottered back to the cockpit, turned down wind and ran for the Straits. *FA* lifted her boom and gave a little tug on the mainsheet: "'s better."

Within a couple of hours we were romping along the Straits and I was sitting at the tiller with my feet hitched up on the coamings, singing as if I hadn't a care in the world. For there was Africa, with great big blue-grey African mountains on one side, and there was Spain with green not so big mountains on the other, and there, yes, there was Gibraltar ahead, not looking the least as I had always imagined, much longer and greener. Achievement, for recuperative purposes, has the wonder drugs beat a mile. A colossal Italian liner overtook us, passing close on the starboard side, playing pom titty pom pom, pom POM on her hooter in a very unorthodox and friendly manner, whilst deckloads of laughing passengers leant over the side and waved, so that I waved back in extravagant good humour.

The strong and constant current flowing eastward out of the Atlantic into the Mediterranean gave us such a boost we were through the Straits and entering Gibraltar Bay in five hours, and there I took in the sails and log line, put up the ensign and Q flag, and started the motor; but the clutch was slipping so badly that we bucked the outgoing stream in the Bay for an unconscionably profitless time.

I entered the Harbour finally with a certain uneasiness, for somewhere in the back of my mind was the notion that you

didn't just wander into a Naval Base like this—there are formalities—and sure enough a little police boat came out of a dock at
the double and fussed towards us, watchdog in every strake.
The clutch was only engaging in fits and starts, but as attack is
the best form of defence, I wasn't taking any chances, and pushed
the lever into neutral so that we swung and drifted helplessly.
As soon as they were within *my* throwing distance, I shouted,
"Good, just the men I am looking for," and threw them a line
before they could say "Now, what's all this 'ere," which I
fully expected, as they were dressed in blue uniform like London
policemen, except for an official plainly the Health Officer. He
stood authoritatively in the cockpit and spread his arms as if he
expected the police to rush *FA* and said, "No one aboard until
I've cleared this vessel."

Drifting about in the middle of the harbour he examined my
papers so carefully that I began to think perhaps I was a schizo-
phrenic and a smuggler in my other life. Then suddenly he
pushed them away and took off his hat and official manner and
smiled and said, "We've been waiting for you. But," he sighed,
"I wish we had met ashore." Then he asked for a photograph
and I was so flabbergasted I gave him one. Then I convinced the
police that the clutch was completely and utterly inoperable (I
was not going to be turned out of that harbour for the Admiral
himself—and I had extracted the information that you had to get
formal permission for entry) and they towed us into the
Cormorant Camber, a quiet, secluded dock, where there were
already a number of presumably legitimate yachts lazing
alongside.

After the police boat had gone I puttered about tidying the
decks in a warm aura of delight, thinking Gibraltar, this is
Gibraltar, the second port we've set out to find and found;
Gibraltar, over a thousand miles from England.

All the fears, all the weariness and misery of the past nineteen days were forgotten. They might never have been. The late sun still shimmered on the quay walls, the water was calm as if water could never be anything else. High above towered the Rock. There were sounds of traffic, of people; somewhere a dog barked. It was as if I had never been hungry, weary, frightened, or desperate for sleep, had never crouched in the cabin pretending to read whilst great grey waves ravaged the ship. This was Gibraltar and what was past had gone.

A large, imposing gentleman in immaculate white uniform and large white knees halted smartly on the quay by *FA*.

"A little trouble, eh?"

"Oh, no," I said deprecatingly, "not really."

"Most irregular," he said severely. "All yachts are required to anchor *outside* the harbour and request entry if they wish to come in."

Oh-oh, wrong tactics. "Actually," I said, "the clutch won't engage at all. She can't move under her own power, but," hesitantly, "I daresay the police boat could tow us out again."

"Most irregular," he repeated, frowning. "Well, since you're here, suppose you had better stay till you get your engine fixed."

He gave me a look that made it quite clear that if I had any notions of taking the Rock single-handed I could shelve them once and for all. Then he looked over *FA* searchingly, taking in the detail from stem to stern and keel to truck.

"From England?"

"Yes," I said.

"Alone?"

"Yes," I said.

"Good trip?"

"Yes," I said. I very nearly said "*Rather*."

"Good show," he said and briskly walked away.

Chapter 10

IT transpired that *FA* and I reached Gibraltar just in time.
Another twelve hours and the St Bernards would have been out
pawing the snow. The British and American air forces would
have been scouring the seas, and I would have looked up at them
and wondered what they were after, and it would have been me.
All because I cannot speak Spanish.

Quite unintentionally I left the Vigo authorities under the
impression I was bound for Casablanca. I intended to go on to
Casablanca because I believed the Stanilands were there. A
letter had come from them the morning I sailed from Plymouth,
saying they were in Casablanca making fishing trips on charter
and did not intend sailing across to the West Indies until the
autumn, and it was in the back of my mind when I set out that if
I did not make Madeira and the ocean crossing in time to miss
the hurricane season, I would go on to Casablanca. By the time I
reached Vigo it was plain that the original plan had gone agley
and that Casablanca would be included in the itinerary *after*
Gibraltar, Gibraltar being a sterling area and the obvious place
in which to reprovision a sterling yacht. Also I wanted to see
the Rock. It is a bit involved in English, and translated into sign
language it got so snarled up that the Spanish officials notified
the Casablanca port authorities of my impending arrival, and of
course I turned up missing. This inspired an American columnist
in Casablanca, evidently short of copy, to institute a scare, and
in due course the Seventh Air Rescue Squadron at Sidi Slimane
began putting rescue wheels into motion. The idea caught on
and the Royal Air Force at Gibraltar decided to have a look-
see as well. Fortunately I arrived in time to prevent any waste
of public money, but an R.A.F. officer told me later it was

93

disappointing as they would have liked a change from the usual training routine.

The Stanilands sent a cable shortly after my arrival saying "Hurry up waiting for you here." And as Casablanca was only about 180 miles just round the corner, I replied bragging I would be with them in a week, allowing three days to turn round and four to get there, which seemed a conservative estimate, averaging 50 miles at 12 hours sailing time a day. I looked forward to seeing the Stanilands with much eagerness, excited at the prospect of joining them in my own boat, for there is a special delight in sharing one's achievements, however small, with one's friends. Yet it was five weeks before I left Gibraltar. Why, it is hard to say. Looking back, it may have been that I was undergoing a reaction after the Vigo passage, but at the time it seemed to be nothing more or less than an inexcusable laziness; an inexplicable giving way to an inertia that prevents your doing even the things you want to do. It was very hot too, a sticky, humid heat that was ideally conducive to lotus eating. Most people on the Rock seemed to be affected with the *mañana* complex to a greater or lesser degree so it was quite easy to drift into a lazy social round of luncheons, dinners, cocktails, and sorties into Spain, taking life as it came and God send Sunday. There were a number of yachts in port bound for distant places —when they got round to it—and we idled about each other's boats, gossiping with the casual camaraderie common to small boat sailors, grumbling at the heat, blaming the local wind, the Levanter, for anything we didn't like, occasionally doing a little work aboard; and the days drifted by effortlessly and unnoticed as we stayed on and on and on.

The Royal Air Force was responsible for eventually getting me under way again. Gallantry is an inherent feature of the armed forces and the R.A.F., so to speak, cast the cloak over the puddle for *FA*, and offered to overhaul her and make any

94

Bert takes some canvas aboard

A. H. Lealand

Felicity Ann departing from Plymouth

INSET ABOVE *Felicity Ann* alongside the Dutch yacht in the harbour at Douarnenez

necessary repairs. All of which they did at the Air Sea Rescue Camber with efficiency and expedition, and so removed any further excuse for delay. At a quarter past eight on the morning of August 20th, with *FA* shipshape and the compass, radio, and clutch in full working order, we set out for Casablanca.

There is one estimable quality about the sea. It has a way of keeping perspective in proportion. Whatever delusions of grandeur I may have acquired at having made Gibraltar were dispelled soon after I left. It took only five hours to come up the Straits, but it took a couple of days to get clear of them again. The east-going current put up a strong resistance, and ten hours after leaving the harbour we were still bucking it just off Tarifa, not much more than half way along. It would have been wise to have put in to Tarifa for the night and renew the battle afresh in the morning, but I had to go plugging on. There wasn't much wind and *FA* was fighting with the diesel, which at one o'clock in the morning coughed delicately and stopped. An air lock. The remedy entails "bleeding" the fuel system, not a difficult operation; but by now we were nearly at the entrance to the Straits, Casablanca was only a step away, and, as even a simple operation has a way of developing into a major project at sea, I decided to carry on under sail and deal with the air lock in the calm of harbour. We spent the next twenty-four hours bobbing up and down in light and variable winds in the region of Cape Spartel.

At midday, August 21st, we were ambling along in a light breeze and a calm sea when suddenly there was a roaring noise, and rushing towards us, from horizon to horizon, was a line of breakers, which reached and engulfed us in a sort of portable shoal. The breeze dropped completely and the little ship flopped about uncontrollably in a maelstrom of wild white water. The waves were short and narrow, but fast and frothing, tumbling over each other in angry confusion. It took about fifteen minutes to pass. Then we were left lying in a flat calm still off Cape Spartel. *FA* drifted at the whim of the current and was carried back along the Straits and caught up in a whirlpool where she waltzed round and round in circles for an hour or two. I considered the possibility of getting the engine going again, but envisaged spanners and nuts slipping into the bilges and took the line of least resistance. Wind was sure to come sooner or later, which it did eventually from the east, when we extricated ourselves, not without some difficulty, from the whirlpool, and set out again for Cape Spartel and the Atlantic Ocean.

Towards dusk the wind freshened and I reefed down instead of using it to the best advantage to get out of the Straits and round the Cape; but a freshening wind at nightfall portended a strong blow before dawn and I was still chary of playing with halyards and reefing gear in the dark. With an excess of caution I rolled down too much mainsail, which had the oddest effect on *FA*, obviously disgusted by my timidity. She sat staring the wind in the eye, refusing to deviate one iota, deaf to any instructions from me via the rudder. I allowed her a little more canvas and she became amenable to direction again. By then it was almost dark and blowing pretty hard. Just as I had forgotten the tribulations of sailing on arrival at Gibraltar, so now I forgot the comparative peace of land life, and was back in the familiar fret of fatigue. It was thirty-six hours since we had left the harbour and I had been at the tiller the whole time.

A yacht came tearing down the Straits, heeled well over and going like a train. I signalled her with my torch. She sailed round *FA* in impatient circles: "What ... do ... you ... want?" Frankly, I did not know. A little comfort—reassurance—someone to hold my hand? Communicating with difficulty against the noise of wind and sea, I shouted something about Tangier, which was not very far away and seemed as intelligible as anything to shout. Sailors are used to communicating in single words. "Tangier?" could mean "I want help getting into Tangier. I haven't a chart of the harbour. I don't know the place. Everything is perfectly bloody and I am fed up."

Someone yelled back, "Follow . . . us . . ." and the yacht departed at a rate of knots, to vanish quickly in the gathering dusk. *FA* lumbered after under too little canvas, and it was not until two o'clock in the morning that we were sailing round Tangier Bay tentatively feeling our way, as I had no chart nor any notion, literally, how the land lay. Sailing round strange bays on a pitch black night in a high wind is not one of the smartest things to do, which dawned on me eventually, so we sailed out again and hove to off Cape Spartel, because I was unable to keep my eyes open any longer.

Two hours later we were under way again, running before a gale of wind under storm jib only, careering down the African coast in the angry dawn through threshing white seas with the wind blowing the log line clear out of the water. But at nightfall the fury died as if it had been turned off at the main and left us sitting on a pond, 125 miles from Gibraltar. It was hard to credit both weathers as belonging to the same day.

I had a wonderful night's sleep—back to fundamentals again when supreme satisfaction is exacted from the simplest necessity —and awoke to bright sunshine and a light northeasterly wind before which we ran with considerable pleasure and inconsiderable speed. A Greek tanker overtook us so closely I called up, "Casablanca?" and the man on the bridge replied, "About feefty miles." Nearly there. All day long the monotonous beat of diesel engines drummed out across the water as numerous tunny-fishermen went about their day's work. The distant coastal scene changed slowly, and we only made twenty miles that day, apparently sailing on our reputation as there was hardly any wind, and by nightfall there was none. Yet the really lazy weather was a welcome innovation, and I revelled in the peace of feet-up sailing. The slowness of our progress did not

97

worry me, as time at sea, outside of navigation, soon ceases to have any significance.

It was a brilliant starlight night and the water was so still even the Milky Way was reflected in it. I sat in the cockpit looking at the lovely night, supremely content, for the first time, it seemed, in years.

The next day was so calm it was only good for a six-mile advance on Casablanca, and the day after that was little better. At six o'clock the white towers and turrets of Rabat and Sali were abeam, looking improbably Moroccan and romantic. The following morning, however, produced a fresh breeze at dawn that bowled us along in fine style, so that when a big handsome fishing boat from Douarnenez on her way to Dakar overtook us I yelled, "Vive Douarnenez," with an enthusiasm that startled her crew.

By midday the wind had tapered off again and we were left rolling in a high westerly swell which I could hear (with some misgiving) breaking with a continuous muted roar on the African shore.

Later in the afternoon there was a curious occurrence for which there seems no explanation. There was a sound, faint at first, for all the world like a brood of chickens chirping and twittering, which grew louder and louder as it seemed to draw nearer and nearer. Interested, I wandered round the deck to see what it might be. But there was nothing to be seen. Louder and louder came the sound, the chirpings of thousands of little chicks, almost deafening. *FA* appeared to be floating right over them. I looked all round, even in the air, but still could see nothing, and gradually they passed us, and the sound grew fainter and fainter and slowly faded away altogether as the invisible chickens floated off on their invisible way; and I never saw them or knew what they were.

Finally, on the afternoon of August 27th, we arrived off

Casablanca, seven days out from Gibraltar, and there I dithered about some miles off shore working up courage to *sail* for the first time into port.

In the outer harbour we encountered a small sailboat whose helmsman evinced some excitement at the sight of *FA*. "Madame Davison?" "Yes . . . oui," I shouted, back in the old language hassel again. Whatever plans he had for an afternoon's sailing were chivalrously shelved as he offered to escort us to the yacht basin, which turned out to be at the very end of the harbour, about three miles from the entrance. The little sailboat herded us anxiously, obviously wishing we would get a move on, but I was not to be hurried; there was a problem confronting me, and I didn't want to face it any sooner than necessary. When we got as far as we could without wings, the sailboat turned smartly to starboard and I followed, and there we were in the yacht basin, alarmingly congested. The first ship I saw was the *Nymph Errant* and the first person, Bonnie Staniland.

"Bonnie," I yelled urgently, "how do I stop this bloody thing?"

★   ★   ★

"Ann: you must be beat. Wouldn't you like to go back to *Felicity Ann* and turn in?" Bonnie's voice was sympathetic and came from far away.

I frowned at the tumbler of rum in my hand because the situation called for concentration. The rum, for instance, was magic. It didn't matter how much you drank, the tumbler was always full. Everlasting rum. Someone had put the glass in my hand when I arrived because there was a party going on; someone was celebrating a birthday, someone else had just got engaged, and Bonnie said I was the third thing that day. The party spirit overlapped on to *FA*. Eager anonymous hands had helped tie her up and put her away, and in the midst of it all Bonnie and John and I tried to exchange news in intermittent shouts. Then we were caught up in the web of celebration and circulated amongst the yachts which were moored in the middle of the basin, two or three abreast and in line, there being no quays or piers where a yacht could make fast alongside, until after a gap of time we gravitated to the saloon of the *Nymph Errant* where a score of voices were being witty with all the stops out in French, English, and clouds of smoke. There were a number of reporters in the party, but they had long ago ceased to register. . . .

I didn't think I wanted to go back to *FA*. There was a lot I wanted to tell the Stanilands if only I could remember it, and I was hungry. A tumbler of rum is too much to drink on an empty stomach. An everlasting tumbler of rum, I noticed, was having the strangest effect on Bonnie's face; it expanded and contracted in the most fascinating manner and would suddenly whirl away and come back again. I stared fixedly.

". . . back to *FA*?" she was repeating.

Maybe it wasn't rum. Maybe I was just tired.

"Yesh," I said, "yessss. HOW?"

We had come here on a magic carpet. *FA* was up the dock some place, two or three boats away, and the schedules of magic carpets are uncertain.

"I'll take you back in the dinghy," she said. "We'll slip out quietly and no one'll notice."

(Huh, bad as that, eh?) I walked out of the cabin, up the companionway, across the deck, and straight into the dock.

Bonnie was calling, "John—quick—John!" as I surfaced, but treading water with all the dignity that the circumstances permitted, I said, "Shhhh. No . . . need to call . . . anyone. I *always* swim home."

And with Bonnie pursuing in the dinghy, I did.

Chapter 11

SOME of the reporters must have survived the party, because Radio Maroc sent a recording van down to the yacht basin the morning following my arrival. The interviewer could not speak English and I, that morning, could hardly speak at all, so John Staniland, much against his will, was co-opted as interpreter. There was no shelter on the dock, and we stood at the back of the van, hopping as we talked into the microphone, for we had gone ashore barefoot and the blazing hot concrete scalded the soles of our feet. The inevitable crowd collected, a mixture of French artisans, American airmen, Arab and West African dock-labourers, all with time on their hands, uncertain of what was afoot, but willing to be entertained by anything that offered. They grinned sympathetically when the recording was played over and John and I showed the first signs of life that day and had hysterics, though they missed the reason why. For it was an interview to end all interviews; the perfect parody of "In Town Tonight." John has the classic English accent; the firm clipped tones that have rung from one end of the world to the other, leading men into battle and directing great naval occasions, that have sworn at the dark little men in jungles and adjudicated the affairs of uncomplicated people in far off lonely islands; whose speakers are constrained for ever to shave in the desert and change for dinner on safari. It is unalterable and in-alienable. Superimposed upon French words it is as if an English country gentlewoman had cast off her tweeds and teetered down the market place in tight black satin and five-inch heels.

My voice came over so blasé, so bored, so unutterably world-weary it was unrecognisable, and reminded me irresistibly of the girl who had come into Gibraltar on a large motor yacht—

"My dear, we were so *bored* with the Atlantic . . . we just had to try the Mediterranean for a change. . . ."

The French interviewer was birdlike and eager, pecking at our indifference with sharp little questions.

"He asks why you are making this trip," said John, and I, stupid from lack of sleep and a delayed hangover, had not the remotest idea. "Oh, one just sails from A to B, you know" (so bored with the Atlantic).

"I don't know," snapped John, in not much better state. "You'll have to do better than that, how can I translate 'ah à beh.' Let's try again. . . . What ports have you called at?"

I strung them off, bored to sobs in every syllable, "Douarnenez, Vigo, Gibraltar."

"Elle dit," began John, falsely bright, to tell the public this deathless information, "Douarnenez, Vigo, Gibraltar. . . ."

The interviewer wanted to know what stores I carried on board, I stared blankly at John. "Come on," he hissed, "What do you eat?"

I hadn't the faintest idea. "Eggs?" I suggested, and casting about wildly said the first edible things that came into my head, "Marmite," and with a sudden flash of inspiration, "Ship's biscuits."

John chanted into the microphone, "Elle dit qu'elle a mangé en voyage les oeufs . . . er . . . marmeete . . . et . . . er . . . et les bisquits de la mer," which came out to sound like mother's biscuits.

All told, it must have been one of the least illuminating interviews ever made. We listened to it again that night when it was broadcast in all seriousness, and nearly killed ourselves laughing. Some of it we missed because Bonnie choked over her drink and we had to resort to back-beating.

Casablanca is cosmopolitan to a degree, thronged with unadaptable people imposing their own outlook and way of life,

European, American, and Arabian, in sharply differentiated layers on an outlook and way of life that has not changed since Biblical times. There are skyscrapers and minarets. There is fabulous wealth and hideous poverty. There are coke stands and ragged old men selling water from repulsive goatskin bags. Camels and Cadillacs. Frenchwomen, groomed and chic, and silent, sultry women robed and veiled to the expressive eyes. The town is white and sparkling, busy, broad, and bustling in the modern section; colourful, narrow, odorous, unalterably anti-quated, slow-moving, and soft-footed in the Medina. A fascinat-ing place. I wished I could have seen more of it, but, somehow, we of the yachts seemed to live a more self-contained life in Casablanca than in most ports, possibly because there were more of us with the common interest of coming from and going to places afar (at least eight of us were bound across the Ocean), and possibly because the basin was some distance from the main part of town. Anyway, we did not enter as much into shore life as usual. Even our shopping was done for us, adequately and more economically than we could have managed, by an Arab boy who called daily for orders. I had fun making out my grocery lists with the aid of the French dictionary. . . . Laundry was even more amusing, though mostly we did our washing at home, so to speak, flying our smalls in the rigging. A Texan yacht whose crew had a proclivity for Florida shirts, claimed to have the most colourful wash in port, a claim that none could dispute. Another factor that confined us to the port area was the inevitable refitting of our ships. The burden of the impending voyage was weighing on me and I worked in a frenzy on *FA*, scraping, sanding, painting, varnishing, oiling, greasing, over-hauling, refuelling, and reprovisioning to the exclusion of almost all else, a devotion to duty regarded as a little excessive by the others, who having so much more experience than I, were able to take the refitting more easily in their stride. But I had to learn how to maintain a ship as well as to sail her. My work was always in arrears because I was not quick enough to see the vulnerable parts going before they went. Everything that turned had to be made free before it was oiled and greased because I hadn't the sense to see how quickly it would become frozen through the corrosive action of salt air and water. John, because of his immeasurably superior knowledge and the fact I had almost been one of his crew several times, regarded me as a protégée for whom he was in a way responsible, and often lent a hand aboard *FA*. He used to become exasperated because "nothing ever works on this bloody ship." Experience is a sound school but a mighty slow one.

An Australian girl joined the *Nymph Errant* for the passage to the Canary Islands and across the Ocean. Winnie had skippered her own fishing boat at home, but a sudden yen to see the world had set her off hitch-hiking and working her way across the seas and continents. Being essentially a nature girl, Winnie neither smoked nor drank, and wore the briefest bikinis compatible with convention. She was tall and long-legged, and her beautiful body was tanned to a golden brown, and the sale of binoculars must have soared when Winnie was in port. She was as efficient a seaman as she was good to look at. Moreover, she did not have to stare at a job and figure it out for half an hour; she saw what wanted doing and did it. It was very deflating and no doubt good for the ego that so many yachtsmen I met had glamorous, efficient wives. The only reason that none of them were sailing single-handed was that they preferred, quite naturally, to go along with the old man. I was almost reduced to pulling the hatch over my head and hiding in shame. Even little Ian Staniland, my godchild with the honey-coloured hair, was an object of my envy, for he started life aboard at ten days old and was acquiring boat lore along with learning to walk and talk.

The next step from Casablanca to Las Palmas, Gran Canaria, in the Canary Islands, was a big one for me. It was to be the dress rehearsal for the real thing, the three thousand mile voyage across the Atlantic. It was not only longer than any of the previous passages, six hundred miles, but navigationally called for more accuracy than I was certain of having attained. To find a port running south along the continents of Europe and Africa was one thing, but to locate a specific island six hundred miles out in the Atlantic was a landfall of quite a different colour, requiring navigation of a somewhat higher order than that obtained by simple dead reckoning. The Canary Islands are mountainous and enormously high, visible in certain conditions from prodigious distances. The twelve thousand foot peak of Tenerife has been sighted from ninety miles away, so it has been claimed; but Dr Alain Bombard, in Casablanca en route for Las Palmas, where he had left the raft on which he had sailed from Marseilles and proposed continuing his experimental voyage to the West Indies, living on the sea without taking any of the normal provisions, cast a blight on this one encouraging factor. The islands, he said, were, more often than not, obscured by thick haze, and he had not sighted Gran Canaria until he was on the doorstep, so to speak, in spite of a six thousand foot mountain reaching up to the sky. So, assiduously I checked the chronometer rate and read up on celestial navigation.

Although the forthcoming voyage dominated my actions and coloured my thoughts almost to the exclusion of all else, there are at least two social occasions unusual enough to be preserved in bas-relief in my recollections of the Casablanca visit. One was a dinner party given by the local branch of the Sea Scouts, to which it must be confessed I did not look forward with any surplus enthusiasm. The Chief Scout, who issued the invitation, was the only one who spoke any English, which was about on a par with my French, and I could not see myself scintillating as guest of honour at a kids' party. But I underestimated the kids. I have seldom been so charmingly or adequately entertained, for, from first to last, from the moment they collected me off *FA* by boat to take me to their headquarters, until they ferried me back again, the evening went like an express train. My hosts, twelve of them, most of whom were still schoolboys, had thought out and prepared the party themselves. The food was well chosen and beautifully cooked and the accompanying wines were delicious. We began with cocktails and rounded off with liqueurs. Conversation never flagged. I had gone armed with a dictionary and, unabashed, referred to it when stuck for a word, which was often enough. The boys did likewise, so the little book was well thumbed. As a conversational stimulant a dictionary may be unusual, but it is certainly efficacious. The following day, in the traditional Scout manner, the boys came along to give a hand aboard *FA*, where they worked with a will and proficiency one learns not to expect from casual volunteers. They went up the mast, too, which enabled me once more to dodge the jobs at the truck, much to my relief. (To this day I cannot reach the cross-trees without being so paralysed with horror that the only thing I can do is come down again. There must be some way of overcoming this height disability, but, up to date, six feet off the ground I am a dead duck.)

The other occasion was not strictly social, and is remembered more with curiosity and embarrassment than with pleasure, for it was nothing less than a reprehensible gate-crashing into a reception given by the Sultan in his palace at Rabat. It was the first time in history that a woman had ever attended such an affair undisguised, and would in sterner times have brought about a summary parting of body and soul; and it all came about because I cannot speak Arabic. When I consider the number of languages I cannot speak, the future is fraught with unlimited possibilities.

There is an annual festival, basically religious but with the strong secular overtone that is apt to develop with the passing of centuries, held throughout Morocco called the Festival of the

106

Lamb. It is a public holiday. Every district closes down, sheep are slaughtered, and a barbecue is held for the delectation of one and all. The peak of the celebration is reached at the palace at Rabat, the capital of French Morocco, where the Sultan holds a reception to which are invited personages of importance, the Governor, consuls, admirals, generals, diplomats, and top level visitors. Speeches of diplomatic intensity are exchanged and the convention of hands across the sea is affirmed. Then in the palace ground the Sultan receives his chiefs of districts, who bring gifts of a material nature as an assurance of fidelity. For the general joy and edification, a bread and circus routine is gone through in the grounds, and Arabs gallop about on steeds appropriately fiery, to loose off long-barrelled carbines in a scurry of noise and dust, whilst fortune-tellers, wrestlers, acrobats, tumblers, and the time-honoured water-seller mingle with the crowds that surge about in a carnival spirit. It is all as it has been for centuries, though as a concession to the times it is now possible to have a coke or an ice cream to lay the dust if the going gets too hot.

A young American reporter assigned to cover the story at Rabat invited me to accompany him. "You won't be allowed in the palace," said Wes. "Women aren't allowed in on this deal; but you won't miss much and you'll see most of the show." We went to Rabat by bus and I fell in love with the place at once. A beautiful, dignified, glittering white town, towered and turreted, of broad restful streets and avenues. We wandered about under the palms admiring the vistas and the Moroccan architecture, and drank mint tea brewed from mint leaves and a load of sugar. It is very sweet and surprisingly refreshing, and is as prominent a part of Moroccan life as tea or coffee elsewhere. Finally we made our way through the Medina to the house of Ali, a Moroccan student friend of Wes's, with whom we were to have lunch.

Ali was a progressive, which meant that we sat in his room eating little chunks of meat roasted on skewers, settling the affairs of the world in a polyglot of tongues. We were joined by his sister who sat with us unveiled. She spoke only Arabic and was training to be a nurse. When she left us to go out, she went enveloped in the customary nun-like white garment, for progress is a heady wine, to be taken slowly. She did, however, allow me to take her photograph on the roof of their home, unveiling for the camera. Few Moroccan women will permit this liberty, as photography is held to be a combination of the evil eye and bad luck, and is something to be avoided at all costs; an influence that appears to affect only the women, for most of the men seemed eager to have their pictures taken and would pose at the drop of a hat.

A number of Ali's student friends joined us after lunch, talkative and intense after the manner of students the world over, and we all set out for the palace, where in the grounds Ali's friends went about their own affairs and we three made for the palace itself. At the gates, as I said goodbye, Ali said it would be all right for me to go with them into the courtyard. He was anxious for me to have a close-up of the palace, of which he was obviously very proud; and it was, in fact, engaging, in the romantic Moroccan tradition with white domes, towers, turrets, and rounded arches. The royal carriage was waiting in the courtyard, with a team of bays in fancy trappings, and wandering about catfooted were hordes of white-robed Arabs, swarthy and hawk-eyed, fierce of mien. Little prickles of ice slithered up and down my spine as we walked amongst them. I could feel them looking after me in a way no woman ever wants any man to look after her. The Mohammedan view does not permit the entry of women into Paradise. Nor, from the general expressions, into the palace precincts.

"Ali," I whispered, plucking his sleeve, "I think I won't go any further." But he only made a gesture that means "nonsense" in any language and hurried on.

Wes said, "If he says so I guess it's all right."

And as I had no wish to return alone through all those dark, bitter men, I went along. We followed Ali through one court-yard after another until we came to one packed close with Arabs, sitting, standing, leaning, waiting for we knew not what, in silence. An enormous official, black-robed and imperious, sprang in front of me with upraised hand.

"See you later, boys," I murmured. But Ali broke into an animated discussion with the black-robed giant, and eventually disappeared through an open doorway after warning Wes and me to wait. We waited, awkwardly and uneasily, pretending, not too successfully, to be invisible to the malevolent gaze of the dark-eyed men. Eventually Ali returned with another black-robed official, who beckoned; and, when I hung back, Ali said, "Yes, you come." We went. We tramped through endless courtyards and corridors and joined the tail-end of a procession at the head of which was the French Governor. "How'd we get in this lot?" I whispered to Wes, who shrugged. We were amongst the press, and I thought we would be herded into a press box or the equivalent of the Stranger's Gallery. The procession marched on through more corridors, and slowly advanced up a long, long flight of stone stairs. Step by step we climbed in silence, round and round we wound upwards, until suddenly we came on to a small landing which debouched straight on to the throne room. One by one, headed by the Governor, the parade marched to the centre of the great hall, bowed low and passed across to the other side where it reformed in line and stood at attention. Consuls, generals, admirals. . . . It came to my turn. No turning back at this point, so I walked across and curtseyed. Way down at the far end of the throne room sat the Sultan on his throne, wearing dark glasses. Safely across without the Red Queen popping up to shout "Off with her head," I joined Wes, who was quietly giggling with delight, for the presence of a female at the reception was causing more of a flutter amongst the newspapermen than the reception itself.

The Sultan made a speech in Arabic which was repeated in French. Then the Governor made a reply in French which was translated into Arabic and told all over again, etiquette of the ages demanding that all official exchanges be made in Arabic. Then the formation of high-ups about-faced and bowed itself out. When it came to my turn, I made a real job of a sweeping curtsey, and most graciously the Sultan bowed in return.

I brought away a memory of a long, high hall, all gold and filigree, so exactly like an illustration of a Sultan's throne-room it is impossible to avoid the feeling one had stepped into a fairy-tale, or a set for a desert movie.

Outside the palace I started breathing easily again, and we watched the reception of the chiefs, a colourful pageant with the Sultan riding a gaily caparisoned white horse which danced and fussed in a popular manner and gave the men trying to keep a sun canopy over the Sultan a hard time. Some of the gifts were presented to the Sultan on their own four legs, magnificent stallions which would gladden the heart of any horse-lover.

When the Sultan retired from the scene we wandered off to find Ali's friends, who were whooping it up in the mob as is the custom of festival crowds everywhere.

What it was that Ali had said that got me into the palace he could not or would not impart, and I shall never know, though there is probably another more interesting account in the archives somewhere.

Chapter 12

ONCE you have done a thing more than three times it becomes routine, and leaving Casablanca represented the fifth departure, so by then going to sea had fallen into a regular pattern. One set out with a mixture of regret and anticipation. The first few days were lonely and uncomfortable and then, imperceptibly, one slipped into the solitary self-contained existence devoid of time, where the only reality is, literally, keeping one's head above water. It is then that life ashore assumes something of the incredibility of the memories of early youth, and one's destination the improbability of a lightly given promise. It no longer matters how long the voyage may last, for the tanks are full and the lockers are stocked, and it is as hard to believe one cannot sail on for ever as it is to realise one will not live for a million years. Which was just as well. Our passage from Casablanca to the Canary Islands took twenty-nine days, a record for tardiness that is likely to stand for some time unless someone decides to swim it. Dr Bombard in his raft slipped along in eleven days.

One of the pitfalls of departure is the celebration that is likely to develop as soon as it becomes known you are sailing. In self-defence I had adopted the technique of announcing I was going on Thursday, say, when my real intention was to depart on Saturday, which gave a day for the farewell party to settle down; but the Casablanca Yacht Club caught me out. In all innocence I went to say goodbye to the Yacht Club officials on the morning of September 25th, and found the champagne corks already firing a salute for my imminent departure. And after a while it was quite easy for Bonnie to persuade me to stay for lunch; a couple of hours seemed an inconsiderable delay in a couple of weeks by then. Lunch aboard the *Nymph Errant* was fried fish, and very good fried fish too, but fried fish and champagne make a horrible mixture, as I discovered later when *FA* rolled with a wicked deliberation in the heavy swell that was running in the open sea. We had motored out of the harbour, and I had intended putting up the sails outside; instead, I simply laid a few more paving blocks of good intentions on my personal road to hell, and stayed unambitiously at the helm immobilised by the quarrel in my stomach. We drove along on the motor until seven o'clock the following morning and for all we had been under way for sixteen hours the log only registered forty-one; for *FA* had her problems, too. During the four weeks she had been in Casablanca she had collected enough fuzz on the bottom, coral, weeds, and barnacles, to stock an aquarium. The speed of a sailboat is governed by her waterline length, and theoretically the longer the ship the faster she goes. With only a nineteen-foot waterline and everything in her favour, *FA*'s maximum speed is a mere six knots. And the maximum speed of a sailboat being cruised single-handed is attained on rare occasions for only short intervals. A large vessel can afford to lose a knot or two off her maximum, but not so a small one. The marine growth on her bottom slowed *FA* down so that it took her an hour to pound out the three miles from the Yacht Basin to the Harbour Entrance. I regretted not having hauled her out for a clean up and repaint, but I had planned to do this in Las Palmas, so that she would be smooth and clean to start out on the three thousand mile passage to the West Indies. Doing this twice I regarded as an unnecessary expense, not realising what a difference it would make until we set out, when of course, it was too late.

The day after I sailed was a Friday, never noted by the superstitious for its good fortune, and for me it was a lost day owing to the chain reaction set up by the fried fish, champagne, and rolling sea combination. *FA* wandered westward, close-hauled, on her own making only a little more headway than leeway as I was too sick to trim the sails properly and she spent most of the time luffing up and playing at being a rocking-horse. I recovered only to go down with dysentery, and it was several days before realisation finally dawned that the water with which the tanks had been filled at Casablanca was slow poison for anyone not inured to its invisible contents. Boiling the water thereafter did not effect a cure, but at least prevented any further intake of belligerent bugs into a pretty shaken system. The dysentery persisted and I lost weight rapidly, which was no great sorrow as it is something I am always trying to do, but I also lost strength which was not so good, so it was fortunate that the weather was limpid and kind most of the time.

Apart from the physical distress, for which the sea for once was not to blame, it was an extraordinarily pleasant voyage, certainly the nicest so far, and I enjoyed the sort of lazy-hazy lotus-eating sea life one dreams of walled up in a city.

Conditions had a delicious dreamy Southern feel about them, calm and unhurried. There were lovely soft pearl-grey nights of a peculiar luminosity and soothing restfulness that were the physical manifestation of contentment. There were sunrises of such crystalline clarity and pristine glory that one could forgive any amount of travail for the joy of beholding those few golden moments when the world was born anew. There were sunsets so lurid, when an orange sun crept down a black and blood-red sky into a smooth lead-coloured sea, that one was convinced there was nothing less than a hurricane in the offing. I would shorten sail and batten down and prepare for the worst, only to discover that all the fuss in the heavens was for a few drops of rain. The weather eye I had acquired through years of flying and farming in England was sadly out in the lower latitudes, where the familiar signs and portents meant nothing at all. The weather could, and did, change with extraordinary rapidity, and the minutest rise or fall in barometric pressure might mean a severe blow, or nothing. As John said in Casablanca, if the glass fell the way it does in England, it would mean the end of the world.

Moreover the alteration in pressure seemed to take place as conditions actually changed. The sky would throw a few clouds together and the wind, sea, and pressure rise at the same time to conjure a squall out of a flat calm with the apparent intention of working up into something big, but in a couple of hours it would all peter out and leave a subsiding sea babbling and gossiping like a football crowd dispersing after a close game. I soon gave up trying to forecast and took the weather as it came. After all, there is very little else you can do in the ocean, with no convenient ports to run to for shelter there, so I gave up reefing until it was necessary, and it was hardly ever necessary on this trip, as most of the time there was either a glass calm or a very light breeze, and our average day's progress was twenty miles.

The snail-like advance was a straight incitation to barnacles to grow on the log line, and they were surprisingly tenacious and difficult to remove. The water was so still and clear that sometimes it was almost as if you could see straight down to the bottom of the sea. Fascinating little striped fish, black and bright blue, swam about in the shade of the ship. A few flying fish skittered across the surface like flat stones thrown on a pond. They were very small flying fish, no bigger than minnows. There were times when rubbish thrown over the side in the morning would still be alongside at nightfall. Then the air was breathless and there would not be the smallest sound from the ship, not even a creak, and the silence was primeval. One might have been alone on the planet where even a cloud spelt companionship.

Most of the time, however, there was a huge swell in which *FA* rolled abominably and flung her boom from side to side with a viciousness that threatened to wrench it clean out of its fastenings. She rattled her blocks and everything not immovably fast below with an aggravating irregularity, so that I was driven to a frenzy of restowing and rigging preventers in an effort to restore peace. An intermittent blop—rattle—crash on a small boat at sea is the nautical version of the Chinese water torture.

Calms permit a little basking, but not much for a single-handed sailor. They provide an opportunity to overhaul gear and repair or renew anything that might give way under more embarrassing circumstances, for if there is one thing the sea will not forgive it is a lost opportunity. I made up and reeved new jib sheets, mended slide-seizings on the mainsail, patched the sails where they showed signs of chafe, and recovered the fenders whose canvas covers had been ruined by oil in the dock at Gibraltar, and felt no end salty at my work, deriving a deep satisfaction in the doing of it, even though the patches on the sails were by no means the finest examples of a sailmaker's art.

For the first nine days out of Casablanca there was not a ship to be seen, and I missed them, grizzling quietly to myself at the loneliness; then we joined the north- and south-bound shipping lane and two steamers appeared on the horizon at the same time, whereon, embarrassed by riches perhaps, I perversely resented their presence. "What are you doing on my ocean?"

Being in the shipping lane again meant the resumption of restless, sleepless nights. I figured out it took twenty minutes for a ship invisible over the horizon to reach us, and as a big ship was extremely unlikely to see me I had to see her, so any rest below was broken every twenty minutes throughout the hours of darkness. Enough practice since leaving England had endowed me with a personal alarm system which rang me out of a comatose condition at the appropriate intervals. Occasion-ally it let me oversleep, and once I awoke to find a south-bound steamer twenty-five yards astern of us. She was deep in Aldis conversation with another vessel, northward bound to west-ward of her, and utterly oblivious of our existence. A miss is as good as a mile maybe, but twenty-five yards is a narrow enough margin in the ocean, and it gave the required jolt to the personal alarm clock. On these ship-watching nights I used to get two hours of genuine sleep at dawn, when it could be assumed that *FA* was reasonably visible, and I couldn't care less by then anyway, but the overall lack of sleep did not improve the general physical condition, already much lowered by dysentery. The thought processes, never on Einstein levels, were reduced to a positively moronic grasp, and I had some rare hassels with navigational problems. However, the balance of nature was somewhat restored in that I was eating better on this trip than on any of the previous ones—the voyage from Douarnenez to Vigo was made almost exclusively on oranges—and there are several references to cooked meals in the log book. I may say that anything mentioned in the log book at this stage outside of navigation notes was a sure indication of an *Occasion*, though they were simple enough meals in all conscience, consisting mainly of scrambled eggs, or an omelette and coffee, or weird mixtures of cheese and onions. One reads of explorers and other isolated people dreaming up extravagant concoctions they are going to eat on returning to civilisation, but quails in aspic were not for me. I had an uncomplicated yearning for plain boiled potatoes and cabbage. As these do not represent a normal taste on my part, I concluded it was a deficiency desire, and stepped up the daily dose of vitamin tablets: a strict necessity for ocean voyagers, as I discovered on the nineteen-day Vigo to Gibraltar run, when I tried to do without them and broke out into reluctant-to-heal sores. The only canned goods whose vitamin content survives the canning process are tomatoes, which probably explains why canned foods lost all appeal for me as soon as I went to sea. Very practically I was learning what stores would be required for the long passage.

One supper was especially memorable, though not for the menu. At 1750 hours, Sunday, October 5th to be exact, I was fixing some cheese nonsense on the stove, for it was a flat calm and I was in an experimental mood, and whilst stirring the goo in the pan I happened to glance through the porthole over the galley and spied a steamer way over on the horizon, the merest speck to eastward of us, going south. A few minutes later I looked out again and to my surprise saw she had altered course and was making towards us. Coming out of her way specially to look at a little ship. Thrilled to the quick, I abandoned supper, brushed my hair, and made up my face, noting with detached amazement that my hands were trembling and my heart was beating, and I was as excited as if I was preparing for a longed-for assignation.

She was a tall, white-grey Italian liner, the *Genale* of Rome, and she swept round astern of us, the officers on her bridge inspecting *FA* keenly through their binoculars. As she had so kindly come many miles out of her way, I had no wish to delay her needlessly, for minutes are valuable to a ship on schedule, so I made no signals, but waved, and the whole ship seemed to come alive with upraised arms waving in reply. She went on her way satisfied that all was well with her midget counterpart, and the night was a little less lonely from the knowledge of her consideration.

The radio worked very well on this trip. Reception at night was excellent and I was able to keep a regular check on the chronometer rate with the G.M.T. signals sent out by the B.B.C., and after the time signals I took whatever offered with an unquestioning enthusiasm practically unknown ashore, for there is a singular piquancy about an essentially domestic programme heard against the background sounds of a ship at sea with one's nearest neighbour hundreds of miles away. It is a little like looking through a window into a warm lighted room on a cold windy night. An assurance of comfort even if one is not able to use it. It must be rare for the B.B.C. to have such an attentive, uncritical listener. They could have recited the alphabet over the air and I would have been delighted.

117

The lazy weather gave ample opportunity to practise celestial navigation, and I spent hours taking sights and worrying out little sums and drawing fantastic position lines on the chart, for the results of my workings were invariably crazy. But not quite crazy enough to convince me they were wrong. They had a tendency to put us near the Salvage Islands, an uninhabited group of rocks with all sorts of outlying horrors north of the Canaries, where I least desired to be, and there was a bad twenty-four hours spent wondering if after all the workings could be right. When you have only yourself with whom to discuss a situation, you can argue from ten different viewpoints and sell yourself on any one of them. Dead reckoning, on the other hand, put us on our course over the Conception Bank, which seemed reasonable as the seas had the shorter, shallower appearance of water over a bank, yet there was this doubt milling about in the back of my mind, so I kept alert and anxious until the evening of October 15th, when a peak of land appeared in the clear light of the westering sun. It was only a shadow, and looked like a dark cloud on the horizon, but the outlines were harder, more definite than those of a cloud and it did not alter shape. I reckoned it must be at least sixty miles distant and felt sure it was the peak of Tenerife. All would have been well except that the following morning we met a Spanish fishing boat whose crew volunteered the information that "Palma" lay in the direction we were going. After they were hull down on the horizon the thought occurred to me, did they mean Las Palmas or the Island of Palma? It makes quite a difference, I pointed out to *FA* as she curtseyed along in a freshening breeze. It was not impossible for us to be further to the southwest of our course than we believed, and for the land to be nearer and to be the peak of some other island—Palma, say—and the more I thought about it the more I was confused. A long wrestle with the sextant revealed nothing useful. The positions obtained were all wildly divergent, and after eliminating all the other errors, I concluded my timing was at fault, and that it was impracticable to work single-handed without a stopwatch. Counting seconds ("one-and-two-and-three") from the moment the sun bounced on the horizon until I reached the chronometer, gimballed in its case and screwed down right forrard in the cabin, was altogether too inaccurate, a hit-and-miss method not assisted in any way by the concern of holding the sextant protectively meanwhile. For it is impossible to lay anything down haphazardly aboard a small ship; it must be held until it is safely stowed, otherwise it is apt to find its way overboard or to be shattered to pieces. Lurching through the companion hatch, clutching the sextant, I would murmur, "One and two and oops and three, no four, and oh-oh, and six, where was I? and—oh damn," and climb out again to take another sight. Resolving to buy a stopwatch at the first opportunity, I sailed on towards the island, now rendered invisible by the day haze, to find out what it was when we got there. But two days later, the winds being slight and fitful, more land showed up in the sunset, which eventually turned out to be Fuertaventura, volcanic and forbidding, but welcome because it was where it should be. Confidently, at last, we continued on our way to Las Palmas, arriving there on October 24th, to be greeted with the unrestrained enthusiasm usually reserved for the prodigal son, or one given up as lost.

Chapter 13

"Don't look now, but I hope we are being followed," *FA* was chattering along under motor, yawing lazily over the swell now coming in from the east. Overhead, little round clouds were forming, small and symmetrical, dark shadows against a pale night sky lightened by an as yet unseen moon. The clouds were low, barely five hundred feet, so low indeed that it seemed one only had to reach up to touch them. They marshalled in serried rows, above and all round, right across the sky to the rim of the sea and remained static and alert as if waiting for a starter's signal.

"Trade Wind clouds," I thought, delighted at having recognised them and thrilled once more at the actual sight of something grown vicariously familiar through so much reading in the past. "About time too, *FA*. We've been looking for them long enough." It did not take much imagination to conjure up a fleet of old-time sailing ships rolling along before the winds that had blown steadily round a belt of the earth since weather began. Imagination was a little premature, however, for although the Trade Wind clouds were forming, the winds were yet to come. . . .

Eleven days out from Las Palmas on a sou'westerly course looking for the Trade Winds, and all we had had were calms and westerlies.

"Sou'west to 20N 30W," John had advised, "and you'll pick up the Trades and all your troubles will be over. It will be the experience of your life . . . there's nothing quite like it . . . running for a thousand miles or more before a steady wind. . . ."

(But the Commodore of the S.S. *Andes* had frowned and shaken his head when he heard this. "20N 30W?" he had said.

"Oh no, you don't want to get so far south. Not this time of year . . . keep north, keep north, and you'll be all right."

Someone said, "Left it a bit late, haven't you?"

And someone else, "Going a bit soon, aren't you?")

It was the twentieth of November, 1952, when *Felicity Ann* and I sailed out of Las Palmas bound for Antigua across the Ocean. A filthy day it was, with ragged black clouds racing before a southerly wind which drove horizontal rain before it and whipped a grey sea into tumbling whitecaps. Not the sort of day one would choose for a departure, but having set a day for going it is better to go. If you stay and wait for weather it is a fidgety performance, like waiting at a station having just missed a train : lost time that belongs neither here nor there. A launch with friends and a Spanish movie cameraman aboard accompanied us to the harbour entrance, where a fishing boat under shortened sail rolled up to wish us farewell.

I felt no emotion, other than the usual one of surprise at having arrived at a point which, although representing a goal, was never wholly related to reality. In a way it was a repetition of the Plymouth departure with, perhaps, a little less practical bewilderment.

FA worked in the short head sea. Her planking had shrunk as usual from her four weeks' idleness in port, and water seeped through the seams. She would take up quickly enough, I knew, larch being a sponge-like wood, but meantime the sea bubbled in drop by drop and welled, like tears of utmost sadness, down inside the hull into the bilges. Rain and spray saturated the decks and percolated through invisible cracks into the cabin, so that within ten minutes everything below was as wet as on deck, with fruit and vegetables rotting in an atmosphere as humid as a hot-house.

Plenty of wind, Miguel, the Las Palmas Yacht Club watchman, had promised as he helped me get ready to leave the mooring in front of the Club. Had warned in fact. Keep away from the southern end of the island, he had begged, nearly falling out of his boat in the effort to convey how far one should keep away from the island: "Múcho viénto," he said, "múcho viénto." And múcho viénto there was that night, as, ignoring his advice, we had turned on to a sou'westerly course at the southern end of Grand Canary. The wind had backed from south to east and we roared before it, carrying far too much canvas, exulting, quite erroneously, at being one of the lucky ones who find the Trade Winds right away.

We ran on all night, and in the early hours of the dark, wet, windy morning, I discovered the bilge pump had choked, and was compelled to lift the floor-boards and spend the better part of an hour upside down in the bilges clearing the pump. I slipped and cut my forehead and dripped blood all over the cabinsole. One way and another it was a discouraging way to begin a long voyage, so it was comforting, in a negative sort of way, to think of Bombard, already four weeks on the way across in his rubber raft—without even an apple aboard to rot— and reflect that, however miserable it might be for me, it would be infinitely more unpleasant for him. Compared with his venture I was making a luxury cruise. This brought me to thinking of the many other ocean crossers who had been in Las Palmas at the same time. Long-distance voyagers appeared to be a minor industry of the port; and I wondered how they were getting on and how far they had got, for they had all left ahead of me by two or three weeks. A regular league of nations we were, going hither and yon in our little ships. There were French yachts, German yachts, American yachts, and a strange motor vessel flying the Venezuelan flag, known amongst the rest of us as the "square-rigged motor launch" on account of an enormous yardarm attached to her stump mast to take a square-sail and eke out her insufficient fuel capacity for the crossing. Her crew included a young Yorkshire fisherman in a constant maze at finding himself where he was—"here's a rum go"—and since no international port is complete without a band of Dutchmen doing something valiant with a small ship, there was a yachtload of Hollanders emigrating on the inevitable, gallant shoestring to Dutch possessions in the West, where they intended to create a new life for their families left patiently waiting in Europe. There was a very modern cutter, *Beyond*, with reverse sheer, and a plethora of gadgets aboard including an electric remote control device to enable her to be steered from the cross-trees and conned through reef-ribbed waters. She was owned by Tom and Ann Worth, who were sailing briskly round the world on a two-year schedule. Ann Worth gave me a frying-pan to replace the one I lost washing up one morning on the way from Casablanca, my washing-up bowl being the ocean. The frying-pan slipped out of my hand and sank in 1500 fathoms. It had never been the same since its beating in the fog off Finisterre, but I was sorry to lose it, as a frying-pan is the most important, if not the only, cooking utensil for a single-hander. It is valuable not only for its intended use of frying, but acts as a toaster, a griddle, and even as a modified oven with the addition of a lid. Ann's pan was an improvement, however, being a much more solid job than its predecessor and less likely to lose its shape in the advent of further fog.

Long-distance voyagers run a sort of free library amongst themselves of paper-backed books, which they unload on to each other on arrival in port, which provides variety in one's sea reading without putting any undue strain on the mentality. Ann gave me a bunch of these books whose lurid covers belied their innocuous contents, and lastly she presented a canned Christmas pudding. Catching my rather wry grin, for it was only the beginning of November, she said quickly, "Not that I don't think you'll make it across before then—but, you never know. . . ." With a rush of optimism I said I would share it with them in Antigua. Tom Worth and I had missed meeting years ago in the Argentine, for I left the ranch where I was visiting way out in the prairie a few months before he arrived. Tom was flying airplanes then, and I had just become infected with the aviation virus. Then, these years later, we have to meet in our own boats in a little Atlantic island, both bound across the Ocean, which proves nothing but that the long arm of coincidence strikes again.

Also in port was the *Nymph Errant*. She left the Canary Islands for the West Indies, two weeks before I, and was, no doubt, I reflected enviously, romping along in those fabulous Trades that I was looking for and John had spoken of so glowingly, making her way across in the smart, seamanlike fashion inevitable under his command. John's parting advice, made a little beseechingly, had been not to loiter. . . . "Make it a good fast passage this time, Ann, don't give them a chance to turn it into a circus again. Not like the last effort. . . ." Sailing was too near to his heart to be brought into disrepute by anything resembling a stunt or false dramatics, and the "last effort," *FA*'s protracted passage from Casablanca to Las Palmas, had come perilously close to doing just that. I had realised of course, that we were taking an unconscionable time to cover the distance, but it honestly never occurred to me that this would cause any excitement. Most of the time we were in the shipping lanes and rarely out of sight of a ship, some of which, as the *Genale*, must have seen us, and I had thought in my simple fashion, that if anyone should raise a question as to our whereabouts, one of the vessels would surely report having sighted us. At any rate the calm weather along the route would be known and explanatory of the delay. It seems this was not so; imaginary gales were invented, and no one asked the right ships the right questions. I daresay if it had not been for the English newspaper, for which I was writing articles, getting impatient at the lack of copy, no one would have bothered to ask any questions at all, but the newspaper took to calling up Las Palmas on the long-distance telephone, a practice that is apt to create a certain interest in the object of the call. So by the time *FA* and I came puttering into port flying our little flags and minding our business, the ponds were on the point of being dragged and we received a welcome as if we had done something remarkable instead of simply arriving—if late. . . . After the news had been cabled to England, the newspaper promptly called me up through a shipping office to ask for the story, at which I was a little aggrieved. Nearly two thousand miles of sailing, five months spent in the doing of it, and they just lifted the receiver and called me as if I had slipped round the corner from Plymouth to Brixham. Those jungle men who shrink heads have nothing on modern communications that can shrink a whole world.

I suppose I should have been delighted by the interest in the venture which appeared to have snowballed whilst my back was turned, but in point of fact I was embarrassed. Fresh from the sea, I was in a pretty humble frame of mind, for whatever the conditions, a week or two on the water under that illimitable dome of sky will deflate any ego, and the concern for my welfare seemed exaggerated and unnecessary. And when the time came to leave again, I was resolved to try to live up to John's injunction to make a good fast passage.

With luck, even with a small, slow ship like *FA*, the crossing could be made in thirty days; it was more likely to take forty, but with what I then considered to be an excess of caution I prepared for a sixty-day trip.

Preparing for this voyage had been in a way unlike preparing for any of the others, although naturally it was a projection and development of them all, and the preparations were more in the nature of a mental strengthening of the skipper than a material provisioning of the ship, a feature with which I was now pretty well acquainted. It was to be a much longer passage than any of the others, and it would be much lonelier; there would not be the comforting knowledge of vast continents only a hundred miles or so to the eastward, and I could not expect to see any ships en route. Once the busiest sea lanes, the Trade Wind belts are now the most deserted, for steamships have no need of following winds, but sail great circle courses direct to where they want to be. And there could be no turning back on this voyage. No change of plan. This sort of certainty was sobering. When there is no way back, no way out, you must be very, very sure of what you are doing. I did not know how I would react to absolute solitude. It is an experience few of us are ever called upon to undergo and one which few of us would voluntarily choose. It is almost unimaginable, because solitude is something that normally can be broken at will. Even being on one's own in undeveloped country, popularly supposed to epitomise loneliness, is not true solitude, for one is surrounded by trees and bush and grass and animals, all part of the substance of one's own living. But the sea is an alien element; one cannot live in it or on it for long, and one survives that little time by one's own wit and judgment and the Grace of God. When a man says he loves the sea, he loves the illusion of mastery, the pride of skill, the life attendant on sea-faring, but not the sea itself. One may be moved by its beauty or its grandeur, or terrified by its immensity and power of destruction, but one cannot love it any more than one can love the atmosphere or the stars in outer space.

For years I had been constructing an armour of self-sufficiency, deluding myself it was strong enough to resist any onslaughts of physical or spiritual loneliness. People—why, I could take them or leave them alone. But the voyage so far had revealed a chink or two in the armour, and my independence was by no means as complete as I had believed. And in previous passages there had been ships at hand and a reasonable proximity of land; the situation, then, was not immutable if it grew untenable, the knowledge of which makes all the difference in the world. That problem was one which could only be answered by time and

Felicity Ann in Casablanca

Felicity Ann on the slip at Las Palmas for cleaning and repainting for long crossing

practical experience. And if that had been all, the future would not have presented so formidable an appearance. I was not really afraid of not reaching the West Indies, although I was certainly concerned as to *how* I was going to reach them, but the how was overridden by the why, the motive for attempting the crossing in the first place. Would there be an answer to that? Would the fears and insecurity that had warped my values, that must have warped them or the *Reliance* tragedy would never have happened, be allayed? Would I be able at last to touch the philosopher's stone; find the key to living? Life since the shipwreck had been of a two-dimensional quality without depth or meaning . . . even the voyage to date had had little more than a travelogue superficiality to it. At least that is how it felt at the time, and it was not until much later that I realised the experience was going deeper than it appeared. Patience has never been my strong point, and I want answers right away, as soon as the question is posed. If there was no answer at the end of the voyage, if life was to continue to be flat and devoid of purpose, the notion of simply putting in time was impossible to contemplate. Some of us never question the necessity for acquiring maturity and insight: life is ordered, and day by day we move along a seemingly predestined groove as a locomotive moves to its ultimate destination. Some of us, the lucky ones, find the key by accident, and smoothly live out our lives unquestioningly, upheld by a balanced philosophy. But some of us follow mistaken beliefs to disaster, as I did, and then we must perish or find the right key. And if I didn't find the right one, what then?

Although the dominating aspect so far as I was concerned, it was certainly the least tangible one of the preparations. There were practical matters to attend to, and they were legion. In these I was helped immeasurably by Ken and Dorothy Park, who selflessly devoted themselves to the project as if the outcome was of utmost importance. The Parks epitomised for me the unrestricted friendliness and generosity I had found, and was to continue to find, throughout the voyage. The kindness that did so much to chip away the rock of cynicism that I had acquired defensively through the years along with those twisted values. Gradually it was being brought home that people, everywhere, regardless of race, colour, or creed, are fundamentally decent and warmhearted, eager to put out the hand of welcome and succour and friendship to another human-being without thought of reward for their actions.

Ken Park was managing director of Blandy's, one of the leading shipping agents in the Islands, and his interest had been roused in the voyage of the *Felicity Ann* by the anxiety of the newspaper for which I was writing, for it was to him that the editor called to find out why we had gone missing. When at last we had arrived, Ken had come out in the firm's launch to greet us, a courtesy I hardly appreciated at the time, and one normally only extended to the commodores of the mightier vessels. *FA* was then put on the lists and attended to as if she had been a twenty-thousand tonner instead of just a no-account sloop. . . .

It might have been irritating for such a busy firm to have the S.S. *Whosit* down for several thousand gallons of water followed by the A/S *Felicity Ann* for thirty-five: for the bunkering requirements of the *Whosit* to run into thousands of gallons of fuel oil and for the one-man-band of the *Felicity Ann* to put ashore a dozen two-gallon cans for filling; for the provisioning department to have to think in pounds instead of tons; but everyone concerned seemed to regard it all as very funny. Even when *FA* went alongside the waterbarge, the waterbarge being far too big to come alongside her in the normal way, the lightermen thought it the best joke of the year, trying to control the giant python pipes designed to fill the water holds of large vessels, guiding the gushing stream into *FA*'s cockpit tank without sinking her and filling the two dozen aluminium quart bottles I had for an emergency supply. A great deal of water was wasted that day, much, much more than was stored for the crossing, and the lightermen wiped their eyes, wet with laughing and wild streams of water.

The Parks were English, as were many of the executives of the various shipping firms, for the Canary Islands, such as Grand Canary and Teneriffe, are in effect giant filling stations at an ocean junction, and consequently international. But the Islands are Spanish and the language there is Spanish and I don't speak Spanish. When *FA* was to be hauled out in the shipyard that was a subsidiary company of the Blandy's, for scrubbing and painting and the removal of her underwater jungle, I had a high old time trying to describe the shape of her underwater body to portly, sunny Juan, the foreman, who beamed appreciatively at everything I said, and understood not a word. The result of this was a team of divers arriving alongside *FA* the following morning at five o'clock to find out just what it was the gal said. Undeterred, I persisted in visiting the yard to see how work progressed, and, of course, persisted in talking to the men, because I don't seem to be able to lose the illusion that if you open your mouth and make sounds someone is going to understand you. The yard manager was a Scotsman, and as long as he was there, someone did, but he was not always there, and he came along to me one day with a puzzled expression. "What's this," he asked, "about welding a tank?" I have often wondered since which of the actions employed in my personal sign language indicated that particular request.

Whilst *FA* was high and dry being overhauled I stayed with the Parks in their cása, which has a more imposing sound than house, and better suits the home of the Parks; and with them I enjoyed an interlude of gracious living that is fast becoming a memory in Europe. The ménage included what seemed a veritable battalion of retainers to one accustomed to the do-it-yourself way of Western living, and all of them appeared to be indigenous to and indissoluble from the household. When the time came for me to leave, they all lined up and shook hands with a moving sincerity. The cook, with tears in her eyes, promised to put up prayers for my safety. I am not religious in the conventional sense, but I found this of peculiar comfort. That a stranger, met only for a few brief days and of an association that might almost be called glancing, with whom there could be no discussion or interchange of ideas except through an interpreter, whose outlook was so divergent that all we shared was our species and the habitation of the same planet, should feel strongly enough to weep and include me in her prayers which had a real and deep significance for her, was an illuminating and very heartening experience.

She was also a practical woman and baked for me a batch of bread rusks which were one of the most appreciated items of the commissariat on the crossing. I stored them in a large biscuit tin and sealed the tin with adhesive tape, and those rusks might have lasted some time if I had not enjoyed them so much at the beginning of the voyage. The cook was also responsible for obtaining me a few pounds of local meal called "gofio," which was simply maize (or corn) roasted and ground to a flour. This was recommended by Dorothy as being very sustaining, and, since it is already cooked, needs no further treatment other than the addition, say, of milk and sugar. Local farmworkers practically live on gofio and their general appearance of well-being can give no better recommendation. Most of the provisions were obtained from Dominguez, who worked in with Blandy's for provisioning ships, and Señor Dominguez was so fascinated by the project that he dealt with my minuscule order himself. I stocked up with citrus fruits, bananas, and tomatoes, all stacked with vitamin C, and they were delivered aboard green and unripe . . . the hope being that they would last a little longer than usual. I took aboard, also, fourteen pounds of potatoes, of the kind that are small and hard and known as "new" in England, and a few pounds of onions, which I intended to allow to sprout so that I could eat the green shoots, and a few dozen eggs, which were wrapped in newspaper, packed in a basket, and hung from the deckhead. Past experience had shown that eggs stowed this way would keep fresh for many weeks, providing they were fresh and had never been refrigerated.

Dorothy Park took me for several trips into the interior of the Island, which like all the Canary Islands has a rather more forbidding than inviting appearance from seaward, but a curious charm once you are ashore. Perhaps because of its special significance, Las Palmas did not slide over the horizon of my consciousness so easily as other places had done after I had sailed. And surely there could not be a more fitting place from which to take a departure in a small ship bound across the Atlantic, for the Canary Islands are perched on the very edge of the Old World, looking out across to the new, and are themselves a stimulating mixture of the old and the new. Ships bound to and from South America and Central America, great vessels with every possible amenity aboard for their particular purpose, steam majestically in and out of the harbours, where the local trading and fishing boats go about their affairs under sail. Few of the Canary boats are fitted with engines and they are charmingly old-world in design, with high poops and pronounced tumblehome, and they are maintained beautifully. You seldom see work-boats that are titivated so continually and enthusiastically.

Grand Canary itself is an arid island of brown mountains with little pockets of fertility tucked away in volcanic crevasses, and geraniums, growing with unexpected profusion in a handful of dust, line the roadsides as they might a private driveway. Bougainvillea, hibiscus, and poinsettia decorate Las Palmas and outlying villages, splashing white walls and buildings with bold brave colours as the pools of paint blaze on an artist's palette. The architecture is generally Spanish-Moorish and the buildings are interspersed with naked areas like the bombed sites in London. There are modern hotels of a quality unsurpassed anywhere, yet if you get up early enough in the morning you will see herds of goats being driven from door to door delivering the day's supply of milk, which no one can deny is fresh.

Old and new. From the old to the new. The sojourn in Las Palmas had been so vivid and real, and a springboard, I hoped, from an old life into a new one. We left the island enveloped in cloud thicker than the mists of memory, the day we set off in search of the Trade Winds, the New World, and a new life. . . .

Miguel's múcho viénto tapered off after twenty-four hours of gusto and by six o'clock on November 22nd the sea was flat calm, a condition that lasted for six days, so that I was compelled to start the motor and drive along under power in order to make any mileage at all. On one of those flat still mirage mornings I busied myself clearing out the cabin, sorting through fruit and vegetables ripening with unprecedented rapidity, throwing the rotten stuff overside, together with the baskets in which they were delivered and stowed. They were fine big containers, those baskets, beautifully woven, the size of old-fashioned laundry baskets, and I regretted their demise, but they took up altogether too much space below. They floated along with the debris by the ship and would have remained with us all day doubtless, but I started the motor and left them.

When I first began cleaning up there was not a fish or a bird in sight, but as soon as the first rotten apples hit the water, dim dark shapes began to lurk in the depths, and overhead gulls wheeled and cried, and petrels fluttered over the surface, conjured into being by my action, apparently, otherwise how did they know?

At the end of a week we had accomplished one tenth of the

journey, and I had the first of a recurring dream that I was fitting out a small ship to sail across the Atlantic. Then we had twenty-four hours of a vicious and quite uncalled-for squall in which we could do nothing but lie-to in huge, remorseless waves, computing our drift in the wrong direction, and listen to the screaming wind. When it eased I turned *FA* and worked south under motor, hoping to find better weather; and on the night of December 1st the Trade Wind clouds started forming overhead. For once the portents were not fooling and the winds quickly followed their heralds, the little round white clouds which might be translated from the Chinese as "heavenly sheep." The log registered 500, and the Atlantic crossing began in earnest.

Part 2

Log of the Felicity Ann
Canary Islands . . . Dominica, B.W.I.

Chapter 14

Wednesday December 3rd 1952

0750 hours. Thirteen days at sea. Have been up since before dawn doing odd chores. Considering only have one meal a day extraordinary how washing up accumulates. Trade Winds blowing quite fresh. Feeling not so good these last few days. Don't know why; eyes have been bothering, sore from salt and glare, and I don't think the crack on the head from the boom last night helps much. Did not realise it had actually split open until this morning when tried to comb hair and found comb all bloody. Lack of exercise also beginning to tell. I don't want to eat, but get low and dispirited if I don't. On course 237 degs. running with full main and working jib. Shall have to do something about rigging twins.

Making 4/5 knots. Will have to wait for this to ease down a bit before trying to put up twin staysails.

1100. Sight first flying fish this trip. Sea growing heavy and confused. If like this all way across it is going to be tough sledding.

1630. One hell of a sea got up. Reefed and changed to storm jib. *FA* carries a lot of weather helm which makes steering very hard work. She fights all the time to turn up into wind.

Shoal of mullet-looking fish just slipped past.

1955. Hove to for night. Very tired. Conditions a bit easier now. (Note. About 1900 hours, saw an amazing meteor thing to the north of us. It went off with a huge bright flash; not a flash exactly, more like the slow blossoming of a white flame; and it slowly fell across the sky like a red hot cinder.) Log registers 580.

Thursday December 4th

Have been troubled since 0400 this morning by dysentery again. Feel lousy in consequence. No sign of wind abating either.

0700.   On course, 237 degs.

1900.   Heave to. With the best will in the world cannot steer more than twelve hours now at a stretch. Tried to set twins but there was too much of a sea. Log 630.

Friday December 5th

0630.   Surface to find flying fish on deck. Felt honour-bound to cook it for breakfast having read so often that this is one of the perks of Trade Wind sailing. The fish are attracted by the lights of a small vessel and fly towards them. Find flying fish good eating, like fresh herring only not so oily. Split it like herring, took out backbone, and fried it in butter.

1040.   Spent up to now setting up twin staysails.

This was quite a task. The jib and main have to be taken in first, and *FA* then wallows broadside, making a fearful fuss and a very unstable base to work on. The twin staysails are hanked to two forestays that are not normally set up but which lead from the upper cross-trees to eyebolts in the deck. These eyebolts are about 3 feet forrard of the mast and about 2 feet 3 inches apart. The stays are made fast to the eyebolts by lanyards attached to the end of the wire. The two booms are then fixed by snap fasteners to brass dumb-bell-shaped fittings on the forrard shrouds, and sheets or guylines from their outer ends led to the tiller through blocks on the aft stanchions and openings in the cockpit coamings. Non-adjustable topping-lifts from the lower cross-trees are then attached; light wires with rope tails which are made fast to cleats in the centre of the booms. The sails are then hanked on . . . (oh, this jargon—this *nautelese*) fastened . . . to the forestays with snap fasteners; lanyards from the tack are made fast to the eyebolts in the deck so that tension on the luff

138

can be taken up or eased as the case may be. The outhaul snap is attached to shackles in the clew, and the foot of the sail is hauled out along the boom.

Then you take courage in both hands and a heave on the halyards, trying to get both sails up at once. This is rarely possible unless it is flat calm, and from then on you are on your own, and the ship goes mad. One sail fills and draws and she starts sailing on it furiously. The other is taken aback and tries to drive the ship in the opposite direction. And whilst you are making frenzied trips from the tiller to the foredeck, the two sails exchange operations, smartly and with precision; but at last you have the ship running down wind with both sails drawing beautifully and the next problem is to attach the guy-lines to the tiller so that she will steer herself. This is a very nice and delicate adjustment, but once made you are rewarded by an automatic and tireless helmsman that can steer the ship with a greater accuracy and sensitivity than you can yourself as long as the winds allow, and without the least fear of an involuntary jibe. There is no such thing as perfection, however, and the motion is fantastically wild.

1140. Making only three knots under this rig. But it is blowing quite hard and what with the look of the sky and slight fall in the glass I think it is wiser to stick to these small jibs than put up the big ones. I had the storm jib duplicated so they could be used as "reefed" twins.

1200. Seas absolutely monumental. Haven't rigged steering device yet—don't feel this is the time to experiment.

1500. Blowing F7.

1530. School of large handsome fish, bright blue, green, and yellow swim up to the ship.

2340. Lying to—have utterly failed to get the twins self-steering. Must sleep. Beat. Log 667.

Saturday December 6th

Surfaced 0645 feeling absolutely scuppered and wondering how on earth to carry on. Get tired more quickly and for less effort this trip—getting worn down, or appalled by enormity of distance? If the big twins won't self-steer either, this is certainly going to be a long, long passage. Sore throat.

0815. Big twins up. Pulling like a couple of horses, dray horses. Blowing F5. Hope it stays easier.

Spent all day dickering with twins and getting *FA* to sail herself. Succeeded after drilling and sawing away part of the cockpit coaming so that the sheets or guylines leading from the booms did so unimpeded. The sheets from block to tiller have a pronounced circular movement which the original fairleads in the coamings did not permit, and the slightest friction destroys any pretence to self-steering. Working with drill and keyhole saw, trying to steer at the same time before a masterful sea, was a tricky operation. Wind fallen away to F4, then 3.

Sunday December 7th

Ship steered herself all through the night and put up 45 on the log. The motion is fierce, very quick and erratic, and the sound of the water rushing past as heard from below is as if it was being poured very quickly from a giant and inexhaustible bottle. At last feel we are getting somewhere . . . if only Trades play fair and don't get too savage again . . . seafaring teaches one never to take anything weatherwise on trust.

1200. Log 759. Took day off and read a couple of whodunits and feel better for rest. Whodunits in middle of ocean are even more improbable than ashore.

Experiment taking noon sights, which difficult in frantic motion. Today's guess, latitude, 19 34 North.

Monday December 8th

Surfaced dawn to find log reading 818. This is *joy* . . . to have her sailing on whilst I sleep. Leap out in morning to count mileage like enthusiastic chicken farmer counting eggs.

1200. Log 835 Lat. 18 35N . . . hm. . . . Day's run 76, from noon to noon. *FA* caught another flying fish. Good-sized one, too. About size of herring. Intended to have it for lunch, but stove gone mad. Ship persists in steering too far south and nothing I can do seems to make any difference. Very annoying. Winds NE and she won't run any other way but dead before them.

Tuesday December 9th

Surface dawn as usual. Delicious morning. F3 wind. No cloud. Hot sun. Fixed primus and went to town with fried potatoes and eggs for breakfast. Passed empty rum bottle—who are we following? Did Bombard cheat? Later, passed lots of jetsam and ship debris. Strange how reassuring a few empty cans can be on the ocean.

Course now 272 deg. Approximately correct for Dominica, which would make a good West Indian landfall being high and mountainous and visible from afar.

Log 911, day's run, 76, Lat. 18 17N. Am not exactly happy about these latitudes as it is so difficult to take sights with *FA* rolling the way she does. No means of checking and only time will tell. . . .

Wednesday December 10th

Small sardine-like fish on deck this morning, hardly food value and didn't feel like fish anyway.

1200. Log 985, day's run 74, Lat. 18 16N.

1700. 1000 just up on the log. One third of journey done. . . .

Thursday December 11th

Three weeks at sea. Blew up to F7 since sunset last evening and it is still blowing about 6; very overcast and cold. Ship steering herself well, but motion wicked, didn't think it possible for it to get worse, but apparently that only another of life's little illusions. Primus mutinies and won't work; can't fix it in this sea.

1200. Log 1071, day's run 86. Far too lively to get noon sight. Wind F6.

Friday December 12th

Gorgeous golden sunrise with authentic golden rays. Fixed primus as wind abated and seas slightly easier. Also hungry. Cooked enormous breakfast of french fries, apple, and eggs. This to cover today and yesterday. The motion never really settles down and I don't think one can ever become used to it the way one becomes used to normal motion, it is quite unpredictable. Curtails activity. Takes over an hour and a half to prepare and eat breakfast, a very exhausting procedure. Sometimes wonder if worth it. Wish nourishment available in capsule form. Still overcast and surprisingly cool. Paucity of bird-life here, which sad, as like to see them around; companionable.

1200. Log 1155, day's run 85. Muddle over time, so did not get noon sight.

Saturday December 13th

1200. Log 1225, day's run 70, Wind F3, warm, Lat. 17 41N. Hot and sunny day.

Sunday December 14th

Time marches on, to coin a phrase. Yesterday afternoon wind fell away to F1-2. This morning sea calm. Wind fl. but glass slowly going down and sky clouding over with alto cumulus. Wind freshening slightly now and most of the cloud cleared away. Weather obviously doesn't know its own mind.

1200. Log 1266, day's run 41. Lat. 17 30N. Beginning to think there must be something in this latitude business. It appears to work out the way it should, more or less. Managed to get slight croak on radio last night. Fading badly. Suspect battery is going to peter out. Hot humid cabin is no storage place for dry cells. Hot day. Reading *Riddle of the Sands* second time this trip and *n*th time since first doing so. This classic has everything. . . .

1340. No wind.

1800. Utterly becalmed. Have taken in log line, it having grown barnacles again. Three large and colourful fish swimming purposefully round ship. Must remember not to fall overboard. Sunset yellow and murky. Glass falling—but only diurnal fall after all.

1920. Lightning to north. Still no wind. Atmosphere oppressive.

Monday December 15th

0750. Light wind from south-*west*, hardly enough to fill these light sails—but why south-*west*? Alter course 332. Log 1270.

1045. Course 290, Log 1271. Have to alter back to fore and aft sails, full main and working staysail. Close-hauled on port tack.

1200. Unable to get sight for cloud. Log 1274, day's run 81. Enormous shoals of flying fish just got up. Flew across water like flocks of birds. Have passed lots more jetsam—makes me think we must be following someone's track pretty closely. Whose, I wonder? Take time off to cook sausages and peas for lunch. For which I feel better, thank you. I must eat more often. The fish watch my washing up operations with evident interest. They don't look so large today. Different fish? They certainly are, the others have just turned up. Four to five feet long, bright turquoise blue with electric blue fins and yellow tails. Gorgeous creatures. They swim close to the surface of the water and give the flying fish hell. Little fish like silver pencil dances madly on its tail on surface just by stern of ship, dodging death by inches, no doubt. Reflect gloomily marine life unequivocally grim.

Two bosun birds visit ship with loud squawks and fly round and round mast shrieking ornithological oaths at one another. Flying appears to be a great effort to them and they seem to be on the point of stall unless flapping furiously with their narrow swept-back wings.

2125. Heave to. Torrential rain. Heavy thundersquall. Log 1288.

Tuesday December 16th

Squalls all night. Continuous lightning and heavy rain. *FA* most prominent thing on this part of ocean. Speculate on effect of ship being struck by lightning.

0500. Deemed wiser to reef and change jibs. Wind *still south-west*. And plenty more squalls to come. This very disappointing. Have to dismantle twins rig—stays, booms, etc.—completely.

0645. Under way, course 290. Filthy morning. Clouds low and black, swirling in vaporous turmoil overhead. Wind screaming. Waves hissing. Beating into short steep seas. Lower edges of cloud trail almost to water. Ahead is black archway of cloud through which sun is shining and sea is blue. As if we were in darkened room looking out . . . feel if only we can get through archway all will be well. Another fallacy. It is even worse "outside."

0900. Take in another reef. Conditions fierce. Wind SW, F8. Have no alternative but to heave to. Barometer has not registered for this at all.

1130. Overcast. Wind fallen away, but left a heavy sea with pyramids instead of waves. Am not to be lured into making any moves until I see what it is going to do.

1150. Everything eased down, but have uneasy notion wind is only taking a breather. Lots more dirt to come in the sky, and I see no way of dodging it.

1600.   Here we go. More squalls. Rising seas. *Enormous* rain-drops hit the water with dimples and splash and make curious sheet of white spray over entire surface. Any end to this that is pleasant?

1800.   One of the most dramatic sunsets I have ever seen. Huge multi-coloured cumulus piled high in the east where lightning plays over it illuminating reflected colours of the sunset. Brilliant gold in the west, against which black anvil clouds stand out in silhouette. Overhead it is clear and Venus glows with a serenity that contrasts with the drama taking place on the horizons. Now it is dark and lightning flickers all round us. Terrifying.

Wednesday December 17th

Wind went round to the east this morning at 0600 hours. But all that fearful weather we have had is heaped up black to east'ard of us and is coming back. Am afraid squalls would blow out those light twin sails if I put them up. Decide those colourful fish are dolphins. They are supposed to be good eating and easy to catch, but although there is a fishing line and strong hooks aboard, I cannot bring myself to try and catch one. They are too friendly and trusting. One comes every morning to see what I have to throw overside, and if I lower the canvas bucket on to his nose, he doesn't swim away but seems to like having his nose scratched. He has an engaging habit of rolling over and studying me searchingly with one eye.

1000.   Squalls broke up and passed over without fuss. Spend an hour setting up twins and then discover wind has gone round to south-west again. By steering myself I can get her to sail 336 degrees, but she will not steer herself on this course. Sickening.

1145.   Back to the old fore and aft. Wind abeam. Full main and working jib. Course 290, Log 1292.

145

1300. Wind SW, F2. Lumpy sea with heavy cross swell which makes it very tiring to no purpose. Making two knots. Blazing hot. Cumulus piled up impressively all round sky.

1500. Wind SE, but with all that heavy cumulus in the offing anything can happen and wind is very fitful.

1745. No wind. What did I tell you? Heave to. Another night of lightning more terrifying than ever.

2112. Had just gone to sleep when awakened by shriek of wind and found the most awful black squall in full blast. Ship lying right over and lightning flashing all round.

This is very bad. Will have to reef.

Reef down on wet deck tilted at incredible angle. Wind takes your breath away like icy plunge. Work in dark as cannot hold flashlight as well as hold on. Lightning darts about apparently looking for us. Idiotically try and pretend not to see it.

Are we ever going to get out of this? And back to some nice Trades?

Thursday December 18th

Four weeks at sea and not half way. Hideous night like those off the Portuguese coast. Leaves one so limp for the next day.

1055. On course 290 deg. Log 1302. Running with reefed main and storm jib. Squalls blow up to F8.

1215. Today's great thought. . . . The secret of love *is* greater than the secret of death . . . and hey presto, the storm clouds clear away and heap up hugging themselves way, way, way over on the horizon.

1700. Heave to. Tired out and gybing as unable to concentrate any longer. Wind has laid off now, but sea still heavy and it has been a rugged afternoon. Arm aches and hand trembles from strain of holding tiller against *FA* who tries to swing up into wind all the time. Yet it is a comforting thought that if I did go

146

overboard she would luff up and wait for me. Now blowing F6–7 but awkward seas coming every which way.

Friday December 19th

0400.   Wake after first really restful sleep for what seems ages, with much surprise that it *was* restful, and that it is calm now. Suggestion of wind from the east-sou'east. But refuse to be taken in by it, so potter about, cook and eat breakfast, figure out position, wash up, etc., whilst waiting to see what wind decides to do.

0905.   Wind east, F2–3. So up twins and on course 290. Well, we are off again. How long for this time? It is no light matter setting up the twins and I have no confidence now in the theory that once they are up they are set for a couple of thousand miles. Jibsheets and mainsheet show signs of wear and tear, which hardly surprising. Don't think they'll see the voyage out unless weather very kind, and with 1700 miles to go this seems unlikely. Lots of dolphins round ship this morning. All sizes.

1200.   Log 1333, Lat. 18 28N, which I think is about right. Took out worn ends of mainsheet, and made baggywrinkle—the ocean cruiser's best friend—all morning.

1245.   Have just taken a look at the bottom, both sides as she rolls; *covered* with barnacles. This in only four weeks. So much for copper paint. Another factor to slow us down.

1730.   Is sunset, which also checks with latitude. Made more baggywrinkle (delicious word) this afternoon so that starboard twin is protected from chafe on the upper lifeline against which it is inclined to rub.

Dolphins have romped round ship all day practising flying and diving at which they are no good at all. They are obviously playing and enjoying themselves, but don't see why, as it must be painful sport. They leap high out of the water and flop back broadside with the most resounding thwack that jars *me* from

147

my toes up. A new type of fish has also adopted the ship, small, flat, and black with prim little mouths. Trigger fish according to illustrations in fish book. One of them likes cigarette ends. Made scones for tea (two meals today!). Wind east F1. Advancing on America majestically at one m.p.h.

Bosun bird, going east, flies past ship without batting an eyelid. This very unusual as these birds take a great interest in *FA*. So I give a piercing wolf whistle, whereon bosun bird wheels smartly round, flaps back to ship, dives and stalls about three feet from my head, looks sharply at me, decides against whatever he had in mind to do and flies smartly away again.

2355. A most unrestful night. Came on to blow just as I was going to sleep and starboard twin started flogging so had to turn out and readjust sheets. Easier said than done, and only achieved after colossal struggle. After which one squall after another until now it is pouring with rain again.

Saturday December 20th

0730. Surface feeling pretty washed out from lack of sleep. Plenty of dirt coming up. Log only registers 1368 and yet it was blowing smartish during the night. Only 35 since yesterday midday, nineteen and a half hours. This is serious.

Bloody barnacles.

0900. More rain. Ship rolling along a bit better. Four knots since last entry.

1200. Log 1375, Lat. 18 11N. Not too happy about that. It was a bad sight. Ship rolling heavily, and intermittent but dense cloud at the crucial moment.

1630. Plodding along at just under two—yet there is a nice breeze that ought to send us along better than that. Touched by despair tonight. If it blows hard enough to get us moving I am worried sick. These twins are only light canvas and not up to much weight; but if it doesn't blow hard we get nowhere fast, and there is a hell of a lot of ocean to cross yet and that worries me more.

1800.   Wind fallen away to F1.

Sunday December 21st

Squalls started again at 2200 last night and continued throughout with very heavy rain.

0730. Surface. Still very squally, but ship bowling along nicely, though wind has gone round to the south-east and is driving us north-west.

0815. Just finished breakfast. Make a rule to have this before doing anything else, for if I don't I am liable to overlook eating altogether since meals have no social significance, and I never feel hungry and generally meals mean time off at the expense of progress which I begrudge. Rarely have the energy to fix anything at night and would rather sleep then anyway, but if one doesn't eat, morale gets very low. There is apparently no end to this filthy weather; more is coming up and the wind shows a definite tendency to veer to the south-west. Am so sick of this.

0920.   Have been dickering with twins for the past hour trying to get *FA* to sail *anywhere* west of north, but wind is all over the shop now and it is pouring with rain.

Everything below is soaked and moulding and rotting, without so far as can be seen any chance of drying out. . . .

1050.   Change rigs again. Log 1421, course 340. Brought chart up to date. 1125 on course, 290 deg.

1355.   Close hauled again and the best we can make is 342. Log 1422. Rigged boom guy which is vast improvement to peace of mind. In these seas with only a light wind the boom swings like a crazy pendulum trying to demolish the gallows . . . and me if I am handy. . . .

Very thick low cloud to which there seems no end.

149

1420. Curious pimply sea and no wind, but plenty of dirt all round.

1425. Off again . . . running . . . course 282.

1630. Exasperated. I've had the wind going round and round in circles. Torrential rain. No visibility. Soaked to skin. Have reefed main and changed to small jib and packed up. I am going below and it can do what it likes. See if I care. Disgusted.

Monday December 22nd

Quiet night. Calm sea. Little wind.

0600. Disappointed to find wind direction still south-west, F1 increasing (ha) to F2, look you. Cooked breakfast, made some baggywrinkle. Washed up. Hell of a thing to be stuck in the middle of the ocean like this.

0855. Under way, course 320, log 1424. Wind SW F3.

1100. Wind pulling round to westward. We are making progress at one knot. ("Trade Wind sailing a wonderful experience?" Phooey!)

1200. Log 1426. Lat. 18 44N. Uncertain sight as cloud intervened at critical moment. Believed approximately correct.

Wind now F2.

Am making northwards in hope of finding Trades. Course 360.

1400. Have made up new pair of jibsheets and put them on. After which it started to rain so came below and made more baggywrinkle (when in doubt make baggywrinkle!) for starboard shroud. Have already fitted some on port shroud. This is where the jibsheets chafe.

1800. Wind fallen away. Reefed down and changed to small jib. Unnecessary of course, but don't want to turn out in the middle of the night to reef in squall, and it was just such an evening as this that I had to do so before. Note wire strand sticking out in main halyard. *FA* making a lot of leeway and probably half a knot. It is really going to be serious if we don't pick up the Trades again soon. Log 1431.

Tuesday December 23rd

Fooled again. You take a chance and get a wind fit to blow the anchors off an admiral's buttons; you reef and nothing happens. Quiet night, but sleep fitful and nightmarish. Consequently feel washed out and weary this morning, a morning that would be wonderful if only the wind was from the east, but there is no wind at all and the ship bangs and slats in shimmering glassy swell. Finish making baggywrinkle and fit same to starboard shroud. Make chart up to date immeasurably depressed by infinitesimal progress. Wash up and bring in log line to scrub off the barnacles it has acquired over last few days. Wish could do same for bottom. Log line appalling sight and it took hours to scrub the little beasts off. Fish life abundant this morning. The cigarette-eating fish is here again, gobbling up the butts I throw overboard, and a blue-and-black-striped job about six inches long is scavenging barnacles scrubbed off the line. Stupid sort of fish, why doesn't he go browse off the bottom? Dolphins much in evidence and am glad to see them.

Suffer much from thirst these days. It is very hot and everything I do makes me sweat inordinately. The water temperature is around 80 degrees and the boat is virtually floating in a warm bath so the cabin is not only hot but humid. I have only to sit on the settee to have the sweat running off me as though I was playing endless games of squash. So I am thirsty. But water is limited. Water is the limiting factor of the whole voyage. At present rate of progress we should make the other side in about one hundred and twenty days from now and there is not enough water for that. Have rationed drinking to one pint per day, and can think of little else but when I can have the next drink.

1115.   Start motor. Must put a few more miles on the clock. Motor starts very well, right away without fuss.

1127.   On course 308. Log 1431.

1500.   *FA* making four knots. Blazing hot day, but nothing in the way of wind as yet. Things look tricky to the north-west where we are going—cumulus massing and banking all round, getting ready for all sorts of oceanic frightfulness I've no doubt.

1915.   Stop engine. Log 1462. Thirty-one miles further on the way. Calm night; half moon; very beautiful. *FA* moves westward close hauled at point two knots which I have calculated from old-fashioned Dutchman's log method. This hardly seems worthwhile, so have hove to and then if the wind changes whilst I am sleeping it won't matter too much. The dolphins were rather amusing when I got going on the engine today. They took up station alongside and swam by the ship like dogs walking to heel. Every now and then they would spot a bunch of seaweed or a flying fish and dart after it just like a dog going into a hedgerow or after a rabbit. Then they would look round to see where the ship was and come scampering back to heel. After a couple of hours they got bored with our straight and steady progress and pushed off and I didn't see them again. Wonder if they'll turn up in the morning—only I shall never know if they are the same fish.

Wednesday December 24th

Another quiet night, which fills me with suspicion, for when things are quiet I have an uneasy feeling of living on borrowed time. This morning, 0700, there is plenty of low and threatening cloud. *FA* waltzes in light and fitful airs coming from all directions. I fill primus and start fixing breakfast before deciding what to do.

Wind suddenly rushes in from south-east with rain squalls. I collect a little rainwater to eke out supply, but find on tasting it that it is brackish and nauseating and for ultimate emergency only.

Wind struggles to come from east-sou'east, which may mean anything or nothing, for there also is the filthiest-looking weather this side of heaven. No fish by the way. But strangely enough a strong smell of dead fish pervades the atmosphere. Later discover porpoise in the vicinity and they sometimes betray their presence in this manner.

1050.   Light wind from the south-west—wouldn't you know—with a very hard bright sky, though the glass is steady. When it comes to inconsistency women simply aren't in the same class compared to weather.

The bottom is solid with barnacles now and the creatures grow visibly in size. I make a not very successful attempt to scrub them off from the deck.

Topping-lift is going to unravel itself, and there is nothing I can do but watch, it being where it is, way up out of reach on the permanent backstay. By light of day I see several more strands have gone in the main halyard. Porpoises are playing all round the ship. We are advancing at the delirious rate of one knot. I have lumbago. Never a dull moment.

1200.   Lat. 19 13N according to noon sight, which is six miles north of position calculated by dead reckoning.

1500.   Running into plenty of dirt ahead again, which of course may mean anything (or nothing I tell myself). Glass slightly down but not more than normal. Back painful. Lumbago ashore is not much fun, aboard a fussy little ship it makes the performance of the simplest task one of the most exquisite tortures this side of hell. We are a fine pair—I am hobbling and FA no longer sails like a smart Bermudan sloop, but lumbers along like turn-of-century box-bottomed barge.

1600.   With the ship pottering along by herself closehauled—what a thing in the Trade Wind area—I have been making intensive researches into the Ocean Passage Book, wind charts, etc., to see where I could possibly have gone wrong, but am no wiser. The Trade Winds ought to be blowing here and why they're not, God knows. They can't have read the book . . . which says they blow steadily from NE through to SE according to the time of year, never more than six knots and never less than three and they blow for 365 days a year. Moreover the doldrums never extend farther north than ten degrees above the equator. We, on the other hand, have never been any further south than 17 30N, and if these are not doldrum conditions they are an imitation indistinguishable from the real thing.

1800. The dirt ahead doesn't look so bad now we have caught up with it. Night seems calm enough. Wind has faded to F1. *FA* stealing along closehauled, probably making half a knot. Am taking a chance and leaving the canvas full, so hope I won't have to turn out for anything drastic.

1925. Managed to get quite wonderful reception on the radio . . . bit of Christmas cheer from the BBC, but it faded right out at the critical moment for the time signal which I wanted for a chronometer check. The announcer said, "In one and a half minutes time when it will be ten o'clock . . ." and the set went dead. Battery I am afraid. As near as I can get, the chronometer is ten minutes slow, and I reckon her average daily rate to be two seconds slow.

Thursday December 25th

What a Christmas. Opened a letter delivered to me at Las Palmas, marked not to be opened until December 25th, and a parcel given me by the Parks, also marked Christmas Only. The letter was a greeting card from home, and the parcel was full of messages and little Christmas objects. Somehow this thoughtfulness did not impart the spirit intended. I feel acutely lonely, saddened, and dispirited, desolated by the sensation of absolute isolation. Try to improve outlook by opening tin of Christmas pudding for dinner, not having any turkey, but my one meal a day is breakfast and Christmas pudding is no good for breakfast, even on Christmas Day.

Dawn breaks fair. Wind still south-west and *FA* plods on at half a knot. There are signs of more wind in the sky, which is sheeting over from the west with mare's tails, but no sign of Trade Winds. Had a go at the radio but will not know whether I have done any good until tonight as reception seems limited to night time. Fear the battery is finished, though, as it has been in use since last June under pretty trying conditions.

0810.   Log reads 1467 but reckon it should read 1474 as it won't register at speeds below two and a half knots.

0925.   Start motor.

1125.   Stop motor. Until we run into Trades or as long as this gorgeous weather—it really is gorgeous now, even if defeating to my purpose—continues, shall run motor two hours daily. This keeps the engine from getting stiff, gives my morale a much-needed boost, and adds some ten miles to the day's crawl. And God knows, every single mile is valuable now.

1200.   Lat. 19 11N which seems reasonably correct. Figure we are making point-eight knots. Heat is stupendous. Sun burning hot without being oppressive. It would be perfect if only we were moving a little faster towards the West Indies. I read with real interest a booklet called *Survival at Sea* presented pessimistically before leaving Plymouth.

1310.   False alarm . . . a little sea without the wind to back it came chattering in from the south-*east* and filled me with wild hope for a moment, but it petered out.

1415.   Start motor . . . so calm, can't resist.

1615.   Stop motor. Really, it has been a beautiful day and my back is much better. I drink to absent friends, pulling faces over the poisonous rum bought in the Canaries. So raw it makes you shudder for half an hour after swallowing. I should have tried before buying but naïvely thought rum was rum all the world over. My mistake, some of it could be used as fuel for a jet plane. Maybe I'll get used to it as have no wish to forgo sundowner institution. It makes a time mark in the day and something to look forward to, though I notice it has a tendency to get earlier and bigger each day. I visualise my friends very clearly as I drink their health. As if they were present. I can even hear their voices. Imagination seems to have a four-dimensional quality at sea, especially when you are on your own, and can conjure up scenes and people in a manner unknown ashore. But it is nostalgic and disturbing. If this was Plymouth Sound now, and *FA* wasn't hampered by these blasted bloody barnacles, what fun it would be.

1815. Calm clear night, calm clear sea. Lightning on eastern horizon. Patched mainsail at the luff and tackled sorting out cabin, which now looks worse than ever. No joy from the radio. Will try spare battery when I get round to locating it in the locker jammed to the deckhead with oddments.

Friday December 26th

0400. Knockdown squall struck ship. Having developed sensitivity in these matters heard it coming in my sleep and dashed out on deck to reef, repeating horrid process of other night, working sideways in screaming wind, driving rain, and vivid lightning. Westerly squall of course. Wonder if I am in the right ocean? The nicer the weather beforehand the worse the squalls to follow, it seems.

0915. Oh, what a beautiful morning—black as your hat as far as the eye can see. Thunder, lightning, and no wind to speak of. *FA* waltzing in stately circles. I am preparing the biggest breakfast ever, a monstrous dish of sausages and batter, which I just couldn't eat when it was fixed. Ah well, there are only 364 more shopping days to Christmas.

1040. Some wind coming in from the north-west, but it is still pouring with rain and heavily overcast. Will wait and see what happens before going out as am getting short of dry clothes. Also getting short of reading matter. Have read all books aboard two or three times, know all the adverts in the magazines intimately and have taken to studying the shipping announcements in Brown's Nautical Almanac. Verse is the most satisfying literature at sea. Always seems to come fresh. Swinburne's *Deserted Garden* has a strong appeal at the moment.

1120. As usual, false alarm, the wind tapered off and *FA* rolls in lazy swell. Rain is continuous and there is no sign of a break above.

1200. No sight, no sun. Just cloud, thunder, and rain. Log 1487.

1410. Wind squalling round in circles. Impossible to do anything with it. Still no sign of any let-up.

1455. Raving wind on the port quarter and away we go furiously on course 308.

1725. Heave to. Conditions are superficially a little better. The bitterness is out of the wind and there is not much force in the seas, the weather has broken to leeward, but there is plenty of rough stuff to windward, and it was quite a party while it lasted. *FA* logged six and a half knots skating over the waves with a fraction of main above the boom and the storm jib, which considering the state of her bottom was no mean effort. It *felt* faster than the speed of sound and was pretty exhilarating.

   The trouble with small ships like this is that you have nowhere to stow wet sails and clothes until you can dry them out.

Saturday December 27th

0630. Quiet morning. Sea calm. Wind, very light, from west. Low cumulus.

0920. Usual chores. Put up main or rather take out reef. Main halyard getting painful to handle and mainsail needs increasing attention. Put up working jib more or less to dry it. Usual conditions of no wind, except hint from west. Shoal of trigger fish haunting ship. One has long white scar just above port eye and is thus identifiable.

If this goes on much longer will have to resort to Bombard's methods. He should be across by now.

0930–1130. Run engine. There is a healthy following swell but no wind. Lots of little low cumulus are forming, round and fat and white, though some of them are rather grubby, the black sheep of the flock, and they appear to be transfixed, immobilised, and waiting, against the blue sky. This is where we came in, yet, if I put up the twins in anticipation the wind like as not will come romping in from the west.

1200. Log 1503, Lat. 19 21N. Water is very dusty here; motes like grass seed are thick as far as the eye can penetrate the depths. Also small insects dart about on the surface, some like minute transparent moths, and some like the familiar "waterboatmen" of farmyard ponds. These must be what the petrels live on. I often wondered what they were pecking at on the water. Normally you cannot see the minutiae of the ocean, only when it is flat calm like this.

1225–1425. Run engine again, but have now only two cans of fuel left which must conserve for landfall. There is every indication of a strong blow to come—swell high and glassy, slight fall in the glass—I just don't seem to be able to divorce myself from noting these signs and portents even though they rarely work out. The clouds have now all retreated in that curious way they have to the horizon where they are crowding together in a watchful manner. The swell runs in from the north-east and there are puffs of wind from the north-west.

1530. A little breeze is sneaking in from the north-west. The Ocean Passage Book says the north-west blows are the worst. . . .

Felicity Ann at English Harbour, Antigua

The Author, photographed from the
bows of *Felicity Ann*

1715. The glass says no, it is not falling . . . on the contrary . . . and you never saw such a peaceful evening. The climate down here has me foxed. Apparently you just pays your money and takes your choice (Trade Winds are extra, though).

FA still ambles along in stockinged feet and I continue with my lifework making baggywrinkle.

Sunday December 28th

0030. Must sleep, so heave to.

0630. Awakened by thunder, but the wind is coming in from the south-east and I take a chance and an hour later have the twins up and drawing. Have a headache so decide to take the day off. Now that I know most of the books aboard by heart have taken to inventing foolish games like "How many of the 48 States can you name?" and "What are the English counties reading from the south-west up?" Must be suffering from softening of the brain as America seems to contain anything from 24 to 53 States and the English counties are strangely elusive. Another game is to study a map of England and go for a drive across country trying to recall the bends and bridges in the road and how each section looked. These games serve the same purpose as Whodunits by providing escapism without making any demands on intelligence. One runs out of things to think about . . . you start on some profundity like the expanding universe and then think, bother, I thought about that yesterday. And sometimes I wish I could just put my brain in cold storage and stop it for it will keep pouncing on any old subject and making an issue of it, seeming to dislike being dulled from worry and needing to find something to get an edge on.

1635. Wind barely noticeable . . . just another false alarm, I suppose. *FA* moving, but only just.

1730. No wind.

1815. No radio either. Tried out spare battery, but that is flat, too. Don't know that I have ever felt lower.

Monday December 29th

This is the thirty-ninth day at sea. Last night was calm with occasional tiny breezes to keep us on our way. Beautiful dawn, and now at 0800 hours there is just enough movement of air to keep us going forward at half a knot, but even that in the right direction is something. According to the chronometer (G.M.T.) and my watch which is kept at local sun time, we are much farther west than recorded by dead reckoning. If this is so it is wonderful, but I am not counting on it, just bearing it in mind for when we get nearer the other side. (Will keep two positions like Columbus: he kept one to comfort his men, I shall keep one to comfort me.) Am not sleeping well these days; up and down all night to see if the wind has changed or if one of those bloody squalls is in the offing. And when I do sleep it is only to dream of sailing a small ship across the ocean.

1200.   Log 1531, Lat. 19 17N.

1715.   The sun glides down in golden splendour and another day of light wind and still cloud comes to an end. The sea has been strangely silent all day and in spite of increasing anxiety I am still capable of appreciation and find something hauntingly beautiful about all this. . . .

Tuesday December 30th

0040.   Light wind coming in from the south-east driving us north-west. The snag about this wind direction is that it invariably goes into the south-west. Self-steering isn't working so well as it did, rudder seems stiff and heavy.

0750.   Wind south-west—what did I say? Sailing closehauled again, and there are all the usual signs of squalls and trouble. Wind F2.

1200.   Log 1542, Lat. 19 23N. Course 323. The dirt passed astern of us and we have sailed closehauled all morning under a cloudless sky with a southwesterly wind of F3–4. It is very, very hot.

1410. Took a sight at 1340 and our position works out at 38 52W, 19 23N, and I guess that is more or less right. Find the stop watch, bought in Las Palmas, a great joy and invaluable aid, but chronometer has to be a certain amount of guesswork since the radio went out of commission.

1500. Threw the air plant overboard. "Something to watch," Dorothy Park had said when she gave it to me, and I have watched it hanging from the boom gallows gradually shrivelling to death. Which is very depressing apart from anything else, and in a venture like this one has an inclination to invent superstition. . . . "If this lives we'll get to the other side . . ." and there is no one to talk one out of it, so I threw the plant into the sea and that settled that.

1835. Throughout today we have advanced at the rate of one knot and at sundown we approached a dirty big bunch of rain clouds, the kind associated with those villainous squalls, but as one knot is one knot only, I did not reef but left *FA* sailing herself closehauled with all sail, and I came below to make supper, having acquired an appetite from somewhere. Made a queer batter from one spoonful of gofio and two spoonfuls of dried egg and ate the result with margarine and brown sugar and liked it very much indeed. *FA* meantime slid between two black and trailing clouds.

1930. No wind, put ship hove-to on port tack and came below again for relaxation.

2055. Turn out again for squall and reef down. Sail her until 2245 then go below to warm up, and *FA* pounds on herself making more leeway than headway in a clumsy sea. Turn out again almost immediately for singularly savage squall and an hour later heave to. *FA* rides awkwardly in a lumpy sea and is knocked down several times by sudden gusts of incredible weight. Lightning plays all round. All the old stuff . . . am getting increasingly more nervous and restless each day.

161

Wednesday December 31st

0600.   Surface reluctantly after wretched night, and the morning does not promise to be much better. Although not in the least hungry am preparing breakfast as it is doing something positive which is the only protection against apathy and despair.

1500.   First opportunity to take a sight, almost an impossibility in this sea. Will work it out tonight.

1700.   Heave to, absolutely beat. Today touched an all-time low.

Thursday January 1st 1953

Woke at 0600 absolutely scuppered, not having been rested at all. I slept all right, but it didn't seem to do any good. Forced myself to eat breakfast and now it lies on my stomach like a log. The glass has shot up to unprecedented heights and the wind shows signs of working round to the north-east. It is as much as I can do to climb out on deck and start the day's run . . . a run that looks pitifully small on the chart.

1800.   Log 1592. Heave to, been running all day with reefed main and small jib and wind on starboard quarter. The seas were heavy and swell monstrous, 30 feet at best. If this is a Trade Wind it has returned very stern and forceful after its prolonged Christmas vacation. Was too tired to cope with changing rigs again, and anyway there was too much weight in the wind for light canvas. Waves, I noted today, break in divers ways. There is the kind that bounces up to you like a large and friendly puppy (down, boy). There is the kind that slams down beside you with the ferocity of a large fat man trumping your ace, and there is the kind that grows bigger and bigger and bigger and topples over with a kind of hissing roar that is like nothing on earth.

Regret not being able to use this wind tonight but am too exhausted to go on. If this is the Trade Wind it will be here

162

tomorrow, and maybe in better shape, both it and me, to allow the twins up. And if it is not the Trade Wind then I won't have used my depleted store of energy for nothing. Feel sick and dizzy tonight.

2100.   Awakened by boom swinging and banging and find it is calm again. This is incredible. How can so much wind be turned off like water at a tap?

Friday January 2nd

0600.   Still calm with just a slight breeze from the north-east. Had a long night's sleep but still feel tired and bereft of energy. Dreamt in nightmares all night long and the horror of them still lingers . . . although I cannot remember what they were about.

1000.   After breakfast took out reef and put up working jib, but only fitful little easterly airs now, so changed over to twins. But it is very calm and even they just flap as *FA* rolls to the monstrous swell that continues to roll in. I don't know what to do about this nervousness. I feel dizzy most of the time and am completely at the mercy of uncontrollable emotional impulses. The least little thing can delight or distress beyond measure. Mostly it is distress and I have wept more in these last few days than I have ever done in my whole life and for such trivial reasons as failing to light the stove with one match.

In spite of meaning to conserve fuel for landfall I ran the engine for a couple of hours this morning and the log now reads 1610. There is no wind worth mentioning. BUT—have discovered a bottle of gin I didn't know I had, hidden at the bottom of a locker. Treasure. CORN IN EGYPT.

Saturday January 3rd

Calm all night. Calm this morning, and now at 0730, it promises to be terribly hot. These are undoubtedly the doldrums, there can be nothing else to account for such conditions.

0830. Glassy calm.

1000. Still glassy calm. Took two sights this morning which gave an incredible intercept, but as both the same it looks as though they're on the ball. Of course there is this doubt about the chronometer and the almanac is out of date which means additional computing (*guess*work on my part) and the margin of error grows with each little sum I have to do, my arithmetic being what it is. It was foolish not to get a 1953 almanac before leaving Las Palmas . . . whatever gave me the notion I would reach the West Indies before the New Year? I do believe however we are considerably farther west than dead reckoning makes out. A noon sight may help by cross checking on earlier position. Am uncertain about ship's time, but if I can get 1200 local from the sun the difference between it and G.M.T. will give approximate longitude.

1200. Lat. 19 30N, and longitude works out to be 45W! I do hope this is true. It can't be too far out surely? What about the west-going current . . . I have never allowed for that. . . . If it is true we have only just about a thousand miles to go. Still glass calm. A cigarette can thrown over hours ago is still alongside.

1730. After sweltering still day in which it was possible to see thirty feet or more into the ocean and watch the fish as in an aquarium, light breaths of air are coming in from the southeast, there is a fine undramatic sunset, little Trade Wind clouds are forming, and *I* am all set for one of those super squalls they do so well out here.

Saturday January 4th

Fooled again. Quiet calm night. A light northeasterly breeze at sunrise, so after breakfast, which was a dead loss as I don't seem to like anything these days, I put up the twins once more, and now at 0925 we are under way. If you can call it that, we are hardly making any advance, but some, and that is better than yesterday's no progress at all. I am worried about my fearful thirst and the fish are worried about our moving, having got used to us as an oceanic fixture. Little Scarface, the trigger fish, is still with us. Am getting quite fond of him as he is the only one I can recognise.

1200. Lat. 19 04N, Long. 25 03W. Log 1611. The log under-registers at very low speeds and there does seem to be an appreciable westerly current (I tell myself).

Wind is only F1 and the sun is blazing hot. . . .

1350. Spending some time trying to take pictures of the trigger fish. They are really very amusing, friendly, and tame, and nibble my fingers without fear when I put a hand in the water. Because of this and their recent habit of chewing at the barnacles on the bottom they have earned immunity. Sometimes in the calms they can be heard scraping against the planking and indeed there are not so many barnacles as there were.

Have been dickering with the cabin flashlight which has ceased to light, because, I fear, the batteries are flat. So have to over-haul the kerosene lantern and prepare it for work. According to the log, we have made no progress today, but I know better.

1700. Wind still very light but swell coming in from north where lots of cumulus and muck lies in wait—if *only* it doesn't go round to the north-west. . . .

Monday January 5th

A nice smart wind got up during the night and we bowled along merrily until dawn when it began to drizzle in the most English fashion and the wind abated to leave us rolling in a brisk chop. Still, we have made a positive move in the right direction.

1100. After making that entry the wind blew up again and it has been blowing a good F6 all morning with F7 in the gusts, and *FA* fairly romped along. At first the tiller was very stiff and did not answer quickly enough, but I hit on the notion of greasing the tiller-bar slit in the aft coaming, which lessened friction and seemed to be the cure. Heavy rain clouds follow and the barometer shows a sharp rise.

1200. Too rough for a sight and horizon is obscured by waves. Log 1645.

1715. *FA* has roared on all afternoon steering herself admirably before pretty fierce seas. Motion fabulous of course. Sky astern looks better and I keep telling myself the seas are easier, but I don't know. It all has the appearance of having once started it is prepared to go on roaring for ever. And what am I griping about—that is what I want, isn't it?

Tuesday January 6th

Restless anxious night as wind and sea continue high and I have developed a chronic worry condition. The twins would keep having flogging bouts and I could visualise them blowing out any minute.

0600. We are running far too fast at times, but I am reluctant to lose any speed as we don't get it often enough, so will carry on as long as possible. Flying fish for breakfast, a good-sized one, too. Deck is covered with tiny baby cuttlefish for some inexplicable reason.

1200. Log 1732, day's run 87. Too rough for noon sight, but— we are nearly off the eastern section of the Atlantic chart.

1700. Another restless night is promised. Low, heavy cloud follows menacingly and wind is hardening. It is quite cold after what we have had.

Wednesday January 7th

Another harassing night. When I do sleep it is only to have these wretched dreams of fitting out a small ship for an ocean crossing, or such horrible nightmares I am afraid to sleep at all. And the twins keep flogging. Seas are savage this morning and although it is clearer immediately overhead there is more cloud sheeting over.

Noon, log 1827, day's run 95.

Thursday January 8th

Seven weeks at sea. A more restful night than usual, but maybe I am more tired—if that is possible—and care less. Living under these conditions, apart from the anxiety, is terribly wearing as the fantastic motion makes the smallest task the most prodigious effort. Some rain during the night. This morning it is blowing brisk again, but without so much north in it so that we are not making so much southing, which is good.

0900. Took sight which seems quite a reasonable one, and hope to get another this afternoon. Have had to make a new decision regarding landfall . . . can carry on like this and go to Barbados, or put *FA* back into fore and aft sails and make for Antigua as originally planned. But if I put the main and jib on again it means steering and only half a day's progress against *FA* steering herself for twenty-four hours and days on end. So Barbados it is. And I reckon that is only 650–700 miles distant, which—whoops!—seems nothing after all we have gone through, but is a veritable voyage none the less.

1200. Log 1921. Day's run 94.

1450. After much trouble in getting an unreliable sight I make our position 13 53N, 49 30W, which seems nonsense. Ship now running on course 272.

Friday January 9th

0850. Log 2001. Observed position 15 00N, 50 08W, which is more like it . . . and it had a nine-mile intercept only. Motion this morning worse than ever. Two of the smallest flying fish ever on deck, one the size of minnow I threw back, and the other gave just a taste of fresh fish.

167

1200. Log 2015, day's run 94. Quietened down a little during the day and smartened up again during the night.

Saturday January 10th

I don't know why the motion seems worse in the morning, maybe one has to get used to it every day. Small flying fish again for breakfast.

0935. Sight with nine-mile intercept seems reasonable. Perhaps I am getting the hang of this thing at last.

1200. Log 2100, day's run 85.

1345. Log 2106, observed position 13 58N, 52 35W. Afternoon sights always turn out queer and I always have a hell of a job getting them for some reason. If this position is correct, we are only 420 miles from Barbados. Broached last bottle of brandy, opened last tin of cigarettes, and finished last of potatoes for breakfast. So we had better be only 420 miles from Barbados.

1615. Feeling rather lousy this evening—too long sea voyage is telling physically as well as mentally. Have painful sty on eye, and sea boils are manifest in spite of vitamin tablets.

Sunday January 11th

Wretched night, hardly any sleep, as eye was very painful and I had to keep bathing it, and this morning it is a most sordid sight. Wind got up during the night, driving *FA* like a scalded cat and the motion was worse than ever, if that is possible. An enormous flying fish was in the cockpit when I looked out, I heard it flop aboard during the night, and there was another smaller one on deck, so it was a very good breakfast indeed, though I am pooped after it as usual; preparing, cooking, and eating being a major operation and equivalent to a hard day's work ashore.

0900. Got a fairly reasonable sight and it appears we are fairly walloping up the distance to Barbados. Wonder how near this navigation is?

1200.   Log 2195, day's run 95. We are certainly moving and the racket is appalling—only hope everything holds together.

1500.   13 00N, 53 50W, or about 330 miles from Barbados. . . . Nearly there! Wish I could get the ship to steer more westerly, we are making too far south. . . . Seas are enormous now. Eye a mess.

Monday January 12th

0350.   An awful night. Awake and on watch most of the time. Squalls really bad and the twins flog violently, yet every time I get set to take them in it eases off. In one of the lulls the wind dropped away altogether as if someone had shut a door, and I heard a roaring sound in the distance like surf breaking on a shore, and looked out of the cabin to see astern and coming towards us at a tremendous rate a line of white stretching across the sea from horizon to horizon. There was no escaping it, and I watched, transfixed, from the cabin, looking aft over the stern. As it drew nearer it grew higher and higher, and as it caught up with us, towering, tremendous, roaring, and breaking, I ducked below and pulled the hatch over. The ship was picked up and thrown on her beam ends, and it seemed for a moment as if we had had it. . . . Then *FA* surfaced, throwing the water off her, and I looked out to find the cockpit completely flooded. But there were no more tidal waves coming along, thank Heaven. The confusion in the cabin was chaotic. After that sea, which I think must have been the result of a sea-quake somewhere, had passed, the wind got up again and went on blowing with increased vigour. And the rain came down in torrents.

Had two hours sleep from 0600–0800, and woke to find *FA* running too hard . . . twins flogging, booms standing up on end, ship skating over seas that reached after and threatened to poop her any moment, so had to get the sails in, the toughest proposition I have tackled aboard yet. She is now lying-to, without any canvas. I tried to put up the twin storm jibs but they

169

flogged so badly it seemed they would tear down the standing rigging.

1200. Log 2287, day's run 92. Blowing a gale now with F9 in gusts. *FA* running before it under storm jib. Seas are gigantic and rolling and the whole surface of the water is white with foam. Spray is blowing off the wave crests in a horizontal stream. And there is no sight of any let-up.

1800. Pack up. Conditions are a little easier, but don't like the look of things at all, and am so tired am turning in. *FA* lying-to quite comfortably without any canvas. There is nothing you can do with these great top-heavy waves, if they get you, they get you.

I keep the hatch closed and the cockpit drains open.

Incessant scream of the wind gets on your nerves so you could scream back at it. I do, and relieve some of the tension. It is much easier to be brave when there is someone to impress you with your courage, but you cannot fool yourself, and on your own you are just plain scared.

Barometer is not moved in any way by all this. Extraordinary.

Tuesday January 13*th*

Slept some last night, I was dead-beat and would have slept through atomic warfare. Awoke at intervals to hear the wind howling and now at 0700 it is still howling, with a fast hurrying sea hissing and crashing over the ship. I haven't the strength to get up the mainsail, reefed, or in fact any sort of sail up. Perhaps I will feel better after breakfast, having had nothing but one of those self-heating cans of soup yesterday midday. Don't want anything to eat but realise it is necessary to do so.

0850. Breakfast almost insuperable task but managed somehow. Pineapple juice, omelette, and coffee, simple enough, but by the time I had finished I was drenched in sweat and worn out. It *looks* a much nicer day now, but haven't the energy to cope with it. If only it would let-up for a while—the frightful incessant motion, the frightful incessant howl of the wind, the frightful hissing seas. . . . It is going to be such a struggle to avoid being swept too far south in this lot, which looks as if it will never stop until it hurls itself on some far inhospitable shore.

0950. Started running under storm jib with wind on starboard quarter.

1200. Tried to take a sight, but it was impossible, apart from the racket, the horizon was completely obscured by waves. Conditions are easing, I do believe . . . though waves are still 20–30 feet and breaking. Wind more easterly.

1820. Folded up for night, not quite so weary today but pretty nearly so. All afternoon the wind faded and swelled and the waves diminished and grew. Now it is comparatively easy. In fact I could put the twins up again, except that I distrust the cumulus lying astern and I don't want to make any more southing if it can be helped. And a new hazard; with the decks being constantly wet, that paint put on before we left is slippery as all get out, and I cannot get a foothold on it at all. It is my fault. I should have seen that it was mixed with pumice before it was put on as I usually do, but I didn't, so now am paying for carelessness. The situation is not improved by the appearance of three large sharks who have taken up stations beside the ship, one on either side, and one astern. One swam right up under the cockpit and rolled over to look at me in that fishy way they have with one eye. We regarded one another steadily for quite a while. I could have touched him easily but saw no reason why I should. They look unspeakably sinister, seeming to emphasise the menace of the ocean . . . this ceaseless, tireless, lonely, loveless sea. . . .

Wednesday January 14th
It blew up worse than ever during the night with very bad squalls and some shocking knockdown waves. I lay on the

cabinsole, jammed there by a couple of sailbags, on top of the big fisherman anchor and a coil of rope, and fretted about the compression strain on the mast. It hardly seems possible that such a little ship can take such a pasting. And I seem to get less and less used to bad weather. Now, morning, it is as bad as ever. I cannot bear to look out at the fury of the ocean.

Our dead reckoning position is 12 45N, 55 53W, which is hopeless progress, all the time we are being dragged further and further south. I wish I knew what to do for the best. It doesn't look as though it is ever going to let up.

0840. Under way on course 290 as near as we can get. Wind F9, running under storm jib.

1200. Log 2311, day's run according to log, 11. Wind has dropped to F7, but seas still huge, 20–30 feet.

1730. Packed up jittering. *FA* lying-to, two warps trailing astern. It has been one hell of an afternoon and a great strain running as the seas have not only been high and heavy but confused as well as the wind eased off.

What it is blowing now I am in no state to judge.

Thursday January 15th

Eight weeks at sea, the maximum time I expected to take for the crossing. Fortunately it is much quieter this morning, in fact it is perfectly all right and I should press on regardless, except there are villainous banks of cloud hanging about and I am so weak the thought of getting those warps in and sail up slays me . . . and those slippery decks. . . .

0800. Got sight which gives position approximately 175 miles from Barbados.

0945. Raked up some energy from somewhere and got under way. *FA* runs with the wind on the starboard quarter, reefed main and storm jib. The mainsail was already partly rolled round the boom so I left it as it was, there being so much trouble in the offing. Now being approached by heavy rain squalls. *FA* like a hurrah's nest. The cabin is all chewed up, and the trailing warps got wound round each other in the night and are now in the cockpit piled high in an inextricable tangle. Life is very difficult.

1200. Log 2324, day's run 13. Heavy squalls and weather continues to look tough and unsettled. Try and take my mind off it by planning a farm in Cornwall . . . even got down to mortising the joints in the built-in furniture in the farmhouse.

1800. Heave to on starboard tack. Squalls continued all afternoon and show every sign of going on all night. After several hours of patient work not indigenous to my character I got the two wet warps unsnarled and coiled—in the cabin as there is no room for them anywhere else.

About 1700, though, I was very heartened and encouraged by the most perfect rainbow I have ever seen; it spanned the sea in a brilliant arch with colours of a pristine purity all the lovelier for appearing after what seems a lifetime of grey. It gave me as big a lift as a landfall.

2100. Here we are again, blowing as hard as ever. Had to turn out and take in another reef, *FA* pitching wildly in heavy seas. Then the jib sheet shackle broke and it was a wet and windy party smothering the jib and replacing the shackle. Wherever we make landfall, Hell, Hull, or Halifax, it will do me.

Friday January 16th

0200. Each night seems worse than the one before. The squalls and waves are wilder than ever tonight, and the glass has started to go down, which doesn't improve the look of the future. This is the hardest hundred miles of the whole voyage.

0700. Dreadful night and still blowing as hard as ever. Glass still low and no sign of a let up. Have just had a self-heating can of malted milk. These self-heating cans have been a godsend

173

in bad weather, and I have lived on them these past few days. You simply prize the cap off the top of the can, thus exposing a taper to which you put a match or cigarette end, and the taper flares and fizzles out and a chemical reaction is set up that heats the can in four minutes flat. It has been impossible to use the stove, but a hot drink has remarkable restorative powers. God knows, I am bad enough with a hot drink, without one I would be flayed. As it is I haven't the strength to go out and fight this, so whilst *FA* seems to be coping quite well, hove-to, I am staying below until it either eases or gets worse and I have to take further steps. Eye still very sore and swollen in spite of care and bathing.

1000. Barometer rising, but no immediate improvement in conditions.

1315. Sky clear at last, and the heat is scorching. The glass is falling again, but conditions have eased somewhat. I have tried to make some griddle scones, and although they turned out all right, I just couldn't eat. Took a sight with much difficulty which seemed fairly accurate having only a seven-mile intercept. It appears we are advancing steadily towards Barbados. If only we can hang on—if only the weather quietens down—if only I can pick up some strength.

Saturday January 17th

0900. Obs. position, 13 00N, 58 03W, or 98 miles from Barbados, and according to my other, secret, reckoning, we may be even closer than that, and could sight Barbados tomorrow morning. . . . It was a better night and I had some sleep at last, but still feel very weak as if arms and legs were stuffed with sawdust, and every move requires monumental effort.

0915. Under way on course 276 with double-reefed main and storm jib. Log 2334.

1200. Log 2342, Jeeze, hard work running in these seas.

1800. Heave to, tired out. Log 2359.

Sunday January 18th
0710. Awakened by fierce squall.
I do believe we have made landfall.
Can't identify it yet as it is only a faint shape on the horizon, part hidden by cloud. Perhaps it is cloud. If it is still there after I have had a cup of coffee it is land. It is! And it couldn't be anywhere else but Barbados. We are now about 15 miles away and we sail westward to clear Harrison Point and the northern end of the Island. As we gradually draw nearer the first ship for forty-eight days comes into sight. A small, grey, long-funnelled freighter rolling heavily across the seas, appearing high on a crest and vanishing quickly into the trough. We round Harrison Point, well off shore, towards the end of the afternoon and I am fascinated by the occasional glimpse of a red roof and a stone wall. The Island looks peculiarly English from the little I can see. . . . None of this is true. . . . We make south towards Carlisle Bay, Bridgetown, and HAVEN.

We cannot make it before dark, though, and I have hove-to on the starboard tack, about eight miles off shore, so I can fill the lamps, tidy the ship and myself, get supper as have neither fed nor drunk today and feel pretty whacko . . . then we can go in in the morning all fresh. . . .

And, anyway, *we have crossed the ruddy ocean.*

2100. Funny to have ships to contend with again. John lent me a huge kerosene lantern with an all-round dioptric lens as a ship-scarer, and I hoist it on the port twin stay with the hope it will be seen without dashing its brains out or doing irreparable damage to the mast, both of which it is trying its best to do. And how I am ever going to get it down again the way it has snarled the downhauls round the stay I do not know. Still blowing all hell. I am inconceivably *sick* of the sound of wind.

175

0330.   Another ghastly night. No sleep on account of ships for I cannot keep the lights on in these conditions—they blow out as fast as I light them, even John's dioptric job, especially that one—and a hell of a lot of stuff is coming aboard tonight so I wouldn't be able to sleep anyway. We are being driven inexorably westward and the lights of the Island are sinking slowly but surely over the horizon. I don't see how we are ever going to beat back across this stuff, for the seas are running mighty high again.

0400.   Tried oil bag experiment to see if it will stop some of these things crashing on us. Made bags out of circular pieces of canvas and filled them with lubricating oil and hung them over the weather bow. Hard to say whether they are any use or not. It seems easier, but it may have moderated, although it is blowing hard enough for the likes of we. A ship passing close on the port hand tempts me to fire a rocket. If it had been daylight I would have flown the "V" flag . . . "I require assistance" . . . being less drastic than an actual distress signal. *FA* may be able to go on indefinitely but I can't.

0715.   I can run in this or remain hove-to. Neither of which gets me to where I want to be, so am still hove-to as the lesser of two evils. As there is no ship in sight and feeling thoroughly ashamed I have put up the V flag. Also made some more oil bags. I think they work. There is certainly a hell of a lot of oil about the ship!

0845.   God knows what it is blowing now. The seas are colossal. *FA* is riding pretty steady. I've made a sea-anchor out of a canvas kit-bag and she is riding to that. I am going to put out another oil bag, and then I think I will make another V flag. How long we can go on like this, I don't know.

1100.   Made the other V flag and put it up, so there is one either side of the mainsail of which there is only about ten feet up the track. Even so it is amazing how it is standing up to the force of the wind, for it is only light canvas. It is a brilliant sunny day with a hard blue sky. The Island is right out of sight, and there are no ships to be seen. The ironical thing is that since the newspapers were so eager to cry wolf before, they are probably just shrugging it off now when I could really do with some help. Keep going on benzedrine.

1125. Rolled up a few more feet of mainsail, hardly any sail showing above the boom now, but fear it should be taken off altogether, and then she won't ride so well. If we run we'll run smack on to a lee shore. Am resolved to signal first ship I see, day or night. Have imperative urge to let people know we have crossed the ocean, nothing much else matters now, but I would like them to know. . . .

It is heartbreaking to have been so close and to have the prize snatched just when it was within grasp.

I don't think I can take much more.

1700. It has eased down a little and having suddenly remembered I haven't eaten anything since an omelette last night have come below and had two Carr's lifeboat ration biscuits with marmalade and a snort of poison rum. *FA* steering herself meanwhile, closehauled. We came here quickly enough but it is going to be a long, long haul back. My eyes are causing some anxiety, they are both now terribly inflamed and I don't see too well. For this reason if no other, I must try and get in somewhere. Am using up reserves . . . everyone has a breaking-point and am rapidly approaching mine. Odd, how ships disappear. There were several last night, now there are none. I would try and get one to radio Bridgetown or somewhere and send out a tug or something. Blow the expense, I've had this. Had this. The last cigarettes went yesterday, but I don't miss them too much, having plenty of snuff aboard which I am beginning to prefer.

1800. Dickering about with the lamps and what with the motion and all the cabin is flooded with kerosene. It is the devil's own job keeping the windward navigation lamp alight and the great dioptric affair goes out at a breath. I haven't put it up tonight. At sunset I saw what I thought might be Tobago astern and the Grenadines to leeward, but am so tuckered out I cannot think straight and they might be anywhere. Anyway I don't want to get too close until I find out. But it is good to know there is something other than sea about. I don't suppose we are going ahead much. It's these bloody big seas that bitch us and knock the way off the little ship.

I see double out of my left eye.

Tuesday January 20th

FA ploughed on gallantly by herself all night, dealing with the seas far better than I could have done. But the motion and racket was incredible, like a drunk driving a fast car without springs over an unmade road.

0750. To my surprise I slept fitfully during the night but eyes ached so abominably this morning I feel limp and more despondent than ever. Had cup coffee, last in tin, cup of cocoa, two biscuits, two vitamin tablets, and a benzedrine for breakfast.

1000. A great dollop of ocean broke over the ship, poured through the hatch and soused everything. I am soaked. Everything's soaked. Blowing hard again and the seas are white. Don't know how long we can carry on, by continuous beating we can do little more than hold our own. There is an extra-ordinary dearth of shipping, haven't seen one since the night of the 18th. Unless I can get some assistance I don't think I can make port. Am stupid with fatigue and my thinking is warped. Am keeping below as much as possible to save eyes from glare.

1030. The big northern mountain, what I believe to be the island of Grenada, bears 311T.

1115. Discover the handbearing compass to be about 20 degrees out. . . .

1415.   Sight ship half a mile away. Fire rocket and hoist V flag on twin forestay where better seen, but she steamed on without taking the slightest notice, although we were less than quarter of a mile apart at one time. Her indifference was like being unexpectedly hit in the face. Can only hope she may report having seen us if there are any enquiries. . . . Today is all right although the seas continue high. *FA* is easily hidden in the troughs, but if the weather gets bad again, God help us, we haven't the sea room to play with now. I have tried several times to get a sight but they all make nonsense. Whether the error of time is creeping up on me or whether I just can't get one in these conditions I don't know.

1700.   Have taken six sights this afternoon and they all give a preposterous intercept of two degrees! I cannot understand it. I've figured and figured and I can't make it out. It was O.K. this morning, and has been up to now, more or less.

2200.   Heave to on port tack. Started to blow up again and *FA* was racketing south for no good reason at all. So we are lying about eight miles off the southern end of this island that I think must be Grenada, and there is a small light there which gives me a clue to our drift.

Wednesday January 21st

0340.   Squalls all night. Now between squalls have *FA* sailing again. Still port tack, no option.

0745.   Christ. I've made a balls of this. Light has dawned at last. How stupid can you get? Those haywire sights were right. Set out this morning to get round the southern end of "Grenada" and to leeward of it in the hope of winning some peaceful conditions in which to wrestle out the next move, and as we approached the Island it obviously did not jibe in with the description of Grenada given in the West Indies Pilot: moreover, there was a vague outline of another island to the south, which certainly did not apply to Grenada. After some cogitation—you could hear the rusty wheels going round in my head—I discovered it to be St Lucia. I had not allowed for the wind veering so much eastward, nor for the north equatorial current which is a fair walloper. The morning started badly with squalls and angry seas, then developed into a lovely soft day and I sailed along the southern coast of St Lucia in sunshine and ideal sailing conditions. The scent of land was sheer bliss and I relaxed and revelled in it all.

Tonight for the first time since the middle of the ocean it is calm and we are lying hove-to off that curious mountain pinnacle that rises for a thousand feet straight up out of the sea, Gros Piton Point, but I don't think we shall stay here after supper, there is a set towards the land, and I would rather not take the boat with me when I go ashore. I feel entirely different now with land and good weather on hand. Fair weather sailor, me. Now wondering how to get into Port Castries, St Lucia, as I haven't a harbour chart and the sailing directions as given in the Pilot seem rather complicated.

Thursday January 22nd

This is really very funny. On account of having to sleep and eat we are now 20 miles westward of St Lucia and have a long beat back. Missed 'im! It looks as though I shall have to try and carry on to Antigua as originally planned. I started sailing at 0630 but find I should carry full sail. It is fantastic but I have not the strength to get the last bit of sail up, and there is still one roll on the boom, but she is sailing along quite nicely in spite of that. And *still* there are no signs of ships of any sort. Not even a native sloop, incredible among islands like this. Around the Canaries the waters are solid with all kinds of local craft. Wish I had more energy. It is ridiculous to be as weak as this.

0900. Had to drop jib and reef main for vicious squall, and had no sooner done this than it passed and all was as serene as if it had never been. I just can't cope with altering sail again. This cat and mouse business is diabolically cruel.

1245. Morning of squalls and impossible conditions. *Bloody* sea. This Caribbean is as bad as the Ocean.

1745. Blowing up *again*. Have been messing about changing jibs and am soaked and now have no more dry clothes. Bugger. We are abeam of the southern end of Martinique, which is about eighteen miles away. *FA* sailing herself closehauled. Took down V flag this morning, and immediately after sighted a ship, but it was never more than a smudge of smoke on the horizon, and anyway the moment of desperation has passed, although I would dearly like to get a message through to Lloyds and let the folks know that the bad penny is liable to turn up again. *FA* in indescribable chaos below.

Friday January 23rd

I even wake tired these days, as the ads say. Absolutely spun in this morning and barely able to make cup of cocoa, coffee being finished, alas, alas. *FA* has done quite well during the night, bless her—she *is* a good little ship—and sailed us almost to the northern end of Martinique, and Dominica is in sight. Only two islands south of Antigua now.

1520. We've cleared the channel between Martinique and Dominica and are about twelve miles west of the southern point of Dominica. Filthy morning of squalls but pleasant afternoon.

1740. I have never seen such a formidable-looking sunset. The sky is green! The glass is steady, but that doesn't signify a thing. If it blows like it does without warning—what can it do when it warns? It is most unnaturally quiet. *FA* carries on alone closehauled and I am going below to rest while I can. Do wish I could make some contact with the outside world.

Saturday January 24th

What is the matter with me? All my life I have wanted to see the West Indies and here I am sailing past island after island—for why? Because I picked on Antigua? Phooey. The description of Prince Rupert Bay and the town of Portsmouth makes enchanting reading in the West Indies Pilot, and there it is, only a few miles to east'ard. . . . So hi-ho for Dominica. . . .

0720. Start engine and turn for Prince Rupert Bay. Nearing the Bay we run into a flotilla of native fishing boats, built-up dug-out canoes heavily overcanvassed with what appears to be flour bags and going like fun. Some of them pass close and the crews wave cheerfully. It is the most extraordinary sensation to see people after so long. It is sixty-five days since I sailed out of Las Palmas and last set eyes on a fellow soul.

1800. At anchor in Prince Rupert Bay, just off the jetty at Portsmouth, a fascinating little tropical town hiding behind the scrub and coconut palms lining the shore and dominated by the densely wooded mountains in the background.

As we taxied in on the remaining pint of fuel I drew up alongside one of the native schooners lying at anchor, and asked how much water there was. . . . "Plenty, plenty," the crew shouted back, and two of them climbed into a rowboat and came out to give me a hand anchoring and putting the ship away. They thought it strange and unnatural for a woman to be sailing about on her own, and right away offered to abandon their own ship and join mine. I pointed out that *FA* was hardly of a size to allow the luxury of a crew. At 1820 the Customs officials rowed out and cleared the ship, charging, very politely, overtime for the privilege.

★   ★   ★

I sat in the cockpit watching the lights of the little village spring out like fireflies in the deepening dusk, and listened to the jungle chorus humming and drumming and ringing in the green-mantled mountains, which were quickly losing their identity in the dark velvet of a tropical night. I had no desire to go ashore. It was enough that it was there, warm and pulsating, solid and real, and belonging to me in a way no legal deeds or titles could surpass or diminish; for I was of the land and to the land had returned. And tomorrow, or the day after maybe, I would go ashore and walk on solid earth, and talk to people and become one of them again, and revert to my problems, none of which had been solved by this preposterous voyage. But that was tomorrow. Tonight I was savouring an experience I had forgotten existed, symbolised by quiet schooners on quiet waters, a peaceful sea lapping a silent shore, the sibilant wind rustling the palm fronds: tranquillity.

Part 3

Dominica . . . Nassau

Chapter 15

How long I would have stayed aboard admiring the palm trees from afar there is no knowing. At least as long as the remaining stores lasted, for I had no wish to break the solitude that had gone on so long it had become a habit; but the spell was broken the morning after arrival by one of the few white inhabitants in the north, Tommy Coulthard, coming alongside in a motor launch, curious to find out what a small sloop was doing in the Bay flying the Red Ensign.

Tommy, an ardent small-boat sailor, transplanted from Lancashire with his wife and young son, built tugboats and lighters for a banana company in Dominica, and their home was only a step away from Portsmouth—wouldn't I come and visit with them and talk about the voyage? Tommy baited the invitation with the offer of a bath. A long spell at sea alone dulls your social instincts so that you are reluctant to mingle again; but after life has been reduced to its lowest common denominator, you would be surprised what brings a glint to the eye. Fresh water is the shortest and most valuable commodity aboard, baths are unknown and urgently desired, so I snapped at the bait and was driven in a jeep to a house on a hill overlooking the blue Caribbean.

The road was rough and crowded on either side by exciting new tropical vegetation. As he drove, Tommy threw out snippets of information, topical, historical, and geographical, which went straight through my head because I was far too busy taking in the sensation of being ashore on my first treasure island to listen. Under waving palms, dark-skinned children stood aside, wide-eyed and flashing broad white smiles as we passed. Scrawny five-toed chickens scattered into the undergrowth. Natives in shaggy straw hats strolled into view armed with formidable cutlasses, the island tool-of-all-work. They were accompanied by their womenfolk, who carried charcoal pots like witches' cauldrons, apparently ready to light a fire and toss off a meal at a moment's notice. They were all followed by thin, sycophantic, terrier-type dogs.

Mrs Coulthard, her son, and Tommy's mother were waiting to meet us in a house with screens for walls and patios for rooms, as though it hadn't made up its mind to stay in or out, as is the way of tropical architecture. Muriel Coulthard's greeting was straight to the point: "The water's getting hot," she said, "we're going down to the beach. Help yourself to a bath and make yourself at home."

Wallowing in a whole bath of fresh water after weeks of doling it out a cupful at a time has a delicious prodigality about it mixed with a certain wicked sensuality, akin to lolling in satin sheets when you know darn well you can only afford cotton, and ought to be getting on with the day's work anyway. No Roman beauty ever lingered over her bath as I did that day, and afterwards I pattered barefoot about the house learning to walk again. A plunge and a lurch will get you anywhere you want to be aboard the *Felicity Ann*, and my leg muscles had almost atrophied from disuse.

The Coulthards returned for lunch and, afterwards, Muriel, her mother-in-law, and son retired to their rooms for the afternoon siesta. Doubtless Tommy would have retired, too, but over lunch I had rediscovered my fellow-men and wanted to talk. Oh, how I wanted to talk. I told every detail of the voyage from Plymouth to Dominica whilst Tommy listened patiently. It would not have mattered if he had been bored to a stupor, nothing would have stopped me. Even when Muriel reappeared and said, "You have talked to Ann all afternoon" (a slight misrepresentation of the facts since Tommy had hardly been able to get a word in edgeways); "now talk to your son,"

I was unabashed. Happy as a clam to be amongst people again, I was merciless in my desire to share living with them. Shortly after this I met Colonel and Mrs Strong who, not knowing what they were in for, rashly invited me to stay on their plantation. I could hardly get the ship closed up and my gear ashore fast enough.

The Strongs' plantation, not very far from Portsmouth, was three thousand acres of mixed crops and jungle. They grew limes for the lime-juice factory in the south, cocoa, bananas, and coconuts, with a little experimental coffee for home consumption. They ran cattle as a sideline, poultry as a diversion, and waged ceaseless war against the jungle. The jungle in Dominica is of oriental density, steaming under a rainfall of nearly three hundred inches in the mountains, and it covers the rugged contours of the island from the coastline to the mountain peaks, except for the clearances made by man, and there the jungle is not defeated, it is simply waiting.

Dominica is unexploited, undeveloped, and underpopulated. The Dominicans refer to it as the Cinderella of the West Indies, adding with a certain inverted pride that it can never amount to anything as the Island is under the Carib curse, for the Caribs, original Indian inhabitants, in their final defeat swore the white man would never succeed in Dominica, and the failure of various grandiose schemes are pointed out to substantiate the claim.

Curses, black magic, jumbies, and evil eyes were no deterrent to the Strongs, however, who pursued the development of their plantation with pioneer vigour. As the result of some slight domestic dissension the cook put the evil eye on Joan, who simply said, "Nonsense, get on with your work." And as nothing happened to her the cook lost a great deal of face and Joan gained a great deal of respect. She is one of those English blondes who look so frail, but who are in fact absolutely dauntless and practically indestructible.

189

Charles, a quiet iron-grey Englishman with none of the bombast popularly associated with the rank of Colonel, had retired from a life of professional soldiering after the War, and embarked on the Island venture as retirement in post-war England was neither practicable, nor, for a man of Charles' resourcefulness and energy, desirable. Pioneer work is rewarding only in the life it gives you—if you like that sort of life. The Strongs seemed to be making out pretty well after three years. "We like it," Joan declared, "and much good it would do us if we didn't."

Without the ties and the responsibility, or the necessity for having to make it work, my interest in Island life was purely academic, and I found it fascinating. Little snatches of local colour were irresistible; lemons and grapefruit growing round the house; orchids draped prolifically in the trees; parrots screaming in the jungle; big black bats flying round my room at night; and exquisite little iridescent humming birds flying into the house to hover over a bowl of red hibiscus. Day after day slipped by very easily in this West Indian Isle so little known in the mother country that much of my mail was directed to the Dominican Republic some eight hundred miles to the northwest. Communications within the Island, or anywhere to and from outside it, were tropically protracted. The highest peaks in Dominica are over 5,000 feet, and the Island is so rugged that a road connecting Portsmouth in the north with Roseau, the capital, in the south, has never been completed. It goes so far north and so far south, but for the bit in between you have to travel on foot, hacking your way with a machete. It took me two days to despatch cables to England, which had to be telephoned through to Roseau. The delay was partly my fault, in that I was an early victim of the local disease—local that is, anywhere below the 26th parallel—"tropical inertia", but even so, sending and particularly receiving cables in Dominica is nothing less than a project. The cables that arrived in answer to mine came to Roseau first, and then traversed the twenty miles to

Nassau Newspapers

Arrival at Nassau, May 1953, after 30-day voyage from
St Thomas, Virgin Islands

Felicity Ann in Nassau

Portsmouth on the small boat that commutes two or three times a week on a somewhat elastic schedule. At Portsmouth the cables made their way to the plantation if someone happened to be going that way, or I picked them up when I was in Portsmouth, which wasn't very often. From despatch to arrival cables took about a week, which maddened editors and delighted me. One editor demanded "stand by for telephone call from New York," and a week later he would get my cable telling him there was no organisation for overseas telephone calls in Dominica. It is quicker to rely on bush telegraph or telepathy. You can have ulcers or tropical inertia, but not both.

Nevertheless, the necessity to get away from it all remains, even in the tropics. Most of the population aspired to, if they did not own, a town house and a country house, and although neither of them may be anything more pretentious than a one-roomed wooden hut, they are far enough apart to give the illusion of a hideout in the woods. The Strongs had their escape hut on a slope by the sea. We all went there, snarling our way along the dazzling white beach in the Land Rover, the day Carnival was held in Portsmouth. We swam and picnicked and gathered exotic shells whilst drumbeats throbbed in the town and echoed in the hills, muted by distance but atavistically exciting. Occasionally a snatch of melody reached us from the steel bands parading the streets.

These steel bands are peculiar to the West Indies and originated in Trinidad. The instruments are fashioned out of oil drums, cans, biscuit-tins, and mechanical cast-offs like brake drums, and are tempered, twisted, and hammered into shape, to give them, when struck, notes of absolute accuracy and unexpected mellowness. A steel band played at a fancy-dress dance in Portsmouth at which I was invited to judge the costumes, a responsibility which I craftily passed on to the wife of a local dignitary. The costumes were home-made and ingenious, also illuminating as to what was considered romantic or bizarre from another point of view. Some of the girls came in native costume, which is colourful and becoming with its fichus, billowing skirts, and headdress, and would have won honours at the Chelsea Arts Ball; but in Portsmouth the wearing of it as fancy dress was considered as showing a sad lack of imagination. A girl who came as an Englishman drew far more applause, and a dark-skinned gentleman, inspired by a magazine ad., brought down the house as a Scotsman. All the details of the Highland dress were contrived out of odds and ends, and the result was cleverly impressionistic. More representational was a girl impersonating a prisoner. Her face was smudged and her arm was bandaged with a red-ink-stained rag. She wore a dirty white uniform and skull cap and carried a bucket and shovel. Refreshingly uninhibited, the masqueraders played in character as they paraded round the dance hall; the Englishman swaggered, the Scotsman jigged, and the prisoner dragged listlessly. The judges were undecided until the prisoner stopped suddenly, upended the bucket and sat on it, one pink-soled bare foot across her knee, and proceeded wearily to munch at a husk of bread; the final touch that tipped the balance in her favour.

Like the rest of the West Indies, Dominica has a history containing many a violent change of rule, and the erstwhile French domination persists in the charming national costume, now worn only on special occasions or as fancy dress, the patois that the Dominicans speak amongst themselves, and place names that become curiously bastardised into English, turning Roseau, for instance, into Rose-oh.

There is no harbour at Roseau, ships have to lie out in the open roadstead or anchor on a sharply shelving sea-bed, and it is no place to leave a ship without an anchor watch; so when I was invited to spend a couple of days at Government House as the guest of the Administrator and his wife, I did not sail down to Roseau in *Felicity Ann*, but went instead in the "crash boat" which was sent up on this special mission. A singular honour, as the crash boat is strictly reserved for the bi-weekly visits of the plane from Barbados. The stay at Government House was delightful, and the welcome from Roseau overwhelming. It seemed, as the crash boat pulled into the jetty, that the whole town was lined up as a reception committee, complete with bouquets. Sir Winston Churchill had recently visited Jamaica where he was presented with the freedom of the city at Kingstown. This struck the Dominicans as being a pretty nice gesture, and even if they could not own to such an illustrious visitor they were not going to be outdone on generosity, so I was presented with the freedom of Roseau.

Islanders are not as a rule much concerned with anything outside their immediate orbit, as island life is a full-time job, but it was surprising the interest Dominicans took in the voyage of *Felicity Ann*. Questions relating to the voyage asked by inhabitants of this little known Isle were often more pertinent than those encountered in more sophisticated countries. Even children, shy little girls with Topsy pigtails, stopped me with their engaging white smiles, in the streets of Roseau to say "Congratulations," as if they really knew what it entailed to sail across three thousand miles of open sea. Everyone seemed to think it was courageous to take on an ocean single-handed, and I returned to the Strongs' plantation embarrassed by allusions to a quality I did not possess, but which I was beginning to suspect was one of the most important keys for living.

Chapter 16

IT wasn't courage that sent me scurrying off across the ocean in a 23-foot sloop. It was a little curiosity and a lot of desperation that went into the making of that particular dream. I had liked the *idea* of sailing about seeing different places and meeting different people. I still liked the *idea*, but not, as yet, the practical application of it. Being at sea was a lonely, uncomfortable business, and very frightening. So I was faced with the problem of what to do with the rest of my life. I would complete the voyage—no Atlantic voyage is complete until you reach America—and then I would write a book about it all, but after that? Go on sailing bigger and better oceans? To what end? I knew what single-handed sailing was like now. The experience was complete. Any more would be repetitive to a greater or lesser degree, and the only gain would be in improving personal prowess as a sailor and navigator, which seemed pointless as I could hardly aspire to be Commodore of the *Queen Mary*, and to become a good sailor simply for my own satisfaction was not enough. I was discovering it is the hardest thing in the world to live for oneself. If one's achievements are of no benefit to anyone else they are certainly not worth making into a life work.

This was a problem to keep me awake at nights; during the day there were lesser problems to consider, such as making up my mind to get *Felicity Ann* ready to sail to Antigua. The ship needed repainting and refitting generally, and from all I had heard, English Harbour, Antigua, still seemed the best place to do this. It was about 90 miles north of Portsmouth, and the last 40 miles, from the northern end of Guadeloupe, the island next to Dominica, was across the open ocean with all the force of

3,000 miles behind it. I had been very impressed by the temper of the Atlantic, and did not look forward to testing it again, so kept delaying departure until John Staniland arrived unexpectedly and shamed me into action.

He blew into the Bay one morning on a small sloop owned by a young Irish doctor, bound the long way round for Labrador, who had made the passage from England single-handed. John had come to Portsmouth on a job, to collect a schooner there and sail her back to English Harbour for refitting.

The *Nymph Errant* had made a good passage across from the point of view of time, all things considered, said John, for it had been the worst crossing he had ever experienced.

"Nothing but dirty big black clouds," he said, "thunder and lightning, buckets of rain, and blowing harry hellers. Began to think we might be running into an out-of-season hurricane. Didn't like to say anything to the girls, but I read up very carefully all about hurricanes in the pilot books when they weren't looking. It wasn't until we got to Barbados that Bonnie said she had had the same thought and had also been reading up about them. Then Winnie confessed that she too had been going into the hurricane question."

"Which makes four of us," I told him. "What happened to all those beautiful Trade Winds you sold me on in the Canary Islands?"

"Don't you start," grinned John. "Winnie was at me all the way across for misrepresentation; but believe me, it is the first time I've known the Ocean to behave like that in the Trades."

They had not suffered the prolonged calms that had hindered the progress of *Felicity Ann*, however, and had reached Barbados in time to welcome the arrival of the indomitable Dr Bombard in his rubber raft. The *Nymph Errant* was now at English Harbour.

"Coming back with us?" asked John, and thus it was agreed, for one is always so brave in company.

195

Once again I went through the bittersweet routine of parting with people whose friendship and kindness had enriched my life and saying goodbye to an adopted life that had been no less real because of its impermanence; and I turned again with quickening anticipation to the prospect of another scene, for one travels with a gambler's incurable optimism. Beyond the horizon lies Eldorado, Shangri-La, Paradise, maybe only a mean little crock of gold, but something new and wonderful to be won one day.

As the passage had no significance other than a movement from one point to another, John took the *Felicity Ann* in tow and it was expected in this way to make Antigua in twenty-four hours. But it turned out to be a hectic four-day trip, which might have been foretold by a superstitious sailor, for we sailed on a Friday morning. A squall struck as soon as we got under way and blew out the schooner's foresail, and it was rough and tumble all the way to the northern end of Guadeloupe, the French island between Dominica and Antigua. There we turned into Deshayes Bay at nightfall, where the schooner dragged her inadequate anchor all over the bay until she finally fetched up just off a reef at the entrance. After the dust had settled, John came aboard the *FA*.

"Enough of that," he said, explaining the reason for anchoring instead of going on as intended. "The old girl's coming apart. I'd rather watch her disintegrate in daylight."

He had two Dominican boys aboard as crew, who had worked on the schooner before.

"Did you see them lie down on the side-decks this afternoon?" he said. "I told them they could turn in. With all that spray coming aboard you'd think they would've been glad to go below. I asked them why they didn't, and they said, 'No, suh. We never sleeps below on dis ship.'"

We sailed independently early the following morning, not realising in the shelter of the Bay that it was blowing a gale. My main halyard parted about the same time the schooner lost her topmast, jibstay, and jib, so we turned about and put back again into Deshayes Bay to sort out our ships and wait for weather. Conditions were not propitious for our delicate vessels until Sunday night. There is only a very small village at Deshayes and we did not go ashore, as it is not a port of entry and the French are fussy about formalities; but hosts of small black boys swam out to us on logs, paddling with arms and legs, who were persuaded to do a little shopping for us, at enormous cost, of course, but we had not allowed for a protracted journey and our stores were stretched to the point of invisibility.

Ever a sucker for novelty, I was enchanted by the sight of turtles swimming in the Bay.

At eleven o'clock on Sunday night we set out again for Antigua, and this time made it without any mishaps. The wind was steady and not too high. Much to my surprise I enjoyed the trip.

English Harbour is surely one of the most beautiful and sheltered little harbours in the world, and it is cunningly hidden from seaward. If you didn't know what you were looking for you would never find it. I knew what I was looking for, but nevertheless had a few nasty moments before the entrance opened on the port hand, for the land ahead was getting disconcertingly close.

Antigua is an entirely different treasure island from those lying to the south of it; the hills are not nearly so high or precipitous, and the terrain is barren and arid, with a determination to grow cactus where someone is not deliberately trying to grow sugar or cotton; yet the island has a gaunt beauty of its own and is rich in colour. English Harbour, landlocked, forgotten, and haunted, where the waters are translucent turquoise and the lower slopes of the surrounding hills are bright with yellow manchineel and green seagrape, once sheltered the proud ships of Nelson's Navy. The dockyard stands as it did then; the parade ground, the officers' quarters,

Nelson's house, the paymaster's and engineer's house, the boatsheds and sail-lofts, the great capstans for careening the wooden fighting ships, are all there, but dusty and decayed, crumbling away under the relentless erosion of time and neglect. Now the harbour shelters only the more ambitious cruising yachts, and American tourists picnic on the parade ground amazed at a country so rich in antiquities it can afford to forget this last tangible reminder of one of its greatest heroes.

There are no facilities at the dockyard, no stores, fuel, or power laid on. There is rainwater to be had from tanks, but otherwise all that is offered to the long-range yachtsman is a good sheltered anchorage, or a stone quay to tie up alongside, and a wealth of historical interest. It would be an austere welcome for a transoceanic sailor, of which quite a number put into English Harbour, were it not for the Nicholsons. Commander and Mrs Nicholson and their two ex-navy sons, after the war sailed their beautiful old-fashioned schooner, *Mollihawk*, from England to Antigua, where they settled in English Harbour to establish a charter business, with the two boys as skippers and Commander and Mrs Nicholson handling the shore organisation, whilst acting on the side as most congenial hosts to the itinerant sailor.

They lived in the upper storey of the paymaster's house, which was approached by an outside and rickety flight of steps. A plant installed by Vernon Nicholson in the engineer's house supplied their house with light, also power to operate the radio-telephone so that they could keep daily contact with the boats out on charter. A hand-operated dumb-waiter in the living-room provided communication with the kitchens below, but might as easily bring up a surprised and sleepy cat as a dinner. Emmie Nicholson effectively used sea-fans, driftwood, and shells as decorations, and was for ever shooing chickens, cats, and indeterminate dogs out of the house.

Outside the dockyard gates, the original monumental

studded doors, a duty-rutted road leads out across the Island fifteen miles to the capital and port, St John's, on the western coast. On its way the road passes through the scattered village of English Harbour, a collection of tiny wooden houses on stilts, all overcrowded and housing up to fourteen people in one or two small rooms. Congestion does not prevent doors and shutters being tightly closed at night to prevent the entry of jumbies, malicious spirits against whom one is defenceless when asleep. The village is very poor, and the arrival of a new ship in the Harbour brings crowds of villagers down to the dockyard to sell beads, bracelets, and mats, or seek employment through laundry work, or aboard in any capacity from galley-slave to deckhand. Emmie had the welfare of the villagers very much at heart, and almost before your boat is tied up you find your washing disposed of, your crew temporarily increased by at least one, and during your stay you employ quite a bit of local labour owing to Emmie's gentle browbeating.

Even my ship was not too small to escape, and throughout my stay at English Harbour I employed a maid for twelve shillings a week who spent the mornings sweeping, cleaning, and garnishing. Elena was a conscientious worker and never before or since has *Felicity Ann* sparkled as she did then. It was the first time Elena had worked aboard a boat and she was fascinated. "All I need," she said one morning, "is to learn to sail, then I could come with you."

I got badly sunburnt one day painting the decks wearing only bra and shorts. Elena was sympathetic. "I know what it is," she said. "I was burnt once, and never dare go without even a hat now." Which was unexpected, as she was a very dark girl.

As usual I had various commitments to meet for newspapers and magazines, but there was no room to work aboard when Elena was busy, so I borrowed one of the upper rooms in the Admiral's house and took my typewriter there. Outside my window a great sandbox tree shook its leaves and rattled the

199

large round sandbox pods that legend has it were used by Nelson himself to blot the parchments upon which he wrote. Below, on the ballroom floor, sailmakers stitched sails, softly singing calypsos. When the sails were finished I employed one of the boys, a coffee-coloured youngster with coffee-coloured hair, called Khaki, to paint the topsides. He also scrubbed the weeds off the bottom, diving without apparatus and holding his breath for a prodigious length of time. Khaki was a keen reader and asked one day for "some old story books," and I gave him a bunch of surplus paper-backs, which I after regretted as it probably gave him an entirely erroneous conception of the world outside Antigua.

As in Dominica, the voyage of *Felicity Ann* caught the imagination of the coloured folk. They used to stare at the boat in speculative wonder, generally too shy to make any remark if I was on deck, but once, when I happened to be reading below, I overheard a delightful discussion amongst a group of boys who had trucked a dinghy over from St John's. Being town boys they were pretty sophisticated, and discussed my venture with considerable assurance, although they were hazy over details. One said I was Swedish, another I was Dutch, and one asked, "Say, how she navigate?" and a voice replied, sharp with scorn, "Why man, don't you know? She navigate by heart."

There were a number of ships in English Harbour when I was there. The *Nymph Errant*, the Doctor with his sloop still on the way to Labrador, the ketch *Trident* that John had helped rebuild in Casablanca, and a little double-ended ketch I had last seen in Gibraltar. There were brief visits by sailing vessels from America and Africa, and charter boats from the Virgin Isles and Florida put in. Those of us who had come a long way and were going a long way and were in no hurry to get on with our going, led a lazy pasha-like existence with all our help, doing a little desultory work on our ships during the day and entertaining each other aboard at night. We swam and fished and made sorties into St John's for stores and equipment. Our daily requirements in the way of food were shopped for us by a huge, inarticulate negro called Sam. He was dark and hirsute, with a misleadingly ferocious demeanour and the mind of a very young child. Sam would make the rounds of the ships in the morning, standing on the quay by your boat waiting to be noticed, for it never occurred to him to attract attention. He could not read, so you told him what you wanted and gave him the money, and away he went on foot into the village with a handful of baskets. He never got the orders or the change confused. When you tipped him at the completion of a mission, and it was a mission for Sam, he would stand for several minutes silently staring at the money in his hand. If he had executed a particularly difficult purchase, such as tomatoes, which were very scarce, and you tipped him more generously than usual, his face would light up and he would laugh out loud, then without a word he would turn and rush away. Emmie explained: "He is not rude or ungrateful, but he can only think of one thing at a time. If you tip him well, all he can think of is what he can do with the money, and that makes him happy so he smiles. When he is very happy he laughs."

Sam adored Ian, the Stanilands' blond baby son, as did all the West Indians. For the first time in his short life Ian was able to run about freely on shore, and he was fascinated by all sorts of new discoveries, especially dogs. For a time Ian was a dog, running about on all fours, barking. As Sam imitated Ian, he too became a dog, and did all our shopping at the run, ki-yiking in a startling manner.

There is a saying that you can take your choice of disadvantages in the West Indies; hurricanes, volcanoes, earthquakes, or fer-de-lance, which is a particularly deadly snake. Each island has one or more of these disturbing features. Antigua has hurricanes, and, I discovered one night, earthquakes. I was dreaming that I was aboard and that someone had started up the generator, which was misfiring very badly for the ship was vibrating like a tuning-fork. Then I woke up. *Felicity Ann* was vibrating from stem to stern in the most fantastic manner, and there was a rumbling like distant thunder. Still stupid with sleep, I thought, "But I haven't got a generator," and then realised it was an earthquake and went on deck. There was nothing to see, only to feel and hear, and it lasted about twenty minutes. John and Bonnie felt it on *Nymph Errant* which was also tied up alongside the quay, but boats at anchor were not disturbed at all.

Contrast is the chief charm of cruising. One day you are scraping beans out of a can, and the next you are dining at Government House: one night you are drinking rum out of a mug aboard a cockroach-ridden schooner, and the next you are drinking gin in the grand manner aboard one of H.M. Ships. The transition is swift and unpredictable, and it is sometimes difficult to reconcile such diversity of living. I stayed over in St John's one night after a dinner party, and slept in a tall four-poster bed which was heavily swathed in mosquito netting. In the middle of the night I woke up leaning out of the bedroom window staring with horror at the flowerbeds beneath, shouting "My God, we're aground."

From some things apparently there is no escape.

Chapter 17

AFTER four weeks in Antigua I realised how much of a physical toll the Atlantic crossing had exacted. Having been at a low ebb of energy for so long I had come to accept it as a normal condition, but now I was not only making plans, I was eager to put them into action. I was even looking forward to going to sea again. No longer content to sit and watch the world go by, I wanted to go along with it. The wheels were a little rusty, but they were beginning to turn again. The Stanilands were restless, too, and as Easter was approaching it was agreed we would spend the holiday weekend at Nevis, an island forty miles on the way to the Virgin Islands, the Bahamas, and the States. For both the Stanilands and myself the States meant the termination of this particular cruise, and the thought was common to both of us now that it was time this one came to an end, so that we could embark on another. Or something else. Accordingly, on the Thursday before Good Friday, the Stanilands sailed, shouting "See you in Nevis tomorrow," as they cast off. They sailed in the morning, but I delayed my departure until night time, for the winds in the Caribbean blow more steadily and with less force then, besides which there was a full moon, and there are few things more pleasant than sailing under a moon.

I got rid of most of my stowaways just before sailing. Being a very small ship, *Felicity Ann* had only very small stowaways. Mice. They had been raiding my stores for weeks and I began to fear infestation, for nesting operations were obviously in force by the way the books were being torn up. They had managed to elude all usual methods of eradication, but fortunately I found the nest, complete with young, under the ballast in the chain locker a few hours before taking off. This still left "Ma" at large, but I felt I could cope with her, and was thankful the invasion had not been by cockroaches, the usual bane of the sailboat in the tropics. Once they get established, there are only two things you can do; sail to Arctic waters and freeze them out, or sell the boat. Against such a contingency I waged a ceaseless chemical warfare, to the point of making the cabin almost untenable.

The moon was high and bright at eleven o'clock that night, and the old familiar excitement tingled in my finger-tips as I said goodbye and prepared to cast off. Khaki and Elena had stayed at the dockyard specially to see me off, and as parting gifts, Elena gave some necklaces and mats she had made out of "jumbie eyes" and Khaki a dozen eggs, unexpected and touching gestures, incorporating considerable sacrifice, for the necklaces and mats represent a return from tourists, and eggs are untold gold around English Harbour.

The trip to Nevis was the most pleasant sail of the whole voyage; the ideal by which all further experiences would be judged. The Trade Winds were steady and gentle, and *FA* rolled before them as if there wasn't a care in the world. The moon made silver day of the darkness and cast a path of light along the water. I sat at the helm all night, happy just to be alive, and sang at the top of my voice to prove it.

At dawn a damp and infuriated little mouse jumped out of the cabin, stumped along the port-side deck, climbed up on to the footrail, gave me a look of utter loathing, put its little paws over its head, and dived into the sea.

My first reaction was to try and pick it up. Illogical, as I had been trying to trap it for weeks. But as I would almost certainly run it down in the process, and deplore misplaced sentiment, I sailed on, not without a sense of uneasiness. The last I saw, the mouse was swimming strongly and straight for the island of Redonda.

The *Nymph Errant* was at anchor off the small port at Nevis and I tied up astern of her. Later we changed into civilised rompers and went ashore to see what the social life of Nevis had to offer. The island is small and conical, barren and sparsely populated, with only a handful of white people living there. Three of them were in the bar of the only hotel in the town when we wandered in for a gregarious beer. "Good evening," we said, pleasantly, we thought. They turned and stared at us dispiritedly, finished their drinks, rose, and silently filed out. Evidently the place was getting crowded.

We took our beer up on to a balcony where we sipped in dreamy meditation until brought to earth by a shout of protest from the street below. Ian, unobserved by us, and unused to shore manners, had mistaken the balcony rail for the side of a ship. . . .

We walked down the main, and probably only, street and drawn by idle curiosity, joined the crowd on the steps leading up to the open church doors. The church was filled to the aisles, and from the congregation came the most glorious full-throated singing, throbbing with a rhythm and a joyousness that can only come from gratitude for being alive. They sang as a bird sings, with all their heart and soul. Ian was spellbound. With his hand in Bonnie's, he walked, step by step, up to the church doors, with a rapt expression that lit with tenderness the dark faces about us as they watched him.

Over the weekend we were elegantly entertained by Mary, an escapist from London society, whom Bonnie and I had met in the market on Saturday morning, where Bonnie had had to buy meat with averted eyes, because she insisted that the carcase quivered. Mary lived on a plantation in solitary splendour, and there we ate good food, and drank good wine, and listened to good music, so that we talked seriously of settling down and enjoying the good life; but on the morning of Easter Monday we sailed again, bound for St Croix in the Virgin Islands.

It was a still, calm day, our sails hung uselessly, and our ships moved along under their engines. The *Nymph* disappeared over the horizon, but at 2130 hours I passed her lying-to with no lights visible except the riding light. I had half a mind to carry on through the night and beat them to St Croix, but changed my mind a few minutes later, stopped the engine and turned in until four o'clock the following morning. There was no sign of the *Nymph Errant* then, she had left me at the post. It turned out to be a sweltering day of no wind, so that *Felicity Ann* had to continue under engine. In the middle of the afternoon the clutch, which had taken to slipping of late, evidently got over-heated, for it slipped out altogether, and there I was with no engine and no wind either. And no hope of making St Croix that night. My immediate reaction was one of acute disappoint-ment. I had looked forward to rejoining the Stanilands, and could not become easily reconciled to the thought of a lonely evening, which showed I had come a long way since that first night in Dominica.

As a matter of fact I was in for a few lonely nights and days, for the next morning the clutch still refused to engage. St Croix was only about ten miles away, and there was enough breeze to fill the sails, but the entrance to the harbour is long and tortuous, and I did not feel capable of tackling it under sail, so set a course for St Thomas, where the harbour entrance is more suitable for a sailor of my calibre. But I did not arrive there until three days later as the winds were from ahead and light most of the time.

The port at St Thomas is Charlotte Amélie, and a delight to look at after the shanty towns in the other islands. It rises in tiers from the harbour like Torquay or towns in the south of France. The buildings are colour-washed in pastel shades of yellow, green, red, pink, or blue, and the architecture is colonial Danish. It has an atmosphere of stability from seaward that is not borne out ashore, for then it is as if Miami and Broadway have gone to the islands for a wild weekend.

The American port authorities were briskly hospitable, and dealt with my papers so efficiently that I was left with a feeling of unwarranted importance. I was vaccinated, and *Felicity Ann* was awarded deratisation papers. The officer who inspected her for this took one look and said, "Holy smoke, their ain't room for a rat *and* you aboard."

Norman Fowler was the first person I met in St Thomas. He came to meet me at the dock and started talking as soon as he was within shouting distance. He had a *wonderful* trip across to Bermuda, well, not exactly wonderful, but they had made pretty good time. Edward Allcard had gone on to New York from there. He had a crew now, a Bermudan boy. A wonderful sailor. *Catania* was fine. Yes, she was a wonderful boat. Not slow at all like they used to say in Plymouth. But he was going to sell her. Oh, he'd buy her back again later, perhaps, but he thought he would go to North Africa, or London, or New York maybe. But of course, St Thomas was a fabulous place . . . wait till you see it . . . and my dear, *what* have you done with your hair?

"You must come along to my place," he said. "They told me to bring you. They'll give you a room, anything you want. They're delicious people. I adore them."

But I had gone all sailor again and refused to be parted from my boat. I did consent, however, to go along to Norman's "place" which I gathered was some sort of hotel, for a shower, a luxury I had now become constitutionally incapable of resisting.

There was a bareback rider, a clown, a lion-tamer, and a gorilla in the bar when we got there. The proprietress, a tense blonde, extricated herself from a heap of bunting, tinsel, and paper hats. "It's the carnival," she explained, and took me to her suite, to shower and change, forgetting apparently to warn her husband, for whilst I was enjoying the frenzied stream of water, a man came roaring into the bathroom and wrenched back the shower curtain, shouting, "Silly woman, she's left it on again, dammit."

I heard him apologising all the way downstairs.

That night I had dinner with Norman at the hotel. The dining-room was an upper level patio where we helped ourselves from a buffet table, queueing up to do so. "Hurry with your soup," whispered Norman, "or there'll be nothing left."

A man sat at the bottom of a flight of stairs lugubriously playing an accordion. Someone tossed a handful of firecrackers out of an upper window, and leant out to howl with laughter at the startled pedestrians beneath. The patio was so crowded that every time you raised your fork you choked your next-door neighbour. Above the clatter of cutlery conversation drummed the latest gossip, which was exclusively devoted to divorce.

After dinner Norman said we must take in a few night spots. We drifted from one to another, all dark and dolorous and unidentifiable, so that it seemed one had simply gone out of one door to come in again at another. "You need radar to move about in these joints," said Norman cheerfully. A blank-eyed brunette talked to us disinterestedly for a few minutes. "She's a lesbian," said Norman after she had gone. We shuffled a few steps on an inadequate floor and groped our way back to our table. "Ah," said Norman as an attractive blonde glittered into the spotlight, "listen to this. This girl *sings*." In point of fact she did, with just the right amount of huskiness, charming French songs that were wholly wasted on an audience mainly concerned with raising the alcohol level in its blood stream. A marine who had been staring glassily at the ceiling, suddenly got up, said, "Take it easy, bub," and fell flat on his face. His two companions, with the resignation of repetition, picked him up and carried him out. A pretty young man with pink cheeks and false eye-lashes joined us. "I just *love* this place," he said, "I'm so *happy* here. Anything can happen; just *anything*." A blues singer with no make-up and empty eyes took over the piano and played it confidentially, whispering gloomy secrets to the smoke-filled air. "Marijuana," said Norman, "when she gets hopped up she *bays*."

The spirit of Carnival pervaded the town and the talk was of little else. I tried to concentrate on getting *FA* ready for the next long passage of a thousand miles to Nassau. But it was no use. I found myself making a Jolly Roger for a schooner that was being disguised as a pirate ship, and on the morning of the Carnival, dressed as a singularly villainous pirate, I was drinking champagne with the rest of the crew, and by evening I was dancing barefoot in the dust to the wild music of a steel band.

The Stanilands came in from St Croix ("What happened to you?") and asked what sort of a place St Thomas was. "You had better find out for yourselves," I said. "Personally I am aiming to put the show on the road."

I baby-sat for them in the evening so that they could hit the town. When they returned, unusually subdued, Bonnie said slowly, "I see what you mean," and we made plans for sailing to Nassau.

Chapter 18

IT was the twenty-first of April when we sailed out of St Thomas, bowling along before a fine following wind. The Island looked calm and remotely inviting as it slipped astern. My stay had been too short and too confined to give anything but an unbalanced picture of the place, and I made a mental note to return one day and see the other side of it.

I sailed first, but the *Nymph Errant* was soon on our heels, then abeam, with the Staniland family waving derisively, and finally she was hull down on the horizon. Enviously I watched her vanish; not only could she make good speed, she could also keep going for twenty-four hours a day. But so can I, I thought, if this wind holds; and as it showed every sign of doing so for some time, I dropped the sails, stowed the boom and set up the twin staysails. An operation that took two hours, as I was stricken during the performance with an unexpected and overwhelming bout of seasickness. A payment for having omitted to take drammamine before sailing; surely by now, I had thought in a burst of overconfidence, I had acquired a staunch sea-stomach that needed no recourse to aids and remedies; but such was not the case.

Felicity Ann romped along all night, steering herself, and making her usual exaggerated fuss about running before the wind. A large black land-bird with a sharply pointed beak flew aboard during the night and perched trustingly but precariously on the boom above the cockpit. I could have touched him, but did not want to frighten him away as he seemed to need the respite. There was a pathetic weariness in the way he clutched the boom, swaying jerkily with the boisterous motion of the ship, balancing himself with an outstretched appealing wing. At dawn he flew away. There was no sight of land.

It was disappointing that the log only registered 37 at daylight, when it should have whipped up a nice round sixty, but the discovery of a large lump of seaweed wrapped round the spinner explained the discrepancy. *Felicity Ann* continued to run all that day and the next, then, on the morning of April 24th, Hispaniola, the great mountainous island that comprises Haiti and the Dominican Republic, loomed ahead. The wind had come round during the night, so that instead of running parallel with the land we had turned and were running towards it, so I had to change back to fore and aft rig again. The weather turned squally and there were intermittent showers. My watch, which had been an exemplary timepiece since the outset of the voyage, began to show temperament, stopping and starting spasmodically. On the 25th the wind blew so hard it was necessary to reef. Jib sheets wore through so that a new pair had to be made up, and little tears began to appear in the seams on the mainsail.

By midnight of the 25th it was blowing with savage fury, but I was too tired to care. *FA* was hove-to, and I slept till dawn, when the wind fell away to practically nothing, only to return in the afternoon with renewed vigour, and it ramped and raged until the following morning.

By eleven o'clock it was comparatively calm, and it was then I discovered the clutch had not after all been cured in St Thomas as I had hoped. It was seized solid in gear. I did optimistic things with oil cans on visible moving parts, acting with more valour than hope. However, next day it consented to work; I did not want the engine then, but it was nice to know that it was available if necessary. To counteract any conceit that might arise from this minor mechanical success, the faucet on the water tank developed a leak. It is simple enough to fit a new washer, which was obviously all that was needed, but the water flowed from the tank to the faucet by gravity, and there was no way of "turning it off at the main." I had to choose between letting it gush out whilst renewing the washer or drip slowly away into the bilges. I let it continue to drip.

On the morning of April 30th I had a stiff neck and the hope of sighting Great Inagua, the first of the Bahama group. A small M.V. *Air Plover,* passed close by and the crew shouted something encouraging about the Island, which, of course, I did not catch—communicating by voice at sea is very frustrating—but half an hour later Inagua obliged and showed up, low and shadowy, on the horizon. Three hours later Inagua light, a long striped structure like a giant stick of candy, was abeam.

As the first of the Bahamas it was disappointing. It was low-lying and unprepossessing. From the navigational point of view it was unnerving, an indication of things to come, for, unlike the other islands in the West Indies, whose towering mountains give ample warning of landfall, these low coral islands are barely visible until you trip over them. The whole huge Bahama area is beset with reefs, shoals, and currents requiring accurate navigation, and from then on, navigationally speaking, I was on pins. Crossing the ocean had done nothing for my arithmetic.

There was a thunderstorm playing over the island and a huge flock of gulls playing over the sea. They swooped and dived and screamed and fought one another. Just ordinary gulls they were, the kind that haunt any fishing port, but it was not until I saw them flying in a tumultuous white cloud over the sea by Inagua, that I realised how I had missed them, for up to then the only seabirds I had seen this side of the ocean had been terns, petrels, tropic birds, and pelicans, which last are almost an affront to seabird life. I shut my eyes and listened to the gulls screaming and laughing their hideous witch's cackle, and I could imagine myself in Lowestoft or Fleetwood for a few precious moments of unproductive nostalgia. In Lowestoft I had spent a happy time with Bonnie and John aboard their previous yacht,

Diadem, and in Fleetwood Frank and I had rebuilt the *Reliance.*
Both were fishing ports, and it was unlikely I would ever see
either of them again.

From Inagua light I set a course for the Crooked Island
Passage, which lies between Crooked Island at the north end
of Aklin Island, and Long Island. Shipping now began to appear,
all sorts of impressive vessels including a monster battleship,
heading for the passage or coming away from it. *FA* had to run
under engine along the invisible length of Aklin Island, but by
eight thirty that night it had to be shut off when we ran into a
line squall. It stretched across our path, low, black, and threatening. On the windward side of it as we approached it was serene
and peaceful, but as we crossed the line, so to speak, all hell
broke loose, and by one o'clock in the morning *FA* was hove-to
just clear of the Crooked Island light.

Whilst making fast the boom guy which I always rigged
when hove-to, my watch strap caught on a lifeline, unhitched,
and the watch went overboard and sank. Although it had been
erratic these last few days I felt as if I had lost a lifelong friend.

It blew furiously all through the night, all next day, and the
following night. Although *FA* was hove-to, it was exhausting,
for added to the anxiety inevitably induced by bad weather,
there was the necessity for keeping constant watch throughout
the night as there was a lot of shipping in the offing. At dawn
on the morning of May 4th, I fell dead asleep until awakened
at ten by *FA* shaking her boom in the most vehement manner.
I turned out to see what it was all about, and found we were
drifting on to Rum Cay, our drift whilst hove-to having been
greater than calculated. I registered low white cliffs and breakers
on the off-lying reefs, and started the engine, whereon the clutch
mechanism disintegrated with a clatter of finality into the
bilges. The wind had eased so that we could sail on it, and it
enabled us to claw clear of the Island. I streamed the log, which
I had taken in as usual when hove-to so that the line would not

chafe on the stern of the ship, but the spinner was no sooner in the water than it was taken by a shark.

On May 5th the wind abated, though the seas continued to be lumpy and aggressive. *FA*, for no ascertainable reason, started to make a lot of water, and regular sessions at the bilge-pump became part of the daily routine.

For the next four days we averaged about twenty-two miles a day. As usual weather conditions were all or nothing.

By the night of May 9th they were unequivocally nothing, and we were becalmed on a sea masquerading as a mill-pond. Thunder rumbled distantly and desultory lightning lit the empty scene from time to time, but radio reception was magnificent. I got a time signal, a play, and the news from the B.B.C., thousands of miles away in England. This was followed by a piano recital that held me spellbound until a sixth sense warned me to take a look outside, and there, sure enough, coming straight at us, were the lights of a large steamer. No wind, no engine, no way to get from under. I lit every oil lamp on board and hung them all over the ship and winked a flashlight at the approaching vessel. At the last moment she altered course, very suddenly, and signalled, slowly and reproachfully, in morse as she passed, "Your lights are burning badly."

Delighted at being able to read the message I was not in the least chagrined at the content, but resolved to make a real study of morse in my spare time, and spent the rest of the night blinking dots and dashes on the flashlight.

Next morning was calm on the surface, but overhead heavy thunderclouds hung menacingly, decanting at intervals dark downpourings of rain into the sea, which responded with a few waterspouts. The jib tore at the luff where the luff wire rope had rusted and broken. Whilst I was juggling with the sailmaker's kit in the cockpit, hundreds of tiny grey and spotted fish swam curiously up to the ship and, not finding what they expected, swam away. Then a pair of tropic birds made dive-bombing attacks on *FA*, shrieking with resentment as if they would drive us off the sea. I only wished they could, for this was turning out to be a tedious voyage.

Calm weather interspersed with squalls continued. The glass fell out of my temporary watch, a no-good timepiece I had carried around in my purse for years, for no better reason than that I had carried it around in my purse for years. The loss of the face glass did nothing to hinder its already erratic running, but it entailed taking protective measures which were difficult to employ aboard *FA*, and was just another irritation. Then the mainsheet wore out in several places and I had to make up and reeve a new one, after which the jib tore again at the luff and had to be repatched. My skill with any sort of a needle being what it is, this was hardly surprising, but it was none the less annoying. Then a really distressing feature appeared. I was gradually losing control of the ship. She would no longer come about, and would only wear round to starboard, and that reluctantly, for the square rudder-head had worn round, and the tiller, keyed to fit, no longer gripped it effectively. This was not of serious consequence so long as there was plenty of sea-room, but was certainly going to add to the interest of our arrival in Nassau. Always supposing we ever got there.

Chapter 19

EVEN after three weeks at sea there was little sign of movement towards Nassau; we seemed to have reached an impasse, for although I reckoned we could not be very far from the North-East Providence Channel that lies between the islands of Eleuthera and Abaco, day after day went by with the scene unchanged except for an increase in the number of ships, which invariably show up in the vicinity of bottlenecks.

The weather was hot and hazy now. At times the glare on the water made it impossible to take a sight, and at nights the haze blended sea and sky into a universal greyness so that it was impossible to distinguish whether a pinpoint of light was a low star or a distant ship. It gave a sensation of being suspended precariously in space, and once again there was an immutable silence. A silence so great it seems as if sound had never existed; as though the world had never begun. You hold your breath and creep about and listen, and if it went on long enough, you would doubt the validity of your own existence and suspect you were the product of some huge cosmic imagination. Fortunately, it never lasts that long. Moreover, the constant presence of marine life ensures the conviction that the world is spinning as usual.

The sea in the Bahaman area is a brilliant turquoise, and when they are still the clarity of the waters is extraordinary. Sharks swam about the ship, at first as dark shadows way down, then with infinite detail just below the surface. They rubbed up against the side of the ship so that their dorsal fins were within reach of the cockpit, and they rolled over to inspect the ship and myself with cold, calculating, pig-like eyes. Then, as if in pursuit of some machiavellian scheme, they spiralled slowly down out of sight round the log line that hung from the stern like a plumb bob. When the sharks were gone, gay dolphin took their place to nose about the mats of golden floating seaweed or hunt flying-fish with joyous abandon. At times the water would be almost turgid with thimbles, tiny pulsating purple-brown jellyfish shaped like little muffs. And I saw a whale at close quarters. At close quarters it was not so much a sea creature as a panorama. My eyes did not take it in all at once, but travelled along it as it ploughed majestically, spouting, across our wake, not more than twenty feet astern.

> . . . "If this should stay for tea, I said,
> There won't be much for us. . . ."

Three weeks at sea and no calculable end to the voyage. I had expected, hoped, and planned on being in Nassau within a fortnight, for St Thomas was lit by the sun of the dollar, which created an embarrassing situation for a Britisher purchasing stores. The best I had been able to do was to provision thinly for two weeks, and had the winds been co-operative and had I been clever, that is all it should have taken me, but now for once aboard the lockers were growing uncompromisingly empty. There was oatmeal left, which did not promise to be particularly appetising without milk and sugar; there were one or two cans of beans. One could fish, of course, but there was no guarantee one would catch anything, and I was not yet in the mood for plain boiled fish. There was a little coffee still, but water was now running out of the tank like crazy and the supplies of kerosene and priming fluid were running low, which severely curtailed cooking and lighting. Naturally one missed the luxuries more than the necessities at first. I drank the last drink and smoked the last cigarette with a melancholy philosophy one sundown. Then promptly built up a chronic anxiety condition. It was growing increasingly important to reach Nassau, so I lost all faith in my navigation. I took sight after sight as long as the sun was shining, and worked out innumerable positions of increasing inaccuracy. By the time the Trade Winds sauntered back to riffle the sea and stir the sails, I could argue definitely that we were anywhere between Cat Island and the Gulf Stream with calculations to prove any spot I cared to choose.

The one intelligent action I managed to take during this time was to devise a plug for the water tap out of oatmeal and gauze, and even this was not due to brains but to a process of elimination. Wooden plugs didn't work, cork plugs didn't work, rubber plugs didn't work because the pressure was too great, but the oatmeal swelled with the moisture and reduced the flow to an occasional dribble. The plugs had to be renewed at intervals and whenever I wanted to draw water, which meant I kept putting off doing so and thirsted in consequence and added one more fret to a growing list of fumes.

The trouble with this state of mind is that even when a good situation turns up you don't believe in it. Throughout my wild calculations ran a little thread that made sense, and when I made landfall one evening as a logical outcome of following this thread, I shied away as if the land was about to explode. Navigation indicated that it was the Eleutheran side of the North-East Providence Channel, and all I had to do was sail through it, set a course for Nassau and be there the next day. But I was in a supposing mood. Supposing I was wrong; I could sail on a reef. It would be folly to attempt the Channel at night; must have plenty of searoom with the ship the way she is. (How much searoom did I want, for Heaven's sake, the Channel was only twenty-two miles wide?)

We drifted so far out to sea that night that we only made landfall again the following sundown and went through the whole agonising process again. But that night we did not drift so far, and the next morning we sneaked up on the tiny shadows of land on the port bow and nearly tripped over a long line of partially submerged islets and rocks on the way. This so shook me that I rushed off out to sea again to think it over. And the upshot was that I dithered about in a state bordering on hysteria for two days until an incident occurred to restore me to a semblance of good humour and sense.

It is extraordinary how distorted your outlook can get when there is no one around to lever you out of the rut of doubt. During those two days I worried and supposed incessantly, refusing to believe the evidence of my sights, the charts, or the compass. I was so rock-happy that when a wave broke, be it ever so mildly, I suspected it of having a rock underneath. I groped back towards where the Channel would be if my sights were correct with the cynical despair of one walking wittingly into an ambush. There had been no ships for a few days, which had further disquietened me, for they always show up in numbers anywhere near a channel or passage. Then, at half-past nine at night on May 18th, a freighter overtook us on a parallel course. Rather as one makes out a last will and testament, I decided to signal her and ask her to report me to Lloyd's. It would be nice for someone to know when *Felicity Ann* was caught at last in the ambush. . . .

There is quite a procedure to signalling at sea, and I had practised assiduously since that night the ship had told me my lights were burning badly and deluded me into believing that merchant ships signalled in a slow and dignified manner so that even I could understand. When the unsuspecting vessel was within about half a mile, I signalled A, swiftly and decisively on the flashlight until she slowed down, turned on her Aldis and replied T, which means, O.K., whaddya want? Then I sent out DE and *FA*'s registered letters, so that she would know who was talking, but too efficiently evidently, for when she replied it was in a blur of light that meant no more to me than the flickering in a neon tube. She stopped abruptly and humbly I asked her to repeat whereon she did it again. Cutting out all the niceties, I begged, "SLOWLY". Impatiently she hove-to and roared "Repeat" on the Aldis. I knew that one, it was only one letter.

I was balanced on one foot on the cockpit coaming, trying ineffectually to steer with the other, one arm was wound round the boom gallows, and a pad of paper was clutched in one hand, the flashlight in the other. I gripped a pencil with my teeth. Meantime, *Felicity Ann*, as if bored to distraction, lolled broadside to a series of joggling little waves trying to row herself with the boom.

"Repeat," cried the freighter, "Repeat, repeat!" And I broke the pencil switching from my teeth to my hand, and dropped the pad into the cockpit.

"Oh, skip it," I wanted to say. "Let's forget we ever started this." But "Repeat," insisted the freighter. "My God," I thought. "Suppose they think I am in trouble and lower a boat——" So very firmly I signalled END and went below and closed the hatch and watched her through the portholes until I was sure she was under way again.

If it did nothing else, this ridiculous incident broke the tension, for I realised that on the course she was taking the freighter could be heading for nowhere else but the North-East Providence Channel; so I pegged away with the reluctant little wind that was blowing until I was too sleepy to carry on any longer. Next evening a very smart steamer, the S.S. *Andyck*, overtook on a course so close to mine she had to alter to overtake, which was irrefutable confirmation of my navigation. There you are, I thought crossly, wasting your time as usual on unnecessary worries.

The unmistakable glow of a town appeared in the sky the following night, and the morning after that Nassau water tower, no bigger than a matchstick, showed up on the horizon ahead.

According to the charts the Channel seemed to be well marked and did not appear to have any unusual complications; but there was a head wind blowing and I did not think *FA* would be able to beat against it, seeing that she had insufficient rudder control to enable her to come about. So I hoisted the Q and pilot flags and jilled about at the harbour entrance hoping the pilot boat would come out and tow us in. No pilot boat appeared. Darkness fell, and undaunted by the experience of the other night, I signalled for a pilot with the flashlight, but drew even less result, for there was no response of any kind.

Nassau lit up with gaily coloured lights and went about its merry business. Headlights bored through the night, twin searchlights seeking their destinations, as people drove home or out for an evening's entertainment. I thought of the homes and hotels and stores; the friendliness and the comforts that awaited, and was taunted by all the food, liquor, and cigarettes that were going to waste, for no one would be appreciating them as I could then. It was too much for me and I tried to sail up the Channel.

There was an unlit nun-buoy at the entrance which had a way of appearing suddenly and far too close, as I tried to bring *FA* on to the range. The range is a guide, two lights on the shore that have to be brought in line in order to traverse the first part of the Channel without taking in any rocks or reefs on the way. With normal steering control it would not have been difficult in spite of the head wind, but with *FA* answering the helm uncertainly or not at all, it was a hair-raising undertaking, especially in the dark. After we had scraped by the nun for the third time I gave up, and stood off and on outside the harbour entrance in company with a couple of steamers and sundry other vessels all night.

At dawn the pilot boat came out and I hovered hopefully, but she swept blindly by, to fuss solicitously about the steamers.

"All right," I thought, "*all* right," and waited until all the other ships had gone ahead. Then, when the Channel was clear,

I made a final attempt at sailing into the harbour. The wind was very light and still from ahead, but it was easier this time, for at least I could see what I was trying to do. Nevertheless, it was probably one of the strangest approaches ever made into any harbour. *Felicity Ann* waltzed along inch by inch, every now and then apparently turning round to go out again as she wore round to come on to the other tack, turning always to starboard as that was the only way she would turn with any degree of certainty. Then at last we ran out of wind and momentum opposite the British Colonial Hotel, about half-way to the anchorage. However, honour was satisfied. I dropped the hook, stowed the sails, and settled down to wait for the Customs boat. Ahead I could see the wharfs and quays, and had no doubt but that in due course someone would see the little sloop at anchor just off the fairway flying the quarantine flag to proclaim she was from abroad.

It was six o'clock in the morning and I figured there would be some time to wait, for there were very few signs of activity ashore. A man walked a horse down the beach and into the sea, where he washed and scrubbed it meticulously. The beaches were white and the casuarina trees rippled silkily in a fringe partially hiding the town, whose buildings were predominantly painted an Elizabeth Arden pink. It was all very peaceful.

Nassau, I thought, looking much flatter than imagined, but very nice. And I would have been here days ago, if only I'd had the courage of my convictions.

You see, said my other self—a carping creature always ready to say I told you so—if you would only learn to depend on yourself, and get it out of your head that a kind Fate is standing by to pick you up when you fall, you would be all right. It is no good blaming the stars or luck or the lines in your hands, your problems are invariably of your own making.

I know that.

And only you can solve them. So you had better remember

Felicity Ann at Daytona, showing how she travelled the Inland Waterways with her mast unstepped

Felicity Ann on slip showing underwater lines

that in future and make an effort, instead of worrying round in concentric circles.

But I can't help worrying, I thought defensively. After all, I might be wrong. . . .

Might be, sneered other self. Might be. You might be wrong about your landfall and sail on to a reef. You think how awful it would be to lose your ship and get into a tizzy about it, instead of thinking constructively how to avoid such a calamity. But you have always taken the easy way out by running away, as you did when you rushed off out to sea.

I grinned wryly. Maybe I needn't have run so far.

Makes no difference, said other self, who, once started, cannot be stopped. Worrying is a form of running away. An escapism. A mental wringing of hands because of a refusal to face, not necessarily facts, but possibilities. When you see I possible consequence you don't like you shy away. That's no good. You have to square up to 'em.

Courage of your convictions, I thought, which is where came in. Courage—why, that's it, of course. That's the answer. That's what I've been looking for. How surprising—but how obvious when you see it.

Only you didn't see it, other self pointed out. You've been hanging by your teeth all these years because you confused courage with the conquering of physical fear. What you need is not the sort of courage that makes a man face danger. Criminals face hideous dangers sometimes, but they are the least courageous of all, for it takes courage to evaluate standards and live by them.

Then what is courage?

An understanding and acceptance; but an acceptance without resignation, mark you, for courage is a fighting quality. It is the ability to make mistakes and profit by them, to fail and start again, to take heartaches, setbacks, and disappointments in your stride, to face every day of your life and every humdrum trivial little detail of it and realise you don't amount to much, and accept the fact with equanimity, and not let it deter your efforts.

I looked at my watch. Seven o'clock or thereabouts, and still there were very few signs of life ashore. A late-rising town, I thought, with the smugness of one who has been up all night on legitimate business, and decided to go below and catch up on sleep until the Customs boat arrived.

The cabin looked homelike and friendly, books on the shelves, kettle on the stove, even the chaos caused by thirty days at sea had a cosy confusion about it. I felt a surge of warmth towards the little ship that had taken me so far. Cruising is fun, after all, I thought.

Now it is nearly over, said other self, you can think it is wonderful. Only another hundred and eighty miles to Miami and it will all be over.

It is over now, I thought, stretching out on the bunk, at least the quest is. . . .

Don't kid yourself, other self said sharply, you will go on muddling and flapping and floundering your way through life as you have always done.

But at least I'll know what is needed, even if I haven't it in me to use——

You've got it in you all right, everyone's got it in them, it isn't a special dispensation from a selective Providence. It is just a question of whether you have the guts to apply it.

It struck me that I must be pretty dumb, for most people come by it naturally, but I had to sail across thousands of miles of ocean to find out that courage is the key to living.

Part 4

Nassau . . . Miami . . . New York

Chapter 20

THE Health and Immigration authorities came out in a motor launch about nine o'clock by which time I was sound asleep in the cabin and had to be awakened by resounding raps on the coachroof, thereby causing the officials much amusement, it being customary for a crew to be hanging over the side in a lather to be cleared so that they can get ashore. After the formalities had been completed, *Felicity Ann* was towed to a private dock belonging to an hotel on the waterfront. There she was besieged by reporters whom the manager interrupted to offer me a room in the hotel. At first I was inclined to refuse, having assumed the mantle of a rollicking sailor for the benefit of the press, but second thoughts suggested it was not reasonable to persist in being rugged to no purpose, so I left the ship and marched through the hotel and upstairs in my seagoing clothes, scruffy shorts and crumpled shirt, digging bare toes into the carpets, eccentricities that were accepted then as being merely run of the mill as the hotel was invaded by a film company from Hollywood shooting underwater scenes in the local waters for this currently popular type of movie.

In the bedroom I had a high old time switching on lights and turning on taps and watching the water run, and marvelling for the *n*th time at the products of progress, concluding once again they are best appreciated after a period of deprivation. Transition from ship to shore was not immediate, however. The plumbing went wrong in the private bathroom and it was not until I had fixed it myself that the thought occurred that it was no longer necessary to be so completely independent.

It was the end of May and the greater rush of the tourist season was over. Nassau was no longer tourist conscious and dressed to kill. She had her hair down and slippers on, so to speak. The people I met and the friends I made were mainly people who lived and earned their living in the islands, so that I was enabled to blend with the background and take on the protective colouring of an inhabitant, which is not only a much more satisfying way of absorbing atmosphere than visiting as a tourist, but is also a whole lot cheaper.

After a couple of weeks I left the hotel, moved *FA* to another private dock, and went to stay with Joan Strong's sister, whose apartment was conveniently situated only two blocks away from the boat. Kathleen Nicholson had also moved out to the West Indies after the war, but had previously lived in Cheshire only a few miles from where I had spent several years during the aviation phase of my career. Although living in the same locale and sharing many interests our paths had never crossed in England. We had to meet in the Bahamas because I made my first landfall across the ocean at Dominica. These little quirks of coincidence, having no significance, never fail to delight, and it constituted a bond at once between Kathleen and me.

The American magazine, *Life*, with whom I had contracted to write the story of the voyage before leaving England, now demanded copy. "We will concede the rest of the voyage," they said, "so far as we are concerned you have crossed the Atlantic." So I sat on the verandah of Kathleen's pink apartment, where moonflowers climbed round the balustrades, and hammered away at the typewriter, reliving an adventure that was growing daily more improbable.

The telephone rang one morning; "For you," said Kathleen, smiling rather obliquely I thought, and I was puzzled as to who the call might be from as I had purposely kept my whereabouts a secret since leaving the hotel so that work on the *Life* story could go ahead without interruption (where writing is concerned I am a very easily interrupted person).

". . . long distance for Captain Davison," said the operator.

"*Captain* Davison? This is Ann Davison speaking."

"Captain Ann Davison?" asked the operator.

"Well, I don't know about the captain," I said, wondering what they would think of that back home, but the operator insisted that that was the way it was, and later I was to find that this is a point of honour on the Western side of the ocean, where a man in charge of anything afloat demands that his status be clearly defined. Captain it is, and no nonsense.

The call was from Philadelphia, from friends I had met in Antigua, and with whom I had not communicated since, and it was interesting to me in that it was my first experience of the way they do things in the States; for the call was of no specific importance, yet they had taken the trouble to track me down and call me up over a matter that could have been as efficiently dealt with by a letter to my agents in New York whose address they already had.

In Nassau I learnt to enjoy sailing for the pure fun of sailing, just hoisting the canvas and puttering about in unhurried calm over sparkling waters, without the necessity of having to get somewhere a long way away before something awful happened. Kathleen had a sailing dinghy, and every weekend, or sometimes of an evening when she had finished work, we went out, either in her little boat (by comparison)—the handling of which made *FA* seem like a full-rigged ship—or in *Felicity Ann*, or in a Bahaman-built sailboat, which had no pretentions but a great deal of comfort, and explored the regions round the islands and islets that abound just off Nassau.

It was on one of these excursions that I discovered for myself, swimming with a mask and snorkel, the wonderful world that exists underwater; an experience that has to be undergone personally to extract the full value, as no amount of telling or picture-showing can convey one-tenth of the beauty and magic of life under the sea, especially in Bahaman waters, where everything promised in a child's dream of fairyland comes true.

The colour, silence, and incomparable peace of the gardens on the seabed is beyond description, and a point which fascinated me was the way fish seemed to accept you as one of them when swimming under water this way. Shoals of little iridescent fish swam unconcernedly past my ears, under my arms, and over my feet. They were of the most entrancing colours, red, gold, yellow, purple, green, and a velvety black with silver spots or stripes of royal blue.

As well as sailing, and swimming in water whose temperature was never less than eighty degrees, there was horseback riding, and dancing, dancing by the light of an unbelievable tropical moon, under silhouetted palms, to the wild mad music of the calypso bands. Sometimes Kathleen and I took our sketchbooks and went painting. There was no need to look for subjects, you had only to open your eyes and there they were, all around you. Kathleen painted freely with a fine flow of colour and her compositions were full of light and vigour, but mine were moody little daubs, because I was daunted by my temerity in trying to portray so much unalloyed life and colour. Colour is the outstanding feature of Nassau. Unforgettable, brilliant and limpid, clear as a spectrum, and haunting as a half-heard melody are the rich reds, yellows, and purples of the hibiscus, poinsianas, poinsettias, oleanders, alamanaers, and bougain-villea, whose very names make poetry; the deep greens of the breadfruit, mango, and seagrape, and the translucent turquoise of the sea; the pastel paints of the buildings, picturesque in splendour and dilapidation; the drab whites of the fishing boats; the satin-brown skins of the natives and the arresting clothes they wear, and the incredible bustling colour of the markets.

Purposeless and pleasurable days slipped off the calendar as I ate my lotus and delayed departure on the flimsiest of pretexts, until I was offered a job for a month as a private and confidential secretary. At first I thought it was a joke; anyone who has read my MSS would agree that as a typist I am a last resort, but apparently in this case I was, and I took the job. It is not often you are offered payment to stay in a place you don't want to leave, and as I had never done anything so normal in my life as take a regular job I was curious to know what it would be like. To one for whom time has no significance apart from navigation, who eats when hungry and sleeps when tired, it was a revelation. It gave me indigestion and insomnia having to keep to regular hours, but the work was fascinating, at times so confidential I hardly dared read my own writing.

Then all too soon the month was up, the job was over, the hurricane season approached, and the future beckoned impatiently. On the ninth of August I hove my gear aboard the *Felicity Ann*, waved a regretful farewell to Kathleen and the stalwarts who had braved the dawn to see me off, and sailed for Miami.

Chapter 21

FROM Nassau to Miami is about 180 miles, which took four days to cover, because two of them were spent at anchor on the Grand Bahama Bank, a huge area of shallow water, where I rested, read, and recuperated after a week of farewells. It was a curiously piquant sensation lying quietly at anchor in two fathoms with not a vestige of land in sight. The water was so clear the ripples in the sand on the seabed were plainly visible, as were the fronds of weed that reached up, waving gently, as if swayed by an underwater wind. It was very peaceful, except that on the second day it blew unexpectedly and with exceeding wrath so that the waters on the Bank were white with foam. "Like shoal," I thought detachedly, watching it through the port-holes, and realised, with mild surprise, that of course it *was* shoal. *Felicity Ann* plunged at her anchor, but did not drag, and I went on reading and resting complacently. Upon arrival in Miami I learnt the pother was due to fringe winds of a hurricane which had passed way up to the northward, but if I had known it at the time my frame of mind would have been a lot less peaceful.

The sun was extremely hot now, hotter than it had been at any time on the voyage to date, and at nights the display of comets and falling stars made a sight to behold. They exploded, a silent white blossoming, and traced fiery patterns across the sky, as if, incredibly, the whole heavens was erupting.

Dramatic too, was the colour demarcation between the Bank and the Gulf Stream where the brilliant jade of the Bank waters cuts sharply against the deep dark blue of the Gulf. To sail across the line from the Bank into the Stream, when conditions are calm and the waters clear, is strangely akin to driving over the edge of a cliff, and the fact that one does not fall into the apparent abyss is a small shock in reverse. Flying over the edge of a cloud when the wheels of the plane are on the upper surface of the cloud gives a similar sensation.

The Coast-guard came out to meet me in the Government Cut at the entrance to Miami Harbour, and led the way to the Q station, an unlooked-for and pleasing gesture. At the Q station a girl was waiting to report the story, and she was in a great hurry to get it and make the evening paper. A journalist, from the same paper, was also waiting to cover the story for England, having been assigned to do so by the group for whom I had been writing all the long, long way along.

After the ship was cleared, a police boat escorted me to the City Yacht Basin. The journalist came too, doubtless to hold a watching brief for the paper on one who was both contributor and news item. At the Q station I had assumed we had arrived; but no; the trip from there to the City Yacht Basin was just a shadow of the vastness of things to come; for although we drove on for an unconscionable time, the tall towers of Miami never seemed to draw any nearer. The tide had something to do with this, too, but it was still a long way, and the little ship plugged on and on in the channel by the Causeway that leads to Miami Beach, the vacation centre where, I was told, there are no less than 600 leading hotels all vying with one another in competitive luxury of a fabulous kind. From seaward it is the skyscrapers of Miami Beach that one sees first, and they materialise in mirage form so as to appear to be suspended in mid-air. After you have been in the States for a little while, it would not surprise you if they were.

Even the palm trees seemed bigger than those in the Islands, and all along the Causeway sped enormous cars, glinting in the sunlight and swinging along in an unequivocally American manner.

The police boat, unable to keep down to *FA*'s maximum, was soon out of sight, but when at last we came up to the waterfront, and I was debating as to which of the docks we should make for, she appeared again, nosing about the water in a puzzled manner like a sheepdog that has lost its sheep. Then she spotted us and turned in our direction, and I, forgetful of every rule of pilotage, turned towards her without a thought as to the channel or the fact she might be drawing less than *FA* and cutting corners. Which, in fact, she was; with a lurch *FA* slumped on to a sandbank and stayed there stubbornly immovable. It was the first time I had run aground, and I was considerably chagrined. The police boat pulled us off in front of a large crowd which had gathered on the nearby quays. A large crowd, it transpired, consisting mainly of reporters and photographers, who have never been known to miss a trick, and they didn't miss this one either. Leering with shame I agreed I sure had hit America, and when we had worked that one to death, they subjected me to a barrage of questions, which I was required to answer without giving anything away that might belong to the *Sunday Chronicle* or losing their good will.

To be on the receiving end of fame takes some getting used to; I had not expected anything like the number of reporters that were there to meet me, or the interest they showed, and felt they must be confusing me with someone else. I was sure the value of the accomplishment was over-estimated, for, such as it was, it was essentially a personal matter, making no direct contribution to society. All the same I could not help enjoying the small glory at first—even if it was undeserved.

The Immigration Officer had some difficulty in deciding how to let me enter the country. A seaman is allowed 29 days, but a visitor can stay three months. I was a seaman, but wanted to stay longer than 29 days. Finally it was decided that as well as being captain, cook, and crew of the *Felicity Ann*, I might also be a passenger. A passenger was a visitor according to the books

234

and eligible for the three months' stay. Accordingly, in this multiple capacity I entered the United States.

Events thereafter were confused and kaleidoscopic. After years of austerity in England which had only eased a little when I sailed, the first thing that impressed me in the United States was profusion. Profusion of clothes, equipment, and particularly food. The first steak that was put before me was served on a serving dish and overlapped the ends. In the days of rationing it would have been an allowance for four people for a week. This was not a special feature of the restaurant either, it was just a normal helping. The desserts were huge, covered in whipped cream, ice cream, meringues, coconut, jelly, and chocolate. Rich beyond imagining, they were delicious, cloying, and, finally, inedible.

There were radio interviews, and television appearances, and always, everywhere, thousands and thousands of questions to be answered. Curiously probing and frighteningly intimate, some of those questions, for there is no mental privacy in the States as known in England, where deeper subjects are alluded to obliquely, if at all, and only among intimates. To be publicly cross-examined in broad daylight on the detailed anatomy of my fears and spiritual values engendered a feeling of outrage at first, and although I got used to it in time I was never happy about it.

Even the hibiscus bloomed larger in Miami than elsewhere, I thought, subdued by the most, the greatest, the apogee of the colossal. To the English, America can never be quite true. It grows and bounds before your very eyes, getting bigger and bigger as if it were a little universe expanding illimitably. It is wholly fascinating and utterly incredible; the never-never land where everything is larger than life. But to the English it is a play, an extravagance, upon which the curtain must fall and it will be over, and the onlooker must go home and there will be the washing-up to do, the floors to sweep, and the train to catch in the morning.

In spite of the fact I had spent two days lazing on the Grand Bahamas Bank and three months living it up and easy in Nassau, and was probably in ruder health than I had ever enjoyed before, it was decreed by the English newspapers that as I had now reached America and so officially crossed the Atlantic, I must be wilting with exhaustion, and must therefore be resuscitated. Accordingly, plaintively but unavailingly protesting, I was swept away by the *Sunday Chronicle*'s American watchdog to an hotel on the outskirts of the town, where I was received with a sort of forgiving tenderness entirely unwarranted by my robust condition. The building looked like a movie set, designed on the lines of a scriptwriter's dream of a Moorish palace, and apparently built of papier mâché. Within, it was dark and cool and very hushed. Everything moved on ball-bearings. Waiters glided and bellhops whispered. Occasionally a white-coated figure flitted down a corridor. Everyone wore a fixed and gracious smile. A wheelchair moved across the lobby bearing a white, waxen figure, attended by a nurse who spoke in low but determinedly cheerful undertones. Another nurse of an unexpectedly sparkling glamour stepped briskly into an elevator and was whisked from view. A man with neat iron-grey hair and impeccably preserved, wearing the glazed jacket and imperturbable geniality of the medical profession in action, nodded impersonally as he passed.

Nurses—doctors—what sort of a place was this? I turned accusingly to the journalist who had brought me here. "We figured you'd need a rest," he explained, "and this is the finest Rest Home in Florida."

And I have no doubt but that it was. But there was I, full of the joys of spring, loaded with superfluous energy, raring to hit the town, shop all day, dance all night, look at the bright lights, ride in fast cars, take the lid off this great United States and see what was cooking within, there I was, cloistered in a rest home.

"Rest is about the last thing I need," I protested, but the

journalist quickly pointed out that it was an ideal place to work out the story for the *Sunday Chronicle*, which had been beating its paper breast for some time, waiting for the hottest and latest from its strangest outside contributor. "And you won't be interrupted," he added, to which I had to agree; and he departed.

The suite in which I was incarcerated—in the kindest possible manner—was spaciously luxurious, so that as I wandered about examining the elegant fixtures, bouncing on the twin beds (Super-Soft Sleep-Well Slumber-Rite mattresses) switching on the concealed radio and the myriad lamps without which the All-American room is incomplete, and gazing out of the glazed upper-level patio, it was difficult to shake off the feeling I had strayed into one of those local-girl-makes-good stories.

I had no idea where I was, having been driven out in a cab through a town I had never seen before. I had not brought any-thing with me but a clean shirt and some writing materials. I had no money, and all the addresses and telephone notes of people I might have got in touch with were on the boat. I thought wistfully of *FA*, secure in her berth at the City Yacht Basin, and of the rum in her locker and the books on her shelves, and with a regretful sigh I threaded a sheet of paper into the typewriter.

It was a vegetarian rest home, where alcohol was not only banned but mentioned in whispers, as if it was a dirty word. Trays of salads and milk and nutburgers, most tastefully arranged, were placed by my side at tactful intervals.

At night, just when I was ready to turn in, a nurse appeared discreetly at the door. To give me my massage. My *what*? Massage. It would soothe me and relax me and make me sleep. Insomnia was not one of my troubles, and until that moment it had never occurred to me that I might be relaxed or tense or anything. I was just me. Tired of writing and ready to go to bed.

"So you came all the way from England in a little boat by

yourself," she said in a vibrant voice. "What beautiful strong arms you have. Such beautifully strong arms."

Acutely embarassed, I shuffled the papers into brisk heaps on the desk.

"How old are you?" she asked. "You would never guess how old I am," she added with pride, deftly removing the cover off the bed. "Lie down now, there's a good girl. A rub is all you need to make those beautiful strong muscles of yours just let go and relax."

"I am sixty-two," she went on complacently. "Look." She took off her cap and with the same smooth movement removed the pins from her hair which cascaded in a rich dark mantle to well below her shoulders. "Not a grey hair," she said, "not one." Carefully, without haste, she pinned it up again as I watched, fascinated and incredulous and completely out of my depth.

"It is lovely hair," I murmured.

She nodded. "Do you swim?" she asked. "I am just learning. Soon I shall be able to swim quite well. I try to learn something new every year. Four years ago I went to Hawaii. I had never been there before—have you?—and it was there I met my husband. It was love at first sight. He is an Hawaiian. Such a kind man. I am very happy. That is what you should do. Find yourself a good kind man. There is nothing like it.

"So we mustn't keep him waiting," she said severely. "You take your rub right now."

Pondering the incalculable consequences of keeping an Hawaiian husband waiting, I submitted to treatment. Every muscle was efficiently pummelled and pulverised into an acquiescent pulp, which I was assured was relaxation, but I slept just as well as on any other night.

An idea that had been forming at the back of my mind for some time finally matured in Miami, and that was to sail along the Intracoastal Waterways to New York, a distance of about

1200 miles. I was really enjoying myself with the ship now, and it was unthinkable to give up the cruise at this stage and miss visiting all the States on the way, Florida, Georgia, South and North Carolina, and Virginia, romance names of compelling attraction. But I did not start out on the voyage immediately. When the copy was complete for the *Sunday Chronicle* and I was released, so to speak, I shot back to the boat, to be engulfed once more by endless crowds of sightseers and questioners, radio and newspaper reporters, until life quickly became an exhausting three-ring circus. As there was a large batch of mail to attend to and a couple of short articles to write before setting out for New York, I moved *FA* up the Miami River to a secluded yacht basin, where Alan and Mercy Stearns, whom I had met in Nassau, lent me their magnificent 90-foot ketch the *Maria Catherina*, laid up for the approaching hurricane season, as a houseboat. The *Maria* I had also met before. On charter she had paid a visit to English Harbour where John and Bonnie Staniland had taken me aboard to show off the lovely ship they had sailed three times across the Atlantic before the Stearns had bought her.

A few sightseers, with the remarkable persistency which marks the American character, tracked me down in my hideout, and when I appeared on the vast decks of the 90-foot *Maria*, their eyes bulged out in astonishment. . . . "You didn't sail *this* across the Atlantic alone?"

From the Miami River I moved up to Fort Lauderdale, twenty-two miles north along the Waterways, which was rather a harassing introduction to what was in store. Pilotage of inland waters was entirely new to me and I found it far more exacting than ocean work. Loaded, *FA* drew over five feet and she went aground once or twice, and I was further dismayed by the number of bridges we had to pass through, all of which had to be opened on account of *FA*'s mast. *FA* had no reverse gear or means of stopping if the operation was tardy or the stream was running with us, and in some places the channel was too narrow or too crowded to allow her to turn and circle whilst the bridge operators stopped the traffic and opened the bridge. By the time we reached Fort Lauderdale I was not at all sure that the projected journey up the Inland Waterways was such a good idea after all, and considered the alternative of sailing to New York by sea. But September was nigh, the open season for hurricanes, and I had no desire to encounter one at sea.

In this tizzy of indecision I stayed for some weeks with the Stearns at their charming home on one of the canals, where *FA* was tied alongside their private dock, her mast nestling among the lazy fronds of overhanging palms. Fort Lauderdale is bisected, dissected, and practically vivisected by a network of canals and is known as the Venice of America. Apart from its waterways, and in truth it is often more convenient to visit someone by boat than it is to do so by car, Fort Lauderdale bears no resemblance to Venice. Miami brought Casablanca to mind, but Fort Lauderdale brings nowhere to mind but itself. None the less, it is a town of singular charm in its own right, and despite its being a resort with a number-one traffic problem, it has a certain quietude.

The local paper ran a column about *FA*; I spoke my little piece on the radio and in no time the whereabouts of the *Felicity Ann* was known and boat trips were run up the canal to see her.

The advent of a hurricane delayed my departure, and decided me against going to sea. Actually the hurricane did not come to anything, as it turned and made off into the Atlantic before coming anywhere near Florida, but the fact that it was in the offing allowed an insight into the way they are handled in Florida, where they take their hurricanes very seriously.

It was A.R.P. all over again. As soon as a hurricane was notified, radio stations issued bulletins of its size, force, rate of travel, and direction, at intervals which closed until the blow was imminent when news of it was broadcast every fifteen minutes, together with instructions to the populace as to what action to take. As most hurricanes made up a thousand miles or so from Florida there was usually plenty of time to get organised. Hurricanes are named officially in alphabetical order, so the talk would revolve round Carol or Dolly or Edna, it being assumed by a predominantly masculine meteorological department that the contrary nature of a hurricane calls for feminine nomenclature. Reminiscences, at this season, of "hurricanes I have known" are on the lines of better bomb stories rife during the war. Meantime, with a preoccupied air, people shutter the windows of their buildings, remove anything that might become airborne and a misguided missile, and gather coconuts, which although known always to fall straight down whatever the wind velocity, are apt to do so with considerable force.

Hardware stores are denuded of oil stoves and oil lamps and candles in anticipation of gas and electrical breakdowns; and the course of the hurricane is assiduously charted on charts issued on sale for the purpose. Although winds in the eye of the storm often blow between 150–170 m.p.h. most of the damage is done by water; huge tidal waves rush in sweeping all before them. When the storm is about to strike people are warned to move to high ground, which is difficult in Florida where anything over six feet above sea level is regarded as altitude.

It was a wind by the name of Carol that kept me hovering at the Stearns' ménage rather longer than is seemly for a casual guest, and finally tilted the choice in favour of travelling north by Waterway. Then there was much discussion as to the best method of tackling the bridge question, which was a real problem, as bridges are legion all along the Waterways, and we concluded that the solution would be to take the mast down, not an onerous task, it being stepped on deck in a tabernacle, and so enable *FA* to slide under most of them without having to have them opened for her. Accordingly this was done, and the mast was laid longitudinally on the deck from the stemhead over the tabernacle and on to the boom gallows. It made *FA* very unhandy, but, erroneously, I felt the major problem of the projected journey was under control.

Just before leaving, the ship was presented with a stout length of line—"In case of hurricanes," I was told, "this'd hold the *Queen Mary*. Just drive her into the mangroves and make fast. . . .

With this injunction in mind, on the morning of September 6th I started the engine, said goodbye, and started out on the long trek to New York.

Chapter 22

A PRECONCEIVED notion is invariably different from the actuality. Without any basis for such imagining, I had pictured the Inland Waterways as the Shropshire Union Canal on a grand scale. They could hardly be more unlike, and in fact there is nothing in England to which the Waterways can be compared. They are ingeniously conceived, providing an inland passage for small craft all the way from the Gulf of Mexico to the St Lawrence River, utilising for the most part natural bodies of water, rivers, lakes, and sounds, but in places where these were not originally connected canals have been made to join them up. Some of the rivers are leisurely, pursuing their winding way between narrow overhanging banks, and some of them are so wide, land on either side is barely visible. Some of the sounds are so large they have to be crossed on a compass course, and on some of them the course to be followed takes you almost out to sea; but throughout the Waterways the channel is plainly marked by beacons, fingerposts, or buoys, with here and there strangely unnautical signs proclaiming "Bear Left For So and So, 160 Miles," for the Waterways are maintained by the Army, the Corps of Engineers, who are for ever dredging and replacing beacons or posts that have been knocked down by the swing of a heavy tow, or capturing drifting buoys and generally keeping the way clear for the thousands of boats, commercial and pleasure, that travel this way all the year round.

The first part of the Waterways, leading directly north from Fort Lauderdale, was more as I had expected, narrow, winding, and pretty urban. The banks were neat and well built up, and on either side long low houses lay under the palm trees, draped in bougainvillea and screened by clumps of hibiscus.

Shaven lawns, of a misleadingly green grass that feels like raffia underfoot, stretched to the water's edge. Each house had its small private dock, and residents, mostly retired folk, could be seen puttering about the garden, their boats, or fishing, or simply lying in the sun soaking up a tan. But they all did a double take at the sight of *Felicity Ann* and raised a friendly arm of greeting. Some of them called to the house to bring out the family to see the boat that crossed the Atlantic ("Well, whaddya know?").

Throughout the voyage the venture of the *Felicity Ann* had aroused keen interest in every port, but this I had put down to the fact that our advent, usually in a small place, was an excuse to break the monotony of living in the outback. The enthusiasm evinced by the Americans was inexplicable; for in the States our venture was a very small incident in a very large place where important events are happening all the time. After our début in Miami, the dust should have settled on a deed that was done, but it continued to rise in gusts and eddies to the end of the cruise.

In the less elegantly residential sections along the Waterway, I noticed a number of small commercial docks with signs exhorting the passing boatman to stop for hamburgers, shrimps, gas, or bait, and it seemed there would be no problem in finding a place to tie up for the night; but they thinned out considerably as we got farther along the way.

There was a rather nasty moment shortly after starting out when we swung round a blind corner and almost into a dredger that was being manœuvred into position. The dredgers that operate on the Intracoastal Waterways bear a strong family resemblance, to the uninitiated, to the Mississippi stern-wheelers, and, when suddenly encountered, seem to be no less than two blocks long and the size of an apartment house. This one was busy with a tug boat, a lighter, and a plethora of piping. What little free water was left between it and the right bank was mainly occupied by sundry rowing and motor boats. There was no room to turn and no way of stopping, so there was nothing to do but go ahead as if all the ocean was in front of us. There was some powerful skirmishing on the part of the small fry and we did no worse than rock them in passing. The occupants cheered wildly.

The Waterway widened into a lake engagingly called Lettuce, where we bumped on and off a sandbank, and then, just after passing under a bridge at Boca Raton, we ran firmly aground. It was very embarrassing as there were a number of people on the bridge, leaning over to shout and wave and take pictures. I was trying to give a seamanlike version of a combination bow and wave when FA ran aground. She lay over at a stubborn angle and refused to move.

Fortunately, there was a skiff in the vicinity, powered by a big outboard and manned by a handsome youth with an authentic Nordic accent, and he was quite easily prevailed upon to pull us off. After a little struggle, we were afloat and ready to go, but the young man was in no hurry to cast off. "You're English," he stated. "I was in England during the war. The girls there they dance fine. They did the jitterbug, too. Do you jitterbug?" Resisting the impulse to say I did very little else aboard, and before I could make any other reply, he suggested I should stop in Boca Raton and he would show me a thing or two about dancing that night. I had no doubt he could, but planned on making more than twelve miles on the first day, so shelved the proffered jitterbug instruction and chugged on until it began to get dark, when I began to worry. There were no signs of those handy little gas-and-bait docks. It is not practicable to anchor in the channel at night as a considerable amount of commercial traffic, heavy tows and tugs, travel then, and there is seldom sufficient depth of water in which to anchor outside the channel in the Florida area. But it is not practicable to carry on in the dark unless equipped with a searchlight capable of throwing a beam of at least a quarter of a mile. The channel is very plainly marked, but you have to be able to see the markers.

There are marinas in the towns where a boat can tie up for the night, but the towns were getting farther and farther apart. I had hoped to make West Palm Beach before nightfall but had underestimated our rate of progress. As we neared a place called Boynton Beach a small boat with four occupants drew up alongside, and they suggested I stop at a small dock they knew of there, and were, moreover, kind enough to go ahead and make arrangements.

The two men of the party were senators, and nothing would do, after I had made *FA* fast and settled her for the night, but that I should join them and their wives for dinner. This turned into a minor function, as the local mayor joined in. It is these switches from the rugged to the smooth, from single-handed sailing to the social whirl, that are at once the fascination and the bane of boating, for the mental agility required for quick adaptation draws heavily upon one's nervous energy.

Back at the boat again, nourished by good food and local statistics, I was waylaid by a reporter and a cloud of mosquitoes. Talking by the headlights of his car and slapping at the insects, I answered the stock questions for the second time that night. Yes, I was often frightened. Yes, I was often lonely. (I remembered, but did not remark, how once I had thought if only there was a rabbit to stroke . . . something reassuringly alive on board. . . .) No, I didn't carry a transmitter; if I had got into trouble it would have been just too bad. Nor did I anchor at night; that would have meant carrying six miles of chain. No, I didn't get enough sleep. And I didn't get enough to eat either, because to do so meant cooking at the expense of progress.

The reporter diligently took it all down in his notebook, thanked me as graciously as if I had done him a real favour, and drove away. I thought as I turned in that night that if this was a sample of sailing the Inland Waterways, I was in for a busy time.

Next morning I took off about eight o'clock, after having learnt from the dock attendant that the *Nymph Errant* had also spent a night there on her way north a few months previously. It was the first news I had had of the Stanilands since we had sailed out of St Thomas together, apart from a letter they had left for me in Nassau, they having left the Bahamas, of course, long before I arrived. Ian, as usual, had caused quite a stir at Boynton Beach, "so young to be sailing all that way. . . ."

Almost as soon as we were under way the clutch began to slip, and I thought of stopping at West Palm Beach to have it taken up; but by the time we got there it had ceased slipping so I carried on, ever loath to stop having started, just as I am reluctant to start having stopped, being a confirmed clinger to the *status quo*.

The Waterways were busy with small boats, whose occupants all waved in the most friendly manner, and as we slid under the Swing Bridge at West Palm Beach, the operator ran out of his house to lean over the parapet and shout, "Mrs Davison: good luck!"

A squall chased us across a lake after leaving Palm Beach, and then followed a delightful passage up a narrow winding river, which in contrast to the suburban travel we had made so far, was wild and lonely. During the afternoon it poured with rain, which blotted out the scenery and made the going in an open cockpit very uncomfortable. As we were passing a small boat basin just off the main channel at Jupiter, where the Loxahatchee flows out to the sea, some people ran out on to the jetty in the pouring rain, bearing a large notice which read "Welcome *Felicity Ann*." It was only three o'clock and I had intended to drive on until dark, but the invitation was irresistible, and I was easily deflected from my course.

News travels along the Waterways fast, the grapevine there operates as swiftly, if not sometimes as accurately, as the telegraph; and the owners of the Jupiter Marina, Bill and Dot

Dunham, knew all about *Felicity Ann* and had the welcome sign all ready knowing she would be passing that way in the afternoon. Bill and Dot were from the north, but were younger than most people when they discovered that living was more important than keeping up with the Joneses, a truth that usually dawns too late if at all. They shipped their family down the Waterways in a cruiser and set about building up a dilapidated marina into one that the passing boatman no longer passed, but stopped at again and again.

The country round Jupiter was quiet and shady, devoted mainly to fruit and cattle farms. Dot inveigled me into attending a meeting of the local branch of the Women's Club, an institution similar to the Women's Institute in England. The meeting was held at the house of Florida's only mayoress, and went with a considerable bang. The chairwoman, young and attractive, handled the meeting with the discipline of a drill sergeant.

"Stand up when you address the meeting," she rebuked a housewife who had something to say but was afraid of drawing attention to herself saying it. "Don't mumble, we can't hear," she told another. "Stick to the point," she snapped at a rambler, and guided the Club's business to completion in the smallest possible compass of time.

The women, whose ages varied from the newly-wed—and they wed very young in the States—to the greatest grandmother, and whose interests ranged from home-making to politics, all showed a lively interest in the voyage, and after the meeting broke up trooped down in a body to visit the ship.

In Jupiter I was shown a shrub whose blooms are reputed to change colour three times a day, and which in consequence is called the Sweetheart Flower, though for the life of me I don't see why. Inevitably, it was not in flower . . . I should have been there last month. . . .

I left Jupiter full of good intentions to cover a lot of mileage that day, for the first week of September was already over and there was still well over a thousand miles to cover before reaching New York. The last part of the journey, from Norfolk, Virginia, to New York, about 180 miles, would have to be made in the open sea, and if I delayed too long in the south it would mean sailing the North Atlantic in winter time, a prospect that held no appeal whatever. But good intentions are not always conducive to practical results. I ran aground three times during the day, the last time just as it was growing dark, when the chances of a boat passing by to give a pull off were negligible.

The radio that night was most discouraging. It spoke in bated breath of a hurricane approaching the coast—"raging towards Florida"—as the announcer put it, adding it would not be until morning that it would be known how serious the hurricane was going to be. There are happier places in which to sit out a tropical revolving storm, I thought, than perched on a sandbank with little more than a sand-dune between you and the sea. The Waterways follow the coast pretty closely in some places, and I could hear the surf breaking on the shore and was much disturbed, especially as the night turned wild and squally. It was a false alarm, however, for the morning dawned calm and clear and the hurricane was no longer a threat, apparently, for the radio made no mention of it.

Disconcertingly, there was no sign of any boat either; the morning passed and the sun rolled over the top of its hill. I had become almost reconciled to staying indefinitely on my perch when a long lean motor boat slid out from the shore and chugged up alongside. The solitary occupant, a stout red-faced salt of the blue-jersey school, leant over and grasped the footrail.

"Bin watching you all morning," he greeted laconically, speaking round his pipe. "Figgered you was in trouble."

Stifling the ready response in the interests of international relationships, I allowed he was right.

With the ease of a man who has grown up with his job too

long ago to wonder about it, he pulled *FA* off the bank and back into the channel, where he explained how to work the markers so that it was possible to stay in the channel at will, and not wander into the spoil bank at either side as I seemed to have acquired the habit of doing.

"You gotta watch them markers astern as well as ahead," he said. "You gotta go from one to the other, but pick one of them big flashers ahead, say on the starboard side and keep her on the starboard bow. And keep the last buoy or marker you passed on the port side on the port quarter. Keep 'em like that and you'll be O.K. . . . . You got charts?"

I showed him the one in current use; he nodded and pointed to the thin red line that indicates the track all the way from the Gulf of Mexico to the St Lawrence River. "Watch it," he stated succinctly, "it means every word it says. When it favours one side of the channel you keep over that side; when it makes a little loop, like here," he pointed with his pipe, "you see you make a little loop."

Later that afternoon, without having run aground once, I pulled into the Yacht Basin at Fort Pierce, and within an hour was making a recording at the local radio station, thinking, as the tape was being played back, that my voice was altogether too mimsey and not at all in keeping with the person I suppose myself to be.

Chapter 23

My good intentions of pressing on with the journey went overboard again at Fort Pierce, where I stayed for three days, partly because there was an article to write but mainly because of charming people, Beany and Patsy Backus. Beany is a landscape painter of his own school, and the exception that proves the rule that a prophet is not without honour save in his own country, for Beany is both recognised and appreciated not only in his own country but in his own time, a remarkable feat for an artist. His paintings of Florida capture its essensce, the brilliant elusive light, and no young couple would dream of setting up house without a Backus to grace the walls. Beany does not look like an artist, but then he has no need to attitudinise, and the only concession he makes to anything that might nearly comply with the popular conception of an artist is in the Backus studio home, which rambles inconsequently on the edge of the waterfront where small fishing boats tie up and nets are hung in geometric designs to dry, and pleasant large-leaved trees and shrubs screen the front of the house. The front door is never locked, for the Backuses keep open house, and the strangest assortment of people, whose paths would never cross in the ordinary way, mingle there in perfect harmony. Both Beany and his beautiful blonde wife, Patsy, seem to have attained a tolerance that is considerate without being in the least patronising. No one's opinions or beliefs are ever derided, however absurd, and a person can talk the most arrant nonsense without suffering the usual guilty aftermath that he *has* been talking nonsense, for though the Backuses may not agree, and even point out the fallacy of the argument, they can do so without impairing self-esteem, and a person leaves their home with a feeling of increased dignity and worth, which is the most priceless gift that can be bestowed upon anyone.

I left Fort Pierce reluctantly, but with my personal batteries recharged, as it were, on September 13th, and made a good run that day of over fifty miles, which was an improvement on previous days' runs of only 25 to 30 miles. Passing through Vero Beach, an extremely pretty section of waterways, crowded with densely wooded little islands, the local yacht marina personnel turned out *en masse* and saluted by dipping the flag.

Pelicans were busy fishing as we chugged along, diving head first into the water with such a crash and a splash they turned head over heels. It looked the most accidental operation in the world, but it seemed to catch fish. They used to fly into the Yacht Basin at Fort Pierce, but never over the quays like ordinary birds. They flew in at the Basin entrance and followed the channels round the jetties until they arrived where they wanted to be, when they landed all of a heap, then sat for a while self-consciously straightening their feathers.

The water towers that stood high over the towns, gleaming silver in the sunlight, and supported on tall thin columns that were invisible from afar, looked like small airships so that when a small airship actually flew over us that day, it was very confusing.

I spent the night anchored just off the channel, where for once there was enough water, between Melbourne and Eau Gallie. It was a pleasant moonlight night and the water was very still, but it was so hot and stuffy in the cabin that I tried to sleep in the cockpit, without much success on account of the mosquitoes. So I set out next morning tired and irritable, having made a very sketchy job of the myriad duties to be performed before departure. Travelling along the Waterways is no sinecure for a single-hander. I found it much harder than being at sea, where long spells at the helm could be broken by heaving-to, or going below, or wandering up forrard for a stretch and leaving the ship to her own devices. She might flounder a bit and lose way, but she wouldn't run aground. If the weather was bad you could take shelter in the cabin, but on the Waterways you had to sit it out, letting the rain blind your eyes and spill down your neck, for once under way there was no leaving the helm until stopped, and there was no stopping until *FA* was docked or at anchor. At sea, one hundred per cent accuracy in steering was not necessary, but in the Waterways it was, otherwise you went aground. And you had to keep the chart before you all the time, ticking off the markers as you passed, otherwise you could find yourself at the dead end of a creek with no way out or back. The spare pair of eyes you kept glued to the markers ahead and astern to avoid straying out of the channel. Everything needed during the day had to be prepared before setting out, and arranged within reach so that it would not roll into the bilges or get wet if it rained. By now I had developed a routine, and my day normally started between four and half past in the morning, when I made breakfast to radio accompaniment. (Some of the early morning shows were most amusing and informal. "If Every Moon was a Honeymoon," quoted a disc jockey changing the record, adding, "What a beat up lot we'd be." To anyone conditioned to broadcasting by the B.B.C. the American radio never ceases to startle and fascinate. A news commentator spoke one night in truly moving tones of the death of a popular governor, and having got the listener into a thoroughly dolorous and sympathetic frame of mind, switched without a moment's pause into a brisk selling voice, imploring the listener to take "Knockout, the Quicker, Easier, *Happier* way to cure a headache.") Then, having dressed and washed and washed-up, a lengthy process in the confines of *FA*'s tiny cabin, I made sandwiches and a thermos of coffee, sorted out the daily requirements of charts, log books, pencils, knives, rain gear, and anything that might be remotely necessary. Then the engine would have to be gone over with grease-gun and oil can, and refuelled, and after it was started, we were ready to go; but by then I felt as though I had already done a day's work, instead of just starting one. I soon longed for the comparative peace of the sea, and looked forward to stepping the mast at Norfolk, going out to sea and returning to normal.

The next stop I made was at a yard where boats are built under benign benevolence; prayers are said before work is begun every morning and employees are not allowed to smoke on the job. Here I learnt that "Dolly," the hurricane that gave me so much anxious anticipation the night I spent on a sandbank, had turned out to sea, but "Edna's the gal to watch now," they warned.

Place names are fascinating in the States, where geography appears to have gone mad. I left the new—and arrestingly unimaginative—Titusville, for the old, Smyrna Beach (actually *New* Smyrna Beach; a concession to avoid continental confusion?) and on the way crossed the Mosquito Lagoon, which has a fine old pioneering ring about it, but which turned out to be a singularly dreary stretch of water, where the clutch started slipping again and the rain poured down.

Although still in Florida there was a distinct feeling of going north now. The Gulf Stream was no longer close in shore but thirty miles out to sea, and the weather in consequence was much cooler; coconut palms had given way entirely to the stubby palmetto, and the scenery green had lost the brazen look of the tropics.

Unexpectedly, there was a large number of porpoises sporting in the Waterway.

From New Smyrna I went to Daytona, which was only a step on the way, but the clutch was slipping so badly by then I

254

Arrival at New York, pier 9, Coastguard Station

Felicity Ann and author at the Boat Show, New York,
January, 1954

had to stop and take it up, and of course, having stopped I had my old trouble of getting started again and stayed there for nearly a fortnight, having, naturally, a bushelful of excuses for doing so. I had a cold. There was writing to do (there was always writing to do). And, anyway, it was just fun being there.

The marina I stopped at was large, with everything laid on that the heart of a yachtsman might desire. Electricity and water to each boat; a garbage can by every tie-up, so that the water would not be polluted by the fantastic rubbish a boat collects. There were boatsheds where a boat could be floated in under cover and worked on in all weathers. The boatworks supplied shipwrights, riggers, engineers, painters, and sailmakers, also a loudspeaker system that called you to the telephone or played soft music in a stentorian whisper. There was a little park where you could walk on the raffia grass through hibiscus bushes, or sit under Spanish-moss-draped trees. There was a restaurant and showers, and even a row of cottages, so that if anyone was stricken with cabin fever, they could go ashore and, mid the soothing surroundings of modern conveniences, forget that anything like boats existed.

A reporter came along as usual to get a story, but afterwards, which was not so usual, he rounded up members of the newspaper staff and threw a party. When the talk died down and the party broke up we drove out to look at the famous Daytona Beach, miles and miles of hard white sand and nothing else. The great thing is to take your car on to the Beach, which people do with joyous abandon, for the lack of road restrictions affects them the way end of school does kids.

A beautiful blonde whose curly hair hung half way down her back, wearing a red shirt and blue shorts and giving a very agreeable representation of the All-American girl, turned up at *Felicity Ann* one day to exchange greetings as from one skipper to another. Mary Jo skippered a commercial fishing boat;

255

not a fishing boat as known in England, but a small cruiser licensed to take out fishing parties; for catching fish, or the attempt to do so, is one of the most popular pastimes along the United States eastern seaboard. These boats make daily excursions from their home ports to the fishing grounds, sometimes on charter, but more often sailing at a set, advertised time each morning with whoever happens along, a practice reminiscent of the old barnstorming days of flying. It was an unusual job for a girl, and Mary Jo said she met with a certain amount of prejudice, which was surprising, for in the States women appear to be in everything, and very few are unemployed from choice, even when it is economically possible. Even the housewife is rare who is just that and nothing more, but it seems there are still limits imposed upon what is considered suitable work.

Mary Jo asked me to dinner, and she could cook, too, for the chicken Maryland she prepared was delicious. "Easy," she said in response to my cries of admiration. "It's all ready fixed with directions on the packet, and they ain't in fine print either. If you can read you can cook. Not that it does me any good," she added drily, holding up her left hand. "No ring. And we've been steady for three years. Something's got to be done about it. Time's going by. I'm twenty-four."

It is a sad thing when failure stares you in the face at the age of twenty-four. Although women must work, they must also marry in the States, and to be unwed over the age of twenty is pretty well disastrous, apparently.

As we washed up, Mary Jo said, "Why don't we take in a Drive-In Movie—or have you seen one?" I said I had not, so we climbed into her car and set out. Mary Jo drove furiously. "We'll need to make a left turn," she said as we tore along. "There's one—no—too late," as we sped by without any attempt at slackening speed. We missed several turns like this and Mary Jo complained, "Just *look* at those side roads skidding by!"

Finally we managed to capture one and arrived at the Drive-In just as the show was about to begin.

At the entrance was a small toll house where we paid for our tickets without getting out of the car, then we drove into a parking lot spaced out to accommodate about 300 cars. By each parking space there was a stand on which hung an amplifier with a long lead. This we hitched on to a side window of the car. The amplifier was equipped with a volume control, a feature that could be advantageously installed in a number of cinemas I know where the sound track does its utmost to blast out your eardrums. A notice flashed on to the huge screen facing us to remind the audience not to forget to return the amplifier to its stand before leaving.

It was a double-feature show which we watched somewhat harassed by mosquitoes, for if we shut the windows and kept them out we nearly suffocated, but if we left them open we were bitten without mercy. At frequent intervals a spray van toured the lot ejecting a cloud of repellent which effectively blotted out the mosquitoes for a while, but equally effectively blotted out the screen. The first picture was a 3D Western viewed through glasses supplied at the pay office, but as they were designed on the lines of pince-nez without any pince, they required a great deal of concentration to keep on. We worked hard to follow that picture. The second feature was an antique of the thirties starring Jean Harlow, whom Mary Jo had never seen, one of those gentle reminders that emphasise the inexorable passing of time. There were protracted intervals throughout the show during which the audience, by means of the screen, was exhorted to buy popcorn, ice cream, hot dogs, hamburgers, pizza pies, and other delicacies deemed necessary to increase the enjoyment of the entertainment and swell the profits. I concluded that the attraction of a Drive-In theatre lay chiefly in its novelty, but in fact, they are extremely popular, being one solution to the baby-sitting problem. The managements, wise

257

to this angle, supply roundabouts, swings, slides, and even pony rides for the youngsters' enjoyment, and as the evening wears on and the children get tired, they simply climb into the back of the car and go to sleep. Tiny babies come in a cot, and older babies in pyjamas. Drive-In shows are late, as, being operated in the open, they can only exhibit when it is dark, but although the pictures displayed are often pretty old, they are not necessarily bad, and they give parents the opportunity of a night out without the worry of leaving the children.

Hurricanes were in the news again whilst I was in Daytona. "Edna" materialised and swept across the northern part of Florida, much to the local relief, for hurricanes tend to rouse an understandable district selfishness. "Sting who you like, but don't sting me," as Arthur Askey used to sing. Then "Florence" followed "Edna", but did not bother us apart from giving us a wet and windy time with the tail of her coat. However, weather or no, the end of September was in sight and I had to make an effort to go, so I rearranged the stowage for getting under way, and went down town to buy one or two provisions that were short aboard, shopping at the local super-market, which was a mistake, for it is almost impossible to go into a super-market for a pound of bacon and come out with a pound of bacon. You are more likely to come out and call a cab to carry your purchases home. These vast self-service stores stock everything from motor oil to steaks. And not only do they carry a wide variety of merchandise, but also a wide variety of each item. I counted no less than nineteen different kinds of baked beans. Everything is so invitingly packaged and displayed it takes a strong will and a very short pocket book to walk out with no more than what you went in for. This time I managed to get away with only twice the intended amount of groceries, a bath towel and a pair of sneakers.

On September 28th, then, grumbling in the teeth of a chilly

wind, one of Florence's left overs, that blew spray high up over the bows, I shivered all the way to Marineland, 35 miles north, and tied up at a long, lonely dock in the middle of nowhere but mangrove swamps. There was no one about to help take lines and the current was running strong, so I felt rather pleased with myself when I managed to make *FA* fast single-handed. No sooner had I done so than the original ancient mariner himself appeared, who persisted in calling me "Miz Dixon" and vanished as quickly as he came. Only one other boat tied up there for the night, a pretty blue yawl, southward bound, whose crew of two invited me aboard for drinks and supper. "We are NOT typical cruisers," they announced with somewhat unnecessary severity. "We are atypical"; and they left the British *Economist* on the cabin table to prove it.

Next morning I walked across the swamp to visit the Marineland Aquarium, which is a research station and public show combined. Although miles from any town, the Aquarium is on one of the main roads from the North to Miami, and as it is rather an unusual aquarium the public support is enthusiastic and almost unlimited. It was still partially under construction when I visited it, but there were two tanks on show. One, viewed from above, was for porpoises only, and the other, viewed from below water level, through large glass portholes in the sides of the circular tank, contained every kind of fish that could be caught in the sea in that area. In this latter tank a nice balance of nature has been established, for all species seem to survive despite inevitable depredations. The porpoises were extraordinarily tame. The keeper could call individual porpoises to jump and take from his hand a fish, and they had a most engaging way of sitting up in the water and looking at you with a grin on their faces like happy dogs. Through the portholes in the other tank one could watch a diver feed the fish from a lidded bucket. The fish were of all kinds, from goldfish-sized creatures to sharks, but they all followed the diver as he walked about on the bottom of the tank with the anxiety that marks a flock of chickens at feeding time.

This diversion made for a late start, and I had gone no more than three-quarters of a mile when the power unit blew up with a cloud of smoke and a noise as of ten tractors in mortal combat. Hastily I switched off and dropped the anchor. After the works had cooled enough to allow inspection, I established that though the engine was still functioning the clutch was finally *hors de combat*, and beyond a simple roadside repair. The dock at Marineland was round a bend and out of sight. The Waterway was invisible from the road. We were surrounded by miles of mud and mangroves. There was nothing to do but wait and hope that a boat would soon pass by.

Chapter 24

IT was very quiet all day; not a boat passed, north or southward bound. I was hoping that a northbound boat would appear that could tow *FA* to St Augustine, 18 miles away, but the nearest place where major repairs could be effected without going back on our tracks to Daytona, which I wanted to avoid if possible as there was still enough mileage to cover to New York without adding any. When the tide started to make I raised the anchor and let the boat drift and she waltzed northwards for a mile or two until deliberately run aground into the left bank. It was dusk by then and not advisable to be at large and out of control with the risk of being run down by night traffic. Later, a tug with a heavy tow ground heavily past, quizzically shining her searchlight on us, and I was glad we were close by the bank, for the Waterway was very narrow at this point, in fact I could have jumped ashore, but it would not have done any good as there was nothing between me and any remote connection with civilisation but miles of mud and mangroves. One boat passed next morning, and although she stopped at my signal the skipper could do nothing as he was nursing a burnt-out bearing to Daytona. He said he would try and drop a message if he had a chance before his own engine packed up. Evidently he was unlucky, for I heard nothing from that source; or indeed from any other. At the top of the tide *FA* floated and I let her drift into deep water again and anchored until the ebb when I let her drift back towards Marineland. Just as we rounded the bend and were within sight of the dock, she ran aground.

Fortunately, she was seen, and two men from the Marineland Aquarium came out in an outboard in response to my signals and towed us in. A call to the nearest service station brought a mechanic along, but, of course, he was unable to repair the clutch; however, he said he would try and contact a boatyard in St Augustine, where he lived, see if the job could be done there, and if a boat could be sent down to tow *FA*, but he was unsuccessful on all counts. And that was the last day of September.

Next morning a youth with a small boat and a 7½-h.p. outboard was prevailed upon for the sum of $15 to give up his day off and make the tow, but *FA* was too heavy for the little motor, which heated up so badly that half-way to St Augustine, he gave up, cast off, and signalled me to anchor, shouting cryptically, being a man of few words, that he was going to call George, whereupon he departed with a roar and a rush. He returned however, with Jack, George being unavailable, and Jack had a 25-h.p. outboard, and within a short while *FA* was tied up occupying the whole of Jack's little dock, a bait and fishing camp hard by a bridge. I paid off the young man who was most reluctant to accept anything for his services, and Jack called up George, who apparently owned a boatworks in St Augustine. George appeared in person just on dusk, a rotund little man with big round eyes. He listened to my account of the breakdown with apparent astonishment, punctuating every sentence by asking, "Is that *right*?" and after a cursory glance at the offending mechanism, said there was nothing he could do with it there, which was no surprise, but that if I could get the boat to his yard he would repair it in his shops. Jack then offered to tow me up in the morning.

Mrs Jack, a pretty blonde in blue jeans, invited me to their house to watch television, and we spent the evening drinking Tom Collinses, eating savouries, and watching the shows, which seemed unable to play for more than ten minutes without switching into an impassioned commercial. Towards the latter part of the evening a tugboat hooted long and impatiently at the bridge without getting any action. Resignedly, Jack rose and went out to wake the operator. "He's stone deaf," explained Mrs Jack, "and it is very aggravating when boats want to go through at three o'clock in the morning."

I returned to the boat to find her way down below the dock and remembered that after so long without them there were tides to contend with again that had a steep rise and fall.

During the night I was awakened by a loud crash and switched on the flashlight to see a panic-stricken rat scrabbling out through the hatch leaving a coffee can it had knocked over rolling about in the galley.

Jack took me along to George's yard in the morning on a side-by-side tow, his 25-h.p. outboard making light of the job. Pouring rain blurred the scenery, which had completely changed and was now reminiscent of the Constable country on the East Coast of England.

We arrived at the Yard tucked away in a broad and reedy creek at the back of the town and *FA* was made fast astern of a shrimper. Jack would not take anything for his trouble but a couple of rums and five dollars to cover the cost of gasoline.

For the first few days I despaired of ever getting *FA* operable again, for the yard, whose work was mainly in connection with the shrimping fleet, was very busy, and naturally the demands of commercial boats anxious to get back to work overrode those of pleasure craft. Whenever I approached George to try to pin him down to action he simply looked harassed and disappeared into the hinterland with a fistful of oily components belonging to some other ship. "Don't worry," said Eric, who owned a lovely old-fashioned ketch then on the ways, "they may be slow starters, but once they get going they whirl about the job like a bunch of eggbeaters."

Eric and his wife Ruth, recently married, were earnestly seeking a new way of life. "Near to nature," they said. With this in mind they had bought the ketch with the intention of cruising the Caribbean. She was a real old-timer, sixty-three years old, with an elegant clipper bow, and Eric was having steel plates moulded on her bottom to defeat the depredations of the teredo worm and obviate the necessity of having to haul out every three months. Eric and Ruth had not much money but a lot of good ideas, and whilst Eric worked and dreamed away at the boat, Ruth gave swimming instruction at a pool belonging to an enormous hotel in the town, then closed as it was out of season, except for the swimming pool, enthusiastically used by residents.

St Augustine is one of the oldest towns in the United States and very old English in appearance. Americans visit it in wonder, marvelling at the quaint old overhanging houses and narrow streets, but to anyone from England it strikes a familiar note from home. Ruth took me over the dust-sheeted hotel one day when swimming was slack at the pool. It was an enormous baroque structure, grand in the Victorian manner and incongruous in the setting of either St Augustine or America.

It was dark and heavy with teak carvings of fruit and curlicues, massive carved doors, and stained glass windows. It was lavish with cupids and painted ceilings. It was brilliant with colossal chandeliers. It was France of the nineties gone mad. It was frightening.

Another hurricane sprang up, Hazel, which struck Tampa on the west coast of Florida, and spread a lot of wind and rain in our area. There were small craft warnings for two days, but George and his henchmen had by then flung themselves upon the clutch and repaired it, nay, rebuilt it in a frenzy of activity, and as it was October 10th I felt it was time to get on the move again. I had been making jokes about having to sweep the snow off the decks before arriving in New York, but the crack was beginning to sound a hollow ring of truth in it. I started out from the boatyard at 0650 in the morning and although it was quiet enough in the creek, as soon as I got into the Waterway it turned very cold and rough. The man at the helm of a ketch going south shouted I was going the wrong way and I was inclined to agree, but it settled down to a pleasant calm evening by the time I made fast to a small private dock at Amelia City where in spite of its imposing name, the only habitation appeared to be a few private houses lurking in the trees and a log cabin roadhouse where I had dinner. As I paid the check the proprietor said, "Tell your friends. Frankly, we need their money."

Next morning we passed through the last—or the first, depending on which way you are going—town in Florida, Fernandina, where a number of large turtles popped up alongside the boat with an expression of grief on their sad grizzled faces. All day long there was an inexplicable plague of bright yellow butterflies evidently bent on doing the lemming trick. A number of them rested decoratively on *Felicity Ann* for a while. We made a record run that day of sixty miles and put in for the night at a marina at Sea Island, not far from Brunswick. This was Georgia at last. The local news correspondent came down to the boat and insisted on taking me home to meet his wife and have coffee. It was Columbus day and the journalist was delighted with the tie-up he could make with this and the story of the *Felicity Ann* . . . there being no limit to the imagination where journalism is concerned.

By now I had got into my stride again, but was unable to make an early start as the owner of the marina and his wife insisted that I should stay for lunch and take a drive round the millionaire resort at Sea Island.

The next two nights I spent at anchor, the second anchorage being taken on the recommendation of a local boatman, but turned out to have less than three feet of water at low tide and during the night *FA* rolled over on her side. Having to wait for the tide to lift her again delayed starting once more, and I made a mental note never to take anyone's word regarding depths without checking for myself. Nevertheless Beaufort, South

265

Carolina, was achieved that night, and Port Royal Sound was crossed on the way where I revelled in the pleasure of deep water and easy steering. A number of turtles and another host of butterflies marked the day. I had dinner aboard a 30-foot sloop which two French Canadians, bound for Miami, had sailed down from Quebec. Next day I tried to make Charleston, but was beaten by nightfall, and anchored in a creek twelve miles south of my objective. For the third time running I made a late start and this time it was on account of fog. It was not until half-past nine that I could get under way and I arrived in Charleston at noon having had to plug against a very stiff current. I would have carried on, but expected to pick up mail at Charleston, and also *FA* had developed a serious leak at the stuffing box which urgently needed attention. A bulldog met me at the dock, wearing a yachting cap and apparently smoking a pipe. His owner swore that the dog was a capable helmsman, and said he used to leave it at the tiller, complete with cap and pipe, and frighten silly the incredulous crews of passing vessels.

With the aid of several enthusiastic helpers and a day's delay the leak was overcome, though it was not the simple operation it should have been, as the stuffing box was located under the 30-gallon fresh-water tank, which had to be drained and raised before the stuffing box was accessible. The tank itself was under the cockpit deck, which in turn was watertight and not too easy to lift.

The manager of a popular show on the CBS national network called up from Los Angeles to try and persuade me to fly out there immediately for radio and television appearances. This was the second time of asking, he had called before at Fort Lauderdale. To his inexpressible amazement I was not to be deflected from my course. I was not interested in publicity, I was only interested in getting *FA* to New York before winter and the remuneration offered was not enough to compensate for the delay such a project would entail. So I turned my back on glamour and chugged off to Georgetown instead, arriving there just on dark to be welcomed by an unexpected crowd. One party insisted on donating the dollar for the dockage fee, which the manager insisted on refunding in the morning, and a party of businessmen on a fishing vacation took me out to dinner. There is nothing quite so determinedly boyish as the American businessman on holiday. They romped roguishly with the waitress, implored one another to tell favourite stories, and ceaselessly apologised in whispered asides for their wholly imagined lack of convention. "We're *Characters*," they confided engagingly.

Fog again delayed starting in the morning but once under way it was very pleasant. The waterways followed a winding river where tall trees nudged one another down to the water's edge. The leaves were turning and there was a nostalgic smell of Autumn in the air. A snake swam up to the boat and coiled preparing to strike, but when I whipped out a camera it uncoiled and streaked for the shore, beating me to shallow water before there was time to take a picture. Afterwards, I learnt it was a water moccasin, a very lethal creature.

The strain of the trip was beginning to tell; I was very tired that night on tying up at a dock at Bucksport, but was unable to resist the generous hospitality extended aboard an elegant mobile houseboat, whose owners enterprisingly divided their interests between farming and deep-sea diving. And I was still very tired on setting out again next morning, but it was a very rewarding run that day, for the river seemed to grow increasingly beautiful. The water was very still, reflecting in detail the heavy foliage of overhanging trees. Leaves burned with autumn glory and fine veils of mist floated over the mirroring surface of the water, although the air was clear and brisk. Eagles, perched like sentinels, watched from the topmost branches of gaunt lightning-struck trees. Black cattle and red hogs plunged

267

about the banks, and tiny turtles, on curiously stilted legs, lumbered in a primæval manner on the mud.

It was very nearly dark by the time I reached Holden Beach and I decided to tie up at the shrimpers' dock there. Just before the dock was a cable ferry which obligingly lowered the cable to let me pass. All the space alongside the dock was taken by fishing boats, but the fishermen ashore, understanding I was looking for a place to tie up, signalled me to turn into a tiny basin, which I hesitated to do as there was no room to turn inside or lose the considerable speed with which we should have to enter, as the tide was making very strongly. I hesitated a moment too long and the current swept *FA* past the entrance and all the way along the length of the dock, where I turned and crept back to reconsider the situation. With care, I decided, making a check line ready, it might be possible to negotiate the basin without ramming anything, and was just nosing at the entrance when the roar of an angry man and the blast of a hooter made me turn. A fishing boat with all way on and every intention of going into the basin, which it was obviously going to occupy completely, was just astern. I pulled the tiller hard over and skipped from under her bows but almost on to the ferry cable which was up and taunt. No time to stop or turn, or for niceties either.

"Drop that bloody cable!" I yelled, and it went "pang" into the water a second before we crossed over. Turn again Whittington, I thought with hammering heart and brought the ship round, crossed the ferry, and crawled along the dock once more. At the very end, alongside the last shrimper, I made *FA* fast, although it left her embarassingly far out in the stream, but it was too late to carry on and look for somewhere else to stop for the night, also I was far too tired. I switched off the engine and every nerve twitched at the cessation of sound against which I had been braced all day. The effect of noise must be cumulative. Long hours of uninterrupted engine bark was far more aggravating at this stage than when the journey from Florida began. I had only one desire and that was to sleep till dawn, but this the good kind people of Holden Beach were not inclined to permit. They did their best to winkle me out of my shell with the long pin of promises; showers, steaks, coffee, a night ashore; but their hospitality called for a sociability that was beyond me. Regretfully, for they talked exactly like hill-billies, which would have been enough to keep me up in the ordinary way, I declined their invitations with thanks, pulled the hatch over my head and closed the doors.

"That's right, Ann," squealed a voice from the shore, "shut your dam' boat."

Until late that night there were hammerings on the coachroof and demands for the personal appearance of the skipper of the *Felicity Ann*, but I slept pretty well in spite of it all, until 5.30 the next morning, when I scamped through the pre-departure chores and took off at twenty minutes past six. An early start which was nullified by a thick white fog that rolled in from the sea and forced me to drop anchor in the middle of the channel where we stayed for an hour and a half. The fog was low, tree tops showed above it. Disconsolately, I sat in the cockpit listening to the surf breaking on the nearby invisible shore and contemplating the extraordinary shape of my feet and ankles swollen up like balloons with fatigue. But at last a breeze rolled the fog away and by ten forty-five we were bucking a ferocious tide up the Cape Fear River making infinitesimal headway. A Coastguard cutter with a lot more power than *FA* caught up with us and drew up alongside. Assailed by an immediate and unaccountable feeling of guilt I wondered what they could want. A junior officer saluted and handed across a board with a blank sheet of paper pinned to it.

"Mrs Davison, would you mind giving us your auto-graph?"

This pleased me for the rest of the day. Fame indeed, I

thought, docking the boat for the night at Wrightsville. Next morning I refuelled and a Maryland senator, with whom I had been chatting about his smart new cruiser, paid the bill and departed for Miami before I learnt of his generous gesture.

We ploughed up forty-five miles that day, working against the traffic which was now pretty dense, for the hurricane season was officially over and the annual exodus to the south had begun. These were mainly the boats of the wealthy and displayed more radio, radar, television, and fishing equipment than it would seem possible to install on a single private craft. They swept down the Waterways at great speed and *FA* plunged protestingly in their arrogant wash. The night was spent quietly at Swansboro where I managed to sneak into a dock without attracting any attention, and, refreshed, made Morehead City the following day. A cold run, but interesting on account of the number of helicopters whirling about the sky. At one time there were six overhead. The next trip was very pleasant and restful. As we motored up a wild and lovely creek a deer swam across the bows. Then a small reddish-coloured rodent swam from one side to the other, and later I watched a squirrel swimming, holding his bushy tail in the air like a comic sail. The weather was bright and sunny and comparatively warm. The creek widened and opened on to a broad river, where land on either side was almost invisible, and here *FA* started making water again through the stuffing box, entailing a lot of exercise at the bilge pump. The night was spent at anchor in the Pongo River, peacefully until midnight, when it began to blow fiercely from the north. This and the leak which was hourly growing worse, decided me to put into Belhaven in the morning, where I spent a gay three days. Informal newspaper interviews were interspersed with parties aboard and ashore and bouts of struggling with the leak. The bilge pump broke down, a vital pin in its not very accessible interior sheered, but some French Canadians, delivering a vast and luxurious cruiser to its owners in Florida, delayed their departure one morning to mend the pump in the workshop they had aboard.

"The trouble with the kind of life you lead," said a member of a large and happy party stopping at Belhaven for the night, "is that you have no time to make those steadfast life-long friendships that are so valuable." With which I could not wholly agree. What is friendship after all? Does it have to be of life-long duration to be of value? It wasn't the impression I had gained on this voyage.

It was October 28th when I left Belhaven to make 45 miles before anchoring three-quarters of a mile offshore in the mouth of the Alligator River, and I would have tackled the Albemarle Sound next morning, but it was blowing very hard indeed and, there being no need for enduring any more discomfort than necessary, I stayed at anchor. Albemarle Sound is the inland counterpart of Cape Hatteras and has the same evil reputation for the inland sailor as the Cape has for the sailor at sea. The delay was worth while for the following day was pleasant with only a mild hangover from the blow, and the Sound had nothing to offer but a feeble chop. In fact, I had more anxiety dodging fishing nets and flying boats on the Elizabeth on the way to Elizabeth City, where I put in at the City Yacht Basin and was met by an unofficial welcoming committee, who insisted upon my dining aboard. They were a mixed and uproarious crew working very hard at being Characters. "You'll have to forgive us," they said, "we aren't like ordinary boating people." The ordinary boating man in common with the Average Man seems very hard to find.

My visa was up and I stayed over for a day trying to get it renewed, but it was Hallow E'en and a holiday and there was no one available to deal with the matter, so I wasted a day from the point of view of progress and departed on November 1st to wander up a gorgeous limpid river to the lock at South Mills where one enters the Dismal Swamp Canal. The canal is dead

271

straight for over twenty miles, but anything less dismal that day would be hard to imagine. A road runs alongside the canal and it was crowded with traffic. At the northern end of the canal I spent the night at the lock gates and sailed next morning through the impressive Navy Yards at Norfolk to a small marina at Portsmouth, where I planned to re-rig *Felicity Ann*, step her mast, and turn her into a proper ship once more.

A tugmaster from the Navy Dockyards did the rigging in his spare time, and when he was presented with the set of tennis balls to replace the worn-out ones that act as chafe preventers on the cross-trees, his eyes bulged. "Jeeze," he breathed, "tennis! Do you have a swimming pool aboard as well?"

Working away at the wire, he said, "You'll be writing a story about your trip. Will you put me in your book? I'd like so much to be in your book."

In due course the rigging was completed and the mast was stepped. *FA* rolled smugly in her berth, and I made preparations for going to sea on the last leg to New York. But before we left Norfolk, Edward Allcard came in on his way south to the Bahamas, sailing the ketch *Wanderer* on which he had been working since his arrival in the States after making the crossing in *Catania* with Norman Fowler.

Edward puts to sea with less fuss than anyone I know. He simply steps aboard and casts off, assured that everything is going to work perfectly or that he will be able to cope with any eventuality that may arise. And he appears to be impervious to temperature for he consults the thermometer in his cabin before deciding whether it is cold enough to refuel the stove or put on another sweater. When the mercury registers the required temperature he damps the fire and removes the sweater.

On the quarter-deck of *Wanderer* lay a tremendous anchor. "What on earth do you want with that?" I asked.

"I don't know yet," mused Edward. "It was given to me, and

it seemed a pity to refuse, you never know when a thing like that might come in handy."

We left Norfolk together on November 17th, a still calm day. "See you in Tahiti," shouted Edward as he turned towards the south, assuming that all small-boat sailors inevitably find their way to the Pacific islands sooner or later.

Dreaming of the tropics, I turned *Felicity Ann* towards the chilly north.

Chapter 25

EVER since I can remember, my interests have been centred in the more masculine fields of endeavour, simply because the feminine ones always seemed to me to be so dull, going round in circles and not leading anywhere. And all my life I have tried to get on with the job, whatever it was, unobtrusively and without attracting those performing-ape leers that so often reward a female whenever she does anything outside the kitchen. Some women can get away with it. But not this one. Some quirk of fate always switches my simple drama of every-day living to wildest farce at the very point of achievement.

I had a private vision of *Felicity Ann* completing our 10,000-mile cruise by sailing nonchalantly up the Hudson to her final dock in New York as though we did it every day, flying the red duster under the shadows of the skyscrapers with unremarkable aplomb. But I might have known we were to follow the usual pattern that day we sailed out of Norfolk, Virginia. *FA* gleamed in her new rigging, everything was battened down, buttoned up and made immovably fast. I, too, was battened down and buttoned up in jerseys and duffle coats and sea-boots, and we were all set to do Battle with Winter North Atlantic. But the Winter North Atlantic was sunny and benign, as calm as a mill pond.

Off the Jersey coast we ran into fog. I was in a reminiscent sentimental mood that particular night for it was November 20th, the first anniversary of our departure from Las Palmas, and here we were, one year later, on the other side of the ocean, chattering northwards on the last leg of our cruise, with the foggy dew dripping off *FA*'s limp canvas. But the fog curtailed my sentimental reminiscing. We proceeded in fits and starts, stopping to listen for the sound of ships and moving on cautiously when they did not sound too close.

We ran into a small silent area where the fog had thinned a little. A small pale glow materialised astern; grew nearer and larger; became a masthead light and developed beneath it the long shape of a tanker going lickety split. She saw us, did a double take and blew a blast on her horn that fairly rocked the welkin (as has been said before, my navigation lights are somewhat unorthodox, for I work on the principle that it is better for the Merchant Service to say, "Good God, what's that?" than to overlook me altogether).

Allowing a decent interval for the echoes to die away, I replied on the little tin trumpet that had been the open sesame for the bridges up the Inland Waterways. It sounded thin and reedy on the night air, but it sounded. Positively bristling with suspicion, the tanker forged ahead, blowing furiously and answered by my thin piping until enveloped in fog again, when she closed down and did not utter again in my hearing.

The following afternoon the fog lifted high enough to allow a peep of the coastline and the fish traps which are a maze of poles and nets constituting a navigational hazard for unwary mariners. By evening we were anchored in 11 fathoms off the Atlantic Highlands, New Jersey, not far from Sandy Hook. With the setting of the sun fog came down once more, and the radio told of unfulfilled train journeys, abandoned cars, people falling down manholes, flights being diverted, and ferries getting into the wrong piers.

During the night I rose at intervals to take soundings, for *Felicity Ann* has a vice. She is a secret dragger. The small circle of water about us was glass calm. Distant ships mooed mournfully at one another and Scotland Lightship. I slept for a few hours and woke to find fog still enveloping us, the water still glass calm, ships still mooing, and *FA* in eight fathoms of water. At 1300 hours the fog lifted, to hang menacingly at 500 feet.

FA without any apparent motivation had crawled quite a lot closer inshore.

It was obvious that we could not make our destination, 79th Street Yacht Basin, before nightfall, but I reckoned we could at least reach the Narrows, from whereon up the River Hudson, according to the chart, there were plenty of piers and docks, one of which could surely provide sanctuary for the night.

It was ebb tide; *FA* chattered slowly past Sandy Hook and struggled across a vast expanse of water to where the Ambrose and various other channels meet south of the Narrows. Suddenly, with a shattering jolt, *FA* struck, and drifting astern of us was a semi-submerged object the size of a floating dock. In no time the ship was surrounded in flotsam that made the water look like a lumber river.

The sun was sinking, and overhead the fog descended slowly and inexorably. Slowly, through the hideous flotsam and against the tide, we worked towards the Narrows, now representing a prize of some value, for neither the charts nor the immediate waters offered the slightest hope of an anchorage. Very large steamers attended by anxious little tugboats began to loom down the river. The sun sank, the fog lowered to fifty feet, lights began to twinkle in the opalescent dusk. It was going to be dark by the time we reached the Narrows and its haven of piers. It was also going to be very thick. Wreaths of fog swirled about the cross-trees, and the large steamers outward bound had become disembodied blasts of sound.

A ghostly fishing boat overtook us and disappeared ahead, heedless of the attitude of wistful, hopeful bewilderment I was trying to portray. If you are a small strange sailboat you are chary of speaking directly to other ships, it being so difficult to avoid being rescued. Especially if the skipper happens to be a lone female, a contingency that rouses all the latent St George in man. And one has one's pride. However, something had to be done if the night was not to be spent bleating in small circles so

276

when another small fishing boat overhauled us I belayed my pride and signalled with a flash light. The fishing boat swerved suspiciously and prepared to go on, but I pulled across her bows and signalled in a very determined manner. She circled cagily and four dim figures rose up in the cockpit—"What do you want?"

"Can-you-tell-me-where-I-can-tie-up-for-the-night?"

"What?"

"Where-can-I-tie-up?—Stranger-here."

A startled silence. A beer can halted in mid air.

"Are you alone?"

"Yes—Where can I tie up for the night?"

"You talk like a limey."

"I *am* a limey. Is there *anywhere* I can tie up—anchor—STOP —for the night?"

"Where do you want to go?"

Not for the first time I concluded these boat-to-boat conversations are very unsatisfactory.

"I don't care!"

"What do you draw?"

"Five feet."

St George came to the fore. With grandiloquent sweeps of the arms they cried in unison, "Follow us!"

I followed them. Through dark and fog. Within a breath of pier-ends, tugs, lighters, and strange nameless shapes. An enormous tugboat loomed up, leant over us questioningly, and raked us from stem to stern with her searchlight. We could not have resembled in the least anything she might have been looking for, and for a wild moment I feared she would run us down in frustrated fury.

The combination navigation light of the fishing boat winked and faded ahead, and *FA* pounded after it as fast as she could go. Sometimes the light vanished altogether, and afterwards I discovered this was because someone hung a cap over it to stop the glare.

We passed through the Narrows, and were travelling north along by the western shore, within a stone's throw of dimly illumined docks, and almost under the tall shadowy sterns of somnolent freighters.

Suddenly, a huge bright glow, barking fiercely, appeared on the starboard hand, moving very fast on a converging course. I slowed down to let it pass ahead. It turned into a ferryboat, blazing with lights, and disappeared into an invisible pier on the western bank. Immediately another, also barking loudly, catapulted out and shot across our astonished bows. Another barking glow then appeared to starboard . . . and another to port. Even the piers were barking. My guide boat had vanished —which didn't surprise me. Nothing, I thought, could live in that lot.

The tide was with us now, and there was no way of halting *FA*, yet we did not have the speed to cross between the endless stream of ferryboats. I drove *FA* round in frantic circles, hoping for a lull and wishing we were peacefully dragging anchor off Sandy Hook. A small red light suddenly appeared very close on the starboard bow, and very suddenly became a green light. I took evasive action too, just in time to see the fishing boat, miraculously restored, skid past. Four figures leant over the side, and shouted something urgently. I shouted back "What?" still circling, still trying to keep from under rush hour in the river. The fishing boat whizzed round astern and came up along-side. "*Mind the ferries*," they yelled.

I cannot clearly recall how we navigated that particular hazard but somehow after desperate manœuvring the stream of ferryboats were astern and *Felicity Ann* was grinding through a comparatively peaceful fog. The fishermen kept romping ahead and coming back to look for us in anxious sheepdog fashion. Finally they rounded up alongside and said, "You're too slow; we'll tow you," and threw a line aboard. I did not like this idea at all, but because I had delayed them so long, acquiesced, and made fast the line, evoking the remark, "Quite a sailor, hunh?"

FA towed like a resentful puppy on the lead, lying back on the tow rope and yawing from side to side. We turned to port round a green-lighted buoy, passed close by a red-lighted buoy . . . remember this, I thought, you've got to get out of here . . . passed along a line of docks and turned hard astarboard into a narrow waterway where weird black timbers and ragged broken hulls of dead ships loomed about us. We passed so close to a towering black shadow that the shrouds brushed along the hull. *FA* started dragging her feet. Knowing the symptoms I called to the fishermen, "We're touching bottom."

"Yoo hoo," they waved back.

Then *FA* slumped back on her haunches and glared, refusing to move another inch. The fishing boat roared fruitlessly for a while and gave up. We were almost within reach of a small boat harbour, but *FA* had had enough and would, I knew, take a lot of humouring to get going again.

"You draw more than five feet," came a voice accusingly from the fishing boat.

"You're right on a sunken barge," said someone else in the triumphant tone that explains everything.

Having had experience of this sort of thing in the Inland Waterways, I went briskly into action. "One of you guys come aboard and stand on the stem here, and you take the tow hard astarboard to bring her head round." I was talking to myself. Someone pleasantly inquired if I had had many storms coming across, and then the fishing boat plunged fruitlessly ahead. I could imagine *FA* snarling. After a few abortive attempts, they cut the motor and stood in contemplative attitudes.

"Tide's going out," said one of them. "Coming in," said another. Of course I had to shove in my little oar. "Coming in," I said brightly. "Look, I've delayed you long enough. I can see where to go now. Suppose you leave me and I'll drift off with the tide."

"No, no," they cried gallantly. "Don't worry, we'll get you off."

A large cruiser eased quietly past. "All right?" she hailed. "Yes," shouted the fishing boat crew, for knights on errantry bent must never be interrupted. So they went round astern and tried to drag her off that way. Well, the tide *was* coming in, which was a comforting thought. Then someone had a bright idea. One of them came aboard and stood on the stemhead, whilst the boat took the tow round to starboard so that *FA*'s head came round, and slowly, reluctantly she slid off into deep water.

As we moved alongside the wooden jetties, past rows of silent cruisers with outriggers and antennæ silhouetted to make them look like giant water-beetles, people appeared from nowhere, attracted apparently by the unusual sight of a tall mast in their midst.

"No water for a sailboat here," cried a scandalised old shell-back. "Don't tie up there—there's a sunken barge," cried another but at last we managed to find a place that satisfied everybody.

When the welcoming and thanking was over and the inevitable reporter answered, I prepared to turn in, then thought of something. "Where am I?" I shouted after the last figure disappearing down the jetty.

"Bayonne," he replied.

Next morning was clear with the clarity that comes with rain. The boat cemetery looked no less eerie for being exposed to the cold, clear light of day. Now, I thought, there is nothing to do but get under way for the 79th Street Yacht Basin to complete the trip. A prospect that was immeasurably saddening. It had been a way of life for so long now I found it hard to imagine any other, and dreaded the thought of having to lay *Felicity Ann* up for the winter and taking to a shore life again. I tried to comfort myself by thinking of spring, when perhaps we would be able to sail again, but at the same time I knew irrefutably the spell ashore would make a difference and it would never be quite the same again.

I got under way at nine o'clock, cleared the sunken barge without difficulty, and found my way back to the River Hudson where I squared away for Manhattan. Alas, the famous skyline was obscured as it had started to thicken up again, the rain having changed to misty drizzle.

Seventy-ninth Street Yacht Basin had been pointed out to me on the chart, not quite accurately, as being just south of the George Washington Bridge, so I spent some time up there looking for it in vain. In the end I got talking to a tugboat belonging to the Corps of Engineers engaged on survey work in the river. In point of fact they spoke to me first, being intrigued by the sight of a small sailboat at large, flying the red ensign, in winter. The crew were very interested in the voyage, and told me I had passed the 79th Street Basin; and after drifting and gossiping for a while we went our separate ways.

Seventy-ninth Street was closed. It said so in no uncertain terms at the basin entrance. Liberty boats from Navy vessels moored amidstream were using it for landings, but it was quite definitely, unequivocally closed to yachts. Now what, I wondered? The tide runs too swiftly in the Hudson for a small boat to lie at anchor, and in any case anchoring would be no solution as I did not have a dinghy aboard. No room. No room anywhere. No room at the inn, I thought wildly. Trying to find a place to tie up a small boat in New York seemed about as hopeful as looking for a landing ground in the Himalayas. So seeking for comfort, if not advice, I turned upstream again in search of the friendly tugboat.

Surveying was in abeyance whilst the tugboat skipper and his crew considered my problem. Seventy-ninth Street, they said, was the only place they knew of for yachts. Never mind about yachts, I said, I only want a place to tie up for the night (let tomorrow take care of itself). This thing was getting out of hand. I had visions of spending the rest of my life trying to find somewhere to tie up for the night. Then the skipper said, "Why don't you tie up with us at our place?"

"Why don't I indeed, where are you?"

Pier 75 they said, the fireboat pier.

So off down the river I went again to make fast eventually alongside the tugboat, and there the voyage might reasonably be considered to be at an end. Not so. Feeling a trifle jubilant at having got ourselves parked for the night, and in New York, too, which was where I wanted to be, I asked the tugboat crew aboard for a celebrating drink, which the skipper and engineer accepted with alacrity, the skipper whipping off his shore-going hat and saying whoops. Then, I having had access to a telephone meantime, a very good-looking young woman presented herself on the dock saying she was my American publisher's publicity director on Operation Welcome, and she joined the party, to the huge delight of the Engineer Corps. But we had no sooner got down to some serious celebrating when a Coastguard vessel taxied up alongside and demanded my immediate departure for Pier 9. Tomorrow would not do, it had to be now. It was very mystifying, as my entry into the States had been cleared at Miami, and all my papers were in order. Later it transpired that, unknown to me, the Coastguards had been alerted to look out for *Felicity Ann* and escort her into port, and they were a little ruffled at my having escaped their vigilance. Now having found me, which must have entailed some pretty smart detective work, they were determined that the original programme should be fulfilled, and I should be escorted come what may to Pier 9, the Coastguard station at the foot of Wall Street.

The party aboard *Felicity Ann* was all set for a boat ride, so we cast off, headed out into the River, and embarked on a wild mad ride, *FA* making a fabulous speed with the aid of a four-knot current. The Coastguard cutter shepherded us anxiously, fearful lest we should be mislaid, and the Engineers were gay but inclined to be aggressive towards the Coastguards, alleging they had found me first, and that the Coastguards had no business to come butting in. . . .

Pier 9 was lined with Coastguard personnel of every degree when we arrived, and the basin was filled with busy little boats scuttling to and fro. Because of the tide we had to enter the basin with a considerable amount of way on, and there seemed a grave possibility of our ramming the pier, the boats, or Wall Street itself if we did not lose some of our speed. I threw a check line to a likely looking mariner, who caught it and wandered off with it in his hand, looking puzzled. I shouted to him to belay, and at that moment there was a splash.

I looked round and there was my publisher's publicity director being hauled, dripping, out of the river, she having stepped ashore when it wasn't there. Which, as a final touch to a triumphal entry into New York, could hardly be excelled.

Chapter 26

FELICITY ANN moved from the Coastguard station to a ship-yard at City Island on Long Island Sound, which, although within the environs of New York City, is really an island and surprisingly rural, and there the little ship was hauled ashore by a great crane and laid up for the winter. Two months later the annual Boat Show was held in New York, and *Felicity Ann* was invited to come out of temporary retirement to appear as a guest artist at the show.

Interest in pleasure boats had grown so much that the exhibition was moved to a new site that year, and was held in the gigantic Armoury in the Bronx, which, none the less, proved only just big enough to hold all the exhibits and the crowds. There was no room for *Felicity Ann* to be shown in the building, which was just as well, for she was in a very rough state at the end of the voyage, and she would have been sadly out of place amongst the sparkling show vessels. But outside the building, just by the front entrance, was an enclosure, and here she was put on solitary display, behind iron railings and floodlit, with a notice telling of her voyage.

I had no part in this, it was *Felicity Ann's* own private party; but I used to go there in the evenings and stand by the railings to look at her and wonder a little. Forgetting all the discomforts, the terrors, and the weariness, I wished I was back aboard, preparing to set out for some other far off magic land. . . .

On their way to the Boat Show entrance the crowd jostled, saw the rugged, dirty little ship illuminated by floodlights and stopped to read the notice.

"Say, how d'ya like that—some dame sails this thing across the Atlantic by herself!"

"Not for me, brother. Christ, I wouldn't cross the river in it."

"Nor me. What'd be the matter with someone they'd do a crazy thing like that?"

What, indeed?

One man turned to me and grinned, nodding in the direction of *Felicity Ann*. "Don't get ideas, honey," he said.

SOME SAILING TERMS

(explained for the non-sailing reader)

ABEAM: At right angles to the line of the boat.

AFT: In the rear or "after" part of a vessel. Abaft: in rear of. (See ASTERN.)

ALDIS: An electric signalling lamp.

ALTO CUMULUS: Small, round, fluffy white clouds, high up.

AMIDSHIPS: The middle of the ship or boat.

ANVIL CLOUD: Generally speaking, a thunder cloud, large, black and top-heavy of appearance.

ASTERN: Behind the boat.

AWASH: Almost submerged. "Floorboards awash".

BACK: The wind backs when it changes direction anticlockwise. A sail is backed or aback when it is sheeted against the wind, thus stopping the vessel instead of drawing it forward.

BAGGYWRINKLE: Lengths of hairy padding made from old rope and wrapped around the rigging to prevent the sail from wearing away where it touches.

BAILER: A kind of "saucepan" for removing water from a boat—any old tin used for that purpose.

BAR: A shallow patch extending across the entrance to a river or estuary.

BAROMETRIC PRESSURE: The pressure of the atmosphere which causes the needle of the barometer to go up or down.

BATTEN DOWN: To fasten down securely any "hatch" or cover over an opening in the deck.

BEAM: Greatest width of a boat.

BEAM ENDS: On her beam ends. Since the beams referred to are those which run diagonally across the boat below the deck (rafters) she would be right over on her side.

BELAYED: To belay a rope. To tie it securely.

BERMUDAN RIG: Tall triangular mainsail, with its foot extended by a boom; and in the case of *Felicity Ann*, one triangular sail forward of the mast, known as jib, foresail or staysail.

BERTHS: Bunks or beds. Also a position or space for a vessel in a harbour or dock.

BILGE: The lowest part of the inside of a boat. Also the curve of the hull, the sides of which merge with the bottom.

BILGE PUMP: Pump for extracting the water which collects in the bilge.

BILGE STRINGER: A long bar running right round a boat at floor-level.

BLOCKS: Often known to the landsman as pulleys; through which run the halliards for hoisting and lowering sails, and the sheets for trimming them. Also large wooden blocks upon which a ship is built.

BLOWING OUT: "Blow out" a sail. When a sail is blown to pieces by a strong wind.

BOOM: The spar or pole which extends the bottom or foot of the sail.

BOOM GUY: Whereas the rope which actually controls the boom is called a "sheet", the "guy" is a rope which braces it and holds it steady.

BOSUN'S GEAR: To a yacht, what a housewife's mending gear is to a home, plus paint, varnish and other stores.

BROADSIDE: Broadside on, beam on, presenting the whole side of the boat, e.g. broadside to the sea.

BULKHEAD: A strong partition dividing one compartment from another.

BULWARKS: A low "wall" or balustrade running around the edge of the deck. On a small yacht it is rarely more than a few inches in height.

BURGEE: A small flag flown from the top of the mast indicating the owner's Yacht Club and showing the wind direction.

BURNT OFF: Having removed the paint by using a blowlamp and scraper.

CABIN SOLE: The "floor" of the cabin.

CANVAS PULL: Referring to the power of sail when set to a breeze.

CAST OFF: To release a rope completely as when "casting off" from a quay or mooring.

CELESTIAL NAVIGATION: Distinct from DEAD RECKONING (see under that heading) in that the position of the ship is found partly by measuring the angle of the sun or other heavenly bodies.

CHAFE: Self-explanatory. One of the greatest problems of the ocean cruiser is the constant chafing of sails and ropes due to the continuous movement of the yacht.

CHAIN LOCKER: A compartment well forward in the boat in which the anchor chain is contained.

CHANDLERS: Ship's Chandler, a store or shop which supplies all the needs of a vessel.

CHOP, CHOPPY: Waves close together and steep.

CHRONOMETER: A highly accurate clock by which the "longitudinal position" of the vessel is calculated.

CLEAT: A "horned" fitting around which a rope can be fastened.

CLEW: The rear lower corner of a sail.

CLIPPER BOW: The bows or "front ends" of the old sailing tea and wool clippers were given a graceful concave sweep which is still seen occasionally in ship design.

CLOSE HAULED: When the sails are all tightened in hard and the boat is sailed as close to the wind as possible, without the sails flapping. See TACK for further elucidation.

COACH ROOF: A raised part of the deck giving extra headroom to the cabin below. Similar to top of a railway coach.

COAMING: A raised rim or edge around any opening in the deck, designed to prevent water slopping over.

COCKPIT: The well or sunken space at the after end of the boat, from which the helmsman steers and controls her, and from which the cabin is entered.

COMBINATION LIGHT: By international law a vessel must carry a red light on the left or port side (facing ahead) and a green light on the right or starboard side. The combination light has the two in one and is permitted for very small craft.

COME ABOUT, TO: To turn the boat or change direction when this involves heading her into the wind during the course of the operation. (See TACK.)

COMPANIONWAY: The stairway or steps leading down into the living quarters.

CON: A vessel is "conned" when the captain or pilot guides her into or out of harbour, through rocky channels, etc.

CROSS TREES: Cross-bars on a mast, to spread and increase the effective strength of the shrouds which support the mast.

CUTTER: A single-masted fore-and-aft rigged vessel setting mainsail and, forward of the mast, two headsails generally called foresail and jib.

DEAD BEFORE: "Running dead before the wind", i.e. with the wind blowing from exactly behind the boat.

DEAD RECKONING: Navigating the boat by using only the simple elements of direction according to the compass, distance measured as the boat passes through the water, and the estimated effects of drift and tide.

DIOPTRIC LENS: A special lens or glass fitted to certain navigational lamps to concentrate the light in one direction.

DOUBLE ENDED: A type of boat which has a pointed stern similar to the bow.

DOWN-HAUL: A rope for hauling down a sail.

DRAUGHT, DRAW: The depth of the boat below water, e.g. she draws five feet, or her draft is five feet.

DRAW: A sail is said to "draw" when it is filled with wind and pulling the boat forward.

DRIED OUT: Left high and dry by the falling tide.

DUTCHMAN'S LOG: A primitive method of ascertaining the speed of the vessel through the water, by timing a floating object along the length of the vessel.

EBB TIDE: A falling tide.

ENGINE BEARERS: Stout beams which take the weight of the engine.

ENSIGN: The national flag of the country, e.g. Red Ensign ("Red Duster").

EYE BOLTS: Metal bolts terminating in a ring or "eye" for attaching wire rigging and ropes.

EYES OF THE SHIP: The extreme forward end.

EYE SPLICE: A loop (or eye) spliced (plaited) into the end of rope or wire.

FATHOMS: A nautical measurement of depth. A fathom equals six feet.

FENDERS: Tough cushions or pads to protect the boat from bumping when alongside a quay or another vessel.

FITTING OUT: The complete overhaul and renovation of a vessel and her equipment, usually an annual event for a yacht.

FLOOD TIDE: A rising tide.

FOLLOWING SWELL: When the sea swell follows, or runs in the same direction as the boat.

FOLLOWING WIND: Wind blowing from aft.

FOOT RAIL: A rail specially fitted along parts of the deck to afford a foothold when the yacht is heeling over in the wind.

FORCE 5: Strength of wind is reckoned according to the Beaufort Scale, "Forces" numbering upwards from flat calm to hurricane force. Force 5 is what is commonly called a fresh wind.

FORE-AND-AFT SAIL: A sail set in line with the boat. A square sail is set across the boat.

FORE DECK: The front part of the deck.

FORE PEAK: Extreme forward space in the boat below deck. Usually a restricted triangular "cupboard" in a yacht.

FORESTAY: (See JIB STAY.) Twin forestays: a modern development which makes changing jibs or foresails easier, and renders possible the use of two at once.

FOUNDERING: Sinking, wrecked.

FULL MAIN: A full mainsail, when the mainsail is fully extended. (See REEFED.)

GALE: Very strong wind. Beaufort Force 8. (See FORCE.)

GALLEY: The kitchen on a boat.

GALLOWS: A support for the boom (see BOOM) when at rest. Also boom crutch.

GEAR: A vessel's equipment.

GENOA: An outsize jib or foresail usually made of light material.

GET UNDER WAY: To start the boat moving.

GIMBALS: A fitment which enables a lamp or Primus stove, etc., to remain upright in spite of the movements of the boat.

G.M.T. SIGNALS: Greenwich Mean Time signals broadcast at regular intervals.

GUY LINES: Lines used to brace or stiffen.

HALLIARD: Rope by which a sail is hoisted and lowered.

HAND BEARING COMPASS: A small compass which is held in the hand to determine the bearing or "direction" of an object.

HANKED ON: The foresail is commonly attached to the forestay by means of self-locking hooks, known as hanks, which slide up or down the stay as the sail is hoisted or lowered.

HATCH: A "lid" which covers an opening in the deck.

HEAD: Or, "the heads". Seafaring term for the toilet.

HEAD (of a sail): The top of the sail.

HEAVE TO: When the foresail is sheeted to windward, i.e. towards the wind, so that it counteracts the effect of the mainsail and renders the vessel almost stationary, she is said to be "hove-to".

H.W. SPRINGS: High Water spring tide. A spring tide occurs twice a month, at the full and new moons, the level rising considerably higher than at neap tides with which they alternate.

HULL: The body of a boat excluding the mast and sails and other superficial structures.

JACK STAFF: A flag pole situated on the stern of a vessel.

JETSAM: Flotsam and jetsam. Strictly speaking jetsam is that which is thrown overboard to lighten a vessel, and flotsam the drifting remnants of a wreck. These terms are commonly accepted to refer to anything found floating in the sea.

JIB: The triangular sail forward of the mast in a sloop.

JIB STAY: Or forestay. The wire stay which acts as the forward support of the mast, and to which the jib or foresail is attached.

JIBE: When a vessel is running "dead before the wind" a slight deviation from the course will cause the mainsail with its heavy boom to slam across to

the opposite side, with great violence if the wind is strong, unless the operation is deliberate and carefully controlled. This is known as jibing.

JOLLY ROGER: The old "Skull and Crossbones" of piracy.

JURY MAST: A temporary mast which is improvised when a vessel's real mast has been broken.

KNEES: Angular strengthening pieces used in the construction of a boat.

KNOCK DOWN: When a violent gust (or squall) of wind strikes a sailing vessel and forces her over on her side.

KNOTS: A measurement of speed derived from a primitive method whereby a line was allowed to run out as the vessel sailed ahead. The line was marked at intervals with knots which indicated the speed by the number counted in a calculated time. A knot is equivalent to one sea mile (6,080 feet) per hour.

LAID DECKS: When the planks forming the deck are "laid" to follow the curved shape of the boat.

LAID UP: When a vessel is hauled out of the water and immobilised and her equipment stored at the end of a voyage or of the sailing season.

LANDFALL: The first sight of land.

LAY OFF: (A course.) When the intended direction or course is decided and drawn on the chart, the course is said to be "laid off".

LEE: The lee side is always "down-wind". The other being the weather or wind-ward side.

LEE-SHORE: When the land is down-wind, i.e. to leeward, of a vessel, it is said to be a lee-shore.

LEEWAY: When the wind blows at a vessel from forward of the beam it tends to push her to leeward or sideways through the water as well as forward. She is then said to be making leeway.

LIGHTER: A type of barge.

LIGHTS (Navigation): See COMBINATION LIGHT.

LINE SQUALL: A violent gust of wind often of some hours' duration found in the equatorial regions.

LINING UP: (An engine.) The procedure adopted when an engine is being fitted in a vessel to ensure that it is in a straight line with the propeller shaft.

LOG: (a) A device which registers distance covered through the water. It is worked by a spinning "vane" towed behind the boat on a "log-line". (b) The ship's diary, written in the log-book.

LOOM: The loom of a light; when the glow is seen above the horizon without the actual light being visible.

LUFFING: Turning the boat into the wind. The front edge of the sail is known as the luff.

LYING TO: See HEAVE TO and SEA ANCHOR.

MAIN SHEET: The rope which controls the mainsail.

MARE'S TAILS: Long streamers of high cloud associated with the approach of bad weather.

MAST TRACK: Similar to curtain railing, running right up the length of a mast, to which the mainsail is attached, and along which it is hoisted and lowered.

MOORED: Attached to moorings, i.e. a set of permanent anchors in a harbour or river; or when a vessel is held between two anchors so that she cannot swing about. Moored to a quay: fastened by both bow and stern ropes.

MOORINGS: See MOORED.

NAVEL PIPE: A hole in the deck through which the anchor chain passes to the chain locker.

NOON SIGHT: Using a sextant, the angle of the sun and horizon is measured at noon when it is at the greatest height of its swing across the sky.

NUN BUOY: A conical buoy.

OFF THE WAYS: Launched.

OUT-HAUL: A rope used for hauling out a sail along a spar or pole.

OVERFALLS: Confused rough waves localised usually near a headland and caused by fast tidal currents.

PARALLEL RULES: A drawing instrument used in navigation consisting of two rulers joined by arms which keep them always parallel.

PILOT BOOK: A guide book giving details of the coast and of ocean currents, tides, etc.

PILOT CUTTERS: Small, sturdy sailing vessels which were once used in carrying the pilots out to sea, where they would transfer to ships needing their services. Pilot cutters are famous for their sea-going qualities. Fine steamships have now taken their place but are still called "cutters".

PILOT FLAG: A red and white flag flown by a pilot boat or any boat having a pilot aboard.

PLUMB BOB: Not a nautical term. A weighted string used to find the vertical.

PLYMOUTH HOOKER: A type of small sailing vessel peculiar to the port of Plymouth.

POOP: The raised deck-level at the stern of old type ships. A boat is still said to be "pooped" when a following sea comes right over her stern.

POPPLES: Broken and uneasy little waves.

PORT QUARTER: The left-hand back wheel of a car is roughly in an equivalent position to a ship's port quarter.

PORT SIDE: The left side when facing the "front".

PREVENTERS: Extra ropes fixed to assist others.

PULPIT: Protective railings fixed to bow or stern.

PUNT: The West of England name for a small open boat or dinghy.

Q & G FLAGS: International Code Flags for "My ship is healthy and I require clearance" (Q), and "I require a Pilot" (G).

QUARANTINE: A ship arriving from a foreign country must be proved free from disease before her personnel may land. Until then she is in quarantine.

QUARTERING BREEZE: A breeze blowing from the port or starboard quarter.

RADAR SCREEN: A kind of television set which shows a shadow of objects within its range.

REACHING: With the wind blowing at right-angles.

REEFED: When a sail is made smaller by rolling or tying it up at the bottom.

REEVED: Threaded through. A rope is reeved through a block.

REFIT: See FITTING OUT.

RIBS: In a boat "ribs" "timbers" or "frames" are comparable to the ribs in the human body.

RIDING LIGHT: A lantern with a clear white light which is hung in the rigging when a vessel is lying at anchor.

RIGGED: The manner in which sails are arranged, e.g. "sloop rigged". "Rigged" the awning, i.e. fitted up the awning.

RIGGER: One who makes and fits wire or rope rigging.

RIGGING: The ropes, some permanent (standing) and some movable (running), by which the mast is supported and sails are hoisted.

RIPE: An expression applied to a boat which is old and rotten. Rotten timber.

ROLLER REEFING: An arrangement by which the area of the mainsail is reduced by rotating the boom so that the sail is rolled round it, and at the same time lowering the head of the sail proportionately.

ROPE TAILS: Since wire ropes are hard to handle, lengths of ordinary rope are sometimes added to one end.

RUDDER HEAD: The top of the rudder which sticks up through the deck.

RUNNING: Sailing before the wind. "Day's run" is the distance sailed during 24 hours, whether "running", "reaching" or "on the wind" (*q.v.*).

SAIL BAG: A bag in which sails are stowed when not in use.

SCHOONER: A sailing vessel usually having two masts, the main mast being the after mast and the taller of the two.

SCUPPERS: The gutters along the side of the deck. "Scuppered": done for.

SEA ANCHOR: A stout open-mouthed bag put out from a vessel at the end of a rope in very hard weather, so that she

"rides" to it, with all sails lowered, the object being to prevent her from drifting broadside on to the wind and sea.

SEA-ROOM: Safe distance from land.

SEIZINGS: When a plant is tied up to a stick, it might be said to be "seized" on.

SELF-DRAINING COCKPIT: (See COCKPIT.) The floor-level being above the water-level outside, any water in the cockpit can drain away through plugholes.

SELF-STEERING: When a vessel is so arranged that she will steer herself. In the case of *Felicity Ann* by a system of sheets from the twin foresails to the tiller.

SETTEE: On smaller vessels settees are fixtures also forming a bed and with built-in cupboards (lockers) below them.

SEXTANT: A navigational instrument used for measuring angular distances.

SHACKLE: A removable steel connecting-link with a variety of uses on sails and rigging.

SHEET: Not a reference to any form of sail, but the rope which controls a sail.

SHIPWRIGHT: A builder of ships and boats.

SHOAL: Shallow water.

SHROUDS: The permanent ropes (usually of wire nowadays) supporting the mast on either side.

SIGHTS: Bearings or angles taken off the sun or other heavenly bodies.

SINGLE-HANDED: Alone.

SISTER-HOOKS: Twin hooks which come together and form a ring.

SITTING HEADROOM: When the height of a cabin enables one to sit upright but not to stand.

SLIDES: Fastenings used in attaching a sail to a mast track (*q.v.*).

SLOOP: Nowadays defined as a single-masted sailing vessel with mainsail and one head sail.

SPINNER: Rotator. (See LOG.)

SPRAY HOOD: Similar to a pram hood fitted over the cockpit to protect the helmsman.

SQUARE RIG: A sailing vessel which has its sails set or arranged across the deck. (See FORE and AFT.)

STANCHIONS: Posts supporting the railings around a deck.

STARBOARD: The right-hand side of the boat when facing forward.

STAYSAIL: A sail forward of the mast, which is attached to a wire stay.

STEM: The curved timber to which the planks of a boat are fastened at the bow. Stemhead rig: a type of craft which has the jib or forward sail attached to the stem ahead, i.e. she has no bowsprit.

STEPPED: "Stepped the mast". When fitting the mast into a vessel, its foot is lowered into its "step" or socket, usually below and through the deck and cabin floor. (But see TABERNACLE.)

STERN ON: With the stern facing the wind or waves.

STERN SHEETS: The stern (or back) seat in an open boat.

STOPPED: In painting or varnishing a vessel, holes and uneven surfaces are filled with a putty-like material called "stopping".

STORM JIB: A small jib, for use in hard weather in place of the normal jib.

STOW: To pack away or secure.

STRAIGHT STEMMED: (See STEM.) Some older vessels have a straight or vertical stem as against the more modern convex stem.

STREAMED: (Log.) To "stream" the log is to trail it behind the boat as she is sailing.

STUFFING-BOX: As the propeller shaft must pass out of the boat without allowing water to leak in around it, a device so called is used which consists of a rope-like wad of packing held right against the shaft and its hole.

TABERNACLE: A hinging device which permits a mast to be "stepped" on deck instead of below, and to be raised or lowered as required, e.g. for passing under bridges.

TACK (of sail): The forward lower corner.

TACK (to tack): Since it is impossible to sail a boat dead into the wind the only way of gaining ground in an up-wind direction is by a series of zigzags. The sails are sheeted in tightly and the boat steered as nearly into the wind as is possible without losing way. She is then "close-hauled" on the port or starboard "tack" as the case may be.

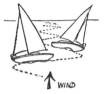

To "tack" is to turn the boat from one tack to the other by means of the tiller (called "going about"), thus bringing the wind on to the other side of the sails.

TACKLE: Blocks through which a sheet or halyard is passed so as to reduce the effort needed to haul on it.

TEREDO WORM: A marine boring worm. A menace to wooden boats.

TIED UP: Fastened to the quay or dock-side.

TILLER: The wooden (usually) bar by which the rudder is controlled.

T.M.: Thames Measurement: a formula giving a ship's tonnage computed from her measurements.

TOP-HAMPER: The above-deck structures.

TOPPING LIFT: A rope from a point some way up the mast to the outer end of the boom; used to take the weight of the boom when the mainsail is being raised or lowered.

TOPSIDES: The sides of the boat's hull above the waterline.

TRADE WIND BELT: Areas about the earth's surface where the wind blows in a regular and known direction.

TRANSIT: An alignment of one object with another which, in navigation, is of assistance in determining a ship's position.

TRIM: Sails are "trimmed" when they are correctly set. A boat is "trimmed" when she is correctly balanced in the water.

293

TRUCK: The "knob" at the mast head.

TRYSAIL: A small, strong sail used in very hard weather in place of the mainsail.

TWIN (Jibs): Two identical sails set together intended to make sailing before the wind easier over long period. (See SELF-STEERING.)

UNDER WAY: In motion, going along, proceeding.

UNDER WATER BODY: That portion of a vessel's hull which is under water.

UP INTO THE WIND: Turning the boat to face into the wind. (See LUFFING and TACK.)

VEER: The wind "veers" when it changes direction clockwise. (See BACK.) Also: to veer some anchor cable is to let some more out.

WARPS: Heavy ropes used for mooring or towing.

WATERLINE: The level of the water around the outside of the hull.

WEAR ROUND: Or "Wear Ship": to turn the boat down-wind and then up into the wind again on the opposite tack; as opposed to "tacking" (*q.v.*). Wearing is only resorted to in difficult circumstances.

WEATHER HELM: Most sailing boats tend to turn themselves towards the direction of the wind. The tendency is corrected by pulling the tiller "to weather", i.e. towards the direction of the wind, and the boat is said "to carry weather helm".

WIND, ON THE: With the wind blowing from forward of the beam.

WORKING: Slight movement of the planking of the hull common in old vessels which causes them to leak.

WORKING SAILS: The sails in normal use.

YACHT BASIN: A dock reserved for the use of yachts.

YAWING: Swerving from side to side when sailing down-wind.

THE SHIP
WOULD NOT TRAVEL
DUE WEST

by

DAVID LEWIS

"But the principal failing occurred in the sailing,
And the Bellman, perplexed and distressed,
Said he *had* hoped, at least, when the wind blew due East,
That the ship would *not* travel due West!"

—LEWIS CARROLL

ACKNOWLEDGMENTS

I CANNOT thank individually all those people, family, friends, colleagues and strangers, who gave me moral support, hospitality, wrote encouraging letters, lent me gear or worked patiently preparing *Cardinal Vertue*. They are too numerous for me to make mention of them all, but theirs was the Atlantic crossing. Their kindness was a tangible force always present aboard, which did not allow me to let them down too badly.

But these I must mention in public acknowledgment of my indebtedness:

The Flag Officers and members of the Royal Western Yacht Club, the Slocum Society, the Royal Burnham Yacht Club, the Little Ship Club, the Sheepshead Bay Yacht Club and the New York Yacht Club.

Lieutenant-Colonel H. G. Hasler and Valentine Howells for their accurate and patient work in completing the medical logs which needed up to an hour a day, and for permission to quote from their published and unpublished accounts.

Commander W. B. Luard, R.N. Retd. for his patient advice and for reading the manuscript of this book at many stages, correcting innumerable errors in spelling and punctuation, and pointing out nautical solecisms and lapses from good taste, and Mr. A. J. Law for helping to remove some of the clichés.

Doctors L. E. Wall, J. J. and L. G. E. De Jode, and Dr. D. J. Gorham, the colleagues who alone made my holiday possible.

The following companies generously donated their products and helped me in many ways: Thomas Walker and Son Ltd., British Nylon Spinners Ltd., Marine Electronics, Stanley Tools Ltd., Pfizer Ltd., John Wyeth and Bros. Ltd., B.C.B. Ltd., Horlicks Ltd., Smith and Nephew Ltd., Scientific Pharmaceutics, Lea Bridge Industries Ltd., Imperial Chemical Industries Ltd., Expanded Rubber Co. Ltd., Jablo Plastics Industries Ltd., Eastwood Plastics Ltd., Minnesota Mining and Manufacturing Co. Ltd.

I have made specific acknowledgment in Appendix Four, "Research Observations", and in Appendix Five, "Treatment of Sea-serpent Stings and Other Ailments", for much valued help and advice in their compilation.

Acknowledgment is also gladly made to authors, their executors and publishers, and the Controller of H.M. Stationery Office, for quotations in text and appendices as follows:

James A. Mitchener: *Return to Paradise* (Random House Inc., New York); D. P. Capper: *The Vikings of Britain* (George Allen and Unwin Ltd., London); "The Orkneyingers' Saga" in *The Icelandic Sagas*, vol. 3, 1894 (H.M.S.O., London); Francis Chichester: *Alone Across the Atlantic* (George

Allen and Unwin Ltd., London) and articles in *The Observer*, July 24, 31 and Aug. 7, 1960; Edward Reman: *The Norse Discoveries and Explorations in America* (University of California Press, Berkeley and Los Angeles); Gaythorne Hardy: *The Norse Discoveries of America* (The Clarendon Press, Oxford); Rudyard Kipling's verses from "Harp Song of the Dane Women" in *Puck of Pook's Hill* (Mrs. G. Bambridge and Macmillan and Co. Ltd., London); Extracts from an article by the author in the *Journal of the College of General Practitioners*, Feb., 1960; *Nova Scotia and Bay of Fundy Pilot*, 1958 (The Admiralty and H.M.S.O., London); *Nantucket Sound: Esso Cruising Guide* (Esso Standard Oil Co., U.S.A.); James Fisher: *Bird Recognition, I* (Penguin Books Ltd., Harmondsworth); Humphrey Barton: *Atlantic Adventures* (Adlard Coles Ltd., Southampton); George Barker: verses from "Galway Bay" in *The Faber Book of Modern Verse* (Faber and Faber Ltd., London); Louis MacNeice: verses from "Bagpipe Music" in *The Earth Compels* (Faber and Faber Ltd., London); Wilfred Noyce: verses from *Springs of Adventure* (John Murray Ltd., London); *North Sea Pilot*, vol. I, 1910, and *Newfoundland and Labrador Pilot*, 8th edn., 1951 (The Admiralty and H.M.S.O., London).

For figures reproduced on p. 440, of *Vertue* with masthead sloop rig: Douglas Phillips-Birt's article "The Vertues" in *The Yachtsman*, Aug., 1960; on p. 442, of *Vertue* plan: Humphrey Barton's *Vertue XXXV* (Rupert Hart-Davis, The Mariners Library, no. 31); on p. 449, of *Gipsy Moth III:* Francis Chichester's *Alone Across the Atlantic* (George Allen and Unwin, London): and also on p. 449, of *Cape Horn:* M. J. J. Herbulot and Soc. Cidevyv, Paris.

Finally, I would single out one among the many unnamed friends to represent the rest: the elderly lady who gave me a cloth and wire wishbone which assuredly brought me luck.

FOREWORD
by H. G. HASLER

THE first public announcement of the impending Single-handed Transatlantic Race was made in August 1957, nearly three years before the race was due to start. In the next eighteen months, a great number of inquiries, requests, and criticisms were received from dozens of prospective entrants, not one of whom subsequently came anywhere near the starting-line.

There was, then, nothing out of the ordinary in the letter that reached me on March 30, 1959, from a Dr. D. H. Lewis, asking for further details of the race on behalf of "some friends" who were "interested", even though it did not need second sight to guess who the "friends" were. I sent him a routine reply, and thought no more of it until six months later, when a second letter revealed that he had spent part of the intervening time in "wandering off to Norway in *Cardinal Vertue*", and that his single-handed passages from Burnham-on-Crouch to Stavanger and back had already been accepted by the Slocum Society as qualifying him to enter the race.

This made me sit up. For the first time, it seemed as if we had a serious entrant on our hands. Ten days later, when he came to see me at Curdridge, I realized that this was an understatement: what we had on our hands was somebody who was going to sail that damned race if it killed him. From this time on, I knew that the race was really going to happen.

David Lewis is not a large man physically, but he has the hard muscular development of an athlete. Mentally, as any reader of this book will discover, he is modest, generous, humorous, dedicated, and painfully honest. There are no heroics here, but many confessions of clumsiness, of stupidity, and of ordinary wholesome fear, that will at once ring true to anybody who has ever taken a small sailing boat across open water. I only doubt whether most of us would have had the moral courage to record them so accurately.

At Plymouth, in the last nightmare days before the start, when David and I seemed to be holding a private competition in unreadiness, he still found time to turn over, as a gift to each competitor, a splendid outfit of medical and emergency stores that he had been assembling for months past. It was typical of him to spend precious time doing this, instead of checking through his own provisions and ship's stores, which later proved, in mid-Atlantic, to be incomplete.

By the time the starting-gun fired, David had already faced and overcome a great number of serious difficulties. Three and a half hours later, I made out—far ahead of me—*Cardinal Vertue* with only the stump of her mast left standing. Surely even David couldn't do much to redeem *that* situation?

This book shows how very wrong I was. *Cardinal Vertue* may well be the only racing yacht that has ever appeared on the prize list after having been dismasted three thousand miles short of the finishing line. After the race, his single-handed passage back from Newfoundland to the Shetlands was remarkable for a succession of heavy gales, and for the way in which the boat and the man stood up to them.

I admire David Lewis both for what he did, and for the way he tells it.

Curdridge, Hampshire.
September 1961.

CONTENTS

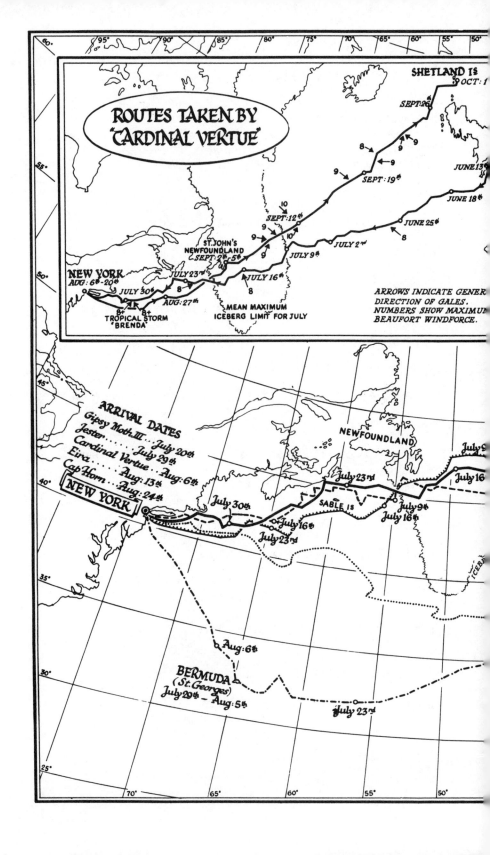

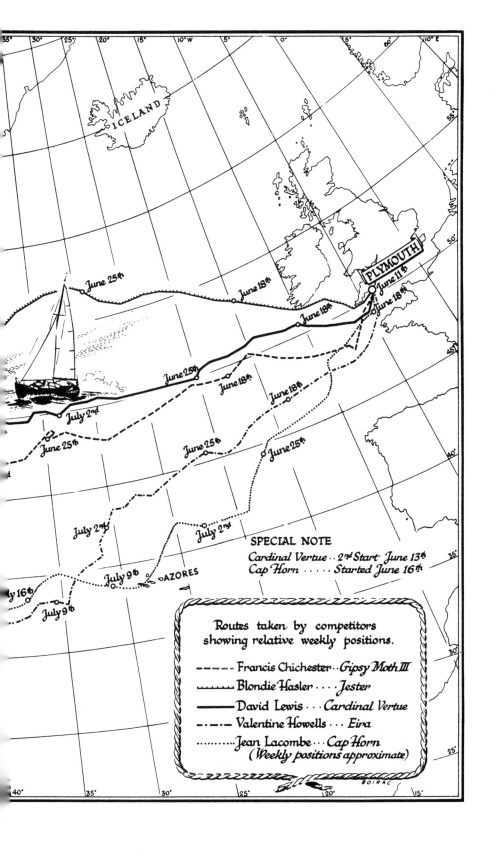

ICELAND

PLYMOUTH
June 11th

June 25th
June 18th
June 18th
June 18th

June 25th
June 18th
June 18th

July 2nd

June 25th
June 25th
June 25th

July 2nd
July 2nd
AZORES

July 9th

July 16th
July 9th

SPECIAL NOTE
Cardinal Vertue · · 2nd Start June 13th
Cap Horn · · · · · Started June 16th

Routes taken by competitors
showing relative weekly positions.

- - - - Francis Chichester · · Gipsy Moth III
·······Blondie Hasler · · · · Jester
———— David Lewis · · · Cardinal Vertue
-·-·- Valentine Howells · · · Eira
············ Jean Lacombe · · · Cap Horn
(Weekly positions approximate)

BOIRAC

PLATES

305

*

[The author's drawings in the text are from
the Log of *Cardinal Vertue*.]

I

FIVE SAILS TO THE WESTWARD

"When the winds blow my mast will go."
East Coast Bargeman's Song.

THIS is not a yachtsman's log-book, nor is it merely the story of a race. It will try to tell something of men's feelings, of their fears and of their laughter as through victory and defeat they test their skill, judgment and endurance against the impersonal Atlantic.

By its nature this account must be an intensely personal one, for only my own experience can be described at first hand. However, the daily records of emotions, sleep, food, and events at sea, which were kept by some of the competitors in the Single-handed Transatlantic Sailing Race to further medical research, have been drawn upon with their authors' permission.

The competitive aspect of the race was outweighed, for me at all events, by the struggle between man and natural forces. The adventure itself assumed greater depth and purpose from the clearer understanding we hoped to gain of man's reactions when he stands revealed, stripped of all outside support, in a struggle, and alone with his soul.

So the problem of scientific investigation into the mental and physical experiences underlying the fight to inch westward towards the Americas, provided its own exciting challenge to the intellect; though for me, the ultimate test was to come after the race itself was over, when I kept a rendezvous, in remote high latitudes, with the storm winds of autumn.

A week before the race four of us were at Plymouth working feverishly on our boats, making last-minute preparations: Francis Chichester with his 39-foot yawl *Gipsy Moth III*; "Blondie" Hasler, who had called his 25-foot modified Folkboat, *Jester*, because she was "such a bloody joke"; Valentine Howells with his 25-foot Folkboat *Eira* and myself with *Cardinal Vertue*, a 25-foot Vertue-class sloop.

Jean Lacombe, caught by heavy weather in the Channel while sailing across from France in the little 21-foot French sloop *Cap Horn*,

307

arrived at Plymouth only on the eve of the race. He crossed the starting-line five days after the other boats.

Arthur Piver, an American, with a most unusual craft, a 30-foot trimaran, sailed over from the United States with two companions, but reached Plymouth too late to compete.

I had been doing a *locum* for the friend who was to look after my patients during most of my absence, so there had been little time to prepare the innumerable things necessary for a three thousand miles voyage. The final week proved hectic; radio transmitters, which had been lent to us, were being installed by the Navy; I had to sort out and pack medical kits and "survival" food packs for each competitor; emergency gear—flares, inflatable rafts and other items had to be collected. These were being supplied by the manufacturers largely through Mr. E. C. B. Lee, Secretary to the Naval Life Saving Committee, who wrote dozens of "baited" letters somewhat as follows:

". . . If there are any items of equipment which you would like evaluated . . . you could get in touch direct with Dr. David H. Lewis, who is co-ordinating the activities. These adventurous sailors also intend to make the return voyage single-handed. The weather is then liable to be stormy so it is *possible that a survival incident may occur*." (My italics.)

A friend and I, under the auspices of the Medical Research Council, had prepared "medical log-books" in which to keep daily records of food, drink, sleep and emotions. Those who agreed to collaborate in this study had to be weighed and their food listed, a procedure to be repeated immediately upon arrival in New York. John Harries, of the Food Science Division of the Ministry of Agriculture and Fisheries, came to Plymouth to assist me in this work but even with his help there was so much to be done that I never did find time to make a list of food I should need myself.

Into the existing chaos there suddenly descended upon us hordes of reporters from the Press, TV and radio. Each morning, soon after we began work on our yachts, we were besieged, and from then on were interviewed almost continuously throughout the day. Although we became hardened to being constantly photographed, it was not until late evening that we were able to continue undisturbed.

I had not fully appreciated the possibility of non-slip decks until I found that Howells' and Hasler's were like sandpaper; you could not slip if you tried. This had been achieved by sprinkling silver sand over an ordinary undercoat while it was still wet and, after it had dried, brushing off the surplus sand and overpainting with a top coat. We scoured Plymouth day in and day out to find some silver sand.

Eventually Cicely, one of my most hard-worked friends, discovered some, not in a paint shop, but in the market, where it was being sold as roughage for canaries! After the reporters had gone she and my son, Barry, spent the evenings, whenever it was not raining, painting and sanding the decks of *Cardinal Vertue*.

There was much discussion among us about which route we would take. The northern one is shorter but runs through the iceberg zone and the winds are contrary. The southern route with the steady favourable trade winds and the Gulf Stream is much longer. We were all very frank about our plans except Francis Chichester, and Francis was being very cagey. We did not know which way he was going until one day he went shopping with Val Howells and bought a great length of fishing net which he said was to drape round the stanchions of his ship in order to catch any flying fish that skimmed aboard. Flying fish frequent the warm southern waters, so this finally convinced us that he was going to take the northern route!

The reporters, photographers and radio and television people who kept coming to see us were very long suffering. One, who was asking me questions, seemed so interested that I became carried away. Holding forth about the tactics of the race, I forgot he was not a sailor. I was trying to explain how a growth of weed on a ship's hull would slow her down and how this would occur more quickly in warm waters than in cold.

"So not only is the northern route the shortest, and not only do you have a favourable current for the last twelve hundred miles, but what becomes most important of all after a month at sea, is the state of the bottom. You see the cold water of the Labrador current is good for it."

He looked startled, and then with a great effort rallied manfully:

"Oh yes—ah—hygiene—so important of course."

Every day now I would climb 34 feet to the top of the mast to become accustomed to the effort and balance involved in doing so, just in case this proved necessary at sea. At first it was difficult. I would cling on so tightly out of sheer fright that I would have no energy left for climbing; but after a time the rhythm of my movements became more automatic until I could scramble quickly up, right to the mast-head, without very much trouble.

The day before we were due to start Jean Lacombe arrived from France. His little plywood *Cap Horn* had bounced up and down in a Channel gale until Jean, who is short, stocky and very, very tough, sailed in exhausted. That night as we sat in a restaurant somebody rushed over towards me.

"The Frenchman has fainted, come quickly."

Jean had not fainted, he was lying with his head on the table, not unconscious but simply fast asleep. He could not get his boat ready in time to set off with the rest of us, so he planned to leave about five days later.

Meanwhile, we heard that Piver's trimaran *Nimble* had reached the Azores from America in three weeks. This was good going, the only snag being that the Azores lie about twelve hundred miles south of England, so it was doubtful whether he could reach Plymouth within the two weeks from the official start allowed by the rules for latecomers. Why did he head so far south? This remained a source of endless speculation, not answered until we met some of the trimaran's crew later in New York. Calms and fogs had delayed their progress for a few days. Then after clearing Nantucket the first north-west gale had struck. Gales and strong winds from the north and north-west had continued for ten days. They were forced to run before or partly across the seas and though *Nimble* surfed across the face of the combers at 15 knots they were carried several hundred miles south of their course. The Azores lay eight hundred miles ahead; America over a thousand miles astern. They made the best of the situation and made their landfall at the Azores. After provisioning, they continued to Plymouth, running before favourable winds. They returned by air after leaving their craft at Plymouth.

A welcome visitor during our preparations was John Pflieger, Commodore of the Slocum Society, but there was hardly time to speak to him in all the bustle. I am afraid I tried my friends sorely. One, a German student, hitch-hiked down from London twice to help with the preparations, yet I do not think I ever found the time to thank him. Another practically made me a radio set. An echo-sounder had been lent to me. Michael Chandler had spent his whole holiday working aboard. There was a sextant borrowed from Tom Moncrief, who teaches navigation at Lerwick in the Shetland Islands. My own yacht club, the Royal Burnham, had noticed my habit of running aground on every convenient sandbank and had sent me some charts. As I had removed the propeller before leaving Burnham to allow the use of the engine for charging the battery during the race, *Cardinal Vertue*, relying on sails alone, had been "on the putty" more often than usual.

Humphrey Barton came and looked over my rigging for me. In 1950 he, and Kevin O'Riordan, sailed *Vertue XXXV* (*Cardinal Vertue* is Vertue XIX) from Falmouth to New York in forty-seven days, encountering a hurricane in which the gallant little ship, lying to a sea anchor streamed from her starboard sheet-winch, was picked up bodily by a sea and thrown down on her port cabin top. The wood split, the glass disintegrated and water poured in. The two men are the only ones I know of who owe their lives to dyspepsia. For Humphrey Barton is highly-strung and thin; thin enough to wriggle through the shattered window to reach the pump in the cockpit. Their voyage was historic in that it showed how a small, modern yacht could sail across the Atlantic in face of the prevailing westerlies. If this was possible on the intermediate route passing near the Azores, which Barton and O'Riordan had taken, then the shorter northern route must be practicable, too.

Barry, my eleven-year-old son, was everywhere. He was fascinated above all by Hasler's boat, with its ingenious Chinese junk rig. As soon as we reached Plymouth he was aboard, full of questions and more questions. I thought:

"Here at last I have my secret weapon against Hasler."

But I had underestimated him. Before five minutes had passed there was an understanding between them. Barry had been rationed to fifty questions to start with, plus five every subsequent hour. "Blondie" kindly but firmly kept him to this agreement.

Barry was incensed to see a newspaper report in which his father was described as a bachelor.

"And what about me?" he asked indignantly.

I tried to explain.

"Well I was married, but I'm married no longer, so that really does count as a bachelor, doesn't it."

He still looked rather doubtful.

"Anyway, don't keep calling me 'Venerable Ancestor'," I snapped peevishly.

Barry was really brooding over the unfair single-handed rule that had stopped him accompanying me.

"But we sailed to Holland together last autumn and we'll sail up to the Norwegian fjords next summer," I said, trying to comfort him.

"Anyway you often complain that I am bad tempered and swear at you at sea."

"The Norwegian Sea isn't the same as the Atlantic," said Barry, still not mollified.

I had expected a friend to drive my daughter, Anna, down, but she had not arrived and one evening after I had turned in tired out by interviews, a man's voice hailed from the quayside.

"Is Doctor Lewis aboard there?"

I sleepily opened the hatch and peered up at two dim figures. Then with considerable presence of mind attained by years of medical practice, I replied:

"I'm sorry but you've just missed him, he sank half an hour ago."

I stepped down and firmly closed the hatch; then was stopped by a patient if somewhat exasperated feminine voice.

"Daddy, it's me."

The night before the start racing flags were broken out from our starboard cross-trees to flap and crackle in a gusty south-west wind. From Howells' *Eira* flew the Red Dragon, the standard of Wales. Francis Chichester sported a Gipsy Moth. Hasler's *Jester* remained uncompromisingly bare. *Cardinal Vertue's* standard, embroidered by Cicely with a kiwi and its large egg, went aloft on a rope and wire halyard. Tomorrow the flags would be at mastheads in place of our club burgees, remaining aloft until we reached New York—or gave up.

Hasler and I were working on board our boats until nearly three that morning. At seven we were picked up by the launches which towed us outside the dock into a small naval harbour, where we attempted to scrub the oil and grease off the hulls.

For weeks we had had fine easterlies, but now it was blowing hard, overcast, dismal westerly weather, with rain squalls scudding across the bay. The forecast was for a south-west headwind of force 7, nearly gale strength. I felt forlorn and miserable. How could the others be so calm? Later, I learnt that each had had the same feeling.

Anna turned up again in time to be press-ganged into cooking me some breakfast. We all felt very tense as I brusquely said goodbye to the children.

Then we were towed outside the little harbour. As we hoisted sail, suddenly everything was transformed. Sailing close past me, Val Howells called out:

"It's all right now, David, isn't it?"

"Yes," I replied, and I meant it.

We were cruising up and down behind the starting-line, sizing up the course down the Sound, watching the signal flags and waiting for the starting-gun, hardly aware of the launches and yachts that rolled and pitched on every side. I saw a burst of flashes from an Aldis lamp at the naval dockyard. It seemed to go on and on, then was answered briefly by a naval launch that swung round, put on speed and pounded towards us. Her decks were crowded with guests. I noticed the Royal Western Yacht Club Commodore and his wife, and Chris Brasher from *The Observer* wearing a grin from ear to ear. As they came near an amused naval officer called through a loud hailer.

"A telegram for you just been flashed across to us—

'*K. M. sends you her love*'."

There were ribald cheers from the launch. I grinned spontaneously. Of all the women I had known in my pleasant "bachelor" life "K. M." was the most poised, the most cautious and the most discreet. It must have cost her great heart-searching before she had sent me a message at all, and here was her indiscretion being broadcast across Plymouth Sound!

Perhaps I remember this incident because my sense of humour was soon to become the first casualty of the race.

Now we began jockeying for position. The five-minute gun sounded and, sheeting our sails hard in, we lay over to the fresh breeze, racing for the line as a puff of smoke from the starting gun drifted over the water, and the starting flag fluttered down from the flagstaff below Plymouth Hoe. Hasler shot away, his hull clearing the starboard-hand buoy by no more than a few inches. After him came the rest of us, out into the Sound, hard on the wind. A quick tack to clear the breakwater, then our ships were plunging as they met the swell of the open sea. Three thousand miles to go now and the land soon began to drop astern.

We had started at ten o'clock in the morning. At eleven-thirty, during a lull, I hoisted the big headsail, the genoa, and now *Cardinal Vertue*, heeling over with water streaming over the lee deck, threshed seawards. The others had gained on me while I was shifting sails, with Chichester well ahead; but soon I passed Hasler and was rapidly over-hauling Howells.

We left the Eddystone Lighthouse, set on its jagged shark-tooth rocks, to starboard. Pressed down by the increasing wind *Cardinal Vertue* was going fast, but, over-canvased, she pounded so hard into the steep head seas that everything down below, even the heavy spare

Calor gas cylinders which had been well lashed down, shook and jumped. Yet she was sailing really well, and Howells' *Eira* was not far ahead. Hasler lay astern but to windward.

At 1.30 p.m., without warning, my mast snapped cleanly 12 feet above the deck, and the upper 22 feet crashed over the port quarter into the sea beside me. I clutched the tiller for several seconds unable to believe that this wallowing hulk, strewn with tangled wreckage, was my beautiful ship which seconds before had danced proudly with the ocean's winds and had seemed so alive. If only she would sink quickly taking me with her!

Then, still shocked, I was acting automatically. The mast had to be brought up on deck before it pounded a hole in the ship's side and tore the sails to pieces. Sobbing with exertion, and with hands cut and bleeding, I tore away the lightning conductor which was attached to the mast by small sharp tacks, until I could slide the broken end far enough along the deck to reach its top and unshackle the mainsail. Next, I slid the upper half of the sail down its track on to the deck and hauled the mast right aboard, until it projected across the pulpit forward, and over the port quarter astern. Then I lashed it down and pulled the sail and the festoons of rigging aboard.

While I was doing this, wading thigh deep in tangled wires and ropes, I was wondering whether the rest of the mast was about to go, in which case I would be carried down, inextricably tangled in a web of rigging, into the tossing sea on which my dismasted wreck was rolling so wildly.

Now I had time to look at the damage. The sail seemed all right, the mast also intact and well stayed up to the broken cross-trees. It had broken cleanly. There must have been a fault somewhere, but exactly where remained to be seen later.

It was clear that there was only one possible thing to be done. This was to set up some sort of jury rig with which to sail back to Plymouth, then to have the mast repaired as quickly as possible so that I could carry on with the race.

I rummaged below for No. 3 staysail, climbed up the wildly gyrating mast to the cross-trees, and clinging on with great difficulty, slipped a block over them and threaded a halyard through it. With this small staysail hoisted the ship had steerage way. So at 1.50 p.m. I was able to turn her nose towards the distant smudge of land.

Hasler now came up with me. He had been sailing slower but further to windward than the rest of us. He circled round, his unconventional rig giving him perfect control in trimming his sheets instantly and in reducing his sail area at will.

"David, can I go and get help?" he cried. "If I sail to the Eddystone they will send for a tow."

"I don't want a tow," I replied. "It's all O.K. I'm sailing back to Plymouth to get this damned mast fixed, then I will see you in New York."

Blondie seemed very doubtful and most reluctant to leave me.

"It *is* all right," I called again. "Look, she is under control already, I'm heading back."

So with a final wave Blondie set out on course again and *Jester* rapidly faded into the grey murk to windward.

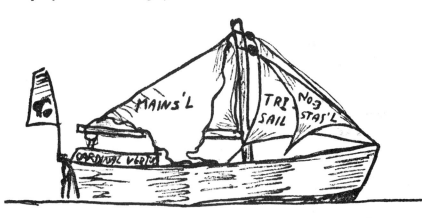

Only twenty minutes had passed between the mast going over the side and the ship again being under way and heading for Plymouth. I climbed the mast once more and rigged another block on which I hoisted the trisail to act as a second headsail. With these two headsails and the lower half of the mainsail, she began to close the dim Devon hills fourteen miles away, moving at about two knots and steering with the wind vane self-steering gear. There was time to drink several mugs of water and eat a bar of fudge and to write in the log:

"Now for Plymouth, a quick repair and on with the race."

I lashed my racing flag with its broken shaft to the starboard rigging as a sign that *Cardinal Vertue* was still racing. It was heartening to see the gallant kiwi aloft again. By 3 p.m. I was abreast of the Eddystone and making good progress. Nevertheless, it was hard to return.

This adventure had started the wrong way round. There had been publicity and praise for what we were *going to* do before we had done anything at all. During the past week we had been speaking on radio and television and giving interviews to newspapers. We had been admired as the clever people who were about to sail the Atlantic; now here was I, after a tremendous send off, returning the same day in a supreme anti-climax. I did not feel at all good about it and swore that I would move the very heavens to have that mast mended quickly.

For the moment there was nothing to be done but to make coffee. *Cardinal Vertue* continued to steer herself in towards the land that still lay shrouded in squalls and low cloud. Two and a half knots now! Some yachts racing nearby passed close, but none seemed to notice anything unusual.

This annoyed me; surely they did not think people went sailing on purpose with such stumpy masts as I had now? It seemed an age until at 7.35 p.m. I passed the outer breakwater and entered Plymouth harbour.

Now I urgently needed a tow to bring me right in. Off Drake's Island a pilot boat threw me a line and brought me into Millbay Docks. I saw we were about to bring up alongside a yacht that was moored there. Suddenly I saw its name, *Cohoe III.*

"Oh no!" I thought, "anywhere but here!"

For Adlard Coles the owner, had sailed his first *Cohoe* from Bermuda to the U.S.A., weathering the hurricane in which *Vertue XXXV* was almost lost, and had then raced back to Bermuda and gone on to win the Bermuda to England race of 1950. His book *North Atlantic* is a classic. Rather than meet a man like this, I felt I would sooner crawl into a quiet hole somewhere to hide. But Adlard and his wife helped me make fast, looked after me, fed me, and protected me from too many interruptions.

As soon as I had touched land I had made frantic telephone calls desperately seeking someone to mend the mast that very night. So one later interruption was very welcome. Mr. Mashford, head of a famous yard at Cremyll, across the River Tamar, came aboard in a flapping raincoat, carefully looked over the damage, and then said in his deliberate, West Country way:

"You will be able to leave by, say, Monday midday."

It was then Saturday night, and to be able to sail on Monday was far better than I had dared to hope for. Yet somehow, this seemingly casual statement inspired more confidence than a thousand flowery promises. Life became worth living again.

316

"I'll pick her up with a towing launch at six o'clock in the morning," he said, and then departed.

Now that I could relax, I realized just how desperately tired I was. But before I climbed sleepily back to my own ship Adlard Coles said something which further lightened my gloom.

"If you ever want to write a book about this race," he said, "come to me for a bit of advice about it and perhaps some help in publishing it."

How could anybody still have such confidence in me after what had happened? Those encouraging words supported me greatly in the days that lay ahead.

I did not wake next morning when Mashford's launch took *Cardinal Vertue* in tow. I was still asleep as we crossed the Tamar, which forms the Devon-Cornwall border, and docked on the other side at Cremyll. When I sleepily came on deck, still early on this Sunday morning, I found that half the employees, and most of the Mashford family, too, had turned out, quietly and purposefully, as if it were the most natural thing in the world and nothing special at all. Within a quarter of an hour the mast was out of *Cardinal Vertue*, the sails were ashore to be checked over and dried ready for repair. The rigging and fittings were being stripped off the mast and the work was well under way.

Soon telegrams of commiseration, greetings and good cheer came flooding in. Friends like Bill Luard, Ritchie Seymour, and people from the Royal Western Yacht Club came over from Plymouth to help.

My daughter, Anna, arrived. It was a delight and comfort to have her there. Barry had already left for London, driving with friends. They opened the Sunday paper that morning.

"My God, David has had an accident!" Barry had turned dead white and snatched the paper, but after a few moments he handed it back, and regaining the unconcern proper to a schoolboy of eleven, remarked casually:

"Oh, it's only his mast, he broke one last year, he is always breaking them."

George Armitage, owner of *Temptress*, the famous ship in which Edward Allcard made several Atlantic passages, took me off to breakfast aboard this wonderful old yawl. I felt much better afterwards and set to work to make the ship ready for sea again.

Meanwhile, word came that Hasler had been sighted closing the Lizard, and had rounded it, in the teeth of a contrary wind of force 7 and, he told me later, in spite of seasickness. There had been no news

317

of the others, but I learnt later that Chichester was by then really tearing along well out towards the western approaches of the Channel. His last sight of the others had been of Howells passing him while he was rolling down a reef, so for the rest of the voyage he was haunted by visions of the "bearded Viking".

But Howells soon met trouble. His 100-lb. battery was lashed firmly in the forecastle. Water, trickling through the forehatch as *Eira* pounded into head seas, had caused the lashings to shrink, so that they had torn away the whole side of the battery. Corrosive acid came pouring out over his fresh vegetables, over clothes, over everything. The battery had to be thrown overboard, leaving Val without lights as the darkness descended on his first stormy night at sea.

Jean Lacombe, unhurried as ever, came to see me. In 1956 he had crossed the Atlantic alone in the 18-foot *Hippocampe* from Toulon to Puerto Rico, and thence to New York. Although the yacht which he was sailing this time was 21 feet long, it was much lighter; so light that it would dance to every ripple, and it was very small. Yet how calm he was compared with me, who was all a flurry of nerves and impatience! He expressed surprise that I was hoping to be away as soon as Monday.

"Me, I will leave Thursday," he said, phlegmatic as ever, unaffected by the excitement and tenseness of it all. And leave on Thursday he did, to face in some ways the greatest ordeal.

2

TO THE WEST—OVER SEA

THIS one day at Cremyll, under the shadow of Mount Edgcumbe, busy as it was, gave me breathing space to become aware of that green rolling Devon-Cornwall border country, to which I was saying good-bye.

A few days earlier, Lord Morley, Vice-Commodore of the Royal Western Yacht Club, had entertained us in his lovely home at Saltram. He had toasted us.

"Four gallant gentlemen of England, adventuring forth westward in your little ships in the spirit of those who set out from the West Country in other times."

Perhaps his words in such a setting had conjured up an evocation of an imaginary Elizabethan England, of some idealized never-never land. Nevertheless, I felt that I was saying goodbye to something of England which was real and part of me, as I had been born here, across the river in Plymouth.

However, my earliest memories are of New Zealand, where I was taken as a baby. It was my mother's country and to it I owe the shaping of my childhood and young manhood. By a strange twist in the skein of kinship, my very first sea adventure had been with my cousin Val Edgcumbe, younger brother to the heir of the Mount Edgcumbe estate, which backed the little port where I now lay.

I can still vividly recall sitting on the bottom boards of a dinghy in the hot sunshine, watching with awe while an almost grown up Val set sail and steered us confidently out to sea. Stark-etched, too, in memory is the look on my father's face after he had rescued us. Years later I mentioned the incident to my mother.

"I suppose Val was about eighteen?" I asked.

She looked at me quizzically.

"Well not quite, you were five and he was eleven."

With some amusement I now remembered a letter from Val written from New Zealand when he heard that I was entering the Transatlantic Race. After a few remarks about the family he continued, obviously following a train of thought inspired by the enterprise on which I was to embark.

"Three New Zealanders were wrecked off Australia last week and lost their craft, and a few months back quite a big yacht, which had set off on a world cruise was caught in a gale off North Cape. Dismasted, she was subsequently rolled over twice in heavy seas, but survived and was taken in tow by a Japanese ship and brought into Auckland. I have had some good fishing lately. . . . I can see by the news that you are having terrible gales in Europe and many ships have been lost with all hands, including a lifeboat on the English coast. The *Holm Glen* was lost with all hands off Timeru last month. No one knows the cause of the disaster. She was 15 per cent. above strength for A1 classification at Lloyds. A new ship and the weather was not particularly bad. Would you please write from New York and let us know how the Race went. We should be most interested to hear of your experiences."

I thought wryly that if my experiences were those he obviously expected, the chances of my arriving in New York at all were remote!

Here in this gentle corner of England I looked back on yet another farewell; a farewell to my father's land, and to the rugged Welsh mountains among which he had spent many happy hours.

During the winter I had twice sought the high hills. Once it was to clamber along airy Grib Goch, the Red Ridge of Snowdon which was thickly covered in new snow at the time and almost Alpine in character. I had been unsteady, unused to the height, for I had not climbed for a long time; but I had decided that my will-power needed toning up. Life in a big city provides little opportunity to test the nervous system's ability to drive us forward against physical fear. It seemed to me that practice in self-control was needed, and would pay dividends in the months to come.

On the second occasion we crossed over Tryfan and Glyder Fawr. When we were descending the Devil's Kitchen—of which my father had often spoken—a great gash in the mountain-side now packed with snow—I untied from the rope, left the others, and kicked steps up into a black cleft laced with monstrous fluted icicles. There I stood alone for a little while looking down the Nantffrancon valley past Bangor, where my father had lived, to the silver gleam of the Menai Straits and the smudge of the Isle of Anglesey beyond. I felt in communion with my father and seemed to be imbued with something of the spirit of this ancient land, and to be granted strength from those wild crags which he had loved.

Back in the valley, I found that a tall, slim girl was staying at the same cottage as my party. Her name, Fiona, held some of the haunting

Celtic sadness of the misty Western Isles. She had intriguing, un-fathomable eyes which quite failed to notice that I even existed. I was still more impressed when she and her girl friend, after a hard day on the mountains in heavy snow, set off gaily to meet friends at Pen-y-Gwryd, six miles away. Six miles! and I was aching in every muscle and could hardly move! Undoubtedly this was a girl who was not meant for me.

In spite of the obvious commonsense of this view, I sought her out back in London and, with other friends, she helped me paint my boat and sailed as one of the crew from Burnham-on-Crouch to Portsmouth on the first lap of the voyage to Plymouth. She learned how to steer and handle a ship and to climb the mast. And after recovering from sea sickness, she played her guitar. I was horrified to find that the stability of my smug, well-organized if rather complex, bachelor existence was beginning to be undermined by a new and disturbing emotion. Yet Fiona's feelings towards me remained entirely elusive.

All that Sunday at Cremyll the Mashfords went ahead with the mast. After stripping it of its metal fittings they sawed off the broken ends and bevelled each stump for about 5 feet. A new middle piece, made up of several planks, was planed to fit exactly, and that evening this rectangular middle section was clamped and glued into position between the halves of the old mast. Was the weather warm enough for the glue to set? This was now the vital question.

In the afternoon I restowed my spare Calor gas cylinders, which had started to bounce about on the cabin sole as the ship pitched. I screwed some eyebolts into the side of the bunks and lashed the cylinders down to them. This seemed to cure the trouble; but not for good, because some five thousand sea miles ahead I was to meet conditions that caused these eyebolts and lashings to prove totally inadequate.

On the morning of Monday, June 13th, I had to force myself to eat in the rush and excitement of the final preparations for departure. The new section, which had been scarphed into the mast, was now planed until round, then varnished, until the joint could hardly be seen. The mast, old sections and new, were held together by glue alone. The fittings were screwed and bolted on and new cross-trees, or spreaders, were made. It was the lower starboard cross-tree which had caused the accident. It had swivelled and snapped, leaving the mast without a major support to windward, so that it had immediately broken just above the spreader socket.

The wire and rope halyards that hoisted the sails had all been labelled before removal. In spite of this, there appeared to be hopeless confusion, for there were halyards to hoist the mainsail, the staysail and the genoa; one to raise the burgee or the racing flag, another for the spinnaker; and one for each of the spinnaker booms. Now they looked like a ball of demented knitting.

The tide was falling fast, too. Soon the ship would take the ground and then remain fixed for another twelve hours. And just as the keel was scraping the bottom, with workmen still tightening the last of the rigging screws, and while I hurriedly cleared the mainsail ready for hoisting, got into my P.V.C. smock and trousers and pulled on my rubber boots, Mashford's launch finally pulled us clear.

It was then a few minutes before noon G.M.T. on Monday the 13th.

"Monday by noon" Mr. Mashford had said she would be ready—and ready she was. At no time had he or his men indicated that there was anything unusual in their starting work at six o'clock on a Sunday morning or going on until midnight, and then setting-to at daybreak the next day. To talk to them you would have thought that this was all in a day's work. To meet these men had been a privilege. I not only owe them a debt I can never repay, but I learnt from them a new humility.

But now there was only room for one thought—to make sail again. A crowd of workmen were clustered on the pier head. A newspaper correspondent was standing among them. As the keel scraped free, while I was shipping the tiller and casting off lashings from the sails in much hurry and confusion, he called out with timing only surpassed by his tact:

"My readers would like to hear your last words, Doctor." Stung by the phrase, I shouted back furiously:

"I'm going to get to New York before those rascals drink all the beer and make love to all the women!"

A shocked hush had settled over the water, but the sails were up now and sheeted in. How good it was to feel the weight of the squalls in the canvas as *Cardinal Vertue* heeled over and raced before them through the smooth water down the Tamar and slipped silently out behind Drake's Island to head down Plymouth Sound towards the outer breakwater. Soon she felt the lift and scend of the living ocean out there beyond the headlands, and she became fully alive once more.

I had been encouraged so often since I had turned back ignominiously, that I thought that nothing more could happen to bolster my morale. I had done nothing to deserve the first send-off, but now I was getting another. Motoring alongside was a launch full of reporters, photographers and friends; the club commodore sailed past in his yacht; ferries, fishing boats and pleasure craft circled around, their crews waving and blowing their whistles in encouragement. How cheering it all was!

The day was overcast, with a strong wind blowing from the south-west, so that as I cleared the breakwater, *Cardinal Vertue* began to lay well over, pounding into the heavy seas.

Outside in Cawsand Bay a naval frigate lay at anchor; trim and seemingly disdainful. Suddenly, in a burst of colour, a string of flags broke from her yardarm. She was signalling me "Good luck". I waved back, deeply moved by their faith in a man who had none in himself at that moment, and carried on with a lighter heart adjusting the self-steering gear, tidying up the halyards on deck and putting things away down below.

Beyond the Eddystone the wind increased until I had to reef the mainsail. In *Cardinal Vertue* this is done by, first, wedging yourself on the steeply sloping deck by the mast, dressed in oilskins and rubber boots against the volleying spray. You slacken off the main halyard and rotate the boom with the reefing handle until the desired amount of sail is rolled around it. Then you slither back to the cockpit to slacken off the mainsheet so that the sail spills wind and you push the helm down to head the yacht up into the wind. Then back you go to the mast again and to set up the mainsail halyard hard. Now you can return to the cockpit and set the ship back on course. This takes seven minutes when all goes well; it has needed twenty minutes and up to nearly an hour on other occasions.

Soon the wind had risen to thirty miles an hour, the top of force 6, and was whining through the rigging. I rolled down another 4 feet of the mainsail, and this time I reefed the staysail, too.

The method of assessing the strength of the wind as different forces was introduced by Admiral Beaufort and is known as the Beaufort Scale. Forces 3 and 4 are good sailing breezes for the average yacht. Force 7 was originally described as "a wind in which a Ship of the Line could sail full-and-bye under all plain sail with the gun ports open, or a wind such as to cause a 30-foot fishing smack to heave to". Force 8 and above are gales.

When I streamed the patent log, which measures the distance a ship covers by means of a spinning rotator towed astern, the distant outline of the Eddystone lighthouse and the hills of England were just dipping below the swells and becoming invisible in the gathering dusk astern. I hoped fervently that this was the last that I should see of the land, at any rate for a long time.

I was still worried about the mast. I trembled with every creak of the timbers, as they strained to the tug of the rigging and the stress of the mast in the mast-step. I was shaking, sick with nerves and unable to eat. I noted wryly in the log-book that afternoon—

"It was a hero's send-off this morning, and now I lie in my bunk shivering with fear."

But the mast held, the ship tramped on her way south-west through the darkness and soon the moon could be glimpsed between ragged clouds, while the sea continued to get up, until sheets of spray rattled

against the sails and the cabin top, and breaking wave-crests thumped against the hull.

Once, through a momentary break in the clouds, like some visitor from a far-off time, I saw a barquentine under reduced canvas running eastward up Channel. Then the clouds came down again and she was hidden.

Midnight on June 14th found me anxiously going round the decks, checking over the halyards and the gear, and keeping a worried eye on the mast. I would try to rest, but soon worry would drive me on deck to inspect the mast and rigging yet again, before going below to lie down. I was too tense and excited to eat anything except some sweets and biscuits and to drink a little water, and later make a cup of coffee. I slept hardly at all that night.

At six o'clock next morning I was clearing seaweed from the deck, unrolling the mainsail and unreefing the staysail as the wind began to fall light, and *Cardinal Vertue*, still on the starboard tack, crept forward ever more slowly.

Just before midday I took a meridian altitude of the sun on the sextant. I had to look up the method in my text-book, because I had never tried it before. In clear weather this is an easy way to find the latitude. You do not need the exact time. A little before noon, you take readings of the sun's altitude at short intervals, until it no longer rises but seems to hang stationary for some minutes and then begins to sink, so that the altitude readings no longer increase but become less. The highest figure obtained is used, and a simple calculation gives the latitude of the ship.

That afternoon the wind was becoming lighter and lighter. Several ships and some fishing boats passed in the distance. I washed and opened up all the hatches to air the ship. Gradually it fell calm, and as the afternoon wore on, the sails, now uncontrolled by the force of the wind, began to slat violently as the ship rolled in the heavy swell.

This was the first of the many frustrating calms I was to meet. For hours, no matter how tight the boom was pulled in by the sheet, there would be the shrill squeak of the blocks as the boom slammed over a fraction of an inch, and the swish, swish of the sail as it was thrown first to one side then to the other. These are the most irritating sounds that a seaman ever has to hear.

I started to make a recording on the tape-recorder I had been lent, describing the start, the repairs and second start, and when I played it back months later I could hear the frightened, tremulous note in my voice. That afternoon I had my first cooked meal at sea—eggs and bacon, bread and butter and coffee. I concluded the recording with the words:

"The sun has just sunk into the Western Ocean. The sky foretells plenty of wind."

June 15th. By midnight the sails began to stir again. It was a calm clear night. So good was the visibility that I could see the loom of the lights on Ushant and Ile Vierge off the French coast, and when looking astern, could count the beams from the Lizard. The Lizard and Ushant are ninety miles apart. It was not so pleasant, when I took a bearing on these lights, to find that I had been swept well back by the tide while I had been becalmed in the afternoon. Slowly the wind increased that night and during the next day. Again I had to reef and to keep adjusting the self-steering gear to cope with the variable winds.

As yet I had not found my sea legs. I was falling about heavily each time the ship lurched and I tried to move, and now I was cut and bruised all over. Towards evening several seas burst across the deck soaking me through gaps in my oilskins. As *Cardinal Vertue* pitched and rolled, I looked up to see a Blue Star steamer going past, as steady as if she were sailing over a lake. Why does one ever go to sea in small boats, I wondered? Gradually in the evening the mist closed down becoming thicker and thicker. The position line I had obtained that afternoon was to be the last for four days.

Each of the five competitors in the race had designed a self-steering gear, or automatic helmsman, to keep his yacht on a constant course in relation to the wind.

Each of us had our own ideas and we had the experience of others to guide us. Michael Henderson had tried vane-steering on several light-displacement craft in the Solent and Channel; Lewis King had made one for his *Jeanne Matilde* to use on his seventeen thousand miles voyage from Singapore to England. It had worked quite well until an inquisitive steamer passed too close and knocked it into the South Atlantic. Ian Major's *Buttercup* used a most successful vane on his Atlantic crossing, and Valentine Howells had made one for a voyage to Spain the summer before our race.

However, none of these was the originator of the method. Three months before the race I had been invited to study at the "source".

"Is that *the* Doctor Lewis, the famous physician?" a voice on the telephone had asked.

"Oh, go away, Francis. I'm busy," I had replied peevishly.

"David, come with me to the Round Pond, Kensington, on Sunday to see how to make a self-steering gear properly! Those model yacht chaps really know how to sail. I go there each Sunday to get hints."

Francis Chichester was right, of course; the model makers first thought of this idea.

My own vane was of the trim tab or servo rudder type and its design and working principle are described in Appendix Two. Its design owes much to several people, especially Val Howells, but its success I maintain, is largely attributable to its true personality—the prim Kiwi painted upon it and watching over it!

Exchanging information about such potentially race-winning gadgets was typical of the spirit of the competitors in this unique race. On Val's good advice I discarded my first ideas on a steering device. Blondie sent round a letter in March:

"I will offer any help I can with vane gears, and *if* you are using a

1. A pre-race trial of *Cardinal Vertue*'s self-steering gear.

2. Looking down on *Cardinal Vertue*'s reinforced doghouse
and self-draining cockpit.

trim tab system, and *if* you are getting oversteering effects, I should be happy to let you study *Jester's* linkage. . . ."

For though we were racing against each other, we were also knit in fellowship in face of our common antagonist, the Western Ocean.

June 16th. Out of the shimmering fog, long slow rollers came from the south-west, like moving downs and pastures of the sea. They had travelled unhindered three thousand miles from America. I washed and shaved; usually I managed to shave every second or third day. After every meal I tried to wash up at once, having long ago discovered that if one leaves so much as a greasy knife, it will butter the whole cabin in an instant. Soon I was almost becalmed and for the first time for forty-four hours I was able to take off my P.V.C. smock, waterproof trousers, safety-belt and rubber boots.

I got out the tape-recorder on which Fiona had recorded some songs, both her own and others from gramophone records. Everything aboard reminded me of my friends. The tape-recorder belonged to Garth and Leslie Harvey. A bundle of burgees had been given by Arnold Greenwood of The Little Ship Club, Cecily's kiwi flag flew at the masthead; there was Ken's echo-sounder, Herbert's radio and Wilfred's compass—or rather Garth's compass that Wilfred had altered for me. Everywhere I looked there were signs of people's kindness: notes on tins and lists of food which Cecily had prepared. I was oppressed by the knowledge that I had not even thanked one of them. I had been so irritable on the morning of the 11th and now I wrote in my log-book that I had better realize I would have no friends at all on my return, and that I did not deserve any either!

During the night the fog became very thick and damp and the first dismal hoots of ships' foghorns became audible. The sounds came closer, until I had to put on my heavy clothing and safety-belt again and clamber out into the cockpit to blow hopefully on a tiny hooter until the invisible ship had passed. Everything was dripping in the heavy banks of fog. At intervals all through the night I listened and peered anxiously for passing ships. I was using the electric navigation lights at this stage of the voyage and also relying on any big ship's radar to pick up my 14-foot metal spinnaker pole which hung down the mast. I had a rather frail radar reflector as well, but it seemed wise to conserve this until later for the Grand Banks of Newfoundland, usually the foggiest sea area in the world.

June 17th. There was no possibility of getting a sight of the sun during these days, but with the radio direction-finder I was able to obtain the bearing of a station at Ploneis in the North of France and another of Mizzen Head in the West of Ireland. I found that I was seventy miles south and a little west of the Fastnet Rock, off Ireland, with about thirty-five miles to go until I was clear of the west of Ireland altogether and out in the open Atlantic. During the night I had crossed the main shipping lanes, so the traffic was now to my port side.

Visibility was a little better in the afternoon so I slept for two hours without my P.V.C. suit and trousers. I decided, however, that for the whole voyage I would wear my safety-belt before laying down to sleep, in case I was suddenly awakened to deal with some emergency on deck. For this was the time when reflexes would be sluggish. It would be no use regretting the one false step during that agonizing last swim! To slip over the side of a yacht steering itself is equivalent to stepping out of an aircraft without a parachute. Any carelessness about this would be inexcusable.

I was awakened that afternoon by the sails slatting violently. The ship had gybed in a wind too light to work the vane, was caught aback, and was now "calling for help". To get her on course again in these circumstances was one of the few things a self-steering vane could not do by itself. *Cardinal Vertue* and her wind vane were both so efficient that I felt less redundant now that I had something to do. As I brought the ship on course I looked alongside to see a shark about $3\frac{1}{2}$ feet long swimming quite near.

Perhaps I should have tested his behaviour with the shark repellent we had been given, but he looked such a friendly little fellow and I was afraid it would work. I did not want him to go away for he made me feel that now we were really at sea, like the people who sail exotic oceans such as the South Pacific. To my disappointment, after circling the ship once or twice, he swam away to the westward.

At the end of a short calm the wind came in from astern so that for the first time I was able to lay the correct course.

It was still foggy, still no sight of the sun, but as the ship ran on, my mood began to lighten and as I looked back out of the cabin at the kiwi painted on the self-steering vane, I felt that he, too, was developing something of a happier personality.

A kiwi is a particularly appropriate mascot for a ship called *Cardinal Vertue*. Not only is he our New Zealand national bird but he has no wings and does not indulge in stupid pastimes, like floating on the sea, or flying, or anything else so silly. Moreover, the male bird has so many domestic virtues; he sits on the huge egg to incubate it; then he feeds and takes care of the young. An admirable creature!

At first he did not know quite what was happening. When the wind was rising and the clouds went scudding by, he used to peer anxiously aloft as if to say:

"Oh dear, whatever next!"—"And the egg, too! However did that get there?"

Now he had an air of smug efficiency! At least he was watching what was happening, and was steering the ship. He looked more confident, too, as if he had realized, at last, that kiwis *should* go to sea.

June 18th. We went on through thick fog through the night of the 17th–18th. By two o'clock in the morning the wind had veered a little so I decided to try out my twin headsails. In the damp mist and the dark, setting them was a slow, dismal job. The wet ropes took on a malicious life of their own, tangling themselves in coils. It took me fourteen minutes to undo one single topping-lift that had been too neatly coiled up by a friend in Plymouth! As I sat struggling with them in pitch darkness on the dripping deck, a foghorn began to blare away somewhere ahead.

Later during the morning of the 18th the wind dropped to a light breeze so that I had to steer. Then the wind backed and I had to change sail again. This time I was able to make a quicker change. For an hour I sat at the tiller composing doubtful ditties about my friends until, as the wind strengthened once more, I could go below and leave *Cardinal Vertue* to herself. Soon it fell a flat calm, the sea undulating in great rollers, a beautiful deep blue, as well it might be, for there were two miles of water under the keel.

But I had no eyes for the beauty of the blue sea nor for the tiny Portuguese men-of-war that seemed to appear by magic every time the wind dropped. Always in these calms a profound depression dominated me. Hour after hour the ship would wallow helplessly in the swell, rolling 20 degrees each way. There was a vicious brutality in the slap, slap, slap of the sails, something of the shock of a hand being slapped to and fro across a face, and on it would go, on and on.

Light airs can be even more trying than calms. With bare steerage way the ship begins to move, then promptly throws herself about. You have to gybe her around on to her course again. In a few moments she is aback once more. Then she is stationary. You are barely moving, yet you cannot leave the tiller. You get up another headsail; try to steer a course; five minutes later the wind peters out again. Sometimes after half an hour's work you come upon the same piece of paper which you threw over the side an hour ago, drifting ahead of you.

At the beginning of each calm I found it very difficult to get down to work. I had not the heart to do any of the jobs that needed doing. But until I started working, and this needed a great effort, it was impossible to overcome my depression.

So now to occupy my mind I plotted the last known position (June 8th) of the ice off Newfoundland. There seemed to be rather less of it than usual. However, the icebergs, which the spring thaw had released from the Polar pack, were being carried by the Labrador current over thousands of square miles of sea, and they could have drifted almost anywhere by the time I passed that way. It was certain that I would have to pass for days, probably weeks, through the area studded with bergs and shrouded with fog.

After this I washed handkerchiefs, shirts, and underclothes, then stripped down in the cockpit and washed myself all over. Next I examined the rigging for signs of chafe.

At 8 p.m. the wind came in from the starboard quarter and *Cardinal Vertue* began to run swiftly and silently, into the mist and gathering darkness, smoothly breasting the long swells. At least we were moving again, but what of the others, I thought dismally? Hundreds and hundreds of miles ahead and surely well out of this damned anti-cyclone with its calms.

Still, for the moment, hard work had proved an antidote to the calm weather depression and the main steamer lanes of the Western Approaches now lay astern. The nervous tension of the last few days was relaxing and suddenly the realization burst upon me that at last I was free from all the complex problems of those months of preparation ashore, and could give myself up to that peace and confidence that the great oceans and high mountains bestow upon those who go upon them.

The adventure, which had for so long been a distant dream, had now begun. Although I was to have cause to know fear, to experience thirst, frustration and bitter disappointment, the unsettled anxious misgivings of the first days at sea were never to return again. Though in every calm I was frantic with helpless irritation, the mood passed when the wind returned.

I slept soundly that night although J had to get up repeatedly between midnight and dawn to adjust the wind-vane to the variable easterlies. Twice while I was in the cockpit, ships' lights appeared in the distance, through momentary breaks in the fog.

On June 19th sunlight came filtering through a thin layer of mist to warm the ship as she rolled along. The air temperature was 68°F. Dressed modestly in just my safety-belt I took the opportunity to open up every locker and hatch to air the ship until the mist again closed down, damp and clammy in the late afternoon. I was happy and relaxed and enjoying the most wonderful holiday. I remembered with horror my irritability and pettiness.

By noon on June 20th I had been a whole week at sea. Now, at last, after four days the fog lifted. A sun sight gave a position line passing within two miles of the estimated position. But I had to wait another day for a further sight by which to fix my position exactly. The estimated position is the calculated position based on the patent log readings, the estimated set and drift of the current, leeway and the compass courses sailed.

Both sight and estimation put me about four hundred and thirty-six nautical miles from Plymouth. The best days' run (from noon to noon) had been only eighty-six miles and the worst twenty-seven. There had been four days and six hours of continuous fog and mist.

I had hoped to make much better time than this, but at least I was on the shortest route to New York, west of Southern Ireland now and passing about thirteen hundred miles north of the Canary Islands. It was not so much the contrary winds that had delayed me. I had expected them; indeed for the last twenty-six hours a following wind had enabled me to set the spinnaker, a huge balloon sail of nylon.

But on four days there had been nine unspeakable hours with no wind whatsoever; many more hours when there had been light airs and zephyrs. These were conditions against which I had no weapon. But in spite of this, the fogs and contrary winds, the week had brought peace of mind. Now, at last, the fear of another disaster to the mast, whenever it creaked, had partly receded, although it was to remain a worry for another month until the scarphed "stick" had proved itself in test by storm.

Before me lay one problem only—how best to handle my craft so that she made the fastest possible progress westward. I was happy now with a renewed sense of humour and a quickening feeling of adventure as we pushed further westward. Between the calms I felt at one with the sea and the sky and even with the grey mist. These were antagonists with which I could join battle using my brains and energy to the full,

331

as befits a man faced with worthy foes. For the vast elements are not hostile or unkind, they are too big and aloof for petty spite.

I was eating properly for the first time for a week; I was sleeping better. But each night I would dream; and the characters in the dreams were always the same—Blondie Hasler, Francis Chichester and Val Howells. Sometimes we were sailing or racing against each other; while on other occasions they were actors in some bizarre dream drama; but until I reached New York all my dreams centred on these three men, the sea, and often the race.

3

ORDEAL BY CALM

The winds have not read
the American Pilot Charts.
—H. G. HASLER

JUNE 21st. A night and morning of calm. Brief panic ensued when a sun sight gave a position line through County Cork, a result which conflicted with the heaving ocean all around! A check showed that I had logged ten minutes to ten o'clock as 10.50 a.m. instead of 9.50. Faith in my navigation was restored.

Whenever the weather was clear I took a morning sight once the sun was over 20 degrees above the horizon, another about midday and a third in the afternoon. The noon sight gave a position line approximating to latitude and the others to longitude. Alternatively, I would take only two sights at a sufficient interval of time to give position lines with a good cut.

I was at last mastering the knack of wedging my hips in the main hatchway so that my trunk remained upright and the sextant could be held steady, while the ship rolled and pitched under me and my body swayed to the sea's rhythm. A lightning glance at the wrist-watch the moment the sun's reflection touched the horizon, then I would clamber laboriously below, clinging on with one hand and guarding the sextant from harm as I was buffeted in the companionway. Next, I would note down the time and the sextant reading, comparing the wrist-watch with the deck-watch that rested in its nest of National Health Service cotton wool on a special shelf. I now knew it gained two seconds a day. It was as well that this error remained regular as the B.B.C. time signals were becoming very faint.

Bracing myself firmly into position beside the chart table with the Nautical Almanac and Admiralty Tables beside me, I worked out the sight in about twelve minutes, plotting the resulting position line on the chart in use.

Perhaps I am making heavy weather of this description; but I had

333

only learnt navigation by attending fortnightly evening classes at the Little Ship Club during the winter. Not the brightest of pupils, I soon gave up trying to learn star or moon sights, concentrating solely on the sun. Nor did I sit for the examination that concluded the lectures, for I did not know enough to pass and failure would have further lowered my already shaky morale. Best, I thought, to learn one simple routine so thoroughly that when sick and frightened and buffeted by giant seas, I could pass the examination that would be set by the grim Atlantic.

Besides, a sailor can be too fussy about details. Joshua Slocum, the first man to sail alone round the world, used a kitchen clock as his chronometer. When it stopped he boiled it in oil. An unsolved riddle is why it worked again! Still earlier, when the 70-foot double canoe *Tainui* sailed from Tahiti on the fourth night of December 1350, all that Taikehu had to guide him—Taikehu who "had charge of the great paddle Huahuaterangi"—were directions handed down two hundred years before by Kupe, The Navigator. "Steer a little to the left of the setting sun in December and you will reach Aotea-roa, the Land of the Long White Cloud." And reach New Zealand the *Tainui* Maoris did— over two thousand miles of open ocean, in company with the canoes *Tokomaru*, *Takatimu*, *Aotea* and *Arawa*.

How true a seafaring spirit that old Viking helmsman, Bard, showed, too, when, a thousand years ago, he led a party of young men from Iceland towards Norway. The Saga tells: "They got so strong a wind from the north that they were driven south into the main; and so much mist that they could not tell where they were driving, and they were out a long while." When a ground swell warned them of nearby land the old man was asked where they were. He answered this silly question with dignity:

"Many lands there are which we might have hit with the weather we have had—the Orkneys or Scotland or Ireland."

They rowed on to recognize the north coast of Scotland.

For hours *Cardinal Vertue* turned slow circles, inert and without life; not even a zephyr stirred. Then, at last, the sea's surface crinkled, changing from glossy to matt as the first ruffling breeze breathed out of the south.

That sunny afternoon, while the yacht was running her westing down, I described on the tape-recorder the rules which trial and error had now taught me:

"First, I must keep the ship sailing as fast as possible on the right course; that is, on the shortest route between my position and New York.

"Then, equipment needs to be maintained in good order; I must never let important things go by the board, yet not exhaust myself by trying to do everything: for instance, when the genoa tore the other day, I mended it as soon as it was dry, without waiting until it was needed again.

"I pump the bilges several times a day to stop water sloshing up behind the bunks at every roll; run the engine every day to charge the battery; keep stock of water and provisions; turn off the Calor gas cylinder *always* after use; write up the logs regularly; and often make notes of tasks still to be done.

"But I do not batten down everything at night. I think one can get into an unnecessary panic about the darkness. It is just the same as day; one should be ready to reduce or change sail, or alter course, and if everything is in its proper place, halyards always on the same cleats for instance, work is easy in the dark.

"Only in bad weather do I lash down the forehatch, fit the wash-boards and make all secure below.

"Similarly, I must be careful not to make a fetish of the safety-belt. A man could become afraid to move without clipping the thing on, and then when he was going from one part of the deck to another and had to unclip it, he could lose his balance and go over. I am well aware that the fundamental rule of single-handed sailing is that one stays with the ship. One must stay aboard, but the prerequisites for doing this are alertness, keen balance, quickness and being generally at home with the boat.

"Not that I neglect the belt. I am now sitting in the cockpit in the sunshine wearing nothing else. We are making three knots and I might have to adjust the vane or go forward, If so, I will clip the belt to something—for I do not think I could swim at this speed!"

The next two days were mainly notable for enteritis contracted through eating the last of my bacon when it had already become mouldy and unsavoury. *Cardinal Vertue* and the wind vane made the best progress they could against light unfavourable winds while the skipper was otherwise occupied.

Then on June 23rd "mare's tails" of cirrus cloud, and a grey, fibrous veil of alto-stratus, began to spread over the sky from the westward. The north-west wind backed into the south; the barometer began to fall.

As I was now outside the sea areas included in the B.B.C.'s weather bulletins (I could hardly hear the radio anyway) I had to do my own forecasting. This was great fun. One of my main sources of information was the section on meteorology that forms part of the introduction to every *Admiralty Pilot.*

In the North Atlantic low pressure areas, or depressions, move towards Europe from Canada. Most pass north of British latitudes. The sequence of events is as follows: high cloud spreads, perhaps forming a "halo" around sun or moon—the "mackerel sky and mare's tails" that made "tall ships carry low sails", of the old sailor's rhyme.

The glass falls and the wind backs towards the south. Then, as the sky becomes overcast, the wind increases; low ragged clouds scud by; rain falls; and the wind veers. When the warm front passes there is a sudden further veer to SW or WSW. Eventually the cold front goes by, accompanied by another abrupt veer in the wind and often by vicious line squalls. The glass begins to rise; the air becomes colder; and the sky clears. The wind, which is now from west or north-west, may blow still harder until the whole system has passed by.

"Lows" are caused by cold Polar air displacing warmer air masses. The winds may be moderate, but depressions are also breeding grounds for gales.

I have written at length about the weather because at sea you live with it; your tactics are dictated by it; you must learn its laws or it may destroy you. So, close to nature, did our ancestors live. True, we have not their belief that we can influence natural forces—Slocum once remarked that he had found praying for a favourable change of wind to be more effective where winds were naturally variable than in the steady Trades. But we can use the accumulated skill and knowledge of centuries to live safely among the winds of heaven.

The sky signs on June 23rd did not lie. The wind gradually veered until I could no longer lay my westerly course, but was forced north on the port tack through damp mist, light rain and overcast; and soon the wind strengthened. I had picked up the mast winch handle to go on deck and reef, but the wind fell right away, and the sea suddenly became "spiky" as little pyramidal waves splashed upward, released from the power which had moulded them into orderly shapes.

When the wind came in again it blew from farther west. Several times this was repeated. Sometimes I did have to reef, once to roll the mainsail right down and change to the tiny No. 3 staysail. Then, as the wind died down before changing to its new direction, the mainsail would have to be unrolled again. The warm front passed in the early morning hours of the 24th, after which I could sail no better course than north-west.

In a bleak dawn the sharply veering squall of the cold front pressed *Cardinal Vertue* hard over. I came about on to the starboard tack which was now the most favourable, but south-west was the nearest she could lie to the proper westerly course.

Gradually the depression passed north, leaving the glass high and the wind dropping. I had only made forty-two miles westward during the past twenty-four hours, at the cost of such frequent changes in course and alterations in sail area that I had had no sleep.

But I would far rather fight to windward than see the glass rise from 1,015 mb to 1,022, 1,024, 1,030, and the sky turn a clear blue, while the sea changed from grey-green to indigo and then became an undulating sheet of burnished copper. *Cardinal Vertue* floated motionless.

"In the middle of an anticyclone," I said on the tape-recorder next morning, the 25th. "I wish to God it would change, but those are all fair weather clouds on the horizon. I have been becalmed since yesterday, I know I am not being very positive about this but I am so depressed. Those damned Portuguese men-of-war are going faster than I am.

"I must try to fight this demoralization that obsesses me because I'm not getting anywhere; give myself a mental kick; make every effort to use each tiny puff of wind to the best advantage.

"I will try to forget how big the ocean is, and how small are the distances between the crosses marked on my chart each noon. I know this is a small ocean compared with the Indian Ocean or the Pacific, but it does seem unnecessarily large to me.

"I find it too depressing to read the accounts of two pioneers of this crossing, Graham in 1934 or Hamilton twenty years later. Their positions moved steadily westward—and that is a damned sight more than mine are doing! I have been at work, trying to lighten my mood by washing clothes and myself; not that I am inordinately clean but it does pay to keep one's skin healthy at sea. Then I checked food and stores.

"The day before the race Cicely asked what I was taking.

" 'Only the basic dehydrated food, I haven't had time to think of anything else,' I had replied. 'Can you   into Plymouth today and buy me six weeks' supplies?' She did it too! But of course there had to be shortages. I have just discovered that I have already used two-thirds of the matches aboard, so will ration strictly until I am farther over. I have decided to use no more than one match a day. This will allow one hot meal and drink until I have built up a reserve stock. No real hardship as the weather is still warm.

"I did not bring enough matches, but to make up for this deficiency I *did* buy a 'gale cheater', better called a 'spoil sport machine'. This hand-held indicator records the wind velocity in miles per hour. The actual reading has to be corrected by adding or subtracting the ship's speed and then by adding 30 per cent. to obtain the corrected wind speed at 33 feet above sea level. All wind speed figures I am giving here are for corrected velocities.

"I am quite sure that without it I would already have been through a couple of gales; *at least* force 8! Unfortunately, with the gadget I knew they were only force 6 winds, so they had to be logged accordingly. I warn other yachtsmen not to take any wind speed device with them: it completely spoils your entries—and the epic stories to be told on return."

But that morning no indicator was necessary in the still lifeless air.

By 2.0 p.m. it no longer needed a forced effort to be of good cheer. I opened the tape-recorder again and exclaimed:

"It is exciting—no, not exciting exactly—exhilarating—a wonderful feeling of freedom! Can you hear the water rushing by as I hold the microphone over the side? Yes; the ship is running. The spinnaker has been up and drawing for half an hour now; blue sea, blue sky with scattered cumulus clouds; and I'm sitting naked in the cockpit with a large gin. Once a shower of little fish came spraying into the air and I thought for a moment that I must be in the tropics among the flying fish. Where are the whales and other exciting sea animals one reads about? So far they are being coy.

"There is one snag; I want to charge the battery but cannot start the engine. Two hours' work has been of no avail, but I will try again later. If it refuses to go for the rest of the voyage it means, at worst, no navigation lights (except for short periods in emergencies), no cabin lights, no radio transmitter or spare receiver, no compass light; I shall have to use the torch for that.

"Possibly if I hang the paraffin riding light in the cabin, when I have caught up with matches, I may still be able to read. We are south of the shipping lanes now; just as well as we are without navigation lights;

338

have been extravagant leaving them on while I slept. If I can keep away from the steamers I should be all right." I was not being pessimistic. The engine did not run again.

The easterly wind steadily increased. At 10 p.m. after I had lowered the spinnaker, *Cardinal Vertue* continued to run at six knots by the patent log, nearly her maximum speed under mainsail alone. Soon I was rolling down 3 feet of the mainsail, but in under an hour I had to close-reef. It was a wonderful sail, tearing away through the darkness leaving a frothing wake, with the seas foaming up alongside.

By 4 a.m. on June 26th I was tired after this exhilarating but strenuous night. The ship would steer herself for about fifteen minutes until a sea breaking against her quarter would slew her round until she broached-to and lay in the troughs of the waves. The wind-vane could not get her back on course so I would clamber out, cursing, and push the helm up.

It was blowing a full gale, force 8, and I lowered all sail, though this was quite unnecessary. *Cardinal Vertue* would have sailed perfectly well under the full staysail.

But the sea and sky were grey and brooding. Great smoking combers came rolling out of the murk to windward. Every now and then one would burst against the ship, throwing her over 40 degrees. The seas, dotted with breaking crests, looked as soft as cotton wool—but how solid they felt as they roared down on the little ship to burst against her.

I pumped the bilge, then wrote in my diary:

"This was to have been a tape-recording but as I laid the machine tenderly in the lee bunk, the ship crashed over on her side and it shot smartly across the cabin. Now it will not work.

"My first gale! Even if it is only a small one, it *is* the first. I am pleased and excited. I was becoming worried, fearing I might be the only person to sail this stretch of ocean without one, as well as making the slowest passage on record. At daylight a fair-sized shark was flopping about near the surface, tail and fin out, brown shadow close beneath."

But the exhilaration passed as tiredness took hold and I became more damp and chilled and bruised all over.

The pitching and rolling of a small ship at sea is generally such that you must either hold on continually with one hand, or brace yourself securely if you have to use both. Even to make a mug of coffee, I would first place coffee, milk, sugar, mug and spoon on the lee side

339

of the cabin sole, then wedge myself on the floorboards beside them. Before I stood up again the ingredients had to be safe in their locker and the mug firmly jammed in another. I could then light the gas. For weeks your home is rolling and pitching violently, and often being dropped several feet with disconcerting abruptness.

But as the motion of a yacht at sea compares with the stillness of a house on shore, so is the fearful tossing about in a gale to normal ocean sailing. You try to eliminate unnecessary effort, but this is sometimes false economy. The log notes laconically how I tried to avoid going out into the cockpit, or making the acrobatic journey forward to "the heads", using the washing-up bowl instead. I was trying to lift it outside between the washboards and spray hood when a sea threw the ship on her beam ends, and over me it went!

Before midday I had set the reefed staysail, and, still grossly under-canvased, was running down my westing over huge swells in a confused sea. The wind decreased until at 7 p.m. I was able to cook baked beans and dehydrated stew with mugs of coffee, still keeping to the ration of one match a day. Then I repaired a rent in my P.V.C. trousers and changed my damp clothes.

Next day at noon I had been two weeks out and was half-way between Plymouth and Cape Race, Newfoundland. Far south lay the Azores and hundreds of miles to the northward I had just cleared the longitude of Iceland. I celebrated with the last of my half-bottle of gin.

"On these days of middle passage," I wrote, "it requires great mental effort to keep up keenness and make it an unbreakable rule to run out westing. The lesson of the previous day's blow is clear. I hoisted the mainsail much too late today. Yesterday, I need never have lowered the staysail. So far I have generally been about right when to shorten sail, but very slow indeed in realizing it is time to make sail again. I must watch this carefully and stop fussing over the mast.

"Where are my companions—rivals? I think of them a lot. They must be a hell of a long way ahead. I hope they haven't had the same calms I have had; but I am human enough to hope that they are not too far ahead. I would like them still to be in New York when I get there."

On that day, June 27th, Francis Chichester, I learnt later, was actually three hundred and seventy-five miles west-south-west of me, his position being 48° 30′ N, 34° 08′ W, and mine 50° 10′ N, 25° 10′ W. Two days before, a severe gale had overtaken him with scant warning. He was westward of, but near to, the centre of a low-pressure system, while I was at its eastern margin. On June 25th, according to the daily weather reports of the British Meteorological Office, a vessel reported winds of force 8, and on the 26th another ship, on the eastern outskirts of the disturbance about one hundred and thirty miles to the west of me, reported winds of forty-seven knots (force 9). Francis found the gale to be stronger still, while I was experiencing my first force 8 blow that morning.

I think my readings of wind velocity were accurate, as they were logged with regard to the state and appearance of the sea and not merely the indicator reading. The instrument was often washed out with fresh water as it repeatedly became clogged with spray. Subsequent comparison of my estimates of wind velocity with ocean weather ship reports, on the two occasions when I experienced gales in their vicinity, showed a close correlation between the figures.

Francis Chichester had spent more than five hours stripping the huge sails from *Gipsy Moth III* before she was running under bare poles. Her mainsail and genoa each measure 380 square feet compared with the 180 of my mainsail, and 230 of my genoa, and Hasler's 240 square foot single Chinese lug-sail. (Conventional Folkboats, such as Val Howells' *Eira*, carry a total of 250 square feet in mainsail and headsail.) *Eira* has 380 square feet when carrying her masthead genoa.

"The din was appalling," Chichester wrote of that gale. "A high-pitched screech dominating everything, spray peppering everywhere and seas hitting periodically with the bonk of a big drum."

To slow down his ship, he shackled a motor tyre on to the anchor chain, which he payed out over the stern, together with twenty fathoms of $2\frac{1}{2}$-inch warp. He filled a tin with oil, punctured it and hung it amidships. The anchor chain left a white wake behind.

June 28th found a battered but indomitable Francis repairing his self-steering gear as the wind fell below gale force.

On the same date Blondie Hasler's *Jester* was at 56° 12' N, 36° 50' W, south-east of Greenland, four hundred and fifty miles north-west of my position. He had passed the half-way mark between the continents and wrote: "Rather restless, tried to do some writing but found it hard to concentrate—partly because *Jester* is doing five knots through fog."

Hasler's log makes his passage sound easy, but he once admitted that it was "A little upsetting to see your mast waving to and fro". Rather an understatement, as his mast was completely unstayed. On the 25th he wrote: "Depressed . . . all sorts of doubts about my rig, provisions and time needed to get to New York. I dispelled this feeling in the afternoon by doing some work aboard."

By this time his rig had really been proved by a three-day gale. On the 26th the weather had moderated enough for him to inspect his ship and find all well. His morale "soared" that day.

I hope I am not picturing Hasler as some iron man, brave only because he fails to notice danger. True, unlike myself, he did not once tick "Very scared" in his medical log. But his courage is that of a bold imaginative mind. Both his wartime exploits and his success in ocean racing stem from planning and logical deduction, leading to definite decision and self-control over fear.

I had never known him so happy and relaxed as at Plymouth, with the enterprise which he had launched about to begin. The day I arrived he had taken me aside:

"David, I have had a little luck and made some money unexpectedly. How are you fixed for dollars? Let me lend you $200 to help out in New York."

There are not many men so ready to share good fortune with their friends. Luckily I was confident by then of getting away without a warrant being nailed to the mast. Not that I was solvent. Two years would be about the minimum to pay for the expenses incurred in the race. But that didn't matter so long as I could take part. So I refused Blondie's offer, as I had $30 of my own for the other side.

"Val has been the sensible one," I said. "He has a metal mast so that no one can nail a warrant to it and stop him sailing." We gazed in silent envy at this evidence of Howell's foresight.

By now, June 27th, Val, who was taking the intermediate route, was nearing the Azores. He completed his first thousand miles that day. I had done eight hundred and thirty, but my route was shorter. "My mind is boggling at the idea of spending another five weeks in this manner . . . feel dirty, have nearly saved enough water for another bath . . . have finished all the reading matter, very very bored," he wrote.

The moment of truth for Val and his metal mast was to come later when he found a second use for it. He was north-east of Bermuda sailing well-reefed through a belt of squalls. None appeared to be moving his way so he went below. Suddenly *Eira* was laid flat by the wind, her mast and sails pressed into the sea. Only the raised cabin coamings prevented her from filling through the main companion hatch and sinking like a stone.

3. (*Above*) *Cardinal Vertue* under mainsail and genoa.

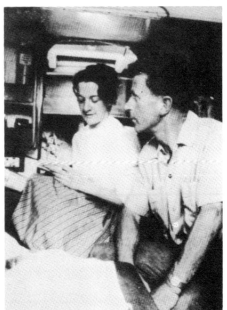

4. (*Right*) Looking forward in the cabin. David Lewis with Fiona.

5. (*Left*) "I would climb the mast . . . to become accustomed to the effort and balance involved . . . in case this proved necessary at sea."

6. (*Below*) The author in the pulpit of *Cardinal Vertue* a fortnight before the race.

"It was hard getting on deck and working my way along to the mast to get the sails down," Howells said afterwards. Considering that the deck was vertical, no one would doubt this.

When at last *Eira* was upright again he wondered how long it had all taken and glanced down at his wrist-watch-chronometer to find it had disappeared during those desperate minutes. He was left without means of finding his longditude and so decided to run his westing down in the latitude of Bermuda.

Jean Lacombe had started on June 16th, and by the 27th was in the latitude of Cape Finisterre, heading towards the Azores.

How had we become so scattered? The course of the Single-handed Transatlantic Race had been laconically laid down in the sailing instructions as, "Cross the starting line from West to East. Leave the Melampus Buoy to starboard, thence to New York by any route." The finish was at the Ambrose Light Vessel in the approaches to New York harbour. There was, therefore, a good deal of scope for the strategic planning of one's route.

We had two main choices; southern or trade wind, and the more northerly direct great circle route. There were also two variations, the intermediate way and the far north track.

We had pored over "Ocean Passages of the World"; the Admiralty chart of sailing ship routes, the monthly Pilot Charts, which contain detailed information about winds, currents, drift ice, fog, etc.; and over the accounts of other seamen.

When I first went to see Hasler, it was clear that we both favoured some variant of the northern route. I preferred the great circle; Hasler, impressed by accounts of 19th-century sailing-ship masters who found they could reach New York quicker from the Clyde than from Falmouth, intended to sail to the north of the shortest track.

At that time we insisted our interest in the race was purely theoretical. I had written to him "On behalf of friends who were interested," and he was "Most unlikely" to enter himself. But as we were saying good-bye at the station, after a discussion over a pint or two of beer, Blondie exclaimed:

"Well at least there will be two of us in this damned race, even if we are the only ones!"

But soon he 'phoned me about Francis Chichester. "The chap who flew the Tasman sea alone in a little seaplane and taught himself navigation to find two tiny islands on the way—then developed the methods the pathfinder pilots used during the war. He is interested."

343

Chichester insisted that he was not really serious about the race, so I was amused to see that "purely by chance" he had in his office about twenty pounds worth of charts which, "by a most fortunate coincidence, happened to cover the course of the race". Here was the man who, in stubborn refusal to accept defeat, had rebuilt his wrecked seaplane on a Pacific island during his historic New Zealand-Australia flight thirty years before. This same tenacity and singleness of purpose had helped him recover from a lung abscess the previous year.

Later we met Val Howells, the huge black-bearded Welshman who had sailed alone to Spain in preparation for his Atlantic crossing. Cuba was in the news just then, and little boys had followed him through the streets of San Sebastian, shouting, "*Ole, Fidelito Castro!*" Val rather favoured the intermediate route.

Jean Lacombe was the only one of us who "knew the way", from his previous crossing. He too, preferred this route.

The shortest way from Plymouth to New York without crossing over land is by sailing a great circle from Land's End to the tip of Newfoundland, roughly two thousand miles, thence parallel with the Canadian and American coasts, west-south-westwards for a little over a thousand miles to the Ambrose Light off New York. A great circle is the shortest distance between two points on a globe and in this case the course is a shade north of west from the Lizard to a position 51° N 20° W, then curves gently south to Cape Race, Newfoundland.

The intermediate route taken by Humphrey Barton in *Vertue XXXV* is some three thousand, six hundred and sixty-nine miles, passing a hundred miles north of the Azores and about two hundred miles north of Bermuda. In their passage from Falmouth to New York in forty-seven days, he and Kevin O'Riordan averaged seventy-eight miles a day, with leading winds for about half the time.

The southern route takes advantage of the steady, favourable trade winds, but is about five thousand miles long. The second *Mayflower* sailed this way in fifty-one days, but she had to average a hundred and five miles a day to cover the greater distance.

The great circle route will always be linked with the name of Cdr. R. D. Graham. To him belongs the honour due to a pioneer. For he had the imagination and courage to sail westward directly against the expected westerly winds. His initiative was rewarded by fair winds. In May 1934 he sailed his 7-ton gaff cutter *Emanuel*, alone, one thousand, seven hundred and sixty-five miles from Bantry in Southern Ireland to St. John's, Newfoundland. Winds were easterly. There were three heavy gales and he saw one iceberg. He averaged seventy miles a day without self-steering gear, an epic performance.

In August 1956 Lt.-Cdr. Hamilton became the second man to sail the great circle route to the New World single-handed. He went still further north in *Salmo*, sister-ship to *Vertue XXXV* and *Cardinal Vertue*. From Glasgow his course curved up to 58° N before slanting south again to Belle Isle Strait. He, too, averaged seventy miles a day also without a wind-vane. For seventeen of the twenty-nine days of his crossing he had to sail close-hauled. He encountered five gales and fog near Newfoundland, which lifted after ten days to reveal a large iceberg.

Cdr. Graham's *Rough Passage*, the deceptively modest article which Peter Hamilton contributed to *The Yachtsman*, and Humphrey Barton's book *Vertue XXXV*, were invaluable to us. Above all we are indebted to Graham, whose initiative led him to become one of the few in each age who have added to the stature of mankind by ripping strips off the tattered concept of impossibility.

There is an earlier sea rover, too, whose name should not be forgotten. Towards the close of the 10th century, one Biarne Hejrulfson was sailing from Iceland towards Greenland when "A north wind with fog set in and they knew not where they were sailing to, and this lasted many days. . . . At last they saw the sun and could distinguish the quarters of the sky. So they hoisted sail again and sailed a whole night and a day when they saw land."

As they were looking for Greenland, "with its great snow mountains", this tree-lined shore, probably Newfoundland, held no interest for the first Europeans to sight the Americas. So: "They left the land on the larboard side and had the sheet on the land side". But the gale increased and Biarne ordered a reef to be taken in and not to sail harder than the ship and her tackle could easily bear".

Eventually they reached Greenland, whence Leif Erikson and Thorfinn Karlsefri made a number of voyages of discovery to America as a result of Biarne's report.

It was another four hundred years before the Viking Greenlanders themselves faded from the pages of history and legend. A 14th-century seafarer gives a clue to how the climate had changed when he reports that: "It is only at peril of his life from ice that a man now sails the old route westward from Iceland to Greenland."

So the grey seas thunder unheeding at their passing, but their story is immortal.

345

On June 28th I was sitting in the dusk listening to the wind dying away and willing with all my soul that there would not be another calm. Then, suddenly, we emerged from under a great black arch of cloud to sail on under a clear pale greenish sky towards a crescent moon poised dramatically ahead. The gentle wind held, driving *Cardinal Vertue* on through the night.

I had fiddled with the tape-recorder until, to my surprise, it began to work. But now the radio had gone dead. I removed the back and stared in gloomy fascination at the incomprehensible maze of wires inside. I gingerly poked and prodded here and there until the valves suddenly glowed and a healthy sound of static crackled through the cabin. I hoped it would keep going but resolved to pay special attention to winding the deck-watch regularly. In any case no radio time signals were audible here, half-way between the continents, but I hoped to be able to obtain them later to correct the deck-watch and also to use the radio direction-finder to obtain bearings of coastal stations when feeling my way through the fog banks off the Canadian coast.

At dawn on June 29th, I hoisted the spinnaker. By noon we had made three consecutive daily runs of over a hundred miles. More than a thousand miles lay astern now. The keel was passing over a submarine mountain range which rises one and a half miles above the ocean floor. I passed a piece of driftwood around which a six-foot shark was lazily circling.

In the afternoon, because it was warm and sunny and the speed had dropped to half a knot, and the water was relatively shallow—only half a mile deep—I decided to have a swim. Tying a line round my waist, I plunged in. The water was cool but exhilarating, and I saw no weed on the ship's bottom. I was swimming about happily, luxuriating in the coolness flowing over my limbs and admiring my vessel, when I recalled the shark I had seen that morning, and a phrase from the Naval Life Saving Committee's shark papers came unbidden to mind.

"They . . . like to pluck legs which hang down from the surface like bunches of bananas. . . ."

An all too apt description that made me climb hurriedly aboard.

I celebrated the record runs with a large cooked meal of dehydrated chips, cold meat, dehydrated vegetables and stewed fruit. After such progress I decided that I could afford to use two matches a day now.

Over the undulating swells a steamer appeared. When she saw me she altered course abruptly to circle the yacht at slow speed. With clothes pegs I attached a notice written on the back of a chart to the dodger *"Single-handed Transatlantic Race. Please report to Lloyds,"* it read, my boat's name being already painted on the dodger. The officers waved from the bridge before the ship turned back to her course.

"Glad my friends will have news now," I wrote in the log. But *Sunetna* of Palermo did not report me.

For the next day, June 30th, this gloomy entry appears in the log:

"Another calm, I can't describe the frustration. Unfortunately, I brought too little fat to cook the dehydrated chips—Never mind. . . . The sights are disappointing, the North Atlantic Drift is holding us back."

Soon a westerly wind set in, increasing in strength. The ever-recurring problem arose. Was it time to reduce sail? After I had lowered the genoa I commented in the log: "I thought so! I was overcautious. . . . The effect of that broken mast. . . . I have lost confidence when pounding to windward. . . . I cannot bear the thought of the dreary trail home with half a stick!"

Another depression was passing north of me; I accordingly came about to the starboard tack in expectation of the wind veering from south-of-west to north-west when the cold front passed. My proper course lay just south-of-west but I could afford to go further south still to miss being caught in an offshoot of the Labrador current which recurved eastward. By such tactics as these I hoped to make the best use of the contrary winds to bring me over the detached submarine plateau, Flemish Cap, and towards Cape Race beyond.

It was hard to make much progress that afternoon against the short steep seas, reminiscent of the Thames Estuary. But in compensation, a school of porpoises puffed and blew as they played alongside. Then, after dark, came one of the ocean's breathtaking moments. I was adjusting the self-steering gear when I glanced down to see the rudder swirling with cold phosphorescent fire and the log line trailing astern like a rapier sheathed in flame.

But in a few hours I was cursing the calm again, and casting a jaundiced eye at the yellow sunrise beneath the edge of the overcast. Gloomily I cooked breakfast; then hurriedly dropped everything to adjust sheets and wind-vane as a breeze from the north stirred the sails.

4

PALE SUNS AND STRAY BERGS

"What is a woman that you forsake her,
And the hearth-fire and the home-acre,
To go with the old grey Widow-maker?

She has no house to lay a guest in—
But one chill bed for all to rest in,
That the pale suns and the stray bergs nest in."
—RUDYARD KIPLING'S *Harp Song of The Dane Women.*

JULY 4th marked the end of my third week at sea. I was terrified of calms now, for out of those twenty-one days there had been fourteen with them. But all that day the wind held, so that the next morning I could write:

"This is what I came for! A squall came suddenly out of the north —the glass had been falling. I dropped the spinnaker smartly and hauled it from the sea, streaming phosphorescence. Soaked through by the driving wet mist, I renewed the tack lashing on the mainsail, then rolled down a third of the sail. After an hour everything had been adjusted, and as *Cardinal Vertue*, no longer overpressed, raced away westward, the stars suddenly broke out overhead, while Venus left a brilliant track over the waves. A glorious night with the spray frothing high! I am celebrating by using an extra match to light the cabin lamp and make coffee."

For thirty-six hours the alternating calms and depressions had not allowed me to sleep. Now I slept soundly until at 4 a.m. I was awakened by the ship wallowing, taken aback by the wind which had fallen light. With chilled fingers I unreefed and set her on course again; the cabin lamp glowed warmly and soon I was nursing a mug of hot soup while a pot of stew was heating on the stove.

I was wearing two pairs of socks, pyjamas underneath corduroys, a string vest, two Norwegian pullovers and a ski-ing anorak now, for the weather was colder as we neared the chilly Labrador current which flows south between Baffin Land and Greenland and then washes the shores of Labrador, Newfoundland, Nova Scotia and the New England States. I would enter the main stream of this current at the edge of the Grand Banks, from where it would help carry me southward.

Meanwhile I was still sailing through the eddies of the North Atlantic Drift, an extension of the Gulf Stream. At the junction of the two currents the sea temperature may change as much as 15°F in a ship's length. This meeting place is called the Cold Wall and here sediment and plankton are deposited.

For untold ages the cod have arrived each spring to feed, and every season for four hundred years fishermen have come to the Grand Banks for them. Many sealers and fishermen sleep here forever, for the icebergs from Davis Strait keep an unholy rendezvous with the rolling fog-banks which form where the currents mingle.

Another depression passed by, building the waves that similar winds might have produced in the English Channel. These steep seas would often stop *Cardinal Vertue* dead in her tracks.

It was becoming easier to tell when to reef. The ship would begin to pound; she would feel heavy and pressed down; sometimes she would luff into the gusts, so that the sails flogged and vibrated, making the whole ship shudder. Then, as the wind increased, she would be pressed down until the lee rail was forced under, and the speed dropped sharply.

I could decide better from down below whether the ship was over-pressed or lifting easier, for my judgment was not obscured by the noise of the wind, the spray and breaking crests and the size of the waves and the greyness of the surrounding murk.

The proper time to make and hand sail is a problem forever demand-ing accurate decision from a small boat sailor if he is to obtain maxi-mum speed without endangering ship or gear. During the race I made eighty-seven major changes of headsails, reefed or unreefed the main-sail eighty-six times and hoisted the unwieldy spinnaker on ten occasions.

I had now reached the region of grey sea and grey skies; sunbathing was at an end. I did not remove my clothes again, unless I had been soaked, for a thousand miles.

For the first time the brown gulls, which often followed me, were joined by delicate black birds with a white stripe across their forked tails. They danced over the waves, flicking the water with beak or claw, daintily as kittens. I never saw one alight and these stormy petrels appeared too fragile to live on the face of the ocean.

349

Cooking had now become a matter of strict routine, but was still fun while some variety of food existed. Everything had to be planned and prepared beforehand, spoons, saucepan, kettle, food, all laid out in a row on the lee cabin side. The rest was a question of balance and anticipation of the ship's next movement. But it was pleasant cooking below at night while *Cardinal Vertue* lifted easily to the seas; the howling wind and the damp mist and spray driving past outside the doghouse windows made the cabin seem a more comfortable refuge.

Orderliness, routine and foresight in little things. There was something feminine about the meticulousness required in matters of detail, feminine too, many of the jobs that had to be done—mending clothes and sails, cleaning, cooking, washing. Too many men who pride themselves on their manliness, and regard "women's work" as beneath their male dignity, manifest their masculinity only in a bedroom; or more often in a bar, describing their exploits. Seamen and small boat sailors, soldiers on active service, explorers, mountaineers—all these spend much of their time, and indeed take pride in their mastery of "women's work".

I have often been asked how the ship remained on her course while I was asleep. The wind-vane kept her sailing at a constant angle to the wind, but what if the wind's direction changed? When this happened the rhythm of her motion across the waves altered. The new "feel" of the yacht, or her pounding when pressed too hard, or the judder of a vibrating sail, would be enough to wake me. In choppy weather I would be lying dressed in oilskins, rubber boots and, of course, the safety-belt. But this was to be avoided when possible as I awoke moist and clammy. The sleeping clothes I preferred in this weather included an anorak and rubber shoes.

So I crawled on westward. Calms alternated with contrary winds. I made desperately little progress.

There was always plenty of ship work to be done—carpentry, care of tools, oiling the log and steering vane, letters to write ready for posting ashore, lists to prepare of jobs to be done in New York in preparation for the return voyage, checking over the rigging, pumping and navigation. Often I had not the heart to tackle them.

Once I wrote "The hours do drag so! The Atlantic is so large! Six weeks is so long. The winds are so bloody unco-operative!" Sometimes I felt sorry for myself when the wind fell away and the spiky wavelets began to plop. "Grey overcast, grey sea! if only I had some butter, how much less like sawdust the biscuits would taste!" But soon my

350

mood would lighten again as I read or preferably did something useful.

On July 8th I could look back on five days of hard struggle to win westing. For four of these days I had sailed on the port tack. At first during the night of July 4th-5th, I could lay my own course, but had to reef and unreef several times as the hours crawled on. No sleep, and next morning, hours of calm. Then another night of reefing, all in grey mist and fine driving rain.

On the 6th, heavy damp fog lay until evening, a day of calms, rain squalls, headwinds and short, vicious seas. When *Cardinal Vertue* plunged her bow into a wave the speed indicator needle would drop from three to three-quarters of a knot; she would shudder, fall away to leeward, then slowly gather way, only to be brought up short again.

Later, when I was hauling the mainsheet hard in, the clew fitting at the end of the boom, to which the sheet is attached, pulled right out. I could barely hold the boom and wriggled down to the wet cockpit floor to prevent it pulling me overboard. Then I clipped my safety-belt to a guard rail, slipped a bight of the mainsheet over the end of the boom and made it fast. It was secure for the moment. As I could not think what to do next, I went below and made tea.

The boom had been shortened before the trip so the deck blocks, through which the mainsheet was threaded, were now too far aft, with the result that the sheet tended to pull the fitting from the end of the boom.

I screwed eyes into the deck further forward, to which I shackled the blocks. Then I spread the clew fitting with Bostik, hammered it back, re-rove the sheet and hoped for the best. The job would have to be completed by fitting a new mainsheet horse in New York.

Cardinal Vertue, headed off course, continued to pound into the seas, sending up clouds of spray, through cold grey white-capped waves beneath a lowering overcast sky. I did not need to reef again until I was cooking dehydrated chips with nearly the last of the butter. The exasperated comment appears in the log that "the wind *always* comes up at the most awkward times. I have little fat of any sort, or milk, or sugar, but am catching up with the matches and can use three a day. It really is essential to make out a food list before starting a jaunt like this."

At 9 p.m. I was trying to light the cabin lamp from the stove, the ship doing her best to stand on end, when a deep "toot, toot" sounded outside. The sound did not register at first, but when it was repeated I dropped the frying pan and sprang up into the cockpit to see *White*

Rose of Helsingfors slowly circling me. I hung out my notice and the great ship came up to leeward going dead slow. A large vessel must keep downwind of a small sailing boat or she will blanket her wind and drift down upon her as she wallows helplessly. This captain was a real seaman who handled his giant as if she had been a launch. When he had read my message he hooted once again then, with passengers and crew waving good-bye, he turned away to the eastward, moving slowly at first so that the wake of his churning propellers should not harm me. I did not know it then, but this was the first time I was reported.

For four days I had been driven north of the proper track. On July 9th I was still unable to lay my course, but this time I was being forced to the south of it, punching head seas which made everything aboard shake and rattle. "On this starboard tack half the damned Atlantic comes into the ship," I wrote. "I think a seam must have opened. I had better fix the leak in New York or some bloody great shark will swim into the bilge. I keep note of the number of strokes with the pump that are needed—forty every few hours now. Still, with the diaphragm pump this is no hardship." This pump had been fitted beneath the cabin sole to supplement the standard one in the cockpit.

Beside the cross on the chart marking the noon position for July 9th is scrawled an unseamanlike, "Oh Mother!" for I had crossed a dotted line marking the mean maximum iceberg limit for July (U.S. Pilot Chart).

"God, it is so cold!" the log-book reads. "This north-west wind is blowing straight off the Barren Lands round Hudson Bay. The thermometer in the cabin reads 57°, but my toes tell me it is far colder. I only wish I could be extravagant with matches now for a hot drink would be welcome. Never mind; soon it will be evening, then a *very* large stew and lots of coffee. I wonder how the others are doing? No one could be as slow as me, not nearly: never, at my most pessimistic had I expected such poor progress as this. In the last twenty-four hours, one of the hardest days of beating to windward I have ever known, we gained eighteen miles! But I *will* get there."

July 13th was eventful. For the first time in ten days the wind was favourable. I was becoming accustomed to the spinnaker, which I was now able to set in half an hour as the vane steered *Cardinal Vertue* down wind. When the wind drew ahead a few hours later, and I had to change it for the genoa, we could still remain on course. I kept the genoa permanently hanked to the forestay when it was lowered, instead of spending time stowing it below, where it could not have dried anyway.

Gowens had made me a new mainsail, and twin staysails of heavy Terylene, before the race; but I had been unable to afford a new genoa as well. After all, working sails had to come before light weather ones. Accordingly I had written to Vertue owners whose addresses appeared in Lloyd's Register, asking for the loan of old genoas. Now, as well as my own elderly sail, genoas from the Vertues *Huzzar* and *Sally II* were aboard, so that I had something in hand when one tore. I had no wish to be like Alain Gerbault who had literally stitched his way across the Atlantic.

When I hoisted the genoa I would let the staysail stand, too, as the two sails did not appear to interfere with each other. The routine of lowering a headsail, as the wind gusted up, was well established. Leaving the sheet taut to stop the sail flogging, I would let go the halyard and allow the sail to drop into the water where it could come to no harm. Then I would lash the head to the pulpit, slacken the sheet, pull the rest aboard and make all fast. No strain on the sail, because it was not allowed to flap, quick, and no deviation from course.

At 5 p.m. fog closed down, thick and impenetrable.

Half an hour later I heard the first foghorn. As I was nearing the Grand Banks and the main Atlantic shipping lanes, I hoisted the radar reflector.

Twenty minutes later I heard the beat of a ship's engine and hurried on deck. A towering shape was looming out of the fog to port, two cables off, moving dead slow. I could hear the crew talking and distinguish their words. There was a moment of panic until I saw that the steamer was passing clear. She disappeared into the fog up wind, her engines remaining audible for a full twenty minutes.

Before the sound had faded, other engines were thumping and foghorns sounding in various keys. A bell was being rung every four minutes from one vessel. On another metal was being struck. These must be fishing-boats at anchor. The one place where they could reach bottom was Flemish Cap, the submerged plateau that rises from the abyss to within twenty-eight fathoms of the surface, and lies three hundred and forty miles east of Cape Race, Newfoundland. It is a rich fishing ground. Here was I, in fog, threading through an invisible fishing fleet and crossing a main Atlantic shipping lane into the bargain! I wished that the fog would lift so that I could see the boats and talk to their crews, but it remained as thick as ever.

Once a siren began to blare very loudly, engines throbbed and a halo of light appeared through the mist. Then it slid by.

For two hours I was becalmed, but by 11 p.m. the genoa was drawing well and the sound of foghorns was growing fainter astern. A long musical note rang out from the topmast stay each time *Cardinal Vertue* curtsied to a swell. She was singing to herself as she climbed the slope of the Continental Shelf which was rising from a depth of two miles, a few days' sail astern, to the hundred-fathom line about forty miles ahead.

At midnight on July 13th it was 10 p.m.! This is no slip of the pen. I had put my watch back two hours—the wrist-watch, that is. The deck-watch or chronometer was always kept at Greenwich Mean Time. So far I had also used G.M.T. for my daily routine, but with every 15 degrees of westing, the sun rose and set an hour later. By now sunset was well after midnight and dawn 9 a.m.! So, as I was nearing land, I decided to fall in line with those on shore.

Another half an hour back would put the clock to Newfoundland Summer Time. Nova Scotian time is four hours behind Greenwich; New York (Eastern Standard Time) is five hours slow. I would now have to note my G.M.T. noon position in the log at 10 a.m. by my wrist-watch. Off New York, G.M.T. noon would be at 7 a.m. E.S.T.!

In keeping with the mood of these two nameless hours a sense of unreality possessed me. With the gentle breeze from the north-west *Cardinal Vertue* tended to fall away to port towards the distant sound of the foghorns, so I dare not relax too much.

The log reads "I am very tired. For more than a week now I have slept only in short snatches dictated by the veering and backing of the winds. I must keep awake in case we sag down wind into that traffic jam. But now we are clear of the actual shipping the tiredness is creeping back. There is a slight ringing and the sound of voices in my ears and the familiar feeling that I am not alone."

The relative lack of hallucinations on this voyage had been a surprise. When I was very tired, and had spent monotonous hours at the helm in winds too light for the vane, I sometimes heard voices. For one whole day in fog the sea appeared to slope up-hill; during a foggy night I had seemed to be sailing on a height with the lights of two passing steamers on a plain far below. But these occasions were rare.

It had been very different the previous summer when I had sailed alone to Norway and back without a wind-vane. Then, after several days at sea, particularly when very tired in the hours before dawn, there came a distinct feeling of having been divided into two personalities, one of which would speak to the other, and sometimes would advise. At times it appeared that another person was at the helm, while the other "part personality" was critically observing his actions and problems.

Slocum describes such an incident during bad weather in mid-Atlantic, when another entity appeared to take charge. He was a good storyteller and with true dramatic instinct identified his "guest" as the pilot of Columbus' ship *Pinta*.

However, one episode of de-personalization occurred during my return from Norway, different from those usually described. A block and tackle gadget, which I had myself rigged up at sea to help me alter course without leaving the cabin, became consistently identified in my mind as of feminine construction.

"While fully aware that he had rigged it up himself," I wrote later; "the subject was never able to accept it as his own work but always distrusted this product of 'feminine' ingenuity, and when it went wrong cursed himself heartily for allowing a 'woman' to meddle with his ship. This attitude persisted throughout the three days during which the arrangement was in use. Is it too fanciful to regard this as a de-personalization in which the feminine-like component of the subject's character stood apart?"

I had seen imaginary rivers flowing through green, bush-clad valleys in New Zealand when, as a boy of seventeen, I paddled a home-made canoe some four hundred and thirty miles along rivers, lakes and estuaries, from my school in Wanganui to my home in Auckland. Solitude, exhaustion and monotony seem to be the common factors underlying these experiences. Blondie Hasler's war-time hallucinations in two-seater canoes during the training period for his "Cockle-shell" raid on Bordeaux tend to bear this out, for the two men, sitting one behind the other, were virtually isolated. After five or six hours' paddling at night phantom ships or buoys would appear. Once Blondie became so annoyed on finding his companion "reading *The Times*", that he was about to remonstrate forcibly when he realized they were creeping through a pitch-dark night without lights! During the actual operation, however, no such phenomena occurred.

I am interested in the effects of solitude and fatigue, because they may throw light on something far more fundamental—the deep-seated urge that drives modern civilized man to seek adventure in the remote places of the earth. I think this has always been part of the essential dynamic nature of the human spirit, but in early ages it found a ready outlet in the individual combat of battle and raiding, in piracy, and along the equally perilous pathways of legitimate trade.

Since about the middle of the 19th century, wars have become increasingly mechanized, impersonal and inhumanly destructive, while the industrial revolution brought relative security, scientific advance and a vast, flat drabness. You could no longer starve or die of plague in civilized countries, but neither could you seek new worlds beyond the sunset. Instead, you might compete with the Jones's in the dullness of your life and the uselessness of your possessions.

Surely it is no accident that this was the period when men began to climb mountains without carrying thermometers, or collecting urine samples for analysis? Nor did they climb for the view, but simply because the mountain was there. The wakes of small boats were soon criss-crossing every ocean. Men like Slocum and Voss did not sail around the world for gold or empire, but simply to fulfil something within themselves. True, Alain Bombard sacrificed his health and risked his life in an attempt to prove his theory and save others, but a less adventurous man would have devised experiments that were not so rigorous (and, incidentally, more effective in finding the answers to still unsolved problems). Adventurous undertakings, not foolhardy ones, have become accepted.

Hasler thinks that people should take controlled risks from time to time to keep themselves up to scratch and be in the best possible physical, mental and emotional condition to react to any sudden emergency. My own experiences as a doctor have convinced me that fully a third of illnesses arise directly from a chronic state of anxiety and lack of courage and self-confidence. Increased social security has not abolished this dread of nameless disaster. Uncertainty, fears and a want of self-respect are rife. Those who have known physical fear, but have learned to control it, seem less prone to these disorders. Of course, security is necessary but security is only one aspect of life— man must also have things to fight and strive for, and so enhance the dignity of his life.

This, I think, was the real reason why we were making this trip. Different as were our natures, attitudes to life, to the sea or to the race, we were driven by much the same force. For each one of us, the problems of getting away, of expense, of learning the skill required, had appeared insuperable, yet something within us had refused to acknowledge the limits of the practical and the possible.

I do not think the concept of escapism applies to undertakings that require so much positive planning and effort. It is true we may simply have been abnormal people, but the encouraging support given to us before the race, and the way in which the idea captured public imagination, revealed that innumerable men and women shared the same feelings and urges and, but for economic and domestic reasons, might themselves have taken part.

It has been argued that endeavour and adventure are of no practical value. But is it more useful to devote one's life to earning money, only to end it by a coronary thrombosis brought on by the effort and worry? I do not know.

Another misconception is that adventurers seek risks. Although there may well be an element of danger in anything worth while, the challenge is in using one's judgment, knowledge and skill to avoid trouble. Two of the finest small boat sailors today are Eric and Susan Hiscock. They know so much—and plan so well—that they have sailed round the world without any serious mishaps. It is those less skilled whose adventures may become rather too exciting for comfort —as I was soon to find out.

Something of the spirit of our race can be caught by the wording of one of the rules. "Yachts must be fully independent and capable of carrying out their own emergency repairs at sea. Crews have no right to expect or demand rescue operations to be launched on their behalf."

In its whole conception the race was supremely an adventure and a challenge. But unlike other single-handed voyages it provided a special opportunity to study the reactions of several men who would each be isolated in similar conditions and perhaps be exposed to fear and hardship. In other words the situation had the makings of a controlled experiment.

I wrote to medical and scientific authorities in England and as far afield as the U.S.A. and Italy. What useful data could the race yield? How best to obtain it?

Eventually I was introduced to Dr. Harold Lewis of the Medical Research Council. He is a quiet South African who had directed the medical research when he was on the British North Greenland Expedition of 1952–1954. There was nothing unusual about his office at the Division of Human Physiology in Hampstead except for files bearing such labels as "Sledging Rations—Antarctic", "Sleep Rhythms

—Greenland", "Fat Thickness—Polar Expeditions". He was now helping to build up a school of Polar physiology, and was interested in all techniques involving field-work. He readily consented to co-operate, for here was a unique opportunity to learn about the eating and sleeping habits, the mental and physical feelings of men in isolation. This sort of information, though very valuable, is usually almost impossible to obtain, and would be particularly applicable in solving problems of survival at sea.

With the blessing of the Medical Research Council we soon had the necessary advisers in psychology, nutrition and statistics. We worked out a plan whereby I (with Hasler and Howells who both agreed to help) would be the advance party in the field, with the team of experts as the base laboratory. It was a pretty wide base because Harold had contacted experts in England and in New York!

Broadly speaking, we were going to study daily changes of mood, the sleep rhythm, food and water intake, using a daily questionnaire. We wanted notes to be made promptly and so we produced for the race competitors a "Medical Log-book", extracts from which are reproduced in Appendix Four.

It was not easy to fill in this medical log regularly when one felt sick or tired, or just bemused by being violently shaken in a boat that lurched and bucked ceaselessly. Yet Howells and Hasler, in spite of their other pressing tasks, spent an hour each day conscientiously completing the record.

My own feelings are pungently expressed in a tape-recording made during our second week at sea:

"This 'brilliant' product of the fervent imaginations of H. L. and myself! How beautifully printed by the M.R.C. and how often I have cursed it these last few days! But it will be really valuable to have a daily record of our feelings because memory of emotions so quickly fades and disappears into the background. I cannot recall accurately my own feelings of a few days ago now. Some memories do remain— How it felt to sail blindly through fog for those four nights—or the other night when I had boomed out the staysails. Damp mist dripped everywhere, the foredeck looked like a battlefield of tangled ropes; a foghorn was hooting somewhere abeam. Then, the moment the sails were drawing, the ship ceased to roll and glided away smoothly through

---

7. (*Opposite*) Blondie Hasler's *Jester* with *Cardinal Vertue* in light airs in the Solent.

8. Race preparations at Plymouth. *Gipsy Moth III* is in the foreground and, facing her from left to right, *Eira, Jester* and *Cardinal Vertue.*

the mist and darkness. That moment, and others like it, will remain with me always."

This is a long digression from my efforts to keep awake. It was not until 2.30 a.m. next morning, July 14th, after the wind had completely boxed the compass and was again blowing from the south-west, that I could come on to the port tack and head away from the faint sound of foghorns. I turned in wearing full equipment but had only an hour's sleep before the genoa had to come in. Ninety minutes later the mainsail needed reefing and in another hour it had to be close-reefed, and the staysail reefed as well. I was becoming more proficient, so that close-reefing the main and staysail now took only seventeen minutes.

At dawn, the sea was wild and beautiful. Crests burst over the ship with surprising violence as she plugged to windward against a force 6 breeze. Sometimes the impact of a breaking sea would bring her up all standing.

I dared not relax with wind and seas increasing, so to stave off my desperate need for sleep I forced myself to cook and eat a little, then washed up, no mean feat with the yacht's wild motion. Encouraged by this success and being unable to stand the reflection in the mirror opposite the companionway, I shaved. Then it was time to plot my estimated G.M.T. noon position, 47° N 47° W—an encouraging day's run of seventy-five miles. But soon the wind dropped completely and we lay becalmed for eight and a half hours.

That evening the fog lifted briefly in a squall of icy rain. The air temperature was 50° as *Cardinal Vertue* entered the zone where fog lies for 40 per cent. of the time in July. We were also crossing "Iceberg track C" (*Newfoundland and Labrador Pilot*), which runs south at the eastern edge of the Grand Banks and is the most usual route along which the bergs drift.

Every time I looked out of the cabin breaking phosphorescent crests momentarily set my nerves on edge. There had not been a satisfactory longitude sight for the past two weeks and for the first time in filling in the medical log I placed a cross in the column "Wish it were all over".

In view of the conditions I judged it appropriate to broach the "Survival Kit only effective west of 35° W", which I had been given at Plymouth and which so far had served as a successful "iceberg repellent" when taken at bedtime—a new use for gin!

Another day and a seemingly interminable night wore on. If my dead reckoning was correct, I should be crossing the edge of the Grand Banks into soundings early in the morning.

It was 4 a.m. on July 16th when I switched on the echo-sounder—it read forty fathoms! Two thousand miles of open Atlantic now lay astern.

As the light grew it showed a sea no longer indigo blue, but a vivid bottle green. Air temperature was 53°, sea temperature 50°. We had crossed the Cold Wall into the south-flowing Labrador current and were over the Grand Banks.

The sea was already flecked with white. The waves increased and grew steeper, until by 7 a.m. the wind was whining out of the east at forty-one miles an hour (force 8) while from a lowering grey sky sheets of rain swept down, penetrating every nook and cranny in the cabin. But what of that! It was a wild and beautiful sight as *Cardinal Vertue* ran before the gale under her boomed staysail.

By midnight the wind had fallen enough to allow me to hoist the mainsail. In the enormous sea that was still running this took an hour. However, wasted time worried me less than the alarming discovery that the gooseneck of the boom, where it pivots against the mast, was badly bent. The boom could still be rotated however, so that roller reefing was still possible.

In the early hours of the morning the topping-lift parted and wound itself perversely round the cross-trees; then the radar reflector sustained damage. Repairs were completed before dawn and then I set out to hoist the spinnaker and free the self-steering gear, which was sticking; tasks occupying another one and a half hours.

The wind died down as the day advanced, until the ballooning blue spinnaker which had been drawing us proudly over the swells began to crinkle, then wound itself firmly about the topmast stay. I tried to clear it but the delicate nylon fabric was foul of the very top of the stay, 34 feet above the deck. Knowing that the longer I put off the inevitable the more frightened I would become, I stripped off my boots and jerseys and went up, over the lower cross-trees, up again until my feet rested on the upper pair, and then on further to the masthead. How that mast swept to and fro across the sky as *Cardinal Vertue* rolled to the oily swells passing under her! As soon as the sail was cleared I slid to the deck to find my legs trembling and my hands shaking with exertion and reaction from fear.

Soon, even the light breeze died away. I was cheered a little to see a whale break surface to port and blow, but it dived again immediately and did not reappear. Then a puffin, a comical little bird with a huge hooked nose and short wings that whirred up and down, came buzzing busily around the yacht, looking for all the world like the animated hub of an aircraft propeller.

That night I made a little progress but was again becalmed next morning. The fifth week had ended. The engine was useless; only three hundred and sixty miles of westing in the last seven days; but on six of them there had been calms and for six days fog.

Cape Race radio beacon was sounding loud and clear about fifty miles to the north-westward. I was nearing Newfoundland, but that day, though I knew nothing of it at the time, Francis Chichester was closing the U.S.A., while Blondie Hasler was approaching Sable Island, off the coast of Nova Scotia.

Blondie's great sweep into the north had helped him little. South of Ireland on June 17th, when he had been six days at sea and I four, he was a little over two hundred miles ahead. When he had regained the direct route a little east of Flemish Cap on July 7th, he was approximately two hundred and sixty miles in front of me. Since then, outside of the worst belt of calms, he had widened the gap.

There was not a ship to be seen; neither fishing smack, nor trawler, nor dory. The Grand Banks seemed deserted as I floated in an uneasy quiet. There was nothing but grey sky and sea and the ghosts of *Bluenose* and the great Grand Banks schooners of yesterday.

But I did not feel lonely, for the old ships which had fished those waters for four hundred years seemed to bear me company, while the wraiths of the dragon ships of Lief and Thorvald and Karlsefni came stealing out of the northern mists across nine centuries.

5

THE THUNDERING SURF

"It is not advisable to approach the coast within the 40-fathom line; it must be borne in mind that this depth may be found within a distance of three miles of some of the most formidable dangers on the coast."

—Nova Scotia and Bay of Fundy Pilot
(Tenth Edition, 1958, page 85).

ON July 19th the log recorded that Cape Race radio beacon still bore a little west of north, much the same as it had two days before; these had been largely days of calm.

Sometimes the speed indicator would begin to register: half a knot, then *Cardinal Vertue* would be taken aback and I would spend a quarter of an hour gybing her back on course again. Usually the tiny breeze would be contrary. Next a puff might come from astern; up spinnaker! But in ten minutes the wind would be hushed again and the enormous ocean swell would be sending everything that was free to move crashing to and fro.

Compass variation had reached maximum and would begin to decrease from now on. At Plymouth the variation had been 10°W, that is, the magnetic compass needle pointed 10 degrees west of true north. As a ship sails westwards towards Newfoundland, the variation increases until it reaches 28 degrees off Cape Race; for the needle indicates the bearing of the Magnetic Pole, which is situated in northeast Canada. Off New York it has become 11 degrees again.

As charts are marked with lines of equal variation, there is no problem for the navigator if he remembers the sailor's rhyme: "Variation west, magnetic best." This means he must subtract variation from compass reading to obtain a true bearing.

Four days earlier, a check on the water showed that with my present rate of consumption and progress there would be barely enough to last to New York. The reasons for the shortage were: calms far in excess of those predicted by the pilot cha..s, and an underestimation of the amount of water needed to reconstitute the dehydrated food. As I had now eaten most of the things I liked best, there was little food left aboard except dehydrated. Furthermore, even worse calms were to be expected in July along the Atlantic sea-board of the United States.

I took the following steps: fresh water was rationed to one and a half pints a day for all purposes. In order to reduce my kidney output to a minimum, I went without any fluids whatever for the first twenty-four hours of rationing. This step is essential when fluid has to be conserved, as the slightly increased concentration of the blood which results automatically signals to the kidneys to "Shut down". The experience was less unpleasant than might have been supposed.

Rain water had to be collected. I emptied all large tins aboard and put them in the cockpit whenever it rained. This was often enough now; so that in the first twenty-four hours I caught four and a half pints, mostly in the canvas spray hood. Some samples were contaminated by spray, but even these could be used for cooking.

The dehydrated food presented the biggest problem. Most solid foods contain 60–80 per cent. water, which has to be added to reconstitute dehydrated food. Some salt water can be used for the meat and vegetables, but the highest ratio I could tolerate was one part of salt water to three fresh. I tried more but it made me sick.

However, I found that if the tins or packets were opened, and their contents were exposed to the moist sea air in the cockpit for about twenty-four hours, they would absorb a good deal of moisture. For instance, the brittle dehydrated "plastic chips" which used to need ten ounces of fresh water, only required two ounces of fresh and two ounces of salt, after twelve hours "airing". I concluded the note in the log by writing: "In case this sounds alarming: (a) By the rules of the race, I *can* put into any port to stock up (St. John's is only a few days away). However, I have no intention of putting in and wasting any more time. (b) I am conserving supplies so strictly that I will soon have some in hand. (c) There are three solar stills aboard which can be blown up and used to convert salt water to fresh, but I am keeping them in reserve for use further south where the sun is stronger. Once in the water, the stills cannot be brought aboard again, and if towed at any speed will capsize and become contaminated. However, these gadgets are ideal for use with a rubber raft. (d) There is an extra two gallons of water in a plastic jerry-can attached to the emergency rubber raft."

363

Rubber rafts were the main items of the emergency equipment supplied to us through the Naval Life Saving Committee. They are normally blown up by CO_2 cylinders, but these did not turn up at Plymouth in time.

When these one-man rafts arrived, they had been piled on my deck. I passed one to each of the others and put another below for myself. There must have been several over, however, because when I had time to sort things out at sea, I found I had no less than three—a miniature armada, I thought, if ever I had to use them!

The rafts had complete covers, for the main cause of loss of life among castaways is cold, aggravated by dampness and wind which soon disperses body heat. So a "fug" must be produced in which heat loss is prevented.

The second enemy is thirst; a man may live fifty days without food but rarely as long as two weeks when deprived of water. About one and a half pints is the least daily requirement to maintain health but with four-fifths of a pint a person's condition will only deteriorate gradually, unless fluid loss is accelerated by a hot climate, seasickness or diarrhoea.

The highest concentration of salt with which the kidneys can deal is 0.8 per cent., but sea water contains 3.5 per cent. of salt. If it is drunk, the excess of salt must be excreted and dissolved in water derived from the body fluids, so that the result is likely to be a net loss of liquid. There is still argument as to whether small amounts of sea water are helpful, useless, or lethal, to castaways. Until more is known, it would be safer to abstain.

The plastic jerry-can of emergency fresh water was tied to a large kit-bag into which had been stuffed my survival gear. The water-can would float, as fresh water is lighter than salt. The remaining contents of the kit-bag, in addition to a rubber raft, were food, a solar still, fishing kit, the lifeboat chart of the North Atlantic, a protractor for gauging the approximate latitude, a compass and a heliograph mirror for signalling. Stored separately were distress rockets.

The food was entirely carbohydrate (sugars and starches), five ounces a day for two weeks. No protein was included because protein foods cause the body to lose water when their waste products are excreted. On the other hand a small portion of the carbohydrate consumed is broken down by the body into water.

"The glass is higher than ever now; will this calm never break?" I wrote on the 19th. "I am trying every plan. Going over the wind roses on the pilot charts, pilot books and tide-tables. Can I work the tides, drifting and anchoring along the coasts of Nova Scotia and Maine? Reluctantly I decide against it. The coastline is too broken and the sea too deep right up to the cliffs for anchoring; nor are the land and sea breezes helpful off Nova Scotia; but I could use the method off Long Island if necessary.

"Graham in *Emanuel* took twenty-five days from Bantry to St. John's. My thirty-two days from south of Mizzen Head (opposite Bantry) to Cape Race (near St. Johns) has been pretty bad. Hamilton sailed from Glasgow to Belle Isle in twenty-nine days. But—neither of these had calms!"

My calms up to noon on July 19th had totalled four days twenty-one hours! I learnt later that Blondie Hasler had made the passage from the entrance to Bantry Bay to off St. John's in some twenty-seven days.

"The problem of morale is all important. I can do nothing about the lack of wind, so let me see what I *can* do.

"Use every zephyr. This means little rest day or night and a lot of steering because the vane does not function under two and a half knots. See to everything that needs doing, e.g. oiling reefing gear—have to force myself out of apathy into activity—but feel the better for it! With the New England coast notorious for calms, I have to expect even more calms now, so must collect rain water. For the past three days have been using rain water only, so am doing quite well. Must avoid slackness, as last night when I kept on the less advantageous tack. The direction was all right but I neglected to look up the pilot chart during the night, so entered a contrary current. I will note down everything that will be needed in New York; replacements, repairs and food lists, *now*, so that I can start back with the least possible delay. And *what* a lot of water and butter and matches the ship will carry! She will be loaded down with books and magazines and have a spare battery, so there will be electric light!

"The last thing about morale is that underneath the bitterness at the calms, the frustration of knowing I have failed in the race, being sorry for myself, and suchlike stupid feelings, plus some real loneliness now, there is gradually emerging a quiet but very grim determination to get there. There seems to be an inner and quite unexpected strength of purpose. It is not melodrama but plain certainty to say that I am going to get to New York in this boat no matter how long it takes and even if I have to arrive there starving!"

Six hundred miles away Val Howells, too, was feeling depressed.

"Progress good, but morale terrible," he wrote that day. "Shedding tears over wife and family."

Blondie also had his troubles. "Over-ate last night," his medical log records!

The evening of July 19th brought wind. "Lord, I am tired!" I had written, after hours of attempting to use largely illusory breezes. But I was to have little sleep that night; just half-hourly snatches, interrupted by having to climb sleepily out onto the transom and squat down, swaying to the ship's rolling, poised over the boiling phosphorescence which swirled off the rudder, to adjust the self-steering gear which needed a lot of attention with a variable wind on the quarter. But the effort was worth while, for by noon G.M.T. next day, 9 a.m. ship's time, *Cardinal Vertue* had covered sixty miles since 9 p.m. the previous night, an average of exactly five knots.

She kept going all day in rain squalls, fog and gathering seas. First the genoa had to be handed, then the mainsail reefed. The glass had fallen to 1,008 mb from its reading of 1,025 mb during the last calm.

Twice the sun broke through the clouds, each time allowing me to obtain a sight. It was a luxury to be able to pin-point the day's position like this, and to have an additional guide in the soundings of the banks below!

During the evening of July 20th we sailed free of the iceberg zone that we had been crossing for eleven days.

"After all that nervous strain," I wrote, "not to have seen even one seems unfair."

I was disturbed that night by an irregular banging in the weather scuppers. Perhaps a halyard was flogging or a stay had parted? I hurried on deck to inspect the rigging with a torch, but nothing seemed out of place. Still the noise continued. Then I shone the torch downwards, to see a glistening blue-green fish, about 10 inches long, with all the glowing colour of the sea in him, flopping about on the deck where he had been cast by a breaking sea. There was a wild scramble before I grabbed him and dropped him down the companionway. I felt rather treacherous towards a fellow sea creature, but I was hungry enough to be ruthless.

Later that night the hourly soundings petered out as we left astern St. Pierre Bank, the westernmost of the Grand Banks, and headed out across the trench scoured by the waters of the St. Lawrence as they emerge from Cabot Strait. The wind now headed us so that we had to plug to windward, unable to lay course against force 4 and 5 breezes and short seas that threw the ship bodily sideways, and still further to leeward. In the open sea without landmarks it is difficult to judge how well a boat is sailing, but I estimated that in these conditions I could only make good sixty degrees from the wind.

"I just can't get used to the motion going hard to windward, especially when she is pressed a bit and leaping about, pounding, swept by spray and shuddering from time to time at the impact of a breaking sea," I wrote. "If the wind does drop a little, I often don't realize, in all the cuffufle of sea and violent motion, especially when I am over-tired and my judgment clouded and my mental processes slow, that it is time to unreef.

"As a result I am often too slow at making sail when the wind is dropping—of course one doesn't want to mistake a lull, after which the wind may blow harder than ever, for a real easing. Sometimes I go on deck two or three times with the mast winch handle, and hold my hand, and am glad to have done so.

"The strain on a ship's gear, other things being equal, is propor-tionate to her displacement. A heavy displacement boat like *Cardinal Vertue* sets up considerable stresses in her mast and rigging in a seaway. Therefore to some extent one has to reef in accordance with the violence of the sea as well as the strength of the wind. However, as I am of a timid disposition, I find that I tend to be too easily overawed by the size of the waves."

Following a new train of thought I continued: "I must say I would be glad to talk to people again. It is five and a half weeks since I spoke to a soul. It is not only people I miss but food and drink, too. That fresh fish for lunch has whetted my appetite; but I can't find the fish hooks!

"I wish the wind would change. It has been right on the nose for twenty-three hours now. But what can I do about it? Slocum thought praying for a favourable wind a waste of time. On the other hand the Vikings, even after their conversion, thought highly of the com-petence of 'Old Red Beard'—Thor—in dealing with such matters as winds, storms and fighting."

My wishes remained unfulfilled, for when the line squall awakened me at 5.30 a.m. on the 22nd and I clambered sleepily on deck, the wind had changed and a row of black clouds lay to leeward, but I still could not lay the course. Swearing feebly, I rolled down 3 feet of the main and came about. Everything got in the way, as it does when one is half asleep.

The glass rose, but the wind was not dropping and the ship was being pressed still harder. This problem of how much sail to carry was presented anew each day. It was the sea's challenge. I held up the windspeed indicator: thirty-four to thirty-seven miles per hour, force 7, and squally too! No wonder she was labouring!

So I rolled down more mainsail until 7½ feet of it had been wound round the boom. This is as much as it can be reefed and still leave enough to function as a sail.

The yacht would not tolerate the full No. 1 staysail and I was grateful for Humphrey Barton's advice to have reef points in this sail, for it is infinitely easier to reef it than to change to a smaller sail. I dropped the staysail into the sea and sat wedged on the plunging, reeling, foredeck with my safety-belt clipped to a stay, tying the reef points.

Once the sail had been hoisted and sheeted in, *Cardinal Vertue* porpoised to windward, thudding and jumping. The wind had not yet had time to raise a big sea, though long lines of foam were beginning to run from the frothing white crests. Now it was blowing at forty miles an hour, force 8. I had not believed it possible for a small yacht to beat to windward in the open sea in a gale, but I now saw that it was, provided the shape and steepness of the seas allowed.

It was a wonderful, bright morning. As the seas built higher, the self-steering vane would be almost becalmed in the troughs between the waves. We were working across the strait between Newfoundland and Nova Scotia. The wind eased towards evening, but rose later, so that I had to reef again at 2.30 a.m. and close reef at 5 a.m. when the yacht was pressed hard over.

I was sleepily beginning to stir when a violent crack sounded from above and a sail began to flog wildly. "My God, the gooseneck has gone!" I thought, as I struggled into my P.V.C. smock and boots. The pawl that engages the ratchet on the roller reefing gear had slipped, partly because the entire fitting had now become loose on the boom. I smeared it with Bostik and hammered it home. Then, with great care, I close-reefed the mainsail and reefed the staysail; while low, ragged clouds scudded by from the westward, beneath a high sheet of alto-cumulus, which was already becoming tinged by the dawn.

It was blowing force 7 on that lowering morning of the 23rd, as the ship crashed her way into soundings across Missaine Bank, the first of the Nova Scotian Banks, south of Cape Breton Island. We had been sailing hard to windward for the past seventy hours, during sixty-nine of which I had been unable to lay course. No sights had been possible for three days. During the night the sky had cleared enough to show stars, for only the fourth time since leaving England. The lights of several ships had passed as they steamed south out of the St. Lawrence. "Every ship passes at night or in fog. I would like the opportunity of being reported," I wrote sadly. The chance was to come only too quickly!

At 4.45 p.m. the silhouettes of four warships in line astern appeared through the murk. One changed course and came towards me, throwing aside sheets of spray as she ploughed through the head sea set up by the force 5–6 breeze.

The Canadian frigate *Swansea* swung round to port of me, on to my weather side, her crew lining the decks as she manœuvred. How excited I was to see so many people!

I told them who I was and asked them to report me to Lloyds. The conversation was direct; the captain using his loud-hailer and myself shouting. My words were relayed when necessary by the crew. The captain acknowledged my request to be reported.

"Do you want your position?" he enquired.

"No, thank you," I answered untruthfully, for I was too proud to admit before such an audience that I had no idea exactly where I was.

They called "Good luck" and started to go ahead; but for some reason slowed again and wallowed to a stop, dead to windward of me. The crew began taking photographs and called more questions; they did not seem to realize the danger in which they were placing me.

In a moment my close-reefed mainsail and reefed staysail were flapping idly, all wind blanketed by the steel monster bearing down upon me. I called desperately for them to go ahead; no one heeded. Then the grey steel hull crashed against my planking, stripping off paint each time we rolled and scraped together. I was sobbing with helpless anger and frustration as I made futile efforts to fend off with a boat-hook.

Much shouting now began from the deck above, where everyone seemed to be giving orders at once, with no visible effect. "Go ahead or to starboard, you idiots!" I yelled furiously.

Then at last they did do something. They went *astern*. As the frigate rasped her way past me the high flare of her bow caught in my rigging and tore the port lower spreader out of its socket, splitting the wood from the thin bolt which held it. Failure of the starboard lower spreader had caused the loss of my mast off Plymouth.

369

Frantically I lowered all sail and throwing off oilskins, boots and jersey, shinned up the wildly gyrating mast to inspect the damage. Thank God, the cross-tree itself was not broken! Down again to collect a hammer, knife and insulation tape and tie them to my wrist. Then up to the cross-trees again where I was able to get a leg over the starboard one and clipped on my safety-belt in case I should be flicked into the sea; for *Cardinal Vertue* was rolling so violently now that at the end of each dizzy swing I had not strength enough to hold on by myself.

I cut the lashing which attached the spreader to the shroud and hammered it straight and back into its socket. Then I bound the inner

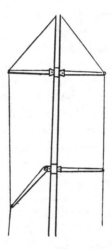

part with insulation tape; the outboard end would have to wait for calmer weather. I slid to the deck and clung to the mast, retching and trembling; wet through with sweat and soaked in spray; mouth open, gasping for breath as I rested my aching limbs.

A hail caused me to look over my shoulder. A pinnace circled near, from which the captain of *Swansea* apologized and asked if I needed help.

"Against the rules of the race, but thank you," I called. "Please report my position."

I hoisted sail at five-thirty. It seemed unbelievable that the whole incident had occupied only half an hour! The wind had dropped a little but we were sailing on the port tack so that the strain came on the damaged cross-tree.

"I only hope to God it holds," I wrote. "My fingers can hardly write from trembling, I am trying to keep dry and get warm, but my torn P.V.C. trousers have been inadequately mended.

"The frigate stood by until I was well under way, then with spray showering over her decks as she got up speed, she was soon swallowed by the mist." She never reported me. "Now the only thing to do is to hang on," I continued. "It is no good reducing sail 'in case'; if the mast is going it will go; I have to know its strength if it is going to last."

I was shivering with cold in my damp clothes and longing for coffee or a chance to crawl between blankets to rest my body which was aching and bruised from the buffeting received on the mast. But the wind had risen to force 7 again, and the ship was pounding and burying her lee rail. I close-reefed to ease her, then wrote doubtfully: "I *think* I reefed for the same wind force as I would have before the accident and was not influenced by my fear—that is something, anyway! I have to live with the damaged spreader, so had best come to terms with it right now!"

Now that there was time to make coffee, the Calor gas cooker jet had burned out. Over a tiny yellow flame I was eventually able to heat one mug of water. I was too tired to eat, even if I could have cooked anything.

I added a postscript to the day's log entry:

"Dead reckoning not going so well tonight. Soundings of banks won't square with my estimated position. Now I wish I hadn't been too proud to accept my position, when the frigate offered it—still, I would do exactly the same again!"

During the night the wind was variable, so that sheets and steering needed frequent adjustment. I awoke after an hour's sleep at 5 a.m. on July 24th, feeling very tired and most reluctant to crawl on deck into a damp fog. I had unreefed the staysail and was trying to decide whether the dying wind and slopping sea justified more mainsail, when a squall screamed out of the mist to windward and heeled the yacht over until she raced along crashing into the seas, with water cascading over her lee deck.

The clew fitting began to slip out again, so feeling depressed, I hammered it home. The stove would not burn, the leach of the mainsail was vibrating where a batten had been lost, the weakened spreader was putting the mast in danger—things seem to be getting on top of me!

"I cut down and shaped a spare batten, only to find that I could not reach to fit it into its pocket without lowering the sail." I noted, then added: "But heave-to unnecessarily in a race such as this I will not do, so am carrying on with the sail vibrating!"

By 6.30 a.m. I had turned my attention to the stove and had it partly dismantled when the squall increased. As I rolled down more mainsail, I found that the bent gooseneck fitting was slipping again. "Nothing I can do about it," I wrote, "Except slacken the sheet for the shortest possible time when reefing or unreefing, because while the sheet remains taut, the boom is held in firmly against the mast."

Back to the stove again to find that by reversing the grill fittings I could use the grill to cook and to boil water. This was a relief, as most of my remaining food would need a good deal of cooking.

With the ship driving through the fog close to her course, and with two large mugs of coffee and the remains of yesterday's curry inside me, the bright side of things began to filter through. I wrote more cheerfully:

"Estimated run to noon sixty miles. Strict water rationing and collecting every possible drop of rain water have eased the position a lot.

"I feel less timid at sea than I was. The essence of this thing is really to overcome difficulties as they arise. To do so brings a profound contentment and self-confidence extending far beyond the business in hand.

"There is no one to turn to for advice or to moan or squeal to. Therefore it requires little effort to tackle anything that goes wrong. It must be seen to, so you just get on and do it, and you find yourself doing things you would have thought impossible."

I sailed on through the fog, taking hourly echo-sounder readings. Sable Island radio beacon, away to the southward, gave an approximate position line showing that I was south of Nova Scotia, but there was no way of telling how far south. The sun and horizon had not been clear enough for sights for four days.

I had to overcome my great tiredness to change headsails as the wind waxed and waned. I tried again to estimate my position; but in the mental dullness of exhaustion I neglected the one important measure of laying off a bearing on the chart, north of which I must not go. So I sailed on through the silent, fog-shrouded world, all the time steadily closing the rock-bound coast of Nova Scotia.

At 1 p.m. we entered soundings once more. This was in order, as I expected to cross a series of offshore banks; but at 3 p.m. the depth had decreased to twenty-eight fathoms, which meant that, one way or the other, my estimated position must be out.

Now I plotted soundings every ten minutes; fifteen fathoms, twenty, fifteen again. Then the monotonous hoot of a foghorn began to starboard. Was it a ship? Or was not the sound being repeated too regularly? I dived below for the light list and tried unsucessfully to identify the signal.

I was still trying when a low rumbling which surged and receded became audible ahead. For a few seconds I did not realize what it was. Then I slammed the helm hard over and jumped for the foredeck to pull the genoa across as we swung round through the eye of the wind. As I wrestled with the sail, I knew the sound for what it was, and I glanced over the starboard quarter to where fifty to a hundred yards away through the fog I could see the lazy ocean swells heaping up and breaking in a frenzy of bursting surf against the iron-bound coast of Nova Scotia.

As we came about, the bolt holding the log inexplicably sheered and it disappeared, together with the rotator and line, leaving the out-rigger still attached by its lanyard. There it lay in ten fathoms, as if it were an offering demanded by the strange gods of that gaunt coast. My knees were trembling as I stood tensed at the helm, for I had seen death that afternoon.

6

UNFRIENDLY COAST

"A tropical depression . . . became designated as 'Brenda' as it moved up the U.S. coast, July 29–31."
                    —*U.S. Dept. of Commerce Weather Bureau,*
        Preliminary report of tropical storm "Brenda": August 1960

*   *   *

"WARNING: This area is exceedingly treacherous, being characterized by numerous shoals and tide-rips."
                    —*Nantucket Sound: Esso Cruising Guide*

BY 6.30 p.m. we were well clear of the Nova Scotian coast. The visibility was still only a hundred yards, but *Cardinal Vertue* was charging the seas and lifting to the swell of the open Atlantic. I pressed on southwards and soon the foghorns of steamers traversing the Canadian coastal shipping lane sounded ahead. We passed through them in light airs until their faint echoes faded away astern.

Midnight found me writing: "Such a trusting little ship! She is 'chuntering' to herself and the kiwi as she bucks and fusses away to the south-westward through the fog and darkness, outside all dangers now.

"I don't want to let her down any more. After all she needs *some* taking care of—come to think of it there are people on shore I would rather not let down either!"

One final radio bearing on Sable Island and a glance at the echo-sounder to make sure we were outside the forty-fathom line and I turned in for two hours of badly needed sleep.

I awoke at 4 a.m. to find the night brilliant with stars and the wind free so that I could lay course. For a time I stood in the cockpit nursing a cup of coffee. Then as day began to break, high and red above a long bank of cloud, I went forward and, holding on to the mast, gazed upwards at the loveliness of the yacht's high sails, now tinged with rose. I was thankful to be alive to see this dawn.

By a tremendous effort I stayed awake until I could obtain a sight

374

9. Four of the five race competitors at Plymouth before the start. *Left to right:* Francis Chichester, the winner, Blondie Hasler, Val Howells and David Lewis.

10. For the race, *Cardinal Vertue* carried 32 gallons of water, much of it in plastic bags stowed in the cockpit.

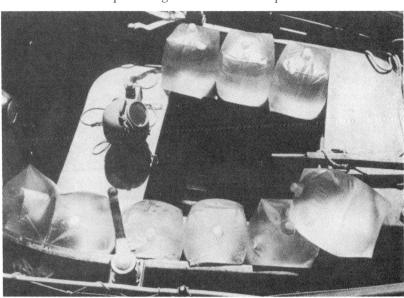

11. *Cardinal Vertue* in Plymouth Sound after the start of the race.

and then retired to my bunk, leaving *Cardinal Vertue* to dance through the sunshine across the blue, white-crested waves. That morning, July 25th, marked the end of my sixth week at sea; a week, as I wrote in the log, that was "not without incident".

Awakening that afternoon, I prepared to work out my morning's sight. The spare log which I had streamed off Nova Scotia was working well; the sight had been a good one—but it was useless. The deck-watch had stopped. In my exhaustion the previous night, I had omitted to wind it!

Would the radio, which was not working well, be able to pick up time signals from WWV, the U.S. Standards station at Washington? I tuned to 2,500 kc and listened anxiously through the headphones; nothing. No!—I could hear the faint voice of the Boston Marine radio operator forecasting calms. Well, I must try again at night, when sometimes reception is better. It was 2 a.m. before, to my infinite relief, the regular *toc, toc, toc* of WWV sounded, and I could start the deck-watch again. I resolved that in future I would compare it with my wrist-watch several times each day so as to have a stand-by time-piece whose exact error I knew. I was lucky to have obtained my time check when I did, for two days afterwards the radio gave up for good.

We seemed to have suddenly reached the south. It was warm for the first time for weeks. Next day, July 26th, we sailed across the Nova Scotia Banks about fifty miles off shore over a sparkling sea.

The metal spring which closes the clip of my safety-belt had rusted and snapped, so I bound the clip with thin shock cord to make a new elastic spring. This worked well for nearly four thousand miles, but I never felt quite at ease in trusting my life to such makeshift handiwork.

There was a relative absence of ocean swell on this windward side of the Atlantic, so I took advantage of the calmer weather to go aloft and put tape around the outer end of the damaged cross-tree and its shroud; it had not shifted an inch!

With a light favourable breeze we glided along under the spinnaker across lines of whispering overfalls. Later, the wind headed us, so I went forward to hand the spinnaker. This sail is set on a metal boom 11 feet long which, in *Cardinal Vertue*, pivots from the mast about 16 feet above the deck. When the sail is set, the boom is suspended horizontally. As I slackened the halyard and topping lift and pulled on the guy, the clip attaching the boom to the sail slipped, so that it swung down in an arc, crashing between my eyes.

I could not have been unconscious for long, because the blood which stained the blue spinnaker and white genoa had not yet clotted. Groggily, I finished lowering the spinnaker, hoisted the genoa and stumbled below. I was a little startled at the apparition reflected in the mirror; but wrote later in the log: "My nose has never been an asset and now that the bridge has been broken it may well be improved when the swelling subsides."

A week later I could summarize the incident. "From the distribution of the bruising tracking across the orbit three days after I cracked my forehead with the spinnaker pole, I apparently not only broke the nasal bone but also the frontal or sphenoid or both" (bones forming part of

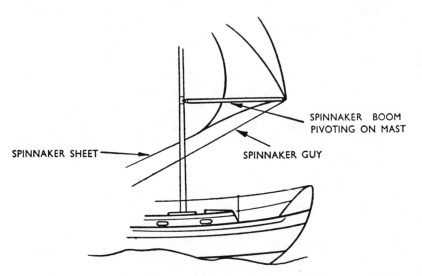

SPINNAKER BOOM
PIVOTING ON MAST

SPINNAKER SHEET

SPINNAKER GUY

the front of the skull). "I was easily tired for several days, possibly due to concussion, but the immediate effect, headache, wore off quickly after three aspirin—in any case I feel well enough now." It was a further week, however, before the abnormal tiredness had quite gone.

The remark that the headache "Soon wore off", was rather an understatement, for it does not tally with the log of the 27th. Due to light winds, I had to steer for most of the night following the accident, and how my head did ache!

But soon my attention was taken by the lights of a power vessel which had appeared ahead. For two hours, as she came nearer, she would yaw about showing first her green light then her red, so that I did not know on which side she would pass. At last all three lights began to glow steadily; she was heading straight towards me. I hastily came about and ghosted away with bare steerage way into the darkness to port, while she went blindly by, two hundred yards away, with diesel thumping and lights blazing.

Dawn broke clear, above the rippling overfalls, to show the first fishing boat I had seen since fog had closed in, south of Ireland. But I felt too ill to take an interest in anything except my own headache and the fact that I was chilled to the bone. So I climbed miserably between the blankets as the wind fell away into calm.

A good deal of thought had gone into making up medical kits and preparing a document to give advice to each competitor in the event of serious accident or illness. None of the drugs was needed, but neither were the distress flares; and I consider that carefully chosen medical equipment should always be carried on ocean passages in small craft. The aim is not first-aid, but fairly long-term treatment. For, especially if a man is alone, he must be able to treat himself and keep himself going for at least as long as it would take to reach a shipping lane; and that might be several weeks.

There are several ways of approaching this problem, which concerns a situation not dealt with by first-aid text-books. The document worked out for the race, and reproduced in Appendix Five, tries to make full use of modern antibiotic drugs and common sense.

On July 28th I rounded Cape Sable which was about forty miles to the north, and in light variable winds headed out across the Gulf of Maine towards Nantucket Shoals light-vessel.

A week before, Francis Chichester had won a well-earned victory by reaching the Ambrose Light.

Hasler was now within a hundred miles of his goal. He was writing:

"Having a great time guzzling butter, jam, etc.—now unrationed!"

As Val Howells neared Bermuda his mood lightened. He had been worried at radio warnings of an approaching hurricane and even more seriously because his boat had been making far "too much water for comfort", and by July 26th things were so bad that he had written: "Will be glad to get to Bermuda (God willing)."

Jean Lacombe was bouncing about, far behind, in light contrary airs, somewhere between the Azores and Bermuda.

But I knew nothing of the others' progress. I was convinced that they would all be in New York already, yet this in no way diminished the thrill of getting out the last set of charts and setting my watch by Eastern Standard Time, five hours slow on Greenwich. I was making up on water too—if only the wind would hold!

377

Since the previous day delicate wisps of high cirrus and veils of alto-stratus had begun to spread over the sky from the westward. Now dark overcast, from which a fine rain was beginning to fall, hung over the sea, hiding the high clouds. The glass began to drop.

As the radio had gone dead, there could be no hints about approaching weather from Boston Marine, but it seemed fairly obvious that a depression was coming. "I will have to tack and reef and sail off course, but at least there will be no calms, and that is worth anything," I wrote.

But I was wrong. The expected "low" did not materialize. Instead the wind dropped right away as a day of disappointment ended in drizzling darkness and the slat, slat, slat, of the becalmed sails.

Midnight brought puffs of wind, which lasted for perhaps half an hour, before giving way to calm again. Later a new breeze would spring up from a fresh quarter only to die out in its turn. All night long, through warm, damp darkness, I steered and changed sails. Sometimes the genoa was needed, at others the spinnaker. The glass continued to fall very slowly.

With daylight came thick fog. I was on the foredeck changing sail when a deep throbbing sound became audible far off in the mist. I stood stock still, my scalp prickling with fear of the unknown. The noise was rapidly becoming louder and nearer. What strange machine could be racing over the water at such speed?

I ran back to the cockpit and sat clutching the useless tiller so tightly that my knuckles showed white, while my eyes strained fearfully into the mist. I was still sitting there when the rumble became an ear-splitting roar and a deluge of blinding rain thundered out of the sky. I have never known rain like it, even in tropical "cloudbursts". I made for the cabin, gasping, drenched and unable to breathe freely; thoroughly ashamed of my fear.

All day in thick fog we worked our way by soundings along the edge of George's Bank, about the middle of the Gulf of Maine. Lines of flotsam marked where currents met—seaweed, sponges, paper cartons, an empty life-jacket—for fifteen hours it was flat, glassy calm. Seagulls "under power" paddled past across that mirror-like surface where we lay helpless.

By midnight, constantly changing sail and steering in the light airs, I had made twelve miles headway in twenty-four hours. For some reason I began to feel less depressed for the remainder of the night, and even sang a little as I hoisted and lowered the spinnaker and adjusted the vane, and we crept onward through fog and drenching rain squalls.

Earlier in the evening I had been so sorry for myself, chafing at the calms and the lack of a compass light, and at my unpalatable food. Now I seemed to have snapped out of it—the slower our progress, and the further we were forced away from our proper course and north of Nantucket Shoals light vessel, the more did stubborn determination come to replace self-pity.

"The sea and winds certainly aren't letting me have this the easy way—but whoever expected that, or wants it?" I wrote then.

At midday on July 30th, the two-day fog parted to reveal a Wellsian structure of domes on stalks about ten miles away. This was Texas Tower No. 2, the first land-based object I had seen (except the Nova Scotia surf) since the lights of the Lizard and Ushant had dropped astern seven weeks before.

The sky cleared, but the glass which had slowly fallen from 1,021 mb two days before, to 1,009 mb, now began to drop so fast that in the next seven hours it fell 10 mb, to 999 mb. Such weather was outside all my experience. I read and re-read the weather notes in the American Pilot and the notes on gales off the Atlantic seaboard supplied by Bruce Robinson, Vice-Commodore of the Slocum Society. What could be coming? If only the radio were working! What a mercy for my peace of mind that it was not; for I was in the "dangerous semicircle" of tropical revolving storm "Brenda", which was now almost upon me.

These storms may or may not reach hurricane intensity (Beaufort force 12, sixty-five knots), and no such great wind velocities were recorded in "Brenda". But they can never be taken lightly. Under the heading "Tropical Revolving Storms" in the *Pilot*, is the ominous phrase — "while small vessels (for example, destroyers) have foundered". This line cannot fail to impress the crew of a yacht about the size of a destroyer's pinnace.

The storm came suddenly out of the south-east. At 5 p.m. *Cardinal Vertue* was still carrying full sail. Two hours later the mainsail was so close-reefed that it set badly. Everything had happened too quickly. Three times I had reefed; on each occasion late; another batten was gone; the phosphor-bronze snap shackle at the leach of the foresail had sheared. "Altogether a sorry performance!" I admitted in the log.

While daylight still lasted the clouds broke. Beneath a pale blue patch of sky we plunged to windward in the rising gale, over a green, white-capped sea, across an amphitheatre surrounded by tiers of great, tossing, black clouds. A stormy petrel was skimming the wave crests.

379

As the sun sank and the moon broke through the cloudwrack I stood on the transom gripping a backstay with each hand, heedless of fatigue, at one with my ship and with the gale; thrilling to the lift and scend as the yacht corkscrewed up and over the seas; every now and then lurching sideways with a breaking crest, or shuddering at the impact of a sea.

My recollections of the remainder of that night are hazy. The storm blew harder still out of a clear sky, and soon after midnight it began to veer, so that I could no longer lay the course for Nantucket light-vessel. The wind continued to increase, so I gybed onto the starboard tack and took in the foresail and lay-to under close-reefed main. But the main was set badly so at times it flogged, shaking the whole ship. According to Boston Weather Bureau Storm Advisory No. 6 of July 30th, the wind in the eastern semicircle within two hundred miles of the storm centre was 40 m.p.h., gusting to 60 m.p.h. I was at that time well in this semicircle, fifty to a hundred miles from the centre.

After all sail was stowed the yacht rolled violently up to twenty degrees to starboard and thirty degrees to port. The cabin lamp had gone out. Feeling sick and exhausted, I filled it with paraffin and lit it. Lowering sail and making all secure, heaving-to and filling and lighting the lamp, had occupied one and a half hours. For a time the fury of the gale increased but I felt too ill and tired to care.

It was still night when the storm left me as suddenly as it had come, to wreak havoc on the nearby coast. As far away as New York, Blondie Hasler who had just arrived, dared not leave *Jester*, even in harbour, for fear she might be damaged.

In pitch darkness making sail on that fantastically tossing deck was an even harder task than stowing it had been. I got under way in a strong south-west breeze; but by daylight I was becalmed once more.

For two days it remained calm. My first sights showed that we had been carried back by the storm and had since drifted up into the Gulf of Maine. No more should be said about these two days. They were one of the times when I was glad to be alone; for I showed up very badly—sorry for myself, depressed and miserable.

The second day of the calms was August 1st, the end of the seventh week at sea, a week during which there had been calms on every day.

That evening a light breeze sprang up, still south-west, and I decided not to round Nantucket Shoals light-vessel, for we had now been set far to the northward and it lay fifty miles dead to windward. Instead, I would set course for Pollock Rip and take the tricky channel into the Sounds which lie behind Nantucket and Martha's Vineyard Islands. For all their tide-rips and shoals, this way would now be quicker. Luckily, I had brought detailed charts of the area to cope with this very eventuality.

At 2 a.m. on August 2nd I awoke and scanned the horizon and saw a flashing light on the starboard bow. A queer noise, rather like an engine blowing off steam, was audible at fairly regular intervals. The chart showed that there was a whistle buoy at Great Round Shoal, which was only a few miles north of my estimated position. Well, I thought, this must be it, ahead. I had never heard a whistle buoy before and the noise did sound most odd. But what else could it be?

Dawn was breaking, and soon by its light I could see two great wet backs, glistening, shot with gold in the first sunrays, come curving out of the water. The whales blew again, then side by side, swam off into the sunrise. So much for my whistle buoy!

Daylight showed a fishing boat not far away, so I altered course to intercept her. As I approached the motor fishing launch *Curlew* one of the two men aboard stepped out from the wheelhouse and waved.

"Good morning," I called. "Can you report me to U.S. Coast-guards, *Cardinal Vertue* out of Plymouth, England, bound towards New York?"

He nodded, replied, "O.K.", and turned back into the wheelhouse.

This casual reception took the wind out of my sails with a vengeance. And just when I was feeling like some budding Columbus! I hardened in the mainsheet viciously and shoved the helm over.

Across the water floated snatches of conversation from the wheel-house:

"That little bitty sail boat come all the way from Plymouth, New England."

"No. He said, Plymouth, *England*."

There was a pause; then the wheelhouse door slammed open and a startled face appeared:

"Did you say Plymouth, *England?*"

"Yes, seven weeks out."

"Man!" over his shoulder to the mate, "This sail boat *did* come from Plymouth, England."

They told me that the light I had seen was Sankaty Head lighthouse on Nantucket Island. Great Round Shoal Channel lay ten miles to the north-west. I thanked them and set off again.

Five minutes later I heard the throb of an engine at full power and

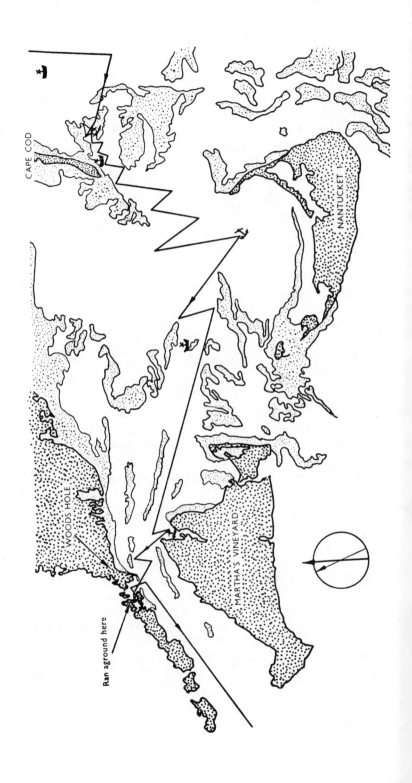

CAPE COD

NANTUCKET I.

WOODS HOLE

Ran aground here

MARTHA'S VINEYARD

looked round to see *Curlew* come surging up, her bow wave creaming high. She slowed alongside and a voice called:

"Did you come all the way from *England?* What sort of weather did you have? Here—you must want some fresh fish!"

It took real self-control to refuse this offer but the rules of the race laid down that we were not to accept stores from another vessel. "I am so damned sick of stew," I wrote in my diary, "and even the biscuit is nearly finished, but I am not going to get disqualified *now*."

As I headed for Great Round Shoal buoy I studied the charts and tide tables but before we could reach the buoy, fog had set in. There was little chance of finding it now, so there was nothing else for it but to keep on until I could hear the fog signals of the two light-vessels which mark Pollock Rip channel, ten miles beyond the Round Shoal. I would miss the tide, but that couldn't be avoided. The only other course, to turn back and go round outside Nantucket Shoals light-vessel, fifty miles out to sea against light variable winds, was unthinkable when I could pass through Nantucket and Vineyard Sounds and then head direct for Long Island. So I watched the echo sounder and studied the charts. A tide rip showed white and broken in the mist to port, then was left astern.

"I will anchor and wait for the tide at Pollock Rip, if this wind holds and I can find it," I wrote. "What a pity the radio direction finder has packed up. But I am so happy to be doing something and getting places. My writing is worse than usual because I am trying to steer in an erratic wind and peer into the fog with fifty yards visibility, and listen, all at the same time.

"The tide turns foul at midday, and then all Nantucket Sound comes sluicing out of Pollock Rip channel which is bordered by shoals, overfalls and tide-rips."

By 9 a.m. I could hear Stone Horse light-vessel towards the inside of the channel and Pollock Rip light-vessel outside, both giving tongue.

The reasons for the decision I took then are recorded in my diary.

"Well, it is half-neaps; there should be enough water over the shoals; the weather is calm. Unless I can make use of the last of this favourable tide, I will have to anchor outside and not begin to negotiate the channel until after dark, with a headwind too. So I am heading straight in over the shoals through the fog, directly towards the sound of Stone Horse."

"God, it was tense!" I wrote afterwards. "Two hours with soundings in feet and the breaking water of the rips splashing aboard!

"Then the sound signals stopped. This could only mean that the fog was lifting around the light-vessel, but near me it was as thick as ever. Then I heard a bell—port side of main channel, bell buoys! I shouted aloud with relief, and a few moments later the low desolate outline of Cape Cod broke through the mist, fronted by a forlorn wreck. One by one the channel buoys loomed out of the fog.

"The tide was already streaming out of the Sound sweeping me back, so I anchored in six fathoms at 1.30 p.m. The tide raced past at 2.8 knots by the speedometer.

"So now the hook is down for the first time for two thousand, nine hundred miles, and I am finishing the gin, drinking to all those who made this possible."

While I was making things shipshape a small whale swam by. "What cheek," I thought—right beside Nantucket Island, the very home of whaling. There was only time for a hurried meal before the tide began to slacken. The wind had risen to force 6 and was blowing from dead ahead. I reefed 4 feet of the mainsail before starting to break out the anchor.

It took one hour and twenty-seven minutes to get that anchor in. Towards the end my hands would not grip any more, so I wound both arms in the chain and pulled by swinging my body backwards. My arms and legs were bruised and I ached all over.

By this time thick fog had descended once more. The wind was far stronger; a "smoking southwester" of force 7, which laid *Cardinal Vertue* far over as we tacked up the channel in sheets of spray, guided only by the blare of Stone Horse foghorn.

"I passed the light-vessel by sound—didn't see it though it was only a few hundred yards off; then hove-to and close-reefed the main and reefed No. 1 staysail," I wrote. "She carried all the sail she could bear even then, as the wind kept rising—force 7—maybe force 8; the fog thick as soup and night closing down, and we beating our way into the shoal-spattered waters of Nantucket Sound!

"What a night! The sea always has surprises and we are prepared to meet them all (except calms), but at each new one you think wryly—whatever can it cook up next?

"But it was wonderful! the challenge and thrill, dashing along like that!—and quite impossible without the echo-sounder.

"What a mess below! Every sail-bag had had to come out to free the anchor chain and now everything that is loose in the cabin is sent flying onto the sail-bags and the floor.

"As the wind rose, I had to gybe round at the end of each board, as she would not come about. Only once, at 7 p.m., when a buoy appeared, did I see anything other than fog and breaking crests.

"So by guess and by lead, we entered the Sound and headed towards the lee of Nantucket Island for one and a half hours. I was very much on edge because of an offlying shoal; there was no way of telling which side of it we were, or whether we were heading straight for it.

"At last we seemed far enough in. I got out the kedge anchor and warp this time, and at 10.10 p.m., threw it over in six fathoms, and sighed with relief because I was soaked to the skin and just about all in. The kedge held as well as a paperweight would have done!

"I didn't finally get the bower anchor's chain untangled and the anchor down until 11.30 p.m.—and could hardly walk then. I changed my sopping clothes and made coffee, and lay for an hour as exhausted as I have ever been.

"After the rest, I cleared the forepeak to have the lashing to hand which attaches the anchor chain to the Samson post, in case she started dragging ashore and I had to cut it quickly. Then I rigged up a handy-billy gadget which I hooked onto the chain over the bow to try to ease the terrific snubbing. By then the fog was lifting, so that I could confirm my position by lighthouses, and the wind had dropped to force 4 or 5.

"And now there is a pot of stew cooking and coffee warming up. Will I be fit enough to make use of the next favourable tide, which starts making at 4.30 a.m.? I rather doubt it."

But at 4.45 next morning I started to bring in the anchor. I had no winch and this time it was even harder than before. So I hoisted sail and lashed the tiller over. *Cardinal Vertue* would gather away, snub hard on the cable, bring up short and swing over to the other tack. This was the moment when, if I were quick enough, I could whip one turn of the chain round the Samson post. One turn at a time only, for after slackening momentarily, the chain became as taut as an iron bar. My hands were swollen and tender, my ankles cut and bruised by the chain, and my back was aching.

This last was my weakest point. Many years ago in New Zealand another student and I had spent ten days in a tent waiting for the weather to clear so that we could tackle an unclimbed peak. Conditions did not improve, but we could not bear to leave without making an attempt and set off up rocks which were plastered in wet new snow.

385

As the sun warmed the rocks and snow slides went sloshing down every gully we realized the danger and began to retreat. My companion was crossing a snow couloir, while I anchored him from the snow-covered rocks above with 60 feet of rope, when a snow avalanche buried him and swept him down the couloir, and the tightening rope plucked me off the rock buttress and flicked me through the air like a fly. I fell clear of the rocks and landed on my bottom on hard-packed snow near my companion, who had been cast aside by the avalanche in the lee of the buttress.

We crawled to safety, my friend clutching the head of his broken ice axe; thankful to have been spared the penalty for our foolishness. Our bruises soon healed, but ever since I have limped a little, and when parachuting during the war, would often feel an excruciating pain in my back. I dared not report this for fear of being thrown out of the Airborne Forces; but after the war I had by back X-rayed and found that in my climbing accident I had crushed a lumbar vertebra. So now if ever I flex my lumbar spine unwisely, the sciatic nerve gets trapped and a tiresome spell of hospital exercises, traction or manipulation and rest are required.

As I tugged away at the chain for an hour, wrapping it turn by turn around the Samson post, and then for another hour, I prayed that my aching back would hold.

At 7 a.m. a fishing boat came up and offered to help. I was sorely tempted, but the chain was nearly in.

"When did you get in here?" he asked.

"Last night, through Pollock Rip," I answered wearily, and he stared across at me in disbelief.

At 7.15 a.m., after two and a half hours' work, the anchor came in. Nantucket Island was still but a dim outline through the mist as I hoisted sail and headed up the Sound.

Then the mist rolled back to reveal a new world. Across sparkling green seas, white yachts were sailing on every hand. In the space of seconds we had passed from the grimness of fog and storm into something resembling the Solent during a sunny Cowes week!

I looked around at my untidy ship festooned with ropes and chain, and at myself, filthy, wet and unwashed, and reluctantly decided that I must clear up.

Soon a five-tonner came up with me, sailed by a pleasant-looking couple I would have liked to talk to. As I jumped eagerly up the companion ladder, I stubbed my toe and cursed aloud in anguish. A look of alarm and consternation spread over the two faces in the approaching yacht, which promptly sheered off and rapidly dwindled to leeward. I was left nursing my throbbing toe and the conclusion that I wouldn't be fit for polite society until I got over the habit of speaking my thoughts aloud!

When I unreefed, everything seemed to go wrong, even the topping lift came adrift and was only recovered after an unseamanlike struggle. Eventually things looked a little more shipshape, so after hurriedly shaving and changing, I could at last hoist the Blue Ensign without shame. Of course by now there were no yachts in sight!

In the early afternoon I entered Vineyard Haven on the last of the tide and anchored with the kedge in still water. A gaff cutter sailed by, which I thought for a moment might be Bruce Robinson's *Picket*. Yachts and fishing boats passed and waved or stopped to talk. A can of ice-cold beer was tossed across, which I had already drunk before I remembered the race rules.

I did not know it at the time, but only a mile inshore of where *Cardinal Vertue* was lying to her anchor, her famous sister, *Vertue XXXV*, was moored.

I was desperately tired, but with so many people to see and talk to I was too excited to sleep. I lay down and tried to relax, but was still wide awake when the tide began to make. At eight-thirty that evening I hoisted sail, hauled in the anchor and set off down Vineyard Sound, tacking against a light south-westerly breeze.

The night was clear with lights everywhere; lights of cars and houses and navigation buoys. I felt relaxed and contented, but had only had one hour's sleep since 2 a.m. two nights before, so that I did not notice when we sailed out of Vineyard Sound altogether and, swept by a four-knot tide, floated rapidly down the winding, sand-bank-strewn side-channel of Woods Hole.

At first I thought the echo-sounder must have gone wrong. Then I realized that we had somehow got out of the main Sound and I turned back. For one hour, then a second hour, I tried to retrace my course. It was after midnight now, the lights of the cars appeared at longer intervals as we crept through the darkness and I scanned each shadow hoping for clues as to our position. Then at 1 p.m. *Cardinal Vertue* slid to a halt and heeled over gently to starboard. We were hard aground.

7

AN END AND A BEGINNING

"This pretty young maiden she said unto me,
There's a fine full-rigged clipper just ready for sea."
—*Sea shanty*

I HAD no idea where we were. The torch showed a clear sandy bottom
with the tide beginning to make. But on which side of the channel had
we gone aground? The torchlight revealed that I had forgotten to
lower the Blue Ensign, so I hurriedly threw it below out of sight. I
had broken one record anyway; by crossing an ocean and running
aground on the way! Jokes that we had made about Jean Lacombe's
centre-board seemed in very bad taste. I could do with a drop keel now!

Overboard went the kedge anchor; down came the sails. Tables
showed that the tide would soon be rising, but I must try to find out
in which direction deeper water lay. I hauled a spare one-man rubber
raft out of the forepeak, laboriously blew it up and, in the darkness,
inserted the plug. Then I hung the riding light on a stay to guide me
back and dropped my unwieldy craft over side.

Carrying the torch and compass, a chart and the frying pan, with
which to paddle, I stepped gingerly aboard. As I pushed off the tide
gripped the oval raft. I did my best with the frying pan, but the raft
would spin round at every stroke so that we were being swept away
by the tide. This wouldn't do at all! I turned back, but even though my
paddling improved with practice, it was a hard struggle to regain the
ship.

Just as we came alongside, an ominous hissing announced that all
was not well aboard the raft. I hastily scrambled over *Cardinal Vertue's*
rail, pulling my rapidly deflating craft after me. At daylight I discovered
that there were *two* plug holes and that the cap closing one had not
been secured. It had been adventure enough for that night and I
decided to wait patiently for the tide to float us off.

At four in the morning, August 4th, wh n there was light enough to
see that we were aground on a sandspit off a sleeping village, *Cardinal*

Vertue stirred and floated free. At almost the same instant the gentle south-west breeze gave way to a quickly rising wind from the north-west which now put us on a lee shore.

There was no time to waste; within minutes the sails were up and drawing and *Cardinal Vertue* was heeling over as the blast pressed her down. I flicked the anchor out of the sand as we passed and drew a sigh of relief as the echo-sounder registered 4, then 6 feet, of water under our keel.

When we were far enough offshore for safety, I reefed the mainsail and set off to find Vineyard Sound again. Four hours were spent in reaching it; and not until then did I know for sure where we had been, or on what we had stranded—Nonameset Island, Woods Hole, Massachusetts.

Back in the Sound once more, I was fascinated by a tide race which was tossing great showers of white water high into the air. I had never seen one so close before. It was not a sight to miss, so I altered course to close it cautiously.

A coastguard cutter, which had been cruising down the Sound, came over towards me to see if I was standing into danger. It was about to turn away again when I shouted across, requesting that I be reported to the New York Coastguards. I should have stipulated New York in my earlier messages for the report of my previous sighting by the fishing boat *Curlew* had not penetrated beyond Nantucket. This was only the second time since I left England that a report of my having been sighted reached New York and London.

While we ran down the middle of Vineyard Sound with a fair wind I was setting the ship to rights. Anchors, chains, spare sails, warp and rubber dinghy had to be restowed. Soon everything was in place, except for the kiwi racing flag which had impaled itself on the lightning conductor at the masthead. I felt rather sad about this, but prudently decided to postpone climbing the mast to free it until we were in harbour.

How good it felt to take final bearings of the land at 10 a.m., to stream the log and watch the hills drop astern, and know we were sailing safely out to sea once more.

"There doesn't seem to have been a soul about this morning," I wrote. "And I was away just as day was breaking—but no doubt some old retired Yankee whaling skipper was up and watching through his bedroom window, and shaking his head!"

The wind held, so that by 8 p.m., Block Island light was abeam, and at 10.30 Mauntauk Point light, on Long Island itself, was flashing over the starboard bow. There was no chance of sleeping for we were running before a most variable wind with the spinnaker set. From time to time we would sail through a rain squall, after which the wind would fall light for a spell.

Next afternoon, August 5th, we passed to port of two proud white liners and a bobbing champagne cork. At 3 p.m. the wind backed, so that the spinnaker had to come down; and borne by this new breeze, fog banks came rolling in. Ships were passing on every side now. From 10 p.m. to midnight we were becalmed, while their lights streamed past on either hand, like street lamps on a misty night. Then we were sailing again. At 3.20 a.m. the fog lifted to reveal a flashing light ahead. I went below, opened the log-book and wrote without emotion:

"Ambrose light-vessel, bearing 290° magnetic."

Then I stared at what I had written. For two whole years the Ambrose light had been the goal of the enterprise which had filled all my thoughts. "I don't believe it is real. I thought it was just a joke!" I said out aloud, and burst into tears. I could not stop crying for long during the next half hour. I would control myself for a few moments; then it would start again. I was still sobbing at intervals, when I rounded the Ambrose light-vessel at 4.59 a.m. E.S.T. on August 6th.

We had covered three thousand and twenty-four miles (three thousand one hundred officially) in fifty-four days' sailing time, fifty-six days since the official start of the race. On thirty-seven of those days there had been complete calms, whose combined duration had totalled seven days and fifteen hours.

Though I blew a foghorn and yelled, no one aboard the lightship stirred, so I signalled to a passing sports fishing launch and asked him to call up the Coastguards on his radio and ask them to tow me to the quarantine station, as it had fallen calm again.

We talked as I coiled in the log line and hoisted the Stars and Stripes at the starboard cross-trees. "Was I going to sell the boat there?"

"How will I get home if I do that?" I asked. There was a moment's surprised silence.

"You are *sailing* back."

"Yes."

"When?"

"As soon as I can repair everything—in a week if I can make it."

12. Francis Chichester's *Gipsy Moth III*, shortly after crossing the starting-line.

13. Blondie Hasler's *Jester* away to a good start.

The skipper of the launch shook his head slowly.

"There'll always be an England!" he exclaimed.

Soon a Coastguard cutter came up. "That big yacht came in first," they replied to my eager questions, for nobody as yet had been able to tell me news of the race, "and we towed Colonel Hasler in from here a week ago."

"But when did the others arrive?" I demanded.

"Well, one broke his mast——"

"Yes, that was me, but the other two?"

"They haven't got in yet."

I could hardly believe it, not last after all, but third!

They took me in tow and soon we were racing past lines of buoys, innumerable fishing launches and half-submerged driftwood. We were going so fast that I dared not leave the helm. I was very tired now that reaction had set in, longing to sleep, wanting a meal and wishing above all else that I could leave the tiller to go forward to the "heads".

In my discomfort, it was without much interest that I watched the fabled skyline taking shape through the mist.

"I don't think much of skyscrapers," I thought, but as we came nearer I could see that these were only the gasometers on Coney Island.

I lapsed into lethargy once more, but roused when a high-speed motor launch came out towards us. The slim, blonde girl who was sitting gracefully on the foredeck with her wide skirt spread out over her ankles was waving. "Trust a girl to wave to a uniform!" I thought cynically, eyeing the trim Coastguard officers up ahead.

The girl reminded me of Fiona and I was overwhelmed by a sudden sick longing for her. If only she could have been here to share this moment with me! The undertaking, planned so patiently for two years, now seemed only an incident in my need to return to her. Even my discomfort was forgotten as I looked over with distaste and irritation at the girl on the speedboat who aroused such uncomfortable thoughts. I kept looking; gripping the tiller unheedingly, while she smiled at me and waved again.

No, it was impossible! I stared ahead once more, but after a moment, I had to turn back. There was Blondie Hasler, grinning from the speedboat's cockpit, and there on the foredeck was—Fiona!

The rest of that day is rather hazy and dreamlike in my memory. Fiona had borrowed the fare and flown to New York a few days before, to meet me. Blondie had called for her at her hotel that morning when the Coastguards had phoned to say I was at the Ambrose light.

At the quarantine station, thanks to Doctor Drescher, the port doctor, formalities were at a minimum. Even across the form headed "List of suspects aboard vessel", was written "Not even one"!

But for a full hour Professor Severinghouse of Columbia University put me through a fearsome psychological test designed by the U.S. space administration doctors. They were interested in our trip because, though they could make ground experiments on solitude easily enough, they could not reproduce fear. They were much too polite to say so, but they obviously also wanted to know whether observations on people like ourselves would also be applicable to really normal humans!

After this, an inventory was made of all the food remaining on board and I was weighed. I could hardly complain, as I had started all this, but I did wish that the American doctors were not quite so thorough. I had lost nineteen pounds.

The Dreschers were described by Blondie as "Running a Marina in which nobody is allowed to pay!" It is hard to find words to describe their kindness and hospitality. John Pfleiger, the Commodore of the Slocum Society, who took us to lunch, is another of the kindest people I have ever met; always unobtrusively ready to help. I had asked him for American charts and light lists before the race—to my embarrassment he would not allow me to pay for them.

Then a launch towed *Cardinal Vertue* to Sheepshead Bay, while a medical correspondent sat below, bravely going through my log and turning slowly green with the heat and unaccustomed motion. Meanwhile Blondie and I swapped experiences in the cockpit.

A number of ships had sighted him, including the *Queen Elizabeth*. There is an unconfirmed story that the officer on watch stared in disbelief and cried out "There's a bloody Chinese junk"; then went straight down below and swallowed half a bottle of whisky.

The other version, that on making his report he was clapped in irons for being drunk on watch, hasn't been admitted either.

When Blondie was in mid-Atlantic, a Russian deep-sea trawler, fascinated by the apparition, closed *Jester*. Her crew lined the rails calling and waving. Blondie's knowledge of the language is not good enough, however, for him to confirm or deny that they were shouting "Long live Mao Tse Tung!"

As we passed Coney Island and watched captive parachutes on

wires dropping from a tower we recalled our war-time parachute training, which we had both done at Ringway, near Manchester. "It all terrified me," remarked Blondie, quite untruthfully, I think. "None of the equipment had any adequate safety margin."

He told me about Francis Chichester's magnificent forty-day voyage and of how Val Howells had just reached Bermuda.

Then we were alongside the yacht club float at Sheepshead Bay, being welcomed by Tom Culyer, the Commodore. The men asked about gales. Their wives had no time for such nonsense; they were full of questions about Fiona. "Doesn't your girl friend trust you with us American girls?" one asked.

I have often been questioned whether the land "rocked" after fifty-four days at sea. The truthful answer, is that it did not; that is, until I had been introduced to a wholesome drink called "Kentucky Cream". Then it fairly heaved.

Next morning at high water we laid *Cardinal Vertue* alongside the club pier so that the propeller could be replaced at low water. I made her fast in what I considered to be seamanlike fashion, so that she would lean well in against the pier when the tide had fallen and left her high and dry.

Then Blondie, Fiona and I repaired to Bruce and Ellen Robinson's sixty-year-old gaff cutter *Picket* for breakfast. Bruce, who is Vice-Commodore of the Slocum Society, had become a friend through his letters before we had even met. He and Ellen had sailed out beyond Block Island hoping to meet me and escort me in, but I had passed them in the dark.

I will always remember that breakfast—pancakes, maple syrup and bacon. Every time Ellen asked if I would like more, I answered truthfully, "Yes". At length, to give Ellen a rest, Fiona took over the cooking until the stock of pancake mixture was exhausted.

We rowed to *Cardinal Vertue*, to find to my horror that she was leaning away from the piles, held only by straining warps attached to cleats which were beginning to twist under the strain of her four and a half tons.

"Do you always lay up your English boats that way?" a puzzled yachtsman asked politely.

"Yes, always," I replied firmly. "She is very stable."

Then I hurriedly made fast extra warps and prayed that they would hold.

Bruce and I replaced the propeller while Fiona scraped off what

393

little weed and barnacles had collected, and filled the gaping seam which had caused the leak on the port side. The club members helped.

The weather was so heavy and humid that Fiona and I spent all our time on the yacht in swimming suits. We never could remember to put on shoes or more respectable clothes before passing through the club-house, but the good-natured club members came to make allowances for us. I was very glad to have remembered to bring some small yacht club burgees, which at least served as mementos for some of our new friends.

There was so much to be done; a Press statement to prepare, radio and TV interviews; magazine articles to be written, and so on. On arriving in New York, I had phoned Chris Brasher, *The Observer's* Sports Editor in London, and heedless of the bill the paper must be incurring, had excitedly told him my story. *The Observer*, besides providing the trophy for the race, had signed a most generous con-tract with the four English competitors in return for prior news rights. Modern publicity may be a nuisance but at least it helps any-one who is not a millionaire to recoup some part of his expenses on trips such as ours. Bruce Robinson firmly dragged me away from the boat next day to stay in his apartment to write and visit editors.

The Press were helpful and took pains to be accurate. The one exception was, I regret, an English correspondent who painted a picture of Fiona being carried off to sea by a pretty seamy character, as vicious as he was senile, who waded knee-deep through ex-wives! My daughter's stock at school had been slightly raised when her father had sailed the Atlantic. Needless to say this report was of far more interest and put it sky high!

Before the race we had made strenuous efforts to interest manu-facturers in supplying us with free equipment. Apart from the Naval Life Saving Committe, a tool firm had been most helpful. My own prize came quite by accident. The invaluable echo-sounder which had been lent me was a new model not yet fitted with a waterproof casing. On my return, I wrote to the manufacturers asking whether a casing could be supplied before I gave back the set to its owner, and compli-menting them on its performance. The manager promptly came to see me.

"It really *shouldn't* have worked all that time without the casing," he said, as he generously presented me with a new set!

Macklin Boettger, who owns a machine shop, welded my goose-neck and made me a new horse. He also arranged for the supply of some wonderful black bread which was sustaining and palatable and lasted all the way to Shetland. I was rather worried about the cost of the fittings, as he is a craftsman who made some of the gear for *Columbia*, the America's Cup winner; but he would not accept a penny.

Macklin's other ideas about food did not seem so practical as his special bread. One evening Ellen had cooked the largest steak I have ever seen. Macklin, who was dining with us, expounded:

"Protein!—poisonous!—forms rivers of toxic mucus!" meanwhile busily shovelling down forkfuls of "noxious" steak!

A week after my arrival, Fiona and I, who were temporarily acting for the Race Committee, were called-up by the Coastguards with a message that Val Howells had passed the Ambrose. After hurriedly phoning the Press, we took a cab to Statten Island Ferry and reached the quarantine station just as Val came alongside. His eyes lit up when he saw me, but after I had handed him his mail he stood balancing on his foredeck, heedless of all enquiries, until he had read the letters from his wife, Eira.

Then with Welsh eloquence he expressed the feelings which every small boat sailor must experience after an ocean voyage:

"Never again! I wouldn't so much as cross the bloody Serpentine in the *Queen Mary!*"

But not more than half an hour later, while his boat was being towed to Sheepshead Bay, and we were sitting in the cockpit drinking rum and eating popcorn, Val said thoughtfully:

"You know, for the *next* Single-handed Race I am thinking of trying a schooner. . . !"

Knowing he would be living close to nature all those weeks, Val had been sensible enough to bring with him a book about seabirds. One passage especially had impressed him.

"Look, I'll show you," he said, rummaging below for the thin volume, which he opened at the section on petrels.

"Mating takes place in a burrow, where for *one night only* in the year (Val's italics) is heard the special mating trill written as 'mmmm, mmmm . . . mm',", he read.

"Just think of it! One night in the year *only!*" He stared out to sea for a moment, overawed by the mysterious ways of nature.

His face darkened when we examined the broken gooseneck that he had repaired at sea.

"Yes there *were* bad times," he admitted. "I used to pray. Yes, I even prayed for you, David!"

"Thanks very much," I replied, nettled.

By this time Francis Chichester had become a veteran New Yorker and was busy writing a book about his trip.* Only Jean Lacombe was still at sea. He had been sighted in the Gulf Stream and was nearing the United States.

It was impossible for us to take advantage of all the hospitality that was so generously offered us, for there was much to be done in preparation for the return voyage and little time in which to do it. My own list of chores, prepared while I was still at sea, reads:

"Charge battery, get spare battery, repair engine, fit propeller, repair leak port side, repair gooseneck and clew fittings, new horse, check up on spreader, charts of Newfoundland and Shetland. New P.V.C. trousers. Fit stainless steel universal joint to self-steering gear. Repair cabin lamp. Repair radio. Gasoline, engine oil, torch batteries, books (borrow from Bruce)."

Among provisions I had specially included were: matches, cooking fat and butter, milk, candies, bread, ham, cheese.

During the fortnight we spent in New York, I was not even able to find time for a haircut. Fiona and Ellen Robinson went shopping efficiently and economically and the radio was repaired after a fashion.

The engine presented a bigger problem. Every electric lead had to be replaced. Damp and corrosion had wrought havoc everywhere. For days it was dismantled, reassembled and dismantled again. As I am one of those people whom engines do not like, I was fortunate in having the help of George Donaldson.

An American had remarked to me thoughtfully one evening, while we were crossing on the Statten Island Ferry towards the grandeur of Manhatten:

"Do you see the statue of Liberty there? When immigrants first see it they cry with emotion. After they have been a few days ashore, they cry again because everybody robs them!"

But my experience was exactly the opposite. For instance, George spent four evenings toiling over the engine after his return from work on the New York ferries. Sometimes he was aboard until well after midnight. Yet all that he would accept was a beer!

Before leaving England, Val Howells had arranged to sell his boat in the U.S.A. He lent me his P.V.C. trousers, as mine were ripped beyond repair, a spare log-line and rotator, and his safety-belt for

* *Alone Across the Atlantic.* By Francis Chichester: George Allen and Unwin, 1961.

Fiona, who was to accompany me on the first leg of the return voyage. He also let me have his surplus food.

Val's impromptu stop at Bermuda had been expensive, so I lent him half my money. I had been expecting to be paid in America for some radio and TV appearances but as the cheques did not turn up until later, in England, Fiona and I had to pool our resources and count our assets very carefully. We could not have managed without the Robinsons' hospitality.

There were several reasons why we must hurry our departure. The doctor who was looking after my patients must be facing an impossible strain for I had never anticipated being away so long. Fiona had to be in London to begin a course at a dancing studio in early September. She would have time to sail with me as far as St. John's provided we did not dally in New York, but she would have to fly the rest of the way from Gander.

"Late August is a bad time of the year for a small boat to be on the Atlantic," Humphrey Barton believes. Yet the very earliest I could hope to set out from St. John's would be the end of August. The route I proposed to follow led far north of the direct steamer lanes to Europe and close to the area of the maximum incidence of gales in the Atlantic in September, where they were about five times as common and far more severe than those usually encountered in August in more frequented parts of the Western Ocean.

But more than a thousand years ago, Norse longships had nosed into the creeks and inlets of Newfoundland, and they had come via Iceland and Greenland, too. I felt an overmastering urge to retrace the "Sea King's Road" from Newfoundland to the ancient Viking islands of Hjetland, which today are called Shetland.

However, even the Skald had chanted, "You cannot go in longships thither," when speaking of an autumn passage to the Faroes. So I must be on my way across the storm centre of the Western Ocean before furious, lashing seas should bar the way.

When, at last, we were ready to sail we had to delay our departure for two days while hurricane "Cleo" passed by. Fortunately, Sheepshead Bay, where we were moored, is a well-protected harbour and easily accessible from the open sea.

Val was experiencing difficulty in selling his boat. The first stock question would be:

"What make of motor have you?"

"None."

The intended buyer would be shaken, but if persistent would go on to the next.

"What's the cubic capacity of your ice-box?"

Again he had to confess the deficiency. Only a most serious yachtsman would put the third question.

"How far does your standing headroom extend forward of the mast?"

The reply that even the maximum headroom only just allowed you to sit usually ended the discussion. But a Texan who had reached this stage in the inquisition placed his hand on Val's shoulder and gently summed up his objections:

"That's a nice little boat you have there, son, mighty nice! But when I buy a boat I want full fornicating space below!"

We were unable to wait for the arrival of Jean Lacombe. He had radioed his position to the Coastguards when he approached Nantucket. As the hurricane was also heading that way, they sent a cutter out to him which gathered him in out of harm's way until the danger had passed.

One remarkable feature of Jean's voyage is that a keg of whisky which had been given him in Plymouth remained unopened. Val helped him remedy this deficiency. In a letter to me Jean wrote:

"Feelings were just the same as on land, too much to do to feel lonesome!"

He had been sighted twice while crossing the Gulf Stream. On the second occasion the steamer *Christopher Columbo* had come alongside to ask if he required help. He had waved his arms and replied in French that all was well. There was nothing unusual about this incident, except that Jean flatly denied that it had happened at all. Nobody took any notice of this, as he could be expected to have been rather "boat happy".

But on November 6th, forty-nine-year-old Daniel Gautier in the seven and a half metres sloop *Isis*, reached New York, a hundred and fifty-nine days out from St. Nazaire:

The mystery of the sighting by the *Christopher Columbo* was now explained, but who could have expected two Frenchmen to have been at sea in the same area at the same time, both in tiny sloops?

The Dreschers and John Pfleiger did their best to look after Gautier.

"Like most single-handed sailors," Pfleiger wrote, "he is a timid and mild-mannered man—five years in a German concentration camp, a tiff with the French Government who put him in St. Anne (the crazy asylum) have left their imprint—he came as it is, without a passport, much money or anything."

In spite of the efforts made on his behalf, Gautier was deported back to France.

After two weeks in New York, Fiona and I set out from Sheepshead Bay in the late afternoon of August 20th. We were flying the Stars and Stripes from the starboard yardarm, with below it, the flag of New York State and the Sheepshead Bay Yacht Club burgee. Our Blue Ensign waved astern. In the cabin hung a plaque from the Slocum Society, inscribed "Third Man Home".

Such a host of craft escorted us that we were terrified lest we should hit one. Launches and speedboats raced round us, horns blaring; yachts and sailing canoes zigzagged by. We missed them all, though later Blondie was not so lucky! Then at last we were alone, outward bound over the lift and surge of the swell as we curtseyed past the Ambrose light-vessel in mist and darkness.

Jean reached New York the next day and with his arrival the first Single-handed Transatlantic Race was over.

The results were:

Francis Chichester:	40 days
Blondie Hasler:	48 days
David Lewis:	56 days elapsed time from official start (54 actual time)
Val Howells:	63 days elapsed time (55 days actual time)
Jean Lacombe:	74 elapsed time (69 actual time).

Chichester's feat was one of unrivalled courage and tenacity; he well deserved his splendid victory.

With his battened lug rig and the many other innovations on *Jester*, Hasler, I think, made what is perhaps the biggest contribution to ocean sailing for thirty years.

A week after our departure he set out for the Hamble where he unobtrusively picked up his mooring the day after I reached Lerwick. His time at sea, thirty-eight and a half days, was exactly the same sailing time as my own. Later, Chichester and his wife also sailed home, via the Azores.

But the contagion had spread. In the early winter, Bruce and Ellen Robinson abandoned their Madison Avenue apartment, and with *Picket* loaded down well below her marks, set off along the coastal waterway for Florida and the West Indies. Bruce ends a letter in which he describes storms, running aground on sandbanks, violent tides, running aground in rivers, bitter cold, running aground in canals: with a note saying that they were "having the time of their lives".

But now in late August *Cardinal Vertue* was heading north and east, towards where I knew, with trepidation but with a strange fascination as well, that I was to challenge the great winds of the Northern Sea.

8

TO BRING ME OMEN

These effigies of grief moved
Like refugees over the water;
The icy empresses of the Atlantic
Rising to bring me omen.
—GEORGE BARKER

THE strategy of our homeward passage was to sail well offshore to take advantage of the steadier winds of late August, and if possible to be helped along by the Gulf Stream; but not so far out that we could not reach shelter in the event of a hurricane warning being broadcast. We therefore aimed to head a little south-of-east until Nantucket Shoals light-vessel was abeam to port, then turn north-of-east along the northern edge of the Gulf Stream, passing outside Sable Island and making our landfall at Cape Race, Newfoundland, just over one thousand miles from New York.

The temperature was near the eighties and sultry. We kept a cotton pullover near the companionway, as the one on watch on deck at night sometimes felt chilly. Apart from this, Fiona wore only her bikini, and I my swimming trunks, day and night.

The vane was set to a good quartering breeze which drove us through the heat-haze. Though we were sailing one of the busiest sea lanes in the world, not a ship did we see during the first two days.

We left Sheepshead Bay at 6.30 p.m. (Eastern daylight time) on August 20th, and by midnight on the 22nd we were passing Nantucket Shoals light-vessel. Only two things marred the perfect peace of those days; myriads of biting flies, and Fiona's seasickness. Once Nantucket shoals were astern the sickness left her, though she was still weak from lack of food. In spite of the lively lift with which *Cardinal Vertue* was corkscrewing over the waves, she decided to have breakfast. What would she like?

"Pancakes, maple syrup and bacon, please."

I groaned and set to work. The ship was jerking so violently that

401

the frying pan soon tossed the pancakes into small piles of blackened debris, the maple syrup spilt, the bacon was burnt. I handed over the unsavoury mess and watched, revolted, while Fiona ate it with relish.

"Whatever is the matter?" she asked solicitously, suddenly noticing my face.

"Damn it to hell, *I'm* seasick now!" I snapped.

Now that Fiona felt better, she began to tackle the problem of finding her sea legs. This required determination, for although as a dancer and rock climber poise and balance are second nature to her, balance is of little use aboard a small bucking yacht, where you must always hang on or wedge yourself securely. Quick moving and impatient Fiona took another two days to adjust herself to this irksome routine; meanwhile she was thrown heavily again and again until she was bruised and sore all over.

But once she had learned to cope with the motion she soon became adept at rolling up the mainsail, changing headsails and managing the vane. She had mastered the traditional skills of an able seaman—to hand sail, to reef and to steer.

We ran one hundred miles on our first full day at sea, ninety on the second; then a weak depression which had been forecast by cirrus cloud and Boston Marine Radio, headed us, so that we only made sixty-seven on the third. That day the wind rose to thirty-four miles an hour, force 7.

The sea these days was a deep vivid blue. Sooty storm petrels, Leach's petrels, kittiwakes and guillemonts flew around us. I knew their names this time as I had been lent Val's precious book.

Once a school of porpoises in line abreast charged out of the face of a wave. Fiona waited patiently with her camera for them to do it again, while I told her not to waste time, for they would have swum miles away. Then out of the spume of the wave-crest, still side by side, they arched into the sunlight once more. Fiona clicked the shutter and replaced her camera without comment.

The next day, against headwinds, we made good only fifty-eight miles, but the following run was ninety-five, and on the day after, August 27th, the last day of our first week at sea, we made our record run of one hundred and twenty-four miles. After a week in which there had been only half an hour of calm, New York lay six hundred and thirty miles astern.

The previous day the log line had parted and gone to the bottom together with the rotator. I decided not to stream the spare one but to keep it in reserve in case of prolonged fog. For the moment we were getting sun sights every day, as well as radio time signals when required, so navigation was easy.

Each day we ran the engine for twenty minutes or so to charge the battery and keep it in trim. To conserve electricity we did not use the navigation lights unless a steamer passed near. One night a coastguard aeroplane picked us up on radar and circled us closer and closer. I deliberately kept the lights off, wondering if he could find us. Sure enough, as he banked overhead, he switched on a searchlight which picked us up immediately.

Ships appeared frequently, often only a few miles away, but they did not see us and the danger of collision was vividly brought home to me one night. I was writing up the log and looking out at intervals; the weather was clear and the visibility good; I had scanned the horizon no more than half an hour before. Suddenly the cabin was illumined by a blaze of lights as a liner raced by at twenty knots only three cables to port.

We still had many things to do for which there had been no time in New York. For instance, only now did we have leisure to open the last of our mail. The prize find was a poem. A friend of mine, with apologies to Lewis Carroll, had produced a magnificent sea-epic which could not be rivalled by even the most technical bar-room discussion in a very nautical yacht club.

> *A Luff Lyric of Vertue and Boaty*
> by Merton Naydler
> 'Twas Plymmig, and the beamsey sheets
> Did gybe and spinnake o'er the beach,
> All burgee were the mizzen beats
> And the stay tack outreach.
> Beware the jurygaff, my son,
> The cleats that jam, the shrouds that stretch,
> Beware the trimaran, and shun
> The clumptions cataketch.
> He took his tiller luff to deck
> Long time the distant main he sought,
> So ruddered he by the gallefry
> And anchored there athwart.
> But as in clewsome fend he keeled
> The cataketch with forestay guide
> Came riding through the gale and heeled,
> All reefed upon the tide.

403

About! About! and in and out
The plimsoll mast went log-a-smack!
He left it barred, and planing hard
He jibbed, abafting back.
"And hast thou slooped the cataketch?
Port to my helm, my boomish buoy!
O freeboard horse! O transom course!"
He portled in his joy.
'Twas Plymmig, and the beamsey sheets,
Did gybe and spinnake o'er the beach,
All burgee were the mizzen beats
And the stay tack outreach.

My last haircut had been in London nearly three months earlier. While I had been able to trim the front and sides with scissors and my neck with a razor, the back had grown ever longer and more shaggy.

"I am going to do something about this now," announced Fiona one day, eyeing my coiffure with displeasure. A mattress could have been stuffed with the result of her efforts!

We did not steer by hand except when the breeze was too light to work the vane, otherwise the kiwi was left in charge. It was only when there was a strong wind and big seas from the quarter that the power of the waves tended to overcome the strength of the vane and broach the ship to. I learned later that this could be completely cured and the ship would sail just as fast if I lowered the mainsail and kept on under the genoa. For this was a larger sail (230 square feet against the main's 180) and as it set further forward than the mainsail, it had much less tendency to drive *Cardinal Vertue* up into the wind.

When I awoke and went on deck to take over my watch on the afternoon of the 27th, the ship was broad-reaching over blue white-capped seas before a force 6 breeze. Some porpoises were playing to starboard and a tiny sooty petrel danced over the foam flecks in the sunlight. But where was the mate? For a moment I knew panic; then I came upon her, dressed in her blue bikini, curled up in the lifebelt on deck, eating popcorn!

That evening, steep phosphorescent seas nine to ten feet high came combing up astern before a wind of thirty-four to thirty-six miles an hour, which sometimes gusted to force 8. Once we were pooped by a breaking crest, but only foam and spray splashed into the snug cabin where Fiona was cooking.

Next day we began to cross Banquereau Bank in soundings. To the

404

north of us heavy fog shrouded desolate, treacherous Sable Island, a twenty-mile crescent of sand, which lies ninety miles off the coast of Nova Scotia. A misty horizon had prevented me from obtaining reliable sights; and just as it had done some weeks before, the radio beacon on Sable Island was giving misleading bearings. On that occasion I had been nearly wrecked on Nova Scotia, but this time we aimed to keep east of the Island. The relevant paragraph in the *Nova Scotia and Bay of Fundy Pilot* was not too encouraging. It says:

"... the irregularity of the currents and tidal streams in the vicinity of Sable Island is probably one of the principal causes of the numerous wrecks that have occurred on the island ... but ... their general trend is to set to the westward; many vessels wrecked on Sable Island supposed themselves to have been considerably eastward of the island when they ran on shore."

Study of the pilot chart only seemed to show that the currents converged on the damned place from all directions! It was also a notorious neighbourhood for fogs; so altogether this was an uncomfortable spot to be without sights, and for radio bearings to be at odds with the estimated position. I began to be touchy as we ran through the darkness; nor was I much cheered to see the pale greenish glow of the Aurora arching across the sky to the northward shortly before dawn.

August 29th. There was still no sight obtainable. According to our dead reckoning we should be well past Sable Island, but radio bearings persistently came from abeam. I decided to discard the radio bearings in plotting our course, but to keep an alternative set of positions based on the assumption that they alone were correct. In either case, unless the wind changed, we would soon pass clear.

About 3 p.m. *Cardinal Vertue* tripped in her stride as the forefoot struck something with a resounding thump. I sprang into the cockpit in time to see a long greenish body just awash, spinning in the wake astern—a dead porpoise or small whale, we thought it.

Two hours later, when Fiona was finding sunbathing a trifle chilly and had donned a pullover, we sighted a small vessel ahead. As we approached, we saw that she was a strange-looking fishing boat, *Janet Irene*, from Liverpool, Nova Scotia. She closed us in the gathering dusk, and hailed to ask where we were heading.

"St. John's, Newfoundland."

"We thought you must be on that course," was the comforting reply.

"What *is* that thing on your bow?" I asked, overcome by curiosity.

"That's for spearing swordfish, but they're getting pretty scarce here this time of the year," came the reply.

During the night the wind backed and increased. I was adjusting the vane when the metal clip on the foreguy sheared and the boom gybed all standing. No damage had been done, but the change in wind direction was forcing us northward, towards where, if the radio bearings were correct, destruction lay waiting in the surf breaking on the drying banks, east of Sable Island.

I became more tense and irritable every minute as I watched the echo-sounder readings and studied the chart over and over again.

It was nearly midnight when I decided to play for safety. By now it

was blowing twenty-six miles an hour, force 6, so before wearing ship on to the other gybe, the genoa had to come in and the main be reefed. The mate steered and tended the sheets, while I struggled on the wet deck in the darkness, and in my worry about our position I cursed her most unjustly, until she was almost in tears.

Neither of us had eyes at the time for the wild beauty of the soaring searchlights and curtains of cold unearthly fire which now began to pulse into life across the northern sky, springing up, arch upon eerie, glowing arch, to reach the very zenith.

Fiona forgave my bad temper when I told her how worried I had been in case we were standing into danger, but I had shaken her confidence in her own seamanship, and this took some time to return.

It was not long before we left soundings on reaching the edge of the Nova Scotia Banks and sailed on over deep water. We need not

14. Val Howells, "The Bearded Viking", takes *Eira* across the starting-line at Plymouth.

15. *Cap Horn*, Jean Lacombe's 21-foot plywood, centre-board sloop, which was a late starter but completed the course in 74 days.

have worried. Our dead reckoning had been right after all and the radio bearings inaccurate.

But there was a deeper reason for the anxiety that had been reflected in my snappiness. All at once we had left summer behind; we had felt the first cold breath of the winter stealing upon us from the northern wastes and Arctic seas, bring me omen of what lay ahead.

Long into the night I pored over the pilot charts. Yes, the percentage of all ships' observations in the Atlantic during which winds reached force 8 and above, rose steeply in September. In the western approaches of the Channel, the July figure was 1–2 per cent., August 1–3 per cent., September 2–4 per cent. But I was bound far to the northward of the Channel, across the stormiest stretches of the whole Western Ocean, and here the gale percentages for September read 5, 7, 9 and 7, until north of the 60th parallel and east of the Hebrides, they fell to 4.

In the early hours of the morning I wrote in the log: "Yesterday Fiona was still wearing her bikini, and I my trunks, but to-night and the night before, the pale lights have been flaring to the northward. Orion hangs high and clear now; and it is a winter constellation. The sun's northerly declination is down to 9 degrees, soon it will sink past the Equator into southerly declination. Signs, all signs, to hurry on. Summer is ending and I am bound towards 60° N, east-north-east over two thousand miles of ocean. Best not to linger overlong!"

On we sailed, north and east through a grey dawn beneath the overcast, to log ninety-eight miles by noon. Later in the day the wire burgee halyard chafed through. Fiona caught a glimpse of the brilliant colours of the Royal Burnham Yacht Club burgee floating tantalizingly close as we drove by, running before the wind with the mainsail boomed right out and pinned by the fore-guy. By the time we had sheeted in the boom and gybed, and headed back to search fruitlessly among the waves, it had disappeared.

The same thought was in both our minds as we came back onto our course once more and hoisted the Little Ship Club burgee on the spare main halyard—the difficulty of picking up a man overboard.

At 6 p.m. we entered soundings once more over St. Pierre, westernmost of the Grand Banks of Newfoundland. Here we crossed my outward track of July 21st.

During the past few days Fiona had occasionally noticed a curious feeling that a third person was on board. The sensation was of a somewhat neutral presence, neither friendly nor hostile; momentarily so real that she would begin to turn round to speak to it. When we compared notes we found that our experience was identical. In my case it usually occurred when I had just awakened and was going on watch. What is the explanation? I do not know, but this is a very common experience in the wilds. Perhaps we are so used to other people around us in everyday life that our senses reflect some echo of their former presence, even when they are not there.

That night the aurora flickered once more. Next day, August 31st, Cape Race radio beacon became clearly audible, sixty-five miles away. Unlike Sable Island it gave an accurate bearing.

As it grew dark again the wind fell light and we had to steer. So silently did we slip forward that we caught a flock of roosting seabirds unawares, until suddenly the air was filled with alarmed, indignant, squawks as they flapped away.

At 4 a.m. on September 1st, a flashing light appeared on the port bow, so I thankfully handed over to the mate, with instructions to call me when she sighted land. I was very soon awakened, when daylight showed the slate cliffs of Cape Pine.

We rounded Cape Race before noon and headed north up the coast with a fair wind. We passed within a quarter of a mile of the famous Cape, which towered across the cold green water in tiers of slaty ledges, backed by barren country. As we went by, mist shrouded the promontory and a fog signal began to blare.

But the land mist gradually cleared until we were sailing up a corridor between the coast on our port hand and a wall of dense fog which hung over the Grand Banks to starboard.

I wished to make all possible speed because the glass had begun to fall quickly, and cirrus cloud spreading from the west foretold an approaching depression.

We tore along through the calm water in the lee of the land, quickly eating up the sixty miles that separated us from St. John's. Bare, rounded hills ended abruptly in great sweeps of stratified cliff. Gullies and sheltered slopes were clothed with pine forest, while at long intervals at the head of some deep inlet there would be a scatter of white houses.

As I sat at the tiller I mused on the "courageous captains" whose schooners had faced the fog, ice and storms of the Grand Banks over the centuries. Where were they now? I feared that, along with the caravelles and longships, they could dwell only in that hall of memory which enshrines the quiet heroism of man. It would have been about this time in the evening that the smaller schooners from the outports would have come sailing out of the rolling fogbanks to seaward, to head for land; booms squared off, brown sails drawing as they ran towards home.

It was a moment before I realized that the four schooners which had just materialized out of the fog were real. On they came; small craft, 30 or 40 feet long. One, towing a dory nearly as long as itself, crossed our bow and disappeared shoreward behind two fantastic rock pinnacles called "The Hares Ears", to enter Fermeuse Harbour.

Near this spot, seventy-seven years ago, a man rowed a dory in from the Grand Banks. His companion sat rigid and ice-sheeted in the stern, where he had been frozen to death.

On January 25th, 1883, Howard Blackburn and Tom Welsh had

been fishing in one of the dories from the schooner *Grace L. Fears*, about one hundred miles off the Newfoundland coast. A storm drove them to leeward in fierce snow squalls, and all through the night and next day they had to bail and chip away frozen spray. Sometimes they tried to row, but usually they had to lie to an improvised sea anchor as their little kedge anchor dragged. Blackburn lost his mitts, so that his hands began to freeze. He bent his fingers over and poured water over them so that they froze into talons which could still grip the oars. Tom Welsh died that night and Howard Blackburn rowed for another day and a half before he sighted land. He had spent three days and nights in the dory without food or water.

As he lost all the fingers of both hands and a half of each thumb, Blackburn had to give up fishing. To enliven his retirement he had a 30-foot sloop built in which, sixteen years after his ordeal, he sailed alone from Gloucester, Mass., to Gloucester, England, making the crossing in sixty days. Not content with this feat, he set sail once more from Gloucester, Mass., in 1901, in a still smaller sloop, the *Great Republic*, only 25 feet long. Again this man without fingers was entirely alone. He reached Portugal safely in thirty-nine days.

After darkness had fallen on September 1st, I wore ship onto the starboard gybe in order to keep well offshore, for lights, either for navigation or of houses, are rare along the Newfoundland coast and the weather was rapidly deteriorating. Then, after putting our watches forward one and half hours to Newfoundland summer time, I handed over to Fiona and turned in.

About 3.30 a.m. on September 2nd I came on watch again to find that Cape Spear light was winking to port. We gybed again and, well reefed, ran towards the land, sweeping in across impressive rollers. Soon mist closed down until we had only a fog signal to guide us.

The wind had gusted up to thirty-four miles an hour, force 7, and our lee rail was pressed under as we raced into calmer water in the shelter of the dim, misty, outline of Cape Spear. Ahead towered a red limestone cliff, split by a monstrous gash, which was flanked on the one hand by an old fort and on the other by a lighthouse. This was the entrance to St. John's Harbour, the most magnificent landfall I had ever seen.

As we entered the narrows, rain was thundering against the rock ledges above and drumming on the painted wooden houses, fish-drying frames, anchored dories and *Cardinal Vertue*. But all wind was cut off by the walls of the defile, so that the sails slatted uselessly.

Soaked to the skin, Fiona lowered sail while I started the motor, and we set off round St. John's harbour in search of a mooring. It was only 7 a.m. and no one was about. Even in this sheltered basin squalls made the leeward piers unsafe. We eventually moored at a coal pier at 7.30, ahead of a Bowring sealer, two trim Icelandic trawlers and an incredibly rusty Spaniard, which had spent all summer on the Banks. We had covered one thousand, one hundred and thirteen miles in twelve and a half days.

We found a better mooring in the afternoon, at one of Bowring's wharves nearer the town beside some sadly cut-down Grand Banks schooners which were now coasters, trading with the outports.

Groups of quiet fishermen and seamen came to look at our boat. This was embarrassing as our deck was a jumble of sails and ropes, and I knew the knots with which I had made fast the warps were not the correct ones. Nor could we afford to buy a Newfoundland or Canadian courtesy ensign. The professionals eyed our slender spars with some mistrust. But I was glad to hear that their opinions were, on the whole, favourable.

We had eaten so well on the trip from New York, thanks to Fiona's cooking once she had had her sea legs, that we now had partly to re-stock the ship.

The grocer had various brands of margarine, canned goods, sweet biscuits and salt cod; Fiona always chose the cheapest. At length he entered into the spirit of the thing and began to hunt out long-forgotten cans from dusty back shelves.

Leaving Fiona only enough money for her hotel bill and the journey to Gander, we spent the remainder on food for me, a post card to Tom Moncrief in Shetland, and rather meagre presents for Barry and Anna. "Be sure and bring me back lots of Yankee chewing gum," Barry had written; and chewing gum was all his father was able to bring him.

A mission launch, which came alongside on Sunday, gave us a pile of books and Canadian magazines, a welcome supplement to those we had borrowed in New York. In the end, I had everything I needed, except that I could not afford enough paraffin. However, the engine was working and should be able to charge the batteries so that I could use electric light. When I did leave St. John's, the currency on board totalled one cent Canadian!

We had arrived in Newfoundland at the beginning of a public holiday and how we blessed the peace and quiet. Derick Bowring, whose family of merchant adventurers have been the owners of fishing schooners and sealers for generations, took us to dinner one evening at his home above the town. Before the meal he drove us up Signal Hill which rises to 500 feet on the northern side of the narrows. The town and harbour were spread out beneath us. Then I turned and looked out over the Atlantic stretching on and on to the rim of the night, and I thought how peaceful it looked. Yet it seemed to me that this apparent peace concealed such forces as would test my resolution to the utmost; I thought of the morrow when I must sail, and I was afraid.

But a Vertue is a confident little ship, and has good reason to be so. Speaking at a dinner the previous winter, Jack Giles, their designer, had said, rather piously I thought, that a hand "other than his own" had guided his pencil when he drew the lines of the first Vertue, *Andrillot*, in 1936. Later the same evening, he said more confidentially,

"As a matter of fact, old man, someone asked me to make him a miniature Bristol Channel Pilot cutter, so I just copied the underwater lines." This confirmed, and rather amplified, his earlier remarks.

In keeping with their descent from such a famous English line, Vertues are heavy displacement craft by modern standards; for 4½ tons displacement on a 21-foot waterline is a good deal. It implies a comparatively easy motion, more room below, more speed in light winds because of a small wetted area, but more strain on spars and rigging due to the greater momentum imparted by the heavy hull. Two tons of the weight is made up of lead in the keel, so like all yachts with ballasted keels, Vertues are self-righting in the event of a knockdown; always provided that the upper works remain intact and waterproof.

The class was given its name after *Epeneta*, in 1939, won the cup donated by M. B. Vertue to the Little Ship Club for the best cruise of the year. Hence the spelling of Vertue. As I was writing the last sentence, I looked at the Vertue Cup more closely, to find with some amusement that the recipient for 1960 had been misspelt *Cardinal Virtue!*

When she was being built at Christchurch in 1948, her original owner suggested calling her *Easy Vertue*. Mr. Elkins, her builder, was scandalized.

"It would be more appropriate to name her after one of the five cardinal virtues," he admonished severely; and so *Cardinal Vertue* she became.

Since *Vertue XXXV's* passage to New York in 1950, Vertues have been as thick as flies upon the Atlantic. In 1952 Dr. Cunningham crossed from Ireland to the West Indies in *Icebird*. In 1955 he sailed from Newfoundland to Bermuda, and in 1957 from Bermuda back to Ireland.

In 1955 David Robertson reached the Bahamas from England in *Nan*. This yacht was originally named *Jonica*; her next owner called her *Easy Vertue*; David Robertson changed her name to *Nan*. Her present owner has called her *Jonica* again.

Next year, John Goodwin in *Speedwell of Hongkong*, which Peter Hamilton had already sailed from Singapore to England, set out from Gibraltar to the West Indies. Two years later he left the West Indies for Brazil and, ultimately, Capetown.

Then in 1957 Peter Hamilton in *Salmo* became the second single-hander to reach the New World by the northern route. He layed up at

Quebec, and the following year continued on his way, with his wife as crew. They traversed the Panama Canal and crossed the Pacific to Tahiti, finally returning to California.

The record is an honourable one, and if any small yacht was fit to meet the September gales of the northern wastes of the North Atlantic it was a Vertue; and *Cardinal Vertue* was now in superb trim.

It seemed a far cry now from when I had bought her in 1959 and asked Humphrey Barton's advice about how best to install a self-draining cockpit with the least expense. He had written back to say that one was unnecessary round the English coast. After receiving my reply, he 'phoned me. Where was I going anyway?

"To Southend Pier, it gets *very* rough there!" I replied shortly.

"Oh, of course, then you *will* need a self-draining cockpit," he replied immediately. Understanding had been established.

The winter of 1959 had seen an incredible number of jobs accomplished and Bob and Sunny Coles of Tucker Brown's, in particular, must have hated the very sight of me. Yet their good temper and helpfulness had never varied. But when we were finally launched and I promptly ran aground opposite their yard, Bob had shaken his head and muttered, "He'll never make it!"

But I must not delay longer. The morning of September 5th was bright with sunshine and a fair wind rippled the blue, red and orange sails which were hanging out to dry above the nested dories aboard three Portuguese motor fishing vessels which had entered harbour during the night. These two-thousand-ton ships had come in to take shelter from hurricane "Donna", which was recurving north from its sultry breeding ground off the West Indies. Though my stomach turned cold when I looked at the great white ships and realized what their presence in harbour implied, I knew that even leaving immediately, it would be October before I could hope to make my landfall, so I could not remain in this haven.

I could not bear to look at Fiona as I rolled down five feet of the mainsail, and at 3 p.m. G.M.T., hoisted sail, cast off and headed for the narrows. Only once did I glance back at the lonely figure standing on the pier. I dared not look again, so forlorn and fearful and doubly alone did I feel now. It was as if a light had been extinguished, leaving *Cardinal Vertue* and I to sail out through the gloom across a grey wilderness.

9

ORDEAL BY STORM

The glass is falling hour by hour, the glass will fall for ever,
But if you break the bloody glass you won't hold up the weather.
—LOUIS MACNEICE

WITH a fair wind *Cardinal Vertue* cleared St. John's narrows and
headed north-east at four and a half knots. On this course we drew
away from the land so slowly that it was nine hours before the last of
the Americas, still clearly silhouetted against an orange sunset, dipped
below the horizon.

That night the moon was full and it was brilliantly clear; it was cold
and the sea choppy. At midnight a breaking crest splashed aboard but
did no harm. I was lonely as never before; frightened and restless, so
that I could neither rest nor sleep.

Our course was a great circle which curved from north-east to
become east in latitude 60°, south of the Faroes. As we would still be
crossing the Grand Banks for a day or so, I got out the *Newfoundland and Labrador Pilot*. I was struck by the unwonted poetic vein of
one phrase: "In the interior (of Labrador) the only law is the
immemorial code of lodge and hunting ground."

I was delighted, wondering when it was written, for the area in
question contains some of the largest iron workings in the world!

By noon next day we had covered ninety-eight miles in the twenty-
one hours since we left port. The large trawler *Santa Elvira* of Coruña
passed close astern and I was cheered to observe that the seas were
breaking across her 'tween decks, the water cascading out of her
scuppers each time she rolled, while my decks were dry.

Towards evening I sighted the Norwegian trawler *Rindenes* of
Florø, which stood towards me and hailed in English to ask whither
I was bound. Neither he nor the Spaniard appeared to be heeding the
hurricane warning. This at least was good to know. "I wish you fair
winds," he called, resuming his course.

For some reason these simple words spoken by a grave, quiet man,

414

put new heart into me. I felt included within a fellowship, and I warmed to this as a great honour, for the men of the distant trawler fleets form a noble brotherhood.

That night the fair northerly wind carried us clear of the Banks and next day there were no more trawlers. I reefed and unreefed, changed headsails and repaired the foreguy when it parted. The P.V.C. trousers which I had borrowed from Val had become so porous and leaky as to be useless. I wrote, with foreboding:

"Temperature 48°F. Got wet. Hands numb with cold—a foretaste?"

Everything on the ship reminded me of the mate's presence, and the loneliness did not seem to be abating. The nights were so long now; twelve full hours of darkness! I began to have disturbing dreams whose content varied but which always ended with a scene that would shock me awake, to lie trembling and sweating with fear until my racing heartbeats gradually slowed to normal.

In the dream we would be sailing towards a gaunt black crag surmounted by a deserted, unlit, lighthouse. The sea and sky would be those I had seen when I last looked out; usually a stormy cold sea, under driven cloud-wrack.

Why this dream should have recurred night after night, and what was the fear that it reflected, I do not know. There was no rock or lighthouse, lit or unlit, for fifteen hundred miles ahead; nor have I any recollection of having known this scene in real life. But every detail is so indelibly printed on my memory that I would recognize it at once should it ever be my lot to gaze upon it.

On our first full day at sea we had covered one hundred and fifteen miles, and by the following noon, September 8th, we had covered another hundred and nineteen miles and were passing five hundred miles south of Cape Farvel, the southernmost point of Greenland. But we would not be able to keep us this pace for much longer.

The WNW wind backed to SW and steadily increased. By two-thirty in the morning of September 9th, it had already reached force 7 and the glass was falling. At 4.30 a.m., when the wind was blowing forty miles per hour, gale force 8, I lowered the mainsail and ran on with the staysail sheeted hard in so that it should not flog.

By noon the wind had risen to forty-nine miles per hour, force 9, and the glass was still dropping.

"Pooped by a crest," I recorded, "but *Cardinal Vertue* is running well, steering by the vane. The seas are marching in all the grandeur of a full Atlantic gale now."

415

"12.30. Pooped again. Canvas dodger torn adrift."

The stout new canvas had split and every one of the brass eyes along the quarter to which it was laced had been sheared clean off.

At 1 p.m. the straining staysail sheet tore out the fairlead, which was screwed into the deck beams. The wind was now fifty miles an hour and I lowered all sail, and with sopping wet jeans clinging round my legs and water swirling round my ankles, steered before the gale. I was wet through and tired for I had not been able to sleep the night before because of the falling glass.

The seas grew larger and steeper now, until they began to curl over and break. Long lines of foam ran. Each time I saw a wave tilt slowly forward and collapse into frothy, snowy, beautiful, cotton wool I wondered if a yacht could withstand such a fearful impact. Soon a giant with toppling crest reared astern and came roaring down upon the ship, to burst over the quarter, pouring over me where I clung to the rail and sending the yacht spinning like a match box. Unscathed, she shook the sea from her deck, while I sat breathless and gasping, with water sloshing around my knees before it had time to drain away out of the cockpit.

I now did what I had read about, and streamed ninety feet of warp in a bight astern. This made the yacht almost unmanageable; she persistently ran with the seas abeam, only being held down-wind with the greatest difficulty. Even then she would repeatedly broach-to. Apart from hindering steering, the warp was ineffective as each large sea would sweep it forward until it lay coiled almost alongside. Whether a longer one would have proved more useful I do not know.

At 3.30 p.m. the wind was still south-west and still blowing at fifty miles an hour. I had been in the cockpit two and a half hours and was now too cold and tired to steer any more. So I put the helm down, set the vane, and hove-to on the starboard tack. The yacht lay well a-hull, tending to luff a little, though more than once she would be spun right round by a breaking wave.

The Calor gas cylinders were still firmly lashed down but the fastenings which had withstood five thousand miles of sailing were not adequate now. One cylinder was on its side, dented and rolling, hitting its neighbours and the sides of the bunks with terrific force. I screwed in more eyebolts and added extra lashings until it was secure. Then I tried to restore some order in the cabin, and pumped. For the second time that day water was up to the floorboards.

I wound the chronometer and stared out through the doghouse

window at the white seas and the streaming foam and spray, now mixed with fine rain, which howled across the sea's face obscuring the division between air and water. Sometimes a comber would sweep sideways across the wind. Above the waves, delicate storm petrels swooped through the grey rain. The glass continued to fall as I wedged myself into my bunk.

I was promptly shot out again as the ship was hurled onto her beam ends and the cabin momentarily engulfed in green darkness. It seemed incredible that wood, glass and metal could withstand such an impact, but *Cardinal Vertue* rode on as buoyantly as ever.

By 8 p.m. the wind had fallen to forty miles an hour, though the glass was still low and the rain had given way to fog. I took in the useless warp and re-rove the staysail sheet through a fairlead in a rope grommet which I had prepared. Then I cleared the spinnaker boom ready to boom out the staysail when the time should come to hoist. Turning to the pump I found that it was partially blocked and sticking, and that the water was again up to the floorboards.

At dusk the wind had dropped to force 7, but it still blew from the south-west and the glass had fallen a further point to 991 mb. I hoisted and boomed out the staysail then, and we went reeling away north-westward through the thinning mist, on the port gybe, making four knots. The glass stood persistently at 991, but it was good to be on our way again and I sang as we crashed and rolled through the night.

After midnight I slept a few hours, waking at 5 a.m. on September 9th to find that the wind had veered to the west-nor-west and we were sailing south-east. Bright moonlight and the glow of the Northern Lights threw the rigging into relief as I unboomed the staysail, gybed, and adjusted the vane.

An hour and a half later, when dawn broke clear and wild, the glass had risen a point but the wind had increased again to forty-one miles an hour, a force 8 gale out of the north-west. I pumped with great difficulty while the wind steadily increased in violence. By 9.30 a.m. it had reached force 9 again, forty-nine miles an hour, and a sea which burst over the quarter broached *Cardinal Vertue* to. I handed the staysail.

"It was just as well I did so," I wrote in the log later, "for as soon as it was down the wind began to blow harder than ever. Heavens, how hard it is blowing. While I was in the cockpit a sea broke over us, turning the ship right round. She seemed to be trying to fall off before the seas, so this time I hove-to a-hull with the helm loose and the vane set to steer her off the wind.

"Have spent the rest of the two hours since heaving-to pumping with the plunger pump in the cockpit and trying to clear the diaphragm pump. Will make coffee if I can manage it and have a try at sleeping. Glass 993–4 mb."

At 2 p.m., a great wave broke over the yacht, spinning her round again and sending books, charts and instruments flying. Water spurted through the thin crack between the washboards and the main hatch cover with such force as to soak everything in the cabin. Gybing round to heave-to on the port tack again and mopping-up operations occupied half an hour. *Cardinal Vertue* was tending to luff now, as she had done in the previous day's gale. I wondered whether the difference in her behaviour was due to the varying size and shape of the seas; there was a big cross sea running at this time.

The frontal clouds began to break up and patches of sunlight appeared. It seemed wrong to waste such an opportunity, so clinging on to the housed boom against the momentum of the ship's dizzy swoops and rolls, I tried to take some photographs. But though I shielded the camera from the spray as best I could I had not much hope for the result. Then I dismantled the pump and tried to clear it. The wind was down to forty-two miles an hour between the gusts.

I noted down at 2.30 p.m.: "Can't sleep, worse luck; too tense, I suppose; slight apprehensive feeling; motion too irregular to cook; lying in the bunk reading and eating dried fruit and sweets. I miss the mate very much and would rather be with her than here! This *is* interesting *and* exciting though! I have every hope, now the glass is rising after this morning's veer, that this will blow itself out soon and enable us to get going again without wasting more time with this lying a-hull nonsense!"

"8.30 p.m. There is a mackerel sky over low hurrying storm clouds, but the glass has risen to 1,002 mb and the wind has fallen to thirty-four miles an hour, but it is gusty and variable and the sea is still large.

"Have spent another hour clearing the diaphragm pump—mostly matches and hairpins! Partial success. Could not sleep this afternoon but rested. Will now have coffee, tinned fruit, bread and cheese; then hope to make sail.

"9.15 p.m. We are away at three knots on port gybe under sheeted staysail."

I had had only four hours sleep during the previous sixty-one hours.

But now that the glass was rising and the ship sailing once more, I could at last relax and I slept an unbroken eight hours. On waking, once I had shaken off the effect of my fear-dream of the unlit lighthouse on the crag, I felt wonderfully rested.

In the awesome swell left by the gale *Cardinal Vertue* rolled sickeningly, developing every few minutes an accelerating rhythmic roll which, at its crescendo, prevented me from doing anything except holding on.

After a further three-quarters of an hour the pump was finally cleared. It is a wonderful pump and this trouble had been my own fault for mounting it against the ship's frames without enough clearance.

Clothes, blankets, all my possessions, were wet. Yet I dared not open the main hatch as every now and then a dollop of water would plop aboard. In these conditions it was with some trepidation that I got out the sextant. What with the height of the seas, the rolling, the spray and the scurrying clouds which often hid the sun, the sight seemed likely to be a poor one. However, its accuracy was confirmed by two others later that afternoon.

In spite of two days when the wind had reached force 9, we had covered two hundred and sixty three miles since our last accurate noon position three days before.

The two gales had evidently been part of a single low-pressure system. The first from south-west with mist and rain and falling glass —typical warm front weather. The second, the nor'-wester, had shown all the cold front phenomena; a veer, rising glass and clearing sky.

Before evening the wind had dropped sufficiently for the genoa to be hoisted, and the rubber-sealed hatch in the cockpit, which gave access to the engine controls, could be safely opened. After some coaxing, the engine started and kept going hesitantly for half an hour. I was not to know when I switched it off that it had run for the last time. For after the drenching it was soon to receive it never started again, and on examination in port was found to be so corroded as to be good only for the scrap heap.

During the night the glass again began to fall. At one-thirty on September 11th the wind backed into the south-west and freshened, causing *Cardinal Vertue* to luff into the wind, her genoa flailing and vibrating. After I had handed it and lashed it down to the pulpit and stanchions, everything was secure and I could relax, to write at two-thirty:

"In spite of the falling glass and rising wind I know she is well snugged down, at any rate until gale force is reached. So I am being very rash and sleeping without boots, or (useless) P.V.C. trousers! Feet, legs and thighs damp for three days now, but at least they are warm in the blankets!

"7 a.m. No luck! Just at first light by the Greenwich time I am using *Cardinal Vertue* was thrown aback and hove herself to. Wind forty miles an hour, force 8. I set her on course again and pumped her dry. What a mercy the pump is still clear.

"At 8.30, a second fairlead was pulled out of the deck by the staysail sheet. The wind was now gusting to forty-six miles an hour."

I lowered the No. 1 staysail and tried to hoist the tiny 45-square foot No. 3 staysail whose sheets were already rove. But the power of that wind! As the sail filled the lee sheet parted and the minute sail took charge like some demented thing of enormous power. The clew made a blurred arc as it flew, and emitted a high pitched hum; the mast shook and rattled with the fearful force of the flogging; the weather sheet wrapped round everything in sight including my legs.

In the half hour that it took to make things fast the wind had risen to force 9 and I hove-to a-hull, with the vane set to head *Cardinal Vertue* up into the wind, as she was tending to luff this time rather than turn down wind.

I considered using the sea-anchor, but decided not to do so for the time being as the ship seemed to give way and slide easily before the breaking waves, and it seemed likely that a sea-anchor might hold her up to the pounding. I would try it only as a last resort.

The sea was combing all ways by this time. Not at all the stately procession of breathtaking rollers of the first gale on September 8th.

By midday the yacht was tending to fall off a little, instead of luffing as she had done earlier. Was this in spite of, or because of, the vane setting? I had to admit that with the irregular sea it was hard to tell how she *was* lying. She was riding easier than in the last two gales, but this meant little as the seas were so different.

"Perhaps the 19 mb the glass has dropped in fourteen and a half hours means that the warm front will soon be passing?" I speculated, and continued: "All my trousers are wet; have managed to make coffee and with this and the heavy black bread and jam, I feel better. At least I have nothing to complain of, after all I *did* challenge the winds by coming this way at this time of year, so now I must just learn to take it!"

The afternoon seemed endless. I made a stew, which was quite a triumph. I tried to read—anything that would take my attention from the sea outside. But neither the *Cave Paintings of France*, nor *Lolita*, nor the magazines given us by the mission launch, nor *Pilots*, nor even Dr. Hannes Lindeman's account of his two crossings of the Atlantic by canoe, could hold my attention for long.

The hiss of an oncoming breaker, its shattering blow as it hurled the ship on to her beam-ends and darkened the cabin, would be enough to distract my attention from anything. Usually reading of Lindeman's dreadful hardships cheered me up by making me feel that I was living in a palace in comparison; but this time I was beginning to feel really sorry for myself.

The wind, which had backed a little towards the south, continued to increase. By 4 p.m. it was blowing at fifty-eight miles an hour, force 10, and harder in the gusts. The shriek of the wind was frightening; the tops were blown off the waves and the whole sea became white.

"Thank God for these changes in the wind direction," I wrote. "They hold the seas down a little, for however frightful the force of the wind it is the waves that matter most.

"*Cardinal Vertue* tends to lie broadside or by the quarter, with a 10–20-degree list; but when hit by a sea she heels to 50 degrees. When will the wind veer and the glass rise, I wonder?

"I felt that I was getting demoralized down below and had better go out and face it. So I crawled about the deck, lashing down the sails more firmly, and took some photographs; doubting if they would survive the spray. I feel calmer since going on deck, but I am still scared."

I pumped again and waited, tense and uneasy. There seemed little I could do, and whatever I did might well be wrong for I had never known the like of this before.

It was *Cardinal Vertue*, not I, that was successfully riding out this gale. Proudly she accepted the challenge as, tossed to and fro like a cork, with reeling spars, she rode the waves. When a sea broke fair across her she would shudder to her oaken soul, then shaking herself free with cascades of water streaming from her decks, she would leap skyward once more, alive and free and whole.

The wind blew consistently at fifty-eight miles an hour up to around 6.30 p.m., when it began to ease a little and to veer towards the northwest. But the waves were still growing higher and steeper, and breaking with greater fury. Twice in fifteen minutes the yacht was hove over and buried by waves that sent us crashing and spinning into darkness, and which really frightened me. I dared not let her battle alone any longer. I must try to help.

So, at about 7 p.m., I took the helm and steered before the gale. We would climb dizzily up and up until the ship would be picked up by the crest and hurled forward. As she began to surf, with eight knots registering on the Smith's speed indicator, the water spouted high above the cockpit on each side, before curving over to fill it with a frothing mill-race of icy water, great sheets of which would be flung out over the stern as *Cardinal Vertue* lurched and bucked and threw her bow high as the crest left her.

It was wildly exhilarating but I was drenched to the skin to start

with, and after half an hour I was too chilled to continue. So at 7.30 I shackled the eye at the end of the sea-anchor warp to the wire strop round the transom, streamed it astern, and adjusted the vane to head the yacht down wind.

Twice big seas hit her, spinning her right round each time. The sea-anchor did not seem to be helping and *Cardinal Vertue* lay almost broadside on. But I was too tired to care. I was learning the aptness of the seamen's saying that when you are in a small boat in heavy weather, for every point the wind rises, your ship grows one foot smaller!

I pumped out the bilge as the water was now above the floorboards and exchanged my trousers for swimming trunks, because corduroys, slacks, jeans, pyjama trousers and underpants were all wet now. "Shades of New York and the Gulf Stream," I wrote. "This rig was more suitable then!"

16. The jury-rig with which *Cardinal Vertue* sailed back
to Plymouth after her dismasting.

17. *Cardinal Vertue* alongside at Mashford's Yard, Cremyll,
with only 12 feet of her 34-foot mast left standing.

18. (*Above*) New York and Third Man Home: *Cardinal Vertue*, in tow of a Coastguard cutter, heads for the Quarantine Station.

19. (*Left*) Blondie Hasler lends a hand on the author's arrival in New York. This cockpit view shows the speed-indicator on the doghouse bulkhead and, aft, the mass-balance of the self-steering gear.

The gale was rapidly blowing itself out now. As the last streaks of yellow stormy sunset faded from the sky, around 9.30, the wind had dropped to force 8 or 9. All lights aboard were fused.

At midnight, with the wind force 8, the glass rising steeply and the air temperature 48°F, I wrote by the light of the oil lamp in the cabin:

"As the pressure of the wind slackens, everything becomes lively. The sea is wildly lumpy now and the ship, no longer pressed down so much by the wind, leaps around like a jumping bean. I have pumped again and am now wearing a folded tartan blanket over my swim trunks, tied around my waist with a piece of rope—like some grotesque caricature of a Scotsman."

I should have made sail during the night, or at least taken in the sea-anchor. But I lay exhausted, and alternately shivered and slept until morning. Water was sloshing over the cabin sole again.

Without much difficulty I hauled in the sea anchor, only to find that the shackle had chafed the wire strop half-way through during the thirteen hours it had been in use, mostly after the gale had abated. Later it was discovered that a rim of paint had cracked all round the transom, where the terrific pull had threatened to wrench the stern bodily off—yet the sea-anchor had seemingly been ineffective in holding the ship stern-on to the seas.

I have since consulted the Daily Weather Reports of the British Meteorological Office. No ships were in my vicinity until September 11th, when a deep depression had formed not far to the north-west of me, and a front was passing. My position on the 11th was 52° 20' N, 39° 50' W, only one hundred and fifty miles west of Ocean Weather Ship C, which was at 52° 50' N, 35° 30' W.

At noon this weather ship reported a south-westerly gale of forty-two knots (force 9) and a mean wave height of fourteen feet. At noon the gale at my position had not yet veered, and I, too, was logging a south-westerly gale of force 9. By 6.0 p.m. the waves at the weather ship's position had reached a mean height of $17\frac{1}{2}$ feet. The largest waves would be 40 per cent. bigger than this, some $24\frac{1}{2}$ feet high.

The next two hours were occupied in disentangling the No. 3 staysail and its sheet, fitting a new fairlead, hoisting the No. 1 staysail, and pumping. It was a cold grey morning and swimming trunks beneath porous P.V.C. trousers offered little protection from the raw wind. The ship's motion was very severe.

I slept for a little while, then lit the stove to dry out the electric wiring and cook a leisurely meal, consisting of two eggs, toast, coffee and biscuits. Over breakfast I read Lindeman's book. What incredible courage he showed! During his second canoe crossing in 1956 he had no room to lie down for the first three weeks until some of his stores were eaten, and could only doze hunched up forward over his canvas spray deck. Twice he was capsized as he neared the West Indies. All he seemed to lack was a sense of humour and I, for one, could hardly blame him for that!

I listed the gale's damage:

A fairlead torn off the quarter and the cockpit coaming cracked by the sea-anchor strop; all lights still *caput*; ship leaking; damage to sea-anchor strop and foresail fairlead.

I concluded by writing, with feeling: "I am so thankful to have an intact boat, mast, rudder, wind vane, navigation equipment and food— My God, I am lucky!"

That grey day, September 12th, ended with the lights still not working. In the week since leaving St. John's we had covered five hundred and ninety-five miles. Our best day's run was one hundred and nineteen miles. We had only been on the wind for twenty-three hours, and had been hove-to in the three gales for a total of forty-two hours. On the debit side, the gales had made me so jittery that I could not take my eyes from the barometer, and consistently under-canvased the ship during the following week.

Though I had tried to be exact in my note-taking during the gales, in case the record should be of value, the strength and fury of the seas, the fearful din and the driving spray, made it hard to tell just what the wind, waves and ship were doing at any particular moment. I was so overawed that my "scientific detachment" failed to run to making some obvious observations, such as the period of the waves as we lay a-hull. Nevertheless, I found that even the attempt to be detached, and to describe everything that was happening, helped to replace fear by interest.

Even though I had become so nervous of the weather, the aching loneliness that I had felt after leaving St. John's had gone. This was my own familiar sea with which I felt content to be alone.

I was able to sleep for the whole of the next night, so that on September 13th, even though the sky was streaked with cirrus and the glass had fallen a little, I felt much better. After some more drying out, and by-passing a sodden fuse-box with a length of wire, I got the lights working once more. It was bitterly cold but the sun was shining on blue white-capped seas and a shark appeared and swam for a little while astern.

Life seemed to have returned to the sea again; the petrels were now joined by terns and gulls which wheeled around the ship.

But I was much less happy to sight two ships; for even though the lights were working again, with the engine dead the batteries could not be re-charged and I could not afford to leave navigation lights burning through twelve hours of darkness. But I drew some comfort from the thought that, unlike icebergs or the drifting logs I had seen off the St. Lawrence, ships did at least have radar. When fog closed in that afternoon I could only trust that they would use their radar scanners even more carefully during such thick weather.

At three-thirty the following morning I hoisted the genoa and realized with annoyance that the ship could well have carried it the previous day. How much time had I wasted? The sail had only been set an hour when, "A wind light as yet, but with strength in the gusts", caused me to lower it hastily, and write, "So here it is again, oh well!"

But I soon realized I was being unduly pessimistic, and to help combat the effects of nerves and laziness, I made the following resolution:

"Have decided in view of my recent reluctance to make sail that I will sleep without my warm blanket-kilt. This way I feel cold, so should sleep lighter. This afternoon my sleeping gear consisted of three Norwegian jerseys, swim trunks, safety-belt, ski socks and wellingtons!"

As darkness descended after a gloomy day of damp mist the sky cleared and for a long time I stood on the transom, holding on to the backstays, oblivious of the cold, feeling the lift and scend of the ship beneath me as she rolled her easting down beneath a cloudless sky.

Next day, September 15th, we ran another ninety miles before a force 5 breeze from the north-west. The ship was leaking much less now as her seams took up after the terrible pounding she had received.

The sun set in dubious orange splendour and the sky was still clear at 1 a.m. when the wake, and every breaking wave crest, were afire with cold phosphorescence. To the northward, cold greenish curtains of light soared upwards. It was a grand and awesome sight which was only marred for me by the unwelcome lights of a ship astern.

When I awoke on the morning of the 16th I found that the wind had backed east-of-south, and we were racing merrily away due northward.

While I was resetting the vane I saw a ship approaching and, hoisting the ensign and the flags M.I.K. (Please report me to Lloyds) which Val had lent me, altered course to intercept her. She was *Mathilda Thordein* of Uddevala and she flew an answering pennant in acknowledgment of my signal before continuing on her way.

I must be on the shipping lane between Belle Isle Strait, the northernmost entrance to the St. Lawrence, and Scandinavia. But as I had been unable to obtain longitude sights for two days I could not be certain. In any case there was nothing I could do about it.

The wind began to head us and for most of that day I set the

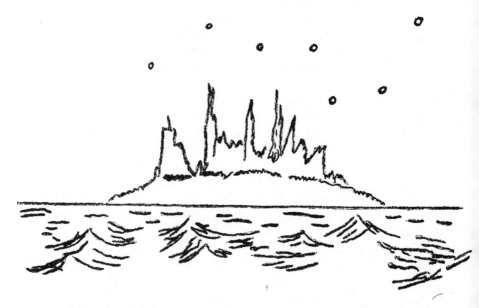

reefed mainsail. Then we sailed through varying winds, calms and rain squalls for the next one and a half days. My clothes and blankets began to dry and I even made pancakes, but not as well as the mate had done. We were now moving clear of the area 9–10 per cent. gales, which lay south of Greenland, and were entering a 7 per cent. gale region. Then there would be a square of 6 per cent. frequency until we had passed north of the prevailing westerlies, in latitude 60°, when we could expect finer weather.

These were busy days, occupied in taking sights, working for hours on the the silent engine, mending a split genoa and checking stores. With a spare battery aboard, I could afford to use the cabin lights if I was careful. This was just as well as paraffin was very short. All other stores were in good supply and I was certainly not losing weight this time.

All was going well; but the sea must never be taken for granted, lest the unexpected catch the unwary off-guard, as it nearly did me.

As I was hoisting the genoa one evening the wind gusted; and when the wind increases, things on the yacht behave quite differently. The usually docile genoa became wrapped about the forestay. The wire part of its halyard wound itself round the forestay the opposite way, while the halyard's rope tail, though cleated, still had enough play to loop over a spreader.

While I was disentangling the muddle the ship gave a violent lurch which pitched me neatly off the lee bow. I was not using the safety-belt but I clutched the wire guard rail as I passed, locking my arms and legs so firmly about it that I was a minute in freeing myself and clambering back aboard. Though the danger was over in under a second the incident left me thoroughly shaken.

In the early morning hours of September 18th, a new gale began to blow out of the north-west. The aurora swept across the northern sky and upwards from east and west to arch, blazing, across the zenith. Between rain squalls, the lights flickered until dawn behind ragged black cloud masses. The wind cut like a knife—as well it might, blowing as it did straight off the Greenland ice cap, five hundred and fifty miles away.

Though the wind was blowing at forty miles an hour I managed, in spite of the wild motion, to boil an egg and laid it down tenderly, wrapped in a cloth. When I turned back to it a moment later it had plastered itself against *both* sides of the cabin! How it did it is a mystery.

At 10 a.m., between the sheets of spray and rain squalls, I managed to obtain a sight of the sun. The log entry: "Calor gas cylinder changed at 2.30 p.m." covers a good deal of effort. Doing anything at all in a gale is unbelievably difficult. I was boiling salt fish and doing my best to stop the water from splashing out of the saucepan, and shampooing my hair at the same time, when the gas ran out. While I was wrestling with the cylinder's locking nut, we broached-to. When the ship had been set back on course, the sheets needed attention. Then the ties on the furled mainsail had to be reinforced; and an opportunity had to be taken to obtain a sight. After all this I could return to the cylinder. By the time the fresh one was in place the gale was howling at

427

forty-eight miles an hour, and a sea, bursting over the quarter, spun us round and broached us to, this time aback. I noted that "The effect of the breaking waves seems to depend on whether they hit the ship forward, or aft, or a-beam. According to where the weight of the blow falls, the yacht spins round accordingly or is thrown bodily sideways. Exactly the same seems to happen whether she is running, or hove-to in some fashion."

The gale died down during the night. For the first time we had not had to heave-to but had been able to keep running under reefed No. 1 staysail.

How stiff the gales had left me! Not bruised so much, because by now I was pretty canny at hanging on, but aching in every joint through being thrown about like a dice in a cup.

The next day, September 19th, was the end of the second week out. The wind had been mainly fair, in fact the mainsail had only been hoisted for eleven and a half hours. We had covered five hundred and ninety-four miles. The best day's run was one hundred and twenty miles.

That night the wind backed to east-of-south and a rapidly falling glass foretold further trouble. I hoisted the mainsail at 4.30 a.m. when the wind was south-east and we could still lay our course. By 5.30 the genoa had to be handed as the wind, which had backed further to east-south-east, was increasing.

Two hours later I awoke to a strong smell of Calor gas, but had no time to investigate as the ship was hard pressed. As I was rolling down the mainsail the topping lift jammed between the boom and its clew fitting and locked solid. Eventually, with a turn of the sheet, I was able to restrain the wildly threshing boom, which jerked me to and fro until my teeth rattled, for long enough to enable me to cut the nylon cord with which I had replaced the topping lift shackle.

When I had captured and made fast the topping lift again it was time to reef the staysail. As I set the ship at the short steep head seas which the force 6 breeze had raised, spray and rain drove over us until I was soaked through my inadequate P.V.C.'s.

Now that I at last had leisure to look for the Calor leak I found that I must have kicked open the valve of an almost empty cylinder in the dark. I did not know if a dangerous amount of gas had escaped, so to be on the safe side I aired the ship at the cost of a good deal of water down the fore hatch.

At 11 a.m. with the wind up to force 7, I close-reefed the mainsail and raised the gallows to allow the boom to set lower, beneath it. The sheet could not function in this position so I lashed the boom down to a cleat. The sail set flatter this way, without flogging, and *Cardinal Vertue* punched her way to windward into the stinging rain at four knots. "It is back to swimming trunks again, I am afraid," I wrote. "Thank goodness I had the foresight to fry an egg at 4 a.m."

By 1 p.m. the wind had reached forty-two miles an hour and the glass was still steadily falling. Two hours later it was blowing forty-five miles an hour and we were continuing to make headway to windward.

But when the wind, blowing persistently from the east-south-east, increased to fifty miles an hour, force 9, at 5 p.m., I hove-to on the starboard tack under the close-reefed mainsail by lowering the staysail and lashing the helm down with the tiller lines.

I thought we had been able to keep going for so long because the gale had come up at right angles to the prevailing westerly Atlantic swell. Now the yacht rode comfortably hove-to.

It was hard to visualize what life would be like without the wind-vane. I became chilled, wet and exhausted after only half an hour on deck or in the cockpit in bad weather; I could never have steered for hour after hour in these conditions.

The wind eased during the evening but it was a foul night with rain squalls, a fearsome cross sea, a falling glass and a wind that neither veered nor backed. What did such weather mean? Was the "low" north or south of us, or where?

Whatever the signs portended, the wind continued to ease until I could no longer in decency remain hove-to; so before midnight I crawled out of my warm bunk and got under way. This was only a matter of hoisting the staysail, freeing the helm and unrolling some of the mainsail. I would have been more reluctant to get under way had there been warps or a sea-anchor to get aboard.

"How easily I could have gone to sleep and missed this opportunity to press on if I had allowed myself to be hypnotized by the falling glass!" I wrote smugly. "Why it is as smooth as a pond outside—or almost!"

I turned over and went to sleep with the wind east-south-east and light, and woke at 2 a.m. to find it blowing a force 8 gale again from the north-west, almost exactly the opposite quarter.

After I had lowered the mainsail and resumed the proper course under reefed staysail, I noted in a more chastened mood, "So *now* I know what the unchanged wind direction, with steadily falling glass followed by a lull, meant. I should have guessed, of course, that the centre of a depression was passing clean over us. But no! the 'clever' navigator had to go to sleep about 1 a.m. and only wake when his ship was luffing hard and sailing in the wrong direction!" This was later confirmed from the Daily Weather Reports of the British Meteorological Office.

The wind continued to blow at forty-one miles an hour between squalls. Twice before daybreak *Cardinal Vertue* had broached-to and been thrown a-back. At 11.30 a.m. the gale was still blowing at forty miles an hour but the glass had begun to rise and the sunshine to break through. I climbed on to the housed boom and up the mast a little way to try to get level with the tops of the waves in order to judge their height more accurately than I could from the cockpit, from where they had seemed enormous. To my chagrin I found that they were much lower than I had expected, only about 14 feet high on average!

According to Cdr. Errol Bruce in *Deep Sea Sailing*, a force 8 gale of unlimited fetch and starting from a calm would raise a sea $12\frac{1}{2}$ feet high in nine hours. On September 21st the north-west gale had been blowing at force 8 for nine hours when I made my observation of wave height, but it had not blown from a calm. It had followed, after a three-hour lull, a nine-hour east-south-easterly gale which had reached force 9 for several hours.

On the other hand, the fetch was not unlimited. According to the Daily Weather Reports the distance from the centre of the disturbance which caused the gale was less than two hundred miles. This distance, and not that from the nearest land to windward, determines the fetch, and therefore the height, of the waves.

At noon, an hour after my note, a ship to the north of me was still experiencing gale-force winds, but I was only logging force 7. Ocean Weather Ship I, in 59° N, 19° W, which was some ninety miles north-east of me (my position was 58° 08' N, 20° 24' W) also recorded a wind which had fallen from force 8 to force 7 (28 knots), and confused waves 13 feet high. My own estimate of 14 feet as the height of the seas would therefore be about correct.

The wind moderated during the day and that night I was able to lie in my bunk looking through the doghouse windows at the Northern Lights, which, between hail storms, illumined the inky thunder clouds with unearthly magnificence, and listening to Paul Robeson singing negro spirituals on Radio Luxembourg. His magnificent voice formed a fitting counterpart to those remote glowing curtains which hung at the edge of space, high over Iceland, three hundred miles to the north.

The next day was notable for the discovery of two packets of mildewed bacon I had overlooked. As it would not keep much longer, I cooked it all and dined sumptuously on bacon, eggs, fried bread and coffee.

On the radio's trawler band I could now hear the fishermen talking to each other from the Outer Bailey or Lousy Banks. How had these banks come by their name, I wondered, and I sighed for a moment at the memory of the Grand Banks, now so far astern.

Ships passed by nearly every day now; far too many for comfort. They were bound to or from Canada, via Pentland Firth, or between the Faroes and the Shetland Isles.

While I had good reason to be concerned about steamers, my other fear was quite irrational. This was of hitting Rockall. This isolated rock spire rises 70 sheer feet out of the depths some one hundred and sixty miles west of St. Kilda in the Hebrides. Over the centuries it had often been sighted but it was not until 1810 that its existence was finally established by H.M.S. *Endymion*. Prior to this time it had often been taken for a full-rigged ship under sail, so steep was it and so white with bird droppings. On one side of the rock dangerous reefs extend for some miles. In New York I had marked these on a chart from the information in Blondie Hasler's *North Atlantic Pilot*. Now I found that I had left this particular chart behind and could not remember on which side of Rockall the reefs lay. But I had nothing to worry about because I had obtained good sights which showed that when I passed Rockall next day I would be sixty miles north of it.

During the morning of September 23rd the weather again deteriorated. The wind backed to the south-east and began to rise; while the sea became shrouded by a dismal fine rain. The high-tension battery of the radio took this opportunity to give out and I found to my dismay that one of the leads of the spare battery had corroded. The delicate work of "pirating" a lead from the used battery was difficult in such a seaway, so that I was surprised and delighted to get the set working. Any day now the B.B.C. time signals should become audible, when I could correct any error in the deck-watch. I had no wish to impale the ship on any of the fearsome Gaelic rocks like Sula Sgeir, whose jagged spires guard the northern Hebrides.

For three hours after the wind had reached forty miles an hour we beat to windward into the driving rain and spray under close-reefed main and reefed staysail.

At 5 p.m. the wind veered to south-east which allowed me to run before the gale. Slipping out of my kilt, I went on deck wearing a hooded P.V.C. smock and three pullovers but with nothing below but my swimming trunks and knobbly knees, purple with cold and goose pimples. It was as well I handed the mainsail when I did for a few minutes later the wind was shrieking at forty-eight miles an hour and *Cardinal Vertue* was running at five knots under reefed staysail alone. Fortunately the sea was confused and relatively small, as yet.

Every now and then the yacht would broach-to or be thrown a-back, so I kept wearing my P.V.C. smock in the cabin, ready to climb out of the hatchway in a hurry and set the yacht back on course; for this time I was determined to keep going if possible.

Between 6.30 and 8 p.m., the wind blew at fifty-three miles an hour and *Cardinal Vertue* tended to luff and run across the seas; the action of her vane repeatedly overpowered by blows from the steep, breaking crests. I steered for half an hour before seas which seemed mountainous to me. The Smith's indicator registered nine and a half knots when we surfed and the cockpit was filled with swirling water. Even though my safety-belt was in use I would grasp the guard rail and hang on whenever a wave steeper and higher than the rest climbed toppling above the stern before cascading over me.

Once, while I was out on the transom adjusting the wind-vane, a sea burst across us, broaching us to. The water swirled around my knees as I struggled for foothold on the after deck, while over my shoulder all that I could see of the ship was her doghouse, part of the weather rail, and the mast.

This was enough steering for me; darkness was falling and the surface of the sea was being blown into white smoke. I retired below and hoped that the vane could carry on.

"I don't know how much longer she can keep going," I wrote doubtfully, then continued wistfully, "The mate would have looked far more becoming than me, dressed like this! Come to think of it, I wish the mate were here!" Then with something less than gallantry, I coupled the last sentiment with: "I wish I had some whisky, too! and I wish the wind would ease; I am being bounced all over the cabin."

I was lucky indeed, for by nine-thirty, the wind had fallen to force 8 and less heavy water was coming aboard. This was the sixth gale; but this time we had made it without having to heave-to at all.

It was true that I had also successfully kept going through the gale on September 18th but it had been a milder one, the wind velocity only exceeding force 8 for a short period.

According to the Daily Weather Reports a "low" had passed over my position on the afternoon of the 23rd. No ships were in my vicinity or near its centre, but the following day a vessel in its track reported winds of forty-seven knots, force 9.

What had been the height of the waves which I had described as "mountainous"? As the disturbance passed clear of Ocean Weather Ship I, no data is available. I would judge the waves to be about the same as those on September 11th, which were recorded by Weather Ship C as having a mean height of 17½ feet, so occasional very large seas might have reached 24½ feet, but such waves would be rare.

The next day I was irritable and drained of energy as always after a gale. Every joint ached where it had been jerked and snapped to and fro. Souvenirs of the gale were everywhere; an overturned saucepan of stew in the food locker, pools of water in incredible places, a violent motion which lingered on in the swell, without the thumps and thundering cascades but also without the inimitable grandeur of the storm.

On consulting the tables, after taking a sight, I found that the sun had now crossed the Equator into southerly declination, abandoning us to the northern winter. We were crossing longitude 10° W, that is, we were passing the extreme tip of Ireland, four hundred and twenty miles south of us. That night, beneath the remote aurora, I obtained the first B.B.C. time signal.

The wind now became fickle and capricious. The reason for this was that the European wind systems were cushioning the Atlantic gales, in particular the westerlies were dissipated against a stable anticyclone which was sitting firmly on the Norwegian Sea.

By morning, the wind was blowing steadily from eastward, dead ahead, and for the next three days we plunged and bucked to windward on the starboard tack.

On the second day I was sighted and reported by the Swedish ship *Ragneberg*, and a few hours later I caught a glimpse of a submarine's conning-tower between the waves.

Next morning the stainless steel lee runner frayed through and had to be joined with bulldog grips and supported by a tackle.

When I reached the latitude of the Faroes, and was north of Shetland altogether, in 61° 13′ N, I could at last lay Sumburgh Head on the

433

other tack. I came about and sailed south-east through a day of sun-shine and a night during which a great black cloud hung over us to port like a cliff, silhouetted first against the aurora, then the dawn. At daybreak a few scattered clouds lay on the eastern horizon but as the sun rose higher on September 29th they scattered—all but one!

"This bloody maritime weeping act is trying to start again!" I wrote, with disgust, in the log. But it was no cloud that lay ahead, it was Foula, first island of Shetland, its cliffs rising sheer, 1,200 feet out of the sea.

The wind died and for the next twenty-three and a half hours I lay becalmed, watching the unchanging shape of Foula, which some say was the "Ultima Thule" of the Romans. The stove was giving up now but would still cook slowly. Though I was able to dry out properly for

almost the first time in three weeks, I still knew little peace of mind until the wind gave the ship life next morning, September 30th, heeling her over on the port tack. "After this long unexpected calm in sight of land," I wrote, "I feel as if my free-will had been 'wrung-out'. Far more than a gale, a calm brings home our smallness before nature."

All day Foula grew larger, until by 4 p.m. West Hoevdi Cliff stood gigantic above the ship. One by one the hills of the Shetland mainland rose out of the sea ahead; hosts of seabirds dotted the water, a dolphin appeared, then a seal.

Through light airs and brief calms I stood on as night fell, revealing the lights of trawlers scattered over the sea. "A wonderful day with some progress and above all some feeling of self-mastery over the effects of what I find hardest to bear—calms," I wrote. "Now the cliffs of Hoevdi are tinged with rose. One feels a special quality in these Norse Isles, as if the old gods still linger here."

At midnight I tried to describe the scene: "The moon stands high to the right, and a most brilliant aurora arches over the sky on the left. Around us is a vast panorama of islands; Foula astern now, Fair Isle to the southward and Sumburgh Head silhouetted against the stars on the port bow with its lighthouse blinking. Ahead, too, lies Sumburgh Röst. Now the wind is falling light again and heading us as we sail on into the October night."

I felt great thankfulness at having passed safely through my ordeal by storm, but as I gazed out at the vastness around me, I wrote, "I wonder when next I shall see its like again?"

Wilfred Noyce in *Springs of Adventure* has expressed my feelings far better than I:

> Who has known heights and depths shall not again
> Know peace—not as the calm heart knows
> Low ivied walls, a garden close,
> The old enchantment of a rose,
> And though he tread the humble ways of men
> He shall not speak the common tongue again.

10

SHETLAND LANDFALL

"This dangerous race in which the sea runs to great heights, and breaks with violence, at times even in calm weather extends ... two to four miles off Sumburgh Head. ...
As in this confused tumbling and bursting sea, vessels often become completely unmanageable and sometimes founder, while others have been tossed about for days together in light weather, the röst should be given a wide berth."

Sumburgh Head Röst—
North Sea Pilot, Part One (1910 Edition)

EVEN though I had no such detailed account as this of the röst on board, I aimed to keep well clear of a place with such an evil reputation. As long ago as A.D. 81, Agricola's Roman fleet "discovered and subdued islands hitherto unknown, which they call the Orkneys. Thule too was seen . . . but they reported that the sea was *sticky and heavy for the rowers.*" This seems a good description of the röst.

Then the Orkneyingers' Saga tells how "Earl Erlend and Sweyn held on south at once into the Isles with five ships and got caught in Dynrace (Sumburgh Röst) in dangerous tides and a storm of wind, and there they parted company. Then Sweyn bore up for Fair Isle with two ships and they thought the Earl lost. Then they held on their course under Sanday and there Earl Erlend lay before them with three ships and that was a very joyful meeting."

I had planned to keep a good offing from Sumburgh Head but the wind veered and headed me, so that the best course I could lay led right through the middle of the röst, barely clearing the headland itself.

But the tide would only remain favourable until 7 a.m. so that if I tacked away southward I could not hope to round the Cape in the face of light contrary winds and a foul tide until some time in the afternoon. Furthermore, when the tide changed it set southwards, away from the land for the first few hours, so if there were any bother in the race *Cardinal Vertue* would soon be swept clear.

436

Nevertheless, I closed the röst with some care and trepidation, writing in the log: "Even the Saga tells of a Viking fleet caught here in a gale; this is no gale; but I am no Viking either!"

Over the stern the aurora still stood like an archway leading from a faery land that we were leaving, as at 5.30 a.m. on October 1st we entered Sumburgh Röst and for nearly two hours were tossed and shaken until I felt sick and giddy. Great pyramids of water would hump up, erupt and topple; a frightening sight, even in that light easterly weather.

In the midst of this wild ride we came upon a sleeping seal lying on his back and twitching his grey whiskers irritably whenever a wave splashed him. He looked for all the world like some old gentleman dozing in a club armchair. An expression of comical alarm spread over his face when he opened his eyes and saw the ship beside him; then he flipped over and dived in a flash of sleek dark grace.

The clouds were pink and orange in the sunrise as we rounded the ness and sailed into calmer water, bearing away for Bressay Sound.

With a fair breeze, *Cardinal Vertue* ran swiftly up the coast of Shetland. By 10.15 we were passing the Pictish Broch on Mousa Island, a round tower, relic of a vanished race, which has provided a prominent sea mark since the first Norse invaders "fed the ravens with the harvest of their spear-storms".

It was 12.35 p.m. when we entered Lerwick Harbour and rounded-to alongside Tom Moncrief's schooner *Loki*; while a Shetland model sailed by like some miniature longship.

St. John's lay one thousand nine hundred and eighty-four miles, and twenty-five days twenty-one hours, astern. For two-thirds of the way we had run before the wind, usually without a mainsail but we had not been off the wind during the past five days. There had been five force 9 gales and one which reached force 10.

I seemed in a daze that afternoon and my impressions are hazy. I remember handing back a battered sextant, and finding kindness and hospitality that I can never forget. I recall Basil Wishart in the newspaper office asking me who had sailed that way before. I did not know; so he took up the telephone. When he replaced the receiver he turned to me, grinning:

"He says, 'No one since Leif Erikson!' "

Tom suggested that I should be broken-in to the land gently by way of a cruise into the Voes aboard *Loki*. As we clambered aboard, his son remarked: "Dad didn't expect you."

437

"Why not?" I asked puzzled. "Didn't he get the card I sent him from St. John's?"

"We got it all right, that's *why* he didn't expect you. When he read your card he said: 'That's the last we've seen of him!' "

As the stately 27-tonner breasted the swells beyond the Sound, I stood alone in the dusk remembering Shelley's lines:

> The wilderness has a mysterious tongue
> Which teaches awful doubt, or faith so mild,
> So solemn, so serene, that man may be,
> But for such faith, with nature reconciled.

For a little while I had been living intimately with things greater than myself. Tom was right in saying that I needed time to become fully part of the civilized world again, for I knew that I had been subtly changed, a man of deeper calm and confidence perhaps, but above all, imbued with profound humility.

THIS BOOK IS DEDICATED TO

FIONA, MY WIFE

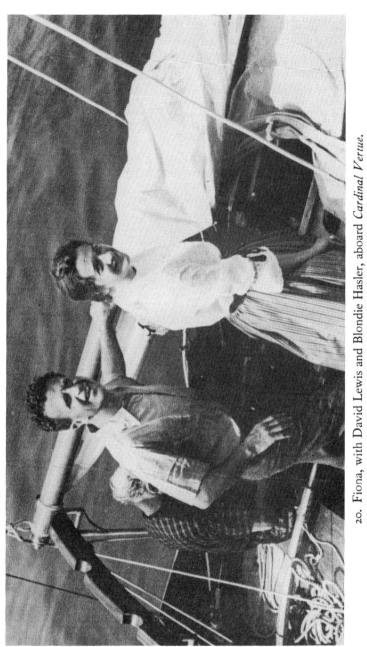

20. Fiona, with David Lewis and Blondie Hasler, aboard *Cardinal Vertue*.

21. H.R.H. the Duke of Edinburgh presents the author with his award. On the right is Lt.-Col. Odling Smee, Rear-Commodore of the Royal Western Yacht Club, the organizers of the race.

APPENDIX ONE

Cardinal Vertue

Cardinal Vertue is a Vertue-class Bermudan sloop, designed by J. Laurent Giles and built by E. F. Elkins and Co. at Christchurch in 1948. Her port of registry is London and her official number is 183341. Principal dimensions are:

Length, overall	..	25 ft. 3 in.
Length, waterline	..	21 ft. 6 in.
Beam	..	7 ft. 2 in.
Draft	..	4 ft. 6 in.
Displacement	..	4.5 tons
Thames measurement	..	5 tons

Sail areas

Mainsail	..	180 sq. ft.
Genoa	..	230 sq. ft.
Spinnaker	..	400 sq. ft. approx.
No. 1 staysail	..	98 sq. ft.
No. 2 staysail	..	68 sq. ft.
(or No. 1 reefed)		
No. 3 staysail	..	45 sq. ft.

Modifications made for the Race

An inner lining of five-ply was fitted to the side of the doghouse between the windows. This was to prevent the mahogany splitting along the grain in the event of a knockdown.

The Triplex windows were covered outside with Perspex, and brass strips backed the grooves in which the washboards slide down. Originally only $\frac{1}{4}$ in. of wood held the washboards in position, and they would have been vulnerable to a bursting sea from astern.

Hand-rails were fitted inside the cabin and proved invaluable.

A diaphragm pump (Mike Henderson) was fitted beneath the cabin floorboards. It was most efficient and would have been unblockable except that I mounted it too low. Far superior, in my experience, to plunger and semi-rotary pumps.

A canvas dodger surrounded the cockpit.

Non-slip decks were obtained by sprinkling a wet undercoat with silver sand, brushing off the surplus when dry, and covering with a top coat.

439

The fore-hatch was bedded on rubber strips, fitted with a hasp and also lashed down, all from inside. It proved watertight.

Heavy insulated cable was used throughout for electric wiring.

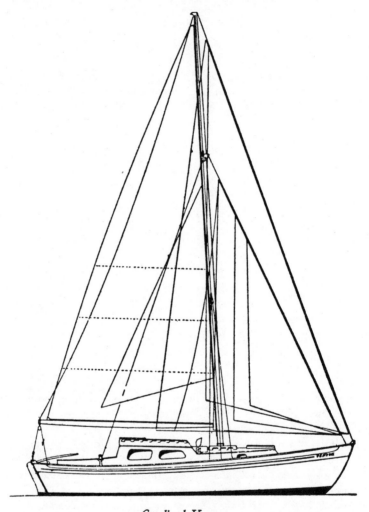

Cardinal Vertue

The self-draining cockpit was reduced in size to standard Vertue s-d. dimensions and two $1\frac{1}{2}$-in. drains fitted. Two-inch drains would have been better. Locker tops were bedded down on rubber strips and fastened with hasps.

Mainsail and twin No. 1 staysails of 10-oz. Terylene were made specially

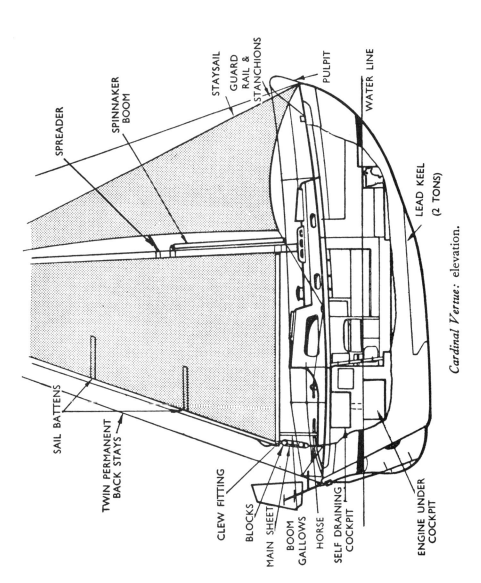

Cardinal Vertue: elevation.

SPREADER

SPINNAKER BOOM

STAYSAIL

GUARD RAIL & STANCHIONS

PULPIT

WATER LINE

LEAD KEEL (2 TONS)

SAIL BATTENS

TWIN PERMANENT BACK STAYS

CLEW FITTING

BLOCKS

MAIN SHEET

BOOM GALLOWS

HORSE

SELF DRAINING COCKPIT

ENGINE UNDER COCKPIT

for the race by Gowens of West Mersea. Though they flogged violently at times there was no damage and only one small area of chafe where the topping lift touched the lower part of the leach of the mainsail. If I had not been so secretive about where I was going, Gowens would have fitted shackles for the slides. These would have been better than seizing. The staysail was fitted with reef points at Humphrey Barton's suggestion and this proved a great success.

The main boom was shortened and twin masthead backstays fitted (alternative Vertue pattern). *Cardinal Vertue* is as fast with her new smaller mainsail as with her larger cotton one.

A main boom foreguy was fitted on the recommendation of Humphrey Barton. It holds the boom down and safe from an unexpected gybe, yet can be quickly released. The disadvantages, which to my mind are quite outweighed by its advantages, are: (i) strain on stanchions, as the foreguy must pass outside everything; (ii) the foreguy easily chafes through.

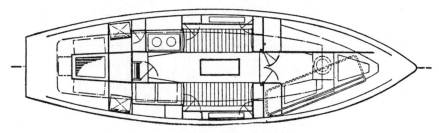

Cardinal Vertue: plan.

The rigging was of stainless steel but I was in error in using too small a block round which the running part of the lee runner had to pass. With a bigger block it would not have been bent at such an acute angle and would not have chafed through.

P.V.C. covering was carried well up shrouds and over the guardrail. There was no chafe of sails or sheets and baggy-wrinkle was never needed.

A permanent gallows was already fitted.

A permanent topping-lift, kept taut by a length of shock cord, had been fitted and I replaced the shackle by a length of nylon cord to facilitate lengthening the topping-lift as the boom dropped lower when close-reefed.

Some Notes on Equipment

Radio D.F. set: I made the mistake of mounting mine too near the hatchway where it was damaged by spray. A model whose loop is mounted on a hand-bearing compass is easier to use when alone, as you cannot take a radio bearing and read the direction the ship is heading on the steering compass at the same time.

Safety-belt: The most useful piece of equipment of all.

Inflatable covered rubber dinghy: The ideal one for the ocean cruiser has not yet been made. Should disaster overtake a yacht on an ocean crossing no one would know anything was wrong for months and even then would

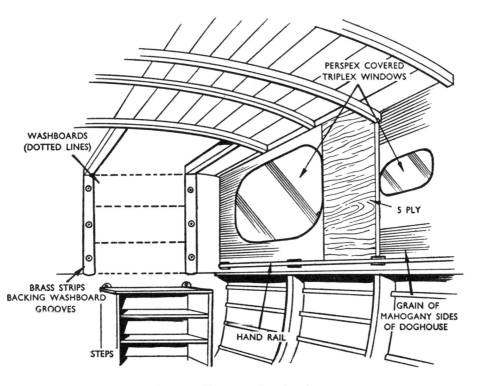

Cardinal Vertue: cabin details.

not know where to look. Ideally, therefore, an ocean-going yacht's emergency rubber dinghy should be capable of sailing into the nearest shipping lane, i.e. it should be oval and have a sail and either a keel or lee-boards.

Echo-sounder: A transistor set is an invaluable navigational aid when in soundings.

Sextant: A micrometer type is far easier to read than one with a vernier. I shall try to borrow one again next time I go to sea.

Navigation: I used Lt. Cdr. Rantzen's book together with the *Abridged Nautical Almanac* and H.D.486. I needed three volumes of these tables to cover from New York to Lerwick. H225A, the sight form for use with these tables, simplifies navigation enormously by listing each step in the process of working a sight, so ensuring that none is missed.

Insurance: The underwriter was most reasonable. Insurance for twelve months, seven in commission including the two-way Atlantic crossing, on a value of £1,800, was the same as for an earlier voyage to Norway, namely:

	£36 3s. 0d.
Third party	1 5s. 0d.
Racing cover	6 0s. 0d.

Total premium £43 8s. 0d.

An excess clause of £100 was in operation for the duration of the race.

Unnecessary equipment: In the light of experience I found the following items to have been unnecessary: (i) Twin spinnaker booms and twin running sails (twin No. 1 staysails)—these were rendered superfluous by the vane; (ii) Sea-anchor and sea-anchor strop; (iii) Tackle for hoisting oneself up in bosun's chair. When I used the chair, it was less effort to hoist it first, then climb up into it.

Desirable additional equipment and precautions include: (i) Non-slip tread on the companion ladder steps and on the cockpit seats; (ii) A stronger gooseneck; (iii) A better spray hood than the present one of my design; (iv) Tapered slats glued along the boom to counteract the tendency of the boom to droop when close-reefed; (v) Better protection of engine from damp; (vi) For a long trip a paraffin cooker would have been better than Calor gas (though less convenient) because bottled gas threads vary in different countries and heavy cylinders have to be carried (surely it is time the manufacturers came to an international standardization agreement!).

APPENDIX TWO

The Self-steering Gear on "Cardinal Vertue"

Cardinal Vertue's self-steering gear was of the trim-tab or servo-rudder type. The design was my own but was based on the advice and experience of others, especially Val Howells. It was made by the brothers Foster of The

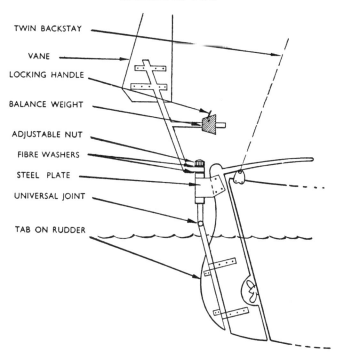

TWIN BACKSTAY

VANE

LOCKING HANDLE

BALANCE WEIGHT

ADJUSTABLE NUT

FIBRE WASHERS

STEEL PLATE

UNIVERSAL JOINT

TAB ON RUDDER

Aries Engineering Company of East Ham, and by Jack Staines of Tucker Brown and Co. of Burnham-on-Crouch, who made the trim-tab.

In operation the ship is set on course and the sheets correctly trimmed. The vane is allowed to trail with the wind and is then locked to connect it to the tab. If the ship moves off course to port, as shown in the diagram overleaf, the wind strikes the right-hand side of the vane, pushing it over to port. This moves the trim-tab to port, too. The water pressure against the trim-tab forces the main rudder to starboard, and the ship, turning to starboard, resumes her course.

The vane itself was made of marine five-ply and was probably unnecessarily heavy. The tab, too, was rather too large in proportion to the wetted surface of the rudder. During trials, a tremendous vibration would develop at certain angles of tab, due apparently to cavitation. This was cured, on the advice of Mike Henderson, by thinning down the tab.

It is essential that the device be as free from friction and as well-balanced as possible. The two ball-races on which the shaft turns are lubricated by a grease nipple and were most satisfactory. The universal joint is of stainless steel and kept freely mobile.

In the light of experience I would now make the following improvements to the gear.

445

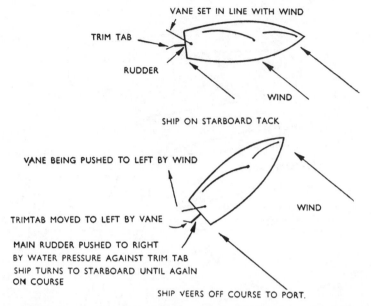

If the ship moves off course to port as shown in the diagram above, the wind strikes the right-hand side of the vane pushing it over to port. This moves the trim-tab to port too. The water pressure against the trim-tab forces the main rudder to starboard; the ship, turning to starboard, resumes her course.

(i) A light vane for gentle winds. My gear, like Val Howells', did not work properly in force 1–2 breezes. I had to steer by hand under $2\frac{1}{2}$ knots, as rudder and vane would be thrown over by the swell and the ship be taken a-back when winds were very light.

(ii) An inboard control in cockpit or cabin, as was successfully used aboard *Jester*.

(iii) A calibrated indicator so that the vane could be set at marked positions.

(iv) A slightly smaller trim-tab and vane.

(v) A wheel locking-nut which would be more convenient than the short handle I used.

Setting the vane: In a normal craft with some weather helm, the vane is not set exactly down wind but with a few degrees bias one way to counteract the weather helm. I can never remember the direction of this bias but, like its amount, it is soon found by trial and error.

Effect of quartering seas: As described in Chapter 6, each quartering sea slews the yacht round, after which she swings back on course by the action of the vane. If, however, the seas are steep, this constant driving of the ship off course can produce a zigzag well to windward of the course required. Val

446

Howells experienced the same trouble, and in both cases our ships maintained their correct courses when the mainsail was lowered and we proceeded under genoa or staysails alone.

Vane steering for other craft: Counter sterns and bumpkins present problems which may be tackled in various ways.

(i) Leaving the main rudder free, the vane can be attached to an auxiliary rudder fitted to the counter. A reverse linkage must be incorporated here. (*See Mike Henderson's article on "Mick the Miller" in* Yachting World, *April 1957 and "Jean Matilde's Gear"*, Yachting Monthly, *June 1959.*)

(ii) A large vane can be made to work the main rudder direct, again through a reverse linkage, as successfully used by Francis Chichester.

(iii) For a counter-stern yacht a trim-tab can be used if there is room to run a shaft down the rudder trunk and connect it to the tab by side arms. Ian Major used this method on *Buttercup.*

Other methods of self-steering: Hamilton used a boomed-out genoa connected to the tiller by its sheet, the tiller being held under tension by shock-absorber cord. The Hiscocks in *Voyaging under Sail* describe various twin headsail layouts but the ever-changing winds of our latitudes make such systems cumbersome for other than trade-wind passages. They do not confer on the single-hander that "freedom of the ocean" which goes with the ability to make self-steered passages through the variables. Whatever the method employed, a balanced hull and sail plan are desirable if a yacht is to steer herself efficiently.

APPENDIX THREE

The Race and the Competitors

The First Single-handed Transatlantic Race from Plymouth to New York, originally suggested by Lt.-Col. H. G. Hasler, was organized by the Royal Western Yacht Club of England, with the Slocum Society responsible for the finishing arrangements. The object of the race was to encourage the development of suitable boats, gear, supplies and techniques for single-handed ocean crossings under sail. Yachts of any size or type were eligible but no means of propulsion could be employed other than the force of the wind, the manpower of the crew, or both. A competitor, to qualify, must have completed a single-handed cruise of a nature to satisfy the organizing committee or produce a certificate of competence endorsed by a recognized yacht club.

The start of the race was from Plymouth at 10.0 a.m. B.S.T. on June 11th, 1960. Competitors could proceed by any route to the finishing line off the Ambrose light-vessel in the approaches to New York harbour and, to qualify as a finisher, had to complete the voyage not later than September 11th, 1960.

Each entrant was required to carry, as safety equipment, an inflatable life raft, radar reflector, portable loud-hailer, foghorn, daylight distress signals and marker dye, flares and pyrotechnic distress signals. No physical contact, except for the passing of written messages, could be made with other craft at sea and no stores could be received from any other ship during the race. Yachts were permitted to put in anywhere, and to anchor or moor for any purpose during the race, but when at sea were required to be fully independent and capable of carrying out their own emergency repairs.

Race awards, presented by *The Observer*, comprised a trophy, consisting of a salver depicting a map of the Atlantic, to the first competitor to arrive at the finishing line, a smaller salver of the same design to the second competitor to finish, and replicas of the salver to other competitors finishing within the specified time.

Gipsy Moth III — FRANCIS CHICHESTER

The winner of the race. Time: 40 days. Yawl, designed by Robert Clark and built by John Tyrell at Arklow, Eire, in 1959. Self-steering gear designed by owner and built by Agamemnon Boatyard, Buckler's Hard.

Length, overall	..	39 ft. 7 in.
Length, waterline	..	28 ft. 0 in.
Beam (max.)	..	10 ft. $1\frac{3}{4}$ in.
Draft	..	6 ft. 5 in.
Thames tonnage	..	13 tons
Gross tonnage	..	$10\frac{3}{4}$ tons
Iron keel	..	$4\frac{1}{4}$ tons

Sail areas

Mainsail	..	$380\frac{1}{2}$ sq. ft.
Genoa	..	380 sq. ft.
Trisail	..	144 sq. ft.
Storm jib	..	65 sq. ft.

Course: Great Circle course, Plymouth–New York, approx. 3,100 miles (4,004 miles actually covered). Averaged $76\frac{1}{2}$ miles per day, on course towards New York, or almost 100 miles per day actually sailed.*

* Methods of calculating daily runs varied among the competitors. Chichester and Howells appear sometimes to have taken their patent log readings (i.e. distances actually sailed). Hasler recorded the shortest line between successive 0900 hours G.M.T. positions. My own method was to note the distance covered in the direction of the objective between successive noon G.M.T. positions. All distances are in sea miles,

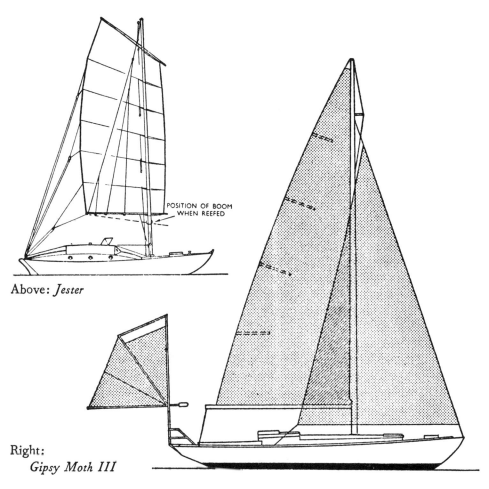

Above: *Jester*

Right:
Gipsy Moth III

POSITION OF BOOM
WHEN REEFED

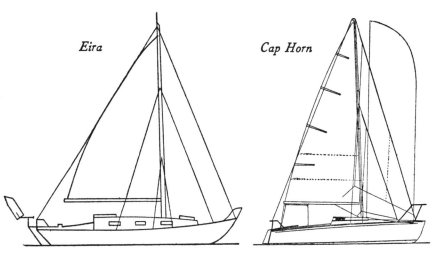

Eira

Cap Horn

On wind, 636 hours (65 per cent. time); Wind free, 288 hours (approx. 30 per cent.); Bare poles, 48 hours; Fog, totalled 336 hours; Calms: says there were not many and they gave him time to sleep.

Sail changes: Reefed main, 16 times; set trisail, 7 times; no main or trisail 24 times; boomed-out jibs, 4 times; major changes headsail, 43 times; Spinnaker not used.

Jester — LT.-COL. H. G. HASLER

Second man home. Time: 48 days. Modified Scandinavian Folkboat with Chinese lug rig on an unstayed mast. Built 1952.

Length, overall	..	25.9 ft.
Length, waterline	..	20 ft. 0 in.
Beam	..	7 ft. 3 in.
Draft	..	4 ft. 0 in.
Iron keel	..	1 ton
Displacement (light)	..	2½ tons
Thames tonnage	..	5 tons
Single sail area	..	240 sq. ft.

Course: Followed northern route—higher than Great Circle route—past SW corner of Ireland, curving up to 57° N, 30° W. Distance, 3,417 miles. Averaged 65 miles per day, or 71 miles per day actually sailed. Longest runs, two of 120 miles. No record available of frequent sail adjustments. Return voyage: Sheepshead Bay, Brooklyn to the Needles, I.O.W., 3,417 miles in 38 days 9 hours; average, 86 miles per day.

Cardinal Vertue — DAVID LEWIS

Third man home. Time: 56 days elapsed time (including return after dismasting); 54 days actual time.

Course: Great Circle course (3,100 miles). Average sailed, 57.4 miles per day; able to lay course only 40 per cent. of time, remainder prevented by headwinds or calms. On wind, 758 hours (70 per cent. of time); Wind free, 286 hours (22 per cent. of time); Calms encountered on 37 days (67 per cent. days of voyage) and totalled 183 hours, or 7 days 15 hours, (15 per cent. of time). Fog, 308 hours. Longest run, 102 miles.

Sail changes: Major changes of headsails, 87 times; reefed mainsail, 43 times; lowered mainsail, 3 times; Spinnaker used 10 times for total of 93 hours.

Remarks: Genoa was always left on stay and No. 1 staysail kept set and drawing well when genoa was set, yet time lost in sail changing was considerable. Had to heave-to during reefing, or unreefing the mainsail for 7–15 minutes (86 times) and when reefing staysail (12 times). Estimating the average time stopped at 10 minutes per operation, total time lost was 16½ hours, in contrast to Hasler on *Jester* who made many and exact sail changes virtually without stopping his ship.

RETURN VOYAGE: NEW YORK–ST. JOHN'S–LERWICK, SHETLAND ISLES

New York–St. John's, Newfoundland

Distance: Sailed with Fiona; 1,113 miles covered in 12 days 10 hours 40 minutes. Best day's run: 124 miles; worst, 58 miles. Average, 88 miles per day. On wind, 49 hours; wind free, 260½ hours; able to lay course, 73 per cent. of time. Fog, 16 hours over 4 days; calms, 3 hours over 3 days.

Sail changes: Reefed mainsail 11 times and lowered once because of wind strength; reefed staysail once, major headsail changes, 6 times.

St. John's, Newfoundland–Lerwick, Shetland Isles

Sailed single-handed, September 5th to October 1st, 1960. Distance, 1,984 miles covered in 25 days 21 hours. Average, 77 miles per day. Best day's run, 120 miles; worst, 10 miles. Able to lay course 408 hours (66 per cent. of time); unable to lay course, 213 hours; on wind, 182 hours; off wind, 419 hours. Calms totalled 30 hours including 23½ hours continuous calm after sighting Shetland; fog, 29 hours over 6 days; gales, hove-to 4 times, total of 48½ hours, all during first three weeks.

Sail changes: Reefed main, 12 times. Sailed without main, 15 days 4 hours, three-fifths of time but never in last 5 days. (This was not always through stress of weather; she sailed faster and steered more easily when broad-reaching or running with genoa alone. The mainsail is less than 80 per cent. of the area of the genoa.); Reefed No. 1 staysail, 3 times; changed headsails, 20 times. Ship was steered throughout by wind-vane except in very light airs (when ship's speed fell below 2 knots) and in winds over about 50 m.p.h.

Total time: New York to Lerwick: 38 days 11 hours.

Eira — VAL HOWELLS

Fourth man home. Time: 63 days, elapsed time (including 8 days in Bermuda). Sailing time: 55 days. Folkboat, sloop-rigged.

Length, overall	..	25 ft. 0 in.
Length, waterline	..	19 ft. 6 in.
Beam	..	7 ft. 2 in.
Draft	..	3 ft. 9 in.
Thames tonnage	..	5 tons

Sail areas

Mainsail	..	200 sq. ft.
No. 1 staysail	..	50 sq. ft.
No. 2 staysail	..	30 sq. ft.
Genoa	..	180 sq. ft.
Total sail area	..	380 sq. ft.

Course: Distance sailed by log, 4,125 miles. Average sailed, 75 miles per day. Average made good on direct route Plymouth to New York (3,100 miles), 56.3 miles per day. Longest run, 129 miles.

Head winds, 58 per cent. of time, mostly early in voyage. Wind free, 35 per cent. of time. Calms, 117 hours (7 per cent. of time) including one continuous calm of 31 hours. Fog, about 12 hours. Self-steering not effective in very light winds; also overcome by big quartering swells.

Sail changes: Major headsail changes, 56 times; reefed mainsail, 11 times; handed mainsail, 21 times, mostly in calms or when running under genoa.

Cap Horn — JEAN LACOMBE

Fifth man home. Time: 74 days, elapsed time (started 5 days late); 69 days sailing time. Sloop; plywood construction with centreboard and 400 kg. ballast keel. Designed by J. J. Herbulot. Self-steering gear designed by M. Giannoli.

Length, overall	..	6·5 m. (21·3 ft.)
Length, waterline	..	6·0 m. (19·7 ft.)
Beam (max.)	..	2·27 m. (7·5 ft.)
Beam (waterline)	..	1·9 m. (6·2 ft.)
Draft (centreboard up)	..	0·6 m. (2 ft.)
Displacement (light)	..	900 kg. (1,980 lb.)
Displacement (loaded)	..	3 tonnes (2·95 tons)

Sail areas

Mainsail	..	12·5 sq. m. (134½ sq. ft.)
No. 1 staysail	..	9·3 sq. m. (100 sq. ft.)
No. 2 staysail	..	5·9 sq. m. (68½ sq. ft.)
Genoa	..	12·6 sq. m. (135 sq. ft.)
Tourmentin	..	2·0 sq. m. (21½ sq. ft.)

Course: Average sailed, 61 miles per day; average made good on direct route Plymouth to New York (3,100 miles), 45 miles per day. The craft was so light and its motion so violent that Lacombe was unable to sleep properly.

In his first two weeks out from Plymouth Jean Lacombe covered 450 and 500 miles respectively. During the third week he passed between the Azores, resisting a strong temptation to call there and fix the self-steering gear which was giving trouble, and by July 13th he was half-way across. At this rate of progress he would have equalled or bettered my time. On July 25th he ran into a severe gale and lay to a sea-anchor, first from the bow, and then from the stern where it proved more effective, even though he was swept by a wave which lifted the hatch and swamped the cabin. Calms followed the gales so that by July 29th he had covered only 250 miles in 13 days. To avoid the August hurricanes he altered course to the north, a most seamanlike decision in my opinion, though it meant being headed by the Gulf Stream.

By August 18th he was off the Nantucket Shoals lightship where he was taken in tow by a Coastguard cutter as he was in the path of hurricane "Cleo". When "Cleo" changed course a few hours later he cast off the tow and reached the Ambrose light on August 24th.

I am indebted for this summary of *Cap Horn's* voyage to Jean Lacombe's account in *Le Bateau* and to John Pfleiger, for the translation.

APPENDIX FOUR

Research Observations

The idea of doing some research during the voyage first came to me as a possible excuse for such a long absence. But before long the prospect of breaking fresh ground in a field that had long interested me became an exciting prospect in its own right.

As a basis for research Dr. H. E. Lewis of the Medical Research Council and I prepared the daily "Medical Log" reproduced below, copies of which were given to each of the competitors with the following introduction:

The Single-handed Race is a unique opportunity to learn about the eating habits, the mental and the physical feelings of men in isolation. This sort of information, though very valuable, is usually almost impossible to obtain. In turn it will help us in problems of survival at sea, especially water requirements.

We have listed a number of "feelings" in the log and would like you to tick off the column that is nearest to your mood. Each feeling is matched by its opposite, so from one end of the line to the other there is a broad span of mood. If you think that the words at the end don't apply, or apply equally, tick the middle section.

Bearing in mind that you will have to attend to many other things, we have tried to keep this daily log down to a minimum. We greatly appreciate the trouble you are taking. Be assured that any personal information will be treated privately and confidentially.

DAVID LEWIS

In collaboration with H. E. LEWIS,
Medical Research Council, London, N.W.3

Many months will still be needed to analyse the mass of data we obtained from these daily Medical Logs, and the following are merely some tentative ideas which the work suggests at the present stage.

Eating and sleeping habits: We studied these because man, being a social animal, is conditioned in his activities by sociological conventions and it is, therefore, very difficult to discover his natural biological patterns of behaviour. Are there inherent sleep rhythms? How much sleep do we really need? Are our meal times dictated by physical necessity or by custom and

453

convenience? These are some of the questions whose answers we do not yet know.

There are two situations where human beings are practically isolated from

1 JULY 1960

A. *How do you feel?*

	Applies very strongly	Applies	Both apply or neither apply	Applies	Applies very strongly	
My normal self						Seeing things
Exhausted						Fresh
Lonely						Completely self-sufficient
Enjoy cooking						Can't be bothered about food
Poor appetite						Hungry
Calm						Irritable
Feelings have been constant						Feelings have changed a lot during the day
Tense and excited						Calm and relaxed
Confident						Scared
Keen to do well						Uncertain, sorry I started
Bored						Not bored: too much to do
My normal self						Hearing things
A new confident mood						Wish it were all over
Sexy						Not sexy
Happy without feminine company						Would enjoy company of other sex

Other moods:

B. *Water:* What did you use today?

   Fresh water: ....Drinking (including beverages)

   ....Cooking

   ... .Washing and waste

   Sea Water: ....Cooking

C. *Food:* What did you eat today? | Times
Underline what you heated and cooked.

the pressure of social convention; in Polar expeditions, and when alone at sea. Polar parties are, of course, groups, so they must conform to a minimum of social organization. On the other hand, they live in conditions of continuous daylight or continuous darkness, so a sense of clock time does not dominate their routine, and they will tend to organize their meal times, and their "day and night", in accordance with convenience and their biological requirements.

In single-handed sailing, extraneous social connections are completely

1   JULY   1960

D.   *Physical feeling*

Do you feel absolutely A.1 ?

If not, what do you feel is wrong, how severe, and which part of your body ?

E.   *Sleep, naps and interruptions*

24 Hours (State whether G.M.T. or Ship's Time)

From Yesterday | 1 2 3 4 5 6 7 8 9 10 11 12 13 14 15 16 17 18 19 20 21 22 23 24 | Contd. Tomorrow

Cause of interruptions :

Did you dream ?

F.   *General comments*   (to give full picture)

G.   *What time did you fill up this form ?*

................hrs.

absent. Food and sleep are taken according to need, modified by the availability of artificial light and fuel, the stresses of weather and working ship, proximity to land, shipping lanes, ice, etc.

Sleep: The experience of four recent Polar expeditions has been that, in spite of great disruptions in sleep, the average is almost exactly eight hours. This figure does not vary significantly whether or not "cat naps" are taken;

nor is it effected by exercise; nor does it differ between the Polar night and day.*

Racing to windward alone in a small yacht, sleep is often broken and at times sadly lacking. I, personally, found my judgment to be so seriously impaired during periods of lack of sleep that I made serious errors, in spite of being on my guard. Two examples were, closing the cliffs of Nova Scotia, and running aground off Vineyard Sound. Our average hours of sleep were 6·7 hours per night. Quality of sleep is as important as its length and undoubtedly varies. But how to measure and study "depth" of sleep is a difficult problem.

Food: Hasler lost nineteen pounds during the race. I also lost nineteen pounds, in spite of heavier physical work, and some food and water shortages. I lost no weight on the return trip.

Our eating patterns varied. Mine, during the race, showed long periods without food, followed by close-spaced groups of meals. This tendency is also present in the records of Hasler and Howells, and of my trip back; but it is less obvious and tends to be masked by "nibbling". Nevertheless, the eating pattern seems to have been dictated more by biological needs and the demands of sailing than by conventional meal times.

Studies of mood: A few tentative conclusions are now emerging.

(i) Solitude is not at all the same as loneliness, e.g. the loneliness that a friendless person experiences in a big city. We were rarely lonely on our voyages. Even during the long, awe-inspiring nights, illumined by the Northern Lights of the homeward journey, I did not feel lonely.

(ii) Observations noted *at the time* are the only valid ones. Memory very quickly plays tricks; usually seeing our behaviour and emotions in a better light than they really deserved. For instance, I honestly forgot that I had been frightened at all during one gale, until I looked up my notes.

(iii) The degree of fear varied with the individual; one (not me), did not suffer acute fear at all. In general there are two types of fear: (*a*) initial tension and anxiety, lasting for the first few days at sea, and then replaced by calm confidence and enjoyment; (*b*) after this we were only afraid with due reason, as in gales.

(iv) A relaxed confidence, a sense of being "at one" with the ocean and its winds, was our main emotional state, after the period of adjustment had passed. This state was often temporarily disrupted by such events as calms, shortages of books or exhausting sail-changing but tended to become re-established when conditions allowed.

(v) Hallucinations seem to occur only when solitude and fatigue are

* *Sleep Patterns on Polar Expeditions.* By Dr. H. E. Lewis. Ciba Foundation Symposium on "Nature of Sleep", 1961.

accompanied by monotonous occupations. Thus, long hours of continuous steering sometimes caused them, but because of the efficient operation of our wind-vanes, they were minimal. This observation may have some bearing on space flight. Possibly the rhythmic effect of monotonous activities tends to induce auto-hypnosis. Whatever the mechanism, I would think that varying tasks demanding physical and or mental effort could be valuable in preserving emotional stability.

Acknowledgments

Grateful acknowledgment is due to the following who have taken part, or are still participating in the work involved in this research project:

Dr. H. E. Lewis, Division of Human Physiology, National Institute of Medical Research.

Dr. D. Hollingsworth, Dr. Neil Beaton, Dr. E. C. Drescher, of New York, Dr. J. C. Lilly of the U.S. Virgin Isles, Dr. W. H. Sebrell, Jnr. and Professor E. L. Severinghouse, M.D., both of Columbia University, and Mr. J. M. Harries, Ministry of Agriculture and Fisheries.

APPENDIX FIVE

Treatment of Sea-serpent Stings and Other Ailments

The following is virtually a reprint of the "Medical Advice to Competitors" notes which were compiled and circulated before the race, together with medical kits and emergency stores supplied through the generosity of the manufacturers.

I feel that the general principles and approach to the question of illness, accident and survival, when alone or short-handed and far from help, are valid. A part of this approach, however, was the full use of modern antibiotics and other powerful remedies; the very progress of medicine soon renders particular products out-dated. The named drugs and dressings, therefore, should be treated as examples only.

For this appendix to be of any use, it should be regarded only as a frame-work, whose interstices may be readily filled in with the aid of some of those innumerable medical men who have become hopelessly infected by love of the sea or the waste places of the earth.

During about two hundred and ninety man-days of solo sailing, apart from initial seasickness, sundry cuts and bruises, and my bump on the head, competitors in the race were fortunate in keeping fit and well throughout their passages.

Medical Advice to Competitors

HEALTH, MEDICAL EQUIPMENT AND EMERGENCY SURVIVAL

by David H. Lewis, M.B., Ch.B.

AIM OF MEDICAL ADVICE

People quickly go to pieces when morale breaks down; it is best maintained by knowing what to do.

Stop short of exhaustion, keep something in reserve; lack of rest warps judgment and impairs efficiency.

Eat and drink what suits you best; sweet foods and drinks are useful when very tired. The only vitamin you need is Vitamin C (anti-scurvy).

Keep the skin clean; severe boils and painful and disabling infections of the skin are caused by ingrained dirt and crusted salt. Fresh water is well spared for washing at times. Bare feet (when practicable) help prevent "Athlete's Foot" (infection between the toes).

A protective cream against sun and salt is provided.

MEDICAL EQUIPMENT

Only a few remedies can be carried, so selection has had to be arbitrary and advice dogmatic. In general, minor ills, accidents and symptoms can best be left to nature and common sense. Some of the drugs here are powerful, so you should show the list to your own doctor to check for individual sensitivity, or to add anything you personally may need.

NOTE

Alcohol. This is a matter of personal taste; it has no medical value.

Stimulants, sedatives and "tranquillizers" vary in their effects with different people and according to circumstances. None is included. If you wish to take any, you are strongly advised to consult your own doctor.

GUIDE TO TREATMENT

Wounds and bleeding. Wash off dirt. Apply an Elastoplast dressing or apply antiseptic cream (No. 10), then a standard dressing (No. 13), or Elastoplast. *Firm* bandaging of a pad over a wound will stop *any* bleeding. Do *not* make a tourniquet, as it will usually increase bleeding by compressing veins but not arteries. If it is applied properly it will cause gangrene, by cutting off the circulation. To close a gaping wound, use interlocking strips of Elastoplast from each side.

In severe wounds, fractures or burns, take the *antibiotic capsules* (No. 1) in a dose of one capsule four times a day for four days (or longer if infection occurs). Take *pain tablets* (No. 3) up to eight a day, or if pain is very severe, take *severe pain tablets* (No. 4) one every four hours, dissolved under the tongue.

Fractures. Antibiotic capsules, if the fracture is associated with wounds (*see above*), and pain tablets (*see above*).

Arm. Strap it to your body with Elastoplast. If you splint the limb, you will automatically use it when you lose your balance, and cause further damage.

Ribs. Leave them alone. No treatment. Do not put Elastoplast round your chest as this will only restrict your breathing and do no good.

Leg. Improvise long splints from floorboards, etc., well padded with clothes, to immobilize joints above and below injury.

458

Burns. Wash clean, apply antiseptic cream (No. 10) and cover with an Elastoplast dressing if small, or with a standard dressing (No. 13) and crêpe bandage if larger. Do not disturb for several days if comfortable. For large burns also take antibiotic capsules (No. 1) and pain tablets (Nos. 3 or 4) as described under "Wounds".

"Athlete's Foot". Painful cracks between toes. Bare feet. Use powder (No. 11).

Pneumonia, bronchitis, infections of the skin and tissues, fractures, burns and large wounds. Use antibiotic capsules (No. 1) one four times a day for four days, and continue if necessary.

Acute appendicitis (and related conditions). There is severe persistent abdominal pain, repeated vomiting and great tenderness, probably constipation. Prop yourself up in your bunk, take fluids only, and take the antibiotic capsules (No. 1) as above.

Severe diarrhoea. Especially if slime and blood is present. Take the sulphonamide tablets (No. 1) three tablets four times daily, for four to six days.

Preventing scurvy. Take one Vitamin C tablet (No. 5) each day.

MEDICAL SUPPLIES LIST

No. 1. Broad-spectrum antibiotic capsules (Terramycin (S.F.) Caps. Pfizer 100 supplied).

No. 2. Sulphonamide tablets (Succinylsulphathiazole tabs. ½ Gm. 50 supplied).

No. 3. Ordinary pain tablets (Soluble salicylate) (Zactirin tabs. (Wyeth) 300 supplied).

No. 4. Severe pain tablets (Aminode hydrochloride. 5 mg. 25 supplied on individual prescription).

Note. Morphia may so impair judgment that, for a lone sailor who has to rely on himself, it is rather a means towards suicide than a treatment. It has been omitted.

No. 5. Anti-scurvy tablets. Vitamin C. (Ascorbic acid, 50 mg. 50 supplied).

No. 6. Eye-drops to relieve pain to allow removal of foreign bodies. (5 per cent. cocaine drops, 2 drachms. on individual prescription).

No. 7. Eye ointment for inflammation of the eye (1 tube antibiotic and hydrocort. ointment).

Note. Sore red eyes due to stinging of salt spray should be bathed with water only. Use neither the eye drops nor ointment.

No. 8. Protective skin cream against sun and salt. (Prepared by Dr. Hughes of Scientific Pharmaceuticals Ltd.).

No. 9. Waterproof Elastoplast dressings. Three Elastoplast 3-in. bandages. 2 lb. cotton wool. Gauze. 6 crêpe bandages.

No. 10. Antiseptic cream. (Preferably an antibiotic cream.)

No. 11. Powder for Athlete's Foot (Amoxal). (Smith and Nephew) 2 oz.

No. 12. WESCO First Aid Kit containing standard dressings, 1 pair scissors, antiseptic burn and wound creams. Codeine Co. tablets (for pain).

IF FORCED TO ABANDON SHIP

Cold, aggravated by wetness and wind, is the greatest cause of loss of life among castaways (*MacDonald Critchley, 1943*). Therefore, a covered life-raft, in which a "fug" can be produced and heat-loss prevented, is most desirable.

A man can live fifty days without food but usually under two weeks without water. He should not drink salt water, because more fluid is lost from the body through the kidneys in getting rid of the excess salt.

WATER

Carry two gallons in a plastic jerry-can attached to the rubber raft. (This will float, as fresh water is lighter than salt.)

Ration: *None on first day.* Minimum of 1½ pints (900 c.c.) per day. However, ⅔ pint (500 c.c.) per day will maintain fluid balance for a time, but you will deteriorate gradually.

EMERGENCY FOOD

Protein and fats are harmful with restricted water. Food should be carbohydrate (sweet food) only. Rations: three to four ounces per day (90 gr.) made up of rum fudge, glucose sweets, glucose lemon in the drinking water, Horlick's tablets, etc.

A solar still is provided for use with your life raft.

RARER CONDITIONS

Such accidents as Polar bear bites or sea-serpent stings are certainly uncommon, but are of such great literary interest that they may safely be left to the imagination and initiative of the competitors.

Acknowledgments

Invaluable advice in the preparation of this document was freely given by many people. Sometimes circumstances prevented it being taken in full and the responsibility for final choice and decisions and any consequences thereof, remain my own. Similarly, while this document could not have been prepared without their help, it does not necessarily represent their views.

I wish to thank especially: Surg. Capt. Baskerville, R.N.; Mr. E. C. B. Lee, Secretary, Naval Life Saving Committee; Mr. F. E. Smith, Assistant Secretary, R.N.F.R.C.; Mr. H. Proctor, F.R.C.S., of Birmingham Accident Hospital; Sir Heneage Ogilvie; Dr. H. L'Etang; Prof. Guide Guida; and Mr. A. B. E. de Jong.

ALONE AT SEA

Hannes Lindemann

EDITED BY JOZEFA STUART

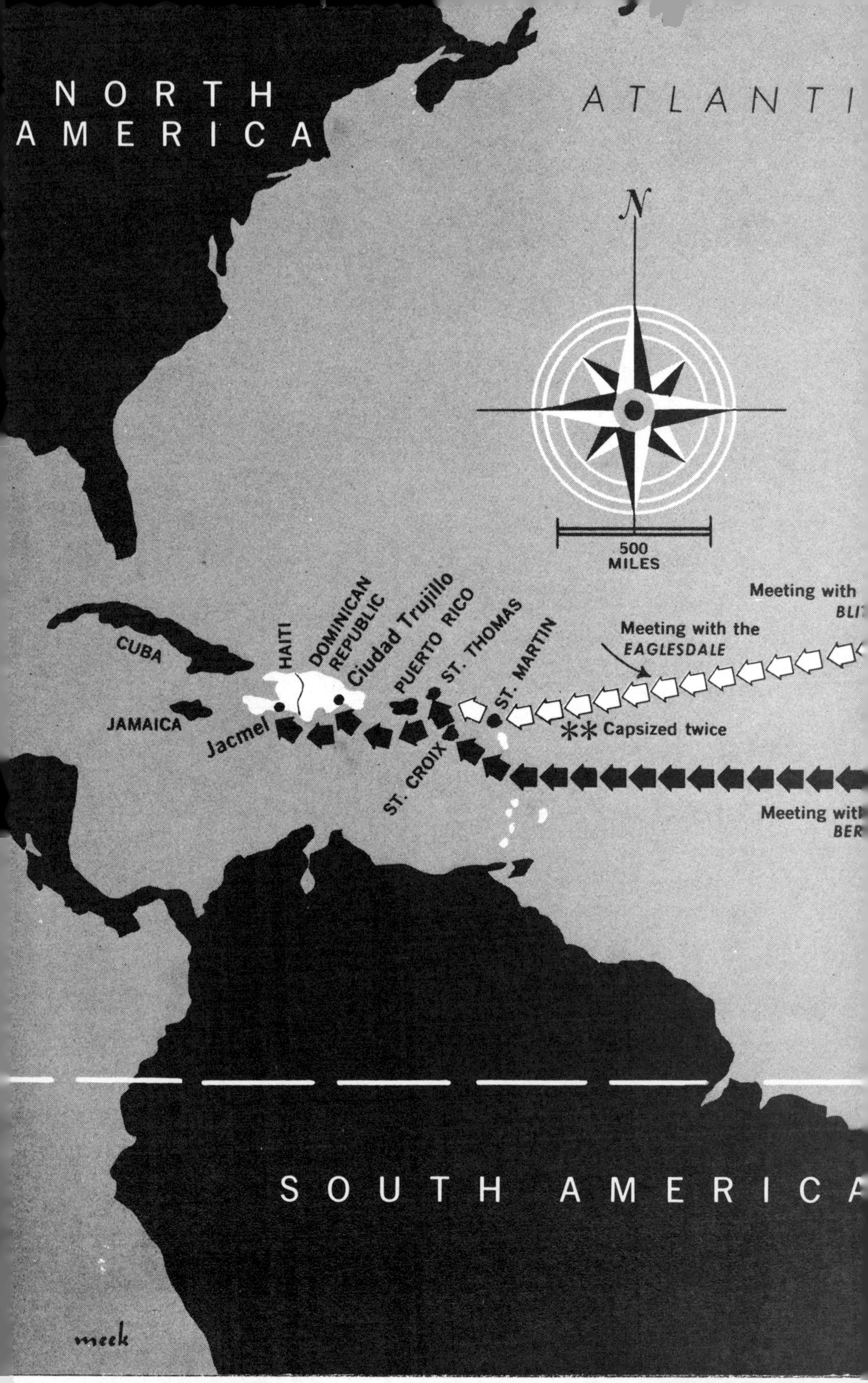

NORTH AMERICA
ATLANTI
N
500 MILES
Meeting with
BLI
Meeting with the
EAGLESDALE
CUBA
HAITI
DOMINICAN REPUBLIC
Ciudad Trujillo
PUERTO RICO
ST. THOMAS
ST. MARTIN
JAMAICA
Jacmel
** Capsized twice
ST. CROIX
Meeting with
BER
SOUTH AMERICA
meek

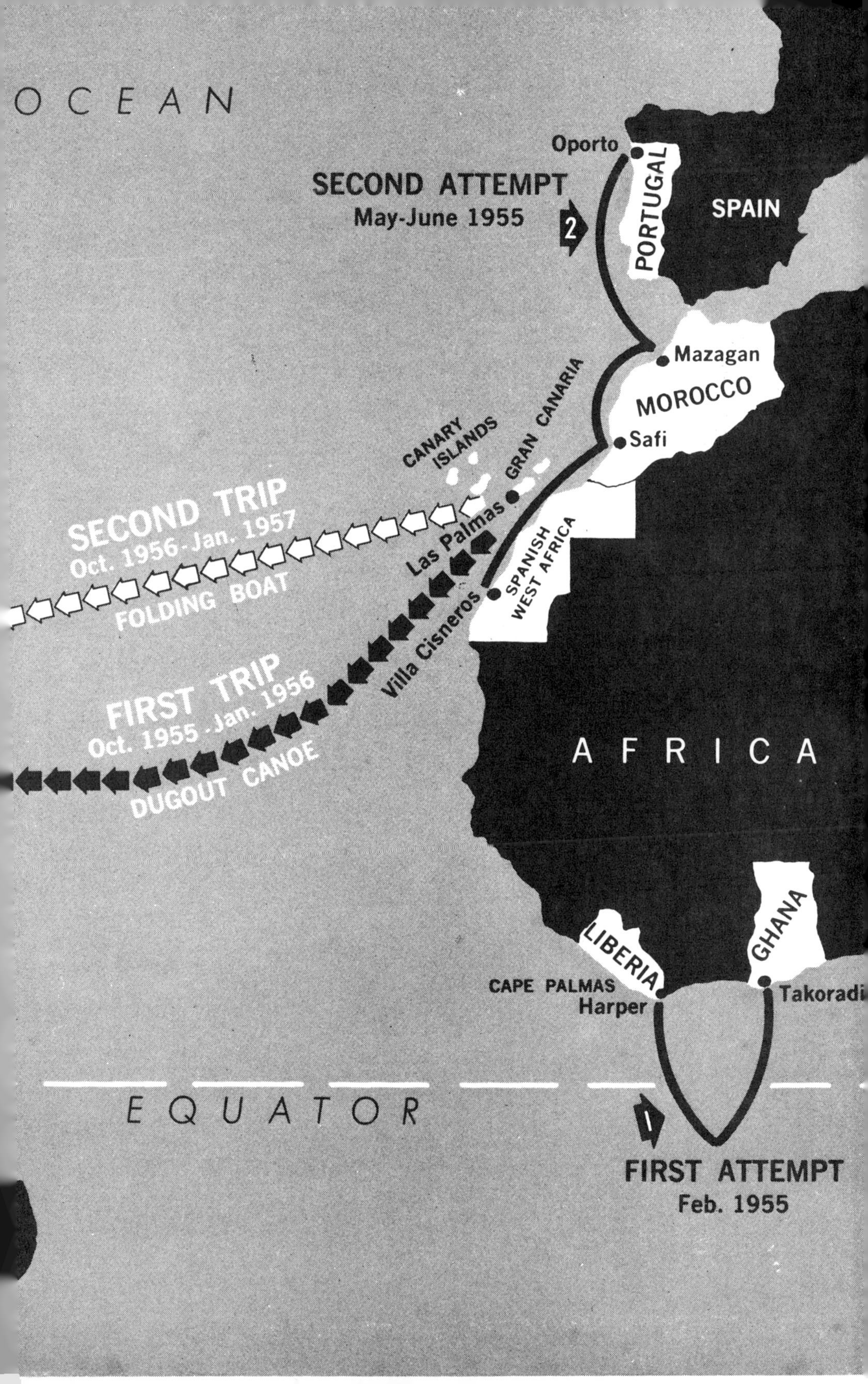

OCEAN

Oporto

SECOND ATTEMPT
May-June 1955

PORTUGAL   SPAIN

2

Mazagan

MOROCCO

Safi

CANARY ISLANDS

GRAN CANARIA

SECOND TRIP
Oct. 1956 - Jan. 1957

Las Palmas

FOLDING BOAT

SPANISH WEST AFRICA

Villa Cisneros

FIRST TRIP
Oct. 1955 - Jan. 1956

DUGOUT CANOE

AFRICA

LIBERIA   GHANA

CAPE PALMAS
Harper   Takoradi

EQUATOR

1

FIRST ATTEMPT
Feb. 1955

photo: Howard Johnson

CONTENTS

First Voyage

1 THE START OF MY VOYAGE

From a very early age I have loved the sea and sailing. When I was a small boy, my grandfather, a captain from the old windjammer days, stirred my imagination with the lore of sailing and the legends of the sea. Under his guidance I first learned how to handle a boat. As I grew up, my interests and activities widened to include long trips in sailboats and in folding boats—small, kayak-like boats with collapsible wooden frames and rubberized canvas covers. I sailed the rivers of Europe, and when my skill and confidence increased, I sought more exciting voyages. Single-handed, I rounded the Iberian Peninsula and sailed through the Mediterranean. Out of these experiences gradually grew the idea for the greatest adventure in single-handed sailing—an Atlantic crossing.

In all of us there is an impulse—though it may be deeply hidden—to leave behind us our ordinary lives and go beyond the morning to seek our fortunes. This urge is usually thwarted in our time by the restricting responsibilities of family or society. Yet some continue to climb almost inaccessible mountains or to explore the distances of the sea, dreaming of other coasts. And the curious thing is that when this impulse comes to the fore in some individual

469

and is acted on, most men are puzzled; so remote and fantastic, perhaps, do their own dreams seem.

I am a doctor by profession, trained in Hamburg, where I always intended to settle down and practice. But restlessness and curiosity drove me instead to travel and work abroad. In 1952, when I was twenty-nine, I found a job at a U.S. air base in French Morocco, and while there I signed a two-year contract to work in the plantation clinics of the Firestone Rubber Company in Liberia.

When I was working in Morocco I had met the Frenchman Alain Bombard who, as a voluntary castaway, had studied the problems of survival at sea. One of his most firmly held convictions (which came to be widely known) was that it is possible for a castaway to survive by drinking salt water. I found it impossible to accept his thesis. I was convinced that acceptance of such advice might easily endanger the life of a castaway, that the human body is not capable of surviving the rigors of exposure and the danger of dehydration without recourse to fresh water. I felt challenged both as a doctor and as a sailor to put his theory to the test myself.

The idea of experimenting with the problem of survival at sea continued to excite me after I moved to Liberia. In my free time, while tropical downpours drummed on the roof of my bungalow, I studied books on boats, sailing and the experiences of other single-handed sailors. By the end of my first year in Liberia, I decided the time had come to plan seriously for an Atlantic crossing. My first step was to acquire a boat. Clearly, I could have done what so many have done before and bought a small sailboat, but, living in Liberia, where the dugout canoe is the vessel of all native fishermen, I was inspired to try one of them. This would be original and exciting: to sail across the ocean in the most primitive of all boats. If, as some scientists believe, an early cultural tie may have been established between the West African coast and the Caribbean Indians by early canoe voyages, I would be emulating the explorers of prehistory. In any case, to test my survival threshold and my seamanship, I would remove myself as much as possible from the crutches of our comfortable civilization.

I had the choice, when I first started making my plans, of buying a second-hand canoe or of building one myself. As I had twelve months in which to make my preparations—I planned to leave Liberia as soon as my Firestone contract expired—I decided to build one. In that way I could be certain of the strength of my canoe, which would have to withstand battering Atlantic waves. Also the boat had to be carefully designed in weight and balance to be able to ride out storms without capsizing. I knew I would have to make certain modifications in the crude coastal canoe of the West African fisherman. So I decided to begin at the very beginning and pick out a tree in the jungle that I could fashion into a suitable dugout.

For its strength and size, and because I knew that the Fanti fishermen of Ghana use it, I chose a kapok, a common West African tree, which can grow to a height of one hundred and eighty feet and a diameter of six to nine feet. Without much difficulty, I found a tree suited to my purposes, growing on the territory of one of the local paramount chiefs. I explained my need for the tree to the chief and offered to buy it from him, but he insisted I take it as a gift.

My troubles began after I had the tree. I started enthusiastically and innocently, unaware of the difficulties that any unusual venture in the tropics is sure to encounter. I offered the job of cutting down my tree to three stalwart young men. After studying the tree, they refused. So towering a giant, they claimed, must be the home of evil spirits, who would revenge themselves for the loss of their tree by taking a human life. I offered more money, but their fear of the spirits was greater than their love for money. I was almost prepared to fell the tree myself when I learned of a village whose inhabitants are professional woodcutters and whose evil spirits do not haunt treetops. Further negotiations with their chief bought their services; one week later, my tree was felled and a thirty-six-foot length cut from the trunk.

I had chosen my tree well; the wood proved healthy and easy to work with. In eight weeks, two young natives, working with axes, chopped out the interior. The trickiest part of hollowing out a canoe comes when one tries to get an even thickness of the trunk walls. Our method was crude and simple: we chopped on the inside with a transversal axe and held our hands to the outside to get a sense of the thickness of the trunk. At the end of eight weeks, we carried my roughly hewn boat to my house on the plantation and stored it under the porch. Once a week I sprayed it with insecticide (a necessary precaution in a tropical climate), meanwhile looking for a skilled carpenter who could finish the job. I found Alfred. His first contribution was to write on the stern: This boat is sixty-four feet long. My two houseboys were very much impressed by Alfred's erudition; I less so, for the boat measured only thirty-six feet. Alfred's carpentry proved no better than his mathematics; so I looked around for a replacement. My next helper was William More; but, as it turned out, he could not work unless he got his daily ration of fermented cane juice. And sometimes he could not work when he did. Despairing of reliable carpenters, I set to work to do the job myself with the help of my two houseboys.

After four months of hard work the canoe was finished, except for the keel. We drew the boat up in front of the house and set to work smoothing the final rough spots. To my consternation our planes uncovered insect holes. Out of my boat crawled fat white maggots, small black bugs, big black wood beetles and bark-colored stag beetles with antennae as long as my finger. Lying for eight weeks in the jungle, the trunk had become a haven for the rich, varied insect life of the rain forest. The insecticide, which I had sprayed and rubbed on the wood with such care, had betrayed me. Hoping that I might be able to smoke out the insects, I asked Sunday, my houseboy, to light a smudge fire under the canoe. The biting smoke forced me away from the house. I returned a few hours later to find the *Liberia*—as I had christened the canoe—and six months' hard work, burning brightly. Sunday slept peacefully beside the bonfire.

I started afresh the next day on my search for a canoe. I was still hopeful of acquiring a new one; so I visited a canoe-building tribe in the interior. I made them the tempting offer of four times their usual price, and they promised to do the job for me. My contract with Firestone had only another six months to run; time was therefore precious to me. But it held no meaning for them; despite my urgings they did not begin the work. I now realized that I no longer had time to build my boat, that I would have to make do with a second-hand canoe. I found one, belonging to a fisherman of the Fanti tribe, which seemed suitable; I offered twice the price of a new canoe for it, only to be disappointed again; the fisherman, who had at first been willing to sell his boat, changed his mind at the last minute.

I had a friend among the local fishermen, a Liberian named Jules. Now I went to him, in desperation, begging him to help me find a boat—no matter what the quality. One week later he found one for me. It had holes in the stern and bow, and in the bottom where it had lain on the ground. Also fungus growth had softened the wood somewhat. Still, the trunk seemed strong enough, and in any case I planned to strengthen it further by covering the hull with fiberglas.

Now, finally, three months before my hoped-for departure, I at least had a boat. The mahogany canoe measured twenty-three and a half feet from bow to stern on the outside and twenty-three feet on the inside. Its width was twenty-nine and nine-tenths inches outside and twenty-eight and seven-tenths inches inside. My house-boys and I made a keel five-and-one-tenth-inches deep and eleven-and-a-half-feet long and weighted it with two hundred and fifty pounds of lead. We planed the underside of the trunk with an electric sander and painted it with a mixture of hardener and resin. Using this mixture as an adhesive, we attached fiberglas to it, and then painted it over several times with the same mixture. This process was necessary to ensure the strength of the trunk.

When the hardener and resin were thoroughly dry, we set the boat on her keel and spanned her width with bent lengths of iron. We made a deck by covering them with plywood, leaving a small cockpit in the stern and a hatch before the mast. At the approximate water line on either side of the hull, we attached corkwood pads—each some ten inches thick—hoping they might lessen the roll of the boat. The canoe now resembled the pirogues of the Carib Indians. We also covered the deck with fiberglas. It afforded additional strength and would also protect the wood against teredos, a shipworm or destructive mollusk prevalent in West Africa.

Bearing in mind the possibility that I might capsize, I took measures to ensure that the canoe stayed afloat by partitioning off the ends with bulkheads, putting empty airtight containers behind them. I attached steering cables to the rudder so that I could control it with either my hands or feet. Then we made a mast of ironwood, which has enough give to it so that the boat could run even in the Gulf of Guinea without a backstay. The boom was made from rare red camwood, which warps even less than mahogany.

The long-awaited day of launching arrived exactly four weeks before my contract expired. Slowly and carefully, we drove the boat on a company truck to Cape Palmas, eighteen miles away. I stood, movie camera in hand, while my friends did the launching. But the canoe would not stay afloat; the shallow keel was too light to counterbalance the weight of mast and sail. We filled three big sacks—provided for this eventuality—with sand and used them as weights. They gave us sufficient stability and, with a three-horse-power motor, my canoe made her first test run. In memory of my ill-fated first canoe, I christened her the *Liberia II*.

I accustomed myself to the handling of the canoe by making short sailing and fishing trips. During these I found that a jib of three square yards, a square sail and a gaff sail of nine square yards gave me sufficient play in varying winds.

I registered the *Liberia* as the first "yacht" in Cape Palmas and loaded her with a three-month food supply. With Haiti, first Negro republic of the world, as my destination, I set sail one hot February day.

2 WHITE SHADOWS IN THE GULF OF GUINEA

I left the little harbor town of Harper, which lies in the lee of Cape Palmas, with two young boys—paddles in hand—perched on the bow of the *Liberia II,* while I sat in the cockpit. Jules paddled alongside in his canoe. He was to take the boys back after we had got my boat out of the harbor. At the sight of my unorthodox craft even the fishermen and dockside loungers were startled out of their usual apathy. Their interest increased when, just as we were making headway on the outgoing tide, cries of "Stop, Doctor," forced me to look back. Customs officers were signaling to me to return. I shouted across the water that my sailing papers were in order, as indeed they were; I had paid my taxes, tipped in the right quarter, and I had no intention now of postponing my departure.

We continued out to sea, to the southwest, paddling past a steep rock that pointed an accusing finger into the open ocean. I noticed three friends waving from the roof of a building on the rock, and I answered by clasping my hands over my head. To the left, high up on the cape, we passed a large building. People breakfasting on the roof garden there looked down on us through binoculars and stretched out their hands in a well-bred, unenthusiastic farewell wave. I was irritated by their superior attitude, which seemed to me to imply a complete lack of faith in my chances of success.

The *Liberia* now faced her first real test of seaworthiness. We had to cross a reef where waves reflected from the rocky coast met the large wind-blown waves of the ocean. Slowly we struggled through a seething, foaming mass of shallow water. The boys on the bow paddled hard, and we made it. I cast a last look at the fishermen's huts that lined the harbor. The water deepened, the waves flattened, and I took deep breaths of the pure air of the open sea, happy to leave behind the typical harbor smell of rotting fish and decomposing rubbish mixed with the salt of surf spray.

But we were still not completely free of the harbor; a channel, lying between the rocky cape and a small island, had to be negotiated. Ocean waves and waves reflected from the shore mingled there, and the tide from the strong Guinea Current struggled around the entrance. Once again, the two boys paddled me through.

The time had now come for me to go on alone. The boys jumped into Jules's boat, I hoisted my after sail and Jules shouted, "We will pray for you, Doctor." I was deeply touched by his farewell, and even forgave him his lapse of the night before. I had asked him to watch my boat for me while I went out for a few last drinks with my friends. On my return I found he had let her capsize in the outgoing tide. The outboard motor was waterlogged and refused to come to life again. Jules's carelessness forced me to leave without a motor.

As I sailed with the current in a southeasterly direction, I sat on the windward side of the boat and gazed back at the sandy beach of Harper. Gray spray hung like a silk curtain between us. After two years in Liberia I had formed a strong attachment to the country and its people. It was not so much the work I did, though it was more responsible and freer than any I had known before, but the warm-hearted, generous people that I knew I would miss. I had chosen Haiti as my destination largely because I was eager to see if the only other Negro republic in the world had the same unspoiled spirit.

Gradually I lost sight of Harper, and some miles east of Cape Palmas I saw the coconut palms which shaded the round huts of

476

the small village of Half Grevy. Columns of smoke from native bush fires drifted lazily to the sky. Hanno of Carthage, who sailed down the West African coast in the fifth century B.C., has left us an account of these same bush fires. There had been little change in the way of living here from his day to ours; the men burn down the bush for new land, women clear the land, hoe it and sow hill rice between logs. After each harvest the land lies fallow for two or three years, and during that time other parts of the bush are burned off.

As the sun stood at its zenith, I passed the southernmost cape of this part of Africa. The rising tide at the mouth of the Cavally River pulled the boat shoreward. The tremendous force of the Cavally as it spews its waters into the ocean changes the shoreline here almost every day. When the tide falls, dirty inland waters mingle with the raging surf over the sandy reef and attract an immense number of barely visible inhabitants of the sea and their bigger brethren. I heard the seething thunder and roar of waves and saw hungry, foaming breakers run rhythmically up the beach and lick the yellow sand. Here the swell, eternal breath of the ocean, has ground the stones of the beach to powder—as though, like Sisyphus, damned eternally to push stones up and down, up and down the beach. I gazed at the inhospitable West African coast from the canoe, seeing what has met the eye of every seafarer who ever traveled here: an unending stretch of waves hurling themselves at a flat beach, unbroken by harbors or protected inlets that can offer refuge to the sailor. The sole signs of human life are the bush fires of the Africans, and only an occasional mangrove swamp or huge gray boulder interrupts the monotony of sea and sand.

It is not an easy coast to sail along, and I was thankful when the time came to leave it. To the north the white beam of the lighthouse in Tabu grew smaller and smaller. A school of minute octopi leaped out of the water with the force of jet propulsion and then—sk-latsh—fell back into the sea. The sun sank behind a chain of clouds with a rare and exciting display of color. It was as if this short, dazzling eruption were to compensate for the monotony of the dark night ahead. My horizon was bounded briefly by a bank of golden clouds and then, with startling suddenness, the bright trop-

477

ical bloom darkened to a threatening blue-black. At the beginning of my first night at sea, I felt as though I were part of an overwhelming natural spectacle.

The first stars shone high above now; shadowy waves raced past the dugout, and occasional small combers lapped against the hull. It was time for me to be practical and think about my first meal. Can a castaway survive by drinking sea water? I intended to find out and, therefore, planned to drink one pint every day. I knew that any amount beyond that would damage my kidneys. I carried canned milk and fruit juices with me knowing I would also have to drink other liquids, or my kidneys would be unable to excrete the high percentage of salt. (I never did accustom myself to the taste of sea water and at each first swallow I came close to vomiting. Thereafter the salty taste would disappear because of an augmented secretion of saliva.) I had not eaten in the twelve hours since leaving Harper, and I was surprised to notice that I was not hungry. My energy level had already lessened and it took me a long time to make decisions. Despite my lack of appetite, I knew I had to eat, and out of my supplies I chose sausage, butter and black bread for my first meal. I managed to choke down two slices of bread, and as I ate I thought back to the days of the old, slow sailing ships, when food for the crew was an even greater problem than navigation.

My meal was interrupted by a sudden burst, an explosion, beside me. A ray hit the water with its hollow wings. I sat quietly but heard no more from him.

The wind weakened. I fixed the tiller, squeezed my body underneath the plywood deck and put on the wind jacket. Meanwhile, the pirogue had sailed through the wind and gone off course, and I had to bring her back with my paddle. Glancing overboard, I noticed with surprise that the bow wake water shone in silver-gray streaks. Even the combers glowed. I hit at the surface with the paddle and produced a new kind of fireworks display: out of the water rose phosphorescent particles, big and small, which shone yellow, orange, green and blue in the darkness. Dense clouds of bioluminescent plankton had risen to the surface; its movement created this nighttime magic.

While I amused myself by slapping the water with my paddle, I noticed the lights of a ship far away. As I sailed closer to it, I took out the flashlight and beamed it onto the gaff sail, hoping to make my presence noted. The ship appeared to be stationary; then suddenly it veered off in a southeasterly direction. Time passed slowly. I sat, tiller in hand, with nothing to do, struggling to stay awake. Because I was on a steamship route and there was a danger of collision, I had decided to sleep during the day and sail at night. In daylight I could be seen, but at night I would have to signal. Even so, I was not now sure that the beam of my flashlight was enough to warn other ships of my presence.

The morning came at last, bringing with it a visit from a shark. It was a nine-foot-long tiger shark, and I was curious to see what it would do. Cautiously circling the boat, it gazed up at me with ugly little pig eyes; it thrashed its dark brown, spotted tail, and drops of water landed on my deck. Several little pilot fish swam nervously back and forth between the rudder and their master the shark, which continued on its way, undisturbed by its excited retinue. After a few rounds of the boat, it suddenly disappeared; I must confess I felt a certain relief.

A calm breeze wafted over the sea now, enough to fill the sail and cool my sweating body. Throughout the morning, shining mackerel jumped out of the water around me. At noon I took my position with my bubble sextant, and found I was nearly sixty miles south of Cape Palmas. At this time of day the intense heat of the sun beat down on the unprotected crew of the *Liberia* with tropical intensity. I draped a wet towel over my shoulders to prevent a serious burn on my neck; I dangled my feet over the edge; finally I decided to try a cooling bath. I slid into the water and swam around the dugout. Unfortunately, I had not brought underwater goggles with me, so I missed the tremendous variety of life that abounds in the ocean. The bath did not refresh me as much as I had hoped it would. Afterward I sat in great discomfort while the sweat and salt water ran off my body, mingled and dripped into the bilge.

All day long I had enjoyed watching the petrels as they fluttered in the swell, pecking at plankton, or held their wings high, seeming to walk on the surface of the ocean with their webbed feet. Sailors

479

of long ago christened them petrels after St. Peter; like him they seem to want to walk on water. (I was grateful to all the living creatures of the sea and air that I could watch from my boat. They shared my solitude and were a steadying reminder of everyday life throughout the voyage. They helped to keep me from total absorption in my daydreams, and later they even dispelled desperation.) As I watched the starling-sized, soot-black petrels I was reminded of the agitated flight of bats. Petrels are known as birds of the night, but I cannot imagine them more active than they were during the day. In the daytime I never saw them sleep and I rarely saw them alight on the water for longer than a minute.

A blood-red sunset ushered in my second night at sea. In the twilight a petrel flew carelessly into the gaff sail but escaped unharmed. The night passed uneventfully. For an active young man the sea was too smooth and too calm; the hours dragged slowly by. I took short cat naps, amused myself with dreams of my future, and sang songs from my college days.

When the third day dawned there was still no wind. I fell asleep and awoke in the heat of noonday, bathed in sweat. I took my position and to my disappointment found I had made only half as much progress as on the day before. My feet were beginning to swell from the salt water I had drunk. I was still not hungry. Perhaps it was because I was worried about the boat. I was beginning to realize that there was something radically wrong with the *Liberia*'s ballast. I needed a heavier keel, more outside ballast. The sandbags put in at the launching were not the answer. Still, I was not yet ready to turn around; I wanted to test the boat in stronger winds. I decided to sail as far as the equator, where I could expect to meet the trade winds, to make a final decision. I knew that my return trip, if necessary, would be easier sailing and would take far less time than the outward voyage.

That day I spent my time watching mackerel. They leaped out of the water with such enthusiasm that I was reminded of myself jumping into a cooling bath at the end of a day's work in the Liberian heat. Their bodies were heavy and muscular, and in the air they lacked the stiff elegance of flying fish or the pliancy of a dolphin. They landed on the water with the full weight of their two-foot-long bodies, sometimes flat on the abdomens, sometimes slightly turned to the side.

Toward evening I noticed albacores for the first time. Albacores are large members of the mackerel family; these were three feet long and had long pectoral fins. The surface frothed from their activity, and the metallic sheen of their bodies and the yellow of their tails produced a fantastic display of color in the gold of the setting sun. They held their bodies stiff and straight when they ventured into the air, as though they feared they might shatter like glass.

Just as the sun sank below the horizon I was startled out of my daydreaming by a light thump against the port side of the canoe. A mysteriously large fish surfaced on the starboard side, touched the rudder cable and then submerged without giving me time to identify it. Despite its size I was not very disturbed, as I knew that even a big fish would have trouble capsizing the *Liberia,* and that fish generally yield the right of way. Of course, a whale, surfacing straight from the depths, could lift a small boat out of the water as Joshua Slocum, who sailed around the world in his famous yawl the *Spray,* reported, but it was one of the least of the dangers I faced on my voyage.

The third night passed uneventfully; I searched the skies in vain for the polestar, which I had never seen in West Africa. I was thwarted by a cloudy sky and a hazy horizon. At intervals during the night I heard the childlike, shrill cries of petrels. They sounded doubly loud, for the wind slept, the moon seemed anchored in the sky, and the smooth swell rose and fell, without a wave marring the surface.

In the morning the wind freshened, and splashes of water fell onto my dirty deck. To make the boat sail faster and to hold her upright, I perched far out on the windward side and braced my feet under the cleats on the lee. I sailed swiftly to the southeast until noon, when it was time to take my position. The opportunity to climb down from the uncomfortable seat on the gunwale of the canoe was welcome. Now, as if to facilitate my navigation, the wind died down and the sail swung loose drawing with it the squeaking line. A blue shark, approximately nine feet long, circled lazily twice around the canoe, then swam away, and for a few brief moments the ocean resembled a quiet mountain lake. Then the surface shivered, dark patches appeared in the water, and an unseen hand painted small ripples on the blue canvas of the sea. The sails filled. In the distance I heard a musical cadence of babbling, chattering and subdued giggling; it floated across the water and I imagined I heard the gossip of water nymphs. It soothed me, and my tired, sweating body was revived by the wind. But soon the pleasant, far-off music changed to an awesome rumble that betokened a storm; combers, large and bold, slapped against the hull, coughing and sputtering on all sides. From afar I heard the roar of ever-larger breakers and I was reminded of the rush of coming rain in the tropics. The wind whistled with force through the sails and beat against the mast. The pirogue was too crank to sail athwart; so I took in the sail and put out the sea anchor. (The sea anchor—a framed cone of canvas, which, when in use, is dragged behind the boat, the larger end toward the stern—held the stern straight to the wind.) The temperature had dropped with the rising wind, and to protect myself against the cold, I eased myself down under the spray cover until only my head was visible. The *Liberia* rode out her first Atlantic storm successfully, and it was not long before the squall was over, leaving only a gentle, southerly breeze.

By nighttime the weather had changed again. Brooding, menacing cloud banks gathered on the horizon, a screen for a colorless sun that slipped quietly behind them. In the rapidly increasing darkness, these clouds seemed to threaten me personally. Soon sky and clouds merged into stygian blackness, through which the *Liberia* sailed haplessly. As I watched the rise and fall of the bow increase, I found myself wishing I were not alone on a dark night on the Atlantic.

I had no idea of the kind of weather that lay ahead, so I reefed the sail by turning the boom. The threatening weather flattened the swell, and neither lightning nor thunder, wind nor rain relieved the tension. Only streaks of glimmering bioluminescence, whirling like dust in the wake of my pirogue, lightened the heavy, suffocating darkness. Profound silence—then, out of the blackness came a strangely human sigh. The sound rose and fell, softer and louder, like the moan that heralds the approach of death: a voice from an unknown, mysterious source. I could not place the sinister sound, and my ignorance made me afraid. I cursed the unholy darkness through which the pirogue sailed silently, as though drawn by the hands of unseen spirits. As we approached the lament, it ceased, and no beat of waves nor fluttering of bird wings broke the silence. I shone my flashlight over the water, but I saw nothing. (It was only much later that I read a description of the moaning of petrels during their breeding season and realized that that was the sound that had frightened me so.)

Gradually the silence around me was broken, first by the moderate whispering of the waves and then by a louder and more distinct gurgling. From afar came the rush of wind, the sail filled and the boat listed heavily. To balance the canoe, I had to leave my shelter and sit on the windward side. I tried to make myself comfortable by putting a cushion under me, but it slipped and was lost in the water. I had stupidly forgotten to tie it. I realized that many of my good intentions had already gone overboard in like fashion. I had meant to keep a detailed logbook and to study carefully the reactions of my body to the ordeal. But what, in fact, had I done? Fallen into reveries of my past and plans for my future, or spent hours gazing dreamily at the sky, the water, the fish and the birds. My primitive environment, my low-calory diet and the continued lack of sleep: all contributed to inhibiting my activity.

Now, I sat in discomfort on the side of the boat. The wind rose, tearing up sinister masses of clouds as it raced across the skies. Soon it swept the heavens clean, and the water shimmered with the reflection of stars. Around me, bioluminescent foam glowed like the last embers of a fire, and looking upward, I saw the polestar for the first time, almost engulfed by the high waves but rising again and again.

My next day dawned on a heavy sea. I held to a southeast course, with a swell so high that I knew it had just left a storm. Water landed on my deck, and I pulled the spray cover up as high as possible for protection. Every hour or so I let the *Liberia* sail a little away from the wind and bailed water out of the bilge.

Slowly the pirogue approached the equator, the area of the southeast trade winds.

On the eighth day the wind strengthened and, changing to the southeast, drove small white typical trade-wind clouds northwestward toward Liberia. I was beginning to need sleep badly, but in such dangerous seas I could not relax my vigilance; so I took pills to counteract my extreme fatigue. Despite the pills and despite the fact that I was precariously balanced on the washboard, I dozed off. Several times I awoke just in time to grab the cleat as I was slipping off my seat. Then I hit on the idea of fastening a line around my body and attaching it to the boat.

At noon the following day I reached a point a few miles south of the equator. The wind still blew with twenty-mile-an-hour force. For three days I had been uninterruptedly on the alert; only cat naps of a few minutes had broken my constant watchfulness. I forced myself to a superhuman effort to keep awake; I sang, I shouted, I screamed at the wind at the top of my lungs; still I dozed off, to be awakened by knocking my head against the hull. I threw the sea anchor overboard and took in the sails. Then I settled into the cockpit and tried to sleep. Because of my overwrought condition, the combers beating against the hull sounded like thunderclaps. The motion of the boat did not disturb me, but my sleeping arrangements were uncomfortable: my shoulders took up almost the width of the hull, and I had to sit diagonally to be able to move at all. I waited for sleep to overtake me, but I found that my nerves were too much on edge. My legs itched, my back needed scratching, it seemed as though an army of ants marched up my arm. I lay there, bathed in sweat, in the rays of the merciless tropical sun. From Phoenician times to Columbus' day, sailors were convinced that the sun below the equator was strong enough to burn men and ships. This superstition, which held back the circumnavigation of Africa for hundreds of years, seemed about to be realized in my case; I was slowly being scorched by the fierce sun. My head ached and buzzed, my eyes burned, and I could hardly breathe. Sleep in this intense heat was impossible; I climbed out of the cockpit and hoisted the sails. At last the sun went down, the wind sank, but the high swell and my headache remained.

Malaria! Was it possible that I was suffering from one of my recurring attacks of malaria? I rejected this dread possibility, but the thought kept coming back. I threw the sea anchor over again, determined to sleep this time. I left the sail up and lashed the boom. The *Liberia* rolled terribly now, for without the guiding hand of the wind, she would not lie in the right direction to the swell; instead, she bucked like a stubborn mule trying to throw its rider.

I sat down, my head sank limply on my chest and I yielded to utter lassitude and exhaustion. The word malaria haunted me. I knew I ought to rouse myself and take some antimalaria medicine. I was so tired that nothing seemed of any importance or urgency; nothing seemed worth any exertion. But the instinct for self-preservation drove me to make one final effort. Slowly and clumsily I groped for the pills and swallowed them. My experience in the tropics had taught me that malaria, a cunning enemy, overtakes men when they are at their lowest ebb. I remembered now how often I had urged my patients, faced with a fatiguing bush trip, not to forget their antimalaria doses; here I was now, caught myself. Of course, lack of sleep could also account for my condition, but as I drowsed in the cockpit, I was plagued with the image of Alexander the Great, who had died of malaria at my age, thirty-two.

At last I sat up and looked over the edge of the pirogue. Darkness surrounded me, and mist hung everywhere in the air. Under me, the canoe rolled and heaved. I was tired, too tired to solve the riddle of mist at the equator. I knew, however, that I had to stop the terrible roll of the boat. The sail was up and flapped emptily from side to side. Without knowing what I was doing or why I did it, I hung my heavy blanket over the starboard side, and on the portside, a seabag filled with cans. Then I sank back into the cockpit. I do not know how long I sat there, but I was suddenly roused to half wakefulness by a splashing and shouting in the water. Where was I? Were people swimming near me? Why did they disturb the quiet of the ocean with their vulgar noise? Slowly I drew

my tired body up on deck. The night was extraordinary. Gray—
everything gray—no sky. I searched the swirling mist for a glimpse
of the noisy swimmers. Then I saw them—blurred shapes, trailing
white veils, coming at me across the water in a *danse macabre;* I
shouted at them, I swore at them, and they danced away. I felt
foolish and ashamed. Why had I driven them off with my curses?

For a night and a day I was held tight in the grip of nightmare
and hallucination. I recovered with the setting sun and with only a
hazy recollection of what had happened, but I realized immediately
that I had been active during the time; crates of cans, a copper
container with flashlight batteries, my last rubber cushion and
other important possessions had disappeared. I had thrown overboard everything that was in my way. It was a cruel awakening.
Later, I came to the conclusion that my hallucinations sprang from
lack of sleep and that even a short cat nap of ten minutes would
have kept me in possession of my senses. As it was, I now faced the
fact that I would have to turn back; too many of my possessions had
gone overboard, the *Liberia* needed work done on her keel, and I
needed rest. I had little chance of reaching Haiti alive if I continued now across the southern Atlantic.

After I had made my decision, I pulled out the map to find the
nearest port on the African coast. I chose Takoradi in Ghana, and
on the twelfth day I turned the *Liberia* around and started on my
homeward sail. The trade winds blew, the dugout sailed to the
northeast at a good speed, while I slept through the night.

The return trip was uneventful, and I was grateful to the fish
and the birds who helped me to pass the time; dolphins and flying
fish jumped and soared through the air, huge porpoises cut the
surface of the water in slow motion, sharks swam in the *Liberia's* wake. I had time to notice that a dolphin jumps from the
water with the easy mobility of a child at play, whereas the flying
fish cuts through the air stiff and straight, propelled by fear of
pursuing fish. The poor flying fish!—hunted in the water by dolphins and mackerels and in the air by frigate birds. I felt at one
with the fish and the sea around as I sailed back; even my hair was
now bleached to the color of sea foam by the tropical sun.

One day I was pleased to discover a new fish that danced in the
wake of the boat; it was bright green, with a long forklike tail and a

dorsal fin that rose more than an inch above the surface. In the sun its colors sparkled emerald, blue and violet, making it an easy prey to its enemies, and only its speed, which was unusual, saved it from death.

I sighted the African coast fifteen days after I had left it. In the fading light of the late afternoon, I saw palm trees and spotted a wrecked ship that lay to the west of an inlet. In the distance loomed a lighthouse. These landmarks told me that I was approaching the Bay of Axim in Ghana, which lies only some forty miles from Takoradi. Then, as the last golden clouds of the evening hung in the sky, a storm gathered; pitch-black walls of cloud overshadowed my pirogue, the wind slapped at the surface of the water. I took in the sails, put out the sea anchor and drew the spray cover over my head. The wind howled and I heard the roar of coming rain, which fell with tropical suddenness on my deck. Like the beating of a thousand drumsticks, huge rain drops crashed on the *Liberia,* thunder exploded over my head and lightning cut across the sky. Despite the storm, the combers, racing ahead of the wind, gave off their bioluminescent shimmer. Secure in my cockpit, I slept through the whole storm.

The wind abated during the night, making it possible for me to sail on. At dawn I started to take in the sea anchor and was pulling in the line when it was suddenly tugged out of my hands. I tried again—one, two, three, four yards came up easily, and then—whoosh—the line shot out again. The canoe listed dangerously; I was afraid I might capsize, so I dropped the line and threw myself against the opposite side of the boat. A ray or manta had attached itself to the sea anchor and trapped me in sight of the coast. I had to make up my mind whether to wait for the fish to detach itself or to cut the line. I was curious to see the creature that had caught me, but my eagerness to proceed far outweighed my curiosity. I cut the line quickly and was on my way, not without regret at missing my captor and photographing it. I have heard many stories of fishermen of the Red Sea and the Canary Islands, whose poorly anchored boats have been dragged out to sea by rays.

With fair winds from the southwest and support from a strong current, I easily circumnavigated Cape Three Points. But it was not until dark that I saw the lights of Takoradi. I cruised west of the harbor during the night, out of the way of incoming steamers; then, in the morning, I began to sail for the harbor entrance. The light breeze barely filled the sails, and I grew more and more impatient at my slow progress. The swell raced with an eerie sigh of death through the hull of a wrecked ship that lay in my path; to the east more than ten steamers waited to load their freight of lumber and bauxite. I came around an easterly pointing breakwater, took in my sails and paddled against the wind and the outgoing tide. I was making so little headway that I gladly accepted the offer of a police boat to tow me in.

It was seventeen days after my departure from Liberia that I jumped ashore in Takoradi. My knees were a little weak and for the first few hours I felt the movement of the sea, but I had no trouble walking. The chief ill effect was the swelling of my legs. Up to the time of the attack of delirium I had drunk a daily ration of four small glasses of sea water, and on the second day at sea my feet had begun to swell. Gradually the swelling extended to my knees. Small broken blood vessels laced the skin surface of my feet, and when I pressed my thumb against my ankles, it left a deep depression. My ankle bones were sunk in swollen flesh; the sensitivity of the nerve ends had diminished. Massaging my legs twice a day for ten or fifteen minutes and daily exercise had not prevented or lessened the swelling; on subsequent trips, when I eliminated salt water from my diet, I found that my legs remained nearly normal in size.

In Takoradi a policeman took me to the immigration office, where I was informed that I would have to find someone to vouch for me if I intended to stay. I was introduced to the harbor doctor, who offered to be my sponsor and allowed me to moor the *Liberia* alongside his boat.

I had no intention of abandoning my plans for a voyage across the Atlantic, but the keel had to be better ballasted or a successful trip was out of the question. I felt less badly about my miscalculation of weight and balance when I remembered that C. H. Voss had made the same mistake when he rebuilt his Indian canoe, the *Tilikum,* for his world cruise in 1901. Because Hamburg had the best facilities for the work that had to be done, I booked passage home for myself and the canoe and left Takoradi within a few days.

488

3 EMERGENCY LANDING

In the Hamburg docks I had the *Liberia* readied for my second attempt to cross the Atlantic. The inner ballast was removed and an equivalent weight in lead placed under the keel. The rudder, which was too small, was replaced by a larger one, and I had a four-inch-wide plank built around the cockpit so that I could sit there in comfort. After a new coat of paint, the boat was ready. I shipped her to Oporto in northern Portugal; from there I planned to sail to Las Palmas in the Canary Islands and make that my port-of-departure for Haiti.

The arrival of my odd-looking boat in Hamburg caused comment and wild conjecture in the papers. One newspaper announced, "A Viking from North Africa awaits good weather to sail across the Atlantic," and then went on to say that the boat had been sailed by an African along the coast of Africa, through the Bay of Biscay and on to Hamburg, without mishap. Another paper reported that I planned to sail first to Norway and from there to America. I ignored the publicity and sat quietly at home until the *Liberia* was ready and shipped to Oporto, when I left to join her. As the train pulled out of Hamburg, I fell into an introspective and melancholy mood; I wished with all my heart that I had never thought of a voyage across the ocean. I tried to analyze the reasons for my mood. Was it this recent contact with my friends, who were all working at steady jobs, or was it the sea's rejection of my first attempt that had brought on my depression? I fell asleep at last, still trying to find the answer.

On my arrival in Oporto, I went at once to the customs house, hoping to clear my boat immediately. But on the basis of earlier experience with Portuguese customs I should have known that my boat would not be released quickly. In true Iberian fashion I wiled away the days in local cafes until the time had come to try again for the release of the *Liberia*. Again I was frustrated by the slow deliberate approach of the officials, who are dedicated to well-thought-out, long-contemplated action. Every day I sat in the cafes and drank coffee in the company of sad little men in dark suits, returning every few hours to the customs house to badger the officials. I discovered that part of the difficulty was their indecisiveness about how the boat should be listed officially. Happily, within a few days the customs chief was struck with the idea of listing the canoe as a "crate of second-hand goods," and the *Liberia* was then released to me.

Losing no time, I drew the boat up on shore in front of town and set to work preparing her for the voyage. I planned on a crossing of about sixty days and I hoped to accomplish it in June and July. I fastened the rudder, rigged mast and sails, stowed away my cans of food. At the end of the day the work was done, and I floated the *Liberia* alongside a barge. As darkness came, I climbed aboard and fell into exhausted sleep.

Early the next morning, I set sail down the Douro River with a light land breeze to help me. I felt a great urgency to outwit time, and therefore ignored the storm warnings of some passing fishermen. I had no time to spare if my trip was to be accomplished before the dangers of hurricane weather made the attempt too foolhardy. So I sailed on, despite the warning, heartily glad to see the mouth of the Douro behind me. My progress was slow; by afternoon the thunder of surf still sounded in my ears, while sinister cloud banks in the west seemed to restrain the sea breeze. To my relief, the wind rose at last and the first small combers left passing foam scars on the surface of the water. I sailed cautiously, under jib alone, as I always do at the beginning of a voyage, until I know the boat.

The Iberian Peninsula is as dangerous to sail along as the West African coastline, and it was important to keep a good distance between myself and the breaking surf. As a long-time sailor I knew that fewer accidents occur on the high seas than near a coast.

It was the 28th of May, but the weather was still cold; not even two shirts, a pullover and wind jacket were enough to keep me warm.

My route lay between the coast and the sea lane used by large ships, so I felt I could safely take short cat naps during the night. But the intense cold prevented my sleeping in comfort; my teeth chattered, my hands were numb and cramped, a cold wind blew directly into the cockpit. The dugout took on so much water that I had to bail every six hours. My spray cover was too short to protect me adequately; in fact, it forced the wind directly into rather than over my cockpit. I had made little holes in the hull, through which I ran cables that enabled me to handle the tiller with my feet as well as my hands; whenever a big wave came along, it splashed water into the boat through these holes. It wasn't much compared to the amount that later storms were to force into the *Liberia,* but it was enough to add to my discomfort.

The second evening out of Oporto, the Portuguese north wind, a well-known wind in that part of the world, strengthened to over fifteen miles an hour, and I crawled into the cockpit to sleep, leaving the canoe in the hands of the sea anchor. I had purposely not brought a mattress to sleep on because a hard surface under me would make me, even in sleep, more susceptible to any change in motion. I lay on two crates of oranges and apples, and with even the slightest change in the roll of the boat, I was immediately awake. (I think this saved my life later in the voyage.) After an uncomfortable hour on the two crates I was always happy to see the beginning of the dawn, and I looked forward all night to the moment when I could hoist the sails.

I awoke on the third morning to a breeze of some fifteen miles an hour. For a big boat this wind strength is only moderate, but for me it was ideal. With it the *Liberia* was able to achieve her maximum safe speed. On awakening, I collected my rations for the day, before hoisting the sail. Once under way, I could only get at them by letting go the tiller, which invariably put me off course. To reach my food I had to crawl headfirst into the stern, and soon my elbows and knees were covered with sores from the roll of the boat. Yet I had done my best, before my departure, to organize the *Liberia* as efficiently as possible, using space with the greatest economy. In the bow, which was separated from the rest of the boat, I had stowed clothes, books, the telelens for my Leica, and my typewriter, all of which I knew I would not use during the trip. To give the canoe buoyancy in case she capsized, I also put in a few empty airtight containers. In the stern, in another compartment, I kept my food, spare parts and two small fluid compasses. In an easily accessible part of the canoe I stowed my drinking rations: four sixteen-liter demijohns of mineral water and two ten-liter demijohns of red wine. I mixed one part wine to three parts water, and this slightly sour mixture tasted good to me. Not only did it help drive off thirst, but the wine had the added advantage of containing easily absorbed calories. On the starboard side of my big compass I kept a brief case with sea books, and on the port, extra line and canvas; to starboard, above the brief case, was a small compartment, which held my logbook, a nautical almanac, a flashlight and photographic equipment. The small items I used continually, like sunglasses, suntan lotion, knives and can opener, I stuck into canvas pockets on the side of the cockpit. I did not shave and I had no mirror with me. I had no wish to look at myself during my torturous voyage.

At noon on the third day I sailed through the passage between the Farilhoes Islands and the Peniche Peninsula. Vegetation floated everywhere on the surface, and murres—small soot-black birds with white stomachs—crossed and recrossed my path. One might say they are the penguins of the northern hemisphere because of their white abdominal shirts, dark jackets and webbed feet, which are planted far back toward the tails.

I approached the mouth of the Tagus River, and for the first time since leaving Oporto, I saw big ships, some sailing toward

Lisbon, others coming from the mouth of the river. I passed a ship from Hamburg and waved to the officer on the bridge. He waved back, little knowing that it was a fellow-townsman who floated near him in the strange craft.

With the last golden rays of the sun I sighted the roofs of Cascais and Estoril, home of exiled kings. I looked up at the hill terraces, where I had often sat in the warm winter sun, gazing down on the Alcántara pier, dreaming that one day I would make a voyage across the Atlantic, like the Portuguese sailors of old. And here I was, full of hope that this time I would succeed.

Night came. The long, thin lightfinger of the lighthouse at Cape Espichel circled above me. Occasionally, ships sailed fairly close to the *Liberia,* so close that I could make out shadowy figures on board. I was on a maritime highway now and could take no chances with sleep, but several times I found my eyes closing, and to keep awake, I resorted to singing and whistling, talking out loud to myself and to imagined friends. Nothing is more monotonous for the single-handed sailor than keeping a night watch.

The next day, as I was taking my noon position, a cormorant, whose sparse feathers gave him the damp, naked appearance of a new-born baby, flew over the pirogue. This bird—whose name is a contraction of *corvus marinus,* sea raven—is a first-class fisherman, a skill that has made him of use to natives in some parts of the world. They force him into the water, a leather ring around his neck, and when he surfaces they remove his catch, which the ring has made it impossible for him to swallow.

On the fifth day I looked across white-capped seas to Cape St. Vincent, the most southwesterly point of Europe, where the dark eyes of large caves have looked for centuries upon shipwrecked sailors and sea battles. Columbus was rescued here, while he was still a young man, after his ship was sunk by a French-Portuguese fleet. From the steep, rocky cape I could hear the dull grumble of surf and swell, and then I came in sight of the rock of Cape Sagres, where, five hundred years ago, Henry the Navigator built his famous school of seafaring and exploration, which helped make his country a first class power for a brief moment in European history.

I sailed on with favorable winds. On the evening of the eighth

493

day I stood before Casablanca, some 450 sea miles from Oporto. Calculating my actual sailing time, I found I had achieved an average speed of a little over four knots, a good performance for my canoe. I decided to wait until daylight before entering the busy harbor, although I knew it well from my work there three years before. During the night a stiff breeze came up from the northeast, an Ithacan counterwind—so called from Odysseus, who was often thwarted by counterwinds when he tried to sail to Ithaca—which blew me away from the harbor entrance. I sailed athwart for one hour, trying to get back, but the *Liberia* shipped so much water that I gave up, deciding instead to head for Safi, the second largest port in Morocco.

As I sailed past the heights of Mazagan on my way to Safi, I was surprised by a sudden stormy wind. It was useless to try to make further progress, so I put out the sea anchor and settled down for a nap. The *Liberia* behaved like a cork on the turbulent sea, rolling and bobbing ceaselessly, but I felt little of this inside and slept soundly, although I had to rouse myself every now and again to bail. The wind drove me back toward the east, but with a favorable breeze the next day I reached the heights again by evening.

The surf near Mazagan breaks at a depth of thirteen yards so that sailing there is dangerous and tricky. My entire attention was concentrated on keeping a safe distance between myself and the coast; I sailed with special care. A feeble breeze came from the west; it seemed wisest to enter the harbor of Mazagan immediately. Very, very slowly I approached the harbor lights. A terrible swell rolled under the canoe; I checked and rechecked my position to make certain that the distance from the coast remained at one sea mile. Through the darkness I could discern the white line of the swell breaking in the black night, a frontal attack of sea upon land.

Then, suddenly, I was caught. Giant breakers rose high above the boat and thundered at me on all sides. It was a sailor's nightmare; I had lost the passage to the harbor; I was trapped in the breaking swell. Small waves broke on the back of the mountainous swell, which raced at me with the speed of an express train. The sail was still set; each time the swell rushed by, the boom struck with such fury that my head was in danger. All at once I was faced with a moving wall of water; dwarfed, I crouched low in the canoe, held my breath, and then, with a roar, the wave struck. I pulled out the paddle. Would it help? I paddled like a man possessed; again I felt the boat shudder as tons of water poured over me. Was this the end?

Another breaker took me, like a toy, in its white claws, rolled under the canoe, and I paddled and paddled to get free. I was lifted into the air, but this time only the crest of the wave broke with a hissing sound as the *Liberia* settled back into the water. I struck desperately with my paddle to avoid the next breaker. A mountain of water hovered over me—would it break? Once again I was lucky, only the white top broke, partially filling the cockpit with water. I paddled athwart the swell, knowing I would not be safe until I had reached the deeper water that lay ahead.

The beam of a nearby lighthouse circled the skies, remote and unconcerned by my plight. In the distance the lights of Mazagan shone elusively through the darkness. I was alone, with no time to think out a course of action, with the paddle the only possible instrument of escape.

After what seemed like hours, I reached a spot where the swell was no longer dangerously high. I stopped paddling and dropped back exhausted onto the seat. My carelessness and myopia had led me into that frightening crisis. In the dark I must have miscalculated my distance from the shore and so been thrust into the giant surf. I was wet through and the dugout was awash—flashlight and books swam in water, and the compass was nearly flooded. But the boat had come through undamaged.

In front of me a fishing boat loomed up in the night. I shouted to it, hoping to be towed into harbor, but only a dog, barking furiously, answered. So I set my course alone on the entrance to Mazagan. A rising tide and steady use of the paddle brought me at about midnight to the dock of the yacht club, where Arabs still fished. Clear moonlight shone on the old ramparts and minarets of the town and turned them to ghosts that hovered over the *Liberia* and the thick clay harbor walls. I spent an hour bailing the boat, changing into dry clothes and setting to right my possessions. Then I sat down on the washboard. I had no desire to go ashore until I had

495

recovered from my terrible experience; I had to be alone, quiet, for my body still shook and I was drained of all strength.

In the morning I reported to the police, who graciously granted me a *permission de séjour* and simultaneously set a spy at my heels. When I came off the boat, my feet were swollen, and the next day blisters developed all over them. During the past eleven days at sea I had drunk a daily ration of seven fluid ounces of salt water and almost a quart and a half of other liquids. By the second day edemata had developed, which soon extended up to my knees. Otherwise, I was all right, except for extremely painful buttocks, where pustulae and then boils had developed. I had started out using a rubber air cushion, but found that it contributed to my discomfort for it pressed my wet clothes to my sore skin and cut off all circulation of air. The hard, wooden surface of the canoe became my favorite seat.

In Mazagan I bought thick canvas and lengthened the spray cover over the cockpit. I added fresh oranges to my provisions, and in two days I was ready to leave. Members of the local yacht club towed me out of the harbor, and after several hours of cruising, I sailed free of the treacherous breakers, which I remembered with painful vividness.

I set my course on the most northerly of the Canary Islands, Lanzarote; with the help of trade winds, the *Liberia* made good time. I felt relaxed and happy in my progress and found time to admire the many Portuguese man-of-war jellyfish, that swam in the water beside me. I watched their pink combs that perch on top of light blue helmets and I thought how deceptively peaceful they appear on the surface. I knew from bitter experience, while underwater swimming, that beneath their surface beauty they carry poisonous tentacles, which can be extremely painful to the unwary or the unknowing.

The first night out of Mazagan there was a fresh wind. I tied the tiller, put out the sea anchor, and slept like a healthy baby. When dawn came, however, disaster jolted me out of my dreams; as I got set to sail again I found the rudder no longer reacted to the tiller. I suspected that the connecting split pins to the rudder pole had broken. I put on underwater goggles, which I had added to my supplies, jumped into the water, only to have my fears confirmed. There was nothing I could do at sea to repair the damage. I had to decide whether to try sailing on to the Canaries or to turn back to the North African coast. The coast was no longer visible, but as I knew it could not be more than twenty sea miles away I preferred to return to the nearest port, Safi. I used my paddle as a rudder, sailed only under gaff sail; luck and the wind were with me, and I sighted Cape Cantu, some ten miles from Safi, at noon. I hoped to reach Safi that day, so I sailed on, gripping the paddle with both hands, thankful that they were sufficiently calloused to prevent blisters. Evening came on too quickly to suit me; although the wind weakened, I continued sailing. At sunset I reached the bay, sailing directly under the huge rocks that guard the harbor entrance of Safi. I made three attempts to sail the *Liberia* into it, but an offshore wind thwarted me every time. I was finally forced to wait until the next morning, when I succeeded on the second try. I landed rudderless but without help, and my sense of achievement almost overshadowed my anger at a broken, useless rudder.

I moored the *Liberia* at the yacht club and set to work repairing my gaff sail, which had torn a little. Suddenly, from above me, a lady called down, "Can I help you in any way?" I explained my predicament to her and was delighted when she told me that her husband was a diver in the harbor and would be able to fix the rudder. The afternoon of that day my new-found friend put on his diving suit and went into the water to unscrew the broken rudder. He made new split pins, welded the hinges to the rudder rod and had the blade made smaller. The next morning he towed me out of the harbor.

During the next few days the boat made good speed, but there followed several days of sultry calm, alternating with the merest breath of wind. My patience was tried to the utmost. I could do nothing but wait and follow my established daily routine, which was as regular and as punctual as the daily round of a banker. I took a bath every morning, I napped at noontime, I ate my meager meals according to the clock. Dolphins passed by; underneath the *Liberia*, small fish made their homes, and a long beard of green algae grew on her bottom and floated out in the water. Flocks of squeaking

terns, sporting dark berets on their bright heads, and solitary petrels flew alongside. Occasionally I heard the snorting of whales;
then the dugout would creep slowly forward for three hundred
yards or so through their slimy, light brown excrement. Curious
shapes were formed by the dung as it floated under the surface;
once I made out the skull of a cow, another time I traced the
outlines of a bare femur. Often the wind blew it into long brown
streaks, in which sea birds found their nourishment, reminding me
of sparrows picking at horse dung on city streets.

I watched flying fish take agonizing leaps out of the water to
escape their enemies. The water was full of plankton—millions and
millions of microscopic plants and animals mixed with the eggs of
larger sea life—and I spotted many swollen fish eggs in it. Small,
dark jellyfish lay on the surface like tiny dust particles; the white
shells of cuttlefish caught the sunlight and shone from the flat, lazy
sea. On the fifth day out of Safi, the hours passed so uneventfully
that all I wrote in my logbook were the words sunrise and sunset.

I do, however, remember one incident that occurred that day
which I did not note in the log. I had nailed a horseshoe to the
starboard side of the boat, a symbol of good luck that was constantly under my eyes as I sailed, but that day, to my annoyance, I
tore my jacket on it. I recalled a sailor's superstition that wishes are
granted when a loved object is thrown overboard; storms, they
believed, could be calmed in this way; so I thought that perhaps,
conversely, a heavy wind could be conjured up. I chiseled the
horseshoe off the hull and, with many heartfelt wishes, threw it as
far as possible into the water.

The next morning my wish was more than granted. The wind
roared, the sea raged, and the pirogue staggered and reeled in
mountains of water; I had just time to throw out the sea anchor and
furl the sails. Big combers rushed over the boat. The hollow interior of the canoe magnified the sounds of the waves as they
crashed against her; I felt as though I were sitting in a drum. Foam
and spray seeped into the cockpit over my spray cover, and heavy
breakers let loose floods of water that found their way to me. I bailed
continuously, until my hands resembled a washerwoman's. There
was no doubt that the horseshoe had outdone itself; this was a real

storm. In spite of it I managed to sleep in short cat naps. By next morning the foam had abated, leaving only trade winds—still stormy enough to send watery messages into the cockpit. On the horizon the sea raged, giant waves rose up and broke up into boiling water. Petrels danced over the waves with such exuberance that it was obvious they prefer a heavy sea to a flat calm.

All day, because of the still-stormy wind, I progressed with the tiller tied and with two sea anchors out to keep from drifting south. Then when evening brought gentler winds, I reached for the tiller and with a shock found that it met no resistance from the rudder. I untied it and stretched out across the side of the boat to find out why. Foam ran down my neck through my open collar and dribbled down my chest, but I felt nothing; I was too intent on my problem. As the stern rose on top of a wave, I could see the upper hinges of the rudder trunk. They were empty. The rudder blade had fallen out of its hinges; it had developed an independent spirit and gone off to join the fish. I was furious, I screamed at the wind, at the empty air, anxiously waiting for the next wave so that I could examine the hinges again. I hoped against hope that my eyes had deceived me the first time, or that the rudder might have returned of its own free will to the copper hinges, like a repentant child to its mother. Whom should I blame for this disaster? The shipyard in Hamburg? The storm? My friend in Safi? Myself? It was my boat; I alone was responsible.

The ocean roared as before; combers rushed over the stern and into the cockpit, glancing off the deck like shot. Rudderless and helpless, I floated on the ocean, trying to keep up my spirits by losing myself in happy memories.

That night I put out two sea anchors and tried to sleep, but the noise of the storm made me restless. I awoke from a nightmare, bathed in sweat. Flashlight in hand, I crawled out of the cockpit and went to adjust the sea anchor. The stern rose and fell, now high in the air, then again completely submerged. With a grappling iron I reached for the line of the farther sea anchor; I found nothing. Damnation! The anchor was gone; I reached for the second one. Again the grapple found nothing. I pounded the seat in rage and frustration; I was going to be destroyed—rudderless and without a sea anchor—in the Atlantic in a bad storm. But I had not time to think; I had to act fast to find something that could go aft to replace the anchors. My knee happened to jab against the balloon sail. It would have to serve. I knotted a line twice around it and hung it into the water.

Morning came at last, and I found some sailcloth and sewed an emergency anchor. My hands still shook with fright from the night before. As the day lightened, a steamer came toward me; I was overcome by a strong, sudden urge to hail it. I had had enough—I was finished. But the ship passed about one sea mile to starboard, without a sign that anyone aboard was aware of my presence. I could see a face, very clearly, peering out of a porthole. The ocean between us raged and foamed. I waved with a white life belt. No answer. I climbed on my seat and waved again. No answer. The man had to see me; I would force him to notice me. But again no response. The boat rocked with such violence that I slipped off the seat into the cockpit. My whole body shook with desperation; at the top of my voice I screamed across the water at the ship, "Stop, stop, I can pay you for this. Please stop," and I held the life belt high in the air. But the tanker plowed on through the raging seas, while the face in the porthole gazed dreamily and sightlessly at the turbulent waters. Sinking down in my seat, I realized that the sea was too heavy and too foamy for anyone to see me. For a moment my will to succeed left me. I was seized by a great depression. Should I jump overboard? Suddenly with a thunderous clap a large wave broke over the cockpit, knocking me over the compass. Water roared and rushed into every nook and cranny of the *Liberia;* my camera, watches and books were soaked. I bailed, I shook, I swore. I bailed again, prayed and bailed once more. When the work was finished, I found it had calmed me, although I was still too tense for sleep. I took five Dramamines and swallowed them dry. They act as a sedative. Then it occurred to me that the wine would help bring relaxation and sleep. I took hold of the demijohn and, leaning against the side, I drank deeply, drank and lay down on the bare wooden boxes—happy that I still had a berth at all. All I wanted was sleep, only sleep.

The next day the wind howled, and breakers hurled themselves like rocks against the hull of the boat. I bailed again and then crept into my cockpit. I was glad the tanker had not stopped to pick me up; my spirits had recovered. I finished sewing two new sea anchors and tied them both with plastic lines.

The furious face of the ocean did not change. Stormy winds whistled; huge waves roared and rumbled. I whistled, too, and sang, and then swore at the unnecessary delay. I hunted for a jar of hard candies I had bought in Oporto because they were called "Good Adventure," but to my disappointment their taste was as bitter as my present situation. I hurt physically. From constant immersion in water, small ulcers had developed on my swollen feet and showed no inclination to heal; my buttocks burned as though a volley of shot had been fired at them.

The storm raged for four days and then the trade winds calmed, leaving a powerful swell. The *Liberia* had stood up well under the ordeal, but I had weakened. I had lost hope and been on the point of surrender. I took my noon position, then, three hours later, my longitude, and realized that I had been blown between the African coast and the Canary Islands, and to sail back against the currents was not worth the attempt. Dakar, the nearest good harbor, lay seven hundred sea miles south, which was too far; after some thought, I chose to head for Villa Cisneros, the capital of Río de Oro in the Spanish Sahara.

As I sailed back I came upon a locust, lying on the water but still alive. Whole swarms have been known to reach the Canary Islands from Africa. Another time a hideous cormorant paid me a visit, he must have been unusually courageous to have flown so far out to sea. To vary my diet, I speared and ate a dolphin. The wind lessened, and the Portuguese men-of-war sailed as fast as the *Liberia*. In a calm sea these jellyfish capsize frequently. They have to keep their combs wet, and in a flat sea they can do this only by listing heavily to one side; in a rough sea the comb stays wet from the spray, and the jellyfish rides out a storm with ease. Throughout the day I admired the constantly lively petrels, which were as much at home in the air as at sea.

After three days of sailing, I heard the sound of breaking surf. Soon the white beam of the lighthouse at Cape Bojador pierced the haze. Later that afternoon, I looked upon a steep coastline that showed me only rock and sand. An unending stretch of beach where trade winds stir up the sands of the Sahara to an orange-red hell.

Rudderless, I had been forced to hold a paddle for fourteen hours a day; my left hand, once partially paralyzed during the war, was not suited to the task. It hurt from sunburn and its palm was covered with blisters.

After I neared the African coast, I was becalmed almost every day at noon; I found it difficult to decide which was harder to bear—a calm or a storm. When my nerves were strained to the utmost by the calm weather, I amused myself by teasing Portuguese men-of-war. I threw water over them, and they withdrew their pink combs, turning indignantly over on their sides. Plankton and fish filled the waters here; every day I met Spanish boats, for this is their main fishing bank. One time I had a sudden, and for me unusual, impulse to talk to someone, so I paddled up to a boat that lay at anchor, the crew angling over the side. I threw a line to them and a dark-skinned boy held it.

"Are you French?"

"No, *Alemán*," I answered.

"Do you have any cigarettes?"

"No"—my reply disappointed him. "But would you like some cans of food?"

Canned food is a luxury for these poor fishermen, and the captain, bearded and tanned, accepted quickly. "Sí, sí, sēnor." So I gave him some of my canned meat, wished him good luck and sailed on.

From the coast came the dull rumble of the surf. Dolphins, who had been my companions for so long, had left me now; in their place were huge schools of herring-like fish. Flat calm weather plagued me; the sea was as expressionless as a death mask; only a light breeze filled my sails. My slow progress tempted me to put the dugout ashore and walk to Villa Cisneros, but when I looked at the sand dunes, I comforted myself with the knowledge that even poor sailing is preferable to hiking through hot sand.

Sailing without a rudder demands great patience; whenever the pirogue fell off wind I had to take in the main sail and paddle hard to return to my course. I woke up one morning—twenty days after my departure from Safi—in a thick fog, brought on by a cold coastal current meeting warm air from land. It was in part because of these fogs that the Romans named this part of the ocean the Dark Sea. At noon a fishing boat came up slowly behind me and with great difficulty sailed past. As it came alongside, we exchanged greetings and I found out that it, too, was bound for Villa Cisneros. When the captain heard we had the same destination, he threw me a rope, which I fastened to the bow of the *Liberia*. It was a lucky break for me, as, in any case, I would have had to be towed up the long archipelago to my destination. I climbed onto the fishing boat and arrived just in time for a cup of coffee. The next afternoon we dropped anchor in front of Villa Cisneros.

My dream of crossing the Atlantic in the summer months had vanished with my rudder, so I gave my provisions to the crew as a token of my gratitude. I had been afloat for fourteen days without a rudder; for two weeks I had steered a barely maneuverable craft with a paddle. During that time, my daily intake of sea water had been ten and a half fluid ounces, which I swallowed in doses of one and three-fourths fluid ounces six times a day, and now my feet and legs were swollen in spite of rest and exercises. I had proved to myself that there is no advantage to drinking salt water; it can, in fact, weaken a sailor's physical condition at a time when he needs all his strength.

Villa Cisneros is a place devoid of natural green; no trees, no shrubs, no grass break the monotonous yellow-brown of this Sahara outpost. A few deep wells provide brackish water, but drinking water has to be imported from the Canary Islands and is extremely expensive. As one approaches the chalk-white houses, one can see a little green, painstakingly cultivated by the owners, who are all, in one way or another, connected with the Spanish Army. The Portuguese once traded here for gold dust, hence the alluring name of the bay, Río de Oro—river of gold; but the river is as illusory as the gold, for it is only a long arm of the Atlantic that washes around the peninsula. The native Arab nomads, *moros*, live in blue tents strung out in straight military lines and swarming with flies and fleas. Dromedaries, goats and sheep loafed around the animal tents. The nomads are unusually hospitable, and often quite unknown faces and voices invited me to share their mint tea. I was amazed at how few children I saw, but learned that the infant mortality rate is exceedingly high.

One day during my stay I felt a longing to see the open ocean again and wandered down to the beach. Even there, I was followed by swarms of attacking flies; sand-colored beetles scurried away, their tails high in the air; dark, lazy beetles burrowed in the sparse vegetation. Trade winds suffocate the sea breezes here. Year in, year out, they howl around the corners of Villa Cisneros and stir the sand. It is an uncomfortable, unpleasant spot, and the only people who live there are those sent for professional reasons, and of course, the nomads.

After three weeks, I was rescued by an ancient mail steamer, the *Gomera*, which carried me and the *Liberia* to Las Palmas in Gran Canaria. After we arrived, the pirogue remained for some time on the dock, suffering the expert inspection of curious fishermen and sailors. Finally, I was able to put her in a small shipyard for repairs.

I spent most of my time in Las Palmas on the beach or in the harbor, spear-fishing slimy cuttlefish, octopi and angry moray eels. I practiced my crawl so assiduously that my friends insisted I was planning to cross the ocean as a swimmer.

The known history of the Canary Islands goes back to the days of the Carthaginian explorer, Hanno, who mentioned them after a West African voyage. The name derives from the Latin *canis* and stems from Roman times when wild dogs roamed the islands. In the centuries that followed, Berbers, Phoenicians, Greeks, Italians, French and Spaniards contributed their part to the beauty of to-day's inhabitants. The island of Gran Canaria has been Spanish since Columbus' day, although Drake—and others—tried to wrest it from Spain. From the air Gran Canaria looks like an island volcano. It is cut through by deep gorges whose sheer sides fall away to the ocean. There is, nevertheless, such a diversity of landscape on this small island that one is forced to liken it to a miniature continent. Deserts with dromedaries, fertile valleys that produce tomatoes and bananas, high plains of wheat fields and pine tree groves give the naked mountains a friendly look. Date palms, coffee, papaya and pineapples are as native to the island as apples, pears, cherries and plums. Still lakes lie at the foot of steep mountain ridges and from an alpine landscape one looks down on tropical valleys. This is Gran Canaria, *continente en miniatura.*

My canoe lay in the boat yard where I was able to work on her in seclusion. Four weeks before my departure, I began the final preparations. I cut a square sail of six square yards, sewed a spray cover and attached an iron stave to the sides, over which the aft part of the cover could be drawn. By raising the level of the tarpaulin I hoped to keep away the heavy splashes of water and avoid the wind whistling through the cockpit. A new and stronger rudder was, of course, my major concern. A blacksmith made me a monster so large that a liner could have been guided by it. I had learned a lesson from the loss of my first rudder, and I took with me all sorts of spare parts, including a new mast of eucalyptus wood and a spare oar. One of the best sailors in Las Palmas happened to notice my gaff sail and remarked that it looked as fragile as newspaper. I was forced to agree with him, but I could not bring myself to part with all my old things. (The sail repaid my trust and stayed with me to the end. My spare sail played a part too as it served as a comfortable dry pillow throughout the voyage.)

The bottom of the boat I painted a reddish brown, the deck an ordinary white. Two days before the intended departure I moored the canoe in the harbor. I left that move to the last, so that barnacles and algae would have less time to grow on the bottom. But then my plans were upset by a storm from the south that swept the island. Palm trees bent like bows, banana trees were uprooted, masses of vegetation were carried to the sea by dirty flood waters.

After the furious south wind had worn itself out, it left the field to timid trade winds. The storm put me another three days behind in my schedule. My nerves were on edge. The day before my departure I knocked my alarm clock to the floor with such force that I had to throw it into the harbor as useless. I cut myself with a knife, and an attack of indigestion reflected my general unease. My last night in Las Palmas I moored the *Liberia* to lobster crates and slept on board. I trimmed the boat—a task that soothed me. On that last night my feelings were numb; no excitement and no fear stirred me. I knew that nothing would ever be as bad as the last storm without a rudder.

That evening, hot and perspiring from my work, I sat on the washboard to rest; shadows of fishing boats made a dark chain in the dead waters of the harbor; from the dock I heard the snores of the night watchman. It was the 25th day of October, 1955. The hurricane season in the West Indies would soon be over. If the trade winds blew with their full strength, I could reach Haiti in two months. But past experience made me wary of planning ahead; only the Atlantic winds could dictate the length and the route of my voyage.

4 THE BIG JUMP

In the morning I sailed from the dockyard over to the yacht club, where I said good-bye to my friends. I had told them that I planned a voyage down the West African coast. I had kept my true destination secret in order to avoid comments and questions. One hour later I left the harbor of Las Palmas, alone and unnoticed; only the cathedral spire of the town and the naked mountains gazed after the canoe for a long time.

Outside the harbor the wind freshened; because I was under square and gaff sail the wake water moved in great whirls. Banana stems and torn cactus plants, remnants of the storm, floated on the surface. A fishing boat, apparently surprised at the foaming bow wave of my little dugout, came from the shore and ran beside me to test my speed. I was doing five knots. The boat came up under motor, and after a friendly waving of hands, she returned to her berth.

From the southeast of the island the Sahara of Gran Canaria loomed yellow and inhospitable. The trade winds ceased. Pityingly, the lighthouse of Maspalomas looked down on the *Liberia,* struggling free of the coast. I was sewing a button on the chin strap of my rain hat to tighten it, when I knocked my pouch of sail needles

507

overboard. With all my needles gone I had no way of repairing torn sails during the voyage. My old standby, adhesive tape—which as a doctor I am in the habit of using on everything from torn shirts to book covers—would not stick to a constantly wet sail. Happily I had been foresighted enough to bring a spare sail along.

By afternoon I had cruised to the south of Gran Canaria. In the twilight a pair of porpoises snorted calmly and swam across my bow in slow motion. Mount Teyde, the volcanic crater of Tenerife, peered over its wreath of clouds like a Velásquez head over its Spanish collar. The clear moonlight gave the bioluminescent waters little chance to glow.

By next morning the current had dragged me back some miles toward the coast. Feeble puffs of wind were suffocated by a burning sun. The pirogue rolled in the dead water; with every swell, the boom menaced my nose, and my nerves were frayed by the aimless flapping of the empty gaff sail.

I took my sun bath, did my daily exercises and waited for the faithless trade winds. The islands would not let me out of their sight. To keep occupied, I took out my new Primus cooker, but in the high swell it would not balance on the bilge board. Instead, I squeezed it into a fruit crate, put a can of meat and an onion into my only cooking pot and lit it. Instantly it flared up. I jumped on my seat, grabbed my measuring cup and poured water over the flames; it seemed to make them worse. As they shot higher, they ignited the crate. Flames touched the deck. "I'll drown you before you burn me up," I shouted and, jabbing the prongs of the fishing spear into the crate, I hurled it overboard. Water suffocated the licking flames. I no longer had a stove; but I had chosen my food so that I could eat it hot or cold, and now the decision had been made for me.

In the late afternoon sun of the second day, I sighted the three southernmost Canary Islands. To the west, a lazy breeze made a fluted pattern on the surface; to the east, ship after ship steamed north or south. On the morning of the third day, a light breeze felt its way toward the African continent; but as I skimmed south I was surprised by a rain squall, which forced me to take in the mainsail. It was over in a few minutes, and I sat in a calm again, swearing at a poor wind which was forcing me into a dangerous steamship route. To the north, the cold, blue mountains of the Canary Islands taunted me with their indifference to my slow progress. On the fourth day I lost them behind the horizon; now at last the west wind freshened and the first combers fell into the cockpit.

To starboard, steamers passed me, headed for South America; to port, they passed bound for West and South Africa. For a single-handed sailor there is nothing worse than knowing he is caught in a steamship route. I, for one, felt as helpless as a seal on Broadway—clumsy and immobile in the face of oncoming traffic. I could achieve some measure of safety by using the system I had followed earlier—sleeping during the day, when the *Liberia* was more clearly visible, and watching alertly at night—but this is easier said than done. Hanging out navigation lights can only reassure a beginner, for it is pure chance if they are seen from the bridge of a steamer. Even here, in a coastal area which was crowded with fishing boats, not all of the big ships kept a watch on the bow. Although I was aware of the danger, there were several times at night when my head fell forward on my chest, and I dozed.

During the first week I ate only fruit and one can of meat a day. I had taken precautions against spoilage by wrapping my oranges and apples individually in paper, but on the fourth day some of the oranges had already begun to rot. Apples kept better. As long as the fruit stayed edible, I wanted it as a substitute for water and a protection against constipation, a condition hard to avoid on a concentrated diet and little exercise.

The west wind blew on the fourth and fifth days. This wind would have drawn a rubber raft to the Sahara. I managed to hold my own and stay in the steamship route, but still I felt a steady pull toward the inhospitable desert coast, of which I still had such clear and unpleasant memories. Rain squalls passed on either side of me, but always missed the *Liberia;* ships sailed by and an occasional fishing boat appeared over the horizon. I was constantly on the alert, and soon I began to long for some sleep. I searched the sky hopefully for some sign of trade winds that would blow me out of my misery. Nothing! No change! Dolphins flashed in and out of the water, chasing flying fishes; petrels fluttered in the high mountainous swell from the north; large shearwaters thrust themselves straight into the air, then shot down in the valleys of water, without seeming to move their wings; and, beside the boat, the light green shadows of fishes darted through the blue water.

On the evening of the sixth day, high white cloud banks sailed across the sky from the north; but at the water level, the wind came, as before, from the west. I remembered an old medical school teacher who used to say to his students, "Do not forget, gentlemen, when making a diagnosis, that you will find the usual more usual than the unusual." Would the trade winds finally obey this maxim and put an end to the unusual west wind? It seemed not. During the endless night the stars glittered, dolphins streaked through moonlit waters, but no breath of wind stirred in the sails. A caravan of steamer lights twinkled on the horizon. I had counted on the trade winds carrying me across the Atlantic. Would my third attempt also end on the sandy shores of the Sahara?

A full moon smiled down on the ocean and gave me enough light to write in my logbook. The next morning, at last, a timid trade wind blew from the northeast. Its harmlessness invited me to take a bath. I inspected the boat bottom and found the first small barnacles but no algae. That whole day the trade winds were so feeble they could hardly force themselves over the horizon, and on the eighth day I still dawdled in the steamer route near the West African coast.

The next morning, November 3rd, the monotony of my days was broken at last. In the many, many years I had dreamed of crossing the Atlantic in a small boat, I had always been certain that I would see something unusual in the ocean. Now at last I did. The sea was as flat as before; an even ripple lay over the surface; no foam was visible: the best weather for observation, the worst for sailing. A huge swell, rising close to thirty feet, rolled from the north; in its deep valleys fluttered Madeira petrels. I was watching them when all at once on the surface of the water I noticed an extraordinarily large brown shape. It disappeared into the next valley and then reappeared, this time in two distinctly separate parts, moving in the foam. On the fore part the sun's rays reflected against two big black eyes. I quickly reached for my camera; but as I was preparing to take a picture, the creature disappeared. Distance in the sea is difficult to estimate, it might have been as much as three hundred feet away; its length, also hard to gauge, looked to me to be at least double that of the *Liberia* and possibly as much as seventy-five feet. Though I saw no tentacles, I felt sure that what I had just missed with the camera was a rarely seen giant squid. Perhaps there were two together, which would explain the stretch of water in the middle. Their immense size has been estimated from tentacle scars left on the skins of sperm whales, who are their bitterest foes. They are shy creatures, like their cousins the octopi, and live in the deep regions of the water, where they can avoid their enemy the sperm whale. It was a bitter disappointment to me that the squid was so camera-shy. I waited for it to reappear, but it lacked any instinct for publicity. Someday, someone will be able to photograph this extraordinary ten-armed mollusk and it will be a real achievement.

On the tenth day the trade winds still husbanded their strength; a mere thimbleful of wind tried hard to push me westward. Yet only with difficulty could the *Liberia* outdistance the feathers, orange peels, corks and bottles that floated on the water. Water striders moved faster than I did. Around noon I heard the loud unrestrained snorts of a whale in the distance. The cameras were ready, and there it came . . . and this time I got my picure. It was Cuvier's beaked whale, a rare specimen, that came to cheer me up after the disappointment of the day before over the giant squid. The solitary whale headed straight for the boat, its dark body patterned by leopard spots, which emphasized its bright beaked head. No one knows whether these light spots on their skin are there from birth, are the result of bites from their own species or are produced by parasites, although I believe that the spots are too large for the last explanation to be the correct one. Then with great swiftness, my visitor turned back as if it had forgotten something, took a deep breath and disappeared into the depths.

Throughout the second week I sat in a flat calm; the wind seldom had enough energy to produce as much as one tired breath. Somehow, I had to pass the time during this waiting period: I paddled, I watched the birds and the fish and I indulged in daydreams. The surface of the water now looked as though a thin layer of oil or dust had been sprayed on it, but it was of course only plankton. I had my first visit from a tropic bird, who flew about my mast, trying to perch; he was unable to believe that I hadn't reserved a place for him. He tried over and over again and each time was frustrated by the small wind-indicating flag atop the mast. The only favor I could do him was to take his picture with my Leica.

On the eleventh day, with a slight wind behind me and the aid of the Canary current, I made my entrance into the tropics. Petrels and shearwaters flew listlessly over the interminable high swell from the north; they appear to need wind as much as a sailboat does, for without it they tire easily. They seemed as melancholy as I in a calm.

Small fish paid short visits to my dugout. On the fourteenth day, the first shark swam toward me; he loitered around the *Liberia* beating a steady tattoo with his tail fin against the cork pads on the side of the boat. I found that all sharks were curious when the boat moved slowly. Dolphins hunted their small victims and at times shot right out of the water in their eagerness. I threw them tidbits, and they rushed at them greedily only to turn away disappointed when they found they were not meat. Dolphins are confirmed carnivores, active day and night in their hunt for meat. During the night I could hear the hard beating of bird wings in the darkness. Before the moon rose, dolphins trailed long gray-white trains of bioluminescence through the water. Sometimes the canoe or the rudder touched a jellyfish or some other plankton form which lit up briefly and darkened again at once. Twice at night I caught glimpses of a dragonfly and a butterfly in the beam of my flashlight. Unfortunately, they did not have the presence of mind to take refuge on my canoe.

Every night now I was delighted by a display of shooting stars. On the sixteenth day a shearwater deposited its droppings in front of my bow and that night a comet swung down from the skies. Were they omens of good luck?

Throughout the long, dark nights I watched, entranced by the bioluminescence in the waters around me. Not enough has been written about this phenomenon of the sea, about the light the inhabitants of the sea make for themselves; for they are afraid of the rays of our sun and make their own sunshine. At night they turn themselves into spirits of light that haunt the surface of the water. They shine through the dark in a profusion of shapes and forms: spotlights, strip lights and floodlights are an old story to marine creatures. Taillights, halos, headlights are their natural inheritance. Nor is that all: plankton forms let other forms glow and shimmer for them; they catch bacteria which will light up at their command, or they grasp at lighted bacteria and bask in their rays. Jellyfish ornament their billowing skirts with shining bacteria and swim like ballerinas through the wet darkness. The fewer the stars that shine at night, the more friendly the light of the sea. Sometimes I found the nocturnal world of the ocean hard to fathom, but its very mystery lent enchantment to my lonely nights.

One night, as I watched the shimmering plankton, I thought I should like to taste it, at least once. It is, after all, the basic food of the sea. I hung out a net of the finest mesh, which had the effect of a sea anchor and made the boat groan over her additional burden. Because of this I left the net out for only an hour and then drew it up to examine my catch. Lighting the flashlight to investigate, I saw some sort of repellent vermin moving at the bottom. After a moment of hesitation, I took a spoonful and nibbled carefully. Immediately my mouth was full of an intense burning sensation. Scooping up a cup of sea water, I rinsed my mouth, and then smeared my lips with heavy cream; but the burning continued for hours. Since then, I have not fished for plankton—although I think it was not plankton that burned, but floating poisonous tentacles from a Portuguese man-of-war caught in the net.

On this trip, as on my two earlier attempts, Portuguese men-of-war often crossed my path. When the sea was calm—as it was during those first two weeks—I could see their light blue, pink-crested helmets across the mirrorlike surface of the ocean. Centuries ago, sailors from northern Europe knew that these jellyfish, swimming as they do in warmer waters, were an indication that their enemies, real Portuguese men-of-war, were close by, and they watched the horizon carefully. The helmet that these jellyfish wear is their sail. It is filled with gas, and when the sun shines strong and their silver-blue sails dry out, a nervous reflex forces them to turn on their sides to wet them. For the jellyfish it is self-defense, for when their helmets dry out, they wrinkle and collapse like empty balloons. It is a singular phenomenon of the sea, this Portuguese man-of-war— *Physalia*. It is made up of a community of tiny animals, of thousands of little individual creatures who have all developed special functions. Zoologists call this type of colony of living forms *siphonophora*—a grouping of translucent, beautifully colored, floating ocean forms. On the surface of the water they show only their beauty, but under the surface the jellyfish carries a field of burning tentacles that turns the Portuguese man-of-war into a floating island of piracy and murder. Not all these tentacles perform the same function; some are there to kill and eat, while others are there to lay eggs and nurture them. This trail of tentacles, or streamers as they are sometimes called, can grow to the extraordinary length of ninety feet, and in a storm it acts as a steadying sea anchor.

On the high seas I watched a dolphin investigate a tentacle field; it hunted a fish that had taken refuge there and appeared to be immune to the stinging streamers. Not so the dolphin, who was burned, and quickly retreated from the field. I would not give one cent for the life of an underwater swimmer caught in a bed of these burning tentacles. I have often been stung by little pieces of these streamers that the surf has torn from the parent body and that have lodged on a coral reef; it feels like boiling tar poured on the skin, and even picric acid applied at once does not alleviate the pain.

After two weeks the ocean was still so calm that I could see, deep in the water, a swarm of dolphins mingling with their pilot fish. The shrouds had rusted and streaked the sail a pale yellow, so I decided to wrap them in sailing yarn. I was standing on the deck, working on this project, when I heard a loud splash before the bow and saw dolphins swimming for cover to the *Liberia*. My eye was caught by the passing shadow of a large fish. Another time, a periscope broke the flat surface, perhaps the arm of an octopus or the head of a turtle. It happened fast, and when I came closer, the periscope was discreetly submerged. The sea was alive; gelatinous masses floated everywhere, mixed with plankton and the excrement of whales. Only the trade winds had died.

I had to wait for my sixteenth day for a change. On that day heavy cloud banks approached from the north, followed by the longed-for wind. Shearwaters took a new lease on life, playing in the water like children and running lightly over the waves on their yellow feet until they were drawn into the air by the wind. Their cry resembled a goat's bleat rather than the song of a bird, and they did not charm me so much as the smaller stormy petrels; but they had the advantage of keeping me busy for a long time trying to classify them. Finally, after checking carefully in *Birds of the Ocean* by Alexander, I decided that my companions were the Mediterranean shearwaters, *Puffinus kuhli,* the largest Atlantic shearwater. Although they stayed near the *Liberia,* they showed no curiosity about her, seldom bothering to turn around and look at her. I did not find it easy to classify shearwaters and petrels from my small boat; if I had had weapons, I could have shot them and made accurate identifications then and there. Instead, I took color pictures and made my identification later.

Now the trade winds blew as they are reputed to, and I sailed westward. Squalls rushed over the sea and forced me to concentrate on handling the boat. I no longer saw much sea life; a few swarms of flying fish leaped into the air, fleeing dolphins, the sea birds became livelier, but plankton and water striders disappeared into the rough seas.

On the eighteenth day, the wind veered to the northwest—often a danger signal—clouds and sea merged and the horizon drew threateningly close. Crests of white foam capped the surface as the old trade winds and the winds of the new storm met and battled for control of the waves. At first the *Liberia* stuck obstinately to the old wave course, but with the help of my paddle I forced her into line. Moments such as these, when two wind directions meet head on with full power, can be extremely dangerous for small boats. I was relieved when the new winds took control of the waves and they became regular. Later that afternoon, the tornado—as squalls are sometimes called on the West African coast—had passed and the trade winds blew again. I was happy to see them despite the acute discomfort they caused. Whenever they blew with any degree of strength, I was wet—water dripped off my beard and ran down my neck, my sunglasses were blurred, and my drenched clothes clung to my body. The continual wet increased the soreness of my buttocks, which burned so intensely that I could hardly bear to put any weight on them.

On that same day—my eighteenth—I threw overboard the last of my oranges and apples; they had all rotted. Up to now the fruit had supplied me with all the liquid I needed. I was never thirsty and my intestines functioned beautifully. After the fruit ran out, I switched to a daily liquid intake of fourteen ounces of evaporated milk and a mixture of one and a half pints of mineral water and a bit less than a half pint of red wine, which I kept cool in a canteen wrapped in wet cloth. The raw onion I ate every day constituted my vitamin intake, and it was evidently enough, for I developed no symptoms of scurvy, such as bleeding gums, throughout the entire voyage. Columbus on his voyages took with him onions from the Canary Islands. Although he knew nothing of scurvy, he knew how to prevent the bleeding gums and loss of teeth that occur on long sea trips. Arab friends once told me proudly that long before the English gave limes to their sailors to prevent scurvy, Arabs always carried them on their dhows.

In addition to my daily ration of a fist-sized onion and a can of meat, I ate two small mouthfuls of honey at nine in the morning and at four in the afternoon. Honey has been prized for its restorative powers since ancient times and, like red wine, belongs to the old-fashioned family doctor's prescription for convalescents. I had brought it with me to give me added strength. Once in a while I ate the barnacles that grew on the *Liberia* or a triggerfish or dolphin I managed to catch. For centuries sailors have known that the sea can supply them with meat at any time. More recently the founder of the Oceanographic Museum in Monaco has added scientific weight to this belief by saying that shipwrecked people need not die of hunger if they have with them fishing tackle and a harpoon. Alain Gerbeault came to the same conclusion after he had sailed alone from Gibraltar to New York in 1923, and the experience of those shipwrecked in wartime tends to confirm this theory. There is for example, the case of Poon Lim, a Chinese sailor, whose ship, the S.S. *Ben Lomond* was torpedoed in the narrows of the Atlantic between Africa and Brazil. He spent 134 days afloat on a raft. His food supplies lasted only fifty-one days, and thereafter he subsisted entirely on fish, birds and rain water. He was eventually picked up by Brazilian fishermen and was still able to walk.

During my days of calms I had sailed through a sea that resembled bouillabaisse from Marseilles or a soup of fish eggs. Now that the trade winds blew, the soup had greasy waves. There were times when I grew alarmed at the violence with which the dugout rolled and lurched in the turbulent ocean. On the whole, however, I felt secure; my new rudder was strong, and the heavy following seas could do no real damage.

On the twenty-third day I spotted a white sail on the horizon. I assumed it was my friend Jean Lacombe, who had planned to sail from Las Palmas a few days after me. We had decided on a southern route and then a westward course along the nineteenth degree latitude in the expectation of a mid-Atlantic rendezvous. My heart lightened at the sight of the yacht and at the prospect of a brief respite from the discomforts of the *Liberia*. At nine o'clock, I prepared for my visit to Jean's boat; by ten, I had begun to wonder; by eleven, I was certain I had made a mistake. Jean's *Hippocampe* was smaller than the boat I saw and did not sail under a double spinnaker. As the yacht drew closer, I saw she was the *Bernina* from Basle. She came alongside under motor, and the crew asked me if I needed anything. After my "no-thank-you" they sailed on. Later I found out that the *Bernina* had made it in twenty-eight days across the ocean from Las Palmas to Barbados—a fine contribution to sailing, because she, too, had been hindered by little wind.

For two more days the wind blew with strength, and then on the twenty-sixth it veered, first to the east, shortly thereafter to the southeast, and finally to the south. Soon the wind died, and the waves, subjects of the kingdom of the winds, flattened—only the ever-present high Atlantic swell remained.

The heart of the swell lies in the storm region of the North Atlantic. From there it is pumped southward throughout the ocean. The swell is dangerous only when it combines with rough winds at the beginning of a storm and throws up giant combers; now all was calm around me and I slipped into the water. My quick trip into the ocean brought to mind the story of the single-handed sailor whose boat had started on an independent course while he was swimming. Fortunately, such independence was not a part of the *Liberia*'s character. She was as attached to me as barnacles were to her. I did, however, take the added precaution of swimming with flippers to give me speed. There were many times during the trip when I raged at my *Liberia*, when she caused me more sorrow and anger than amusement or pleasure, but still I admired her. She was beautiful and she had character.

There was no wind from the east, no wind from the south and only an isolated, infrequent gust from the west. Occasional local squalls swept over my shaky boat, so that I had to handle her carefully, but not until the twenty-ninth day was there any real change in the weather. On that day, a menacing wall of cloud gathered its forces in the west, swept quickly toward me with ominous aspect. I took in the sails, put out the sea anchor and sought refuge in my hole.

I was awakened by a noise like thunder. My first sleepy reaction was that I was being called upon as a doctor to help in an emergency; then I realized I was in the *Liberia* in mid-Atlantic. A shark had wakened me by banging against my boat. Like a comfortable citizen, disturbed at his noonday nap, I was enraged at the shark's lack of consideration. I pulled out the Leica and took his picture. He was not impressed. He slunk along the starboard side, a little on one side and inspected the boat. He disgusted me with his wide, cynical mouth and small pig eyes, which seemed the essence of greed. He was nearly fifteen feet long and such a giant that he appeared heavier than the pirogue. I pulled out my movie camera, pressed the button . . . but nothing happened. I tried again with no result; the camera had rusted and filming for this voyage was finished. The shark slunk off, taking with him my following of little pilot fish. As a farewell gesture, he splashed the bow with water with a flip of his huge tail. I watched my faithless pilot fish dart nervously around their new host, thinking to myself how human they were with their characteristic of attaching themselves to those that can give them the most. When I began to steer again, I found the rudder did not work. The shark's blows had broken both port-side cables that controlled the steering. If my rudder had been less secure, the blow might have had more serious results. I replaced the torn cables with strong wire, an easy job now that the storm had passed, and no wind blew. Later I strengthened the other cables, in case another shark should decide to use the rudder as a target. From now on I gave up steering with my feet, as I could only do it in calm weather when I had no need to. In windy or stormy weather, I had to sit on the washboard and hold the tiller to balance the boat. To keep my boat as dry as possible, I closed up the small holes in the hull that I had made for the foot-steering cables.

Still the wind came from the west. I decided that the pirogue would make better time on its own, riding the westward current, so I let the sea anchor take over. The halyard to the square sail was frayed, and to keep myself occupied, I decided to replace it. I tied the ends of the old and new halyards together, but the old one broke near the top and fell to the deck. What was I to do now? I couldn't take down the mast because its base had swollen fast in the deck. If I climbed the mast, the pirogue would capsize. Finally, I came up with a solution. I tied the halyard loosely to the grappling iron and wrapped wire around its end to stiffen it. Then, standing at the base of the twelve-foot mast, I reached up and threaded the line through the block with ease. But to my irritation, I found I could not free the iron. "Patience," I counseled myself, "there is more than enough time." The canoe bobbed about in the high swell, but after several hours of painstaking, steady concentration, I finished threading the halyard through the mast block; I pushed with my left hand and drew it through with my right. The job, performed under a broiling sun, had taken every ounce of will power and patience I possessed, and when I had completed it, I rewarded myself with a double ration of wine and water.

I was now close to the middle of the Atlantic. Only the swell disturbed the absolute calm of the ocean. I sailed through a gigantic aquarium of floating plankton, of water striders that zigzagged around me, and of triggerfish that nibbled at my barnacles.

None of the fish I saw gave me greater pleasure than that funny creature the triggerfish. I had my first visit from triggerfish when I sailed into the tropic of Cancer, and they consoled me for the lack of wind. I had been watching, with mounting irritation, the sail flap idly to and fro, when my attention was caught by these little fish popping out of the water. They waddled around the *Liberia*, matching her clumsiness. Triggerfish do not hunt other fish, but subsist on parasites or any flotsam and jetsam they find. From my boat they had luxury meals of barnacles, but their usual source of food is plankton. They followed me all the way across the ocean, waddling along behind the canoe in calm weather, like baby ducklings behind their mother.

Alone and bored in mid-Atlantic, I talked to the triggerfish, at times in friendship, at times in anger. My attitude toward them depended on the weather: "Good morning, my friends, and how is everything with you today?"—but then, when the trade winds refused to blow, I screamed at them, called them thieves for stealing the barnacles from the *Liberia* and ordered them to leave. That they neither heard nor understood did not bother me; it was enough for me that I had someone to talk at, I did not need an answer. Sharks and dolphins grant triggerfish a safe-conduct pass and never attack them, but I was not so kind and killed them with my spear whenever I could. When they are in danger, triggerfish push up their dorsal fins—it is from this trick that they derive their name—but they do not fight back. If they are fished out of the water, they turn pale and give one shocked grunt; because of this sailors have nicknamed them "old women."

I did not kill for the sake of killing but to enrich my knowledge of the sea; all of us who have sailed the Atlantic can add to man's knowledge, if only in small details that may eventually form the basis of a scientific formulation of our combined experiences.

Triggerfish meat has reputedly poisoned people, so I approached mine cautiously. I ate a little less than an ounce the first time, gradually increasing the amount so that within a few weeks I was able to eat a whole one-pound fish. I suffered no ill effects. Fishermen of the Caribbean islands know that poisonous triggerfish are caught on one side of an island and harmless ones on the opposite side of the same island; it seems likely, therefore, that these fish are safe to eat unless they themselves happen to have eaten poisonous plants or fish. I know that barracuda, which we ate as a delicacy in West Africa, is considered unsafe to eat in the Antilles or the Pacific. Also, the fact that poisonous fish are less likely to occur on the high seas gave me confidence in my experiment with triggerfish meat.

Although my primitive way-of-life on the *Liberia* had coarsened my taste buds, I could still detect a difference between the flesh of a dolphin and that of a triggerfish; the former is tender and tasteless and the latter is tough, salty and slightly bitter. Of course, since the loss of my Primus stove at the beginning of the voyage, I had to eat everything raw. I had no aversion to raw meat; as a matter of fact I found that the organs tasted better raw than cooked. Sometimes I added flavor to my fish with salt water in the Polynesian manner.

Every speared triggerfish had in its stomach barnacles from the bottom of the boat, most of them still bearing traces of the supposedly poisonous red paint. Sometimes twenty or more congregated under the *Liberia,* excitedly nibbling the barnacles, then surfacing with a quick, explosive "tsh-tsh," either a belch or an expression of pleasure, before they returned to their meal. After I had speared one, his companions craftily stayed close to the rudder or bow where I could not reach them.

During the first seven weeks on board, while the calm weather lasted, I spent a great deal of time in the water with goggles and flippers. I was careful to keep a look-out for sharks, but they were busy elsewhere; I substituted as host to two small shark-following pilot fish. Groups of these nervous little fish were often to be found swimming around the boat, changing daily, so that one day my following would be tiny blue-striped fish and the next larger green pilot fish. There was only one faithful pilot, who stayed with me for fourteen days, making his home close by the rudder. When I swam in the water, he entertained me with his antics, but was careful to stay at a safe distance.

I had heard many stories in my life, about the ravages of man-eating sharks. I had only half believed them on dry land, but once in the water—and vulnerable—everything seemed possible. As I swam around the *Liberia* one day, a dark shadow on the starboard side of the boat caught my eye, and I drew myself quickly up from the fearful regions of the water into the shelter of the cockpit.

On the thirtieth day I had the pleasure and excitement of seeing my first school of small whales. I watched them surface and blow water-laden air from their lungs. Even in the humidity of the tropics this warm water vapor is visible to the naked eye. Each variety of whale has its characteristic spout, which enabled whalers to tell them apart. When whales surface from a great depth, they take several shallow, quick dives to enrich their blood with oxygen, and this is exactly what my group of little whales was doing. They took deep breaths and disappeared for several minutes. Large whales can stay under the surface for over an hour and dive to the depth of half a mile or more, but, like men, they are vulnerable in the water. I remember an incident that occurred in 1932 off the coast of Colombia, when a sperm whale got caught in a telegraph cable at a depth of over three thousand feet and drowned.

The next day the wind from the northwest was still slight, although clouds, pulled into long strips by the wind, appeared here and there in the sky. A painful boil had developed on my neck and caused my glands to swell. Smaller boils appeared on my thighs, due, I think, to dampness, and I had to take aureomycin for three days before they disappeared.

During this calm weather, that tried my patience and hindered my progress, I kept to a set daily routine that helped pass the time. Every day, at midday, I took my noon position—next to staying afloat, the single most important job on a boat—and then put the sextant, that precious instrument, very carefully back in its wooden box. Sometimes splashes of water had wet it, and then it had to be dried in the sun before I packed it away again. It took me only a few seconds to figure out the latitude and then another few minutes to arrive at the longitude, by means of the time difference between Greenwich time and my time. The accuracy of my calculations reflected the condition of the sea: the higher the waves, the less accurate the results. In calm spells my logbook frequently noted the same latitude for several days. With my navigation completed, I took a sun bath and spread out around me my brief case, books, cameras, clothes and blanket; even my valuable onions shared the sun with me. Despite these precautionary drying-out periods, my cameras rusted.

The sky was seldom the azure blue it is over the Mediterranean; in fact, the intense humidity often turned it into a leaden gray. On windless days the rays of the sun pierced the overcast with tropical intensity, and I sat with a wet towel draped over head and shoulders. Still, I sweat more than was good for my health. My skin began to show the effects of dehydration, and on dry days I increased my ration of liquids. Although I was not necessarily more thirsty than usual, I knew that thirst is not an accurate measurement of a body's need for liquids, and under conditions like mine, one has to drink more than one thinks necessary.

At four o'clock I ate—a can of meat and an onion. To relieve the monotony of my diet, I served myself beef one day and pork the next; I always drank an apéritif of wine and water. In the evening, as the hours dragged by, I sat and licked at my weekly ration of honey. On days that brought discouragement and loneliness, I cheered myself by eating a whole pound of honey at one sitting. With the setting of the sun, the temperature would drop and I would put on more clothing; when the wind was strong I even wore a cap for protection against the cold. In the last light, I would write my final entries into the logbook.

My narrow canoe rolled and yawed so badly that I usually took in the gaff sail and went under square sail at night. The sun pointed his last golden finger into the sky, the evening star appeared and there—suddenly—the *Liberia* and I floated alone in the tropical night. The air cooled, and no matter how much clothing I piled on, I shivered and rheumatic pains shot through me. Tropical nights are long, and at sunset I faced a long period of inactivity; on my tiny boat there was nothing to do but sit and think. These night hours, therefore, seemed doubly long, lonely and frustrating; I could only wait in enforced inactivity for them to pass. But I delighted in watching the drama of the clouds; I traced pictures in their shapes. I watched as dogs and horses were chased across the sky by gnarled and twisted apparitions from Hades, to be replaced in a few minutes by magnificent cloud trees. Then, as a mass of clouds streaked across the sky, shapes, pictures and outlines would dissolve into pitch-black night.

During the night my subconscious—constantly aware of potential danger—exaggerated everything: shadows of great waves menaced me; breakers loomed high, frighteningly large; and the *Liberia* sped too fast through the water. When the combers overwhelmed me by their size, I did not sail at night; instead I threw over the sea anchor, took in the gaff and square sail and lashed them to the deck. I drew my spray cover over the iron arch I had built to keep the wind from blowing around my bare toes and crept onto the packing cases, put my head on a seabag and slept; that is to say, I napped in short intervals, depending on the weather outside. Even in sleep, I was alert to possible danger and always awoke at the first splash of water into the boat, as a mother wakes at the first cry of her child. When the wind was favorable and allowed me to sail I never slept more than five and sometimes only three hours. When the waves were fierce or the wind contrary, I managed twelve hours of sleep—with breaks for bailing, of course.

I knew from past experience that my life depended on sleep, that without it I was incapable of being sufficiently alert for safety. My attack of delirium in the Gulf of Guinea had taught me that lack of sleep is often the biggest single danger a lonely sailor faces. I was determined not to allow it to happen to me again.

Everything I did on the *Liberia* depended on the wind. When no progress was possible because of stiff winds or a calm, I slept until dawn. With favorable winds, I was up at two in the morning. My first morning chore was to bail. Then I hauled in the sea anchor, whose line was often covered with particles of bioluminescent plankton. The next step was to set the square sail. This was no easy job in a strong wind; the sail had to go around the shrouds in the forward part of the boat so that the wind would suddenly fill the six square yards of canvas. Then the canoe would respond by lying over on her side. Sometimes I was afraid I might capsize, and now and then I was forced to drop the sail into the water to right the boat. A near miss like this in the middle of the night always startled me, and I usually waited until daylight to hoist the gaff sail. I had resolved at the beginning of the voyage not to lose my temper or shout when something went wrong, but often after a misadventure I had to remind myself again of my resolve.

During the morning, my mind and body refreshed by sleep, the

524

hours passed quickly; I observed the life of the sea around me, daydreamed and did my exercises. I did knee bends, massaged my legs and executed a—albeit stationary—walk in the cockpit. At nine every morning I drank a fourteen-and-a-half-ounce can of evaporated milk.

A whole month went in this fashion: small squalls, calms broken by an occasional good wind. I waited, hoping for a good wind that would take me across the Atlantic and, at last, on the thirty-second day, November 27th, the trade winds came to my rescue. The red-billed tropic birds and petrels took a new lease on life. Mediterranean shearwaters paid me their last visit; I saw them no more for the rest of the trip. In the evening a shark swam close to the pirogue, dousing me with a flip of his tail. In the pale moonlight he looked as evil as his reputation. Perhaps he sensed my revulsion, for he said his good night quickly.

The trade winds blew vigorously for two days. Night sailing became dangerous, so I put out the sea anchor and went to bed with the start of darkness. The waves pushed me forward. I thought of them as my persecutors; powerful and mighty, they attempted again and again to change the course of the *Liberia*. They were especially dangerous and importunate going down wind; then the canoe yawed and rolled, moved from starboard to port, luckily never making a real sideways jump. I knew the *Liberia* well by now and would not tolerate any tricks from her. I kept my hand steadily on the tiller, ready to yield or to oppose as the occasion demanded. I allowed her very little freedom because I knew she could not handle it.

I remember a completely unforeseen moment of danger that occurred during those days, as the sea roared and stormed and foam danced on the surface. Swell and wave met, and giant mountains of water rolled under the pirogue, broke head on with a loud roar and left a flat foam-scarred surface behind them. I exulted in my speed and in the frothing wake of the *Liberia*. The boat skimmed over the seas, and I had her well in hand, I thought, as she sailed flat before the wind. I was careful not to look back. The noise and froth looked more dangerous behind me than ahead of me. So I sat still, keeping my eye on the square sail and on the passing seas. Then it happened. A giant sea heaved the stern higher—higher—higher, and the bow dug deeper—deeper into the water. I clutched the tiller. I held my breath. The sea broke aft with a crash and the *Liberia,* for one frightening instant, stood on her head. Then she righted herself, and the sea passed under her. I was safe, but the fright that had gripped me left me weak and nauseated. My stomach refused to settle down. I knew how easily a small boat can capsize. To calm myself I threw out the sea anchor, took down the sail and breathed deeply. Although the average height of the waves was only eighteen to twenty-four feet, occasional larger ones, measuring anywhere from thirty to forty feet, rolled by, and when these mountains of water broke, the resulting roar chilled and shook me.

I had been afraid that, as the voyage progressed and I consumed my food stores, the *Liberia* might become too light. As a precautionary measure, I had put all empty bottles, jars and cans in the bilge water behind the aft seat. The constant and terrible roll of the dugout made the empty containers glug and gurgle as the water in them rose and fell. To me they sounded like the voices of men and women; they shouted and whispered, laughed and giggled, tittered, coughed and mumbled. Their voices became so clear that I finally joined in the discussions. But no one seemed to care very much for my opinions; they laughed at me and kept on in their own strange language. Hurt, I no longer added my voice to theirs; I was convinced I had been wronged. Later I had my revenge. I took the water out of the stern bilge and thereafter only an infrequent sad, quiet sigh floated up to me.

The trade winds that blew at the end of my first month at sea brought with them quick, scurrying squalls. Menacing banks of clouds, reaching down into the horizon, would darken the sky and hurl buckets and buckets of water at me. I began to dislike the sight of these clouds that portended rain, not because I dislike rain, but because it fell upon us with such force that the pirogue lay over to one side. I was always forced to take down the sails. I hated and dreaded these mid-Atlantic squalls that exposed the weaknesses of my boat, leaving me impotent in the face of their brutal strength. Not a day went by that I was not menaced by one; sometimes they enveloped me; at other times, in a kindlier mood, they left me out of their play.

On the thirty-fifth day red-billed tropic birds flew over me ceaselessly. The next day only one came, and then for seven days, they left me alone. I missed them. Their unabashed appraisals of my boat always gave me pleasure; they never flew over the *Liberia* until they had given her a careful scrutiny. Then they swooped over me in curves, yip-yapping back and forth to each other. I was sorry I could not understand their comments on myself and the boat. These birds, who limit their flying range to the tropics, were to me the most charming of all sea birds. I could recognize them from afar by their high flight and the steady pigeonlike flapping of their wings. As they approached, I was even surer of their identity; for they sport long tail feathers, and a salmon red touch on their wings, a lobster-colored beak, a black band near their eyes and black stripes on their wings—easily distinguishable markings. They are the same size as gulls, but unlike them, they fly high above the water's surface, flapping their wings in untiring energy. Only once did I see a "son of the sun"—as Linnaeus, the eighteenth-century Swedish botanist, named them—rest on the water.

On the thirty-seventh day, the wind veered from northeast to northwest. Such a change could mean danger, and I put out the sea anchor to give me stability. The sea roared, water rushed into the boat and I bailed frantically. I worked hard and worried hard all through the day. I was concerned not only about the weather but about my health, for my intestines were not functioning as I knew they should. I swallowed half a bottle of mineral oil in an attempt to solve this problem. In vain. Then I realized that my concentrated food did not contain enough roughage; my system knew exactly what it was doing, and I should stop interfering with its functioning.

That night the seas calmed and I was left rocking in a high swell. Triggerfish again harvested barnacles from the *Liberia*'s bottom, a new variety of shearwater performed in the sultry air, and water striders tried to scramble from the corkwood pads onto the side of the dugout. I came across these little insects of the sea quite often during the ensuing calm days. They are common, even in mid-

Atlantic. Their ability to stay on the surface of the water reminded me of childhood experiments when we floated an oil-covered needle on top of water.

The *Liberia* and I had now been afloat for forty-one days and the time had come to take stock of my situation. Back in Las Palmas I had estimated—and thought myself generous—that forty days would see me in the Antilles. But now I knew my generosity had been inadequate, for here I was, still bobbing around in the middle of the ocean. For seventeen days I had had contrary winds that had done their best to push me off my westward course, and ten days of only slight wind had afforded an excellent opportunity for a closer acquaintance with the life of the sea, but had brought me little nearer to my goal. The Atlas of Pilot Charts had promised me trade winds, but as I found out later from other sailors who made the crossing at the same time, the wind conditions that particular year were not normal. They forced me to relinquish my plan of a non-stop voyage from Las Palmas to Haiti and to decide on a closer goal. I chose St. Thomas in the Virgin Islands. I did not feel easy in my mind about the rest of the voyage, for I was haunted by a fear of further contrary winds that would strain my calculations to the utmost. But there wasn't anything I could do to alter whatever the weather had in store; certainly brooding and worrying would not get me one mile closer to the Americas.

I vented my anger and frustration at the delay by spearing dolphins, and cutting them up. At one point I had tried catching them by throwing out a metal fish lure, but the dolphins were far too wise to bite. So I invented another game to play with them that would occupy my mind; I cut up a speared dolphin, strung its vertebrae on a nylon thread and threw it into the water. Within seconds, its living brethren had devoured the meat. I hung out more and the dolphins followed me, like a swarm of begging children behind a tourist; I held a piece in my fingers over the water, and—snap—the most courageous bit it right out of my hand. I kept on at this game; my canoe followers were insatiable. In their excitement their dorsal fins moved up and down, and they fell furiously on their prey, oblivious to all danger.

The trade winds blew unenthusiastically for the next few days.

Little drops of fish blood on the tarpaulin smelled so badly in the tropical heat that I had to scrub it thoroughly. I enjoyed a cooling bath in the waters of the mid-Atlantic. I watched tropic birds fly by and wondered if they could be my first messengers from America. I wasn't sure. They could have followed me from the Cape Verde Islands or they could be welcoming me to the Caribbean. As their numbers increased in the following weeks, I began to be certain that they were messengers from the New World.

On my forth-sixth day I was shaken by an untoward occurrence. The trade winds blew stiff, and I had not dared hoist the sails during the night. At intervals I crept into the cockpit and bailed. Suddenly, only a few hundred yards away, a great lighted steamer came across my course. The sea anchor aft with some thirty yards of line plus the length of my boat made a vulnerable "beam" of about thirty-eight yards. It was a bad moment for myself and the *Liberia*. The danger passed, but it left me in a brooding mood. I thought with envy of the crew—of their dry clothes, their foam rubber mattresses, and of their dreams of their next shore leave. In contrast, my *Liberia* offered no physical comfort and demanded a constant watchfulness; at a moment's notice my whole being had to be ready to do its utmost to keep her from capsizing. The steamer, plowing powerfully through the water on its way from New York to Capetown, so solid and secure, depressed me. But I knew I was there—alone—of my own free will. Even during my worst hours, when I felt most deeply discouraged, this knowledge helped me.

Again I was persecuted by squalls. I would not have disliked them so much if I could have caught their rain, but my boat rolled too much to make that possible. One must have a beamier boat to be able to collect rain water. Once (unfortunately, only once) I found two tiny flying fish on my deck in the morning. My boat was also too narrow for this excellent source of free food. Occasionally other flying fish "flew" onto the deck or sail during the night, but they always fell back into the water.

My hands were in bad shape; the calluses had worn off and left them sore and open. I was forced to wrap them in a towel or a sock before I could touch anything. My skin mutinied, too, by breaking out in boils. Two of them made it impossible for me to sit in comfort, and one on my thigh made my foot swell. For three days I took two aureomycin capsules every six hours. My physical condition and my concern over the weather led to moments of deep depression and frustration. During my worst moments I found myself singing—songs from my childhood and student days; when the sea was rough, they turned into monotonous chants. I often heard myself repeating, for hours, the opening bar of one song. I had come to a point where the world beyond my horizon no longer existed. Here at sea other forces ruled my life; I was alone with God, alone with nature, alone in remoteness and solitude. Yet I experienced none of that sense of loneliness—that "cosmic feeling of solitude" as it has been called—that can afflict us in the presence of other human beings. Loneliness weighed on me no more than it does on a healthy child. Like a child, I peopled nature with my friends. I talked with tropic birds and addressed remarks to water striders skating over the surface. Conversing with nature calmed me.

Now the trade winds blew briskly and night combers raced by the *Liberia*. Even my stomach churned at times. Squalls darkened the foaming waters, while banked clouds scurried across the sky in all directions. My fish deserted me in the heavy seas.

In those days of stiff wind, the setting of the square sail required a great deal of patience. A couple of times I had to let it fall into the water in order not to have the canoe capsize. Despite the high seas, I took my noon position; I had to be sure that I was not drifting too far to the south, where trade winds blow up storms that last much longer than those in the north.

On the morning of the fifty-fifth day my flashlight went overboard. I had put it inside the life belt which was lashed onto the deck in front of me, but at a roll from the *Liberia*, it fell into the water. The speed with which this occurred made me realize, with a sinking sensation, how easily it could happen to me. With my flashlight gone, I had to hoist the sail in darkness without being able to check the lines. The results were unhappy; the jib fell into the water, its line broken. Instantly I threw out the sea anchor and cut down the sail. The new blocks I had put on the mast in Las Palmas, to save weight, had frayed the line. I sailed that day with only a gaff sail; but the best gaff cannot replace a jib, and I found the sailing very tricky. Despite the trade winds, wind and waves came at me from more than one direction, and the high swell, surging from the north, combined with the wind from the northeast and rocked the canoe athwart. Then a sudden breeze would blow from the southeast, throwing the boom from port to starboard. It was dangerous sailing that demanded constant and exhausting care and watchfulness from me.

The wind died down the next day. I was then able to replace the broken line. My previous experience with a similar task helped me, and I did it much faster this second time.

In mid-Atlantic I had had petrels with me constantly. Now I was leaving them behind. At twilight on the fifty-eighth day, in a symbolic gesture of farewell, the last one flew against my sail. I never saw any again, although they are not unknown in the Caribbean. Early on the fifty-ninth day, as I was setting the sails, the jib line ran out of my hands. It hung in the air, and as I climbed to the bow to catch it, I looked up and saw my first "Americans," two frigate birds, circling in the air above me. They were the first sure messengers from the continent that lay ahead. I knew that these birds are seldom seen more than one hundred miles offshore, and their presence raised my hopes. Was it possible that I might reach Antigua by Christmas?

In the soft light of early morning these frigate birds or man-o'-war birds looked even blacker to me than their plumage and their reputation warranted. Like eagles, they circled menacingly in the sky, ready, when they spotted their prey, to plummet to the surface of the water, with their fork-shaped tails spread, grabbing for their food with long hooked beaks or sharp claws. I watched them hunt dolphins and catch flying fish that had been chased into the air. The long-winged frigates are sea birds that cannot rest on water, for they need an elevation to rise into the air. They generally spend their night on shore, where they sit, vulture-like, gathering their strength for the next day's hunting.

At noon on the fifty-ninth day the trade winds failed. What little strength they had appeared to derive from occasional rain squalls. This delay as I was nearing my goal became almost insupportable to me.

On December 24th the winds remained unchanged. Here I was

531

in the most accurately predictable weather system in the world, but, as elsewhere, the forecasts proved false. Morning brought eight frigate birds, and at noon I heard the drone of a plane. I knew then that I would reach Antigua the same day. My Christmas present to myself. I sailed on with renewed hope and vigor until late that night. But no welcome lights rose through the darkness before me. I began to doubt the accuracy of my chronometer. I wondered if my longitude were wrong. Still, I sailed on. At two o'clock the next morning a squall brought thunder and lightning; at three, the storm ended, and I saw two lights rise and fall behind the high swell. Steamers? Fishing boats? I could barely see them through the enveloping darkness. Were they, perhaps, the two lighthouses of Antigua? According to my noon position, they lay before my bow. Then, at four that morning, I saw lights that shone from a high point of land and I knew I had reached Antigua. Behind those lights, I thought to myself, someone is celebrating a tropical Christmas; so I set the sea anchor, took in the sail and looked around for some way of celebrating on my own. All I had left was canned milk and honey, but in my jubilant mood it was enough. I was the first to cross the Atlantic alone in a dugout canoe, and I had achieved my goal at Christmas. I could not imagine a more welcome present.

As I drank my cocktail of milk and honey in my dugout paradise, my thoughts turned to Christmas, to Antigua and to the people who sat behind the bright lights while wet trade winds hurled through the night. It was now five in the morning. Were they still awake in their homes? At least their lights shone at me through their windows. And it was America and Christmas morning. So I began to sing "Silent Night" and "O Tannenbaum."

I listened for the welcome sound of surf, but the trade winds carried it to the west. I left the decision whether to sail north or south of Antigua in the hands of the current. It took me south, so in the early dawn I set sail for the southeast cape of the island. It lay before me, cloudless in the sea. Then slowly the hills collected a white cap of cloud and anchored it there. These island clouds are visible for many miles, for they rest, immobile and heavy, on the mountains; unlike the light, fast, white trade-wind clouds, they are not easily driven off by the winds. Only a bad storm has the force to move them.

When the sun rose on the chain of Caribbean islands that stretched before me, I noticed a curious phenomenon: these islands were linked by clouds that ran from Barbuda to Antigua, and from there to southwestern Montserrat, which suffocated in heavy clouds.

I sailed close to shore, hoping to see the famous harbor where Nelson had anchored, in hiding, for several years. I was unable to catch a view of it, but I admired the green hills, pretty bungalows and white beaches that lead down to cobalt waters. The sight—my first sight of land—awoke in me a mood of irresponsibility; I felt childishly gay and playful. Around the *Liberia* floated pieces of wood, put there by fishermen to mark their lobster pots; to me they symbolized human life and activity, a sign that I was no longer alone in the world.

As I sailed southwest of Antigua, the wind brought me the smell of balmy land air, reminding me of dry grass and hay. I was suddenly overwhelmed by a longing to set foot on land. I started to calculate when I could expect to reach St. Thomas. With mild trade winds, I thought, I might arrive in time to celebrate my birthday on December 28th. But the wind, refusing to cooperate, took a holiday. In the meantime, I hunted for a can of rye bread I had stowed aft. I had brought it with me to eat shortly before reaching land, in preparation for a fuller, richer diet. It served its function, for later changes in my diet brought no intestinal complications.

The *Liberia* wove her way slowly to the west. The following morning I stood south of Nevis, which lay before me, bare of clouds; but as I watched, a fresh cloud cap collected over the three-thousand-foot crater and, within minutes, grew into a beautiful white wreath. As I sailed east of Nevis I saw all the more northerly islands; even the farthest, Saba, was visible in a murky spot of cloud. I sailed on slowly, passing St. Kitts, shrouded in mist. To the north, St. Eustatius, which had profited greatly during the American Revolution as a neutral free port, became clearer and clearer. Then I reached Saba, a crater rising sheer and sharp out of the water, and here I slept. It took me a whole day to get out of sight of this island; the trade winds were evidently uninterested in my idea of a birthday celebration in St. Thomas.

That night a West Indian sailing ship, bound for St. Kitts,

sleeked by. Then, on my birthday, I came in sight of St. Croix, but St. Thomas lay still further to the north. When I was northeast of St. Croix, the wind changed to the northwest, driving away all hope of reaching the other island. It became apparent that a storm was brewing; wind clouds rushed high into the blue sky, and the waters darkened. I held course as far west as I could, thereby gaining a favorable position for entering the harbor of Christiansted, the largest town in St. Croix. During the night the wind stiffened and the sea roared; at dawn I was happy to set my course for the harbor entrance. Slowly, slowly the deep, dark water changed to a shallow, light blue. Rocks gave the impression of lying only a few inches under the keel in the clear water, and I had to reassure myself by checking a special chart before I dared sail on. Before me the town straggled up the side of a hill; to starboard, a small island in the harbor grew bigger and bigger, sheltering in its lee some twenty yachts.

I sailed up to a wharf where Caribbean sailing vessels were loading and unloading, handed my line to the usual crowd of dockside loungers and stepped on shore.

5 THE LAST STORM

As I jumped ashore I was surrounded almost immediately by a large crowd. "Where do you come from?" they asked. "From Spain, from the Canary Islands, in sixty-five days," I answered. I was interrupted by the arrival of the harbor master, who asked me the same question. He found my answer hard to believe. "In *that?*" he asked incredulously, pointing at the *Liberia.* I explained to him that it had taken me nine weeks, but I could see that he still found it difficult to believe.

I now moored the canoe alongside a coastal freighter, changed into more suitable clothing and, identity papers in hand, set off for the harbor master's office. My knees were weak; the ground under my feet felt as liquid as the sea; I found I had difficulty walking a straight line. But, on the whole, I felt extremely well and, above all, jubilant at my safe arrival. A deep sense of well-being and achievement made it possible for me to ignore minor physical discomforts. The crowd that followed me asked several times if this were really my first landing, for I walked fast, carried myself well, even managing the steps up to the harbor master's office. I was examined by the doctor there, who certified that my general physical condition was good and that I had arrived without edemata. I was surprised

535

to find that I had lost only twelve pounds; I had counted on losing at least twenty. I attribute the smaller loss to the fresh fish I ate, which enabled me to stretch my canned rations.

That same evening I found myself strolling through town in the company of four new-found friends. In local fashion, we shuffled down the narrow streets to the rhythm of a marching steel band. I ate my first steak and, later, sat at a bar surrounded by elegantly clad tourists. And I found myself thinking, "How strange!" I had the feeling that I had been in those surroundings for weeks, whereas, for the past sixty-five days my life had been so different. I had been rolled and battered in a dugout canoe, utterly alone. My beard, a painful boil on my thigh and the many questions I had to answer were all that reminded me of my voyage.

I spent ten days in St. Croix, enjoying good food, good weather and human companionship again, while the *Liberia* rested at anchor in the harbor. Then, my brief vacation ended, I prepared for the departure; the sails were overhauled, the ropes spliced, and fresh onions stored on board. I had planned to slip quietly out of the harbor, but my kind and hospitable friends insisted on towing me out in full view of all the anchored boats in the harbor, so that my leave-taking was public and noisy. We were hailed by cheers and shouts of encouragement, by the banging of saucepans and blowing of whistles; not accustomed to such excitement, I was terribly embarrassed. I was further discomforted when, as we were pulling out of port, the old towline broke—my reward for being too penny-pinching. However, the damage was quickly repaired, and I was towed to one mile beyond the coral reef. Here, in a dead calm sea, the towing boat and I parted company. As I left, someone on board shouted across to me: "We will see you again soon!" This aspersion on my boat forced me to paddle for several hours, until I was sure that we would not meet again.

Yellow-brown sargasso weed floated on the surface. Though I had looked for it before I reached the Caribbean, it was not until I was south of Antigua that I first saw some. I had crossed the Atlantic just south of the Sea of Sargasso, so named from the Portuguese word for seaweed, *sargaçao*. In that giant area, forgotten by the trade winds and by the Gulf Stream, which cuts across the ocean just north of it, the weed grows in profusion. Millions of years ago, when life was only starting on land, it grew there, and it is more likely to survive a castastrophe of the earth than we are. During these millions of years, an animal world of its own has developed in the sargasso weed, and I was eager to observe what I could of it. I fished some out of the water. My attention was caught by the many little blisters that grew on the weed, for I could see no animal life. I chewed some of the berries and found that they tasted disappointingly like very salty slices of potato. I took another bunch out of the water, shook it out over the deck and found what I expected; an evil-looking caricature of a fish and some tiny dirty-yellow shrimp. Their ancestors had had sufficient time to develop protective coloring and to mimic the grotesque shapes of the weed itself; it was the art of camouflage at its best.

Among those Caribbean islands I made my first acquaintance with the American booby birds. They wear a milk-chocolate brown coat with a white shirt. They are coastal birds, bad swimmers but excellent divers, who shoot like arrows deep into the water to catch harmless, unsuspecting fish. I have been told that they sometimes miscalculate the depth of their dives and smash their heads on rocks below the surface. I was disappointed in their flight, which was solid and unimaginative, lacking the aerial gymnastics of the shearwaters. They are often the victims of the frigate birds, who swoop down on them and force them to regurgitate their catch.

Finally, a gentle breeze came up, and I was able to set the main-sail. The boom, swinging from side to side in the high swell, knocked my sunglasses into the water, but, for fear of losing the *Liberia,* I did not dare dive into the water after them. Two small sharks, barely the length of an arm swam curiously in the soft wake water. Irritated at the loss of my sunglasses, which resulted in my having to look directly into the sun, I was ready to vent my annoyance on the sharks. "Come closer," I commanded. Obediently, one of them drew nearer—and there—I ran my iron directly into his muscular head. But the fish, not in the mood for my game, hit the water dizzily with its tail fin, as if to rise in the air, and thrashed itself free. As the other shark approached, I smashed my spear down on its head. It was knocked out, but as soon as I had hauled it

537

on deck, it came to its senses and slipped into the water, where it paddled wildly around and then disappeared. I was horrified by what I had seen, but it bore out what I had heard of sharks' tenacity. They have been drawn out of the sea, disemboweled, returned to the sea, their intestines put on a fishing hook—and whom does one pull out of the water again? The very same animal, eagerly devouring its own intestines. This is no fishermen's yarn but an authoritative account by a leading ichthyologist.

My present goal was Ciudad Trujillo in the Dominican Republic, but that evening I was thwarted by a shift in wind from the east toward the southwest. Disappointed, I put out the sea anchor and lay down to sleep. By next morning the wind blew so vigorously from the southwest that I was forced to take down the mainsail. After I had shipped a great deal of water, I decided to change course and sail to the more northerly island of St. Thomas. Despite a rough sea, the next morning found me in front of the wooded mountains of St. Thomas. Above me, planes took off or landed every few minutes; to port I sailed past uninhabited rocky islands. The seaport of Charlotte Amalie lies deep in a bay, protected by several small islands. As I rounded one of them, using the western entrance to the harbor, I had my first view of red roofs climbing up the sheer sides of mountains, of white palaces, of mansions built of native stone, of gaily painted villas, surrounded by palm trees. Directly in front of me, a fishing smack docked at a quay. I slipped in beside it, berthing the canoe.

A palette of painted frame houses clustered around a small green-and-blue church facing the quay. Fishermen arrived and threw down their catch. The scene was picturesque, but I needed a less active anchorage. Finding none, I sailed on to the yacht basin in the eastern end of the large harbor. There I found friends from St. Croix, with whom I settled down to a long, chatty lunch. Most of them were yachtsmen who had sailed across the Atlantic in large yachts and could imagine, therefore, what it was to have been at sea for more than two months in a hollowed-out tree trunk. During a lively discussion of sailing and sailors, someone remarked accurately that "it takes a damn fool to sink a boat on the high seas." I was flattered when these knowledgeable yachtsmen made me an honorary member of the Virgin Islands Yacht Club; their yellow emblem with three red crowns, is one of the most valued souvenirs of my trip.

For a whole week the wind blew from the southwest. When it finally righted itself, I sailed off during the night, thereby avoiding another noisy send-off. Outside the harbor I met an east wind that carried me through the Virgin Passage toward the northwest. The United States has military bases here, which make it advisable to steer clear of the many little islands that dot the passage. With a perfect wind of fifteen miles an hour, I was able to sight the lights of San Juan by early evening. But there my progress ended, as the wind died. I was unable to enter the marvelous harbor. Instead, I lay down in the canoe, only poking my nose over the edge every few minutes to make sure no steamer came too close. The following morning the surface of the sea still looked as if it had been lacquered, so I made myself comfortable and slept. Awakened in the early afternoon by a gentle rippling, I found that the wind had come up from the northwest. This shift, which could be a portent of bad weather, made it advisable for me to sail through the ill-famed Mona Passage between Puerto Rico and the Dominican Republic as soon as possible. The present wind would blow me through.

That night the *Liberia* sailed westward toward the passage under jib alone. I think this was the third and last time during the whole voyage that the wind did me this rare favor. The canoe gained only a few miles, but that was not as important as the wonderful feeling that while I slept, the canoe worked for me. The next day I sailed around the northwest cape of Puerto Rico, which was brightly illuminated by an airport. Planes roared constantly over my head, and the lights of steamers passed to starboard.

That night the wind gods wished me well, pushing me through the tricky Mona Passage with a speed of four to five miles an hour. As I sailed, I was haunted to starboard by the small rocky Desecheo Island; sometimes it loomed close by, only to vanish suddenly and mysteriously. This was the only night of the entire voyage that I was unable to sleep or rest at all.

At dawn, standing south of Monito Rock, I could make directly

539

for the southern tip of the Dominican Republic. Gannets and tropic birds kept up a busy traffic between the two Spanish-speaking islands. The next night the *Liberia* entered a lagoon that lies between the island of Saona and the Dominican Republic; the waves flattened, the water changed from deep blue to cobalt and then to light blue cut by streaks of yellow-green and turquoise. There was so little depth here, that the rocks, coral sand and plants on the floor of the lagoon were clearly visible. A handful of huts stood at the entrance to the lagoon, and the inhabitants came out to gape in amazement at my strange craft. Several times my keel crunched on the sand, until I finally ran aground. At that point I was struck with the idea of getting a photo of my boat. I took my camera, stepped into knee-deep water and took the first picture of the *Liberia* under full sail.

As the darkness increased a cold north wind came up, forcing me to put on every available stitch of clothing. Lukewarm water splashed in my face. The next day the *Liberia* seesawed her way farther along a coast that gave the appearance of being untouched by human hand. The shrill cries of royal terns filled the air above me; frigate birds hovered patiently above them, waiting to snatch at their prey. Late that evening the lights of Ciudad Trujillo emerged behind a projecting cape. I threw out the sea anchor in the lee of the cape and lay down to sleep, only to awaken a few hours later to find that I had drifted far toward the west. The rest of the night and the following morning were spent tacking toward the entrance of the harbor. An ugly pelican, perched on a telegraph pole, sent pitying glances at the *Liberia* as she sailed up the Ozama River.

A harbor boat came alongside and offered to tow me in. "Not till the wind dies," I answered. The wind died away almost immediately after my proud answer, and I was forced to paddle upstream. A uniformed official, standing on the dock, ordered me over, and with the help of a rowboat, I managed to put the canoe alongside. I had been warned by American yachtsmen that officials in the Dominican Republic were likely to be obstructive and rude; so I was not surprised when the customs official shouted at me. In a few minutes, his chief arrived—dark-blond and slim, resplendent in a blue uniform complete with gun and holster in genuine wild-west style—and ordered me to his headquarters, where I proceeded under heavy escort. I kept my temper with difficulty, telling him that I had come to see the famous peace exhibition of Ciudad Trujillo, but that I would prefer to sail off at once if I was to be treated with such rudeness. The atmosphere became friendlier after the arrival of an acquaintance of mine, who vouched for me. Then the press came to interview me; curiously, the newspaper men appeared more impressed by my prowess as a linguist than as a sailor. In the meantime, smartly uniformed customs officers had examined my *Liberia* from stem to stern, inspecting empty fruit crates, canvas bags, and food supplies, even glancing through my books. After they left, I made order in the chaos, rescuing my underwear from the bilge water where it had been dropped, and closing up the bags. I berthed the canoe upstream, near a gaily painted shed marked, Club. From there I set out on a leisurely walk through the town, pausing in the harbor to admire a tree to which Columbus reputedly chained one of his caravels. In the center of town a guide steered me through the cathedral, Santa María, la Menor; he pointed out Columbus' bones, a point on which I was careful not to question him too closely, as I knew that Sevilla, in Spain, also claims the honor of their possession.

As I was eager to investigate the city, I hired someone to clean the boat, to remove the green algae beard and the long-necked barnacles from the *Liberia*. He also removed my watch, cans of food and clothing—a loss I noticed only later. After four mosquito-tormented nights, I left Ciudad Trujillo with a fresh land breeze, bound for Port-au-Prince, on the last lap of my adventure.

Outside the harbor the wind sprang up; in the east the weather cleared, and the lights of America's oldest city disappeared quickly. Terns squabbled in the air between the *Liberia* and the rocky coast; waves broke around me, their foam leaving light blue scars on the water. Although only under square sail, the canoe sailed dangerously fast, so that later that evening I put out the sea anchor and lay down to rest. In the middle of the night, disturbed by the shadows cast by the mountain tops in the moonlight, I hoisted the sail despite the wind. Late the next afternoon I sighted Cape Jacmel, a few miles to the north. Streaks of mist soon engulfed the coast, but

541

every now and then mountain peaks pushed their heads through mist and cloud as if to observe the progress of the *Liberia*.

The next morning the sun swept away the fog, brutally exposing the barren mountain slopes. The wind died; malicious small waves climbed up the back of the high swell, which swept past the canoe in a great hurry, seemingly afraid the rocks of the Haitian coast might leave before it reached them. It ignored the wild, uncontrolled splashes of water from the smaller waves around it. Soon the last pitiful breeze died away, and only the majestic swell remained.

The *Liberia* seesawed so violently that I was afraid I might go overboard; my nerves were no match for this balancing game, so I took refuge in my hole after I had squirted the deck with water to cool it. At that moment I was standing approximately fifteen sea miles off the coast, to the south of Jacmel; my sea charts indicated a westward drift, but I found that the flood was actually shifting back toward the east. Optimistically, I peered out over the edge of my hide-away every few minutes to see if a breeze had come up. No sign. A long-armed garfish approached cautiously, showing off its blue coloring; triggerfish waddled around the canoe.

The next day brought another nerve-racking dead calm. Fishermen of Haiti, on these occasions, blow on a large sea shell—a request to the spirits of the wind to fill their sails. I was uneasy in the windless sea. The swell had kept its high, cunning character, sometimes appearing quite frankly to threaten me with its foam teeth. The swell I had encountered in the Atlantic had been gentler and more regular.

To the north of me, the mountains of Haiti disappeared into a blue mist, and the following morning brought decisive action from the weather. The first intimations of change came from the south, where a blue-black bank of clouds hung over the sea. As I watched it, it seemed to me that its aim was to devour me and the *Liberia*. I looked to the north and met another unfriendly aspect: mountains bathed in a dark sea of cloud that merged with the water. Only directly overhead did a blue sky still smile down on the *Liberia*. The two weather fronts approached, neither yielding to the other; it became evident that I had been chosen as arbitrator. On either side of me, clouds spouted forth torrential rain and the remaining blue sky above me turned hazy as small white, fluffy clouds were drawn southward by the wind. The storm, of which the high swell had been an omen, was on its way.

Nature could restrain herself no longer; to the west the sea bared sinister white teeth. The roar of the approaching storm rang in my ears. I readied the *Liberia* for her coming struggle by hanging the sea anchor astern, fastening the sails and pulling up the spray cover. Then the first breakers converged on the stern while the wind howled in the shrouds. The waves were short and hard and broke faster than in Atlantic seas. Within seconds the surface was a raging mass; crowns of waves raced furiously after one another; their foam turned to a high, thin spray. The *Liberia* became their top. In their excitement these raging, wild, gigantic creatures threw themselves blindly onto the canoe, shook her, threw her from port to starboard, finally crashing and thundering onto the deck. I bailed whatever the sponge could absorb, but as I bailed, repeated waves brought more water with them. Then, slowly, the turmoil died down and normal storm waves took over. The sea is often more agitated when a storm starts than it is later. Now I was able to stop my frantic bailing; I even snatched a few minutes' sleep.

But I was wet through and through. Salt water burned the sensitive skin of my thighs. Although the roar of the storm continued, the whining and the roaring were too regular to disturb my sleep. I awoke instantly whenever breakers threw water into my hole; my system was so attuned that eye, ear, even stomach, reacted to these emergencies. Instinctively, I crept out of my hole into the dark night, groped for the sponge, sopped up water, squeezed it into a small pot and then emptied it overboard. A glance at the compass and I was ready for further sleep.

All that night, off Haiti, my floating log was flung wildly back and forth by the storm. In the morning the water foamed only a little under a clearing sky, but the seas were as tremendous as before. Off and on, giant, mountainous waves still broke over the *Liberia*, underlining the sinister, dangerous atmosphere around me. I could see the coast distinctly, even the high point of land behind Cape Jacmel. Tomorrow, I hoped, I would sail out of its range of vision. My hopes were dashed that night, when the sea roughened.

543

I now had to bail again, a sure sign that I could not yet expect to sail on. I was trapped. There was nothing I could do to escape. Jacmel lay to the north in front of me; the wind blew as before; the seas roared and raged, thundering against the deck and hitting the port side with special force, as though they wanted to smash the canoe. But in this respect I had total confidence in the *Liberia*. I knew she was strong.

Later that night as if to taunt me, the *Liberia* suddenly developed a suicidal passion to lie athwart the waves. As I loosened the rudder, the boat vanished into a huge breaker, and it was only after a struggle that she emerged again. I adjusted the rudder so that the canoe lay once again with her stern into the wind. During this operation, water poured into my collar and down my body, leaving me drenched and miserable. I was again forced to bail, sometimes every five minutes, sometimes only every hour. The storm roared on; I lost count of the days I spent in this one spot, bailing, watching, hoping for a break in the weather.

Little by little, this delay so near my goal exhausted me. With these winds, sailing to Port-au-Prince was impossible. I would have to make Jacmel my goal. But even that lay tantalizing and unattainable ahead of me.

I checked on the sea anchors to find that the canvas of one of them, although only three months old, had been torn out of its iron frame by the furious seas. My new, spare, sea anchors had been twisted so much by the force of the waves that the lines were almost frayed through. Only my plastic lines had held. I made myself a new sea anchor by fastening my last remaining steel cable onto a box cover, a blanket, some rusted iron spare parts and a full bottle. In fact, my last dispensable possessions were turned into a new anchor.

The fury of the Caribbean continued unabated, turning my impatience at my lack of progress into pity for my boat. Battered and rammed by storms, the *Liberia* was no longer a sailing boat; she had become a coffin with a lump of lead below and a sodden handkerchief for a sail above. Yet she had withstood the test better than I had. I was the captain, and her mistakes stemmed from my negligence or my ignorance. Then and there during that storm, it came to me just how reliable my canoe was, and, at the same time, how absolutely necessary it was for me to keep a constant check on the sea anchors—for on these rags, hanging astern, depended my boat and my life. Between curses and prayers, I trembled at the thought of any mistake I might make.

Implacable forces roared outside; breakers hammered and rapped loudly against the deck; the grim sea grumbled and broke, pushing and pulling at the boat. Vito Dumas, one of the most famous single-handed sailors of all time, faced seas like these when he sailed his yacht through some of the stormiest seas of our globe.

Dark clouds, engulfing the Cape of Jacmel, opened to give me an occasional glimpse of the shore; at intervals the sun pushed its rays through a barrier of black mist, but the raging of the sea continued. The canvas was torn to shreds by the rushing breakers, my skin sodden and tender from constant wetness. How long? how much longer? rang continually in my mind. I bailed. As I bailed, I was seduced by the idea of deserting the *Liberia*. I new I could swim ashore with goggles and fins, but I could not bring myself to do it; I had to have patience and sit out the storm, it could not last forever. I sang my familiar songs until my throat was hoarse and dry. Outside, triggerfish cleaned the last of the barnacles off the *Liberia*, dolphins played happily among the infamous waves, the canoe rolled and shook and took on water.

On the eighth day after sighting Jacmel for the first time, the wind and the waves calmed, allowing me to set my sails for my last harbor. With the open ocean behind her, the *Liberia* entered the dirty tidal waters of the Gulf of Jacmel. To starboard, I sailed past a small fishing boat, whose crew—completely West African in appearance—gaped at me as though I were a ghost risen from the sea. Ahead of me Jacmel grew in terraces out of the water, like a Gothic fairy-tale town. I climbed onto my seat and peered at the shore line, trying to find an anchorage that would please the *Liberia*. I saw nothing. The drift pulled to the west, making it necessary for me to use the paddle as I cautiously approached the wharf. An audience had already collected there, watching me paddle desperately to avoid a last-minute shipwreck. With sail and paddle I made progress. A policeman, standing on the wharf, whistled at me, indicating that I should dock near him. Sail furled again, a few strokes of the paddle, a rope thrown to the crowd on the wharf— and the *Liberia* was moored.

I was unhappy with the anchorage: the high swell broke only a few yards behind the canoe, so that she staggered wildly from side to side, slamming the rudder against the wharf. I climbed ashore to negotiate for a better anchorage and was advised to take my possessions out of the boat and anchor her outside the harbor. In a few minutes, with the help of the crowd, my meager baggage had been transferred to the customs house. In contrast to his neighbor in the east, even the chief of customs lent a hand. The *Liberia* was soon bobbing in clear water, safely berthed, while I found shelter at the local hotel, the Excelsior. I took a bath, with water that came from gasoline drums on the roof. Then I had time, at last, to think over my past three months.

I thanked God that He had allowed me to make the voyage, bringing it to a safe end. My goal, Haiti, sister Negro republic of Liberia, was attained. My adventurous voyage had proved that primitive vessels, although unable to sail against the wind, can not only cross the ocean but can reach their goal. Was mine the first African canoe ever to touch American soil? I doubt it. But the *Liberia* is the first canoe ever to be sailed *single-handed* across the ocean, and I am certain from my reading she is the narrowest ever to have achieved it.

I was satisfied with the physical preparations I had made for the voyage: my food supplies were well chosen, my navigation satisfactory. From a sailor's point of view everything had turned out well. But as I examined my experiences of the past three months, I realized that physical preparedness was not enough; spiritually, emotionally, I had not been ready for my adventure. When danger struck, I lost heart too quickly and doubted the outcome; I had allowed fear to take hold. At the time of the disastrous loss of my rudder, I had even contemplated giving up the voyage entirely. Would it be possible, I wondered, to be so disciplined and in command of oneself that fears and doubts could not weaken one's resolve? For the time being I pushed the question aside, but I was determined to give it more and serious thought once I was home again.

During the last, wet, stormy days before Jacmel, ulcers had formed on my body. Doctors at the local hospital obligingly gave me penicillin injections against these rebellious skin eruptions. This last trace of my discomfort soon disappeared.

A few days later, my possessions dry, my skin back to normal, I left the unpretentious charms of Jacmel for Port-au-Prince. At ten one morning I said good-bye to the *Liberia*, which was to follow me some days later by an overland route, and took my seat beside the driver of the bus that was to take me across the mountains of Haiti.

During the two months I spent in Haiti, enjoying new sights, sounds and a most hospitable people, I found much that reminded me of Liberia. At that time, 1955, Haiti and Liberia were the only two black republics in the world. Now there are many others, and tomorrow there will be even more, which will have an easier time achieving stability and prosperity than the early pioneers of Negro independence. Liberia and Haiti suffered from a prejudiced world, but survived their many years of isolation and struggle. Liberia, before World War II a primitive backwater, now has a stable economy and is justifiably proud of its progress. The history of a country is always one of ebb and flow; the strength and potentialities of the black people were underestimated by the rest of the world because it was unaware of the disastrous effects which a tropical climate and a strong belief in magic have on man's progress. Today, with the help of modern medicine and education, Africans have proved to us that they can handle pen and scalpel with as much skill as they have handled spears. The mere fact that Liberia and Haiti survived the rain forest, the mountains, the malaria-carrying mosquito—all so hostile to progress—gives proof of skill and faith without parallel in history.

Second Voyage

6 RESOLUTIONS AND PREPARATIONS

I returned to Hamburg in April, 1956, already contemplating a second voyage across the ocean. While sailing the dugout canoe, I had often thought back on the years when I had sailed a rubberized canvas folding boat at sea, and I found myself slipping into daydreams of a folding-boat crossing of the Atlantic. But it seemed an impossible dream and nothing more. It would be too difficult, too dangerous, too much would be demanded of me—my experience in the canoe told me that.

It was not until I learned something of voodoo in Haiti that I began to give really serious consideration to my new plan. Through voodoo I learned that one can, by deep concentration, a kind of self-hypnosis, change one's fundamental attitude toward a problem, that, ultimately through voodoo, one can rid oneself of fears and doubts. "Impossible is not Haitian," runs the motto of the newspaper in Jacmel, owned by my friend M. Brun, and this motto I took for my own.

Therefore, on my return to Hamburg I read everything that could teach me how to develop self-mastery and conquer my anxieties, for I knew that self-doubt and hesitation were my worst enemies in danger. My first step was prayer, the invisible weapon of man, which brings him healing power and relaxation, recovery and renewed energy. True prayer penetrates the unconscious, bringing peace to the individual and thereby helping him to overcome disturbing traits in his character. Without self-mastery, achieved through prayer and through concentration, I knew my voyage would fail.

The problem I had to tackle, first and foremost, was sleep; my experiences on the first crossing proved to me that lack of sleep leads to delirium and hallucinations and from there to deadly danger. If I wanted this second voyage to succeed, I had to train myself to sleep in short intervals, to exist for a whole week without regular, long stretches of rest. I remembered the system—a form of self-hypnosis—advocated by a German psychiatrist, Dr. J. H. Schultz, which he called autogenic training, whereby one concentrates to such a point of relaxation that the environment is forgotten and the self is found. I had made good use of this method before when I had trained myself to snatch a few minutes' sleep riding home from work. So now I began to accustom myself to short intervals of sleep which would enable me to renew my physical and emotional strength when at sea.

Of major importance in my preparations was the need to create within myself the assurance of success. I had to rid myself of all traces of fear and self-doubt, so for three months I concentrated on the phrases: "I shall succeed" and "I shall make it." I hoped to make these thoughts second nature. At the end of the three months my whole being was permeated by a strong conviction that I would succeed; that, no matter what happened, I would survive my trip. It was only then that I decided definitely to carry through my plan.

I only told my closest friends of my intentions. I bought a folding boat, planning to make the necessary changes in it myself. The plywood framework of this boat can be folded like the frame of an army cot, its hull is made of strong five-ply rubber and canvas, the deck of clear, royal blue canvas. Air tubes, built into the hull at the gunwales, give the boat added buoyancy. Its length is seventeen feet, one inch, and its width only thirty-six inches. It weighed approximately fifty-nine pounds. The little harbor town of Las Palmas in the Canary Islands was to be my point of departure again. I chose it because of my many friends there, because of its favorable weather conditions and to avoid a dangerous and time-consuming coastal trip. When I arrived I found that nothing had changed since my previous trip; the employees of the hotel were happy to see their *navegante solitario* back. I was given the same room and slept on the same lumpy mattress. It was comforting to be in such familiar surroundings; I knew the shoe-shine boy in the Santa Catalina Park, I knew where to find the best pastry in town, and the members of the yacht club were all my good friends. A newsreel with scenes of my first trip had been shown a month before, so that I was recognized and spoken to on the street more often than in Hamburg.

My boat had not yet arrived, so I spent my time reading the case histories of castaways to gain insight into their psychological problems. I came upon the report of a French ship's doctor, Jean Baptiste Henri Savigny, who with other castaways had spent thirteen days at sea after his ship sank in 1816. What happened during those thirteen days is hardly credible. Desperation and mass hysteria took over; suspicion and panic spread among the survivors, some committing suicide, others jumping overboard in a useless attempt to swim to safety. Murder, even cannibalism, gained the upper hand. Human excrement was eaten. Out of the one hundred and fifty men who survived the shipwreck only fifteen were left. Those who died, died because of a moral breakdown that could have been prevented by disciplined leadership.

The observations of another ship's doctor confirmed the importance of morale; the castaways of his ship, the *Ville de Sainte-Nazaire* which went down in 1896, were adrift for seven days in an open boat. By the second day delirium and hysteria had taken hold of every one of the survivors. And one year later, when the *Vaillant* sank, only one quarter of those saved survived the six days in a lifeboat; here again death was due to a breakdown in discipline, for we know now that castaways can survive for nine days in the temperate zones, without food and water. Why did so many die unnecessarily? It was due, I believe, to their inability to adapt themselves to new conditions; the crumbling of morale and discipline was followed by physical calamity. One can cite many instances from the last war of castaways who could not survive the trauma of shipwreck or who, through ignorance, handled their food supply with suicidal stupidity. We see what men can endure as castaways when we consider the voyage of Captain Bligh of the *Bounty;* with eighteen men and a mere handful of food he sailed 3,600 miles in an open lifeboat under the tropical sun. His knowledge and his tremendous discipline brought the boat safely to Timor, after forty-two days sailing across the Pacific.

As I read the histories of castaways and shipwrecks, I became more convinced of the importance of morale, discipline and calm to the single-handed sailor. Friends who have sailed the Atlantic in yachts have told me of finding encouragement and peace in prayer during moments of danger. I, too, prayed, but I felt I should do more to prepare for my second voyage; I had to drill my whole being—conscious and unconscious—to accept my plan. So I continued what I had begun in Hamburg. I repeated to myself, "I shall make it," and I added new autosuggestions, "Never give up, keep going west," and "Don't take any assistance." Gradually I felt my doubts and fears disappearing, yielding instead to a really positive optimism and confidence.

I congratulated myself on having chosen a folding boat, or foldboat as they are often called, for now I would be able to relive exactly the feelings of a lonely castaway; I would share his suffering, his hope and his despair. I would know his thoughts during the long nights at sea. I would, in fact, have to contend with even greater discomfort than a person afloat in the life raft of a plane or a ship's lifeboat. By suffering to the utmost from the elements, I could test the durability of the human machine, and in a cockleshell like mine I would learn much that we need to know about survival at sea.

Experience had already proved to me that in challenging the sea I had picked an implacable adversary. But it is in the nature of man to better his own achievement; it is normal and healthy to strive continually for new records. Each newly established record, after all, makes a positive contribution by setting the limits of human achievement. Thus the athlete who has run the one hundred meters in 10.1 seconds is only satisfied when he has run the distance in 10 seconds. But it is a fact well-known to all good athletes that only the man whose past performance justifies it should try to break new ground. What is true for the athlete is also true for the sailor; I was able to challenge the Atlantic in a foldboat because of the experience and knowledge I gained during my first voyage in a dugout canoe.

At last my foldboat arrived in Las Palmas and I was able to make my physical preparations. I christened her the *Liberia III* . My old friend, the sailmaker, sewed me two square sails, reinforced the stern by sewing canvas over it and brought the canvas on the starboard side, from which I could expect most of the winds and waves, as far forward as the foremast. The mast was reinforced by two backstays, and I made a mizzenmast by putting a paddle in a wooden socket-stick and slicing off one third of the blade.

President Tubman of Liberia stopped in Las Palmas on his way to Europe. He and his fellow-countrymen had shown a great deal of interest in the ocean crossing of a canoe of the Kru tribe, and the *Liberia II* is now in possession of President Tubman in Monrovia. For my second voyage he wrote a message of good luck in my logbook.

During my final preparations I continued my self-hypnosis. The last weeks before departure I fell into a mood of complete self-confidence. I had a feeling of cosmic security and protection and the certainty that my voyage would succeed.

7 AN IMPOSSIBLE VOYAGE

Departure: October 20, 1956

"Hey, Hannes." A friend's voice, hushed so as not to disturb the early morning quiet of Las Palmas, woke me.

"Coming, coming," I answered, as loudly as I dared.

I had spent the last night on the *Tangaroa,* a double canoe owned by friends, Jim, Ruth and Jutta. As I awoke slowly, I heard footsteps from above, and Ruth's voice came down to me questioningly:

"Are you awake, Hannes?"

"Beginning to be," I answered and forced myself out of my bunk and onto the deck.

My friends were already up, waiting for me in the dawn. I expected to sail in about an hour. In the last days I had exuded self-confidence; yet, despite my techniques of self-hypnosis, I felt tension. I could not avoid an inner questioning: "Am I really doing this? Am I really crossing the Atlantic in a small rubber folding boat?" I countered these questions and calmed my nerves by repeating, "I'll make it, I shall make it. Stop worrying."

"You act as though you were about to cross the harbor," my friends teased me; so perhaps my tension did not show.

A few last-minute touches were still required. The under water spear gun had to be fastened to the starboard side; Jim tied plastic material around the mast to keep it dry; Jutta sewed my spray cover; and Ruth handed me last-minute items from the *Tangaroa*. She also prepared a traveler's breakfast for me, fried eggs swimming in butter to give me a last boost of energy this side of the Atlantic. These three friends, convinced of my success, did everything to help and encourage me. Jim had advised me—as had friends in Germany—to use an outrigger when I was undecided between that and air tubes around the water line. I finally decided on an outrigger made out of half of a car inner tube, sealed at both ends.

Then the sun came up; everything appeared to be taken care of, although I knew that I could spend another day in the harbor making changes in this and that, altering the trim of the boat in one way or another. But I knew I had to draw the line somewhere. This was it, now. The moment to leave had come. My friends tactfully spared me the painful emotions of a leave-taking; they climbed into their small dinghy and rowed over to the Santa Catalina wharf, a good spot for last good-byes. I paddled the *Liberia* through hundreds of fishing smacks over to a lobster crate on which stood two other friends. "You'll make it," they shouted.

I set the square sail forward and paddled slowly from the fishing harbor, passing the Santa Catalina wharf, where a handful of curious people stood watching me. Jim, Ruth and Jutta, motionless, were among them. I could well imagine what was going on in their hearts and minds, I was far from cheerful myself. They had their little dog with them, whom they had saved from drowning, and even he seemed nervous and anxious. Few people knew my exact destination, but many must have had an inkling. They remembered that before my last voyage I had told everyone that I planned to sail down the African coast, and instead I had gone across the Atlantic. This time, when I first arrived at the yacht club, my friends asked, "Hannes, are you sailing down the coast again?"

"Claro"—but, of course—I answered, only to be openly laughed at.

In the harbor basin I hoisted the gaff sail. Trade winds had blown strong for the past few days, but in the protected harbor I could not feel them. The clouds above me sailed northwest. It was now nine in the morning. I could hear cars honking from the shore and the whistle of steamers from the water. To hasten my progress, I took up the paddle again. It is an old rule for motorless craft to sail out of sight of land as quickly as possible. As I left the protected harbor behind me, the first gusts of wind flowed over my rubber and canvas craft, the swell heightened and the first waves wet the canvas. I passed Las Palmas on the right, in the shadow of the old cathedral spire.

Then from behind me I heard the sound of an approaching engine. In the high swell I made out a white object. "Aha! they are probably looking for me." A moment later I recognized the local pilot boat, and my hope of leaving without official obstruction was dampened. They were definitely heading for me. I left the sail up, but the boat came closer, and the men on it waved me back toward them. I ignored them. They came up alongside, the pilot shouting, "The harbor master wants to see you."

"Why?"

"I don't know. All I know is you're supposed to come back."

"I am sailing to Maspalomas, and for that I do not need anyone's permission."

Maspalomas is a beach to the south of the island, and it was true that I had thought of going ashore there to make some necessary changes in the trim of the boat. I sailed on. The pilot boat came up once more, this time on the port side, where I had attached my outrigger with a paddle. They drove right over it, breaking the paddle, and bringing me close to capsizing. I immediately took down the sail, trembling with rage at their carelessness. They threw a line to me. Furiously, I threw it back at them. The paddle blade was broken and would have to be fixed, so in any case I would have to stop somewhere for repairs.

"I'm going to paddle back," I shouted at them and they left.

I felt limp, tired and depleted. My paddling was too weak to get me back to the harbor. The pilot boat disappeared while I was still trying to paddle against the wind. I was only about three miles from the harbor, but somehow I didn't have the strength to get there. Perhaps it was the impact of my first disappointment, my first setback, and the sudden realization that I might not be allowed to make my voyage. No! I would not allow that to happen. My plans and preparations wasted because of a harbor master's whim? My savings, my hard-earned money thrown away? A voice inside me repeated, "I'll make it, I'll make it," and on a quick decision I turned around, hoisted the sails and set off again with a fine wind.

The trade winds freshened up, combers sprayed and splashed me. Nearly all the seas swept over the entire length of the boat, so that it became clear that she was too deep in the water. But as yet I had no time to take care of the problem. First I had to get the feel of the sea again and find out how to handle the loaded boat. The pointed bow lacked buoyancy, plowing the water to such a depth that at times the seas came to my foremast, while aft they ran to the mizzenmast.

I felt a little queasy. That morning Jim had reminded me to take pills against seasickness, as I do at the beginning of every voyage. Although the foldboat with its outrigger did not roll much in comparison with the dugout canoe, the motion bothered me, and I was glad I had taken the pills.

As I left the protection of the island, in whose lee lies the harbor of Las Palmas, the winds blew more strongly. Soon I took down the one-and-one-half-square-yard sail from the foremast and sailed with the three-quarter-square-yard sail of the mizzenmast. The aft mast was a paddle that sat on the aft washboard. I had arranged the steering as on the *Liberia II,* cables ran from the rudder to where I sat and I could control them with my hands or feet. Also, I had arranged the boat so that I could sit relaxed, leaning back against the aft board, with my knees straight out in front of me while I steered with my feet. I could also sit closer to the front with bent knees, still using my feet for steering. It was only later in the voyage, after I had eaten some of the canned food and the boat was roomier, that I could stretch out my legs completely and then only on windless days when I did not have to steer. My friends had overestimated the speed of the *Liberia;* the loaded boat did not make more than three and a half knots. Now the little square sail on the mizzen was taking me south at two miles an hour. But as long as the trade winds blew I was satisfied.

At twilight I reached the beach of Maspalomas. As the wind blew directly toward the coast, the surf was too high for a landing. I remembered previous expeditions to the beach with my Spanish friends, when we had gone there to picnic and swim. Early that evening I rounded the southeastern tip of Gran Canaria. The sea was calmer, so I took the opportunity to check the outrigger and the paddle which had been cracked by the pilot boat. I took off the paddle and lashed the inner-tube outrigger to the deck, while I tried sailing for two hours without it. But it was too difficult. The boat rolled and my discomfort was acute. I had been rolled to last a lifetime during my first voyage. Ideally, I should have had an outrigger on both sides, but the boat was not strong enough for that. To keep her afloat in case she capsized, I had stored the inflated other half of the inner tube in the bow and several empty airtight containers in the stern.

October 21st

While I worked on the outrigger, the night passed quickly. In the darkness I heard an occasional clap from flying fish. I was worried by the spray cover, which I had made and waterproofed myself in Las Palmas, for water leaked through its two layers of canvas. Water washed continuously over the deck and the spray cover, leaking through to my knees despite my oilskin pants. At nine that morning I wrote in the logbook, "The torture has started." Of course, no one knew better than I what awaited me, but even so I had forgotten that my skin was extremely sensitive to waterproofing ingredients. After these few hours of exposure it hurt badly; when I touched a spot on my body the whole surrounding area burned as though hot tar had been poured on it. It was impossible for me to change clothes in the heavy sea, and the pain became so great that I seriously considered turning back or trying to reach the African coast. But I had to keep on. I reminded myself of the phrases I had continually repeated in Las Palmas: "Keep going west; don't take assistance; never give up." I had hammered these words into my very innermost being back in the hotel when my heart and mind were calm. Now, in this moment of near-panic, I needed them. In my first anger at my skin trouble, my weakness came to the fore, but the often-repeated words kept me going.

During the day the wind came from all points of the compass; flat calm alternated with contrary winds and choppy seas till evening, when the old trade winds blew again. Butterflies fluttered over the water. I pulled a locust out of the sea, and wondered if some day someone might not do this to me.

Water continued leaking through the spray cover. With a little rubber syringe, the kind a doctor uses for cleaning ears, I drew it out. Then at last I found time to concentrate on a quiet meal. I had eaten nothing the day before except my hearty breakfast, but I had drunk twice my usual amount of liquid to prevent dehydration. I had deliberately avoided food for thirty-six hours, hoping to dull my senses by fasting and thereby to make the discomforts of the journey easier to bear. Now I drank my ration of unsweetened evaporated milk and ate several oranges. Suddenly I noticed that my leeboard had fallen off and was floating away. It would serve no purpose to worry over the loss; the ship's doctor of the *Liberia* had forbidden worry, for it could only sap my strength. I was better off in this one respect than most single-handed sailors: I had my own physician aboard. I knew myself well and knew that after the problem of thirst would come the problem of morale. I had to keep my sense of humor and a relaxed outlook; I had to remain cheerful, unconcerned and emotionally stable.

As the second night approached, I tried hard to concentrate on relaxation so that my strength would be renewed for the coming day. I had to learn the art of sleeping while sitting. This is an easily acquired skill, but I was forced to check on the course at the same time. I felt empty, drained of thought, my feet hardly able to control the course. Then, for a fraction of a second, I fell into a dream. A wave awoke me. In the morning I discovered that my head had sunk onto my chest in sleep several times. I realized that I was a simple man with simple needs, a tired creature who needed sleep urgently!

October 22nd

Yesterday I lost sight of land. Now I was really alone. For how long? I counted on seventy days. As I left the protection of the Canary Islands, wind and seas became heavier. In the morning a steamer passed two miles to port, unaware of the little *Liberia.* I sewed a plastic layer over the deck so that less water would come through the spray cover. Because my freeboard was too low, water washed over the boat. The wind was only twenty miles an hour, but even this was too much for the *Liberia.* I had to throw something overboard to lighten her. First went the quinces, lovely, sweet Canary Island quinces, twenty-two pounds, quite unspoiled, floated off into the Atlantic Ocean. But the boat was still too heavy, so, very reluctantly, I got rid of another twenty-two pounds of canned food. The boat sailed better now, and I was less worried. The sea would replace what I had lost, as long as I had the means of catching sea life. I sailed on, carrying 154 pounds of food and drink for the seventy days that might still lie ahead. Despite my previous experience, I might have miscalculated. But it did not matter. What I had read of castaway reports from the last war convinced me that there is enough food in the sea to ensure survival.

I suffered intensely from the oversensitivity of my skin under the sun that day. It was so bad that I began to despair: "Jump overboard. Who cares about you? Who knows where you are? Not even at home do they know of your new voyage." These thoughts ran through my head, taking hold of my senses, until I drove them off by repeating, "Never give up. Keep going west."

My finger tips were swollen, the skin raw from handling wet articles and bailing the boat. In Las Palmas I had painstakingly developed calluses on the palms of my hands and a tan on my nose, but I had overlooked the need to toughen my finger tips.

As the sun set, the first curious birds inspected the foldboat from above. These creatures all seemed bigger than I remembered from the first crossing. Was it perhaps because I felt so minute in my rubber boat?

And then again night came. The mizzen sail was set, demanding constant watchfulness from me to ensure that I stayed on course.

Under the most favorable conditions a boat as flat as mine has trouble keeping on course with aft winds. I concentrated on putting myself into a state of dozing in which my feet would still control the rudder, but no actively conscious thought would disturb my rest. On a clear night, when the stars were visible, I had no trouble steering with my feet, but with cloudy skies I had to use the flashlight to light up the compass.

My pulse that night had sunk to the slow rate of forty-two beats a minute; hunger, inactivity and my physically good condition played a part in keeping my pulse slow. My whole system was influenced, I am sure, by my total concentration on relaxation.

October 23rd

The weather improved, making it possible to dry out my drenched clothes. Above all, I wanted to expose my skin to the sun. My whole lower body felt as if someone had been sticking pins into it. I could hardly wait for the noonday sun to start my cure. At midday I put a paddle over the washboard, forced myself out of the opening in the spray cover and sat down cautiously on the palm of the paddle. I steered with my hands. Slowly, I peeled off my thin rubber jacket, oilskin pants, shorts, thick sweater and undershirt. Everything was soaked through. With a few clothespins I fastened my wardrobe to the shrouds of the mizzenmast. How superb to feel the sun warming and drying my skin! From then on the noon hour was devoted to health; it became my "hour of hygiene and preventive medicine." I sat high on my little seat, bailed water from the boat, dried the kapok cushion in the sun and made myself very comfortable. At the end of the hour I dusted my clothing with talcum powder, rubbed my body with a washcloth and dressed. Then I settled down again in the shadow of the mizzenmast.

The mild wind made a pattern of shingles across the surface; the *Liberia* rocked gently in the swell; and the ocean showed me its friendliest aspect. I felt peaceful.

I noticed a plank floating in the water. It was overgrown with barnacles, and two small crabs fell into the water as I picked it up.

Again the night put a dark veil over the sea. In small boats, nights at sea are disagreeable and uncomfortable. Fortunately the mizzen sail, which had been up since Las Palmas, protected me from the cold wind. My hope and ambition was to leave it up till I reached St. Thomas. Contrary winds, of course, could force me to take it down. I had chosen St. Thomas as my final destination. I felt an obligation to the yacht club there, of which I was an honorary member, so my bow pointed straight to the Virgin Islands.

I was beginning to feel that dozing and emptying my mind of all conscious thought, that concentrating on nothing, would not, in the end, be a sufficient substitute for sleep.

October 24th

I passed an agonizing night, knowing there would be many others like it to follow. It was cold. When the sun finally shone I cut up a large seabag and sewed it aft over the spray cover. I was delighted with this accomplishment. The wind blew favorably from the east and my skin burned less. But my buttocks were uncomfortable; I could only hope that the condition would not worsen.

I found that I daydreamed a great deal. Girls appeared in my dreams, but I knew that in a few days they would be banished for the rest of the trip. A hungry man generally does not think too much about women.

On land I pray regularly; at sea I prayed for alertness and for comfort. I found that praying, which can be a sort of sinking away, a forgetfulness of the outside world, strengthened my morale. The night was clear; the moon outshone the stars, so that I could barely recognize the planets. Inside the boat everything was soaked. The trade winds, as they had done a few days before, came from all directions; one minute from the north, the next from the east and a minute later from the northeast. In a small boat wind irregularities are much more noticeable than on a yacht. Crosswaves slapped the foldboat, giving me the feeling that we were running athwart the sea. But the compass showed that it was the waves, not I, that had veered.

October 25th

On that morning I was pleasantly surprised to find a bottle of orange juice that Jim had hidden for me. Later on, as I took my noon position, I found a photograph of Jim and his two friends, Ruth and Jutta, stuck into my nautical almanac. He had written across the top, "Dear Hannes, keep going west. Your friendship meant a lot to us." And Ruth's message, "Don't worry, you'll succeed," strengthened my determination.

I knew I could rely on the accuracy of my noon position. I measured the longitude only approximately, from the difference between Greenwich and local time, but I had tested my chronometer, and I knew it was trustworthy.

A little later I discovered a locust, clinging to the block on top of the mizzenmast. I christened him Jim in honor of my friend and then worried about how to feed him. The butterflies that fluttered by the *Liberia* had never thought of taking refuge on her.

Once that night I fell into deep sleep, to be awakened by the flapping of the mizzen sail. In my sleep I had dreamed that a friend had taken me to the safety of a harbor where I could sleep without fear of capsizing. The dream was nothing but a rationalization of my weakness in falling asleep.

October 26th

My first concern that morning was for my locust friend, Jim. He was still alive, and a little later I photographed and took movies of him from every angle. The wind still blew from the east. My luck was holding at the beginning of this voyage. By now I was completely familiar with the outrigger and knew its reactions in all weather conditions. I had fastened it to the port side, the side that is more on the lee during a crossing like mine than the starboard. The Polynesians carried their outrigger on the weather side but mine was not like theirs. I, at least, preferred it on the lee. I had had great difficulty setting the sails on the dugout, but now, with the stability given by the outrigger, it was simple.

In order to lighten the boat, I ate only from my supply of canned food for the first week. My only uncanned food was garlic and some oranges. I took garlic along because it keeps so well under the worst conditions; not even salt water spoils it; it is also a better aid to digestion than the onion, although it contains fewer vitamins. In the morning I drank a can of evaporated milk, in the evening a can of beer, together with my meal of beans, peas or carrots and a few slices of garlic. Milk and beer raise the energy level of a hungry man. I have sometimes thought that on steamship routes, where rain can supplement the water supply, lifeboats should also carry milk. It is true that water is the beginning and end of a castaway's existence, but milk is more than a liquid, it is a food. It helps control the factors in a hungry man's body chemistry that make for panic and delirium. The ability to stay calm and in control of a situation is of paramount importance to the castaway. Expressed in simple terms, one can say that hunger creates an imbalance in a man's metabolism which may cause moments of delirium. The alkali content of milk and beer, as well as their easily absorbed calories, can counteract this condition.

In spite of my knowledge of the dangers of dehydration and the care that I exercised to prevent it, I noticed its symptoms in the cracking and peeling of my skin folds. Because man's thirst does not reflect his need for liquid this is a constant danger.

October 27th

Jim disappeared from the top of the mast. I looked everywhere for him, but he was gone. A pity! The wind weakened. The night before I had slept a little. I managed it by changing the sails so that the wind was freer and I could handle the boat more easily. Then I lay down on my left side, with my knees bent and my feet still controlling the rudder, my head resting on the washboard. It was no luxurious bed, but the sleep strengthened me. I slept for half an hour on one side, sat up and then turned onto the other side. I felt I had found a solution to my sleep problem and was only sorry that it could not be done when the winds were stronger.

Last night Madeira petrels danced around the boat. Mediterranean shearwaters, which regularly accompanied me during the day, were seldom visible at night. I wondered why it was so difficult to catch sea birds in these zones. Castaways from other regions of the sea have told of catching quite a few. The castaways of a Dutch luxury steamer that was torpedoed in 1943, hold the record; they caught twenty-five birds in eighty-three days afloat below the equator. It is possible that sea birds prefer to rest on floating rather than sailing objects.

The sun burned with pitiless intensity on my mizzenmast. I sprinkled the sail with sea water and found its shade cooler after that. I took the noon position, then sat down on the paddle seat for my "hygiene hour." I was amused at the thought of a steamer suddenly seeing a man take a sun bath on the edge of a foldboat in mid-ocean.

Before my departure I had developed a method which aimed at disciplining the blood vessels of my buttocks. For three months I spent fifteen minutes a day relaxing and repeating to myself: "I am quiet, I am quiet, my body is relaxed, completely relaxed. My thighs and buttocks are warmer, much warmer. Pleasant, warm blood flows through the buttocks." This was no cure-all for my problem, which came from the fact that I had to sit for so long in wet clothes, but perhaps it helped to heal my salt water sores. I found it difficult at first to do this on the boat; possibly I was disturbed by my new environment, and in heavy seas I did not try it at all.

Now I began to see small fish under the boat. I had painted her underside red, just as I had the dugout canoe. Little fish were attracted by the shadow cast by the boat, hoping it would afford them protection from their enemies. I am not sure as yet whether large fish, like sharks, will avoid the color red. I had brought with me certain other preventive measures against sharks; first in the line of defense was a piece of shark meat to throw at them in case of necessity (after three days it stank so horribly that I had to throw it away). Secondly, having heard that sharks are frightened by metallic sounds, I had tied together some pieces of old iron to throw at them in case of attack. I knew that sharks do not intentionally attack boats. Other big fish follow the same rule. Despite this knowledge, I was still worried; after all, the fish might feel that here was such a cockleshell of a boat they had nothing to fear from it.

October 28

That morning, looking for something on the boat, I found two presents from my friends of the *Tangaroa;* a bottle of rum about the size of a finger and a copy of the *Bhagavad-Gita,* one of the world's great religious works.

The trade winds freshened. Far too much spray and far too many combers washed over the spray cover, but in a foldboat these are as impossible to avoid as dust on a motorcycle. I felt myself as safe and sure on the high seas in a foldboat as a bicyclist on the road. In fact, in some respects I was safer; I did not run the risk of being pushed into a ditch. I owed this feeling of assurance to my previous trips in a foldboat and to the knowledge that the air tubes built into the hull of the *Liberia* would keep her afloat if she capsized.

My noon latitude that day was the twenty-sixth degree north. As I was returning the sextant to its waterproof bag, a dolphin took the bait I had hung over the starboard side. My first fish of the voyage! I hauled it on board and killed it with a knife. First I drank the blood, then I ate the liver and roe, which actually tasted better than the flesh of the fish, as well as being richer in vitamins and minerals. Later I ate part of the meat, putting aside the remainder in the shade of the compass for the next day's meal. I was pleased at having saved a whole day's ration.

The seas had grown stronger, bending the wooden framework of the boat with each wave. Because the air tubes were not fully inflated, there was a creaking, groaning sound in the boat. I began to feel that my own bones were making these unhappy sounds. Yet the foldboat sailed better now than earlier; sometimes she ran before combers like a Hawaiian surfboard. The *Liberia III* had certain advantages over the *Liberia II;* I found it easier to set her sails, and in calm weather I could read because she rolled less. Now the trade winds blew with full power, and the whole ocean appeared to move toward the west.

Fortunately for me, the nights were quieter than the days. At night I skimmed through a sea of bioluminescence, which enchanted me with its beauty and variety and reassured me of the ocean's fertility.

October 29th

Around midnight, the wind, calming for an hour or so, allowed me a little sleep. Then it returned, from the northeast, blowing with a force of twenty-five miles an hour. The outrigger slipped, and in the dawn a big breaker pushed it completely out of place. I waited for more light before repairing the damage. Then I took down the sails, forced myself out of the spray cover, readjusted the course and stretched out over the outrigger. I was pushing it back into position when suddenly an enormous, steep green wall towered above me. It hovered briefly and then crashed over me and the boat. I gasped for air. Because I had all my weight on the outrigger, the boat did not capsize, but it was half swamped with water. I climbed back in during a few seconds of calm and sat down in water. I adjusted my course so that the bow soon pointed west again; then I hauled out my little pot and bailed. I got up the last of the water with the rubber syringe. One hour later the inside of the boat was drier, but I was still soaked through.

The sea roared and stormed with such violence I was unable to take the noon position. A school of dolphins passed by, but I lost sight of them quickly in the rough water. Later that morning I spotted a few albacores.

I reacted to my enforced inactivity like a schoolboy; I squirmed on my seat, I wriggled, I moved first one way, then another, changing positions every few minutes.

For ten days the trade winds had blown steadily. Had I hitched a ride with them that would take me directly to St. Thomas? In that case I could expect to make the crossing in fifty-five days. That evening rain squalls hit the *Liberia,* and with the help of the mizzen sail I caught three quarts on a plastic layer of my spray cover. I drank one quart immediately and put the rest aside in an aluminum container.

October 30th

Eleven days at sea. Now the trade winds appeared exhausted. The night was calm. An Atlantic swell of more than twenty-four feet rolled under the boat, heaving the *Liberia* up to a peak, from which she slid gently down into the next valley. At noon I enjoyed a thorough "hygiene hour." I washed all my clothing in the sea, drying it on a quickly installed clothesline. My knees and thighs were covered with small pustulae. I opened them with a needle, removed the pus and let them dry out in the sun. I fished purple snails from the water. As I crushed them, they stained my fingers with the dye that was once used to color the togas of emperors and kings.

October 31st

I had my first night of flat calm. The cans still took up too much room for me to stretch out my legs in sleep though. The rudder already had a free play of more than twenty degrees, considerably more than I expected from my previous experience at sea. From the southeast a few small breaths wafted over a lazy ocean. I noticed a great deal of plankton, but as yet I had seen no triggerfish or water striders. The wind veered to the south, and a rainfall brought me more drinking water.

November 1st

My thirteenth day at sea, and the winds, of course, were contrary. My watch stopped working, but it was no great misfortune for the chronometer would replace it. A bad squall, coming from the southeast, broke the boom, as I laughingly called the stick no thicker than a finger to which the sail was attached. I repaired it with ease, but the sails no longer fitted as exactly. Before the twenty-four hours of the thirteenth day had passed, I suffered an attack of stomach cramps. My relaxation exercises brought some relief.

That afternoon the contrary wind stiffened. I had no sail up, but I was still blown back toward the east. So as not to drift too rapidly off course, I took down the paddle that served as a mizzenmast. For the first time on this voyage I threw the sea anchor out over the stern. The boat held herself surprisingly well, hardly swinging around at all. I attributed it to a good job of trimming the boat.

November 2nd

For a whole day I lay to on the sea anchor. The boat shipped a great deal of water, since we were no longer sailing with the waves or before the sea. Big waves ran pitilessly over the deck. I bailed at least once every hour, until I was so tired of it that I pulled up the anchor, so that I was again before the wind. I now faced the direction I came from. The only advantage was less water in the *Liberia*.

Around noon, the wind calmed. The latitude showed me that in two days I had been driven almost forty miles northward. But when I compared it to the three thousand I had to cover, forty did not overly disturb me.

A giant swell, indicative of a real storm, rolled down from the North Atlantic. I perched proudly on the washboard, enjoying my "hygiene hour" and watching a little dolphin, hunted by three larger brothers, take refuge in the shadow of my boat. The little fish, not much longer than my foot, waited quietly under the air tube, but his hunters spotted him. One attacked but the little fish escaped. Now I watched a life and death chase. They swam around the rudder, showing very little respect for my boat. Finally one succeeded in capturing his prey. It was hardly an evenly matched contest. The three older dolphin measured three and a half feet to the little fish's paltry inches. However, they must have enjoyed the chase, for they started beating the bottom of the boat with their tails. They approached, turned on their sides and smacked the keel. Although they in no way threatened the safety of the *Liberia,* I was indignant over their lack of respect. In a momentary rage I grabbed my grappling iron, stabbed and wounded the first, then I thrust at the second, but broke the aluminum point of the iron in the process. The third dolphin continued his cavorting until I drove my knife into his body. I could have caught them easily with my underwater gun, but they were really too large to bring aboard without damaging the boat.

November 3rd and 4th

The trade winds returned during the night. The sky was cloudy and later a roaring, blustering and hurling squall poured rain on the sea, ironing it flat with its force. I caught fresh water in my spray cover. In the past sixteen days I had collected more than I was able to throughout the first crossing.

The next day I spotted a squid of some thirty inches. Its red-brown coloring resembled that of the giant squid I saw the year before, and like it, this fellow appeared to have no tentacles. They must have been related.

The wind whistled through the shrouds, and at night I dozed only from time to time. I was beginning to feel tired. During the night of the sixteenth day I had the strange impression that the ocean ran towards the east. I could not rid myself of this kinetic illusion. I put my hand into the water, and, sure enough, it ran eastward. The clouds stood still, and I believed that my boat was being carried back to the African coast. I shone a flashlight on the compass. It showed west. I knew who I was; I knew where I wanted to go, but heaven help me, how was I to rid myself of this certainty that I was going backwards? Everyone has experienced the same kind of sensation, sitting in a stationary train, when the train beside him moves, and he has the illusion that he is moving. But this hallucination in a small boat was unexpected. Then a comber washed over the boat, sweeping away with it this mysterious sensation. With complete assurance I knew now I was sailing west.

I almost always kept the mizzen sail up. Sailors will wonder why, but it afforded me such fine protection against cold winds that I overlooked the less advantageous steering.

The wind was still fresh, so the night was unpleasant. But the sea birds enjoyed it, for it made their flight easier and freer. I saw several Manx shearwaters. There were more of them this year than last, and this time I had no trouble identifying them. Because of their skillful aerial acrobatics, I nicknamed them "the mad flyers." My good friends from the first crossing, the Madeira petrels and the Mediterranean shearwaters, joined me once again. I saw only isolated tropic birds. On my previous voyage I had sailed closer to the Cape Verde Islands, where they appear more frequently. A trained zoologist, by looking at the sea birds and at fish, can roughly tell his location on the high seas without recourse to the stars.

The rough sea had forced me to do without my daily "hygiene hour." Without a sun bath to dry the pustulae on my thighs, I had to wipe them off with a handkerchief. I used my thigh muscles less than any others and properly I should have massaged them daily. However, the erupting exanthema made massage too painful, even though I realized that without it the muscles might shrink. Between my two voyages I intentionally gained weight so that I would use up excess fat rather than muscle tissue at sea.

"How much weight will you lose?" Jim asked me in Las Palmas. "About ten pounds?"

I told him I expected to lose at least forty-five pounds, and he pointed out that I could afford it, whereas with his skinny frame he could never stand such a loss.

November 6th

Finally the wind abated; the first trade wind clouds appeared in the sky. I put out all my wet possessions to dry in the sun: books, cameras, sea charts and, of course, my clothes. I knew I had sufficient drinking water to avoid dehydration and could afford the luxury of a long exposure to the sun. I noted with interest that this slight exertion brought my pulse up to forty-eight beats per minute, whereas before it had been thirty-four.

So far nothing unforeseen had occurred. The voyage had gone as I expected, based on my previous experience, except for less stable weather. My natural optimism took over; I planned new voyages or daydreamed of a farm in the tropics, always a pet idea of mine. During the first two weeks a woman appeared in my dreams of the perfect life, but as the voyage continued I rejected her completely; I was even baking my own bread. Food—I thought mainly of food, mostly of sweets; my special favorite is a cake with whipped cream. There, in mid-Atlantic, food played the foremost role in my daydreams.

November 7th

The trade winds lay dormant; only rain clouds and soft gusts remained unchanged. As I bailed the boat, I discovered that one tin of milk had corroded. In the afternoon a swarm of triggerfish plundered the first barnacles off the boat bottom. It was an odd sensation to feel them under me, first snapping at the barnacles, then diving deeper and slapping the boat with their tails. My body was so much a part of the boat that I had the sensation they were attacking me.

November 8th

To one who uses his eyes, life at sea offers endless variety. Very seldom is one day like the next, but my twentieth day differed not at all from the day before: weak winds from the northeast, the same birds and the same swarm of triggerfish rolled under the keel.

I am an optimist—I have to be—so I celebrated the end of the first third of the voyage. Celebrated with what? There was not much choice; I could either drink an extra can of milk or an extra beer. I chose milk. I had also taken with me a pound of honey for each week of the crossing. I had not touched it yet, but as soon as I remembered its presence on the boat I pulled it out and in minutes half a week's ration was gone. It was difficult to hold to the rations I had planned for. During the first week I was sometimes hungry, but after that, hunger left me and I suffered only from thirst. Surely I took with me the least amount of food of any boat that has ever made the Atlantic crossing, at least much less than Alain Bombard.

November 9th

As long as the nights were calm, I was always able to catnap and renew my strength. During these naps my feet controlled the rudder; although I sometimes found myself off course, still the foldboat managed to stay with the waves.

I saw my first water striders. It is not unusual to find them in the ocean far away from land, although these were a different species from those I had seen in the Gulf of Guinea. The first swarm of flying fish swam and leaped alongside the boat.

I was approaching the tropics and expected to be south of the tropic of Cancer that night. I made several attempts to spear some triggerfish with my knife but only succeeded in wounding them. In the evening the wind freshened. Shearwaters' activity increased, while petrels behaved with the abandon of children released from school. Heavy seas in the early evening forced me to sail with care, lest the boat broach.

573

November 10th

The entry into the tropics brought no visible change; wind gusts were still fierce, identical birds and fish accompanied me and the sea—the sea was, as ever, full of twists and surprises. The wind had beaten the surface, stirred it up, finally turning it into a boiling inferno. Trade winds drew their breath of life from squalls and gusts, which every now and again rushed over the water. My heart felt for my boat, which had to make its way over a sea as rough and as full of bumps as an ancient cobblestone road.

I had to replace the bulb of my flashlight that evening, but my boat was so well-organized that I was able to find it at once. Day or night, I knew exactly where to find every spare part.

November 11th

Sunday, and my thoughts turned to the coffee and cake being served at home. Familiar church bells rang in my ears. Warm air wafted toward me from the southwest. I had decided to indulge in a Sunday treat of canned carrots; when I opened the can I was overjoyed to find Danish meat balls. My mistake came from the trademark on the outside, which looked like two crossed carrots. I had suffered horribly from boils during my first crossing, and thinking they might have come from a meat diet, I took no meat with me on this trip. I had also chosen to take beer, hoping its vitamin B content would help prevent furunculosis.

Later that day I fell into a flat calm. With a quiet surface I was always made aware of the plankton "dust" that floats near the surface of the water. I caught a little pilot fish with seven dark rings around its body; a good start for an aquarium, but unfortunately not in my present situation. Triggerfish returned. I hung a thin nylon line from the paddle support of the outrigger. It barely touched the water, and the triggerfish were fascinated by this dangling object. Every one of them wanted to snap at it, giving me a fine opportunity to catch some. I tried spearing them with my knife, but only succeeded in inflicting wounds. My hand proved more agile, so with a quick scoop I caught one around the head. At first it stayed motionless, but after a few seconds, it grunted a little reproachfully, as if to say, "You broke the law of the sea. I am taboo as food." But it was mistaken. Its organs had a wonderful flavor. Under their fins, triggerfish have red meat which tastes like meat from mammals and which I preferred to their white meat. I ate the brain of the poor creature, although it was not much bigger than the tip of my little finger. When we eat protein such as fish our body needs additional liquid to excrete the salts and urea, but there is no available liquid in meat, unless it is pressed out. The eyes, the brain, the blood and the spinal fluids do supply us with some water, but it is not enough to carry on the process of excretion. Therefore a castaway should not eat protein if he is dehydrated, for it will aggravate his condition.

An abscess had formed on the base of the exanthema on my thighs. I punctured it with a small incision.

November 13th

I noticed a new variety of petrel, with feathers so black that at first glance it looked like a crow. But its flight was as graceful as that of other petrels. I identified it as Bulwer's petrel. Three tropic birds paid me a visit, and one tried vainly to perch on the mast. Every bird gave me pleasure; I admired and envied their way of handling the wind, their easy, free and unaffected flight, their playfulness with the sea.

During the night one of the rudder cables broke. It was replaced at once.

November 14th

For four days the wind blew from the west. It was not strong, but I knew it was delaying my progress considerably. I was no longer alone on the *Liberia*. A crab had made its home on the port side of the boat. At noon every day he came out of a little hole and warmed himself in the sun. But he was a cautious companion, scuttling for shelter whenever I bent over to have a closer look at him.

I caught another triggerfish with my hands; this fellow had little transparent long-tailed parasites on his fins. A pilot fish popped out as I slit his stomach. With fresh bait I caught a dolphin. I sent an arrow from my underwater gun through his body, but could not pull him up on deck until I had killed him with my knife. I could only haul in a fish as big as this one when he was dead; otherwise, he would damage the boat. This fellow had many dark spots on his skin that looked like bugs. They were parasites, and under them the fish's skin had retained its light color.

I threw more bait overboard and caught another dolphin. But then my attention was attracted by the behavior of the rest of the swarm, that suddenly collected on the port side. A shark! Only three yards away from the boat a shark waited, and halfway between the shark and the boat my poor victim dangled from the line, fighting for his life. It looked as though the shark would attack the fish, but he was evidently afraid of my strange craft and did not dare approach. So I pulled the dolphin into the boat, killing him outright with a knife thrust between the eyes. The shark, lolling behind the boat, had obviously been attracted by the struggles of my victim. It was a fully grown shark, about twelve feet long, easily twice the weight of my boat, contents and crew. As the shark seemed as timid as I, I was less nervous, although I was glad to see it turn away. I looked over my catch. In the stomach of one I found a remora, a sucking fish, and in the other fish only my bait. I ate their organs first, then drank their blood mixed with a little rain water.

When I curled up to nap in calm weather, I could feel the snaking movements of my boat right through the rubber. But I trusted to the strength of the material. At that point in the voyage my mood was one of utter confidence; no disaster could touch me. I asked myself, "Why should I concern myself with something that has not happened yet and that I could not change anyway?" Although the calm dampened my hopes, I still expected to arrive in St. Thomas by Christmas.

November 15th

A warm breath blew over the ocean from the west. The atmosphere felt sticky; unlike windier days the air was empty of birds. Probably they were resting on the water, storing up strength. I ate some more of my catch. It stayed edible for twenty-four hours if I kept it in the shade; thereafter it soured. Fish can be kept longer if it is sliced and dried in the sun, and no water is allowed to touch it.

My attention was attracted by the snorting of a single whale.

Then I saw his body, a black patch in the high swell. Occasionally a Madeira petrel fluttered listlessly in the humidity. Only two tropic birds retained their energy, flying high above me. Then once again a loud snort sounded across the water, and I saw a huge spout shoot into the air. I heard the whale take several shallow breaths, then one loud, deep breath; with that he plunged into the depths, his tail fin erect in the water. There is a whale skeleton on display in the Oceanographic Museum in Monaco, into whose abdominal cage the *Liberia III,* with hoisted sail, could fit quite comfortably.

Slowly, slowly I paddled against the breath blowing against me from the west. The sea boasted a pretty shingled pattern; I did about one knot with my paddle. I tired quickly and rested often. Without warning, a shark appeared beside me. It was about nine feet long, the average size for a high-sea shark. It stared at me out of its round, pig eyes, so close I could have reached out and touched it. I found my camera and took pictures while the fish dawdled under and around the rubber canoe. I had time to get at my movie camera, because the shark continued circling around the air tubes, surrounded by a host of pilot fish. I was neither particularly eager to have a shark near me, nor very sure of how to get rid of it. Watching it closely until it came within reach, I hit it on the head with the paddle. My action had no effect whatsoever. After a while, however, it swam off, leaving me convinced that it had no bad intentions toward me. It behaved as a zoologist would have expected.

My sea-anchor line was no thicker than a pencil, but it never occurred to a fish to bite through it. They do not destroy for the sake of destroying, nor do they plan or reason. They never thought of capsizing the boat and then attacking me.

I was worried about my right knee, which was swollen just below the knee cap and very sensitive to the touch. A similar swelling in any other place would have caused me less concern, but the knee joint merits special care and attention.

For the first time since the beginning of the voyage, I trimmed the boat; I took twenty-five pounds of food from the front and stowed it behind my seat. As I still had a west wind, the bow now went better into the wind.

I drew an empty bottle, smelling of gasoline, out of the water, cleaned it carefully and stored it away.

November 16th

Again the wind came from the west. For nine days I had now had contrary winds. The air was heavy, my body dehydrated, my saliva thick and sticky. My tongue stuck to the roof of my mouth. I was roused by seven Mediterranean shearwaters, flying on the starboard side. I had never heard them make such a loud noise before, and the harsh metallic sound of their wings frightened me. Seven in a group—I had never seen so many together.

The swelling on my knee had gone up. I injected penicillin into it.

The terrible west wind frustrated my whole being. It tried my patience, made me nervous, ill-at-ease and irritable. I was ready to start an argument with myself. Of course, I knew these symptoms to be common to people in a state of starvation or to castaways, but knowledge did not help me. Again dreams of a farm and of pastry, topped by mountains of whipped cream, brought release from tension. Nothing else interested me just then. In my mind I was either working on my farm cleaning out the chicken coop, eating marzipan cake, planting trees or whipping cream. My God! What a Philistine I was at heart.

Another bottle, covered with big barnacles and crabs, floated by. It must have spent weeks in the water. I ate two crabs, thoroughly chewing the hard shell to protect my mucous membranes. A huge swarm of pilot fish had adopted the foldboat. They made daring side trips to the outrigger, behaving as nervously as though they were crossing an ocean.

In the afternoon I spotted a sea serpent; I heard a quiet snort on the port side from a comber. I looked and behold! the fabled sea serpent. The swell took me to the exact spot, and there I saw four black curves, the first curve had a black fin. After the next swell I saw three more fins. Four little whales or porpoises, swimming after each other, made an impressive sea serpent. Soon they disappeared behind the high swell, and with them went every sea serpent legend I had ever heard of or read.

November 17th

During the night the wind freshened. I dozed for only seconds. The weather did not look promising; a dark, ominous wall of clouds concentrated in the east. My eyes turned to it constantly. Thunder rumbled across the water; lightning zigzagged through the cloud bank. I was still at twenty-one degrees north and at a longitude of around thirty west. I had sailed more than one thousand miles from Las Palmas.

Darkness came too fast and too early for my taste; in a few minutes I sat in a pitch blackness, through which white foam caps glowed, ghostly and insubstantial. The wind strengthened. I had already taken in the foresail. Now it thundered and lightninged all around me. The wind was more powerful than ever before on this trip. I still felt confident but no longer as cheerful.

November 18th

I passed a cruel night. Every few seconds I had to beam the flashlight at the compass to check on my course. I experienced the darkness of the blind, the thunder of the gods. I was battered, cold, wet and exhausted. The morning found me as empty and lifeless as a doll. Looking at the heavy seas I was afraid they might devour me. It was only fear—the fundamental fear of death—that forced me to stay awake, to use every last possible reserve of energy. Tropical rains smashed down, pounding the boiling sea. It was a storm of major proportions. Threatening clouds obscured the sky. I peered behind the mizzen sail, hoping to find a small crack in the gray sky, but the blue of the sky seemed to have vanished forever, and even the sun no longer existed. The wind raged at more than forty miles an hour. As soon as the rains stopped, the seas reared up to a height of twenty-five to thirty feet; some of the waves that rushed under me seemed even twice that height. I was surprised but pleased to discover that my mizzen sail was just the right size for such a storm.

My average speed through this boiling sea and frequent rain squalls was close to three knots, a good speed for the *Liberia III*. Most of the breakers, when they came from aft, pushed me for-

579

ward without washing over me. On the other hand, when they came from starboard or port, the *Liberia* disappeared into a mountain of water. She could only go with the waves. It was an amazing spectacle of nature: the beating rain, peppering and battering at the water, turned it from green to white. When the rain ceased, giant combers overlaid the surface with white froth and foam. I felt I was in a supernatural elevator that descended rapidly to an inferno at the bottom of the sea, to rise again, with incredible speed, into the sky. But the rubber boat wound her way through all danger. It was impossible for her to keep a straight course with rear winds and a mizzen sail. After each rise and fall I had to look out like a watchdog to keep on course. Cross waves washed over the boat, but her buoyancy brought her up every time. My shoulders were battered by mighty combers hitting from the rear, they broke and foamed over the deck, stopping thirty to sixty feet in front of me. Any nerve-racking backward glance showed me combers capable of knocking down a house. A forward glance, onto the backs of waves, was less discouraging and dangerous-seeming. The trick was to hold to the westward course! Waves could not destroy a rubber-and-canvas boat as long as it went with the wind. The waves coming from aft had less power to do damage as long as they could carry the boat on their backs. Waves broke under the boat, oblivious of the four hundred and forty pounds they carried. I had the feeling that I swam in a cigar-shaped life belt.

The spray cover took on a great deal of water in this raging hell. I bailed every hour. My hands were soon bleached to a snow-white from rain water, the calluses on them soaked and swollen. When I did little repair jobs, my hands were easily scratched, but later the cuts healed without complications.

Despite the storm I had time to give thought to my companions; Mediterranean shearwaters flashed high in the air, dashed down again, rushing at the wave crest and making me think they had never felt better in their lives. Madeira petrels danced on the waves, touched the surface lightly with small black claws and obviously enjoyed the weather. Two big dolphins jumped out of the water, then let themselves fall back in, bending their bodies sideways in a fashion that always astonished me. My little triggerfish were busy cleaning barnacles off the boat bottom. These creatures behaved as always, taking delight in the storm; only the man in the rubber boat was ill-at-ease and worried.

The rudder had a free play of about forty degrees. This, combined with the mizzen sail, made it difficult to hold to the western course. I thought about the advisability of throwing out the sea anchor. I absolutely had to sleep in the coming night; without sleep I could not survive the storm. But I could never wholly forget the great danger of capsizing if I did not stay constantly on the alert. Then, there was a strong possibility that I might lose the rudder in such high seas, for the line of the sea anchor, stretching behind the boat, could simply lift it out. It was a difficult decision, but finally I threw out the anchor, and in a few seconds the boat lay in a good position. I took in the mizzen sail, drew the spray cover up high, leaving only face and chest free. I never fastened the cover over my stomach, as some foldboat users do in mountain rivers; it would have given me a trapped feeling and made it difficult to free myself if I ever capsized.

I thought about the famous voyage of Franz Romer, another story of suffering at sea. In 1928 he sailed in a foldboat, especially made for him, from Lisbon to San Juan in Puerto Rico. He was the first to do it. He left Lisbon at the end of March, shortly afterward was thrown ashore by a storm in the south of Portugal. He sailed from there to the Canary Islands in eleven days and from there made the voyage, in fifty-eight days of unbelievable torture, to St. Thomas. In St. Thomas he had to be pulled out of his boat. During the roughest part of his trip he could sleep—or better catnap—only between crests of high waves, then he was forced to awaken to control his rudder. To me the story of Romer's voyage is the greatest of all sea stories.

Franz Romer in his foldboat and I in mine had to control our boats every minute. They were very narrow and had no keels, so without control they would have capsized. But I had the advantage of setting out a sea anchor, which Romer did not dare to do for fear of damaging the rubber of his boat or the rudder.

Only a man who knows these foldboats can imagine the torture that Romer must have withstood. Eight weeks of sitting or lying, almost always wet, with never a possibility of standing upright, surrounded only by waves and combers. Eight weeks condemned to a cockpit, to suffering, shouting and prayer. In 1928 Romer did not have the medicines of today against pustulae, ulcers and boils. He had only one asset: the patience of a yogi and the energy of a man possessed by an idea. Anyone who has ever tried sitting for twelve hours in a foldboat knows of the cramping pain, but he has no idea how this aches when one's body is covered with ulcers, which don't heal, which exude pus and burn like the fires of hell. Whenever Romer wanted to eat or adjust his sails, he had to open his spray cover and—splash—a bucket of water was flung in his face.

At the very end, Romer, a former ship's officer, made the fatal mistake. He left San Juan in September, the hurricane month of the Caribbean. He had been warned, but he was determined to go farther. Shortly after he left, a bad hurricane swept the area. Romer was never heard from again, nor did any part of his boat drift ashore.

Now I lay behind a sea anchor, more exposed to the combers than when I went under sail, because the boat did not go with the waves. Romer's spray cover was destroyed by a breaking comber. I had protected myself against a similar disaster by laying thin planks over the washboard and putting air cushions over them.

The night was black and stormy, but I felt an unusual exhilaration as I lay in the boat, listening to the roaring, howling and boiling that went on around me, while I sat inside, curled up for a short nap. I fell asleep in a few minutes. Then I awoke, all my instincts working, and without conscious thought, I bailed.

November 19th

The night was endless. Heavy dark storm clouds would not let the daylight through; only rain squalls, thunder, lightning and bailing kept me alert. As I expected and feared, I lost my rudder. The steering cables responded heavily to my feet; then suddenly they turned light to the touch, letting me know the rudder had left me. Fortunately I had brought a spare. I dug my chronometer out from its rubber bag and checked the time. Daylight was half an hour overdue.

It came at last, but the monotony of dark-gray skies between masses of heaving gray-green water remained unbroken. Without a rudder, the *Liberia* could not hold a course to the waves, so I shipped even more water. My hands looked bad. I peeled off the sodden calluses.

The rise and fall of the boat during the night had made it hard for me to rest. I was still very, very tired. I crouched and laid my head on the washboard, too frightened to sleep, and as I lay there I heard the spray cover whisper to me.

"Now come," it said, "be reasonable and lie down. Forget everything. Leave it. Let others do something. You don't have to do everything."

At first this conversation seemed perfectly normal, until I remembered I was alone on board. Often, as I awoke, I looked around for my companion, not realizing at once that there was nobody else with me. My sense of reality had changed in an odd way. I spoke to myself, of course, and I talked to the sails and the outrigger, but the noises around me also belonged to human beings; the breaking sea snorted at me, whistled, called to me, shouted and breathed at me with the rage and fury of a living being.

I had to wait for the storm to lessen before putting on my spare rudder. The sky still threatened. From time to time it thundered and lightninged; tropical downpours and combers emptied buckets of water into the boat. I bailed mechanically and patiently. I gave up worry and thought. The storm had shown me that I could have confidence in my boat. It is only after a man has lived through a storm with his boat that he knows exactly what to expect from her.

November 20th

This was my thirty-second day at sea. The night was restless, but the wind had weakened. I decided to replace the rudder. With the wick of the rudder between my teeth and the blade tied to my right wrist, I slipped, fully dressed, into the water. The waves were still fifteen to twenty feet high, the temperature of the water lukewarm. With difficulty I swam to the stern. One moment I was under the stern, then the boat hit my head, and the next instant the stern was before me. So I took the stern firmly under my left arm, changed the rudder blade into my left hand, when suddenly a big wave tore it away. I cannot describe the shock; it was unimaginable. I reacted quickly, grabbed for the blade and luckily caught hold of the string attached to it. I could feel the sweat of delayed fright coming up inside me. The next attempt was successful; with my right hand I pushed in the wick, fastened it once more with string and crawled back into the boat. I tried to undress, but the seas, with winds still blowing at twenty-five miles an hour, were too high. Water had entered the boat while I worked on the rudder, dragging the cushions out of place. I righted them and sat down again. With the steering cables I again controlled the rudder. My new rudder was the standard size, whereas the one I had lost in the storm was only two-thirds as big. Back in Las Palmas I had decided that my heavily loaded boat did not need a whole blade and that a standard size would exert too much pull on the rubber stern. I pulled in the sea anchor, fastened it behind the mizzenmast and set the little square sail.

Now my legs shook from delayed shock. It would take time for my nerves to calm down. But I felt as though I had won a battle, and after the bailing was finished, I treated myself to an extra portion of milk. The seas still roared around me, the wind blew furiously across a slightly clearer sky. The sun was circled by a big rainbow, a sign of intense humidity in the atmosphere.

November 23rd

Little by little, the wind eased. I hoisted the gaff sail. But the weather did not improve. Squalls chased each other across the water, squeezing rain out of the clouds onto the suffering foldboat below. Every few minutes I looked behind the mizzen to be sure that no bad squall approached, which would force me to take down the big sail. A chart of my course would have looked like the movements of a snake. I was thirty degrees too far to starboard one minute; in the next, a wave pushed me thirty degrees to the south on the port side; but on the whole I managed to keep west.

Two great big dolphins had followed me for several days. Whenever the wind abated, they beat their tails against the bottom of the boat and then swam slowly off. They could easily be caught, I thought, especially when their heads came above water. Though I knew they were too big for my boat, I had a strong desire to get one. I loaded the underwater gun. My first shot was a bull's-eye. The arrow landed on the fish's skull. He jumped, he leaped into the air and lifted the outrigger as he did so. Quickly I jerked at the line and held an empty arrow in my hand. The hooks of the arrow had not taken hold in the hard skull. Perhaps it was better this way!

As the sun went down—1,400 miles from the Canary Islands, I saw a butterfly flutter in the air. Only the trade winds could have brought it this far.

My knees had improved!

November 24th

Tropic birds, Mediterranean shearwaters, petrels and Manx shearwaters flew around me again. The wind was very tired, and all my sails were hoisted. Suddenly, the port-side backstay broke. I took down the gaff sail and, to my horror, saw a huge, dark box only a half mile away. A ship had come up on me without my hearing anything. I had no idea what they wanted. Had they stopped to pick me up? I waved my hands and signaled that I was all right. Evidently they missed my hand signals; I was too far away. They made a turn around the *Liberia*. Stubbornly, I kept the sail hoisted. As the freighter came port side for a second time, I could even distinguish faces on the bridge, crew and a few passengers following with interest my boat's maneuvers. I took pictures and shot film. A young officer jumped from the bridge to the main deck, megaphone in hand.

"Don't you want to come alongside?" he shouted.

"No, thank you," I answered, without giving myself time to think.

"Do you need food?" came the next question, and again I replied, "No!"

He asked my name, and I asked him for the exact longitude. After giving orders to have the bridge reckon the position, he inquired where I came from.

"From Las Palmas. Thirty-six days at sea and with course to St. Thomas," I informed him.

"Would you like me to announce your arrival at the yacht club there?" he wanted to know.

I told him, yes, and gave him my nationality. He gave me the exact position: 56.28 longitude, 20.16 latitude. The young officer found it hard to believe that I didn't need food, but at my insistence the freighter slowly got under way. The captain shouted a last "good luck" from the bridge; the engines started carefully so as not to endanger my fragile boat. Then the steamer, the *Blitar* from Rotterdam, took up her western course.

The meeting left me dizzy. My quick decision to refuse food was unnatural. Evidently my mental discipline combined with the auto suggestions, "Don't take any assistance," had forced my out-of-hand refusal. I thought about their reactions on the freighter as they stumbled on my funny, small craft—which obviously could not hold enough food for a crossing—in mid-Atlantic. The ready offer of help from the captain made me happy. It showed me that men are never alone, that castaways can always hope and that there are men all over the world who help others.

My latitude was exact, my longitude was a few degrees too far west. Thus even in a foldboat one can take the latitude accurately, although I knew that in a high swell and with heavy weather, it is not absolutely correct.

Tropical rains came down in torrents that night. I caught five quarts of fresh water, perhaps to compensate a little for my firm "no."

November 25th

A steamer passed at nine in the morning within three miles but with contrary course. In the high seas and winds of twenty-five miles an hour, they could not see me.

I wondered when the famous stable and sunny trade winds would start. Only at noon did the weather clear for a short time. Another butterfly lay on the water. Dolphins hunted flying fish, and tropic birds circled above the boat.

For the past two weeks some of my canned milk had been sour, but only a little had really spoiled. I discovered some cans with small holes in them and decided that the metal was too thin. The sour milk turned into an excellent aid to my bowels. On a small boat, a badly-functioning digestive system can become a real nuisance. Somehow or other, I had to solve the problem every five to seven days. When I found that my turned milk helped, I no longer worried about the taste.

November 26th

I counted my pulse rate at night; that night it was thirty-two, lower than the usual thirty-four. My body adapted itself more easily to the hazardous ordeal than did my mind. I was still convinced of a successful crossing, but sometimes I became restless and dissatisfied, cursing at the unstable weather conditions. On my thirty-eighth day, a typical stormy squall rushed to the west. In the northeast, explosive masses of dark clouds gathered.

November 29th

Yesterday was calm. I shot triggerfish, happy to save more of my food supply. During the night I hung fresh bait into the water; it soon gave off such a strong bioluminescent glow that I could read by its light. In contrast, the meat lying on my deck stayed dark and lifeless.

In the clear blue morning sky, little trade-wind clouds piled up into huge banks of fine weather clouds. The day was warm and windless. On the flat surface, water striders glided over the plankton "dust." A dark remora, the length of a finger, tried to get free passage under the outrigger. It was shy and nervous, darting to and fro between the boat and the outrigger as though denying its stowaway intentions. A little triggerfish showed interest in something on the deck; it turned on its side repeatedly as it swam alongside, looking up at me with curiosity. But it was as cautious of me as I was eager to catch it, and it never came too close for safety.

I was right in the middle of the Atlantic now.

At dusk a swarm of triggerfish swam over to me. I shot two, while the rest stole my barnacles. It was the first time they had eaten off the *Liberia* at dusk, and I thought it might be a school that felt at home with me and my boat.

November 30th

With a hard, metallic beating of their wings, a Manx shearwater and Bulwer's petrel passed near the boat. The weather was still calm. Now and then a gentle sigh passed over the water. I tried to catch it in my gaff sail and to achieve paddling speed. Again triggerfish came for a visit. They seemed to be less cautious in a swarm. I was able to catch three. Curious to find out how one can squeeze fluid from a fish, I cut up a few slices of meat, put them into a handkerchief and squeezed. I chewed on the handkerchief, but still no liquid came out. I ruined a perfectly good handkerchief by the experiment. I tried again with a plastic bag, first poking a few holes into it with a sailing needle. Then I chewed it and in a few minutes had a mouthful of purée of fish but no fluid. I cut holes into the fish—again no liquid. Later I tried collecting water from the morning dew, but I discovered it was not possible on my boat.

The little remora finally found a spot under the outrigger. I wanted to tease it—a little—so I put my weight to starboard, the outrigger rose in the air, providing my little stowaway with an involuntary air bath. Evidently it did not care for the excursion into other spheres, for it detached itself from the outrigger when it hit water and went back under the boat.

Some hundred yards off to the north, a waterspout reached from the sea to the dark cloud banks. If it came down on the boat, it could sweep everything off.

December 1st

A tropic bird, a last farewell from the east, circled the mast. The dull, weary weather remained unchanged. It had the one advantage of curing my skin eruptions by permitting protracted "hygiene hours." I grabbed a triggerfish, but my stomach reacted against its flesh. I imagined that my breath smelled horribly of raw fish. But I was saving the food for worse times ahead. Early in the afternoon a ship passed by within two miles. The high swell made it impossible for me to determine whether she was a tanker or a freighter. I felt so well-prepared for what lay in front of me that I saw no reason for concern about passing ships. Sunday sailors who stop ships at sea and ask for position and food are like the man who pulls the emergency cord unnecessarily on a train.

The air felt thick enough to cut with a knife. I had hoped that a black cloud wall would bring a little freshness, but it brought only five drops of rain and fierce winds. That evening, however, the rain did come, filling all my containers. I put the aft sail over my head and the rain water poured from it onto the plastic layer of the spray cover. From there, using a sponge or a syringe, I transferred it into bottles.

December 3rd

The sea roared again. A stiff breeze blew from the northeast. Occasional, dangerous squalls sped by; the air echoed to a rumbling and howling, reminiscent of a first-class storm. A tiny fish landed on deck. I ate it, but it was very fatty and tasted as though someone had injected rancid olive oil under its skin.

December 5th

Two bad nights. Several times waves struck the boat crosswise. I sailed the correct western course. Heavy seas coming from the beam nearly capsized me. I was saved by my outrigger. The whole foreship plowed the water in heavy seas, sometimes taking water over as far as the mast, though the narrow bow projected far out of the sea. It was good I had a mizzen sail; with a foresail the bow would have dug deeper into the water and I would have run the danger of somersaulting. Rain squall followed rain squall, while the wind, coming powerfully from the north, drove tons of water over the westwardly running *Liberia*. Another day's ration saved by eating fish.

December 6th

For five days the weather belonged to the wind. My body was constantly wet. Everything ached: knees, elbows, shoulders and—as one would expect—buttocks.

My attention was caught by three small articles floating on the water, one of which looked like a mouse trap.

589

December 7th

I was too exhausted to sail all night as I wanted to. Once again I heard voices speaking to me from various parts of the boat and I answered them.

"Where are you?" I asked the knife. "Come on, don't hide from me. I've got work for you to do."

To the outrigger, as a heavy cross sea tried to push it out of place: "Great! Show the sea what a half tire is worth. Don't, please, make a fool of me. And don't forget, you and I have to stick together in this. If you go, I go."

The imagination plays extraordinary tricks on tired ears; the breaking waves shouted, praising or cursing me. They whispered and talked to each other, to the boat, to the lonely sailor. It was clear I needed sleep. I put out the sea anchor and curled up to take cat naps.

In the morning the weather looked no friendlier; stormy squalls rushed over me, some wet, some dry. A northern wind took command and pushed me south. I tried to sail west, but it became dangerous. I was lucky I had not yet capsized; several times the outrigger plunged deep into the water. I touched wood and took the precaution of putting out the sea anchor so that I could sleep a little.

December 9th

The sea calmed; I shot at dolphins; one struggled free, another flew off with my arrow, which slipped from its nylon line. I had a replacement but decided not to try for big fish any more. I enjoyed a meal of triggerfish meat.

I developed an abscess on my right hand, where a triggerfish had bitten me; the wound healed very slowly, and my local lymph glands reacted by swelling up.

I ate the last piece of garlic. From now on raw meat would have to be eaten without flavoring. My thoughts ran in one consistent groove—food. I decided to stop in Phillipsburg on St. Martin Island—a Dutch West Indian possession—and shop there. I planned a menu down to the last detail: a big loaf of crusty French bread, slices of Swiss cheese and ham, sweet butter and a dessert of applesauce with cookies and chocolate candy. Of course I preferred a cake, but I was sure I would not find it in the tropics. Who knows? Perhaps my Christmas would be spent there.

December 11th

The weather did not change; dangerous clouds gathered in the north; the air was sticky and the wind sleepy. Sargasso weed floated past me but I did not allow myself any false hopes, although in these latitudes it is generally found near the Caribbean. My longitude measurements were rough but reliable, and I knew where I was. My noon position indicated a climb to the north. Menacing weather from the north interrupted my "hygiene hour." My practiced eye discerned a siege of bad weather ahead.

At three that afternoon it was still calm and flat. At six the clouds exploded.

The sea roared and tropical rains hammered at the water. I felt like giving up on the trade winds. Should I said southward? In a vile humor, I threw over the sea anchor. A nylon line, no thicker than a pencil, held it to the boat. A shark's bite and the line would be finished. But I knew this was unlikely. I remembered with amusement the statement I had read in an old book in St. Croix about a shark's taste buds. The author, stating that in the Caribbean sharks attack a Frenchman rather than an Englishman, gave as his explanation the fact that the fish were repelled by the latter's meat diet. I was sure that a fish with such epicurean tastes would never be interested in a nylon line.

December 13th

The trade winds blew at thirty miles an hour. Feelings of discouragement and disappointment took hold of me, and I found myself wishing for a taste of the fine favorable winds I had had during the last three weeks of my previous trip. I comforted myself with the knowledge that these ugly winds would have to stop sometime.

Twenty dolphins, flashing blue and green in the water, gathered around the *Liberia*. There was no time to watch them. My rudder needed my full attention; again it had too much play, and I had to concentrate to stay on course. I was surprised to see so many dol-

591

phins at once. Were they chased by a shark and looking for protection?

I avoided backward glances, for they showed me terrifying seas and towering breakers heading straight for my frail *Liberia*. Once I narrowly missed disaster. An enormous breaker, coming from the rear, left me gasping for air as it poured water onto the boat. We were taken thirty to forty-five feet high into the air and then flung down with a hard bump. It was my first experience with such violence, and I had no desire to repeat it.

To what did I owe the fact that I was still afloat? Luck? Was it only luck that I still lived? I refused to answer my own question. I knew I was well prepared, well trained, and beyond that, I would not analyze my situation. But I had to admit that these giant breakers caused me concern. They did not come often: in a span of twenty-four hours they might pass only once, perhaps twice, with full strength—but the mere prospect unnerved me.

In the dusk I spotted a red light, a little later a green light and then both together. At first I could make neither head nor tail of them, when suddenly I realized that a steamer was bearing straight down on me. In a panic I flashed my flashlight on and off against the mizzen sail, put the paddle beside me ready for use. The ship gave the impression of coming at me head on. I watched with extreme relief as she passed about fifty yards away. I noticed that she rolled even more than I in the heavy seas.

December 14th

I sailed all night through. I had no recollection or feeling that I had ever slept. I knew only that I was tired; terribly tired! Often during the day my eyes closed and my mind wandered. A tropic bird from the western Atlantic, approaching that morning, gave me comfort. The first American to greet me on the voyage. Though I knew, of course, that they fly far from land, I welcomed him and cheered up. The wind blew from thirty to forty miles an hour. I forgot the beautiful white bird and thought solely of my discomfort and my fears. I felt so small, so insignificant and so helpless in these powerful seas. The unusual name that a Fanti fisherman in Liberia had given his canoe repeated itself endlessly in my mind. "Who are You, Seapower?" My God, Fanti fisherman, I thought, come and look at these waves, and you will feel as small as I. All at once a huge steamer loomed to port; it had come up without my noticing it. What do they want, I asked myself, and waved at them.

"Everything is fine here," I shouted. Then I saw a man, megaphone in hand, calling to me.

"My dear Lindemann," rang across the water, "don't be a stubborn fool . . ." And the rest of his words drowned in the roar of the waves. The words were spoken in German, and the voice was familiar. And then I knew who he was. It was the voice of a newspaper man whom I had met when I returned from my last trip. I remembered him clearly because he had arrived before the others to interview me. He was a former ship's officer, but I could tell at the time from the manner in which he questioned me that he hated the sea. And why was it this voice that shouted at me from the steamer?

The ship made a circle around me, putting oil on her course. But I continued sailing, passing by the oil slicks. The small breakers lessened, and the surface appeared smoother; but the huge combers were not impressed by the oil and thundered on. Another squall swept the sea and kept my hands and feet occupied steering the boat in a westerly direction. The steamer, circling around, confused me. I forgot to head west. I took pictures of it, and then there it was, alongside once again. A young officer made a despairing gesture in my direction. Could he not help me? Smiling, I waved a "no" at him, but my smile was a parody, a horrible grimace. I had begun to realize that anything could happen to me in such stormy trade winds, that factors I had not reckoned with could overtake me. The ship veered off close to the boat, its waves mingling with wind waves and splashing over my deck. Then I found myself in its wake, forcing me to be on my guard to avoid the log line of the ship. On her stern I read, *Eaglesdale, London*. The meeting cheered me, for it was fine to know that people wanted to help even though I would not give them the opportunity. Perhaps I should have accepted. Give up after eight weeks, after fifty-five days at sea? I had to succeed by myself. I would make it all right. I was determined.

The German voice coming to me from an English steamer puzzled me. Had I really heard it? Could the man have resolved his hate-love for the sea by returning to it? I would have to write to the ship and find out who had spoken. (After my arrival in St. Thomas I wrote the captain of the *Eaglesdale,* who replied with a friendly note, congratulating me on having survived "such bad weather." But the German voice was a hallucination. My eyes had reacted correctly, but my ears had deceived me.)

As the ship left she put oil out to calm the seas and prolong my life.

December 15th

I passed a night of hell. Again I had no sleep. I was afraid to throw out the sea anchor because in these heavy seas its line would threaten the rudder. I knew I must not lose it, but I also knew I simply had to have sleep. I must not overestimate my energy; I had to be fresh enough to stay on course. On the other hand, I could not afford to sleep even for an instant in that boiling sea. The problem looked quite different here at sea than it had on shore. At sea I could only stay awake for four days and nights; on shore, with short cat naps, I had managed it for longer stretches. And now I felt my eyes closing. I dozed, I dreamed, I became the prey of imaginings and hallucinations. And then I put my last energy into staying alert. I began to sing. Slowly, I ground out a tune, only to find that something in my body cut off my voice. Then I counted, one . . . two . . . three . . . four, and suddenly I could not find the next number; it was lost; it was simply not there any more . . . I knew only one thing; the boat had to go into a garage; somewhere I had to shelter her and lie down beside her and sleep. . . .

The mizzen sail beat against my shoulders. A warning? I flashed the light onto the compass and found I was headed too far north.

I had the feeling that behind me stood a barn in whose lee the waves were flatter, while farther out on both sides, the sea still raged. As soon as I left the protected lee, masses of water washed over the deck. Ah yes! The barn would protect me . . . stay in its lee . . . where it was calm, cal—me—r and then . . . water . . . I swam . . . what was it? The shock awakened me, I flashed the light onto the compass; too far south. I did not hear the breaker that swamped me, it was simply there. I bailed, I had to bail . . . I must bail. Why wasn't I doing it?

I was invited on a hunt. A Negro servant called for me. Lovely! I trusted him, he knew where we had to go. I sat comfortably in a kind of rickshaw. I saw big white lines ahead, and they worried me a little.

"Boy," I asked, "where are we going?"

"It is all right. We have to go through the surf," he answered, and as he spoke we plunged through. The deck was under water and came up again. I looked at the boy to the left. He wore black and snorted like a whale or horse, but he worked without talking back.

"Boy, where do you boys live?"

"In the west."

West! The word reminded me of something. I knew it, and then I remembered the compass. Again I was off course. I looked at the boy on the left, but he had gone. A black horse rode there now, pushing the boat. Horses know the way home. I could rely on a horse . . . satisfied, I relaxed—then suddenly I seemed awake, slowly and instinctively I came to myself. But who was I? No answer. What was my name? No name. What was happening? West, west—and no more stayed with me. Again I remembered the compass. The flashlight lit it up. Again, off course. Then a sound came into my consciousness, the sea still roared. I was cold, although sail and spray cover provided ample protection. Then I clearly heard the voice of Mephisto: "I do not see your water lies." I looked for my black boy and black horse at port side and saw only black outrigger. It must be more than a lifeless object. It had to have spirit and soul.

During the morning a real storm with winds of forty miles an hour had developed. I looked with disbelief into the face of the waves. "Such waves cannot exist," I thought.

A little later I screamed and shouted, "I will get through. I will make it, I will make it."

As if to confirm my optimism, I saw a frigate bird, an American frigate bird, sailing high through the air. According to my calculations, I was still four hundred miles from the Caribbean islands; but frigates rarely fly more than one hundred and fifty from their land base, and I could have made a mistake. What a lovely mistake! It meant landfall within four days. This called for a double ration of food right away. I had starved myself enough. Now began the good life; every day I would eat double rations from now on. I would celebrate Christmas on land. Lucky, lucky man. When I threw out the sea anchor I did it with happiness and a sense of relief. My secret aim was to celebrate Christmas on shore. I bailed and dreamed of Christmas pudding. The storm was at its peak. The boat had trouble sticking with the waves. As she had lightened considerably, she might now be badly trimmed. I should have done something about inner ballast, but both water containers, provided for that purpose, had developed holes. So I forgot it.

I woke up and bailed, napped again. I sat, the spray cover drawn over my head. The time was nine in the evening.

All at once a huge wall rose starboard . . . nothing more . . . out . . . empty . . . dead? No, I gasped for breath, beat with hands and feet, and then they were free. I had capsized, was in the water. "I must reach the boat, the waves must not separate us," went through my head.

The hull stood high over the surface. It felt slippery. My mouth tasted of salt. At last I caught hold of the outrigger. The boat lay across the waves. I pushed her into the right direction. Would the storm ever stop? What could I do? I thought back to the time when my boat had capsized near Madeira, on one of my shorter previous foldboat voyages, and I remembered the difficulty I had had then in righting her. I found myself between outrigger and boat, with only my head out of water. The storm showed no sign of subsiding. The waves rumbled, roared and thundered as before, mercilessly. In the sea, my body felt bitterly cold. Then I climbed onto the hull, my right hand on the paddle to the outrigger, the left cramped to the edge of the boat. The wind hurtled over the hull, comber after comber washed over me. Still I was terribly cold. Only my head, protected by a woolen cap with a hood over it, stayed warm.

Was this the end? No! I would not allow it to be the end. I willed the *Liberia* to stay afloat. Would I sail the rest of the way to the islands, perched on the hull? Waves, warmer than the winds, broke over my back. I glanced at the stars. Orion was not even in the zenith, so it was not yet midnight. I knew I had to wait till daybreak to right the boat. I faced seven hours precariously balanced on the hull. The stiff winds chilled my body, I slipped back into the water. My body curled, and with cramped hands I held tight to the outrigger paddle. Every movement stirred up cold water between my skin and clothing. I forced myself to remain motionless. During the night the sea calmed, but big waves still made giant shadows. I felt sick. I vomited—I must have swallowed sea water. My hands clutched the paddle. How strong they were! To keep my body in the right direction, I had to tread water constantly. I froze.

I thought of home and of my parents; they knew nothing of this voyage. They could not imagine what had happened to their child. Self-pity engulfed me.

December 16th

It was midnight. Nothing had changed, except that I was even colder than before. Then one of my feet kicked against something. What was interested in my feet? Anxiety attacked me. I scrambled up onto the hull, my legs gripping the westward-pointing stern.

Two A.M. Orion descended in the west. I had slid back into the water, forced there by the extreme cold. The pitiless winds had reduced me to a shivering, chattering skeleton. I thought back to a voyage I had made in the Straits of Gibraltar one winter, when the wind blew so cold that my hands were unable to hold the paddle. The wind, that time, blew me into a harbor around midnight, and I had been offered a drink. That was what I needed now.

Suddenly I heard the sound of bells. They reminded me of church bells at home, the same bells that I had rung as a child. Did they ring now for my funeral? They must know, surely, that I could not die now, that I would get through? I was quiet, my muscles held on, instinctively, and demonstrated that deep in my subconscious there was still life. What did the heavy, brutal combers want of me? Didn't they realize that they could not touch me? That I was taboo? That I would survive, that I would make it, must make it? I had not lost my faith, nor had my subconscious or my instincts betrayed me.

At four A.M. Orion was about forty-five degrees west. I dozed on the hull. Once a voice invited me to go to a nearby farmhouse, to have a drink and sink deep into a feather bed.

"Where is the house?" I asked.

"Over there, in the west, behind the hill," came the answer.

Then I awoke. My sense of hearing had returned, I could feel the numbing cold again. I heard myself repeating aloud: "Never give up, never give up, I'll make it." I dared not sleep. Deep sleep meant certain death. I knew the sea devours everything, leaves no trace, draws even the dead downward. In the water again, I floated, dead, empty of feeling, at times delirious. But something survived, the lighthouse that guided me was my determination to succeed. As long as I had that, I lived. Sometimes, the lighthouse darkened— then there was nothing—only muscles—an animal without thoughts—all instinct, until the lighthouse suddenly lit up for me again. Loud and bright, it warned me not to give in, to keep on fighting. It shouted at me, "You will make it." Then I awoke, my senses returned, first hearing, then feeling, then speech. I heard death in my ears, sea and storm beat upon my body, salt stung my eyes, cold shook my bones. I was grateful for my lighthouse, it made me a slave who was not allowed to die, a slave to an idea.

I lay on the hull, my head pressed against the slippery rubber. I thought at times that I belonged to another world but knew not which. A happier world, where no one froze, where salt did not sting the eye. But my hands clung to this world, and for this I thanked God.

Finally, a shy dawn came to my rescue. For the past two hours I had lain on the hull. Hands and legs held fast while my mind wandered. I could no longer control it: dreams and thoughts, reality and hallucination, I could no longer tell the difference . . . a concentration on nothingness . . . but still I stayed alive.

The wind had not lessened its force, but I had to try to right the boat. I could wait no longer. I fixed a long line to the outrigger and pulling from the opposite side, I managed to right her. As the stern pointed westward, I pushed it east. Waves filled the boat. I found to my relief that the compass and my bailing pot had stayed on. The bow pointed far out of the water, the stern just floated. The mizzenmast was broken at its base, the sea anchor lost. I climbed into the boat as waves washed over my face. I looked for three air cushions to push them under the stern. I found the first, inflated it and pushed it far back of the aft washboard. There were the two others, and they followed the first. I began to recover, I drew the spray cover up to my shoulders, untied my pot and bailed. The boat was not yet stable, and I had to sit close to the outrigger.

Big waves ran over the deck, but slowly I put myself in control. I continued bailing. My pot, which held quite a few quarts, struck me as a most useful object. Then I set the course for the west. I bailed until the pot no longer scooped up water, and I finished the job with a sponge.

An hour later the boat was empty, but for some fifty quarts that I left in for ballast. Then I checked the sails, which were in the water on the starboard side. I put them on deck and fastened them. I checked the inside of the boat; every single one of my cans of food had gone, my food supply for the last part of the voyage, had vanished. I had had emergency rations of eleven cans of milk, which I kept in a bag tied to the mast. Where was the flashlight? One had gone, but I found my spare and beamed light at the bow. Clothes, watertight rubber bags lay in chaos. My beam picked out something red. It was the bag full of milk cans. I looked for the two bags that held the Leica, one with black and white film, the other with color. They were gone. The bag with my spare parts was gone. My night glasses, my fluid compass (although I found it later in St. Thomas), the toilet articles, the grappling iron, all these now floated somewhere in the Atlantic.

The port-side shroud of the mainstay was torn from the deck canvas, the lines for the foresails were in such bad shape that I could not use them without repairing them first.

The frigate bird that had consoled me earlier flew over again. I had to be close to shore. Then I remembered to check my sextant and found it wet in its bag. The chronometer was also full of water but ran the minute I touched it. I took my position before it was too late. The trade winds still blew the storms of yesterday, the storms they might continue to blow for many days to come. The nautical almanac was soaked through; I handled the pages carefully. My latitude was approximately eighteen degrees and twenty minutes, it could not be too far off. My good knife had disappeared. My cans! Gone, too! But I was alive and well, and what more did I want? I did not hoist the sail, as storm and wind pushed me to the west. In the late afternoon I shot a triggerfish with the underwater gun. Its meat tasted better than ever before—and my bottles of rain water had stayed with me.

December 17th

The weather did not change; the sea roared, the storm howled, fish and birds gathered around me again. I was dead tired. During the night my body had shivered uncontrollably. Now at last it was warmer, and the sun shone. Shortly before noon, a wave whistled beside me, reminding me of an old sailor's legend my grandfather had told me when I was a child. The legend of the disaster that a whistling wave brings, springs from the story of a shipwrecked sailor, the sole survivor of a ship that went down shortly after a whistling wave had gone by. The sailors heard it, just as I heard it then. Was the whistling wave an omen for me, too? What did I have to lose? Only my life. But I'll make it.

Under the water I could see living creatures move; two dolphins. They were small but edible. I shot them, jerked them up on deck, beat them to death with my round knife and devoured them whole. My stomach was still in an unsettled condition, but I ignored its complaints.

Air . . . nothing . . . air at last. I was capsized again! Again I clung to the boat; it was slippery from long thin algae and the few barnacles that were left did not offer much hold. I pushed the boat in the right direction, and there on the bow was a small bulge on the rubber. It was the line from the outrigger, which I had deliberately left there, under the boat. It was easy to right the *Liberia* with the line. Soon I was climbing inside again. I bailed while my elbows held the spray cover high. How had it happened again? My underwater gun had slipped away. I had not had a chance to fasten it after the last dolphin. That was bad. I continued bailing. The islands had to be close by now. Even without the gun I would succeed. I realized that I had capsized over the outrigger each time.

Were the Polynesians right when they put it on the windward side? Both times I had felt no shock. It could have been such a sweet death. Bail, Hannes, bail! There was a bulge in the rubber. It must have been made by something pointed. I decided to try leaving more water in the boat, if the wooden frame could stand it.

I still sat in water. It was not cold; I felt nothing. I had to rig the mizzen sail. It would give the boat speed and lessen the danger of being capsized by angry waves for the third time. With my knife I sharpened the point of the mizzenmast and put the paddle mast on it. It was shaky, but it held. Then I hoisted my sail, relieved to be under sail again and ready to celebrate Christmas then and there.

December 19th

It still stormed; I was empty, a shell, unthinking, kept going only by a complete concentration on the words, "Keep going west, never give up, I'll make it." I dozed. Sometimes, while meditating, I felt happy; I was somewhere where I could take refuge in irresponsible happiness, where I could escape my ego and my consciousness.

Then I had to find my eleven cans of milk in their red rubber bag near the foremast. Only eleven cans! I felt like drinking two a day. The islands had to be close, I told myself, but these cans were emergency rations and they had to remain that. There was always the possibility that I might capsize again, that I might have trouble with the rudder; I had to save my milk. I would have to drink the water in my bottles; there was still enough to last for a few days. I knew of castaways who had survived more than fourteen days by drinking only one glass of water a day.

A sudden shock awakened me. The steering mechanism no longer worked, I looked back, drew at the steering cables and—to my horror—found the rudder blade barely hanging on. With a paddle I guided the port-side cable over the stern and pulled the rudder in starboard out of the water. Now I urgently needed a sea anchor. The rudder wick was broken; small wonder in such weather, but I now faced the problem of a new wick. My spare parts were all gone. Inspiration came to me when I remembered the small wire on top of the mizzen that kept the sail in shape. It was the very thing I needed. With my paddle I kept the boat more or less on course, pulled the wire into the right shape for a wick, slid fully clothed into the water and fastened the rudder blade. My clothes were now completely drenched, but then they had not been fully dry for days. A pathetic afternoon sun occasionally dried me out here and there. At night I invariably sat in water. It was a miracle that my buttocks were not more painful. Was my skin accustomed to the constant immersion?

Clearly before me, in a mind's eye sharpened by danger, I could see the red roofs and green palms of Phillipsburg.

December 21st

I made a sea anchor of my last pieces of string tied to a seabag. But I did not use it, and I hoped I would not have to, for it could only hold me back. A terrible sense of urgency took hold of me, forcing me to calm my nerves with consoling speeches.

"I'll make it; keep going west," I repeated endlessly.

When my mind wandered I felt gay and lighthearted, whereas my conscious moments brought tension and worry. There were times when I forgot everything, when I removed myself to a place where there was nothing but an eternal stillness, where I hardly existed and the noise of the storm could not follow.

Frigate birds, circling the *Liberia,* announced my imminent arrival; I knew I was not far from the islands.

My strength lay in my foldboat. Taunting the sea, she resisted all combers that sought to destroy her. The sea sensed the *Liberia*'s defiance, and the giant waves hounded me for it, doing their best to catch me.

"As long as the mizzen is hoisted, you won't get me," I shouted at them.

Yesterday I drank a can of milk, and today I was greedy for a second. I scanned the sky for clouds that would indicate an island. Nothing! Tomorrow might bring better luck.

During the night I froze; my teeth chattered, my arms shook and I suffered from terrible cramps. "I will make it," I repeated, as I prayed for alert senses. All my life I have prayed and meditated; now, in meditation, I concentrated on my arrival in St. Martin, with its colorful houses and fat, green palms. But the picture that developed before my mind's eye was gray.

Why not take a can of milk? I would still have nine left. But what if I had another accident? On a sudden impulse, and with the indifference of an exhausted man, I grabbed for a can, beat with my knife at the edge and sucked out the milk. Only after I had emptied the can, did I have the strength to feel ashamed of my weakness.

December 24th and 25th

The days seemed shorter, the nights longer; nighttime belonged to the devil, while the days belonged to hope. Trade winds blew at thirty to forty miles an hour, bringing with them towering waves. How long had I sailed with no sleep? Many, many days, and God alone knew how many nights. It could have been weeks. The passage of time no longer held meaning for me. Time, Philistine word, a modern, sick word; time, the disease of today!

And today was Christmas Eve. Last year I had discovered my America on this very night. I felt certain it would happen again. "I am lucky," I thought, "and twice I will arrive on Christmas Eve." Royal terns squealed and quarreled around me; my Christmas present, a frigate bird, flew by. I sang Christmas carols.

I wondered which island lay ahead. I could be near Antigua, of course, as I had been last year, but I desperately wanted to arrive in St. Martin. I had set my heart on Phillipsburg.

I checked the sextant; it had rusted and was out of order. Still, I intended to land in Phillipsburg. I was determined. I could not put my hand on the movie camera, but as it was probably useless by now, I decided it didn't matter. I had wanted to take beautiful pictures of waves, to show a storm, even take a picture of a wave running over the boat. What difference did all my lost plans make now?

Christmas Eve. I thought of Christmas trees, of all the great variety of trees I had seen in my lifetime of travel, decorated as Christmas trees. In Liberia, one friend had taken a dead tree, decorated it with seaweed, making, in this fashion, one of the prettiest Christmas trees that I had ever seen. I decided on my Christmas present for that night: a can of evaporated milk. I would drink it at dusk, to remind me of my childhood, when I had always received my presents at twilight on Christmas Eve. I still had seven cans. Should I drink two? After all, I might reach Antigua during the night.

The rudder! Something was wrong. I looked back and saw the rudder was gone, empty hinges stared back at me. The paddle! I had to steer the boat with a paddle, as I had done off the coast of the Sahara the year before. Why, why did this have to happen on Christmas Eve? Better not ask. I did not dare ask. My feet were free for the first time since my departure from Las Palmas. They had accustomed themselves to holding the westward course and were unused to their new liberty. With the paddle my speed decreased considerably. One shoulder felt the brunt of the wind side. The seams of my jacket had burst there, and rheumatic twinges shot through my upper arm, necessitating a change of paddle from starboard to port. It was difficult to keep on course—more so now than ever.

Dusk set in. I punched a small hole in the milk can, nothing came out when I raised it to my lips. The milk had curdled. I banged the can against the metal tip of the paddle and enlarged the hole. The end of my paddle smelled of walnut. How I love walnut cake! Walnut cake with marzipan will always send me back to Germany.

A streak of light glimmered in the sky. The lights of St. John's in Antigua? One voice said yes, urging me to take another can of milk. Another voice urged caution; don't be rash, it counseled. At least, at St. John's I would find English toffee. Then the lights went out, the sky darkened. What a pity, for my sake, that the inhabitants went to bed so early; they could have stayed up a little longer. Tomorrow, I would hit St. John's. Tomorrow—all day long—I would chew on English toffee.

The boat ran backwards. I could not understand it, right there, before Antigua. I was attacked by a dizzy spell; with cramped hands I held the flashlight over the compass. West, it answered me. Then I knew nothing could go wrong. Two flying fish fell into the boat. Should I eat them? No! Not on Christmas Eve, tomorrow I would have all the food I needed in Antigua, so I threw them back into the water. A big comber pushed me forward—then another pulled me back—with both hands I clung to the washboard. The world spun around me. Through my dizziness I could not hear, but knew I was still going back and back. Again two flying fish landed on the boat.

"I warned you," I told them, "not to try this again," and I bit into one. It was full of scales. I scraped them off with my thumb and ate both fish. The sensation of sailing backward was confirmed when I put my hands into the water, although I knew it was an illusion brought on by weariness. My course was west. Again a big comber rushed over the boat, shaking my senses into some kind of reality.

The African had returned.

"Where are we going this time?"

"To the west," he reassured me.

I threw the sea anchor. Everywhere I saw the flat shadows of shrubs and bushes. . . . It was flat there, the surf washed over the boat, once, twice . . . oh God! how many times . . . yes! it was so flat there that land had to be somewhere near. My eyes saw what was not there to be seen; my ears heard sounds that did not exist. Suddenly all was quiet. I heard no crash of surf or sound of waves. Why this silence? Why? Why? Only when I talked with my boy or when he answered did I hear anything. How hard he worked. I was happy, endlessly happy, in another world. In a world where the sun shone, where neither body nor spirit existed, a world of ether that surrounded me with irrational joy. I sank even deeper into my mind.

Then I heard again the roaring of the sea, first from the distance, but coming slowly closer. Now it was fresh, menacing and rumbling in my ears. I no longer saw any lights of Antigua. I was awake, alert as never before. My sextant was not working. I concentrated with all my powers on thoughts of Phillipsburg—on the great bay—and the roaring of the sea dimmed. I saw the church, a little church with its roof just over the water and men taking shelter under it. Gray—gray—everything looked gray. Why?

December 26th

I awoke with a dismal sense of oppression. Could I have passed the islands without noticing them? I would not be the first to have missed them. There ought to be land near by. The day before I had seen nine frigate birds and royal terns, a sure sign of land. It had to

605

be somewhere. Should I change course? But how? For a long time now I had not known my exact latitude. I knew I could not be too far to the north, for the trade winds had continually pushed me southward. Still, I decided I would turn south on the first of January. I gave myself five more days to reach St. Martin on the present course.

I still had five cans of milk and a little rain water, brackish but drinkable. Under my skin there still lay a little fat. Oh! I was rich! I could reach the mainland, if necessary. I would make it. Sargasso weed floated on the surface. I caught some, shook it out over my spray cover and feasted off the delicate sea food I found. Several small crabs and two sargasso fish also fell out of the weed, but even in my present situation they had too little flavor to be palatable. However, I enjoyed some little shrimps that I wiped off the plastic cover with my sponge.

Trade winds blew in gusts of twenty-five miles an hour. The easing of the stiff wind made me strong and happy, confident that even without a sextant, I would hit Phillipsburg.

December 28th

There was no longer any doubt that I had missed the islands; frigate birds and terns decreased in number, sargasso weed thinned out. I saw few Madeira petrels or tropic birds. A booby visited me. I tried hard to find out where these birds came from, but I never succeeded. They simply arrived.

December 28th was my birthday. I was hardly aware of it except for passing thoughts of my birthday cake. Cake and Phillipsburg chased each other through my mind.

December 29th

I sat on the *Liberia,* nursing four cans of milk and a hope that never faded. Trade winds had softened to twenty miles an hour or less, the sun shone. It was unbelievable after the long period of stormy seas. Was the sea, at last, becoming reasonable? Soon I expected to sit upon the washboard and enjoy my "hour of hygiene" again. During the day I bailed until my seat was dry once more. But it did not really matter; I was happy—full of hope—and buoyed by the certainty that I would succeed.

Close to noon I noticed a shadow on the horizon to port. A shadow of a cloud, such as I had seen before. No? Yes? I was sure, suddenly, that it was an island. I could see the island, but I could not be sure which one it was. It lay, solitary, on the horizon. I could see it and no other. Strange! I continued sailing through the night, although the island disappeared behind a bank of clouds.

December 30th

I passed a quiet night. I had to sail athwart and to the south to be certain of being in position for the island I had sighted. I was overwhelmed at the thought of seeing land. The island emerged with the sun, bare and broken up by rocks. To starboard lay great, bare rocks; to the north I sighted my actual goal. In the background I could make out another shadow, which I recognized as Saba, the volcanic island. That meant that St. Bartholomew lay ahead of me.

I would land in the bay of Phillipsburg. Now at last I was sure. To the west of St. Martin lies the Anegade Passage, which I would have to cross to reach St. Thomas. It is not easy sailing, and I knew I would have to put my sails and equipment in order, before attempting it.

A last squall stirred the surface of the sea. Slowly I paddled toward St. Martin; rising ahead of me I saw the reality of my dreams: a little church, red roofs and green palms behind a gray veil of rain. I looked on peace and calm. It was late afternoon as I entered the harbor, paddling close to the wharf where a crowd was sheltered from the rain. I sailed straight through the surf up onto the beach.

Forgotten were my seventy-two days, forgotten my discomforts, my fright and my despair. As I climbed out of the boat, a breaker poured a bucket of water into it, my knees buckled, and I held onto the edge of the boat. Turning her on her bow, I tried to pull the stern out of the water. I went to grab the bow, but I stumbled and fell into the last licks of surf. I tried again, and again I fell, until at last people came over from the wharf and carried the *Liberia* ten yards up the beach to where the water could not reach her. They asked me where I came from. "Las Palmas," I answered, but it meant nothing to them and they ran back to their dry shelter.

I made a stab at clearing up the sails, until I was interrupted by a voice from the pier; a police officer wanted to see my papers, so I drew a watertight bag from under the forepart of the spray cover and stumbled over to him. I handed him my passport and answered his questions. The crowd listened to my story and, after they had grasped the extent of my voyage, insisted on escorting me to the hotel. But the boat was still my first concern. I made my way awkwardly back to her, fastened the sails, closed the spray-cover opening and took out a few of my possessions. Then, very slowly, I walked to the hotel. Questions were thrown at me from all sides, but I hardly heard them. "Seventy-two days at sea, seventy-two days at sea!" repeated itself rhythmically in my mind. I could not believe that I was finally and at last stumbling through the streets of Phillipsburg. Although I walked shakily, like an old man, I did not need support from anyone.

At the hotel, the manager told me that word of my arrival had reached the Governor, who had made me a guest of the island. Someone found clothes for me, and I was led to a shower. Staring back at me, from the old cracked mirror, was a face I did not recognize: sunken eyes, hollow cheeks and unkempt blond beard. Good Lord! Was that my face?

I showered, and then, prepared to face a barrage of questions, I returned to the main room of the hotel, which was crowded with visitors. I sat down to eat and was offered—a cake! a beautiful coconut cake! I gulped three slices. As I ate, more and more people crowded into the room, stared at me shyly, shaking their heads in disbelief.

Later that day I investigated my movie camera and found it had corroded, although I hoped to be able to save some of the film. I spread my possessions all over the hotel room to dry before I lay down to sleep. But, still in the grip of immense tension, I could not sleep. At midnight I got up and walked down to the beach, where a small, dark lonely shape lay on the sand. The *Liberia,* a nothing without me. So I sat beside her in unspoken companionship, listening to the surf, whose endless roar calmed me more than the unusual stillness of the hotel bedroom.

The next day a mechanic fixed the rudder, I rigged the boat, stowed away new food supplies and, after another night's rest, left the hospitable island of St. Martin. After fifty hours of comfortable, relaxed sailing, I was before St. Thomas, exactly seventy-six days after I left the Canary Islands. As I paddled into the yacht basin, against the wind, I saw my friends ready to welcome me. They had evidently seen me coming into the harbor. Their first teasing words of greeting reached me as I pulled up alongside the mole. Slowly, with their help, I climbed out of the boat. Someone came over, whispered in my ear, "Didn't you tell me last time that you never intended to do this again?" but as she said it she took my right hand in both of hers, as if to say, I understand you.

8 CONCLUSIONS

I heard later how my friends happened to be gathered at the St. Thomas Yacht basin to see me arrive. I had sent one of them a letter from Las Palmas in which I mentioned that I expected to be with them around Christmas but without saying how I planned to get there. And then one morning a cockleshell sailed from the ocean into the bay of Charlotte Amalie, someone spotted it, and word went around at once, "Here comes Hannes. Have your cameras ready." Thus not only was I warmly greeted on my arrival but I now have in my possession two treasured unposed pictures of myself at that moment.

I spent a few weeks in St. Thomas, regaining my strength and avoiding the present-day Caribbean pirates, who saw a way of making money out of my voyage. For the first few days I had to take antibiotics against abscesses around my knees, but soon they disappeared and I swam and danced again. At the hospital I spent my money in check-ups only to find that there was nothing extraordinary in my physical condition. My weight had gone down by some forty-three pounds. But as the hospital examination occurred five days after my arrival, I think I probably lost nearly fifty pounds, most of them during the last few days of the crossing.

I retain fond memories of my interview with the chief of immigration in St. Thomas. I had to go to him to obtain a visa for the United States, which entailed filling out an official questionnaire for Washington. "How would you describe your boat?" he asked, "motorboat, freighter or steamer?"

"Just put down 'other,'" I told him.

"What was your position on the boat? Master, mate or ordinary seaman?"

"Put down 'other,' again."

"What is the boat's tonnage, and how much water does she draw?"

"She weighs fifty-nine pounds, full she draws eight inches, empty about two inches."

Despite my startling answers I was given a visa, and shortly thereafter the *Liberia* and I flew to New York.

I sat in the plane, looking down on the blue canvas of the sea, on which the wind painted white foam ridges. How harmless they looked from above! But I knew what these combers meant. The motors of the plane ran smoothly and rhythmically, passengers read and dozed, a pretty girl came down the aisles, carrying coffee to the pilots. But what, I wondered, would happen to these people if the motors failed, and the plane was forced to ditch?

During my two trips—two hundred days and nights alone at sea—I had learned a great deal that could help castaways. I know now that the mind succumbs before the body, that although lack of sleep, thirst or hunger weaken the body, it is the undisciplined mind that drives the castaway to panic and heedless action. He must learn command of himself and, of course, of his boat, which is often his strongest and most resilient ally. Morale is the single most important factor in survival. Prayer, which brings hope and with hope optimism and relaxation, is a powerful aid in self-mastery. I cannot overemphasize the importance I place on auto-suggestions such as those I repeated to myself during the second voyage. Hunger brings on quarrelsomeness, suspicion and irritation in people, so it is well to remember to watch one's neighbor, who may suddenly become the victim of dangerous hallucinations. He may think he sees a food store near the boat and jump overboard to reach it. I had this urge myself several times.

Stimulants are harmful for they are usually followed by a break-down. Sleep is a vitally important factor, for lack of it leads to delirium, as I know from experience. The castaway should try to sleep, if only for a few minutes at a time. Seconds of sleep may save his life.

Fresh water is another key to survival. Research has been done that proves that a man can survive for three days in the tropics and nine days in temperate zones without food and water. We know that in the last war, a man survived for eleven days in the temperate zone under these conditions. I feel very strongly that no one who wishes to survive should drink salt water. If there is sufficient fresh water on board, a small amount of salt water may be drunk as a salt replacement, but that is all. Salt water is never a substitute for fresh water. If a castaway should happen to have milk or beer on his life raft, he can consider himself fortunate, for both these fluids will give him necessary calories. A skilled fisherman can keep himself supplied with all the solid foods he needs on a life raft, but he must be careful to balance his solid food intake with liquid intake. Only the eyes, blood and spinal liquids of fish supplied me with fluids; to extract liquid from the rest of a fish's body one needs especially built presses.

Above all, my advice to the castaway is never to give up hope; on my second voyage, for example, I met two steamers in regions that are not crossed by shipping lanes.

Many of these thoughts about my own survival crossed my mind as I sat in the plane from St. Thomas to New York, traversing in a few hours a large stretch of the Atlantic Ocean. And why, I wondered, had I felt challenged to cross the Atlantic in a dugout and a foldboat, when I could have done it with ease and safety in a plane or a steamship? What drove me to test my strength of mind and body to the utmost? I realized that no one answer would satisfy me; the urge for adventure, the quest for scientific knowledge—both played a part. I told myself that man has always searched for the new frontier, pushed for further boundaries and that I, as a man, would have to accept that for my answer.